CW01655987

The Wallace Collection
Catalogue of Pictures
III

The Wallace Collection
Catalogue of Pictures
III

French before 1815

by John Ingamells

The Trustees of the Wallace Collection, Manchester Square,
London W1M 6BN
1989

Board of Trustees

The cover shows a detail from
P387 *Harlequin and Columbine* by Watteau

British Library Cataloguing in Publication Data
Wallace Collection
The Wallace Collection: Catalogue of Pictures.
3: French before 1815
I. Painting, European – Catalogs
I. Title II. Ingamells, John
759'.94'074 ND450

ISBN 0 900785 35 7 (softback)
ISBN 0 900785 36 5 (hardback)

Catalogue designed by Graham Johnson
and printed by The Westerham Press

Contents

Foreword

This is the third volume of the series which will together replace the sixteenth edition of the *Catalogue of Pictures and Drawings* published in 1968. It describes 144 paintings and 8 drawings and water-colours, and of these 152 works 140 date from the eighteenth century.

While this volume was being compiled the study of French eighteenth-century paintings was considerably advanced by a series of exhibitions held at the Grand Palais in Paris (and shared with other locations) devoted to Watteau (1984–5), Boucher (1985–6) and Fragonard (1987–8). They were the work of several scholars, of whom Pierre Rosenberg was the inspiration and principal contributor, and to whom I want to express particular gratitude. Each exhibition was handicapped to a degree by the absence of pictures from the Wallace Collection (the consequence of the Founder's not altogether imprudent Deed of Trust), but perhaps this volume, with its discussion of some of *les grands absents*, may be regarded as an expiatory supplement. My further indebtedness to the kindness and to the published work of other scholars is expressed in the catalogue itself.

Several of the paintings described have been conserved by Herbert Lank, for whose skill and scrupulous advice I remain profoundly grateful.

For permission to use their libraries and archives I am grateful to the Directors of the National Gallery, London, the Warburg Institute and the Courtauld Institute of Art. Much kind help has also been received from the British Library, the British Museum Print Room, the library of the Victoria and Albert Museum and from the London Library; and in Paris from the Archives Nationales, the Archives de Paris, the Service de documentation des Commissaires-Priseurs, the Cabinet des Estampes and Département des Imprimés of the Bibliothèque Nationale, the Bibliothèque Doucet, and the Cabinet des Dessins and Service de documentation at the Musée du Louvre. Mme. Anne Blankert of the Rijksbureau voor Kunsthistorische Documentatie in The Hague has again been most helpful in answering sales queries. Christie's generously allowed access to their archives. The photographs used in this volume, including the colour plates in the hard-back edition, were specially taken by Gordon H. Roberton.

Of my colleagues in the Wallace Collection I owe a very special debt to Richard Beresford, who not only compiled the entries for those pictures by Champaigne and Poussin, but undertook valuable research in French archives and has been closely involved with the editing of this volume.

I want also to thank Ruth Cowell for finding and verifying countless references in sale catalogues and periodicals, and John McKee for constant general help. In more general terms, I must acknowledge the ever-willing assistance of a small but dedicated staff who have variously made pictures available for inspection, administered a complex programme of photography, and helped in the preparation of the typescript. My most grateful thanks go to them all.

This catalogue maintains the elegant format of earlier volumes, due to the continued and generous support of The Monument Trust. They have contributed to the cost of the paper-back edition and entirely financed the production of a limited, cloth-bound edition containing seventeen colour plates.

John Ingamells

Introduction

This account of the fourth Marquess of Hertford's collection of French eighteenth-century pictures may be supplemented by reference to the genealogical table on p.18, to 'Inventories' under Abbreviations on p.20, and to Appendices I, II and III, which give the chronology of the collection and the distribution of pictures between London and Paris, and list those pictures acquired by Lord Hertford which did not form part of Lady Wallace's bequest to the Nation in 1897.

The Wallace Collection has always been distinguished both by the number and the quality of its eighteenth-century French paintings. The first edition of this catalogue in 1900 listed 26 Bouchers, 21 Greuzes, 14 Paters, 11 Lancrets, 9 Watteaus and 8 Fragonards, 89 works of which the present catalogue questions the autograph quality of twelve. At the same time the National Gallery catalogue listed one Boucher, four Greuzes (of which one is now considered to be by a follower) and four Lancrets; Fragonard, Pater and Watteau were not represented at all. Nearly all the Wallace Collection paintings had been bought by the fourth Marquess of Hertford (1800–70) – the remainder were acquired by his illegitimate son, Sir Richard Wallace (1818–90). Exceedingly rich, without professional responsibilities, from 1829 the owner of luxurious appartements in the fashionable rue Laffitte in Paris and from 1835 the propriétor of Bagatelle, a Louis XVI château in the Bois de Boulogne, intelligent and knowledgeable concerning the fine arts, Lord Hertford seemed in many respects a survival from the *noblesse* of the *ancien régime*. In the field of the decorative arts his taste was indeed centred on that period, but with pictures he was more catholic (as the other volumes of this catalogue show), although his Dutch, Flemish and older French paintings would have been (indeed were) admired by such eighteenth-century collectors as Blondel de Gagny and the duc de Choiseul.

His eighteenth-century French paintings were acquired steadily through thirty years of collecting[1] and came to represent a significant part (perhaps a quarter) of his total collection. His earliest purchases were two Watteaus in 1827 (see Appendix III, nos. 144–5) – of which nothing is known save the invoice – but his collection did not begin in earnest until 1841, just before his succession. Within the first decade he acquired fine paintings by Boucher, Fragonard, Watteau and Greuze. The little Fragonard, *Dites donc s'il vous plaît* (P404), came, it appears, in 1841, and *The Musical Contest* (P471) was acquired as a Boucher in 1842. The large early Bouchers, *The Rape of Europa* (P484) and *Mercury and Bacchus* (P487) followed in 1843. Two of his best Greuzes, *The Votive Offering* (P441) and *The Broken Mirror* (P442), were bought in 1845, and two of his best Watteaus, *La perspective* (see Appendix III, no.143) and the little *Gilles* (P381), in 1846. Two more Watteaus, each showing the same subject on a different scale, the little *Champs Elisées* (P389) and the large *Divertissements champêtres* (P391), were acquired in 1848.

Most of his finest Bouchers were bought in the 1850s. From the Prousteau de Montlouis sale in 1851 came the remarkable *paravent* with four Boucher panels on one side (P429, P432, P438 and P444) and four Lancret pastorals on the other (see Boucher P429 note 2), together with two Boucher ovals, *Jupiter and Callisto* and *Angelica and Medoro* (see Appendix III, nos.17–18), and two fine compositions by Boucher's teacher Lemoyne, *Time saving Truth* (P392) and *Perseus and Andromeda* (P417). In 1852 he bought the two large *Pastorals* by Boucher (P482 and P489) and four overdoors by Oudry (P625, P627, P629 and P631), all originally commissioned by D.-C. Trudaine for the Château de Montigny-Lencoup. The finest of all Lord Hertford's Bouchers, *The Rising* and *The Setting of the Sun* (P485–6) from the collection of Mme. de Pompadour, were acquired in 1855, and he continued to buy decorative panels in 1857 with the Boucher overdoors, *Spring* and *Bacchus and Erigone* (P445 and P447), and two Desportes *buffets* (P594 and P628). The former Lord Hertford described to his agent as 'a couple of Bouchers to put over my great doors if ever I finish my Piccadilly house', the latter as 'a little rubbish for the country . . . beautiful of the sort & perfect for my shooting place'.[2] By 1859 he owned at least 16 Greuzes (whose sentimental heads were becoming something of an obsession), 15 Bouchers, 9 Lancrets, 6 Watteaus and 4 Paters.

When, in 1857, Lord Hertford came to choose 44 of his best pictures for the Manchester *Art Treasures* exhibition, he included two Greuzes (*The Broken Mirror*, P441, and the *Girl with Doves*, P428) and single works by Watteau (*Les divertissements champêtres*, P391), Lancret (*Italian Comedians by a Fountain*, P465) and Pater (see Appendix III, no.118). Boucher was not then familiar to English collectors, and his best Bouchers were, in any case, very large. To Martinet's second *Tableaux de l'école française* exhibition, held in the boulevard des Italiens in 1860, he lent six large Bouchers (P482, P484–7 and P489), two Desportes (P594 and P628), a portrait by Nattier (see Appendix III, no.113) and a small, indifferent Pater, *Le plaisir de l'été* (P472).

In the following (and last) decade Lord Hertford bought ten other pictures from that exhibition, of which seven came from the duc de Morny's sale in 1865, including Watteau's *Rendez-vous de chasse* (P416, the pendant to *Les divertissements champêtres*, P391, acquired in 1848) and two Fragonards, *The Souvenir* (P382) and the celebrated *Swing* (P430). He had been slow to buy Fragonard, but he now acquired a select group; the enchanting *Petit parc* (P379) came, apparently, from the Koucheleff collection in St. Petersburg (together with a *turquerie* by C. A. van Loo, P451, and, probably, the Lancret, P448) and *The Triumph of Love* (P394) was bought in 1870. This last was one of several pictures which hinted at a change in Lord Hertford's taste in his last years, away from the more ebullient rococo towards a more staid, classical style. Examples of such purchases include several works by Boilly (P435, P473 and P479) in 1861–3 (and see Appendix III, nos.1–14), two portraits by Vigée Le Brun (P457 and P449) in 1862 and 1868, *The Sleep of Venus* (P348) by Mayer in 1866, and an overdoor by Chardin *fils* and a reduced version of David's whole-length portrait of Napoleon (see Appendix III, nos.43 and

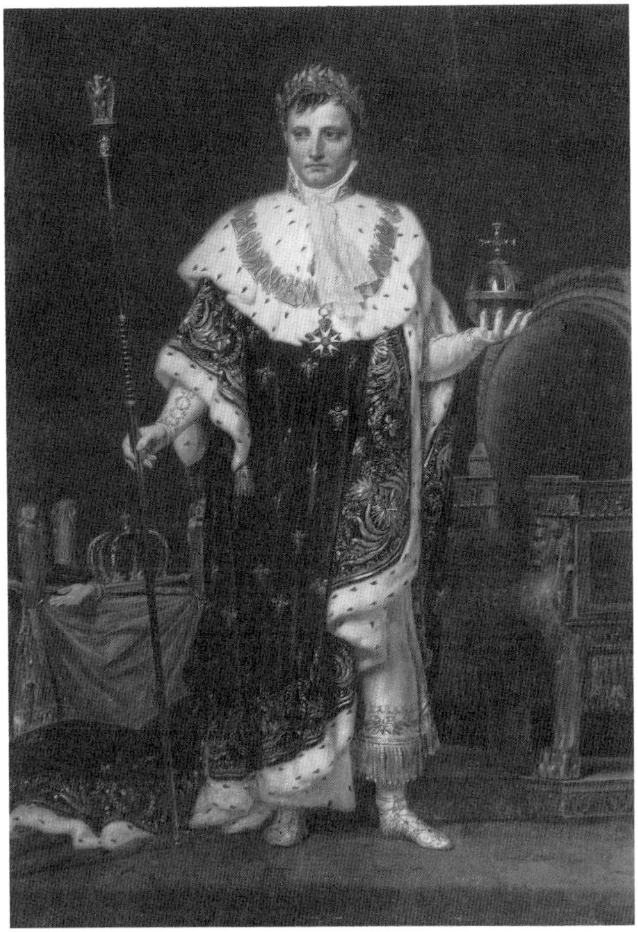

David: *Napoleon I* (see Appendix III, no.51). Fogg Art Museum, Cambridge, Mass.

51) in 1867. Lord Hertford's last years were spent in Bagatelle where perhaps Bélanger's Louis XVI architecture helped to induce his new attitude. But it was not exclusive; his lasting enthusiasm for Greuze was expressed in the spectacular purchases of *Innocence* (P384) in 1865 and *Les oeufs cassés* (see Appendix III, no.78) in 1870, and his love of rococo decorative panels in his purchase of Oudry's fine *buffets*, P626 and P630. Two of the best purchases of his last years were the small Watteau, *La toilette* (P439), and Boucher's fresh yet modest little portrait of *Mme. de Pompadour* (P418).

Although Lord Hertford had acquired a distinguished collection of French eighteenth-century pictures (together with a number of fine Beauvais and Gobelins tapestries after designs by Boucher, Leprince and J.-F. de Troy),[3] he seems not to have been concerned with its display. In the rue Laffitte old masters were mixed up with the contemporary;[4] the six great Bouchers shown in Martinet's 1860 exhibition, the two large Watteaus, *Les divertissements champêtres* and *Le rendez-vous*

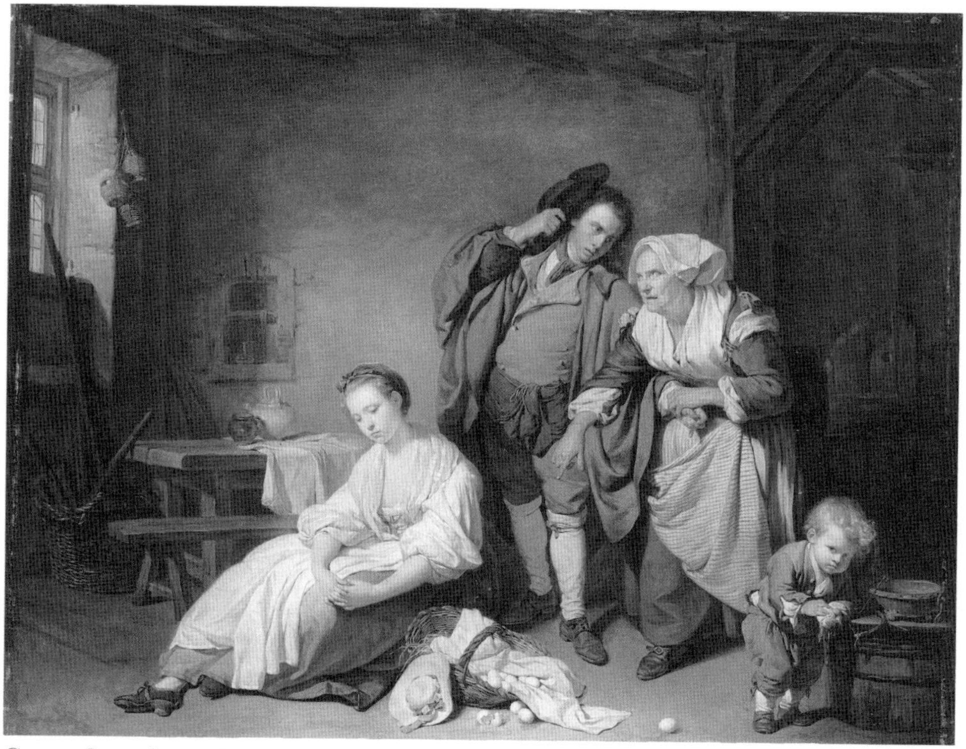

Greuze: *Les oeufs cassés* (see Appendix III, no.78). Metropolitan Museum of Art, New York

de chasse (P391 and P416), and five Oudrys were amongst the thirty French eighteenth-century pictures in the *grande galerie* which contained 116 pictures in all, and otherwise included works by Delaroche, Papety, Guardi, Champaigne and Veronese; in the rotunda four Bouchers were displayed in the *lambris* flanked with portraits by Velázquez and Hals and views by Potter, Hobbema and Willem van de Velde. At Bagatelle Boucher's *Cupid and the Graces* (see Appendix III, no.15) was set in the ceiling of the west boudoir, four Lancrets were used as overdoors (see Appendix III, nos.85–8) and four more Bouchers ('*quatre panneaux de décoration*') were, apparently, set in the walls (possibly P385, P399, P481 and P490); the inventory otherwise lists works by Boilly, Lépicié, Vigée Le Brun, Greuze, Nattier and Watteau (*La toilette*, P439) amongst paintings by Gerrit Dou, Delaroche, Landelle and Meissonier.

After Lord Hertford's death in 1870, Richard Wallace added, amongst others, the large, late Boucher, *Jupiter and Callisto* (P446), two sentimental Fragonards, *A Boy as Pierrot* (P412) and *A Young Scholar* (P455), the charming Lancret of *Mlle. de Camargo Dancing* (P393) and the large, but already decrepit Prud'hon, *Venus and Adonis* (P347). But the character of the collection of French eighteenth-century pictures in the Wallace Collection is due entirely to the fourth Marquess of Hertford.

Charles Yriarte, writing in 1897, claimed that Lord Hertford was '*un précurseur*', one of those who had revived the taste for eighteenth-century French painting after it had fallen from favour with the onset of the Revolution and David's neo-classicism.[5] But he belonged rather to the second generation of such collectors, who confirmed the market, as a glance at the provenances and prices of his pictures will demonstrate. In 1847, just after Lord Hertford had begun to collect in earnest, Balzac published *Le cousin Pons*, whose plot was based on the rapidly rising prices commanded by the art of the *ancien régime*; having acquired a Watteau fan for 12 francs at the beginning of the century, cousin Pons, the poor relation, was by 1843 an object of interest to his family. '*Vous ne connaissez pas Watteau?*', Camusot de Marville asks his wife.

> – *Je connais David, Gérard, Gros, et Girodet, et M. de Forbin, et M. Turpin de Crissé . . .*
> – *Vous auriez dû . . .*
> – *Qu'aurais-je dû, monsieur? . . .*
> – *Savoir ce qu'est Watteau, ma chère, il est fort à la mode . . .*

And Camusot de Marville was one who '*suivait la foule pas à pas*'. During the thirty years Lord Hertford was buying, 1840–70, interest in French eighteenth-century painting increased considerably. Before him, a few collectors, such as the miniaturist Daniel Saint (1778–1847) and his pupil A.-J. Carrier (1800–75), the marquis de Cypierre (1784–1844)[6] and Dr. Louis La Caze (1797–1869),[7] had been able to buy Boucher and Watteau cheaply, with little competition; none of them was particularly rich and all could be described as dedicated.

The advent of such moneyed collectors as Lord Hertford, baron James de Rothschild (1792–1868), the duc de Morny (1811–65), and the brothers Emile (1800–75) and Isaac (1806–80) Pereire, changed these circumstances. They seemed to regard such paintings less as neglected masterpieces than as symbols of luxury and refinement.[8] The consequent rise of interest was otherwise variously reflected: in publications such as Blanc's *Les Peintres des Fêtes Galantes* in 1854 and the Goncourts' famous *L'art du dix-huitième siècle* between 1857 and 1875; in Martinet's exhibition (already mentioned) of 1860; in the Empress Eugénie's addiction to *le style Louis XVI* (her portrait by Winterhalter of 1854 showed her *à la Marie-Antoinette*), and at the Salon, where the visions of Watteau and Boucher recurred in the works of Cabanel, Bouguereau, Chaplin, Jalabert and Roqueplan. But the most direct measure of rising interest lay in the sale room, where the increasingly high prices paid by Lord Hertford were frequently the subject of amazed or angry comment.

Although Lord Hertford had been able to purchase two Watteaus in 1827 for 390 francs (see Appendix III, nos. 144–5), by 1846 he was paying 3,800 francs at the Saint sale for *La perspective* (see Appendix III, no. 143) and 5,000 francs for the little *Gilles* (P381). When he paid nearly 25,000 francs (900 guineas) for the small *Champs Elisées* in 1848 there was an outcry:

> The most astonishing occurrence in the [Morny] sale is the outrageous price, given by the Marquis of Hertford, of 900 guineas, for the small picture by A. Watteau. It would be the climax of imbecile judgment to say that such a picture was worthy of the sum.[9]

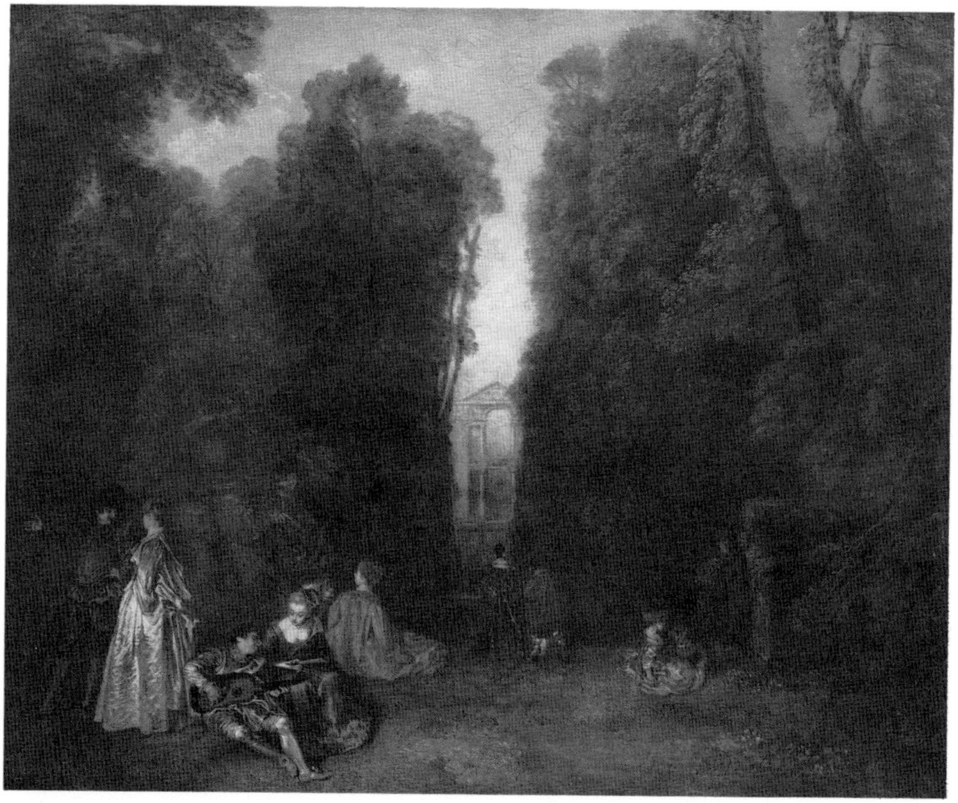

Watteau: *La perspective* (see Appendix III, no. 143). Museum of Fine Arts, Boston

At the same time he paid 30,000 francs for the much larger *Divertissements champêtres* (P391), which had sold for half that sum in 1845 at the Fesch sale in Rome.[10] Lord Hertford had attended that sale but had passed over both the *Divertissements champêtres* and its pendant, *Le rendez-vous de chasse* (P416); the latter he passed over again in 1848, finally buying it in 1865 for 31,000 francs. There are few other instances of such inconsistency in his collecting. One Watteau he failed to get was the celebrated whole-length *Pierrot*, now in the Louvre, which was lent to Martinet's 1860 exhibition by La Caze. When he announced the gift of his pictures to the Louvre (they were bequeathed in 1869) La Caze said he had refused an offer of 300,000 francs from an English collector.[11] That this was Lord Hertford seems clear from a report later printed in the *Times*:

> [The Marquis of Hertford] appreciated and coveted the *Gilles* [as the *Pierrot* was then known] but M. La Caze was proof against the large offers that he made for it. At last the Marquis offered to appeal to the hazard of the card-table, and to play La Caze at écarté for his Gilles, staking against it another Watteau and giving his adversary points. But M. La Caze, says the French chronicler of the transaction, refused . . .[12]

Though neither Lancret nor Pater was generally regarded as the equal of Watteau, they proved equally expensive. Lancret, wrote Blanc in 1854, was '*un Watteau amoindri et refroidi sans doute, mais aimable, civilisé et historique*'.[13] In 1853 at the Louis-Philippe/Standish sale Lord Hertford paid 18,000 francs (700 guineas) for Lancret's *Italian Comedians by a Fountain* (P465), which was catalogued as by Watteau. His appreciation of the picture, as well as his determination to have it, was reflected in letters to his London agent, Mawson:

> I depend upon yr. getting the Lancret (Watteau in the Catag.) for me. I have no doubt it will sell for a good sum, most likely more than it is worth, but we must have it, as I suppose it will not dépassé 3 thousand pds. [75,000 francs]. I mention this to make you comfortable & you are the only person to whom I wd. say as much. I leave it to you, but I must have it, unless by some unheard of chance it were to go beyond 3,000 Gns. [82,000 francs]. Of course it will not, & on all that is honourable, don't mention one word of what I have just said.[14]

Pater's works had been described by Blanc as '*les produits d'une industrie . . . pour les gens de robe et pour les bourgeois de finance*'.[15] When Lord Hertford paid 17,800 francs for *Les loisirs champêtres* (P460) at the Demidoff sale in 1863, both the price and the artist were ridiculed:

> *Quoi! 17,000 fr. une telle peinture! . . . c'est prendre un ver luisant pour une étoile! . . . Autant Watteau est poëte et artiste, . . . autant Pater est faux et ignorant, bouffi et vide. Ses terrains n'ont pas de plans, ses personnages pas d'os, ses poupées mal habillées, point de caractère, ni d'esprit. Ses femmes ont des mines de souris apoplectiques, ses petites filles des yeux en forme d'accolades –, ses lointains sont ternes et sec. M. Pater est un écolier qui a regardé par le trou de la serrure dans l'atelier de Watteau!*[16]

Two other Paters cost him particularly dear at the Morny sale in 1865: *Les amusements champêtres* (P424) 29,000 francs, and *Le bal* (P420), then catalogued as by Watteau, 37,000 francs.

Lord Hertford's Bouchers were cheaper than his *fêtes galantes*. In 1843 he bought *The Rape of Europa* (P484) and *Mercury and Bacchus* (P487), large and beautiful early works, for 2,820 francs (or half the cost of Watteau's tiny *Gilles*, P381, in 1846). In 1855 at the baron de Commailles sale he paid 20,200 francs for *The Rising* and *The Setting of the Sun* (P485–6), Mme. de Pompadour's greatest Bouchers; the baron had bought them in 1827 from a Paris dealer for 380 francs, but considered, quite reasonably, that the sale-room price was disappointing. When Lord Hertford paid 14,500 francs for a pair of overdoors, *Spring* (P445) and *Bacchus and Erigone* (P447), at the Patureau sale in 1857, he was criticised by Blanc:

> *Il y a trente ans à peine, on eût obtenu ces deux toiles pour quelque chose comme cent écus* [300 francs]; *. . . fallait-il . . . faire des folies d'argent pour ces folies de peintures? . . . N'est-il pas scandaleux qu'un Boucher se paie autant et plus qu'un Titien?*[17]

The oval *Shepherd and Shepherdess reposing* (P431), valued at 30 francs in 1799 and sold for 54 francs in 1811, was apparently bought for 4,100 francs in 1860.

Fragonard and Greuze were dear. Although he paid little for the Fragonards acquired in the 1840s (*Dites donc s'il vous plaît*, P404, 385 francs in 1841, and *The Musical Contest*, P471, 721 francs in 1842, as by Boucher), Lord Hertford paid over

30,000 francs each for the three he acquired in 1865 and 1870 (*The Swing*, P430, and *The Souvenir*, P382, in 1865, and *The Triumph of Love*, P394, in 1870), which were more substantial works from the respected collections of the duc de Morny and Anatole Demidoff. Greuze's reputation had not suffered in the earlier nineteenth century; *'c'est une puissance que Greuze! il règne depuis longtemps sur les âmes sensibles'*, commented Bürger in 1860.[18] Lord Hertford had to pay 35,000 francs at the Fesch sale in 1845 for *The Votive Offering to Cupid* (P441) and 19,000 francs for *The Broken Mirror* (P442), two of his best Greuzes, but the most sensational of all his French eighteenth-century picture purchases in sale-room terms were the Pourtalès *Innocence* (P384), 100,200 francs in 1865, and the Demidoff *Les oeufs cassés* (see Appendix III, no.78), 126,000 francs in 1870. The former represents twice the cost of any other picture described in this catalogue, while the latter was the second highest price Lord Hertford ever paid for one picture.

It is not easy to characterise the collection of French eighteenth-century paintings which Lord Hertford had thus acquired. The omission of Chardin seems surprising, and there is a surfeit of sentimental Greuze.[19] The number of Paters and Lancrets overwhelms the few Watteaus,[20] of which one would not rate the large Morny pendants (*Les divertissements champêtres*, P391, and *Le rendez-vous de chasse*, P416) amongst his best, and of which the charming *Harlequin et Columbine* (P387) was a Wallace and not a Hertford picture. Amongst the Bouchers and Fragonards, however, are some extremely distinguished pictures, and the overall quality is very high. D. S. MacColl (later Keeper of the Wallace Collection) rigorously asserted that

> The big net of the limitless purse could not fail to rope in a number of masterpieces, but when we look at the whole take, what can we conceive the collector to have gone fishing for? . . . if he buys Greuze and Watteau, and more Greuzes than Watteaus, I argue that Greuze was the real taste unless both were factitious.[21]

One might counter that, of his twenty Greuzes, half had been kept in London virtually out of sight (see Appendix II), but MacColl's point concerning Lord Hertford's elusive and somewhat inconsistent character as a collector remains. That was also, it seems, the character of the man.

[1] It will be seen from Appendix I that the dates of acquisition of some pictures are not certain, including several Bouchers, two Greuzes, three Lancrets and five Paters.

[2] *Letters*, no.77, p.98 (Hertford to Mawson, Paris, 28 April 1857).

[3] For which, see R.A. Cecil, *The Burlington Magazine*, XCVIII, 1956, pp.116–18. Since they do not appear in the inventories of 1870/1, the tapestries were probably not displayed, but stored.

[4] The following descriptions are taken from the inventories and W. Bürger, 'Les collections particulières', *Paris Guide*, I, 1867, pp.537–9.

[5] C. Yriarte, *La Revue de Paris*, II, V, 1903, p.411.

[6] For whom, see *Connaissance des Arts*, August 1974, pp.34–5.

[7] For whom, see S. Béguin, *La Revue du Louvre*, 1969, pp.115–32.

[8] Cf. F. Haskell, *Rediscoveries in Art*, 1976, p.103; the rise of French rococo taste is described on pp.57–64, 75–7 and 102–3.

[9] *Art Union*, 1848, p.257.

[10] The increase was commented upon by Bürger in the *Gazette des Beaux-Arts*, 1ère, VII, 1860, p.269, where he also alleged that Lord Hertford had refused an offer of 52,500 francs (2,000 gn.) for *Les divertissements champêtres* (P391) at the Manchester *Art Treasures* exhibition in 1857.

[11] Cf. F.J.B. Watson, *Apollo*, LXXXI, 1965, p.437.

[12] *The Times*, 2 February 1889.

[13] C. Blanc, *Les Peintres des Fêtes Galantes*, 1854, p.46.

[14] *Letters*, no.25, p.40 (Hertford to Mawson, Paris, 25 May 1853).

[15] Blanc, *op. cit.*, p.59.

[16] *Chronique des Arts*, 18 January 1863, pp.82–3.

[17] C. Blanc, *Le Trésor de la Curiosité*, 1858, II, p.524.

[18] W. Bürger, *Gazette des Beaux-Arts*, 1ère, VII, 1860, p.349.

[19] The *Pall Mall Gazette*, 14 August 1900, commented: 'The nation now stands possessed of a much greater number of silly pictures by Greuze than any nation under good instruction ought to wish for. In like manner the public has grown rich in Boucher, much beyond the desires of the judicious'.

[20] MacColl commented in the *Saturday Review*, 30 June 1900, that 'the net result of hanging, for example, Pater and Lancret alongside of Watteau is the dry judgment that these men are second rate . . . No-one who can afford to possess a Watteau should buy a Pater unless for export to Watteau-less lands'.

[21] *Ibid.*

The Seymour-Conway Family
Earls and Marquesses of Hertford

FOUNDERS OF THE WALLACE COLLECTION

Francis Seymour-Conway (1719–1794; Earl of Hertford & Viscount Beauchamp 1750; Earl of Yarmouth & *Marquess of Hertford* 1793)	m. 1741 Lady Isabella Fitzroy (1726–1782) d. of 2nd Duke of Grafton

seven sons and six daughters, of whom

Francis Ingram Seymour-Conway (1743–1822; Viscount Beauchamp 1750; Earl of Yarmouth 1793; *2nd Marquess of Hertford* 1794)	m. 1. 1768 Alice Elizabeth (d. 1772) d. of Viscount Windsor m. 2. 1776 Isabella Anne Ingram Shepheard (1760–1834) d. of 9th Viscount Irwin

only surviving child

Francis Charles Seymour-Conway (1777–1842; Viscount Beauchamp 1793; Earl of Yarmouth 1794; *3rd Marquess of Hertford* 1822)	m. 1798 Maria Fagnani (1771–1856)

two sons and a daughter, of whom

Richard Seymour-Conway (1800–1870; Viscount Beauchamp 1800; Earl of Yarmouth 1822; *4th Marquess of Hertford* 1842)

one illegitimate son
(by Mrs. Agnes Jackson, *née* Wallace, 1789–1864)

Richard (Jackson) Wallace (1818–1890; name changed to Wallace 1842; Baronet 1871)	m. 1871 Amélie Julie Castelnau (1819–1897)

Lady Wallace bequeathed the major part of the family's collection of works of art to the Nation as The Wallace Collection

Explanation

Pictures are catalogued alphabetically by artist; for each artist pictures are described in order of their inventory numbers.

Attributions	*After:* derived from an identified work by the named artist *Ascribed to:* there remains an element of doubt concerning the traditional attribution *Studio of:* produced in the named artist's studio, probably under his direction and after his design
Right and left	the spectator's right and left, unless otherwise indicated (e.g. a sitter's left hand in a portrait)
Medium	oil, unless otherwise stated
Measurements	Normally the size of the painted area (often less than the size of the supporting stretcher or panel) in centimetres, height before width; for panels the depth is also given; French eighteenth-century measurements have been converted into cm. (1 *pied*: 32.64 cm.; 1 *pouce*: 2.72 cm.)
Condition	notes list previous restorations as recorded in archives, and are otherwise generally confined to a description of visible imperfections, e.g. repaired damages, retouchings and *pentimenti*
Drawings	preliminary and/or related graphic works by the named artist
Versions	replicas and closely related compositions, generally attributable to the named artist; the support is canvas unless otherwise stated
Provenance	prices: as a comparative guide for nineteenth-century prices, the pound was worth approximately 25 French francs, and the guinea (gn.) 26 francs
Exhibitions	in London or Paris, unless otherwise stated

Abbreviations

See also following artists' biographies (e.g. JR under Boucher, WL under Lancret, IS under Pater, CR and DV under Watteau)

AAF	*Archives de l'Art français*
AHAA	*Annales d'Histoire de l'Art et d'Archéologie* (Université Libre de Bruxelles)
Bagatelle	see Inventories
Bethnal Green	Paintings, Decorative Furniture and other Works of Art lent by Sir Richard Wallace to the Bethnal Green Museum, 24 June 1872–April 1875. Catalogued by C. Black, 1872 and 1874, the second edition showing that Wallace added material after the exhibition opened (listed as Bethnal Green 1874–5)
BI	British Institution, London
Blanc 1865	C. Blanc, *Histoire des peintres de toutes les écoles, Ecole Française,* 3 vols., 1865
boulevard des Italiens 1860	*Tableaux de l'Ecole Française, principalement du XVIIIe siècle, tirés de collections d'Amateurs et exposés au profit de la Caisse de secours des Artistes Peintres, Sculpteurs, Architectes et Dessinateurs,* 26 boulevard des Italiens, September 1860 (see Introduction)
BSHAF	*Bulletin de la Société de l'Histoire de l'Art français*
Dorchester House	see Inventories
Evans invoice	two invoices in the Wallace Collection archives from W. & P. Evans, 18 Silver Street, London, to the 4th Marquess of Hertford for work on pictures in Hertford House – restoration of pictures and frames and 92 new frames; the first dated April 1857 (in connection with the *Art Treasures* exhibition at Manchester), the second February 1859
Hertford House	see Inventories
Inventories	preserved in the Wallace Collection archives, unless otherwise indicated: *Bagatelle,* Bois de Boulogne, Paris, residence of the 4th Marquess of Hertford 1835–70; bequeathed to Richard Wallace; inventory 1871, objects removed from Bagatelle on death of the 4th Marquess and stored at 3 rue Taitbout, Paris (Archives de Paris, D48E^{3} 62) *Dorchester House,* Park Lane, London (demolished 1848), leased by the 3rd Marquess of Hertford 1829–42; inventory 1842 on his death *Hertford House,* now the Wallace Collection, acquired by the 2nd Marquess of Hertford 1797; leased as French Embassy 1835–50; rarely visited by the 4th Marquess who kept works of art there (principally those acquired in Paris before 1848, and those acquired in London); residence of Sir Richard and Lady Wallace 1875–97; inventory 1870 on death of 4th Marquess, and 1890 on death of Wallace

	rue Laffitte, no.2, Paris, residence of the 4th Marquess of Hertford 1829–70; bequeathed to Richard Wallace; inventory 1871 on death of 4th Marquess (Archives de Paris, D48E^{3} 62)
	105 Piccadilly, London, given to the 3rd Marchioness of Hertford by the 4th Duke of Queensberry; used by Wallace 1872–5; sold 1876; schedule of part contents insured by the Sun Insurance Co. (policy no.2498155), 23 April 1874–25 March 1875
	rue Taitbout, nos.3 and 5, acquired by the 4th Marquess of Hertford 1856–9 (these properties adjoined 2 rue Laffitte, see above, and had been occupied by the 4th Marquess's mother, d.1856, and step-brother, d.1859); inventory 1871 on death of 4th Marquess (and see Bagatelle above) (Archives de Paris, D48E^{3} 62)
Letters	*The Hertford Mawson Letters*, ed. J. Ingamells, 1981
Malmaison 1867	*Objets exposés sous les auspices de Sa Majesté l'Impératrice, et provenant de la collection privée de Leurs Majestés, des Magasins de la Couronne, ou des communications faites par des particuliers*, Château de Malmaison, 1867 (cf. H. de Lescure, *Le Château de Malmaison*, 1867)
Manchester, *Art Treasures*, 1857	*Art Treasures of the United Kingdom*, Old Trafford, Manchester, 5 May–7 October 1857; the 4th Marquess of Hertford lent 44 paintings which were housed in a special room (saloon H) with their own numbers
NAAF	*Nouvelles Archives de l'Art français*
105 Piccadilly	see Inventories
RA	Royal Academy, London
rue Laffitte	see Inventories
rue Taitbout	see Inventories
Thieme-Becker	U. Thieme and F. Becker, *Allgemeines Lexicon der Bildenden Künstler*, 37 vols., 1908–49
Waagen I–III	G.F. Waagen, *Treasures of Art in Great Britain*, 3 vols., 1854
Waagen IV	G.F. Waagen, *Galleries and Cabinets of Art in Great Britain*, 1857 (published as a supplement to the *Treasures of Art*)
Walpole, *Correspondence*	Horace Walpole, *Correspondence*, ed. W.S. Lewis, 43 vols. + 5 vols. index, 1937–83

Catalogue

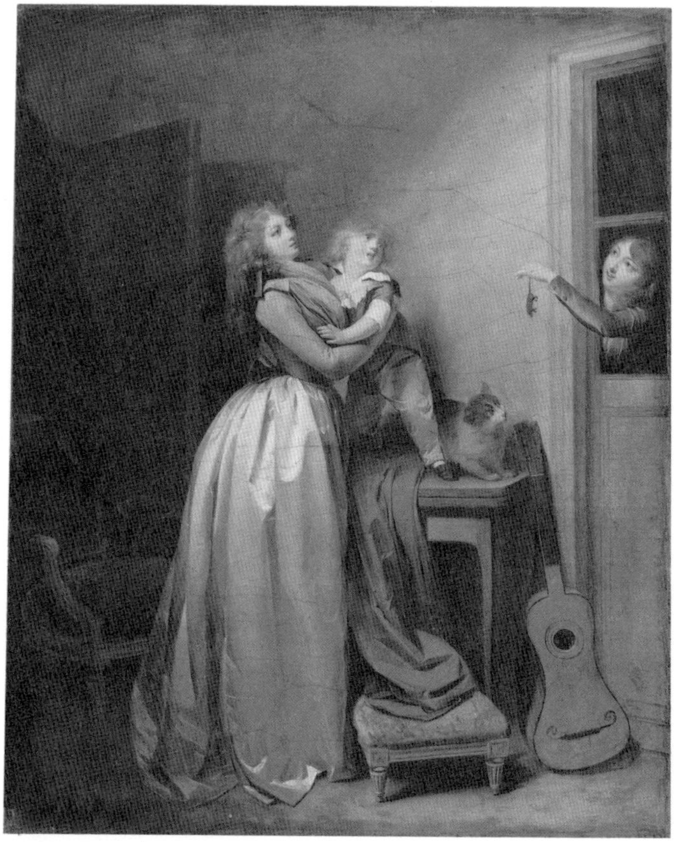

P435

Louis-Léopold Boilly (1761–1845)

Born on 5 July 1761 in La Bassée, near Lille, the son of a woodcarver. Self-taught, he practised in Douai and Arras before coming to Paris in 1785. He exhibited at the Salon between 1791 (when it was first opened to non *académiciens*) and 1824. His earlier subjects of bourgeois *galanterie*, such as those commissioned by Calvet de Lapalun 1789–92 (cf. P473, P479), were denounced to the *Société républicaine des Arts* in 1794 and he immediately painted *Le triomphe de Marat* (Lille) and turned to the illustration of Parisian life. His carefully finished, small paintings recall the Dutch *fijnschilders*, such as Dou, ter Borch and Mieris (examples of each were in Boilly's sale, Paris, 14 April 1829), and his talent for *trompe l'oeil* subjects (such as the *Crucifix* on loan to Magdalen College, Oxford) brought him popular acclaim in the Salon. He published a set of humorous lithographs, *Les grimaces*, in 1823. He was made *chevalier* of the Legion of Honour in 1833, but his work fell out of fashion after the Restoration. He died in Paris on 4 January 1845.

Abbreviation

Harrisse H. Harrisse, *L.-L. Boilly*, 1898

P435 *The Dead Mouse*

The mother wears a white satin skirt and pale blue satin jacket; the little boy a lavender jacket over a pale blue suit; the girl holding the mouse wears dark green; a dull red drape on the table and a dark green curtain on the left.

Canvas, relined 40 × 31.2

The edges were made up during relining to 41.2 × 32.5. A broad overall craquelure, first noted in 1861,[1] has been retouched on the background wall and in the screen. There is a damage between the boy's legs and a *pentimento* on his left hand. The varnish is discoloured.

P435 may be dated c.1793 by comparison with *L'optique* which was shown at the Salon that year.[2] The same three models recur (with the footstool, guitar and chair) in *L'enfant au fard*;[3] the mother and boy recur in *La promenade* (Agnew's 1951; Harrisse, no.460) and *La crainte enfantine* (Cognacq sale, 14 May 1952, lot 6) and (with the stool) in *La tourterelle chérie*;[4] the mother alone recurs in *La dame au manchon*.[5] The chair reappears in P479,[6] and the red drapery in P473. The painting of the satin skirt recalls ter Borch or Mieris.[7] The mother's head seems disproportionately small.

Provenance

M. L [afitte], Madrid; his sale (by order of M. Best), Paris, 7 March 1861 (14, *La souris prise*), 690 fr.; the 4th Marquess of Hertford; rue Laffitte inventory 1871 (370); Hertford House inventory 1890.

Exhibition

Bethnal Green 1872–5 (586).

Reference General

Harrisse, no.515.

[1] The copy of the L. sale catalogue (see Provenance) in the Victoria and Albert Museum is annotated opposite lot 14: *'joli tableau dans la manière un peu dure de l'auteur/craquelé dans le haut'*.

[2] Harrisse, no.6; exh. *Boilly*, Musée Marmottan, 1984 (7), lent by a private collector.

[3] Harrisse, no.185, illus. f.p.100; coll. Meyer 1930. A smaller version exh. *Boilly*, Hôtel de Sagan, 1930 (29), lent by the baronne Gérard.

[4] Harrisse, no.1181; exh. *Boilly*, Musée Marmottan, 1984 (68).

[5] Harrisse, no.253, illus. f.p.106; exh. *Boilly*, Hôtel de Sagan, 1930 (84) lent by the baron Henri de Rothschild.

[6] Doubtless one of the *'fauteuils sculptés gris foncé recouverts de velours d'Utrecht cramoisi'*, listed in the *inventaire après décès* of Boilly's first wife, 13–17 June 1795 (BSHAF 1929, p.22).

[7] Paintings by both these artists were in Boilly's sale, 14 April 1829, but the 1795 inventory (*ibid.*, p.24) listed a Cornelis Bega as the only Dutch painting.

P473 *The Visit Returned*

The visitor wears a pink satin dress with a muslin overskirt and a pale blue bodice; her maid is in pale green; the gentleman has a brown coat and blue breeches, his blue silk-lined hat and russet cape on a red chair; there is a portrait on his desk and a dog by his feet; a dull red drape in the left foreground.

Canvas, relined 45 × 55

Relined in 1878 by Vallance. There are retouchings on the walls above the man's head, above the door on the left and by the hat on the chair. A *pentimento* shows the maid's right foot was redrawn. The varnish is discoloured.

Mabille de Poncheville described the subject as the unexpected visit of a lady to her lover whom she finds writing to her; she appears from behind the *paravent* as if saying *'ce n'est pas un rêve, c'est bien moi'*.[1] The subject was devised by the marquis de Villefranche (see below).

A label attached to the back of the stretcher reads: *Visitte Rendue/peint par Louis Boilly en 1789*.[2] The same hand wrote the label on the back of P479 and has been identified as that of Calvet de Lapalun of Avignon who commissioned eleven *galant* genre scenes from Boilly in 1789–92.[3] The first four subjects (which include P473 and P479) were devised by Alexandre Tulle, marquis de Villefranche (b.1741), then living at Saint-Denis and acting as intermediary between Lapalun and Boilly; the remaining seven were devised by Lapalun himself. This curious episode of provincial patronage has recently been studied by Hallam,[4] who published Lapalun's *'Rôle des tableaux de Boilly'* listing his commissions chronologically. P473 and P479 appear as:

> *2 La visite rendue, inventée par M. de Tulle, peint par Louis Boilly, 1789.* (see note 6 below).
> *4 Les malheurs de l'amour, inventé par M. de Tulle, peint par Louis Boilly en 1790.*

Hallam suggests that P473 formed the pendant to *La visite reçue* (see note 3) which shows a girl entertaining a soldier and secretly sending off a letter, probably to the gentleman she visits in P473. Lapalun's Boillys were otherwise unrelated, except for their general concern with gallantry.

The bureau[5] and fire-place in P473 recur in *La famille Gohin* of 1787 (Musée des Arts Décoratifs), the red drapery in P435, and the fire-place and the two female models in P479.

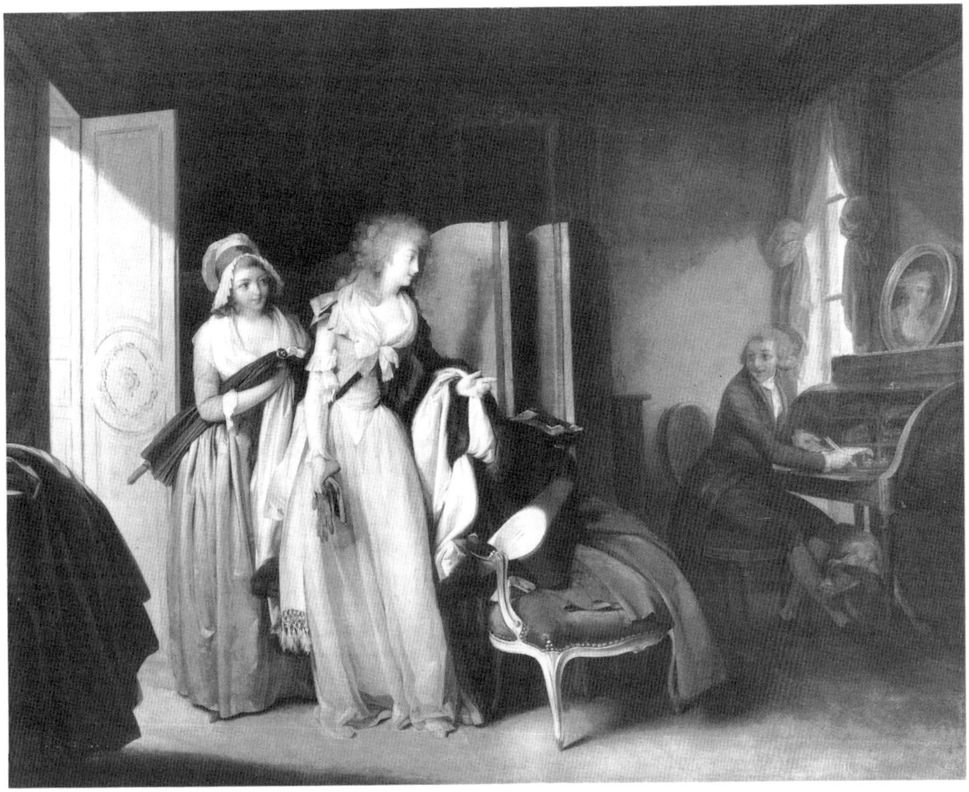

P473

Engraving

See Provenance.

Provenance

With P479: A.-J.-F.-X. Calvet de Lapalun (1736–1820), Avignon;[6] Robert Voisin, *receveur général*, Maine-et-Loire; his sale, Angers, 27 July 1863 (270, '*La visite rendue, Les chagrins de l'amour, ces deux toiles sont gravées et forment pendants. Bordures en bois sculptés et dorés*'), bt. by the 4th Marquess of Hertford, 2,100 fr.; Bagatelle inventory 1871 (942, '*la mauvaise nouvelle*'; 943, '*la visite*'); Hertford House inventory 1890.

Exhibition

Bethnal Green 1872–5 (492).

Reference General

Harrisse, no.565.

[1] A. Mabille de Poncheville, *Boilly*, 1931, p.25.

[2] Part of the label (the top right-hand corner) has been neatly cut away; conceivably it related to that on P479, q.v.

[3] Apart from P473 and P479, these were:

date	price	size	Title (location) Harrisse no.
1789	gift	45 × 55	*La visite reçue* (Saint-Omer) 564
1790	–	–	*Le moraliste* (–) –
1790	390	45 × 55	*Le concert improvisé* (Saint-Omer) 139
1790	336	45 × 55	*Ce qui allume l'amour l'éteint* (Saint-Omer) 117
1790	350	50 × 65	*Le retour de l'infidèle* (coll. Portalis 1952) 475
1791	330	44 × 55	*Le vieillard jaloux* (Saint-Omer) 553
1791	320	64 × 53	*Les avis maternels* (coll. de Bozas 1930) 143
1791	320	45 × 58	*La mère philosophique* (coll. Dadvisard 1930) –
1792	320	64 × 53	*L'amant constant* (coll. de Bozas 1930) 57

[4] J.S. Hallam, 'Boilly et Calvet de Lapalun, ou la sensibilité chez le peintre et l'amateur', BSHAF 1984, pp.177–92. His account largely supplants that by the baron Joseph du Teil, *Les Arts*, 76, July 1907, pp.22–32, although the latter had access to Boilly's account books. Lapalun left Avignon for England in 1793 but returned in 1795.

[5] Perhaps adapted from the '*secrétaire en acajou à cylindre garni de deux tiroirs par le bas et d'une bibliothèque vitrée par le haut*' listed in the *inventaire après décès* of Boilly's first wife, 13–17 June 1795 (BSHAF 1929, p.22).

[6] Lapalun paid Boilly 318 fr. for P479 in 1790; his accounts for 1798 are lost (cf. du Teil, *op. cit.*, p.22), but Hallam, *op. cit.*, p.188 n.7, (quoting P. de Guilhermier 'Les Calvet de Lapalun', *Mémoires de l'académie de Vaucluse*, 5e, VIII, 1959–60, pp.104–5) says P473 was given to Lapalun by Tulle, like *La visite reçue* – the first two Boillys of the series.

P479 *The Sorrows of Love*

The swooning lady has a yellow satin skirt, white blouse and powdered hair; her knitting is thrown on the floor; her companion wears a silk *gorge de pigeon* skirt, a taffeta redingote and her hair is unpowdered; the departing servant on the left has a russet coat and blue-grey breeches, the maid a black shawl and brown skirt; on the mantelpiece a clock with the figure of Psyche.

Canvas, relined 45 × 55

Relined in 1878 by Vallance. There are minor retouchings on the wall in the centre and to the left. *Pentimenti* show the swooning lady's right foot and her maid's right hand were redrawn. The varnish is much discoloured.

The lady's portrait is returned by her lover with a letter of adieu.[1]

A label attached to the back of the stretcher reads: *Les malheurs de l'amour. inventé par/M. de T[u]lle peint par Louis Boilly/en 1790*, for which see P473. The models for the two ladies on the right-hand side appear to be those used in P473; the furnishings include the chair and guitar seen in P435 (and see P435 note 6), and the fire-place from P473 and *La famille Gohin* of 1787 (Musée des Arts Décoratifs) which also shows the work box seen on the floor to the right in P479.

Engraving, Provenance

See P473.

Exhibition

Bethnal Green 1872–5 (500).

Reference General

Harrisse, no.375.

[1] Cf. A. Mabille de Poncheville, *Boilly*, 1931, p.26; previous editions of this catalogue have suggested the letter was from the lady and is being returned unopened and torn; either reading is possible.

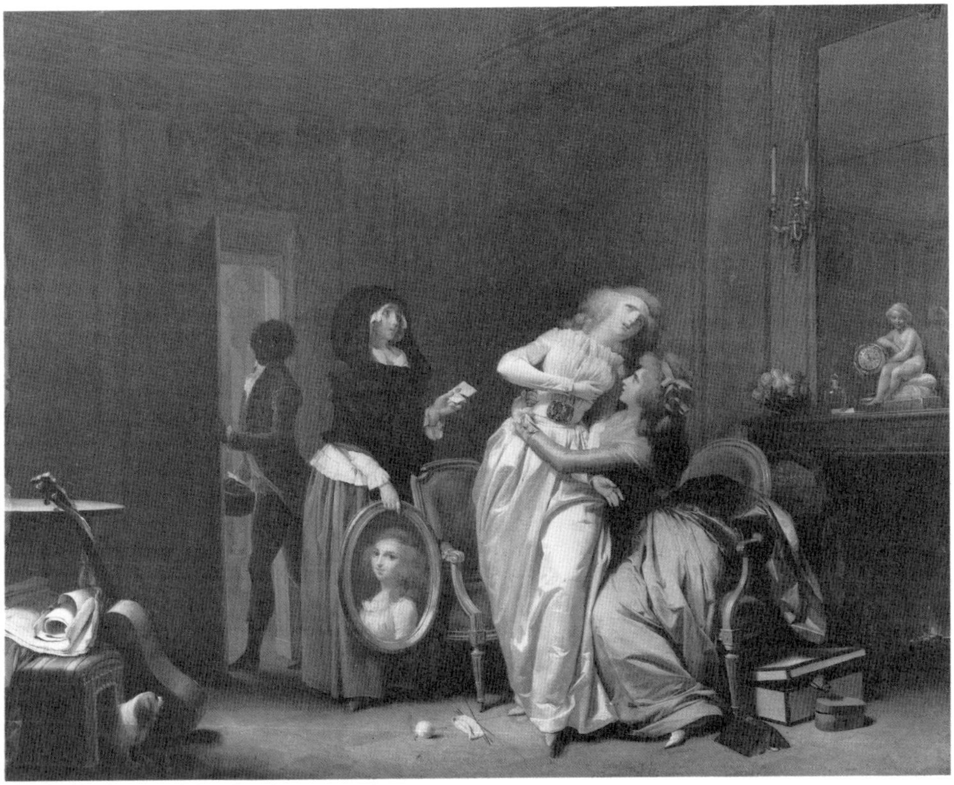

P479

François Boucher (1703–1770)

Born on 29 September 1703 in Paris, the son of a minor painter, Nicolas, by whom he was probably first taught. He studied briefly under François Lemoyne before winning the *prix de Rome* at the Académie in 1723 (*Evilmerodach and Joachim*; unlocated[1]), but there was then no place for him at Rome. Until 1728 he worked for J.-F. Cars, providing drawings for engraving, and made etchings after Watteau for Jean de Jullienne, continuing meanwhile to paint small historical and religious pictures. In 1728 he went to Rome, probably at his own expense, with Carle, Louis-Michel and François van Loo; Vleughels, Director of the Académie de France, found him modest quarters. Although not in good health, he seems to have looked at works by Reni, Albani, Cortona, Correggio and Sebastiano Ricci, and he made a number of landscape drawings (in 1735 he was to publish twelve etchings of figures after Abraham Bloemaert, *Le livre d'étude*). He was in Paris in 1731 when he was *agréé*, and his *morceau de réception, Rinaldo and Armida* (Louvre) was accepted in January 1734. In 1735 he was made *adjoint à professeur* and in 1737 *professeur*. His industry and facility rapidly brought him success, at home and abroad. His first commission from the Crown, paintings for the *chambre de la Reine* at Versailles in 1735, was followed by others for Versailles (between 1736 and 1756), Fontainebleau (1737–53), the *Bibliothèque du Roi* (1741–46), Choisy (1741–7) and La Muette (1748–9). His first tapestry designs were made in 1736 for Beauvais, whose output he dominated over the next twenty-five years, and he provided stage designs for the Opéra (1737–9, 1743–8). By 1750 he was painting for Madame de Pompadour (see P418) whose lavish patronage enhanced his later career. He continued to supply stage designs for the Opéra and Opéra-comique and his work inspired porcelain figure groups for the Vincennes and Sèvres factories, 1749–56. On the death of Oudry in 1755 he became *inspecteur* at the Gobelins. Although in his later years his work was less vigorous and attracted some criticism at the Salon (essentially for its profligacy), his official career was unimpeded. At the Académie he was made *adjoint à recteur* in 1752, *recteur* in 1761 and Director in 1765 (a post he resigned in 1768). In 1765 he was appointed *premier peintre du Roi*. He visited the Netherlands with Randon de Boisset in 1766. He exhibited at the Salon between 1737 and 1769 (excluding 1741, 1744, 1749, 1751, 1755 and 1767), and died in Paris on 30 May 1770. His collections, which included all kinds of curiosities,[2] were sold in Paris from 18 February 1771.

[1] Previously mistakenly identified with the *Joseph presenting his Father to Pharaoh* (Columbia), but see Laing, no. 5.

[2] When Horace Walpole saw Boucher's collection (24 February 1766) he remarked upon 'great quantities of shells, mosses, Japan, china, vases, Indian arms and music, etc.' (Walpole, *Correspondence*, VII, 1939, p.304).

Abbreviations

A	A. Ananoff, *François Boucher*, 2 vols., 1976 (A numbers refer to the catalogue, A doc. numbers to the documents in vol. I)
AD	A. Ananoff, *L'oeuvre dessiné de François Boucher*, I, 1966
cdA	A. Ananoff, *L'opera completa di Boucher*, 1980 (*Classici dell'Arte*)
JR	P. Jean-Richard, *L'oeuvre gravé de François Boucher dans la collection Edmond de Rothschild* (Musée du Louvre, inventaire général des gravures, Ecole française, I), 1978
Laing	A. Laing *et al.*, *François Boucher*, exhibition catalogue, New York, Detroit, Paris, 1986–7 (English ed.)
Slatkin 1973	R. S. Slatkin, *François Boucher in North American Collections: 100 Drawings*, exhibition catalogue, Washington, Chicago, 1973–4
SM	L. Soullié and Ch. Masson, *Catalogue raisonné de l'oeuvre peint et dessiné de François Boucher*, in A. Michel, *François Boucher*, 1906

P385 *Daphnis and Chloe (Shepherd watching a sleeping Shepherdess)*

The shepherd has red and gold drapery, the shepherdess blue and white. Signed, below right: *f. Boucher / 174* [*3* or *5*].

Canvas, relined 109.5 × 154.8 with rounded corners

Restored and partially cleaned by Vallance in 1965 when the spandrels, formed by the rectangular relining canvas, were painted flat grey. There are several discoloured retouchings, most noticeably in the landscape above the shepherd's right arm, in the craquelure on the shepherdess's flesh, in the tower and bushes on the right, and in the trees above the sheep on the left. The sky is disfigured by unevenly discoloured varnish.

The shepherdess's sandals, the draperies, the shepherd's pan-pipes and the Italianate buildings indicate a classical subject which may be identified in Longus, *Daphnis and Chloe*, the pastoral romance of two foundlings (who turn out to be from noble families):

> Once when he was playing his pipe in the middle of the day and the flocks were lying in the shade, Chloe fell asleep without realizing it. Noticing this, Daphnis put down his pipe and . . . began to gaze insatiably at every part of her (I, 25)[1]

Boucher has added the dog. *Daphnis and Chloe* was a popular subject at this time; between 1737 and 1745 Jeaurat showed six scenes from it at the Salon, and Natoire one. See also P2 attributed to G. B. Bertucci.

The figure composition is based on a seventeenth-century Italian bronze statuette (last recorded in 1912),[2] though a study for the sleeping shepherdess is known (see Drawings). The distant tower recurs in many Boucher landscapes from the late 1730s onwards (cf. P431, P447, P489), while the trees on the left are particularly reminiscent of Pynacker.[3]

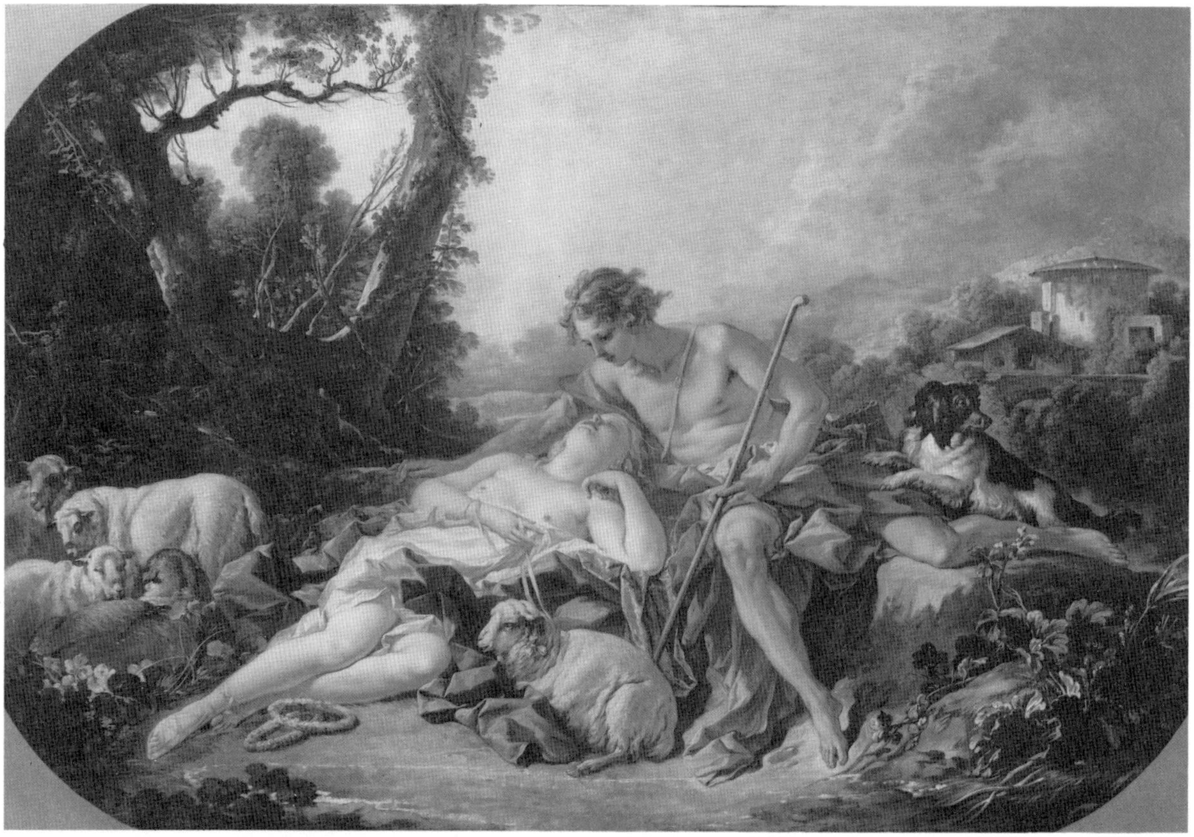

P385

Drawings

PARIS H. D. sale, 31 March 1943 (1); compositional study with the shepherd's crook on the ground and differences in the landscape (AD216; A292/2, fig.850).

A study for the sleeping shepherdess was engr. L.-M. Bonnet as *La dormeuse* (JR382).

Version

An upright version of the composition appears in the background of *Le blasphème surprenant* by A. Landini (1847–1911), sold Sotheby's, Torquay, 14 October 1981.

Provenance

Koucheleff-Bezborodko collection, St. Petersburg;[4] c.1865–9, bt. by the 4th Marquess of Hertford;[5] possibly Bagatelle inventory 1871 (927, as one of '*Boucher, quatre panneaux de décoration*', with P399, P481, and P490); Hertford House inventory 1890.

Exhibition

Bethnal Green 1872–5 (396).

References General

A292; CdA303; Laing, p.223, and *Revue de l'Art*, 73, 1986, p.60.

[1] Trans. P. Turner, 1956.

[2] Illus. W. Bode, *The Italian Bronze Statuettes of the Renaissance*, III, 1912, p.13 as with Durlacher. A. Radcliffe (letter on file dated 30 March 1987), judging from this illustration, considers the bronze to be mid or second half seventeenth century, possibly by Francesco Fanelli (fl. 1609–c.1665). Laing, p.224, plausibly suggests that Boucher may also have been quoting a seventeenth-century bronze figure in the *Retour de chasse de Diane* of 1745 (for which see P445).

[3] Boucher owned at least one landscape by Pynacker, cf. Boucher sale, Paris, 18 February 1781 (20, 31).

[4] The seal of Koucheleff-Bezborodko was identified on the stretcher of P385 by A. van de Put in 1915; see P399 note 6.

[5] See P399 note 7.

P399 *Shepherd piping to a Shepherdess*

The shepherdess wears a white satin dress with red panels and a blue-laced blouse; the shepherd a yellow shirt with white cuffs, blue-grey jacket and red breeches.

Canvas, relined 94 × 142 *chantourné*

The original canvas was made up to a rectangle at the time of relining. A vertical seam 24 cm. from the right-hand edge has been retouched. There is a pronounced craquelure by the shepherdess's feet, and the varnish is discoloured.

The subject, a sentimental scene with bare-footed, elegant rustics, reflects Boucher's close involvement with the contemporary *pantomimes* by his friend C.-S. Favart, which combined the sensibilities of pastoral poetry with the rustic characters of popular theatre.[1] Boucher is known to have taken some of his subjects from Favart's *Vendanges de Tempé* (first performed in 1745);[2] scene v opened with the Little Shepherd playing his flute to Lisette,[3] and may have been the source of P399. See also P431, P482 and P489.

P399 may be dated c.1747–50. The subject first appears in *Le joueur de flageolet* of 1746 (sold Palais Galliera, 17 June 1977; Laing, p.236), and the costumes compare with those in the two versions of *Pensent-ils au raisin?* (another scene from the *Vendanges de Tempé*) which Boucher painted in 1747 and 1749 (see P482). The figure of the shepherdess recurs, reversed, in J. Huquier's engraving after Boucher, *La bergère assise* (JR 1157). Although the shaped canvas of P399 would indicate that it was part of a decorative scheme, no companion piece is recorded; previous editions of this catalogue associated it with P385 (see above) but, though they apparently share the same provenance, they match neither in size nor subject.

Copy

PARIS art market 1976; 88 × 150, showing slight variations and the composition reduced on the right-hand side; ex coll. Barrieutort (A283/3).

Provenance

The comte du Barry (1749–78); his sale, Paris, 21 November 1774 (90, '*un tableau agréable & du bon temps de ce Maître, il représente une pastorale composée d'un berger assis qui joue du flageolet à côté de sa Bergère qui tient de la main droite une couronne & de la gauche un panier de fleurs; dans le coin à gauche un grouppe de moutons* . . . [94.8 × 140.8]'), bt. Villetaneuse, 600 *livres*;[4] anon. sale, Paris, 14–16 April 1784 (75, '...*de la vente de M. le comte du Barry, no.90 de notre catalogue*'), bt. Constantin, 321 *livres*; probably de Polonceau sale, Paris, 26 February 1787 (10);[5] de Crisenoy sale, Paris, 29–31 March 1841 (63, '*assise devant un massif d'arbres, une jeune et fraîche bergère, un panier d'une main, une couronne de l'autre, s'appuie légèrement sur son berger, couché à côté d'elle, et occupé à jouer de la flute* . . . *92 × 140 cm.*'); Koucheleff-Bezborodko collection, St. Petersburg;[6] c.1865–9, bt. by the 4th Marquess of Hertford;[7] possibly Bagatelle inventory 1871 (927, as one of '*Boucher, quatre panneaux de décoration*', with P385, P481 and P490); Hertford House inventory 1890.[8]

Exhibition

Bethnal Green 1872–5 (387).

References General

SM 1499; A283; cdA293.

[1] This association has been discussed at length by Laing, pp.67–72, 223, 233–6, and *Revue de l'Art*, 73, 1986, pp.55–64. See also H. Lemonnier, *L'art moderne: Essais et esquisses*, 1912, pp.215–31, and G. Zick, *Keramos*, 29, 1965, pp.3–47.

[2] Cf. F. et C. Parfaict, *Dictionnaire des Théâtres de Paris*, 1756, VI, p.70: '*M. Boucher, fameux par ses compositions gracieuses, en emprunta l'idée de quelques-uns de ses tableaux, & ce n'est point le moindre honneur qu'ait reçu la* Pantomime *des* Vendanges de Tempé'.

[3] Cf. Laing, p.236.

[4] P399 is identified by a Saint-Aubin drawing in the margin of a copy of this sale catalogue (A283/1, fig.838, and see E. Dacier, *Catalogues de ventes et livrets de Salons illustrés et annotés par Gabriel de Saint-Aubin*, III, 1910).

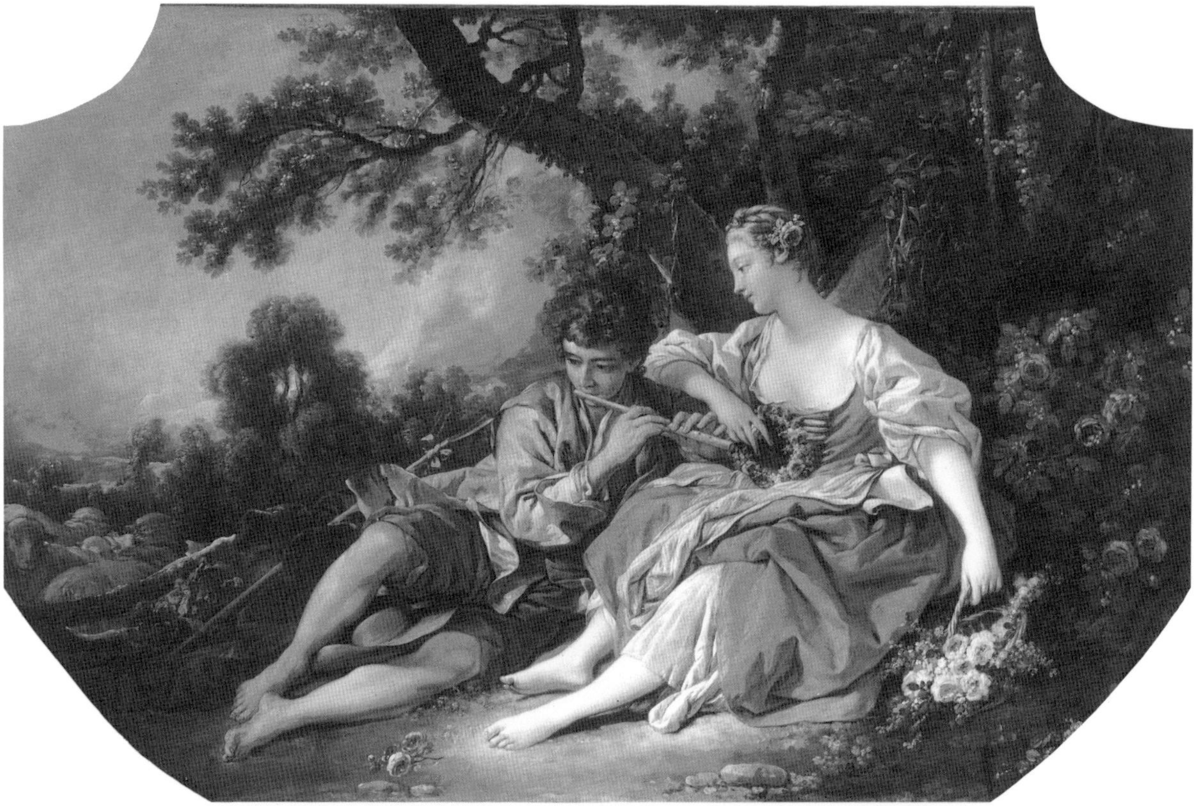

P399

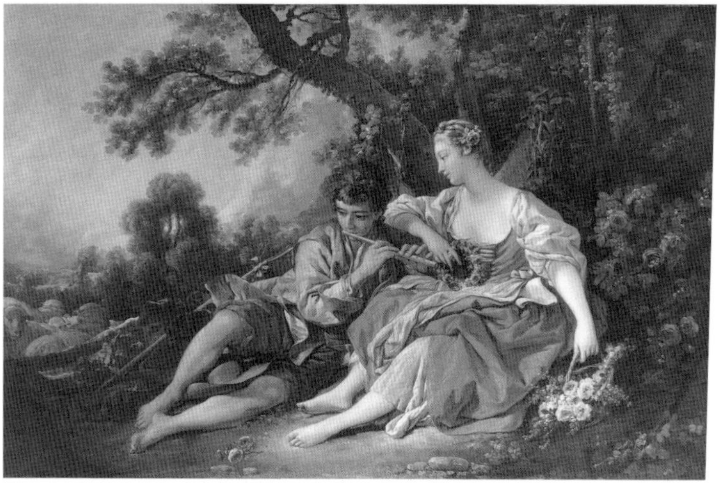

P399 with additions

[5] *'Un paysage agréable, sur le premier plan duquel est une bergère assise et son berger près d'elle qui joue du flageolet . . . proportion de petite nature H. 35p.; L.52p.'*, i.e. the same size as that given in the du Barry sale catalogue, 1774. Ananoff associates the de Polonceau sale entry with *L'aubade à la bergère* (A284) but it probably describes P399 as Laing has suggested (letter on file dated 20 May 1987).

[6] The seal of Koucheleff-Bezborodko was identified on the stretcher of P399 by A. van de Put in 1915 (cf. P385). This collection was formed by the comte Alexandre Andreevich Bezborodko (1742–99) and expanded by his great-nephew, Alexandre Grigorevich Koucheleff (1800–c.1862) and his son, Nicolas (1832–62); his second son, Grigory, sold some of the collection in London and Paris in 1869 (cf. Vernet P135; see F. Lugt, *Marques de Collections*, 1921, p.294). Other parts of the collection were being sold in St. Petersburg in 1865 and 1867, see note 7 below.

[7] P399 (and P385) could have been bought in either St. Petersburg or London. Notes in the Wallace Collection archives show that the dealer Frederick Davis was buying from the Koucheleff-Bezborodko collection (with Hertford's connivance) in 1865, and there are three receipted bills from comtesse Katherine Koucheleff at St. Petersburg to Richard Wallace: for 28,860 roubles on 28 July 1867, 23,116 roubles on 30 September 1867, and 1,000 roubles on 21 October 1867; only the second concerned pictures, mentioning works by Fragonard, van Loo and Watteau (see Fragonard P379, Lancret P448 and C.A. van Loo P451) and none mentioned Boucher. The comtesse Katherine Koucheleff (*née* Vasilt-chikov; b.1811) had m. the comte Grigory Grigorevich Koucheleff-Bezborodko (1802–55); I am grateful to Mark Everitt and John Simmons for this identification.

[8] Ananoff associated P399 with the Rossi sale, Paris, 26–7 March 1847 (39), but the description (*'Bergères assises tressant des couronnes: près d'elles un berger jouant de la flûte'*) does not agree.

P411 *Venus and Cupid*

Venus has a blue ribbon in her hair, pink drapery and a pink rose in her hand; there is a pale green drape behind her; Cupid proffers a golden apple.

Canvas, relined 79.2 × 139 curved top and bottom edges[1]

An inscription, *Boucher/1754*, bottom left, was found to be an addition and was removed during cleaning by Lank in 1987. The original canvas was made up to a rectangle, 82.5 × 139.5, in the course of relining in the nineteenth century. There are losses in the sky, upper right. *Pentimenti* show that the lower left drapery, the two doves and Venus's left shoulder and left leg were redrawn.

For the subject cf. P444 and Charlier P474.

Pendant to P423. Though some areas, notably Cupid's head, the doves and Venus's flesh, display a heavy touch (contrasting with the finish of P423), P411 is perhaps an autograph, if pedestrian, work. The original shapes of both canvases would indicate they were conceived as part of a decorative scheme.

Version

Vénus caressée par l'Amour, engr. L.-M. Bonnet after a drawing by Boucher (JR386), showing Venus holding Cupid with her right arm and without the doves.[2]

Provenance

With P423: probably acquired by Sir Richard Wallace; Hertford House inventory 1890.

References General

A433; cdA454.

[1] The stretcher is inscribed in chalk, *verso*: *M Pauck*[?], and numbered *2* (in chalk) and *33* (in red paint).

[2] An engraver's drawing for this plate was published by Slatkin, *Master Drawings*, x, 3, 1972, pl.33b.

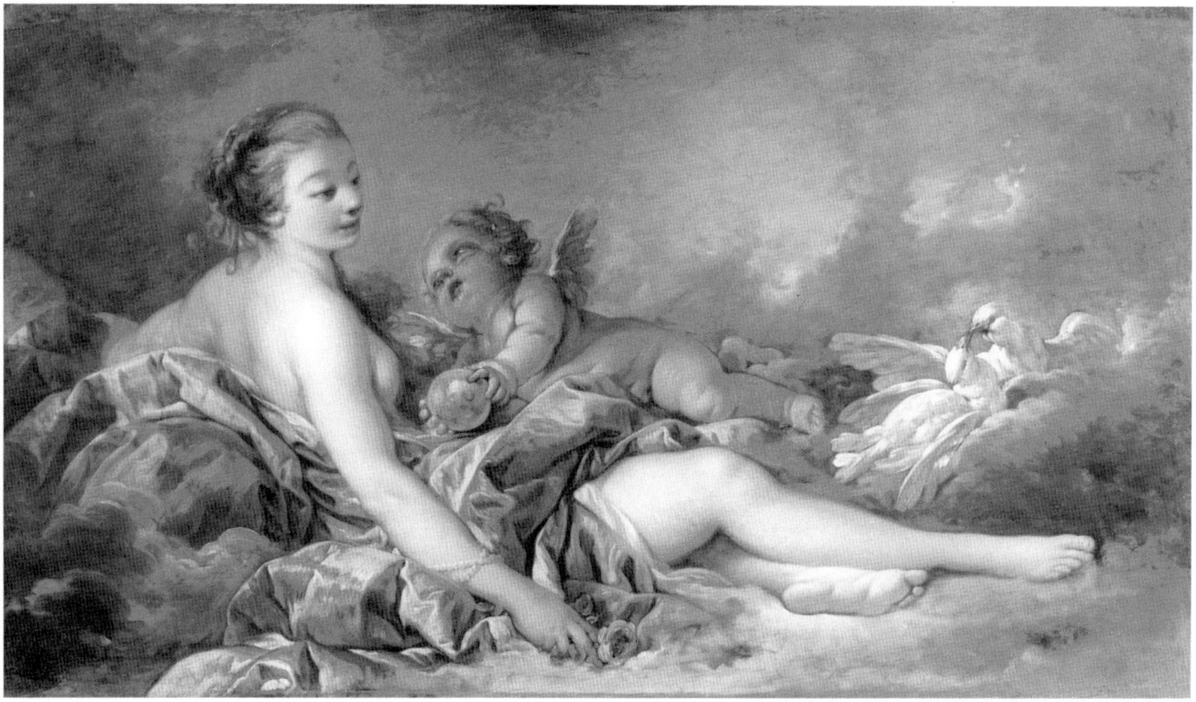

P411

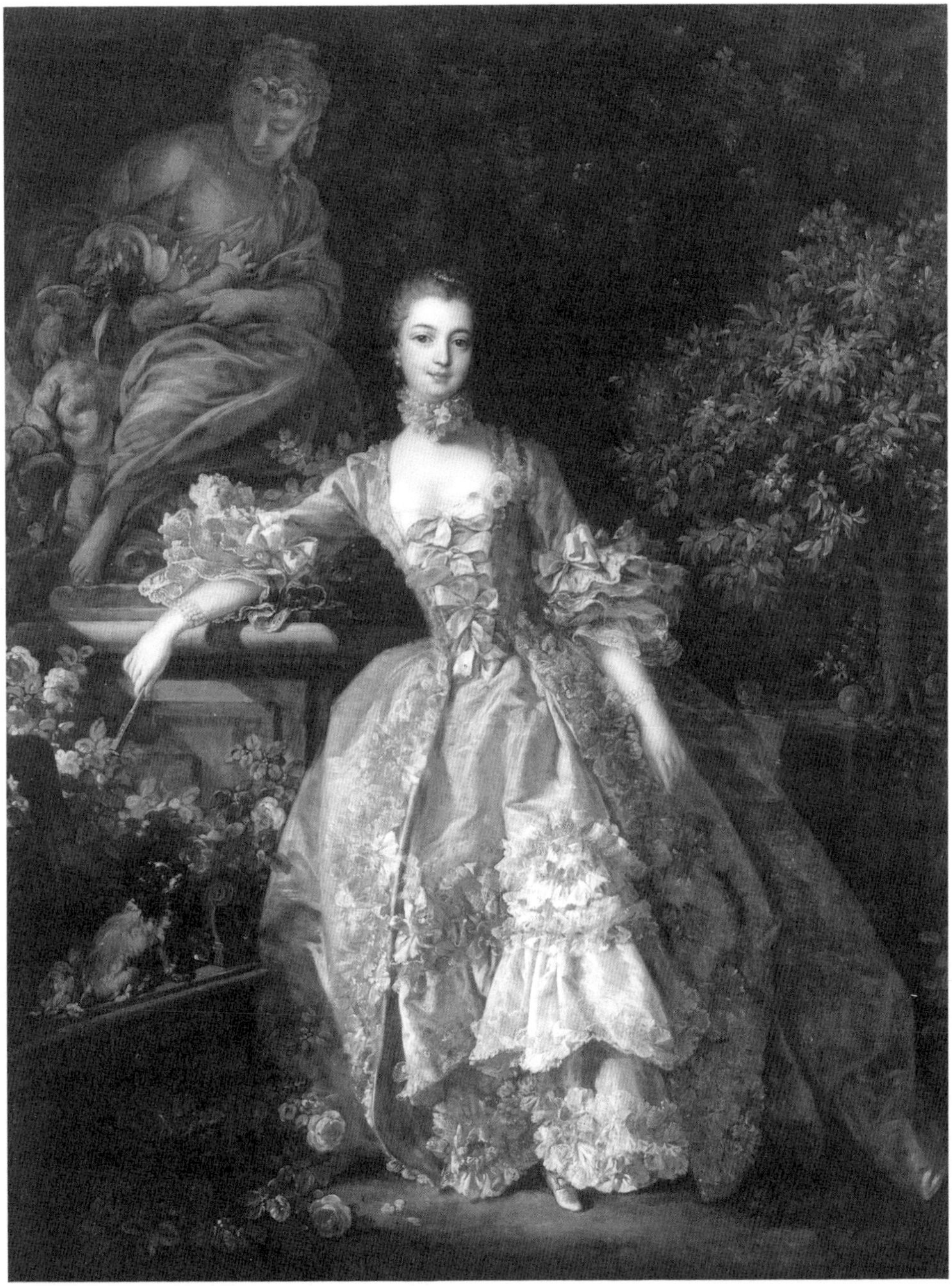

P418

P418 *Madame de Pompadour*

Powdered hair, blue eyes, wearing a *gris-rosé* taffeta dress, a rose in her corsage; a black and white spaniel sits on the green bench. Signed, bottom left: *F. Boucher 1759.*

Canvas, relined 91 × 68

Relined and heavily ironed by W. Morrill after 1870.[1] Cleaned by Lank in 1981. A horizontal seam 2.5 cm. below the top edge (touching the head of the sculpture) has been retouched and there are losses either side. Further losses appear by the right arm of the woman in the sculpture and to the right of the dog's head, lower left; minor losses occur by Pompadour's left arm, in the tub on the right and in the forehead of the woman in the sculpture. The paint on the left and right of the skirt is thin, revealing flowers and foliage painted beneath. Other *pentimenti* show that Pompadour's left hand was originally open, the left-hand ball on the tub was moved slightly to the left, and the sculpture was painted over trees and foliage.

Jeanne-Antoinette Poisson (1721–64), m. 1741 Ch.-G.-B. Le Normant d'Etioles (nephew of M. de Tournehem) by whom she bore Guillaume-Charles (d. in infancy 1741) and Alexandrine (1743–54); cr. 1745 marquise de Pompadour and *maîtresse en titre* to Louis XV; in 1752 accorded the privileges, but not the title of duchesse. Her brother, the marquis de Marigny, succeeded de Tournehem as *directeur des Bâtiments* in 1751. Her lavish patronage of the arts followed the rococo fashion, and for the diversion of the King she created a series of richly decorated and furnished interiors in her châteaux at Crécy (1746), Champs (1747) and Bellevue (1748–50), and in the Hôtel d'Evreux (1753) in Paris. Her vital interest in the Sèvres factory[2] and her extensive patronage of Boucher (see P485, P486) were amongst her greatest enthusiasms. She exhibited a talent for private theatricals and, taught by Cochin and Boucher, became an engraver of some ability.[3] The 1st Marquess of Hertford, who began The Wallace Collection, met her in Paris in 1763 and found her 'most polite and obliging, with a great deal more sense and conversation than I expected'.[4]

After 1750, when he painted the *Lumière du monde* (Lyon; A340) for her private chapel at Bellevue, Boucher became Mme. de Pompadour's most favoured painter, a privilege facilitated by their shared enthusiasm for the decorative arts and a certain affinity of temperament.[5] Boucher was not an instinctive portrait painter, but of the twelve he certainly painted (all between 1743 and 1759), seven were of Mme. de Pompadour.[6] She described the earliest, in 1750, as '*tres-jolis, mais peu ressemblens*',[7] although her bland beauty, as described by contemporaries, was not, perhaps, easily translated:

> *d'une taille au-dessus de l'ordinaire, svelte, aisée, souple, élégante; son visage étoit bien assorti à sa taille, un ovale parfait, de beaux cheveux plutôt châtain clair que blonds, des yeux assez grands, ornés de beaux sourcils de la même couleur, le nez parfaitement bien formé, la bouche charmante, . . . la plus belle peau du monde donnoit à tous ses traits le plus grand éclat. Ses yeux avoient un charme particulier, qu'ils devoient peut-être à l'incertitude de leur couleur; . . . l'ensemble de sa personne sembloit faire la nuance entre le dernier degré de l'élégance et le premier de la noblesse.*[8]

Portraits of her by Carle van Loo (1754) and Drouais (1764), whose likenesses were admired by contemporaries,[9] do not obviously resemble Boucher's.

P418, probably the last portrait Boucher painted of Mme. de Pompadour,[10] recalls the elegant small portraits of Caspar Netscher. The setting recalls the bosquets at Bellevue, where '*des roses, des jasmins, des orangers mêmes . . . semblent sortir du sein de la terre*';[11] the painted garden seat may be identified in the Pompadour *inventaire*;[12] the King Charles spaniel appears to be Inès, whose portrait by Huet was engraved in 1756 by Fessard and Saint-Aubin as *la Fidelité*; the sculpture, clearly portraying Friendship consoling Love, seems a deliberate evocation of Pigalle's *l'Amour et l'Amitié*, completed for Mme. de Pompadour in 1758 and regarded as an expression of the platonic relationship which latterly prevailed between the King and his *maîtresse en titre*.[13] Its presence in this richly contrived Arcadia, together with the carefully posed solitary elegance of Mme. de Pompadour, lends the portrait a certain pathos.

Copies

PARIS private collection 1972; 130 × 100, omitting the bench, dog and orange tree.
A drawing, inscribed *1745*, was in an English private collection 1974.

Provenance

Mme. de Pompadour, probably at Versailles;[14] her brother, the marquis de Marigny (1727–81); his sale, Paris, 18 March–6 April 1782 (25, '*Boucher, Le Portrait d'une Dame en pied, vêtue d'une robe de taffetas garnie de gaze; elle est dans un bosquet, le bras droit appuyé sur un piedestal qui porte une figure de femme assise, & arrêtant l'Amour qui veut l'embrasser, toile* [97 × 65]'), bt. by the duc de Chaulnes (1741–93),[15] 154 *livres*; anon. sale, Paris, 19 April 1869 (1, and only lot, identified as no. 25 in the Marigny sale), bt. by the 4th Marquess of Hertford, 15,000 fr.; rue Laffitte inventory 1871 (363); Hertford House inventory 1890.

Exhibition

Bethnal Green 1872–5 (470).

References General

SM1065; A522; CdA549.

1 The stretcher is stamped, *verso*: W. MORRILL; he is recorded in London from 1866.

2 In the Wallace Collection a garniture of three vases (C248–50) and a tea service (C401–6) come from her collection of Sèvres porcelain.

3 She made 70 plates, bearing dates between 1751 and 1759; see A. de la Fizelière, *Gazette des Beaux-Arts*, 1ère, III, 1859, pp.139–51; E. and J. de Goncourt, *Madame de Pompadour*, 1888, pp.365–91; JR1478–1514.

4 Hertford to Walpole, Paris, 28 October 1763 (Walpole, *Correspondence*, XXXVIII, 1974, p.218).

5 Cf. P. Nolhac, *Boucher*, 1925, pp.109–10: '*L'artiste et la grande dame improvisée sont également brillants, pimpants, admirés; . . . La petite bourgeoise, élevée dans un milieu de traitants et de banquiers du Roi, . . . restera avide, avant tout, de luxe et d'hommages; . . . Le peintre . . . ambitieux, ardent à réussir, cherchant le succès par une audacieuse flatterie du public . . .*'.

6 His other sitters were his wife (1743; A263), Mme. Bergeret (1746; A301), Philippe-Egalité as a child (1749; A332) and Mme. Sireul (1754; A427). His other portraits of the Pompadour are:
1750 60 × 45, sketch, whole-length standing in an interior (Louvre; Laing, no.59, proposed this dating, see note 7 below)
62 × 46, sketch, similar to above (English private coll.: A520)
1756 201 × 157, Salon 1757, whole-length seated in an interior (on loan to Munich; A475; a signed replica of 1758 is in a Swiss private coll.; A504)
1758 81 × 63, half-length seated at her dressing table (Fogg Art Museum; A497)
72 × 57, whole-length seated in a landscape (Victoria and Albert Museum; A496)
There is an element of doubt concerning the identity of the portrait in the Portland Art Museum (A334 as 1749) and concerning the original of Watson's mezzotint of Pompadour (A592 as 1764).
A fine pastel head of the Pompadour by Boucher, signed and dated 1754, is in the National Gallery of Victoria, Melbourne (no.1482.5; illus. A, I, p.101, fig. 143).

7 *Correspondance de Mme de Pompadour*, 1878, p.55; Pompadour to her brother in Rome, 28 April 1750. She had earlier told him (26 April): '*Je vous envoye enfin la copie de mon portrait de Boucher; elle ressemble beaucoup à l'original, peu à moi; cependant assez agréable*' (*ibid.*, p.50).

8 *Portrait de Mme. de Pompadour* by Ch.-G. Leroy (1723–89), quoted in *Correspondance de Mme de Pompadour*, 1878, pp.xxv–xxvi (and Goncourt, *op. cit.*, p.10 n.4).

9 The van Loo portraits appear in *Sultanes travaillant à la tapisserie* and *Sultane prenant du café* (Hermitage; M.-C. Sahut, *Carle Vanloo*, 1977, nos.148–9); the likenesses were remarked upon at the 1755 Salon (Goncourt, *op. cit.*, p.332). The Drouais (National Gallery, London, no.6440) was described as a '*ressemblance . . . des plus frappantes*' by Bachaumont (*Mémoires secrets*, II, 1777, p.85).

10 See note 6 concerning an alleged Boucher portrait of 1764.

11 M.L.R., *Curiosités de Paris*, 1778, II, p.269.

[12] There were *'soixante bancs, tant à deux qu'à trois et quatre places, de bois de chesne, peint de verd'* at the Versailles *Ermitage* (J. Cordey, *Inventaire des biens de madame de Pompadour, rédigé après son décès*, 1939, p.105, no.1423); but a similar bench appears in Boucher's portrait of Mme. Bergeret (A301; see Laing, p.232).

[13] On 2 February 1751 d'Argenson recorded that Pompadour *'jure ses grands dieux qu'il n'y a plus que de l'amitié entre le roi et elle'* (*Journal et Mémoires*, VI, 1864, p.351). For the Pigalle sculpture, see S. Rocheblave, *Pigalle*, 1919, pp.192–4, and L. Réau, *Pigalle*, 1950, pp.153–4; see also K.K. Gordon, 'Madame de Pompadour, Pigalle and the Iconography of Friendship', *The Art Bulletin*, L, 1968, pp.249–62.

[14] P418 may perhaps be identified with *'un portrait de la ditte dame Pompadour, peint en petit par M. Boucher'* in her Versailles *appartement* (Cordey, *op. cit.*, p.92, no.1248–97).

[15] Marie-Joseph d'Albert d'Ailly, duc de Chaulnes, had been the intended husband for Pompadour's daughter, Alexandrine (cf. Goncourt, *op. cit.*, p.68).

P423 *Venus*

Reclining on turquoise and coral-pink draperies. Signed or inscribed, lower left: *Boucher/1754*.

Canvas, relined 79.2 × 138.7 curved top and bottom edges[1]

The original canvas was made up to a rectangle 82.5 × 139.5 in the course of relining in the nineteenth century. Cleaned by Lank in 1987. There are some losses round the left-hand *putto's* left hand, above his head, and in the green drapery below Venus's elbow and above her left thigh. *Pentimenti* show slight alterations to Venus's left arm and the drapery by her left hand.

Venus, goddess of love, with a dolphin, emblematic of her birth from the sea, and a burning torch and doves, emblematic of love.

Pendant to P411, q.v., P423 is in better condition and shows a higher degree of finish; it lacks vitality, however, and is a similarly pedestrian work.

Drawings

LONDON Sotheby's, 25 April 1978 (66); sheet with studies of hands, one of which appears to have been used for Venus's right hand in P423; ex coll. Daniels (Slatkin 1973, no.74; A501/1, fig.1396).

Le repos de Vénus, engr. L.-M. Bonnet after a drawing by Boucher (JR384), variant with doves instead of *putti*.[2]

Versions

PARIS anon. sale, 28 May 1931 (90); 20 × 27, variant without the dolphin (A434/3).

Provenance

See P411.

References General

A434; cdA455.

[1] The stretcher is inscribed in chalk, *verso*: *M Pauck*[?], and numbered *3* (in chalk) and *34* (in red paint).

[2] Slatkin published two drawings related to this plate, one by Boucher, the other an engraver's drawing (*Master Drawings*, X, 3, 1972, pl.35 and 34).

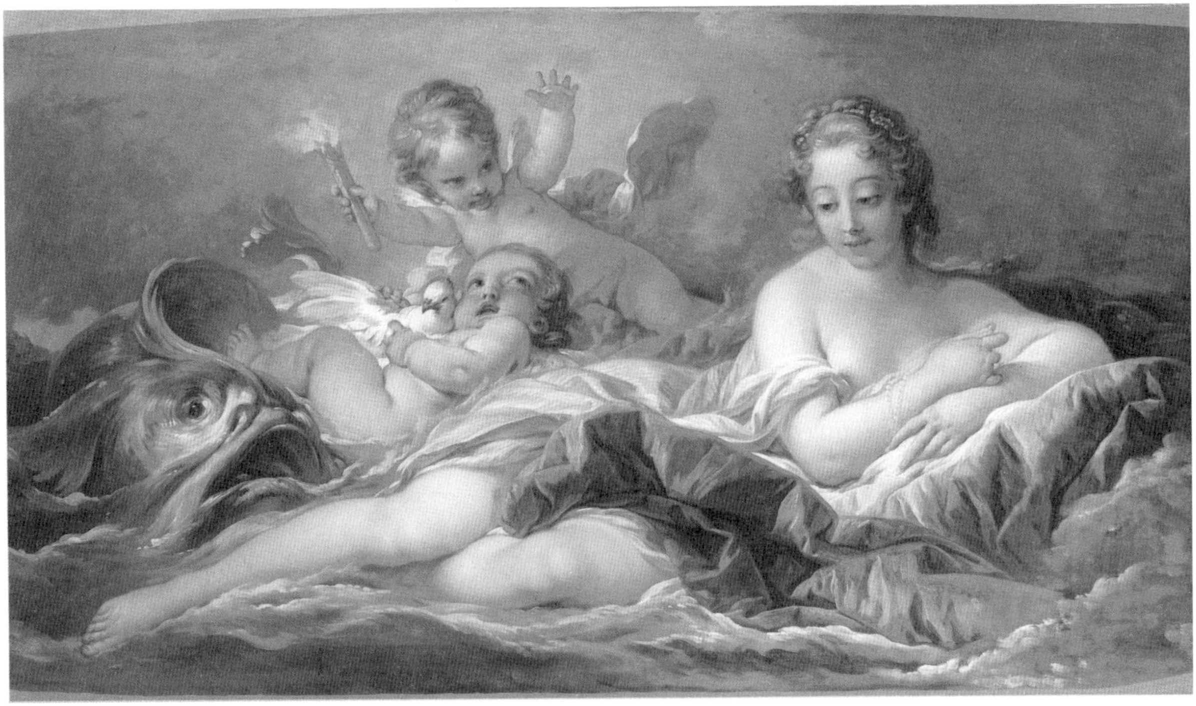

P423

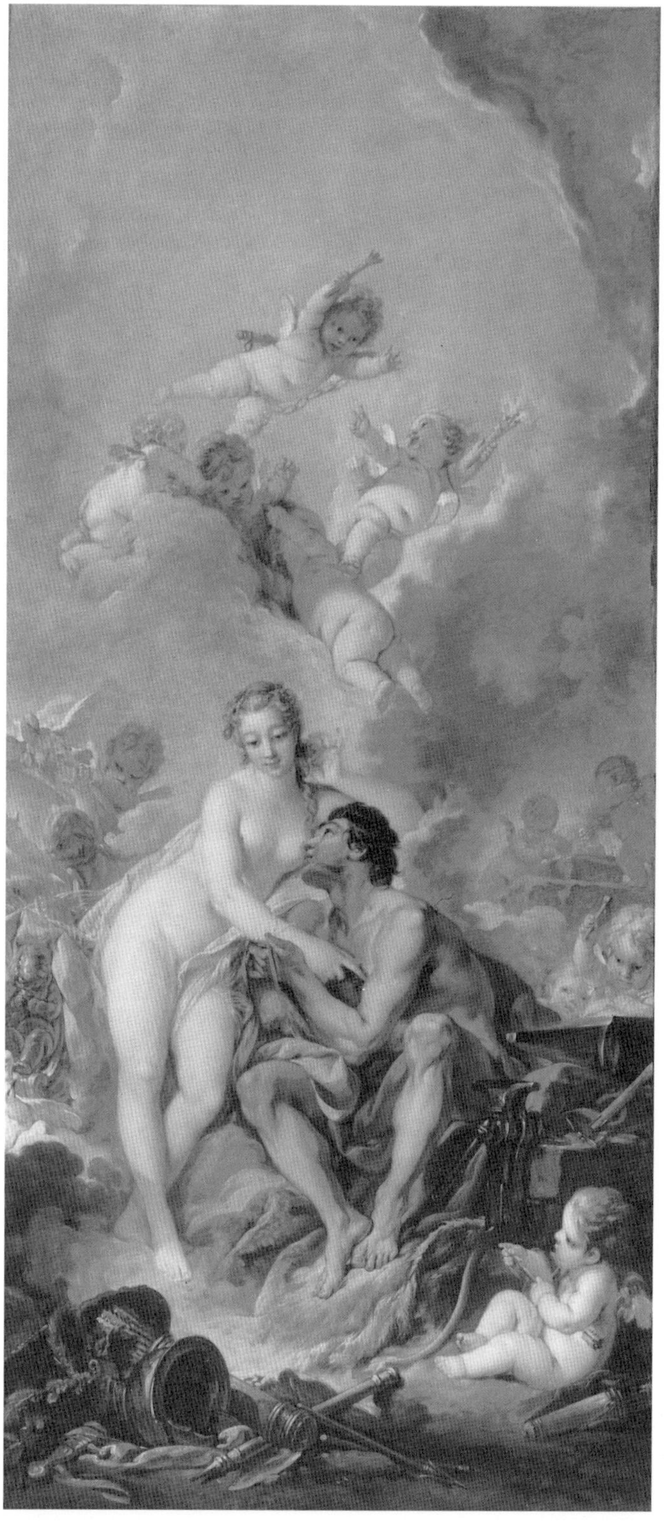

P429

P429 *Venus and Mars*

Mars has red drapery and holds a blue ribbon; Venus wears a satin-striped voile with a diaphanous green and yellow drapery, her hair dressed with pearls and a blue ribbon; on the left her chariot; in the foreground the helmet has a rich blue plume and the quiver is red. Signed, bottom right: *f. Boucher/1754.*

Canvas, relined 164.5 × 71.5

In the course of relining, probably before 1851 (see Provenance), the canvas was made up to 164.5 × 82.5 with additions of 6 cm. on the left and 5 cm. on the right (see below). Cleaned by Lank in 1986. There is a diagonal tear in the sky, upper left, and there are small losses in the sky, centre right, by the heads of the two *putti* above Venus's chariot, centre left, and along the bottom edge. A number of *pentimenti* show that Venus's legs, left shoulder and left hand were redrawn, and other modifications were made to Mars's left upper arm and the drapery at his back, and to the *putti* by the anvil, lower right.

The subject was described by Homer, *Odyssey* VIII, 266–367, and Ovid, *Metamorphoses* VI, 171–89. Venus, goddess of love and wife of Vulcan, god of fire, blacksmith and armourer, with Mars, god of war: when Vulcan learned of Venus's

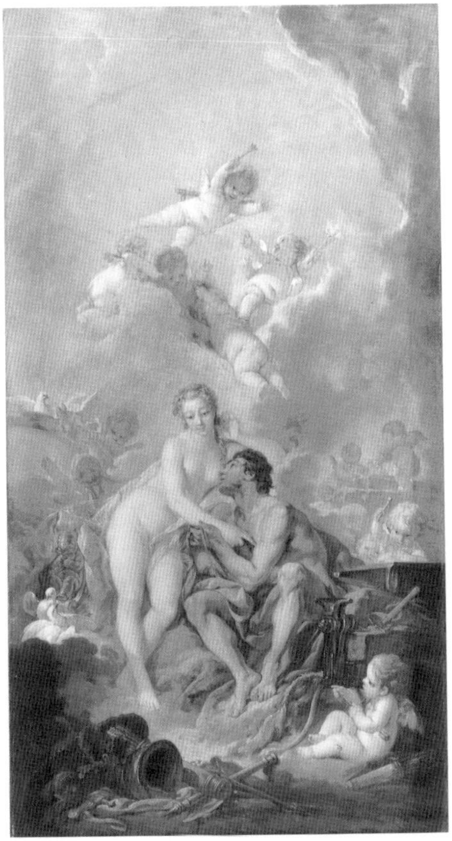

P429 before cleaning

infidelity he made a fine metal mesh which he draped round the marriage bed before announcing his departure for Lemnos; Mars then hurried to Vulcan's forge, where he is shown with Venus in P429. Venus undoes her hair, while Mars, his feet on a lion's skin, has discarded his armour; above them *putti* already bear Vulcan's net, one with an extinguished torch wears a yoke, another with a burning torch wears a quiver full of arrows, while others make arrows in the neglected forge. Their actions and Venus's attitude would seem to indicate that it is not Vulcan but Mars who sits by the forge;[1] he has similar features in P438 (which shows the conclusion of the story). Previously called *Venus and Vulcan*.

By 1851 P429, with P432, P438 and P444, was mounted on a *paravent* on the back of which were affixed four scenes by Lancret (see Provenance).[2] The four Bouchers then formed a set, each exactly the same size, but it is now apparent that P429, P438 and P444 had been made up to conform with P432.[3] P429 must originally have been paired with P438 (they were the same size and their subjects complement each other). P444 was originally 5 cm. wider than these two, but it was, apparently, folded to conform with them; it shows another episode from the story of Venus and is also dated 1754 (cf.P429); though it lacks some of the quality of the other two, it was probably always associated with them. P432, with its different tonality, enclosed composition and generalised subject, was evidently not originally part of the set.

Drawings

LONDON British Museum (no.1885–5–9–1395); study for the two topmost *putti* holding torches (A428/1, fig.1221).
(no.1885–5–9–1396); study for the group of three *putti* who hold the net in P429 (A428/4, fig.1223). Ananoff lists a copy of this drawing in the Musée des Beaux-Arts, Lille (A428/8).
NEW YORK C.E. Slatkin 1966; compositional study, closely comparable to that in Vienna (see below); exh. Slatkin, *Drawings, Pastels, Watercolours*, 1966, no.63, pl.59.
PARIS Polo sale, 30 May 1988 (22); study for Venus, signed and dated 1754, her right hand pointing to a target; ex coll. Stralem (A428/2 and 7, fig.1226).
VIENNA Albertina (no.12130); compositional study with Mars's left leg and hand differently posed and goddesses (?) in the sky (A428/3, fig.1233).

A drawing of a comparably posed Venus leaning on a broken column was engr. G. Demarteau no.321 (JR816), and the figure recurs, reversed, in several miniatures attributed to Charlier (cf. Wallace Collection M52).

Provenance[4]

With P432, P438 and P444: P.-C. Prousteau de Montlouis (1763–1851); his sale, Paris, 5–6 May 1851 (10, '*Quatre sujets mythologiques de la plus belle qualité . . . ayant fait partie d'une décoration d'un boudoir sous Louis XV, peut-être celui de Mme. de Pompadour, dont les traits nous semblent répétés dans la figure de Venus, qui figure dans ces compositions. Ces sujets sont tirés de la Fable et représentent les amours de Vulcain et Vénus, Vénus et les Amours, Mars et Vénus que surprend Vulcain, et le Jugement de Pâris. Ces tableaux sont signés et datés 1754, ils ont été arrangés en forme de paravent, et il se trouve au revers de chacun d'eux une composition pastorale de Lancret*'), bt. by the 4th Marquess of Hertford, 10,600 fr.; rue Laffitte inventory 1871 (635, '*Boucher, quatre panneaux de décoration*'); Hertford House inventory 1890.

References General

SM73; A428; CdA449.

[1] The *putti* apparently symbolise a loveless marriage and the strength of love. Boucher frequently painted Venus with Vulcan by his forge under the title of *Venus imploring arms for Aeneas from Vulcan* (Virgil, *Aeneid* VIII, 370–406), the goddess a little apart from Vulcan and pointing to the armour he has made (cf.A85, A302, A351, A478, A484 and A675).

[2] Previous editions of this catalogue have suggested that these Lancrets were the four lunettes formerly at Bagatelle (see Appendix III, nos.85–8) and now at San Francisco; but their size (61 × 130) and shape suggest otherwise (e.g. the screen could only have had one fold, with the Lancrets as two pairs, one over the other). P. Rosenberg and M.C. Stewart, *French Painting 1500–1825*, Fine Arts Museum of San Francisco, 1987, pp.204–8, also reject the idea. Only one other set of four pastorals is known to have been in Lord Hertford's collection, the Paters P383, P386, P397 and P400, q.v., whose nineteenth-century provenance is not known; see P383 note 2.

[3] Previous editions of this catalogue, and Ananoff, have assumed the four pictures were always pendants. See also P444 note 1.

[4] The four paintings were associated with a romantic provenance first published by C. Blanc, *Les Peintres des Fêtes Galantes*, 1854, pp.79–80 (and repeated in Blanc 1865, II, *Boucher*, p.10): '*La favorite* [Pompadour] *inquiète demanda à Boucher un boudoir magique où fussent exposées toutes ses plus voluptueuses images. Boucher composa sur-le-champ un petit poëme érotique en plusieurs tableaux. Le premier acte se passait sur le gazon, naïvement, en idylle, sous les branches d'un arbre ou roucoulaient des tourterelles. Au second tableau, la jeune bergère faisait voir comment l'esprit lui était venu, et par des transitions délicates, bien menagées, le spectateur était conduit au dernier acte, imitation effrontée d'un bas-relief du musée secret de Naples. Groupes sans voiles qui devaient être enchâssés au milieu de tentures destinées à faire valoir les séductions de la peau, et de glaces pour multiplier les agréments de la forme. Le tout fut posé, en panneaux richement encadrés, dans un sanctuaire de l'hôtel de l'Arsenal, habité alors par madame de Pompadour . . . A la mort de Louis XV, quand Louis XVI prit possession de l'héritage monarchique, Maurepas le conduisit au boudoir . . . "Il faut faire disparaître ces indécences," dit le nouveau roi. Le vieux courtisan trouva naturel de confisquer à son profit les peintures . . . qui, lors de l'émigration des nobles, furent emportées en Allemagne par M. de M. . . . Revenues en France récemment, elles ont été achetées par un Anglais* [Lord Hertford]. *Comme qualité de peintures, dit M. Thoré, à qui nous empruntons ces faits curieux, comme adresse de touche, charme de couleur, ce sont les plus beaux Boucher du monde*'. These comments were identified with P429, P432, P438 and P444 by, for example, Michel (*Boucher*, 1913, p.50), G. Geoffroy (Thieme-Becker, IV, 1910, p.431) and, with various qualifications, in previous editions of this catalogue. But it is apparent that the subjects were not those of the Wallace Collection pictures, while J. Guignard, *conservateur en chef*, Bibliothèque de l'Arsenal, said there is no evidence that Mme. de Pompadour ever lived there (letter on file dated 16 January 1980).

P431 *Shepherd and Shepherdess reposing (The School of Love)*

He wears a red coat with pale blue breeches, she a white dress and blue-laced bodice; a rich blue drape by the straw hat in the foreground. Signed, bottom centre left: *f. Boucher 1761*

Canvas, relined 76.6 × 63.6 oval[1]

An old lining canvas was replaced by Bobak in 1988 when P431 was cleaned by Lank. There are small losses round the edges and along the impress of the stretcher. *Pentimenti* show alterations to the shepherdess's feet.

Costume and setting suggest a theatrical pastoral, and the distant Italianate tower (which recurs in P385, P447 and P489) hints, again, at Favart's *Vendanges de Tempé* (cf.P399, P482 and P489).

P431, a reworking of the *School of Love* of 1760 (see Version), was one of Boucher's last essays in this pastoral genre;[2] it was one of the *Pastorales & Paysages* he exhibited at the 1761 Salon,[3] where it was commended:

> *. . . que de graces & que d'art embellissent ce léger sujet! Les caractères de tête y sont d'un agrément infini . . . Le grouppe des deux figures est facile & légerement enchaîné. Les étoffes sont vraies, drapées gracieusement & sans affectation. Le fond du Tableau est frais & riche dans son espèce; et le coloris y est d'un accord, dont les Connoisseurs peuvent seuls appercevoir tout le mérite, mais dont tous les yeux sentent l'effet.*[4]

The two right hands in P431, however, are weak. The pendant pastoral, *L'oiseau mal défendu*, signed and dated 1761, is in an English private collection (A544).

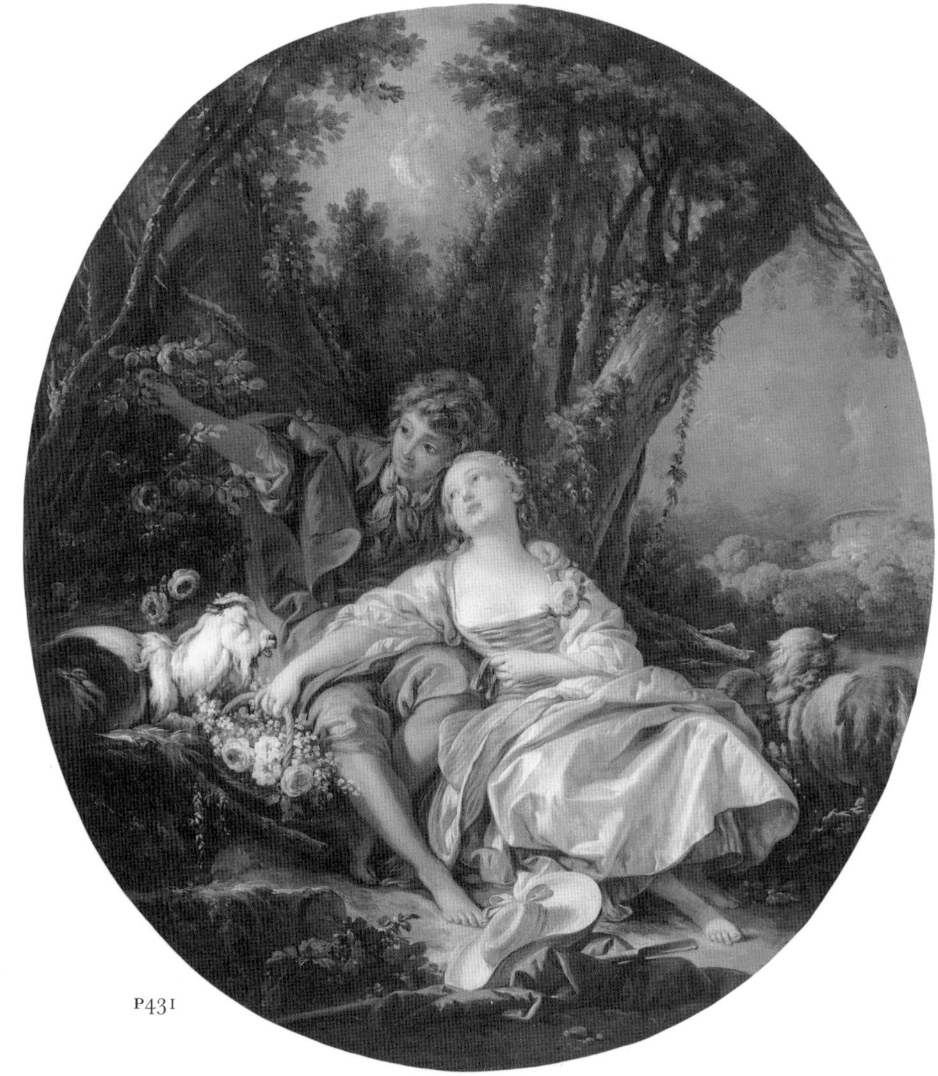

P431

Drawing

Ananoff (A543/1) cites a study for the shepherdess's head (Louvre, no.24764) which, however, relates more closely to the Karlsruhe version (see below).

Version

KARLSRUHE Staatliche Kunsthalle (no.479); 64.5 × 81, signed and dated 1760, showing the same figures as P431 but in a different landscape; painted for the Margravine of Baden (A542; Laing, no.71).

Provenance

P.-L. Randon de Boisset (1710–76), *receveur général*; his sale, Paris, 27 February ff. 1777 (191, *Une pastorale* [73 × 65]) bt. Desmarest, 1,180 *livres*;[5] the marquis de Livois (1736–90); Livois catalogue 1790, no.215, as '*Boucher, une pastorale composée d'une bergère assise à côté de son berger . . . du cabinet de M. Randon de Boisset, no.191 de son catalogue . . . Toile* [73.4 × 65.3]'; the collection was dispersed in 1799, when P431 was valued at 30 fr. and sold to Gamba; his sale, Paris, 17 December ff. 1811 (54), bt. Le Brun, 54 fr.[6] Probably Lord Henry Seymour (1805–59), and his sale, Paris, 2nd day, 14 February 1860 (65, *Le galant villageois, ovale*), bt. Laboureau, 4,100 fr. The 4th Marquess of Hertford; rue Laffitte inventory 1871 (713?, '*Pastorale*'); Hertford House inventory 1890.

Exhibitions

Salon 1761 (9), see above; Bethnal Green 1872–5 (485).

References General

SM1546; A543; CdA571.

[1] The oval carved wood frame decorated with laurel and a ribbon bears the stamp of H. LETONNE, *maître menuisier* in Paris 1773–91. Cf. note 6 below.

[2] Laing, p.287, quotes a letter from J.H. Eberts to the Margravine of Baden, Paris, December 1759, saying that the pastoral Boucher was painting for her (the Karlsruhe version described above) would be 'all the more precious because this charming artist is hardly going to do any more of these subjects'.

[3] P431 is identified at the Salon by a Saint-Aubin drawing (A543/2, fig. 1496, and see E. Dacier, *Catalogues de ventes et livrets de Salons illustrés et annotés par Gabriel de Saint-Aubin*, VI, 1911).

[4] A doc. 798 (*Mercure de France*, October 1761 and '*Observations d'une Société d'Amateurs sur les tableaux exposés au Salon*', in *L'Observateur littéraire*, 1761, p.15). Diderot was critical, suggesting that Boucher's exhibits '*doivent captiver les petits-maîtres, les petites femmes, les jeunes gens, les gens du monde, la foule de ceux qui sont étrangers au vrai goût*' (*Diderot Salons*, ed. J. Seznec and J. Adhémar, I, 1975, p.112).

[5] A second drawing of P431 by Saint-Aubin (cf. note 3 above) is inscribed *m. boucher mars 1777/pastorale/tres beaux*; the sheet also contains sketches of four other paintings, annotated: *Vu chez remy* [the auctioneer of the Randon de Boisset sale] *4 peintures par m. boucher griffeur et m. fragonard éleve qui ne les aime point Remy dit que l'invention est de deshays 46p 7p*, and of the marble group, *Boreas and Orithyia* by de Marsy and Flamen; sold Christie's 28 March 1972, lot 123 (A543/3, fig. 1497; *Gazette des Beaux-Arts*, 6e, LXI, 1963, p.7).

[6] Information concerning the Livois provenance taken from letters on file from R. Planchenault, dated 19 November 1921, and D. Cordellier, dated 15 January 1981. Cordellier states that Livois's frames were often made by E.-L. Infroit (1720–94), but cf. note 1 above.

P432 *Cupid a Captive*

Cupid lies on a golden cloth; behind him a nymph in blue and white drapery holds his lavender-coloured quiver; the right-hand nymph has pale green and white satin-striped drapery; the left-hand nymph red, pale green and white. Signed, bottom centre left: *f. Boucher*.

Canvas, relined 164.5 × 84.5

Probably relined before 1851 (see P429). There is a damage above the two *putti* in the central tree trunk and small losses below the central nymph's right shoulder, and in the right-hand nymph's drapery behind her right upper arm; there is a tear by the foreground roses, centre right, and two scratches behind the right-hand nymph. The bottom edge has been retouched and the signature appears to be reinforced. *Pentimenti* show alterations to the trees: a distant tree to the left of the sculpture was erased, the tree trunk behind the central nymph disappears unnaturally, and it is now apparent that the central nymph's right arm was painted over the trees. The varnish is discoloured.

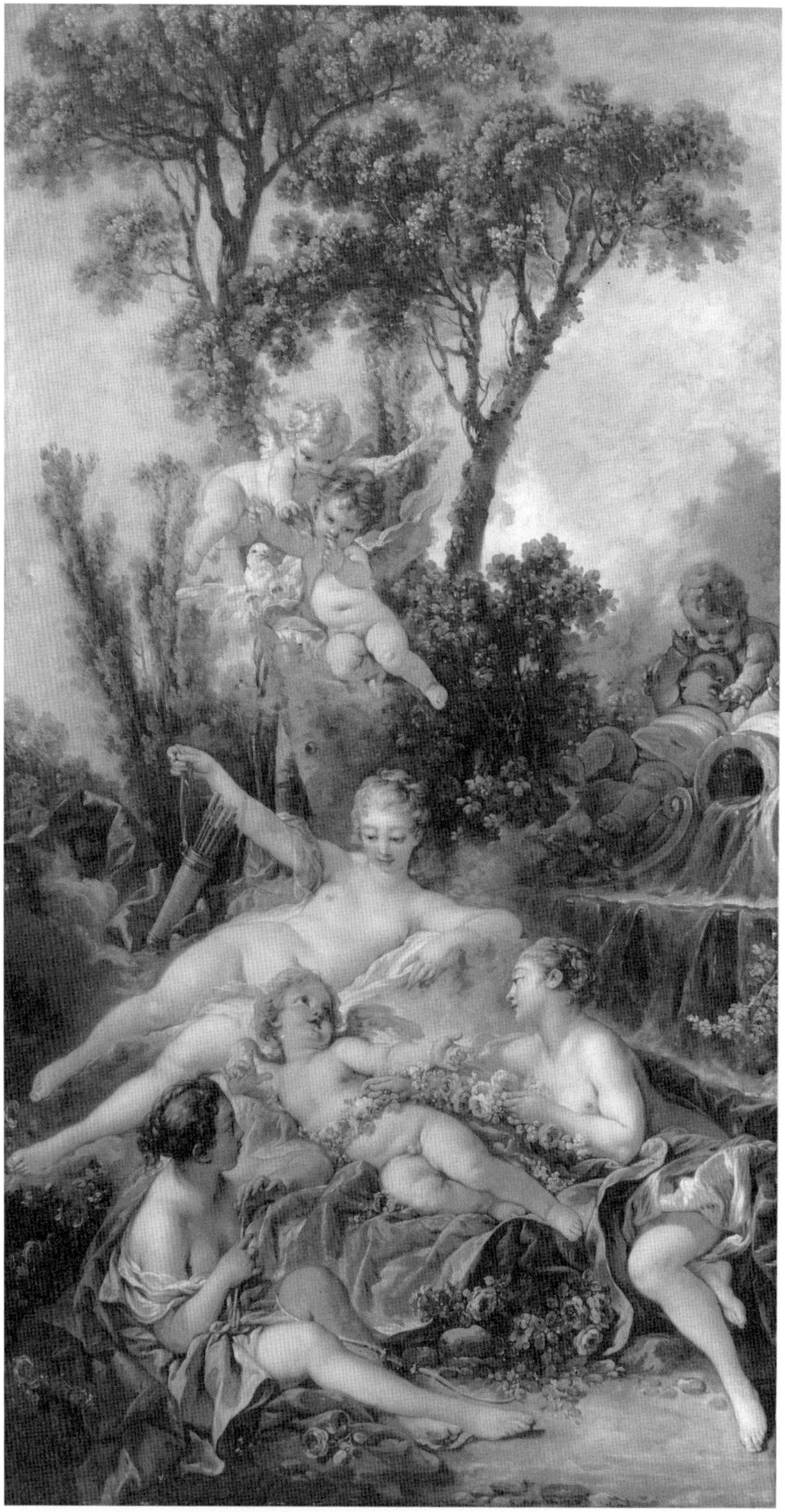

P432

The subject, which Boucher had previously used in 1738 at the Hôtel de Soubise (A162), probably derived from Anacreon, Ode xxx, *L'amour captif*:[1] the Muses bound Cupid with flowers and Venus, his mother, could not attract him back, since

> *... s'étant fait une habitude*
> *De sa douce captivité,*
> *Il prefere la servitude*
> *Aux charmes de la liberté.*

P432 may be dated c.1754,[2] though it may not be exactly contemporary with P429, P438 and P444, the panels with which it has previously been associated; see P429 for further discussion. The model for the central nymph recurs in the *Toilet of Venus* (Metropolitan Museum of Art; A376) and the *Bath of Venus* (National Gallery, Washington; A377), both painted for Bellevue in 1751,[3] and, with the model for the right-hand nymph, in a drawing perhaps of 1750 (Paris, private collection; A351/6; A, I, p.47, fig.90).

Drawing

MONACO Sotheby's, 20 February 1988 (210); study for the central nymph.

Provenance

See P429.

References General

SM73; A429; CDA450

[1] Cf. *Les Odes d'Anacreon et de Sapho, en vers françois*, 1712, p.212.

[2] The Prousteau de Montlouis sale catalogue implied that P432 was dated 1754 (see P429 Provenance).

[3] See Laing, p.256 (under no.60, *The Toilet of Venus*).

P438 *Mars and Venus surprised by Vulcan*

Mars has a yellow bow in his hair; Vulcan wears a red drape; above, a coral-pink canopy; a rich blue drapery, bottom left, and a bright blue plume on the foreground helmet; a gilt-bronze perfume-burner in the right foreground.

Canvas, relined 164 × 71

In the course of relining, probably before 1851 (see P429), the canvas was made up to 165 × 84.3, with additions of 7.7 cm. on the left and 5.6 cm. on the right (cf. P429). Cleaned by Lank in 1986. There are losses and some abrasion along the bottom edge, a damage below Vulcan's ear and a scratch by his shoulder. There are a number of *pentimenti*: the canopy was originally lower and supported by a single *putto* (just discernible by the left-hand edge, on the same level as the dove); a third *putto* with his left arm raised appeared between the two now seen at the top of the canopy; in front of Vulcan, on the bed, there was another *putto* (holding a helmet?); the head of the kneeling foreground *putto* was moved slightly to the left, and the area to the left of his back, and above the central *putto's* right arm, was reworked.

P438 completes the story begun in P429. Vulcan, who had only pretended to leave his forge, surprises Mars and Venus *in flagrante delictu* and traps them in his net. He then summoned the gods from Mount Olympus to enjoy the spectacle.

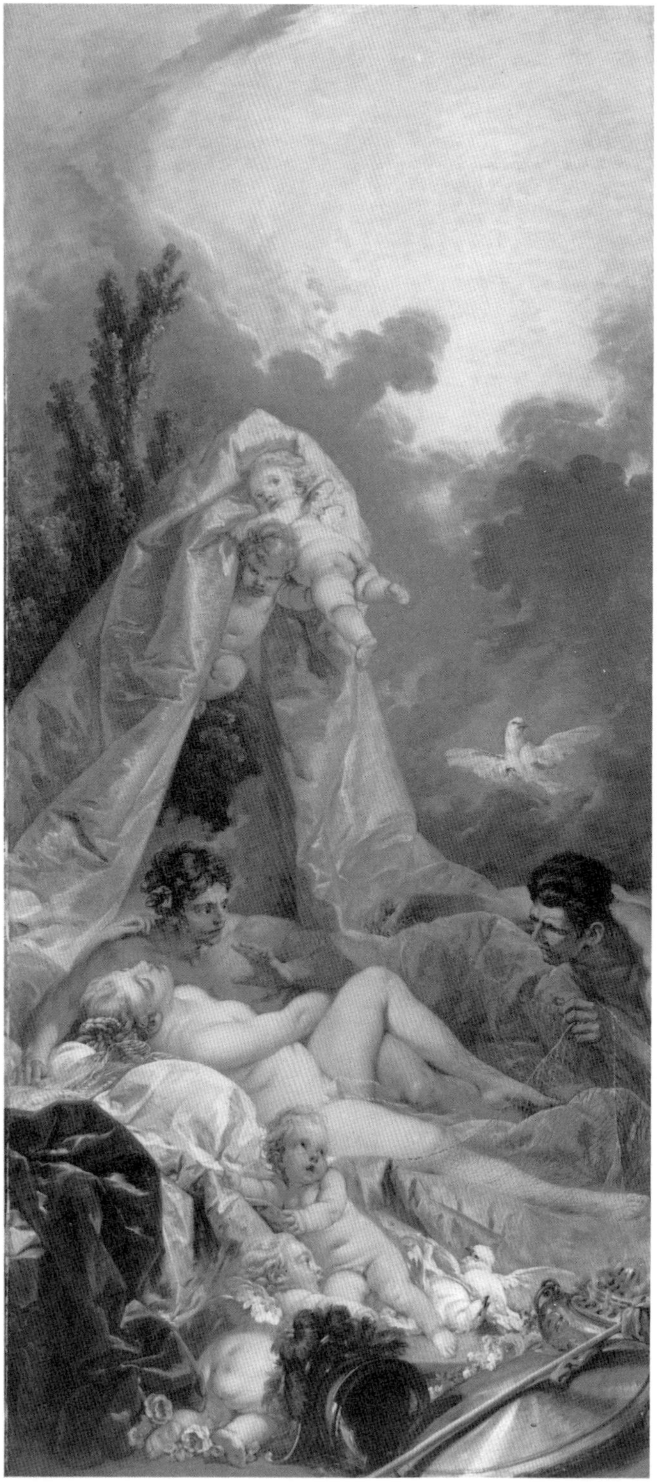

P438

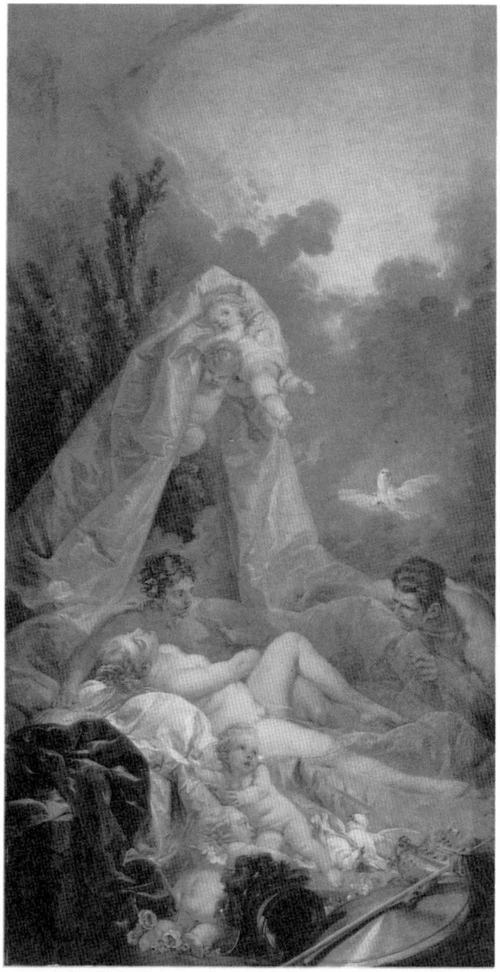

P438 before cleaning

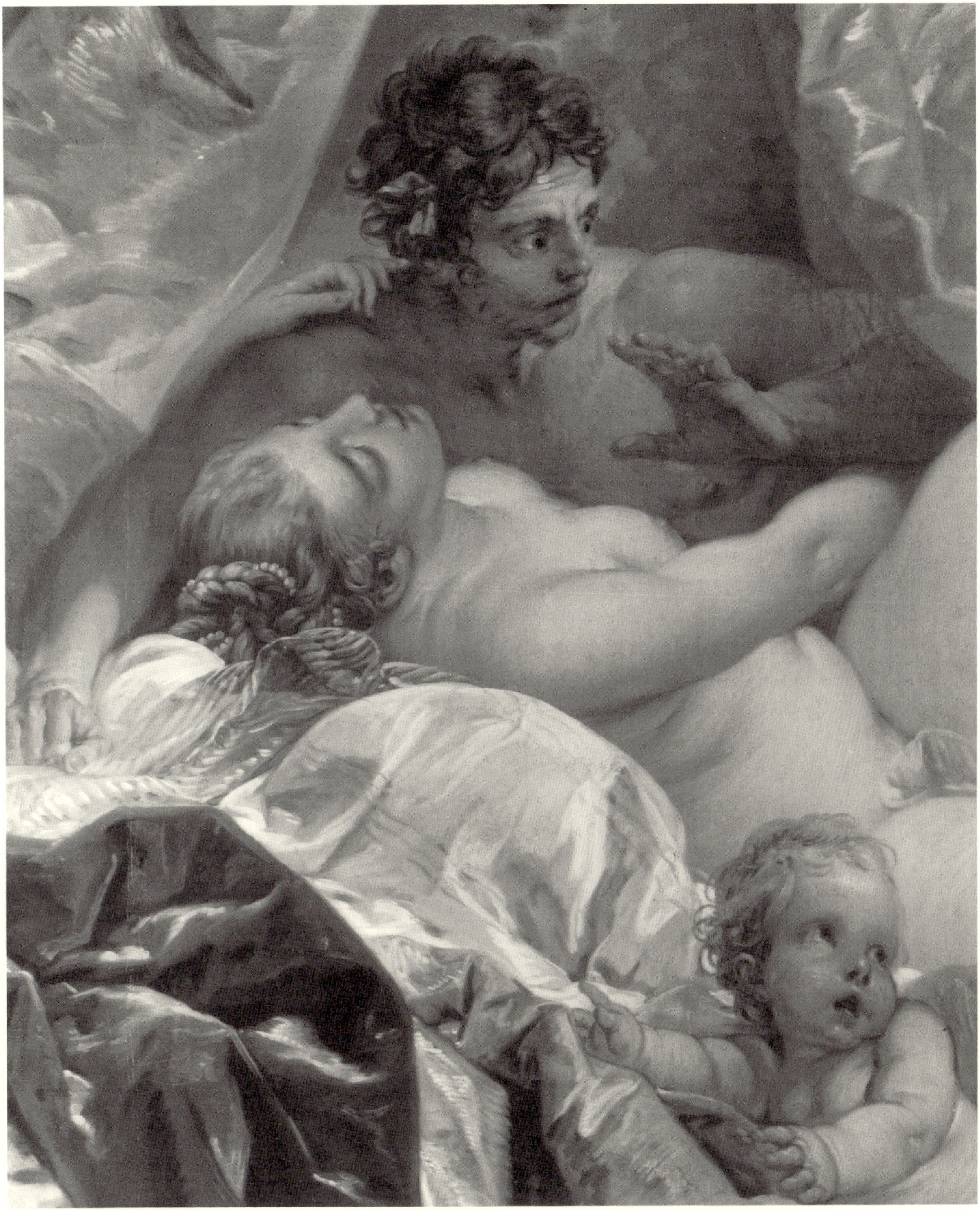

P438 detail

P438, which may be dated 1754 (as the pendant P429),[1] demonstrates Boucher's fluency at its height. The lights on the flesh are stroked in with brilliant whites and yellows, and the canopy scintillates with pinks, golds and reds; the *pentimenti*, described above, suggest that the composition of the ancillary subject matter evolved with a certain spontaneity. Only the drawing of Mars's right arm and Venus's left hand seems weak. The heavy features of Vulcan, on the right, would confirm that he is not represented in the pendant P429.

Drawings

PARIS private collection; study for the figure of Mars (A430/1, fig. 1235).
WASHINGTON Mrs. G. Laughlin Chanler; study for Venus; exh. Washington, National Gallery, ... *Drawings from the* [*Chanler*] *Collection* ..., 1982 (6). A weaker version of this drawing is in the Rijksmuseum, Amsterdam.

A pastel study for Venus, larger than the Chanler drawing, was formerly in the Fenaille coll. (AD759; A430/3, fig. 1229).

Provenance

See P429

References General

SM73; A430; CdA451.

[1] The Prousteau de Montlouis sale catalogue implied that P438 was signed and dated 1754 (see P429 Provenance).

P444 *The Judgment of Paris*

Paris, a leopard skin over his red drapery, proffers the golden apple to Venus; the dark-haired Minerva has a red-plumed helmet and, above, Juno reclines on a golden drapery by her two peacocks. Signed, bottom left: *f. Boucher/1754.*

Canvas, relined 164 × 76.6

In the course of relining, probably before 1851 (see P429), the canvas was made up to 166.7 × 84.5, with additions of 3.7 cm. on the left and 4.2 cm. on the right (cf. P429). Cleaned by Lank in 1987. A horizontal seam runs 50.7 cm. below the top edge, and there are traces of an old vertical fold 6 cm. from the left-hand edge. There are small losses along the bottom edge and by the right-hand edge opposite Minerva's feet, and there is a vertical tear to the right of the doves by Venus's feet. Craquelure appears upper right (following a linear pattern) and in Paris's red drapery and right shoulder. *Pentimenti* show alterations to the area round Paris's head, to the left of Venus's right arm and in her draperies, in the head of the *putto* by her side, and to the right of Juno's peacocks.

The subject was described by Ovid, *Heroides* XVI, 57–88, and Lucian, *Dialogues of the Gods,* XX. At the wedding of Peleus and Thetis, Strife let fall a golden apple, inscribed 'For the Fairest', which the goddesses Venus, Minerva and Juno each claimed; Zeus asked Paris, son of Priam and Hecuba, to judge between them. Juno, wife of Zeus, offered him greatness; Minerva, goddess of war, success in battle, and Venus, goddess of love, the love of the loveliest woman. Venus received the apple, and Paris abducted Helen, wife of Menelaus, thereby precipitating the Trojan War. See also Charlier P476.

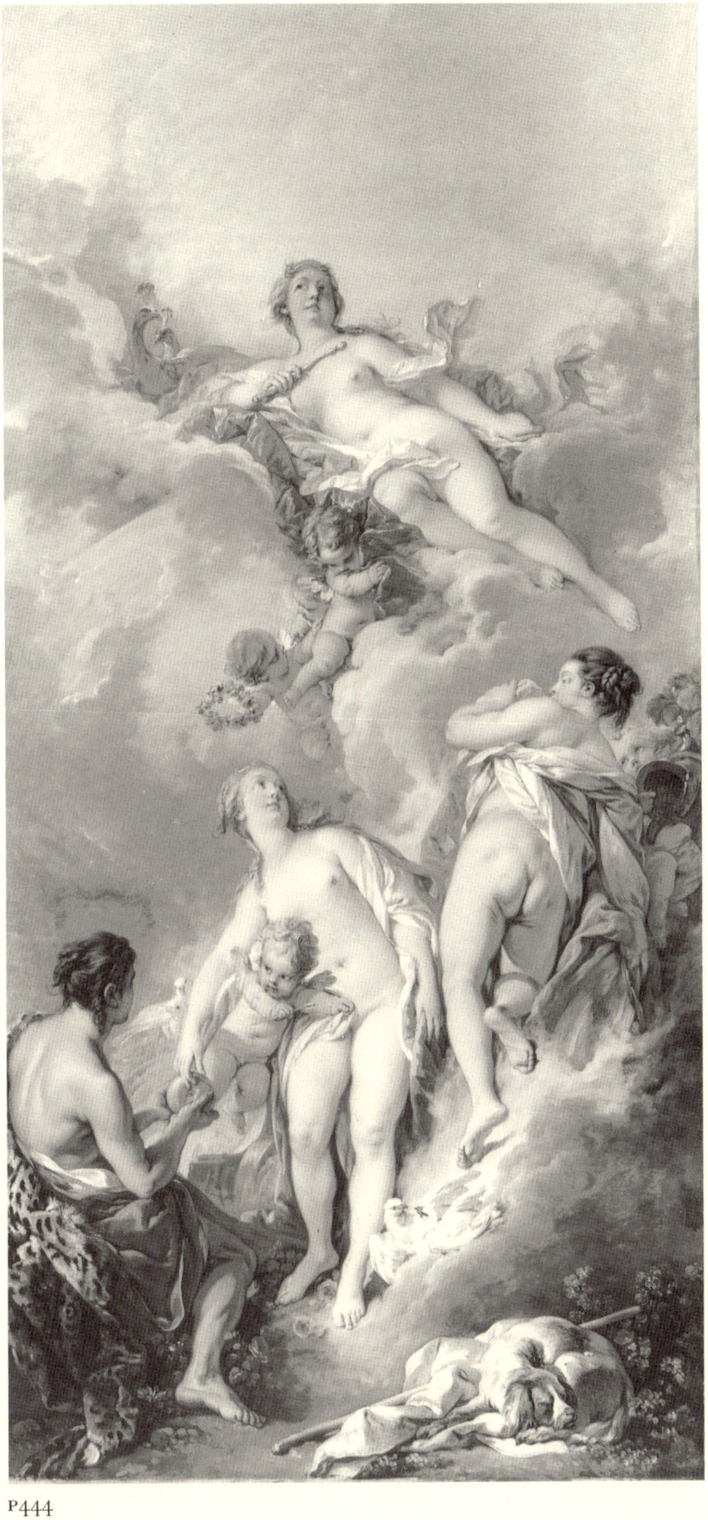

P444

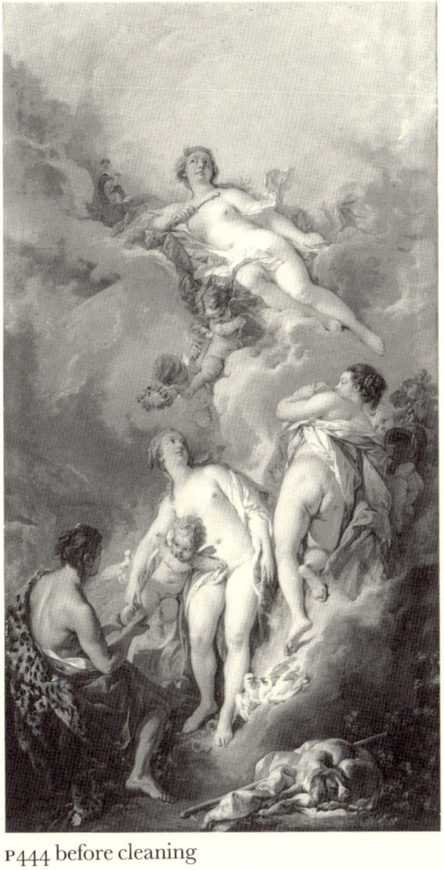

P444 before cleaning

The old fold, noted above, might indicate that P444 was, early in its history, framed *en suite* with P429 and P438, all three being then 71 cm. wide[1]. For further discussion, see P429.

Drawings

PARIS baron Janssen 1964; study for the head of Venus (A431/2, fig.1237).
M. Polakowitz 1975; a less finished study for the head of Venus.
SAN FRANCISCO Fine Arts Museum; study for Minerva (Slatkin 1973, no.71; A431/3, fig.1238).

A drawing probably made from the figure of Paris in P444 was in a private coll., London, 1969.

Provenance

See P429.

Exhibition

Palais Bourbon, *Ouvrages de Peinture exposées au profit de la colonisation de l'Algérie par les Alsaces-Lorrains*, 1874 (719) lent Wallace.

References General

SM73; A431; cdA452.

[1] The composition may be compared with that of the oil sketch attributed to Boucher, called the *Birth of Venus*, in the Detroit Institute of Arts (175 × 76; A619); W.R. Valentiner, *Bulletin of the Detroit Institute of Arts*, XI, 1930, p.50, suggested it may originally have been associated with the Wallace Collection 'series' and could be dated in the early 1750s. For further discussion see Charlier P475.

P445 *Spring (La toilette pastorale)*

The left-hand nymph has red and gold drapery over a white gown, and a pink hat and sandals; the right-hand nymph has blue and white drapery. Signed, bottom left: *f. Boucher/1745*.

Canvas, relined 98.5 × 132 *chantourné*

The canvas was made up to a rectangle in the course of relining. The frame, which probably belonged to Patureau (see Provenance), does not reveal the original shape. There are discoloured retouchings in the sky and some small losses, lower left. *Pentimenti* show small changes to the left-hand nymph's draperies over her right foot, in the feet of the foremost *putto*, and on the further *putto's* left arm. The varnish is discoloured.

P445 and the pendant P447 belonged to a set of four paintings which are identified by their original shape and size and by the set of engravings by Duflos published in 1751 (JR917–22). The original location of the set, evidently intended as overdoors, is not known.[1] The other two paintings are the *Retour de chasse de Diane*, signed and dated 1745, in the Musée Cognacq-Jay (A279; Laing, no.49) and *Les confidences pastorales*, signed but not dated, in the Los Angeles County Museum (A280; Laing no.50). The subjects suggest Boucher's progress from classical to contemporary pastoral (cf. P385, P399 and P482 and P489 of c.1745–50).[2] Two of the four subjects are mythological (the *Diane* and *Erigone*) and two generally Arcadian, but including straw hats, pet dogs and ornate wicker baskets. In each, one figure wears classical tied sandals, and all the figures are richly but loosely draped. Duflos's engravings were published in two pairs, in February and May 1751: the first pair illustrated the Arcadian subjects, the second the mythological.

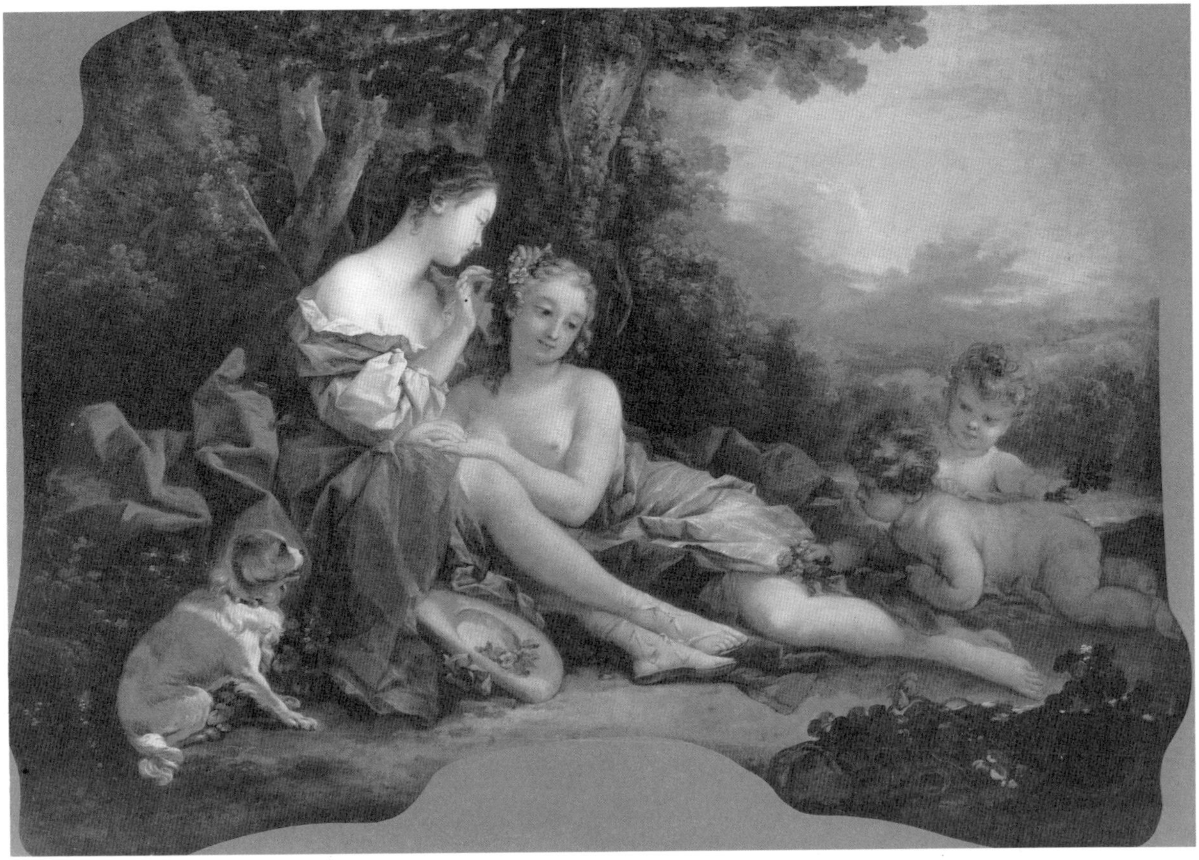

P445

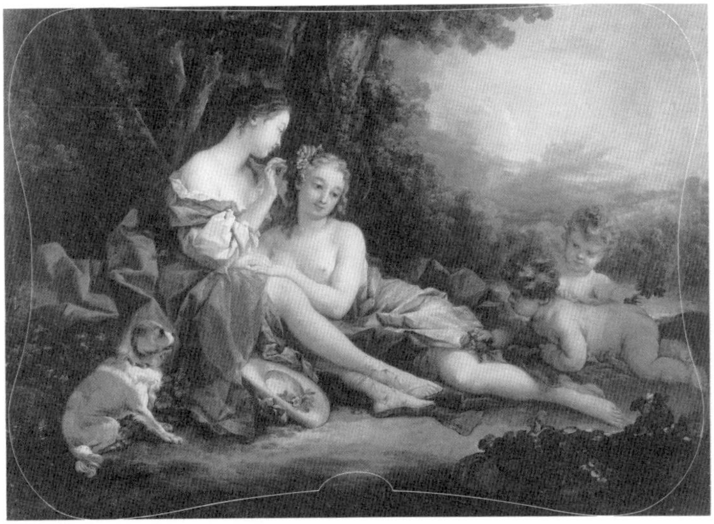

P445 with additions, showing present framed size

The dog in P445 recurs in *La collation* of 1736 (Beauvais tapestry design; A135/5; Laing, no.88), in *La lettre d'amour* of 1745 (A286), and in *L'heureuse fécondité* of 1764 (A583).

Drawings

LONDON Sotheby's, 6 July 1978 (11); compositional studies related to P445 and P447, reversed, possibly ex d'Ivry sale, Paris, 7–9 May 1884 (80, 81); Laing (p.221) suggests they were made by, or for the engraver Duflos.[3]

For a study showing the dog and hat as seen in P445, see P447 Drawings.

Engraving

C. Duflos 1751, *La toilette pastorale* (JR917–18), with verses:

Loin des ornements pretieux
Dont la coquette emprunte sa parure,
Philis à la simple nature,
Doit tous les agréments qu'elle étale à nos yeux.
C'est ainsi que semant des fleurs toujours nouvelles,
Agréable Boucher, Peintre cheri des Belles,
Tu nous fais admirer dans ce charmant Tableau,
Les attraits séduisants de ton brillant pinceau.

Copies/Versions

MONACO Sotheby's, 20–1 June 1987 (677); 85 × 113, attributed to Boucher; without the dog.
NEW YORK Le Royer sale, 8–9 December 1950 (50); 79 × 129, one of a pair, *chantourné*, with tower in right distance and only one *putto* with a basket of flowers; ex De Backer sale, Paris, 1 June 1908 (32).
PARIS galerie Cailleux c.1955; 74.3 × 94.6, signed and dated 1748, with doves instead of *putti* and a quiver replacing the dog and hat; ex Vaile sale, Christie's 23 May 1903 (23) and Sedelmayer coll.
VERSAILLES Salon de la Pendule; copy, acquired in 1894 from the Ministère des Finances, one of a set of four after the original set.[4]

Provenance

With P447: Théodore Patureau, Brussels; his sale, Paris, 1st day, 20 April 1857 (50 [P445] and 51 [P447], both *'forme médaillon'*), bt. Laneuville for the 4th Marquess of Hertford, 14,500 fr.,[5] possibly Hertford House inventory 1870.[6]

Exhibition

Bethnal Green 1872–5 (388).

References General

SM1834; A281; cdA291; Laing, pp.221–3.

[1] Ananoff associated the set with three sales prior to 1857: anon. sale, Paris, 12 October 1798 (53, *'Quatre dessus de portes, de forme chantournée, par François Boucher, différents sujets de Bergères et jeunes filles, dans le genre pastoral et son premier temps'*); Folies de Chartres sale, Paris, 28–9 November 1834 (15, Boucher . . . *'quatre magnifiques tableaux . . . représentant des nymphes couchées . . . [provenant] des Folies de Chartres, où ils décoraient le boudoir des appartements du duc . . .'*), and Stacpoole sale, Paris, 1–3 March 1852, cf. Boucher P482, P489; Oudry P625, P627, P629, P631 (2, Boucher *'quatre dessus de portes faisant pendants . . .'*).
None of these descriptions allows a firm identification to be made (cf. Laing, p.221, and T. Burollet, *Musée Cognacq-Jay: Peintures et Dessins*, 1980, p.49); the 1834 sale pictures were probably those once in Harlaxton Manor (A287–90), and the Stacpoole pictures had been in the Château de Montigny-Lencoup from the eighteenth century. The earliest certain provenance for the *Retour de chasse de Diane* and *Les confidences pastorales* is the Chaillou sale, Paris, 2 December 1911 (1 and 2).

[2] This point is made by Laing, *loc. cit.*, and in the *Revue de l'Art.* 73, 1986, p.60.

[3] Duflos's engravings were based on drawings supplied by Boucher's studio, according to the *Mercure de France*, March 1755, pp.145–6, and May 1755, pp.131–3 (A doc. 617, 618).

[4] These copies are exhibited as shaped canvases (cf. G. van der Kemp, *Versailles*, 1978, p.117, illus.), but these are not the original shapes.

[5] The *Revue Universelle des Arts*, v, 1857, p.188, remarked that *'on ne retrouve pas, dans ces tableaux, l'esprit, la touche enlevée, qui distinguent les ouvrages de Boucher, peintre spirituel par excellence'*. For Blanc's comments on this purchase, see Introduction, p.15.

[6] Lord Hertford told Mawson that he had bought P445 and P447 as overdoors for his house in Piccadilly (see Introduction, p.10), which suggests he may have sent the pictures to London. The 1870 inventory lists *'Boucher, A Pair of overdoors, pastoral'* which were either P445 and P447 or another pair listed in 3 Connaught Place in 1903 (see Appendix III, nos.27–8).

P446 *Jupiter and Callisto*

Callisto, on the left, lies on rich blue drapery; Jupiter, as Diana, wears gold and white drapery round his shoulders and a pale purple cloak; to the right a red quiver with a blue sash lying on a leopard skin. Signed, bottom centre left: *f. Boucher/1769.*

Canvas, relined 160 × 129 oval

There are losses above and behind Callisto's head, below her left hand, at the edge of her drapery by her quiver, below the head of the right-hand *putto* in the sky, and on the raised right hand of his companion. A marked craquelure in the lower central area is tending to lift. There are retouchings on Jupiter's left wrist and by Callisto's profile. *Pentimenti* show that Callisto's left hand was redrawn (see below) and that the tree behind her originally grew much higher (related dark shapes now appear above the eagle); in the sky the left-hand *putto's* right arm was also altered. There is a drying craquelure round the eagle, which seems to have been painted over the tree. The varnish is unevenly discoloured.

The subject is described by Ovid, *Metamorphoses* II, 417–40: Callisto, one of the hunting nymphs who accompanied Diana, goddess of the chase and of the moon, is seduced by Jupiter disguised as Diana. Ovid described Callisto resting, her head on her quiver and her bow beside her; on Jupiter's approach she raised herself to greet him, as seen in P446. Boucher has added Jupiter's eagle in a sinister sky (cf. P484). Callisto subsequently bore a son, Arcas; she was dismissed by Diana, persecuted by Juno (wife of Jupiter) and turned into a bear; eventually Jupiter turned both Callisto and Arcas into stars.

P446 displays the blander handling and colour of Boucher's last years. The *pentimenti* and signature suggest it is entirely from his hand, although studio collaboration has previously been suggested.[1] Boucher had painted several closely related versions in the 1760s (see below), one of which, showing a large tree behind Callisto, no eagle, and the index finger of Callisto's left hand raised (features which appear as *pentimenti* in P446), was commissioned for the Gobelins (see Tapestry).

Versions

FONTAINEBLEAU *petits appartements* (*deuxième salon*); 394 × 234, '*copie agrandie*', studio replica made for the Gobelins, showing Callisto's left index finger raised, no eagle and the *putti* placed higher; it does not agree exactly with the tapestry (see below); ex Château d'Eu; installed at Fontainebleau 1862[2] (A639/2, fig. 1679).
LONDON Sotheby's, 1 November 1978 (35); 39.5 × 21.5, oil on paper; showing identical figures and eagle in a variant landscape (A639/1, fig. 1680).
PARIS Gobelins Manufactory (formerly); 146 × 124 oval, '*d'après Boucher*', dated 1767 by Ananoff and Engerand,[3] and described by Fenaille as stolen in 1870,[4] cf. the Raleigh version below.
Galerie Cailleux 1958; 160 × 130 oval, with Callisto's left index finger raised; ex coll. de Beurnonville (A639/7).
RALEIGH North Carolina Museum of Art (G.55.8.1); 142.3 × 114.3 oval, replica of P446 with minor differences in the eagle; ex coll. Behn (A553/3, A639/6 as copy; cdA674 as autograph).

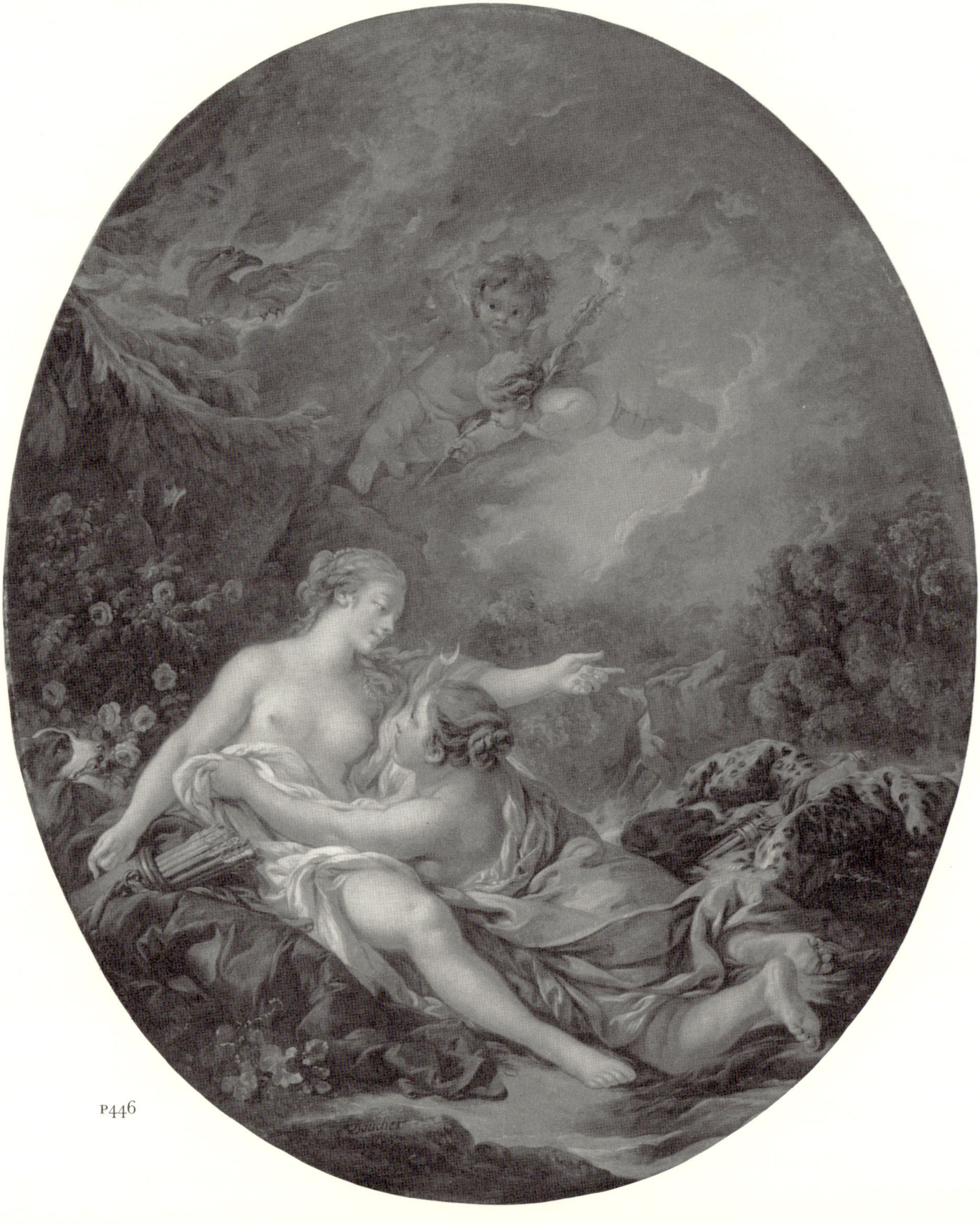

P446

A variant is in the MacDonald collection, Geneva (76.2 × 63.5 oval, signed and dated 1760; A533).[5] Reversed variants are in the Metropolitan Museum of Art (see Appendix III, no.17) and in an English private collection (89 × 68, grisaille; exh. RA 1968, no.65; A535).

Tapestry

Gobelins, by Nielson, 1776–8, *'pièce a deux médaillons'* with Vertumnus and Pomona, made for the comte du Nord (later Tsar Paul I) and displayed in the Pavlovsk Palace; without the eagle and with a large drapery over the tree behind Callisto.[6]

Provenance

Probably Canot sale, Paris, 17 February 1872 (6), 1,700 fr.; bt. from Nieuwenhuys, 27 February 1872, by Sir Richard Wallace, £700;[7] Hertford House inventory 1890.

Exhibition

Bethnal Green 1872–5 (390).

References General

A668; CdA706.

[1] In the previous edition of this catalogue.

[2] See B. Lossky, *Le Musée national du Château de Fontainebleau*, 1970, p.164, and illus. pp.162–3.

[3] A639; F. Engerand, *Inventaire des Tableaux commandés et achetés par la Direction des Bâtiments du Roi*, 1900, p.55.

[4] M. Fenaille, *Etat général des Tapisseries de la Manufacture des Gobelins*, IV, 1907, pp.232, 239, 287.

[5] Exhibited at Leggatt's, *The MacDonald Collection*, 1970, no.2, as dated 1769, although it is identified convincingly by Ananoff (A533) as the picture exhibited in the 1761 Salon.

[6] Illus. Fenaille, *op. cit.*, f.p.284, and discussed pp.232, 239, 285–90.

[7] A note of this purchase is in the Wallace Collection archives. It seems impossible to establish the earlier provenance, given the number of versions of similar size. In the *cabinet* of the duc de Caylus in 1772 there was *'un tableau ovale. . .* [174 × 141], *représentant Jupiter metamorphosé en Diane et Calisto'* (A, II, p.326; A639/5 and A668).

P447 *Bacchus and Erigone (Erigone vaincue)*

The right-hand nymph has blue and grey draperies, her companion a gold drapery and pink sandals; the two winged *putti* bear grapes. Signed, bottom right: *f. Boucher./.1745.*

Canvas, relined 99 × 134.5 *chantourné*

The canvas was made up to a rectangle in the course of relining. The frame, which probably belonged to Patureau (see Provenance), does not reveal the original shape. There are discoloured retouchings, upper left, and beneath the tree, centre left.

The subject, identified by Duflos's engraving (see below), was mentioned by Ovid, *Metamorphoses* VI, 125: Bacchus, disguised as a bunch of grapes, deceives the nymph Erigone, daughter of Icarius.

For further commentary, see P445.

Drawings

LISBON C. Gulbenkian; compositional study including the right-hand figure in P447, reversed, and the dog and hat from the bottom left of P445; ex Sotheby's, 2 May 1923, lot 51 (A282/6, fig.835).
VIENNA R. Schmidt 1976; study for the right-hand *putto* (A243/10 and A281/4, fig.832).

See also P445, Drawings.

Engravings

C. Duflos 1751, *Erigone vaincue* (JR920–1), with verses:

A Bacchus comme amant Erigone infléxible,
Ne répond que par des mépris;
Mais en se transformant ce Dieu la rend sensible,
Et de ses soins reçoit le prix.
En amour comme en guerre, il faut de l'artifice:
De l'objet de ses feux qui veut être vainqueur,
Doit épouser ses goûts et flatter son caprice,
C'est là le vrai chemin au coeur.

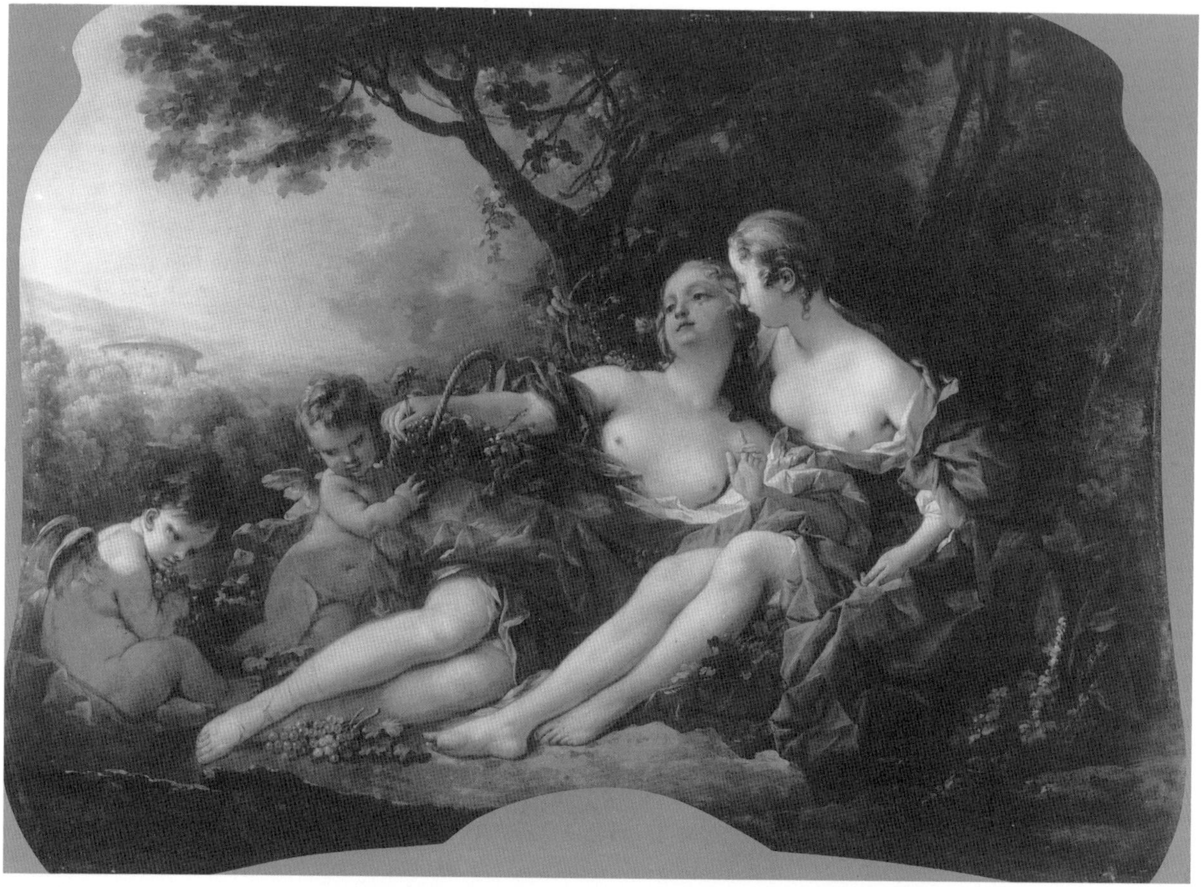

P447

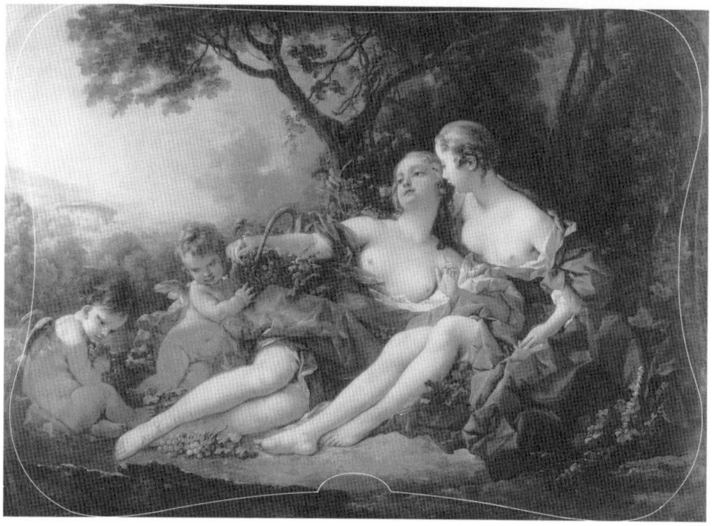

P447 with additions, showing present framed size

Copies/Versions

PARIS De Backer sale, 1 June 1908 (31); 80 × 130, a weak version.
Le Dart sale, 29 April – 4 May 1912 (25); 78 × 127, the composition reduced in height.
VERSAILLES Salon de la Pendule; copy, acquired in 1894 from the Ministère des Finances, one of a set of four after the original set (see P445 note 4).

Provenance

See P445.

Exhibition

Bethnal Green 1872–5 (392).

References General

SM 1834; A282; cdA292; Laing, pp.221–3.

P482 *An Autumn Pastoral (Les raisins Pensent-ils au raisin?)*

The trees bear autumnal foliage; the youth wears golden brown breeches and a pink jacket; the girl a blue skirt, yellow sleeves and white cuffs. Signed, bottom left: *f. Boucher-/1749.*

Canvas, relined 259.5 × 198.6 with rounded corners

The paint surface was transferred onto a fine muslin, supported by a rectangular double lining canvas, probably soon after 1852 (see Provenance). The second lining canvas was replaced in the course of cleaning and restoration by Vallance in 1969–70. A vertical seam runs 119.5 cm. from the right-hand edge and the join has been retouched, together with an area below the girl's feet. A tear runs through the youth's right knee. *Pentimenti* reveal a radical reworking of the lower area to the right of the fountain, where infra-red scanning shows there was originally a donkey laden with baskets of grapes (closely comparable to that seen in the *Retour du marché* of c.1732 in the Chrysler Museum; A83); the little boy in a straw hat was added after the donkey was erased.

The subject derives from Favart's pantomime *Les vendanges de Tempé*, scene vi, in which the Little Shepherd feeds Lisette with grapes; Boucher had painted other versions of this scene in 1747 (Nationalmuseum Stockholm, A309; Art Institute of Chicago, A310). For a general discussion of the subject, see P399.

Painted for Trudaine's new château at Montigny-Lencoup (see Provenance and notes 2 and 4), P482 and the pendant P489 are perhaps Boucher's finest theatrical pastorals, as well as the largest. The landscape settings are broadly painted and both were modified in the course of execution, suggesting a certain bravura. The little dog in P482 recurs in *Le sommeil interrompu* of 1750 (Metropolitan Museum of Art; A363) and the *Pastoral* of 1760 in the Staatliche Kunsthalle, Karlsruhe (A542). A comparable fountain appears in *Le lever du soleil* of 1741 (A181); like the Italianate tower in P489, it was doubtless intended to evoke the Vale of Tempé of antiquity, the setting of *Les vendanges de Tempé*. The boy with the straw hat, on the right, recalls a figure used by Watteau (in *L'indiscret*, CR140, and see P381).

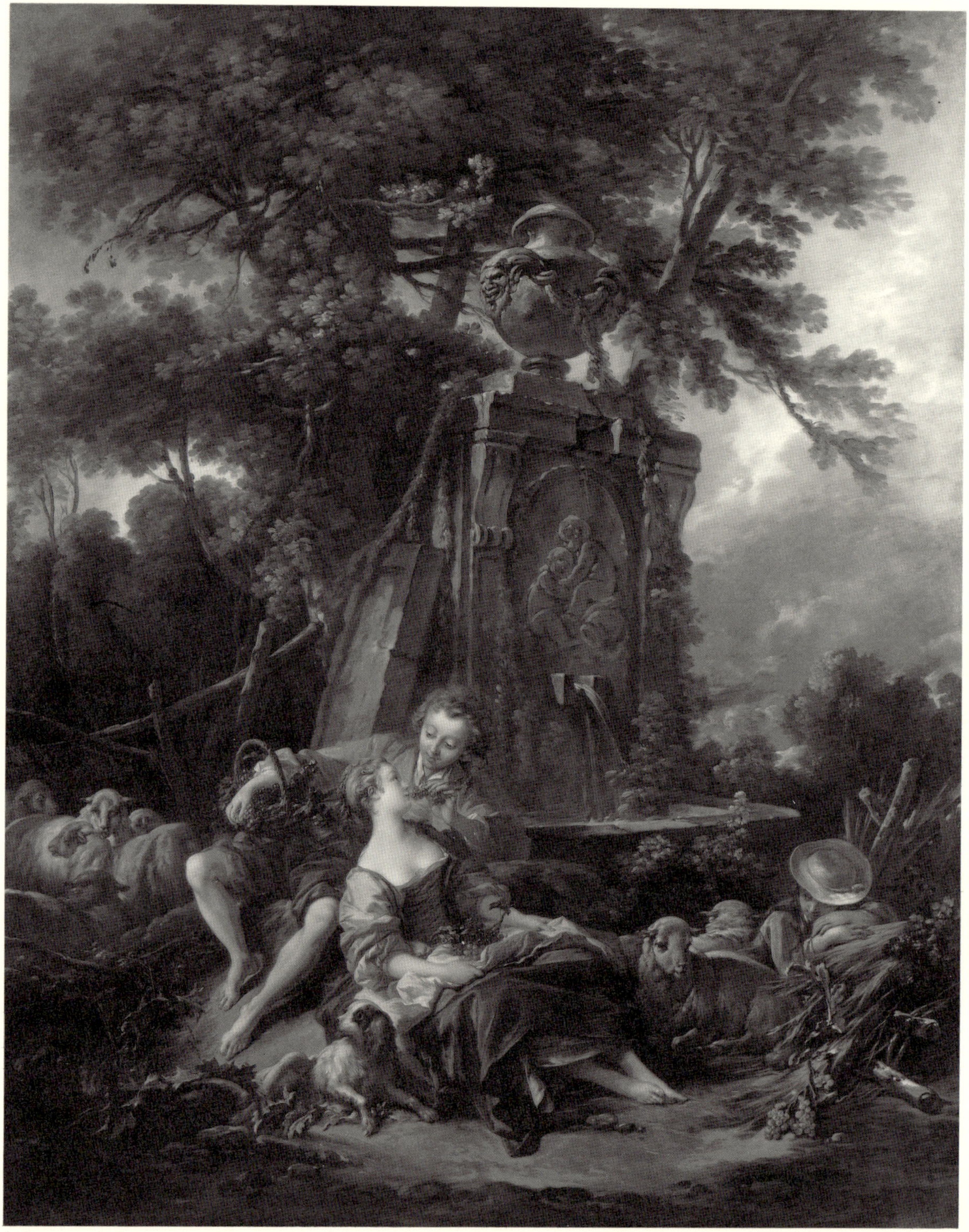

P482

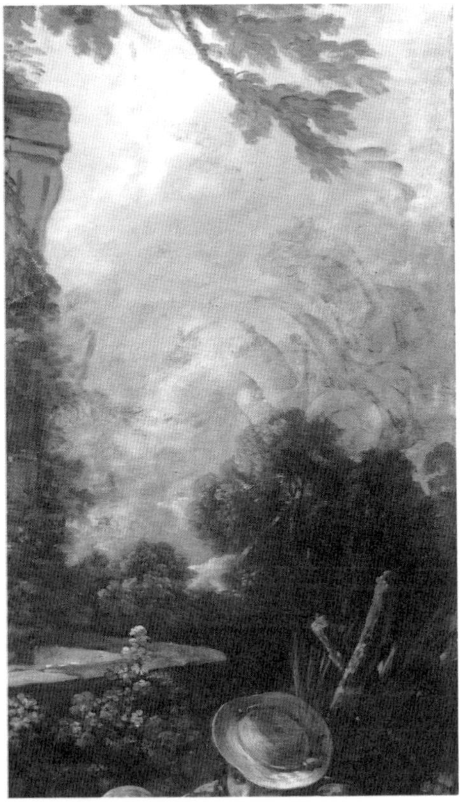

P482 after cleaning, before restoration; detail showing traces of the donkey on the right, later erased

Drawings

Ananoff lists two drawings for the figure of the girl, one for the head (A336/2, fig. 969) and one for the whole figure (A336/1, fig.967), but gives no location for either.
A third drawing relating to this figure was engr. L.-M. Bonnet (*Buste de femme, la tête renversée en arrière*, JR321).

Copies

BAVARIA Linderhof; copy by Ch. Jank, 1870–9, adapted to imitate tapestry (and see P489).

Ananoff lists a copy in the coll. of Ch. Loveland 1962, 105 × 132 (A336/3).

The main figure group in P482 inspired a biscuit group at Vincennes c.1752 (Laing, no.100), and was adapted for the decoration of a Sèvres vase c.1779 (Wallace Collection, C265).[1]

Provenance

With P489: Daniel-Charles Trudaine (1703–69), *intendant des finances*, Château de Montigny-Lencoup (Seine-et-Marne), *grand salon du rez-de-chaussée*;[2] in 1818 the château was bt. by the comte George de Stacpoole (1736–1824)[3] and passed to his son Richard Stacpoole (1797–1848, cr. duc by Pope Gregory XV, 1831); his sale, Paris, 1–3 March 1852 (1, Boucher, '*deux grands panneaux représentant des scènes pastorales . . . [qui] ornaient le grand salon du rez de chaussée*'),[4] bt. by the 4th Marquess of Hertford, 12,400 fr.; rue Laffitte inventory 1871 (430); Hertford House inventory 1890.

Exhibition

Boulevard des Italiens 1860 (82, *Les raisins*) lent Hertford.[5]

References General

SM1566; A336; cdA350; A. Laing, *Revue de l'Art*, 73, 1986, pp.60–1.

1 Since P482 was not engraved, and the Vincennes group is in the same direction as the painting, the factory probably worked from a copy (a drawing?) of P482 (cf. Laing, *Revue de l'Art*, 73, 1986, p.64 n.74); Trudaine was connected with the Vincennes factory (cf. E. Bourgeois, *Le biscuit de Sèvres au XVIIIe siècle*, 1909, pp.21–2; R. Savill, *Wallace Collection Catalogue of Sèvres Porcelain*, I, 1988, p.228).

2 The Stacpoole sale catalogue described the château as '*bâti par M. de Trudaine, ancien sous-intendant des finances sous Louis XV, et rendez-vous de chasse de ce roi*'. Four Oudrys in the Wallace Collection, also from Montigny-Lencoup (P625, P627, P629, P631) are dated 1747–8, which suggests that the château was being completed between 1747 and 1749 (the dates of P482 and P489). For further items from the Stacpoole sale, see *Catalogue of Furniture*, F208–18, F233–8.

3 For information on the Stacpoole family I am grateful to Miss Valerie de Stacpoole (letters and notes of 1984 on file F208). See also D. S. MacColl, *The Burlington Magazine*, XLIV, 1924, p.69.

4 The sale catalogue explained: '*C'est par suite du décès de M. le duc de Stacpoole, dernier possesseur de cette riche demeure* [Montigny-Lencoup], *que ces toiles et ce superbe mobilier ont été enlevés de la place qu'ils occupaient depuis si long-temps pour être livrés aux enchères*'.

5 Cf. W. Bürger, *Gazette des Beaux-Arts*, 1ère, VII, 1860, p.344: '*Ces tons variés font comme un bouquet de couleur sur le vert azuré des arbres et du gazon*'.

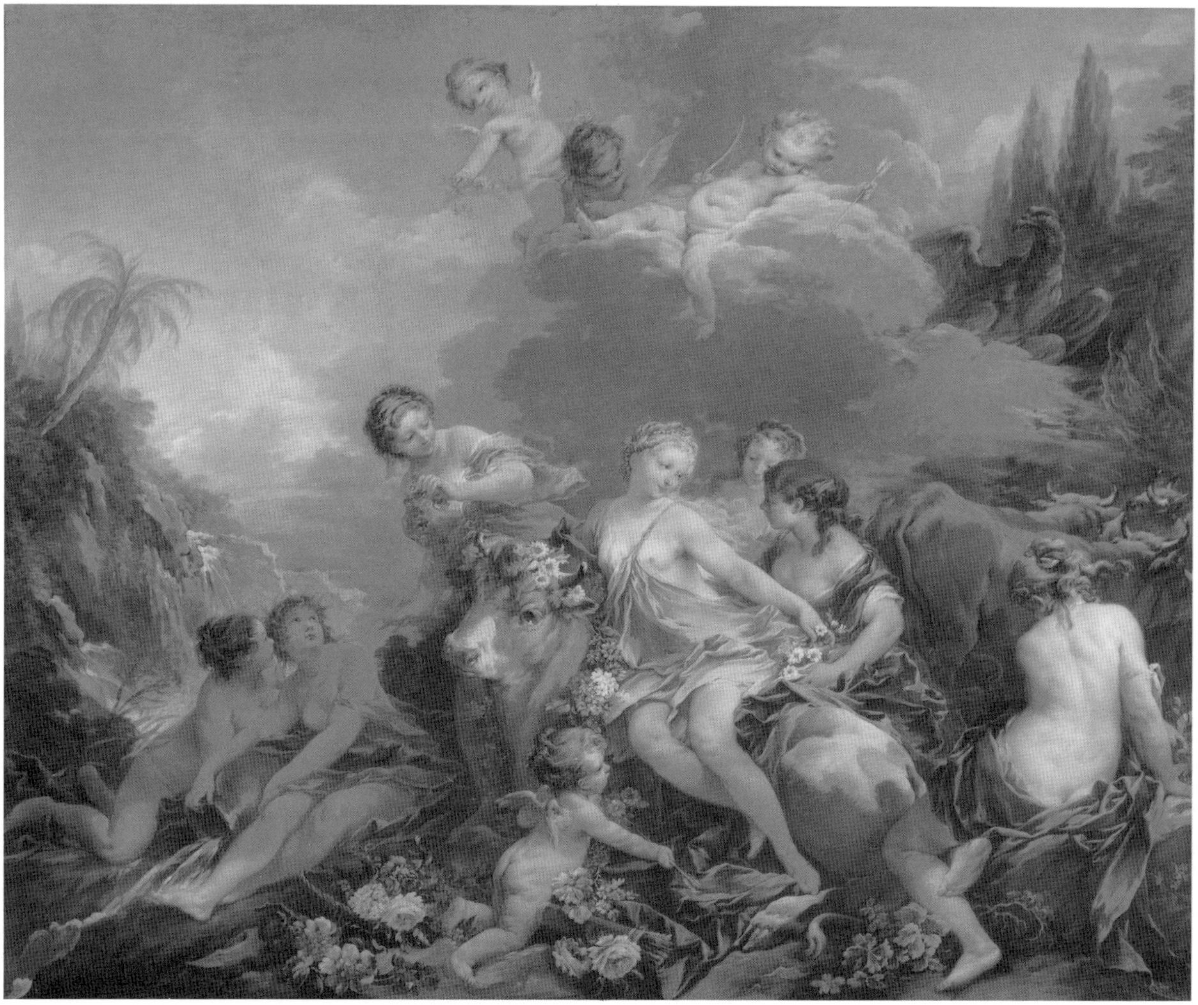

P484

P484 *The Rape of Europa*

The fair-haired Europa has coral-pink drapery; to the right a dark-haired girl in an orange dress, and on the extreme right a nymph seated on a turquoise drape; the quiver, centre foreground, is deep blue.

Canvas, relined 230.8 × 273.5

Varnished by Buttery in 1882 and cleaned by Lank in 1981–2. There are a number of small losses in the sky, upper left and centre, in the basket of flowers, lower left, along the bottom edge and along the horizontal seam 120 cm. above the bottom edge. *Pentimenti* show that the area between the herd of bulls and the eagle, on the right, was reworked, and there are several alterations to the right wrist and hand of the girl by the bull's head, the drapery above her left arm, and to the right arm of the seated girl, extreme right. Painted on a pink ground.

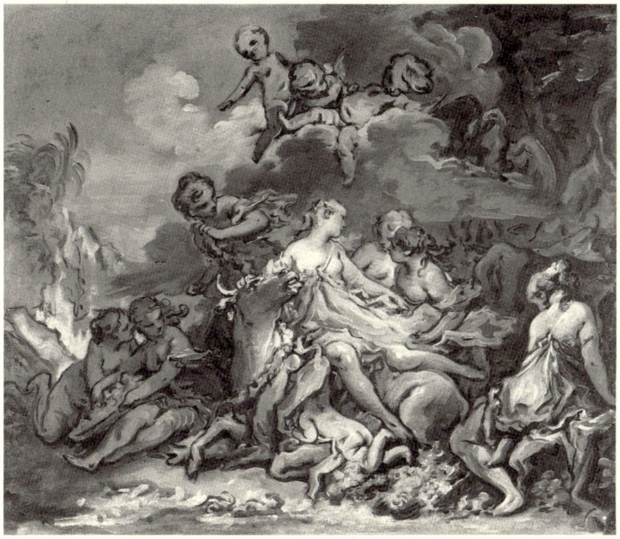

Boucher: *The Rape of Europa.*
Musée de Picardie, Amiens

The subject is described by Ovid, *Metamorphoses* II, 835–75 (and Lucian, *Dialogues of the Gods* XV, see note 1): Europa, daughter of Agenor, King of Sidon, is abducted by Jupiter disguised as a bull. P484 follows Ovid's text closely: the bull looks placid and has small polished horns which Europa has wreathed with flowers before sitting on his back, holding one of the horns with her right hand; the cattle are those of King Agenor, driven to the beach by Mercury that Jupiter's disguise might seem less extraordinary. Boucher has added the flying *putti* and Jupiter's attribute of an eagle on a thundercloud[1] (cf. P446).

With its pendant P487, P484 was among the set of at least eight large pictures which Boucher painted, probably c.1732–4, for François Derbais, an *avocat au parlement* who died in 1743.[2] Mariette later recounted the circumstances: Boucher, he wrote,[3]

> *est né le pinceau à la main. Il ne faut que voir ce qu'il a peint dans sa jeunesse, et en particulier cet enlevement d'Europe qu'a M. Watelet* [P484] *et qui faisoit partie du nombre de grands tableaux qu'il avoit fait pour un sculpteur marbrier nommé Dorbay*[4] *qui en avoit garni toute sa maison, ce qui lui avoit été très-facile, car Boucher, ne cherchant alors qu'à se faire connoître, les auroit, je crois, faits pour rien, plus tost que d'en laisser manquer l'occasion. J'admire ce tableau toutes les fois que je le considère. Tout y est admirable, et surtout un pinceau aussi ferme qu'il est gracieux.*

Mariette implied that Boucher used Derbais's house in the rue Poissonnière as a means of self-advertisement;[5] he would have had less need of such publicity after 1735 when he received his first commission from the Crown, and in 1737 an annual Salon was revived.

P484, perhaps the most elaborate and accomplished of the Derbais pictures, may be dated c.1734, as was first proposed by Voss.[6] Several figures in the composition relate to slightly earlier works by Boucher; the model for Europa recurs (in a comparable, but reversed pose) in the *Rinaldo and Armida* of 1733 (Louvre; A108), the left-hand *putto* may be compared with a half-length figure in *Putti playing with a*

Goat of 1732–3 (A60), the right-hand *putto* recurs, reversed, in *L'amour moissonneur* engraved in 1734 (see note 2), and both *putti* are echoed in the *Aurora and Cephalus* of 1733 (Nancy; see note 2). The dark-haired girl, to the right of Europa, resembles a figure in Boucher's etched frontispiece for the *Figures de différents caractères* of 1728 (JR1). Laing (p.159) points out that the landscape anticipates that of the *Leopard Hunt* of 1736 (Amiens; A125).

The vigorous grisaille sketch for P484 (see Versions) shows the bull turning to look at Europa who looks away to the right, the central *putto* buried under her drapery, and the right-hand nymph of the left-hand group looking down; the flowers, so prominent in P484, are scarcely suggested. In P484 the composition has become more balanced and the action less violent; the richly decorative effect and shimmering lights suggest Boucher was drawing upon Venetian examples of the subject, such as those by Sebastiano Ricci (Palazzo Taverna, Rome) or Veronese.[7] The vigorous execution and strong colour distinguish P484 from the works of Lemoyne to whom, however, it was attributed, with P487, between 1860 and 1925.[8]

Drawings

Related drawings for this composition were in the de Vries sale, Amsterdam, 24–5 January 1922 (67); Masson sale, Paris, 7 May 1923, lot 17 (A104/12), and on a fan (A104/5, fig.413) associated by Ananoff with the Lempereur sale, Paris, 24 May 1773 (538).

Drawings of the same subject, attributed to Boucher, which may have referred to P484 (or to other Boucher versions, see note 1), were in the Lempereur sale (see above), lot 534 (A104/4), the Clisorius sale, Paris, 31 March 1795 (Laing, p.157), the Sireul sale, Paris, 3 December 1781, lots 86 and 87 (*ibid.*). The Boucher drawing in the Louvre, RF40958, shows a different composition.

Engravings

P. Aveline 1748, reversed (JR248–9) with verses by Moraine in Latin and French:

L'Amour est, belle Europe, un insigne imposteur.
Redoutez, croyez-moi, ce Taureau si flateur:
Sa douceur vous pourra causer quelque infortune;
Fuyez, et de ces fleurs cessez de l'embellir.
J'entrevois qu'il ne veut que vous en ravir une,
Qu'aucun printems jamais ne fera revenir.

E. Bovinet (JR392). A variant, *La Terre*, engraved by L. Jacob (d.1802).

Versions

AMIENS Musée de Picardie; grisaille sketch, 51 × 61, see above (A103; Laing, no.25).

A grisaille on paper of the same subject was in the Bardou sale, Paris, 23 June 1783, lot 6 (Laing, p.157).

Copies/Versions[9]

Collet sale, Paris, 8–10 November 1880 (9); 62 × 80.

Anon. sale, Brussels, 15 May 1888 (8).

Schouten sale, Amsterdam, 20 September 1938 (10); 83 × 160, lunette.

The composition was reproduced in part by F. Lainé on a gold box by A.-J.-M. Vachette of 1777–8 (Louvre, OA2223) and, reversed, on a gold box formerly at Mentmore (*Catalogue*, 1884, I, p.171, no.63).

Provenance[10]

With P487: F. Derbais (d.1743, see above); Paris; C.-H. Watelet (1718–86), Paris, probably by 1750;[11] his sale, Paris, 12 June 1786 (12 [P484] and 13 [P487], each 277 × 212), bt., with an *Enlèvement d'Europe* by Pierre (lot 14), Saubert, 3,423 *livres*;[12] Bruslé and de Morny sale, Paris, 16–17 December 1841 (60, *La naissance de Bacchus, gravé*; 61, *L'enlèvement d'Europe, gravé*); Paul Périer (1808–49); his sale, Paris, 16–17 March 1843 (56), bt. by the 4th Marquess of Hertford, 2,820 fr.; rue Laffitte inventory 1871 (428 [P487] and 429 [P484]); 105 Piccadilly 1874–5 (as two of '*four fine mythological subjects*'); Hertford House inventory 1890 as Lemoyne.

Exhibition

Boulevard des Italiens 1860 (86*bis*, '*dans le catalogue provisoire sous le nom de Fr. Lemoine*', see note 8) lent Hertford.

References General

SM140; A104; cdA105; Laing, under no. 25.

[1] Boucher included these elements in later versions of the subject – the painting shown in the 1747 Salon (no.8, the source quoted as Lucian) and now in the Louvre, and the illustration to Ovid of 1767 (JR1556). They were also used by Pierre for his *Rape of Europa*, painted for Watelet in 1750 (see Provenance above and note 12 below).

[2] This provenance was first published by Laing (p.57), following the discovery by G. Brunel of Derbais's *inventaire après décès* dated 2 March 1743. Though it lacks artists' names, Laing has identified in it eight paintings by Boucher: apart from P484 and P487, listed in the *salle de billard*, these are:
L'amour nageur (illus. *The Burlington Magazine*, XCV, 1953, p.90, fig.E; Laing, p.128)
L'amour vendageur (engr. E. Fessard, JR962; A65)
L'amour moissonneur (engr. B. Lépicié 1734, JR1378; cf.A63)
L'amour oiseleur (engr. B. Lépicié 1734, JR1377; Laing, pp.128–9) (these four were listed as two pairs of pictures of children on the staircase, cf. Laing, p.135)
Venus and Vulcan, 252 x 175, dated 1732 (Louvre; A85; Laing, no.17)
Aurora and Cephalus, 250 x 175, dated 1733 (Nancy; A86; Laing, no.18) (these two pictures were in the *salle de billard* with P484 and P487).
In addition Laing suggests that a *Birth of Venus* in the *salle de billard* may have been the large canvas, 250 x 300, formerly with the comtesse de Béhague (Laing, pp.57,159; A180) and the overdoor of *Amours* in the same room the *Bacchanal* by Boucher illus. *The Burlington Magazine*, XCV, 1953, p.88, fig.57.

[3] P.-J. Mariette, *Abecedario*, I, AAF, II, 1851–3, p.165.

[4] Mariette seems to imply here Jérôme Derbais (see S163 and S164 in the Wallace Collection) who, however, died in 1715 (cf. Laing, p.133). There was also a Michel Derbais, *marbrier et sculpteur en marbre*, active in 1722 (cf. NAAF, 2e, IV, 1883, p.268). But there can be no doubt, following the discovery of François Derbais's inventory, that the Derbais in question was François, son of Jérôme (cf. Laing, p.135).

[5] Cf. Laing, p.158–9. Boucher's success seems partly born out by a letter from Bachaumont to Boucher (n.d., but concerning a Boucher commission of 1737): '*Vous faite le Paysage comme un Ange. J'entends d'icy le bruit du torrent; souvenés vous bien de tout ce que vous avés fait ché M. d'Herbais*' (A doc. 130). Laing, p.159, first associated this letter with P484.

[6] H. Voss, *The Burlington Magazine*, XCV, 1953, pp.86, 89. His dating was followed by Ananoff; J.-L. Bordeaux dated P484 c.1733–4 (*François Le Moyne*, 1985, fig.398) and c.1735–6 (*The First Painters of the King*, exh. cat., Stair Sainty Matthiesen, New York, 1985, p.36). P484 and its pendant P487 have otherwise been considered somewhat later, e.g. M.L. Bennet and A. Mongan, *Drawings from the Daniels Collection*, 1968, under no.20, as c.1738; Slatkin 1973, p.65, as 'forties and fifties', and J. Cailleux, *Sanguines*, exh. cat., galerie Cailleux, Paris, 1986, under no.7, as 1742–5.

[7] Boucher could have known the reduced version of Veronese's *Rape of Europa*, once considered the *modello*, in the Orléans collection from 1727 (and now no.97 in the National Gallery, London). It is not known whether Boucher visited Venice, where the original Veronese remains in the Doge's Palace.

[8] The error first arose in the provisional catalogue of the boulevard des Italiens exhibition in 1860 (see Exhibition); it was corrected in the revised catalogue by Ph. Burty who explained: '*par suite d'une erreur accréditée, nous avions enregistré ces deux tableaux dans le catalogue provisoire sous le nom de Fr. Lemoine*'. W. Bürger, *Gazette des Beaux-Arts*, 1ère, VII, 1860, p.343, commented: '*On ne s'explique pas comment* [P484 and P487] *pouvaient être attribués à Lemoyne dans la galerie de* l'amateur *qui possède tant de gracieux Boucher . . . Boucher s'y reconnaît d'ailleurs au premier coup d'oeil*'. The Lemoyne attributions were revived in the 1890 Hertford House inventory and maintained in the first thirteen editions of this catalogue, before being corrected by D.S. MacColl in 1920; they appear last to have been argued by P. Nolhac, *Boucher*, 1925, pp. 9–10 (although cited, for example, in Pigler, *Barockthemen*, II, 1974, pp.44, 87).

[9] The version mentioned by Ananoff in the George sale, Paris, 2 June 1891, lot 68 (A104/11) relates to the Louvre composition (A350).

[10] Earlier editions of this catalogue gave the Provenance as 'Cabinet Basan 1779', which seems to have been a misunderstanding of the fact that one of Aveline's engravings (see Engravings above) appeared in the *Recueil de Basan*, VI, 1779, no.83 (cf. JR249 and the catalogue of the boulevard des Italiens exh. 1860).

[11] Pierre's *Rape of Europa* of 1750 was described in the Watelet sale catalogue as '*fait pour achever l'ornement du salon de feu M. Watelet*' rather implying that P484 and P487 were there already (and see note 12).

[12] Lots 12, 13 and 14 were sold together '*attendu qu'il semble. nécessaire de ne point désunir ces trois ouvrages capitaux & si parfaitement d'accord dans tous les points du bel art de la Peinture*'. Pierre's picture, 244 x 275, is now in a private collection, New York; exh. Stair Sainty Matthiesen, New York, *The First Painters of the King*, 1985, no.18. Watelet also owned Boucher's *Venus and Vulcan* and *Aurora and Cephalus* (both lot 11 in his sale) from Derbais's collection, see note 2 above.

P485 *The Rising of the Sun*

Above, *putti* push back the clouds of night and Aurora, with roses on her fingers and crowned by the Morning Star, sets out to announce the rising of the sun god, Apollo, who stands, fair-haired and with a coral-pink drapery, being dressed for his journey, surrounded by Tethys and her nymphs and Tritons; on the right, white horses prepare to pull Apollo's chariot through the sky.[1] Signed, bottom left: *f. Boucher/1753.*

Canvas, relined 318 × 261

P485 was varnished by Buttery in 1882, surface cleaned and retouched by Haines in 1903, 1910 (twice) and 1920, and cleaned and restored by Vallance in 1949. In 1980–1 many discoloured retouchings were treated by Lank who, in the course of cleaning and restoration, strip-lined the already double-lined canvas, using a new stretcher. A horizontal fold with nail holes 25 cm. below the top edge (through the head of the topmost *putto*) indicates P485 was once on a smaller stretcher. There are vertical seams 26 cm. and 145 cm. from the left-hand edge. There are some losses and tears along and above the fold, some losses along the seams and small tears in the dark clouds on the left (by Apollo's right hand) and on the right foot and buttock of the nymph reclining in the right foreground. Numerous *pentimenti* have become more prominent with time:
1 The group of horses on the right was radically redrawn; the raised head of one of the earlier group appears above the present group.
2 Aurora's drapery originally spread wider, and the attendant *putto* by her right leg was redrawn.
3 Two *putti*, one with a flaming torch, originally pushed back the clouds at their narrowest point on the left, but were subsequently replaced by the pair upper left, of whom one has a redrawn leg (see Drawings).
4 Tethys's left hand, holding the reins, and her right sleeve have been redrawn.
5 Apollo's hair was longer and his right leg is redrawn.
6 The lyre offered to Apollo has been shortened; a second lyre appeared in the waves below Apollo's left foot.
7 The head of the bottom right-hand nymph, and the seated *putto* in the centre, were redrawn.
The greyish half-tones seen in the nymphs to the right of Apollo, in Aurora and the reclining nymph, can hardly be taken to indicate an underpainting in grisaille, as has previously been suggested;[2] P485 and P486 have comparable umber grounds.

The mythological subjects of P485 and of the pendant P486 were loosely described by Ovid, *Metamorphoses* II, 1–160: from the river Oceanus which surrounded the flat earth, where Tethys, wife of Oceanus, lived with her sons, the Tritons, and daughters, the Oceanides, Phoebus Apollo drove each day in his chariot of the sun, to return at sunset. But the iconography would have been more familiar to Boucher from French art celebrating *le roi soleil*, and Boucher doubtless intended his pictures to achieve a certain majesty from this association.[3] At Versailles, for

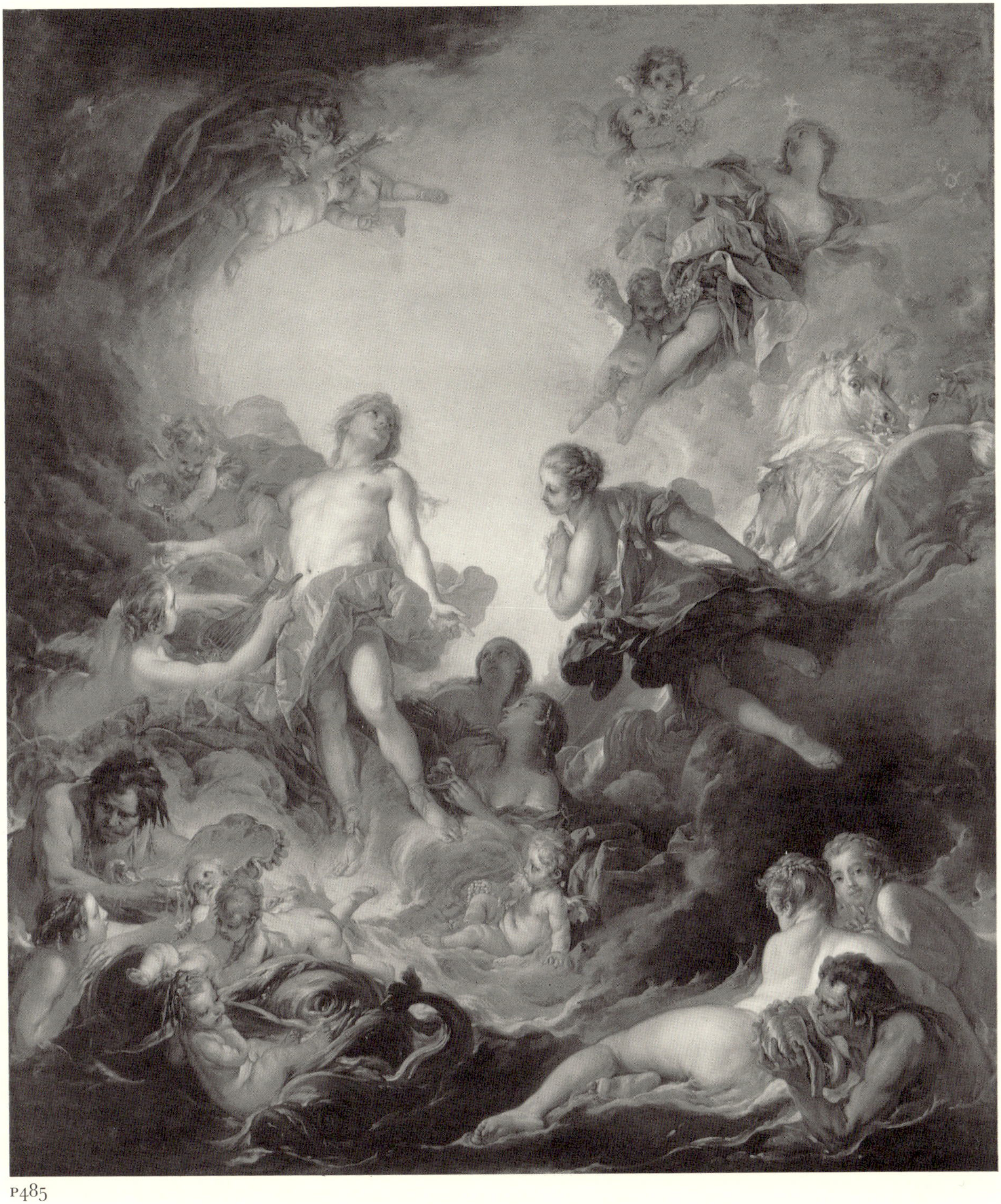

P485

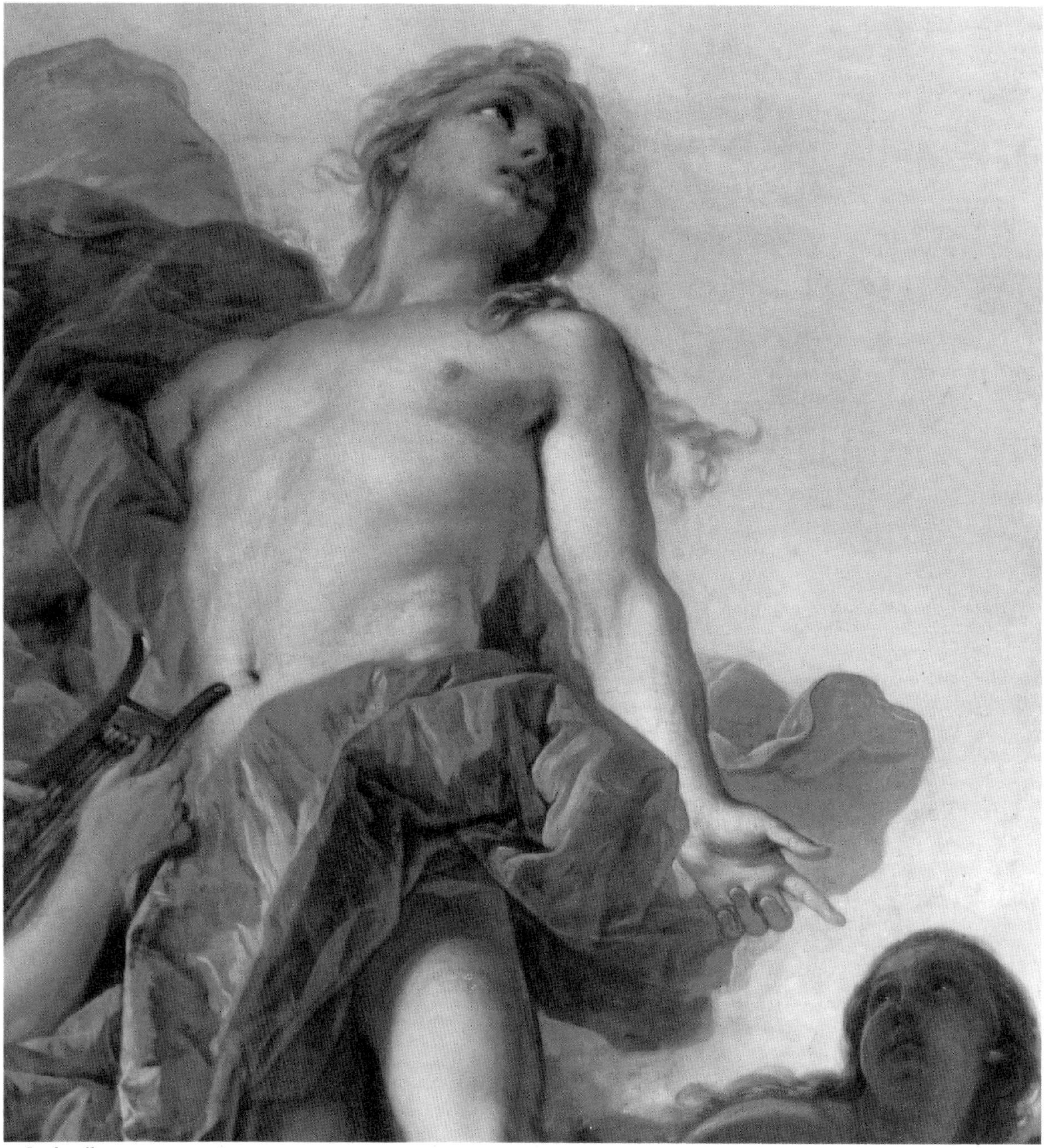

P485 detail

example, he would have known Girardon's *Apollo and the Nymphs of Tethys* and Tuby's *Rising of the Sun*, as well as La Fosse's *Rising of the Sun* and *Apollo and Tethys*.[4] Near the Hôtel de Soubise, where he had worked 1737–9, at the Hôtel de Rohan was Robert Le Lorrain's bas-relief of the *Horses of the Sun*.[5] Earlier, in Rome, he would have seen the celebrated renderings of the comparable subjects by Albani (Palazzo Verospi), Guercino (Villa Ludovisi) and Reni (Palazzo Rospigliosi-Pallavicini).

The figure of Apollo in P485 is reminiscent of the *Apollo Belvedere*, as Slatkin noted,[6] and that of Aurora recalls a figure in the *Rape of the Sabines* (Capitoline Gallery, Rome) by Pietro da Cortona who probably exercised some influence on Boucher's composition.[7] But his overall originality is emphasised by the number of surviving life studies for the figures (see Drawings).[8] The two *putti*, top left, had appeared in his *Rape of Europa* of 1747 (Louvre; A350) and the nymph handing Apollo his lyre is adapted from a figure in the *Rape of Proserpine* (Beauvais tapestry design; A345); the reclining nymph, bottom right, recurs in a drawing at Stockholm (A,I, p.147, fig.173, engr. Sauveur le Gros, fig.174). It has been suggested, most doubtfully, that the nymph's face, bottom right, is that of Mme. de Pompadour.[9]

For further discussion, see P486.

Drawings

CHICAGO Art Institute (inv. no.71244); study for the Triton, bottom right (Slatkin 1973, no.69; AD907; A422/12, fig.1194).
LILLE Musée des Beaux-Arts; preliminary study for the reclining nymph, bottom right (Slatkin 1973, fig.35).
LONDON Wallace Collection Library (PA2); study for the left-hand Triton; presented by the National Art-Collections Fund 1941 (A422/7, fig.1190).
Christie's, 1 April 1987 (136); study for, or from, the two nymphs, bottom right, probably made after P485 and not by Boucher.
Christie's, 6 July 1987 (53), study for the left-hand Triton, a superior version of the drawing in the Wallace Collection Library (see above).
PARIS Louvre (RF29327); study for the two nymphs with a Triton, bottom right; engr. G. Demarteau no.53 (Slatkin 1973, fig.36; AD910; A422/11, fig.1199; JR622). A version of this drawing was in a private coll., Brussels, 1982. A drawing after Demarteau's plate is in the Petit Palais (cf. JR622).
Bourgarel sale, 15 June 1922 (17); study for the two *putti*, top left, probably made for the *Rape of Europa* of 1747 (see above) and showing the legs as originally painted in P485 (A422/13, fig.1187).

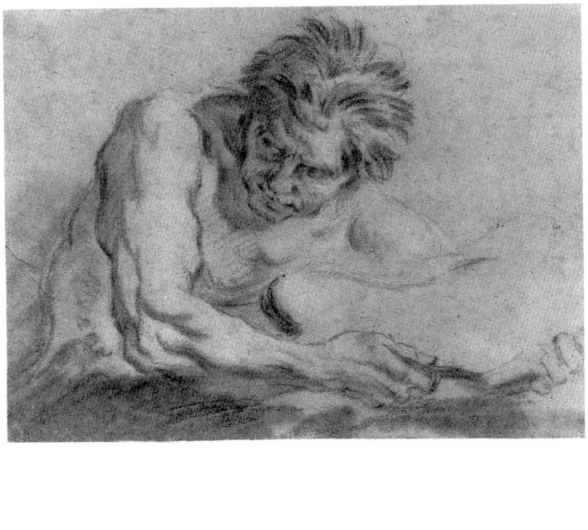

Boucher: *A Triton*, study for P485.
Wallace Collection Library

ROTTERDAM Boymans-van Beuningen Museum (no.138); study for the head of the left-hand nymph with her head on her hands (Slatkin 1973, fig.34; AD908; A422/8, fig.1188).
SWITZERLAND Dr R. Koela (formerly); study for the nymph offering Apollo his lyre, probably made for the *Rape of Proserpine* (see above) (A422/9, fig.1189).
WASHINGTON National Gallery (no.1980.64.1); study for the figure of Apollo with the right foot turned out, stamped: *Ecole Accademique de Dessin d'Orleans*; ex coll. Daniels; engr. L.-M. Bonnet (JR370) (Slatkin 1973, no.68; A422/10, fig.1201).

A study for the two *putti* behind Aurora, top right, illus. A422/15, fig.1197, without location.

The following drawings survive in engraved form:
Study for the group of three *putti*, bottom left, with the dolphin, engr. G. Demarteau no.133 (A422/2, described in error as JR849, fig.1191).
Study for the head of the nymph tying Apollo's sandal, engr. G. Demarteau no.155 (A422/4, fig.1193).
Study for the central nymph looking up at Apollo, engr. G. Demarteau no.149 (A422/5, fig. 1195).

Versions

PARIS comte Boni de Castellane (formerly); a reduced version in oil.[10]

An '*esquisse coloriée, Le Lever du Soleil*' by Boucher, 65 × 51, was lot 75 in an anon. sale, Paris, 28 December 1785, possibly the '*levé du Soleil, esquisse de M. Boucher sur toile*', lot 111, anon. sale, Paris, 13 May 1765. See also P486 Versions.

Tapestry

Gobelins *haute lisse*, by Cozette and Audran 1753–4, 316 × 275; ornamental borders, designed by Boucher, were added in 1760 making the size 435 × 387. For further discussion, see P486 Tapestry.

Provenance, Exhibitions

See P486.

References General

SM200; A422; cdA444.

[1] E. and J. de Goncourt, *Boucher*, 1862, pp.16–17, vividly described P485 as follows:

Des amours au haut du ciel écartent le voile de la Nuit & plient l'ombre comme une tente. L'Aurore, portant au dessus du front l'étoile du matin, effeuille du bout de ses doigts les rayons & les roses dans la lumière qui s'éveille. Sous la caresse du jour qu'elle répand, le jeune Apollon se lève dans sa gloire naissante; la pourpre lui vole en écharpe autour du corps; sous ses pieds, l'écume des flots se brise en vapeur & s'écroule en nuage. Une déité volante lui tend les rênes de son quadrige & la bride de ses chevaux qui piaffent dans l'éther, tandis que les filles de Doris, les nymphes de la mer, à mi-corps dans l'onde qui leur bat les reins, nouent sur les jambes du dieu les rubans de ses brodequins. Au devant du lever de Phoebus, un amour joue avec le collier de perles tombé du cou de l'Aurore; des tritons interrogent, dans un coquillage, le murmure des mers, le flux & le reflux de l'écho; des dauphins aux yeux & aux narines de rubis, balancés au branle de la vague, bercent les néréides accoudées sur l'oreiller de leur tête & tournant au public, qu'elles provoquent d'un sourire jeté par dessus l'épaule, leur dos humide où le flot pleure encore en gouttes de nacre.

[2] Cf. previous edition of this catalogue; Ananoff A422 and cdA444, and M. Levey, *Art and Architecture of the eighteenth century in France*, 1972, p.113.

[3] A drawing relating to the head of Apollo in P486, engr. G. Demarteau no.579 (JR862), has been called a head of Louis XV (see P486 Drawings).

[4] For the sculpture by Girardon and Tuby see, for example, G. Van der Kemp, *Versailles*, 1978, pp.156, 172–3; for La Fosse's paintings, see M. Stuffmann, *Gazette des Beaux-Arts*, 6e, LXIV, 1964, pp.43, 71, 73, 100 (no.18), 103 (no.31).

[5] Cf. M. Beaulieu, *Robert Le Lorrain*, 1982, no.215, pl.lxii.

[6] Slatkin 1973, p.89; she also observed that Boucher's Apollo in P485 is 'undoubtedly the most beautiful male nude he painted'.

[7] '*Pietre de Cortone fut encore un des Peintres célebres qui excita chez M. Boucher le plus d'émulation . . .*' (Antoine de Bret, *Nécrologe*, 1771; A doc.1082). See also *Galerie françoise*, 1771 (A doc. 1081) and the letter from Lépicié to Marigny, 14 July 1753, describing Boucher's Fontainebleau ceiling, showing the *Rising of the Sun*: '*un tout que Piètre de Cortone, suivant moi, ne désavouerait pas*' (A doc.536).

[8] Slatkin 1973, p.89, supposes that P485 may have been the 'very large picture' which Reynolds saw Boucher working on in Paris 'without drawings or models of any kind' (Reynolds, *Discourse* xii, 1784). Reynolds was in Paris in September/October 1752 and September/October 1768; his comments make no sense applied to P485, but may well refer, for example, to the two large pastorals of 1768 (Metropolitan Museum of Art; A654–5) for which no drawings are known (this is also suggested by Laing, p.308).

[9] Pompadour's presence in P485 and P486 seems first to have been suggested in the Commailles sale catalogue in 1855 (see P486 Provenance) where she is identified as Tethys (the only appropriate role for her to play); the statement was taken up by Soullié and Masson (SM200). Nolhac (*Boucher*, 1925, pp.142–3) associated Pompadour with the Tethys in P486, and supposed Miss O'Murphy to have been Boucher's inspiration for many of the nymphs in P485 (those reclining, bottom right, leaning on the extreme left, and offering Apollo his lyre) and one in P486 (lying prone, bottom right). Ananoff (A422/14) compared the head of the bottom right nymph in P485 with Boucher's pastel of Pompadour (A, I, fig.143; now National Gallery of Victoria, Melbourne), without drawing a conclusion.

[10] Letter on file from the baron de la Raudière, dated 15 January 1962, refers.

P486 *The Setting of the Sun*

The dark clouds of Night are pulled across the sky, preceded by the Evening Star; Apollo, fair-haired and with coral-pink drapery, dismounts from his chariot to be received into the arms of Tethys; she has grey and green drapery and is surrounded by her nymphs and Tritons.[1] Signed, bottom left: *f. Boucher/1752.*

Canvas, relined 318 x 261

P486 was varnished by Buttery in 1882, surface cleaned and retouched by Haines in 1903, 1910 and 1920, and cleaned and restored by Vallance in 1949. In 1981–2 many discoloured retouchings were treated by Lank who, in the course of cleaning and restoration, strip-lined the already double-lined canvas, using a new stretcher. A horizontal fold with nail holes 26 cm. below the top edge indicates P486 was once on a smaller stretcher. There are vertical seams 26 cm. and 145 cm. from the left-hand edge. There are some losses and tears along and above the fold and down the seams, along the bottom edge, in the sea round the prone nymph, bottom right, on her left buttock, and by the head of the prone *putto,* centre left. Numerous *pentimenti* have become more prominent with time:

1 The top centre group was redrawn: the head and shoulders of the left-hand figure (who seems to be winged), the left leg of the central figure and the left leg and body of the *putto* on the right.
2 Apollo's left hand was redrawn, and he originally wore sandals (cf. P485).
3 In the centre foreground, the reclining nymph's right hand was redrawn.
4 The prone *putto,* bottom left, was redrawn below the waist.
5 The shoulders of the nymph resting her head on her hands, bottom right, were redrawn.
6 Tethys's shell was originally much smaller and her profile was modified (her features remain somewhat contorted).
7 The area round the Triton holding the reins, bottom left, has been reworked: the horses appear to have been prancing.

For the subject, see P485.

Previously described as dated 1753,[2] P486 is dated a year earlier than the pendant (and see below). It shows a simpler, but more subtly luminous composition, which may be seen as a grand development of La Fosse's *Apollo and Tethys* (see P485 note 4) and as an elaboration of the *Apollo and Issé* of 1750 (Tours; A355). But, as with the pendant, the number of surviving life studies (see Drawings below) emphasises the originality of the composition. For the supposed identification of models, see P485 note 9.

The early history of P485 and P486 was published by Fenaille.[3] On 4 January 1752 Cozette was directed by Mme. de Pompadour to make tapestries for the Château de Bellevue from P485 and P486, '*dont le premier* [P486] *doit estre fait à la fin de ce mois*'.[4] Fenaille said she had obtained the paintings from the King, but such a commission is not recorded in the *comptes des Bâtiments.*[5] P485 was finished by mid-1753.[6] It is probable that both paintings and tapestries were at Bellevue between 1754 and 1760, when the tapestries were removed.[7]

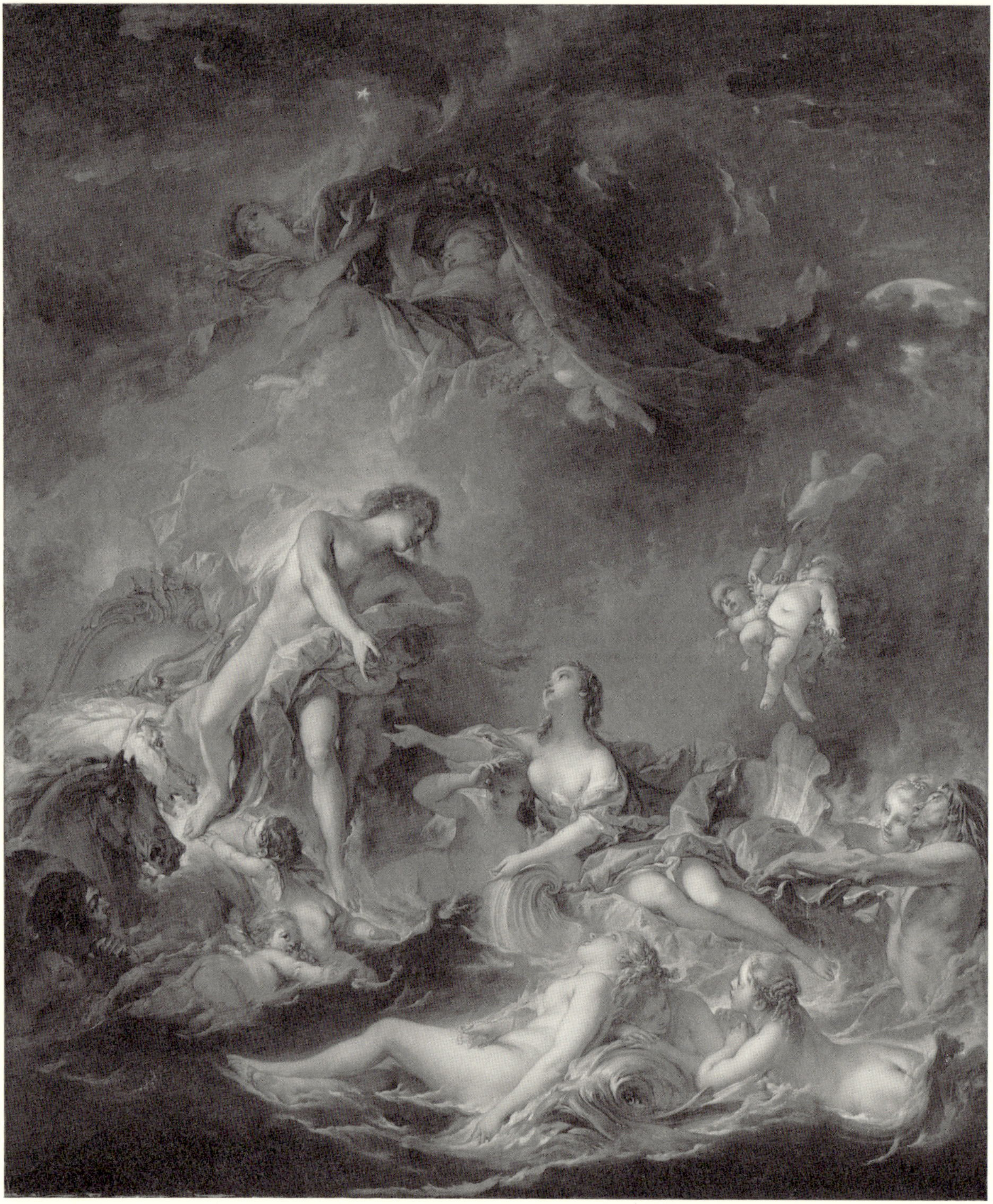

P486

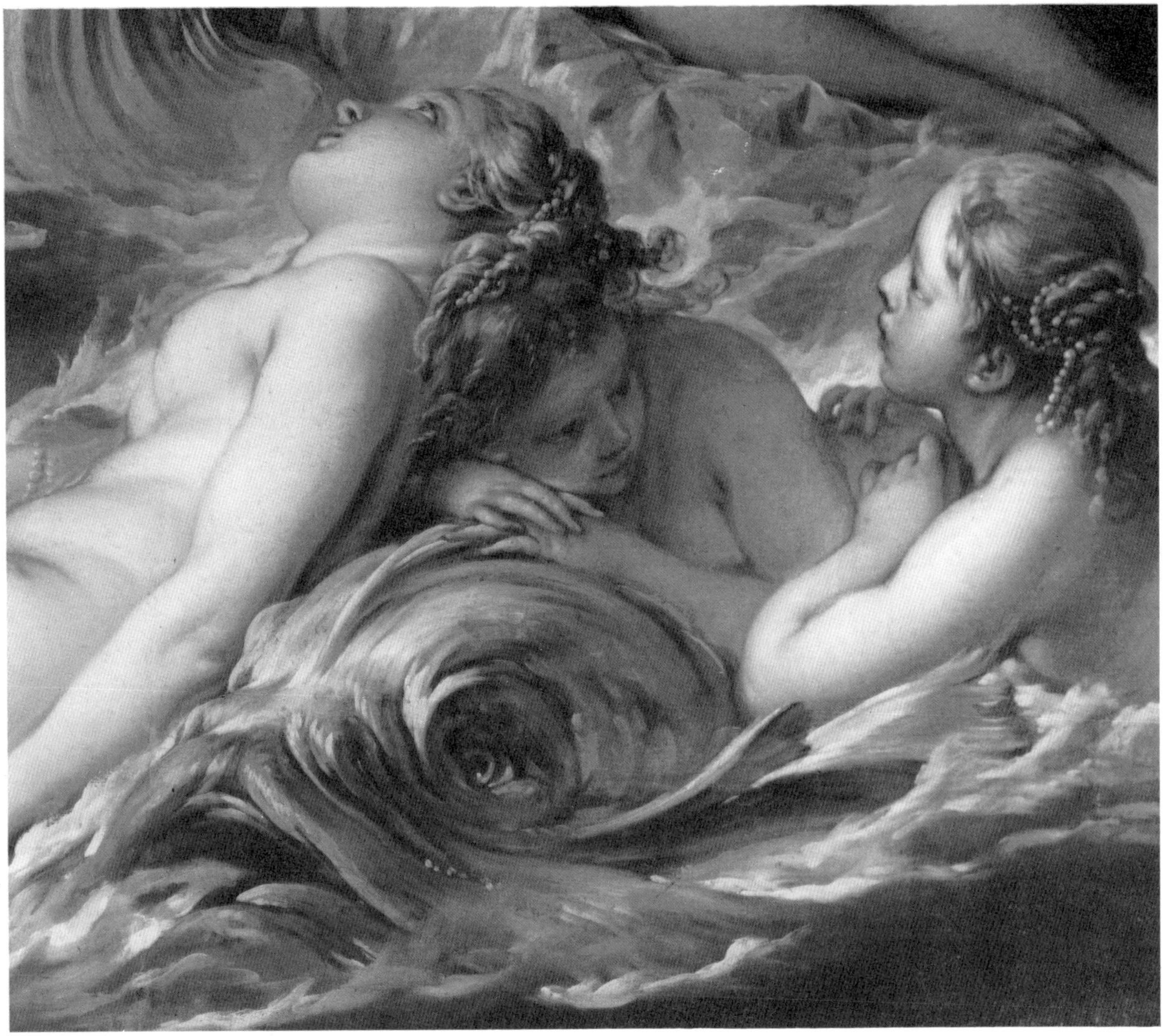

P486 detail

Though P485 and P486 are pendants, their compositions are not closely balanced. Apollo appears on the same side and Tethys looks in the same direction in each, suggesting that the designs were intended to hang opposite each other. Boucher considered them amongst his most satisfactory paintings (see Provenance) and, while they incurred some criticism at the 1753 Salon for a certain lack of decorum – Apollo as god of the Sun should not carry the lyre and arrows, and the nymphs and Tritons are behaving irreverently[8] – they were then generally acclaimed. Cochin, for example, found in them '*une richesse de génie admirable, soit pour la composition poétique, soit pour l'agencement pittoresque*'.[9] When the pictures re-emerged in the mid-nineteenth century (see Provenance) Bürger considered both Apollos '*terriblement maniérés . . . Boucher n'était pas fort sur le masculin – mais les fillettes plus ou moins divines sont délicieuses*'.[10] Two years later the Goncourts delivered their classic appreciation (see note 1, and P485 note 1), which has remained substantially uncontested:

> *Ce sont là les deux pages triomphales de Boucher. Elles ont le rayonnement, le flamboiement, la magnificence de ce char du Soleil versant dans les* Métamorphoses *le feu des chrysolithes & des pierreries. Elles sont le plus grand effort du peintre, les deux grandes machines de son oeuvre. Elles ont excités l'enthousiasme; elles sont demeurées éblouissantes.*[11]

Drawings

LONDON private collection; study for Apollo; exh. RA1968, no.73 (A423/8).

MONTREAL private collection; study for the Triton, bottom left; ex Sotheby's, 5 July 1976 (81); exh. New York, Stair Sainty Matthiesen, *Boucher*, 1987, no.30 (Slatkin 1973, no.70; AD904; A423/7, fig.1210).

PARIS Louvre (RF29005); study for the prone nymph, bottom right (AD910; A423/3, fig.1203).

Baron de la Raudière; finished study for the reclining nymph, centre foreground (AD469; A423/5, fig.1205). A counter-proof was in the Ryaux coll., Paris, and a less finished and weaker version was exh. Washington, National Gallery, . . . *Drawings from the* [*Chanler*] *Collection* . . ., 1982 (5). A similar figure, accompanied by a *putto*, appears in miniatures attributed to Charlier in the Wallace Collection (M55 and M63).

M. Lévy (formerly); study for the head of the nymph by the Triton, extreme right; engr. G. Demarteau no.217 (A423/10 and 11, fig.1207; JR782).

VIENNA Albertina; reversed study for the horse's head (A423/4, fig.1212).

WEIMAR Staatliche Kunstsammlungen; study for the standing Triton, extreme right (Slatkin 1973, fig.37; A423/6, fig.1204).

A study for the head of Apollo was engr. G. Briceau (A423/1, fig.1214); it compares closely with the drawing for Apollo in *Apollo and Issé* (A355), engr. G. Demarteau no.579 (JR862), sometimes called *Tête de Louis XV* (A355/6, fig.1043).

Ananoff loosely associates P486 with further drawings:
a recumbent nymph, somewhat resembling in part the nymph resting her head on her hands, bottom centre right (Palais Galliera, 1 December 1966, lot 108; A423/14, fig.1209, and A515/6, fig.1426); another comparable with the figure of Tethys (Louvre, inv. no.24763; AD892; A423/9, fig.1211), and a third related to the head of Tethys, engr. G. Demarteau no.91 (A423/12, fig.1208; JR663). Another drawing loosely connected with the figure of Tethys was engr. E. Fessard (JR997; A423/16).

Copy

PARIS baron de la Raudière; 60 × 50 (see P485 note 10).

Versions

PARIS comte Boni de Castellane (formerly); a reduced version in oil.

A '*très belle esquisse*' by Boucher, '*Apollon qui descend chez Thétis*', 62 × 51, was lot 6 in the Delaborde sale, Paris, 16 May 1783. Two oval pictures, '*L'aurore et le soleil couchant: paysages avec figures*', allegedly from the Pompadour collection, were in the d'Orlémont sale, Paris, 9 February 1833 (32), see also note 13.

Tapestry

Gobelins, *haute lisse*, by Cozette and Audran, 1752–4, 316 × 264; ornamental borders, designed by Boucher, were added in 1760 making the size 432 × 372.

The Gobelins tapestries from P485 and P486 were commissioned by Mme. de Pompadour for Bellevue (see above) where they hung 1754–60. When she leased Bellevue to the King in 1757 she was considering moving them to the Hôtel d'Evreux in Paris, and the borders were commissioned that year with this new site in mind. But in 1760 Pompadour exchanged them for a set of six *Enfants jardiniers* tapestries. They stayed at the Gobelins factory until 1768 when they were sold to an unknown client by Nielson.[12] Only the two were made, and nothing more is known of them.

Provenance[13]

With P485: Mme. de Pompadour (1721–64), Château de Bellevue (see note 7); her sale, Paris, 28 April ff., 1766 (14, '. . . *La composition ingénieuse, les grâces, & tout ce qui peut contribuer à rendre des morceaux de la première distinction, se trouvent réunis dans ces deux tableaux. J'ai entendu dire plusieurs fois par l'Auteur, qu'ils étoient de nombre de ceux dont il étoit le plus satisfait. Le jugement d'un Artiste aussi modeste & aussi peu prévenu de ses talents que l'est M. Boucher, doit être cru . . .*'), bt. d'Ennery, 9,800 *livres*;[14] by 1771 with L.-P.-S. Marchal de Syncy [Saincy] (d. 1771), Paris;[15] his son, L.-R. Marchal de Syncy (d. 1789); his sale, Paris, 29 April ff., 1789 (15, . . . *deux tableaux . . . les plus beaux connus de cet artiste, que l'on sait les avoir fait pour feu Madame de Pompadour*'); c. 1827 P485 and P486 were bt. from a French dealer by the baron de Commailles [Caumail], 380 fr.;[16] his sale, 25 rue du Faubourg Saint-Honoré, Paris, 2 August 1855 (6, '. . . *ces belles toiles, qui ont longtemps orné la galerie de Mme de Pompadour, semblent avoir été faites pour la favorite elle même, dont, par une adroite flaterie, Boucher a reproduit les traits gracieux sous ceux de Thétis*'), bt. by the 4th Marquess of Hertford, 20,200 fr.; rue Laffitte inventory 1871 (377); 105 Piccadilly 1874–5 (two of '*four fine mythological subjects*'); Hertford House inventory 1890.

Exhibitions

With P485: Salon 1753 (10, '. . . *ces tableaux doivent s'executer en Tapisserie, à la Manufacture Royale du Gobelins, pour les Sieurs Cozette & Audran*'); boulevard des Italiens 1860 (77, *Le Lever du Soleil*; 78, *Le Coucher du Soleil*) lent Hertford.

References General

SM200; A423; cdA445.

1 E. and J. de Goncourt, *Boucher*, 1862, p. 17, vividly described P486 as follows:

> *Des amours & des génies apportent & déroulent en haut du tableau le manteau sombre & bleu de la Nuit. Le jour meurt en reflets sous leurs pieds qu'il éclaire. Au milieu des vapeurs violettes & roses perdues là-bas dans un fond de ténèbres où se dénoue, au dessus du clapotement des vagues vertes, une guirlande d'amours, l'Apollon rayonne dans l'apothéose du crépuscule. Son char rocaille, autour duquel bourdonne une ronde d'amours, entre doucement dans la mer & coule à l'abîme; de ses coursiers blancs, aux naseaux roses & fumant des derniers feux du jour, l'un est encore argenté de lumière, l'autre a déjà plongé dans l'ombre. Le dieu, svelte comme un éphèbe, s'élance en étendant les bras vers Thétis. Allongée dans une pose d'accueil amoureux, la déesse vogue vers lui sur une conque, parée des couleurs de la mer, la robe teinte des nuances d'une vague, les cheveux gris-argenté & comme poudrés de l'écume des flots. Une néréide, réfugiée contre elle & s'appuyant à sa conque, se gare, avec sa main jetée coquettement devant ses yeux, du dernier rayon du dieu; & tout autour de Thétis, sa cour de tritons & d'amours fatigue l'eau du sillon de ses jeux, jusqu'à ce groupe de femmes enroulées, ondulantes, que la mer baigne, chatouille & renverse sur son sein qui palpite.*

2 Cf. W. Bürger, *Gazette des Beaux-Arts*, 1ère, VII, 1860, p. 343: 'Le Lever *et* le Coucher du Soleil, *signés en toutes lettres et datés 1753*'.

3 M. Fenaille, *Etat général des Tapisseries de la Manufacture des Gobelins*, IV, 1907, pp. 174–87. See also A docs. 532–3, 537, 540, 686, 767–8 and 770.

4 Fenaille, *op. cit.*, p. 174 n. 1.

5 Fenaille, p. 174. Fenaille describes, pp. 173–4, a commission of 1748 from the King for two large paintings by Boucher, the subjects from the *Fêtes Vénitiennes* and the *Fêtes de Thalie*, as designs for tapestries intended for the Château de la Muette. By 1749 Boucher had made oil sketches and begun the large paintings, but no further progress was made (see also F. Engerand, *Inventaire des Tableaux commandés et achetés par la Direction des Bâtiments du Roi*, 1900, p. 56; A docs. 320–1, 393, 479, 514; Laing, p. 244). Did these become *Le Lever* and *Le Coucher*?

6 On 22 July 1753 Lépicié reminded de Vandières [Marigny] that Boucher's two paintings, P485 and P486, were required for the Salon scheduled to open on 18 August (Fenaille, p. 177; A doc. 537), but P485 must have been completed some months before. On 1 May 1753 the King had commissioned the ceiling decoration for Fontainebleau, of which Boucher showed four panels at the same Salon, and by November had completed the main panel, *Le char d'Apollon* (the subject, of course, directly related to that of P485; cf. A417–21).

[7] That the tapestries were at Bellevue is clear from Fenaille. In the *Salle des Officiers des Gardes* at Bellevue Pompadour had *'de grands tableaux qui ont servys à faire des tapisseries'* (P. Biver, *Histoire du Château de Bellevue*, 1933, p.48) which very probably included, or were, P485 and P486; they had been acquired in 1753–4 when Pompadour was completing the decoration of Bellevue (cf. Fiske Kimball, *The Creation of the Rococo Style*, 1943, p.195). P485 and P486 do not appear in J. Cordey, *Inventaire des biens de madame de Pompadour, rédigé après son décès*, 1939.

[8] Cf. La Font de Saint-Yenne, *Sentimens sur quelques ouvrages . . .*, 1754, pp. 37–8; Esteve, *Lettre à un ami sur l'exposition . . . dans le Grand Sallon du Louvre*, 1753 (A doc. 549); Grimm to Diderot, 15 September 1753 (A doc.556). An anonymous reviewer preferred the *Setting* to the *Rising of the Sun* in which the pose of Apollo *'est forcée . . . et . . . le dessin en est peu correct'* (A doc.545). For a survey of such criticism, see M. Fried, *Absorption and Theatricality*, 1980, pp.36–9, and note 9 below.

[9] A doc.550; T. Crow, *Revue de l'Art*, 73, 1986, p.11. Other favourable critics included Le Blanc, Caylus, La Combe and Laugier (cf. A docs.544–54, 558; Crow, *loc. cit.*; Nolhac, *Boucher*, 1925, pp.139–40).

[10] Bürger, *op. cit.*, p.344.

[11] Goncourt, *loc. cit.*

[12] Fenaille records (pp.183–5) that in 1766 both the comte Schouvalov and Mme. Geoffrin expressed an interest in buying the Bellevue tapestries which , however, remained at the factory where they were examined on 18 August 1768: *'il faut observer que ces deux Pièces sont faites depuis 10 ans, et qu'elles ont servy et qu'elles ont beaucoup perdu de leur fraîcheur'*. Neilson sold them in October/November 1768 to an unknown client whom Fenaille supposed may have been either the 6th Earl of Coventry, the 2nd Earl of Fife, the 1st Duke of Northumberland or Sir William Weddell (all of whom were buying from Nielson at about that time).

[13] Soullié and Masson (SM200), and previous editions of this catalogue, associated P485 and P486 with the d'Orlémont sale, 1833 (see Versions above), but the descriptions do not agree.

[14] D'Ennery, *écuyer*, rue Neuve-des-bons-Enfants, bought seven Bouchers at the Pompadour sale (lots 14, 16, 18, and 19); see also Laing, p.244.

[15] P485 and P486 were listed in Syncy's collection in two of Boucher's obituaries in 1771 (in the *Galerie françoise* and by Antoine de Bret; A docs.1081–2). He also owned two Boucher overdoors (cf. A487–8, P490 Studio of Boucher, and Appendix III, no.19), three pastorals of 1761–2 (A554–6, now National Gallery of Scotland) and another of 1765 (A615). Syncy, an *'économe général du Clergé'* lived in the rue Fossés-Montmartre, where his son's posthumous sale took place. For the Syncy family, see M. Roland-Michel, *The Burlington Magazine*, CXXVIII, 1986, supp., pp.546–52. I am grateful to C.M. Clarke for help over this note.

[16] Cf. *L'Artiste*, II, 1857, p.235: *'M. le baron de Caumail, riche amateur, acheta il y a trente ans, à un brocanteur, 2 tableaux de Boucher, le* Lever *et le* Coucher du Soleil. *Ces tableaux ont 10 pieds de haut. Le marchand n'en savait que faire; il les ceda à M. le baron de Caumail pour 380 francs. Le marchand crut sincèrement les avoir* bien vendus. *Boucher était foudroyé alors par l'école de David; personne, à aucun prix, ne voulait de Boucher. A la vente de la galerie de M. de Caumail . . . ces deux tableaux ont été* vendus *près de 23,000 francs! . . . Tout le monde, excepté M. de Caumail, trouva qu'ils étaient* bien vendus. *M. de Caumail n'en fut pas satisfait . . . Il trouva qu'ils avaient été* mal vendus.*'*

P487 *Mercury confiding the Infant Bacchus to the Nymphs (La naissance de Bacchus)*

The central nymph has light blue drapery, the reclining nymph on the left green; Mercury wears a steel-blue winged helmet and winged sandals.

Canvas, relined 230 × 273

Varnished by Buttery in 1882 and cleaned by Lank in 1981–2. There is a tear across the left leg of the central nymph, and there are a number of small losses: along a horizontal seam 119 cm. above the bottom edge, across the upper arm of the reclining nymph on the left, in the infant's hair, along the bottom edge and in the top left-hand corner. An old fold mark runs 4 cm. inside the right-hand edge. *Pentimenti* show that the area behind, and to the right of Mercury was reworked (there was probably a rock there originally); the profile head of the nymph second from the left was redrawn and Mercury's caduceus enlarged. Painted on a blue-grey ground.

The subject is briefly described by Ovid, *Metamorphoses* III, 314–15: Bacchus, son of Jupiter by Semele, was persecuted by the jealous Juno; for his safety Jupiter had him delivered by Mercury to the nymphs on Mount Nysa (where Bacchus was to discover the vine). In P487 the central nymph points to the vine which flowers on Bacchus's arrival, an incident related by Philostratus, *Imagines* I, xiv.[1]

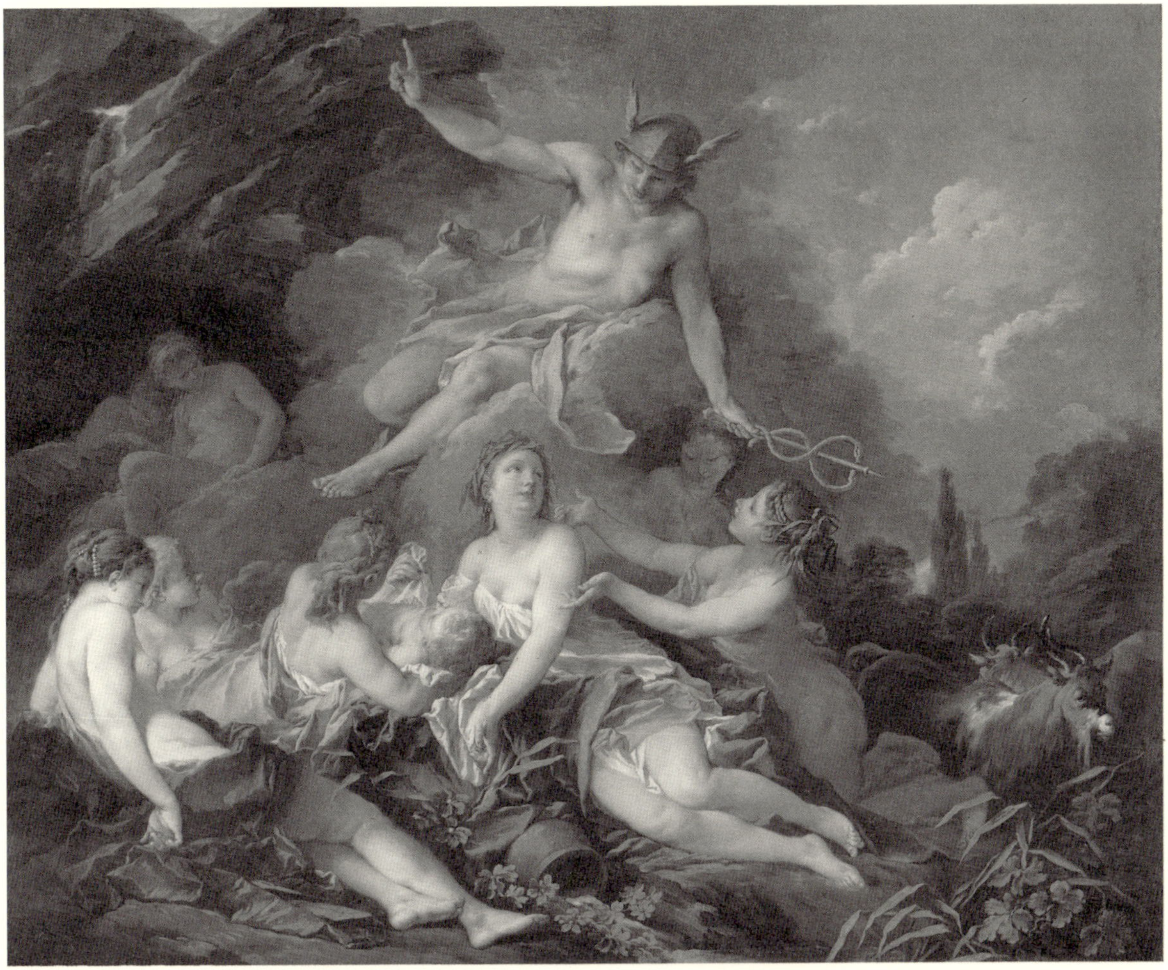

P487

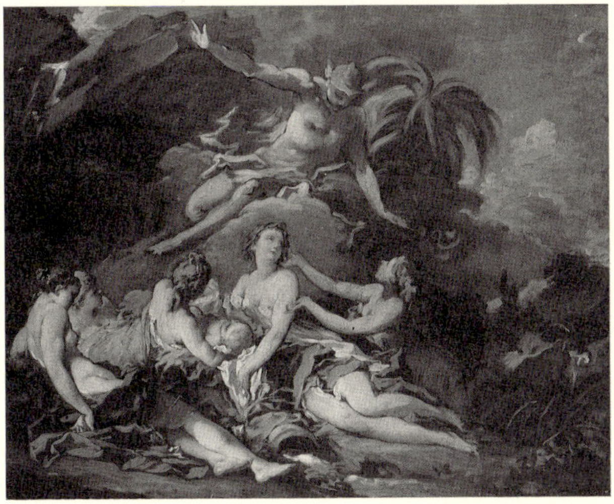

Boucher:
Mercury confiding the Infant Bacchus to the Nymphs.
Private collection,
New York

P487 may be dated c.1732–4; for a general discussion of this dating and of the commission from Derbais, see P484.

Although P487 has generally been dated somewhat later than P484,[2] it is probably earlier, as Laing (p.159) has hinted. The composition is less ambitious, the colour more restrained, and there are weaknesses of drawing (e.g. in Mercury's right leg and shoulder, and the right leg of the reclining nymph in the centre). Laing also indicates that the spirited oil sketch for P487 (see Versions) probably preceded that made for P484.[3] The pose of the reclining nymph seen on the left in P487 recurs several times in Boucher's early work: *Les enfants du fermier* (A2), *La naissance d'Adonis* (A38), *Le moineau apprivoisé* (A57) and *Le repos de Vénus* (A97). The goats and landscape recall the work of Castiglione and Rosa da Tivoli which Boucher would have seen in Italy. The pose of Mercury somewhat resembles that of the same figure in the bas-relief by Nicolas Coustou of c.1726 (formerly Hôtel des Douanes, Rouen).[4]

Between 1860 and 1925 P487 bore an attribution to Lemoyne, see P484 note 8.

Drawings

LONDON British Museum (no.1933.10.14.22); study for Mercury's head, attributed to Boucher (A105/3 and A676/7, fig.1766).
PARIS galerie Cailleux 1978; study for the figure of Mercury, ex coll. Daniels; exh. Cailleux, *Sanguines*, 1978, no.7 (Slatkin 1973, no.50; A105/2, fig.418; see also P484 note 6).
TOURS Musée des Beaux-Arts; study for the three left-hand nymphs (A105/1, fig.417).

Engraving

P. Aveline 1748 (JR247) with verses by Moraine in Latin and French:

Venez, Nymphes, venez recevoir de Mercure
Cet enfant qui sourit d'un air si gracieux.
Conservez bien le fils du Souverain des Cieux:
Quelque jour il sçaura payer sa nourriture;
Et donner pour son lait un nectar precieux;
Qui fera le bonheur des hommes et des Dieux.

The engraving shows a more dramatic sky than P487 and the waterfall on the left is more prominent.

Version

NEW YORK private collection; 59.7 × 73.7, oil sketch for P487, showing Mercury in a red helmet looking to the right, a palm tree behind him, and omitting the flowering vine; exh. Tokyo, *Boucher*, no.9 (A105; Laing, p.159).

Copies/Versions

MONACO Sotheby's, 5 March 1984 (1060) and 23 February 1986 (538); 133 × 143.5, full-scale copy of the lower-left figure group of nymphs with the infant.

The composition was reproduced by D. Chodowiecki on a gold box attributed to D. Baudesson (Louvre, OA7683).

Provenance

See P484.

Exhibition

Boulevard des Italiens 1860 (86*ter*), see P484, note 8.

References General

SM102; A106; CdA107.

[1] The goats in P487 may refer to Jupiter's having once turned Bacchus into a goat to avoid Juno's attention (Apollodorus, *The Library* III, iv), or to the tradition that the goat was sacrificed to Bacchus (Virgil, *Georgics* II, 380–1); they may equally have been a token of Boucher's admiration of Castiglione. There were, according to Hyginus (*Fabulae*, XCII) five nymphs, where Boucher shows eight in P487; he showed five in his later version of the subject (1769; Fort Worth, Texas; A676).

[2] Cf. H. Voss, *The Burlington Magazine*, XCV, 1953, pp.86, 89 ('about 1740'); J.-L. Bordeaux, *The First Painters of the King*, exh. cat., Stair Sainty Matthiesen, New York, 1985, p.36 (1737–8); and see P484 note 6.

[3] Laing, p.160: the grisaille sketch for P484 anticipates Boucher's mature practice, while the sketch for P487 'is executed in a technique more reminiscent of the early finished pictures . . .'.

[4] Cf. F. Souchal, *French Sculptors of the 17th and 18th centuries: the reign of Louis XIV*, I, 1977, p.175.

P489 *A Summer Pastoral (La couronne accordée au berger)*

The standing shepherdess wears a white bodice with red ties and golden yellow sleeves, and a deep plum coloured panelled skirt; the seated girl wears a blue jacket over a white blouse, a silver and blue striped underskirt with a red overskirt; the musette-player wears a silver-blue jacket with light purple breeches. Signed, lower left: *f. Boucher/-1749*.

Canvas, relined 259 × 197 with rounded corners

The paint surface was transferred onto a fine muslin, supported by a rectangular double lining canvas, probably soon after 1852 (see Provenance). The second lining canvas was replaced in the course of cleaning and restoration by Vallance in 1968. A vertical seam runs 78.7 cm. from the right-hand edge and the join has been retouched. Lifting paint in the bottom centre and right areas was treated by Lank in 1980. There are small damages above the tree, top centre, above the back of the central sheep, on the musette-player's left knee, and along the top and bottom edges. *Pentimenti* reveal alterations to the standing shepherdess's right foot, and the foliage from the tall tree originally spread further across the composition to the right; a second tall tree, reaching to the top of the canvas, stood to the right of the present tree; the distant round tower was moved slightly to the right. Infra-red scanning shows that areas behind and to the left of the top of the present tree were reworked.

The subject probably derived from Favart's *Vendanges de Tempé*, like that of the pendant P482; Laing suggests that the two shepherdesses may be the cousins Babet and Lisette from that *pantomime*.[1] The distant Italianate tower, like the classical fountain in P482, may have been intended to convey a Mediterranean setting. The model for the recumbent shepherdess recurs in P482. For further commentary, see P482.

Drawing

Bust-length study for the standing shepherdess, engr. L.-M. Bonnet (JR320). A related drawing is in the Bibliothèque Nationale (Est., B.6. *Rés.*, t.II, format 3; see JR320).

Copies

BAVARIA Linderhof; copy by Ch. Jank, 1870–9, adapted to imitate tapestry (and see P482).
PARIS Mme. Besnard 1904; exh. *L'art français au XVIIIe siècle*, Brussels, 1904, no.3, *La bergère écoutée* (illus. H. Macfall, *Boucher*, 1908, p.92).

Version

HAMPSHIRE private collection; 76.8 × 51.4, oval, signed and dated 1748; without the seated shepherdess; exh. Salon 1750, RA1968 (44); engr. R. Gaillard, *Le berger recompensé*, reversed (JR1032) (A319 as *Berger accordant sa musette*).[2]

Provenance

See P482.

Exhibition

Boulevard des Italiens 1860 (83, *La musette*) lent Hertford.

References General

SM1541; A337; cdA351; A. Laing, *Revue de L'Art*, 73, 1986, pp.60–1.

[1] Cf. *Revue de l'Art*, 73, 1986, p.64 n.74. The résumé of *Les vendanges de Tempé* in the *Dictionnaire des Théâtres de Paris*, VI, 1756, pp.70–82, does not describe such a scene exactly; the Little Shepherd plays the musette in scene i and again to the sleeping Lisette in scene iv.
[2] Gaillard's engraving was one of a set of four (JR1026–32). The other three subjects being identifiable in *Les vendanges de Tempé* (*Le panier mystérieux* A320, *Les amants surpris* A341, and *L'agréable lecon* A311).

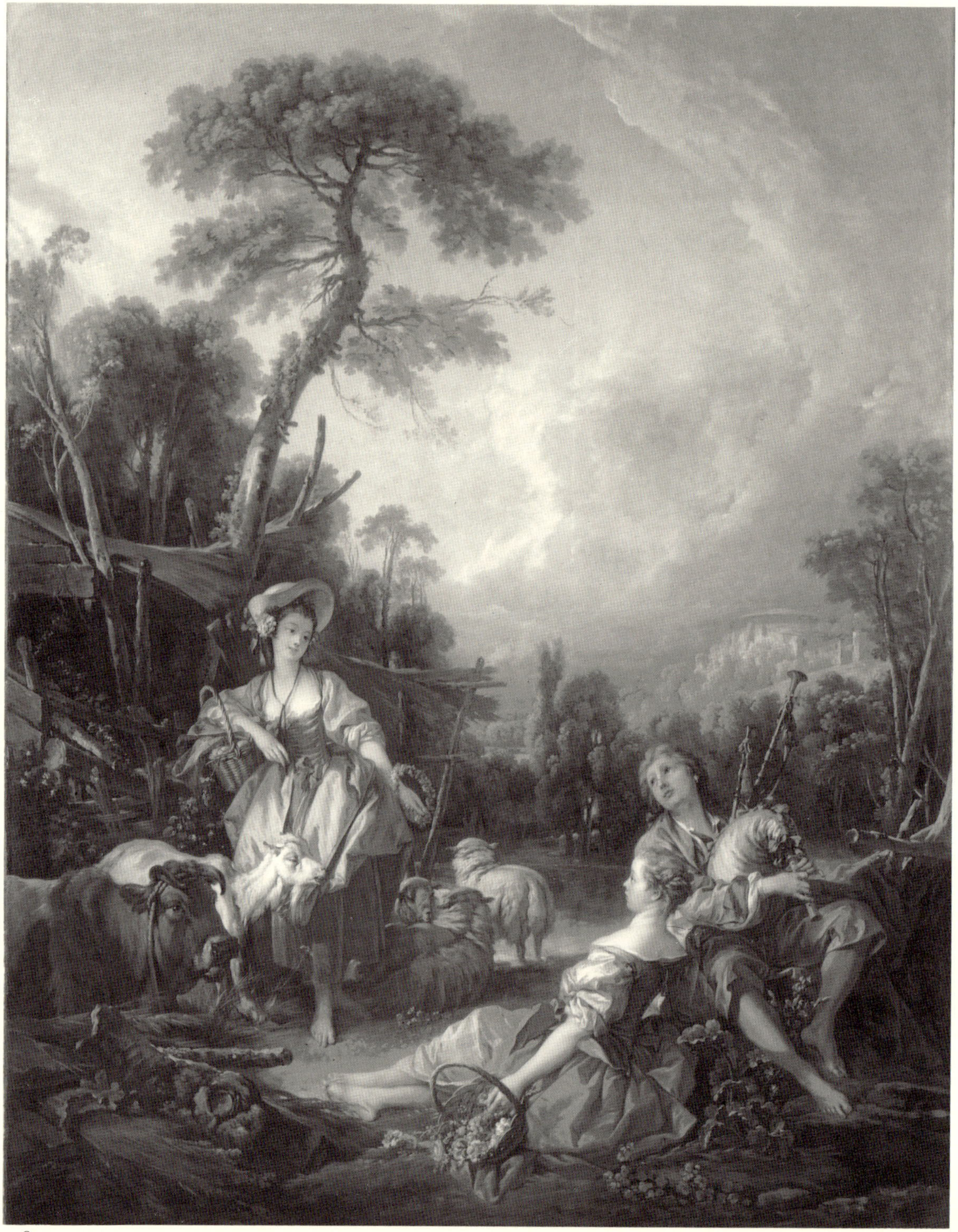

P489

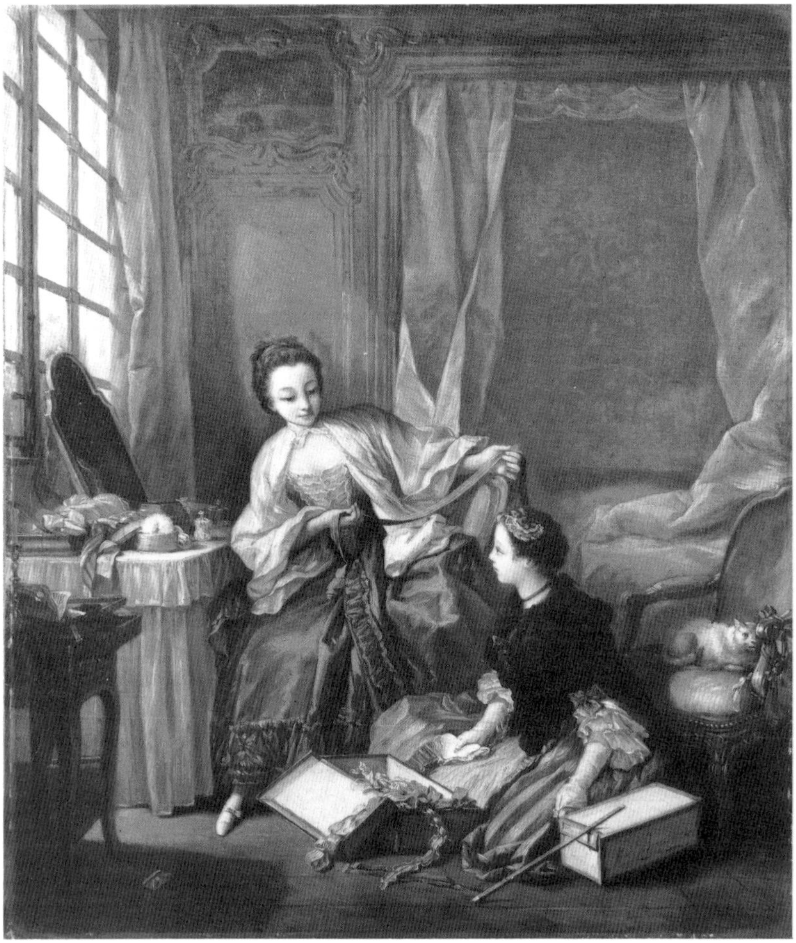

P390

Ascribed to Boucher

P390 *The Modiste (La marchande des modes Le matin)*

The seated lady wears a white wrap over a blue gown; the milliner a black jacket and a blue-striped overskirt; the curtains are pale purple. Signed, or inscribed, on box, lower right: *f. Boucher.*

Canvas, relined[1] 63 × 51.8

The surface was heavily ironed in the course of relining in the nineteenth century. There are small losses in the window and mirror, and to the left of the seated lady's right shoulder. The varnish is discoloured.

The subject was intended to illustrate the first of the four *Times of Day,* but the other three pictures were never completed (see note 3). P390 shows one of four elegant, contemporary interior scenes painted by Boucher between 1739 and 1746,[2] and may be compared with his drawing *La sultane* made for *Moeurs et usages des Turcs* in 1746 (A, I, p.29, fig.66; JR883).

P390 is a repetition of the painting commissioned in 1745 by the Crown Princess Louisa Ulrika of Sweden and delivered to the Swedish Envoy in Paris in October 1746 (see Versions).[3] The differences between the two pictures are slight, which suggests that P390 was painted with the original to hand, i.e. in 1746; they are:

1 The ribbon in the seated lady's hands is red and blue in P390 and yellow and green in the original.

2 Her eyes are more hooded in P390.

3 A blue ribbon in the milliner's box in the original is yellow in P390.

4 One of the cat's eyes is half-hidden in P390, but visible in the original.

5 The floor is faintly squared on the right in P390, but not in the original.

6 The curtains and the colours of the skirts differ slightly (though some of this is due to the discoloured varnish on P390).

7 The neat signature and date on the milliner's box in the original is replaced by an uncharacteristically cursive script in P390.

Practically indistinguishable in content from the original, P390 provided an entirely satisfactory model for Gaillard's engraving published in 1755 (see Engraving).

There are differences, however, in quality: P390 lacks the lively surface of the original (and, of course, the *pentimenti*). Probably made for Prousteau, it was described in his sale in 1769 as *'d'après Boucher'*[4] (see Provenance; he also owned another Boucher studio piece, see note 10). P390 has since been called a *copie ancienne*[5] and a *réplique d'atelier,*[6] as well as an autograph replica (in previous editions of this catalogue, and by Laing, p.227). Boucher often made autograph replicas of pictures destined for foreign clients (see Laing, nos.40, 53 and cf. P431), but P390 seems rather to be a thoroughly competent studio production.[7]

Engraving

R. Gaillard 1755; *La marchande des modes* (JR1024),[8] reversed, after the painting '*Tiré du cabinet de Mr. Prousteau Capitaine des Gardes de la Ville*', with verses by Moraine:

Les Dieux ont pris plaisir à vous rendre parfaite,
Et ces vains ornemens qu'à tort vous empruntez,
Ne servent qu'à cacher de réelles beautés;
Quites donc pour toujours, Philis, votre toilette.
Voulez-vous exciter les plus vives ardeurs,
A vos aimables loix soumettre tous les coeurs,
Ainsi qu'en l'âge d'Or sans fard et sans parure,
Montrez-vous dans l'état de la simple nature.

Versions

STOCKHOLM Nationalmuseum (NM772); 64 × 53,[9] signed and dated 1746 on the milliner's box; the original picture, see above; exh. Manchester, *Boucher,* 1984 (P3) (A297; Laing, no.51).

A version was in the Febvre sale, Paris, 19 March 1852 (5, *'Boucher, coquette dans son appartement, une marchande lui offre des rubans'*), and another was in the Jaeger collection, Stockholm (Laing, p.224).

Provenance

S.-P. Prousteau (d.1781)[10] by 1755; his sale, Paris, 5 June 1769 (53, '. . . *tableau peint d'après M. Boucher . . . on trouve une estampe gravée d'après ce morceau par Gaillard . . .*'), bt. Basan,[11] 45 *livres*; the duc de Morny (1811–65); his sale, Phillips, 1st day, 20 June 1848 (10, Boucher, *La Marchande à la Toilette*, engraved), bt., almost certainly, by the 4th Marquess of Hertford, 55 gn.;[12] Hertford House inventory 1870.

Exhibition

Bethnal Green 1872–5 (421).

References General

SM under 1216; A297/4 and CdA308 as *réplique d'atelier*; Laing, pp.227–8.

1 The relining canvas is marked in chalk, *verso*: *10 x 3297*.

2 The other subjects being:
Le déjeuner 1739, 81.5 × 65.5 (once owned by Prousteau; Louvre; A165)
Woman fastening her garter 1742, 53 × 63 (coll. Thyssen-Bornemisza; A208)
Madame Boucher 1743, 57.2 × 68.3 (Frick Collection; A263).

3 The subject was described in a letter of 17/27 October 1745 from Carl Reinhold Berch, Secretary to the Swedish legation in Paris, to Count Tessin in Stockholm: '*Le Matin sera une femme qui a fini avec son friseur, gardant encore son peignoir, et s'amusant à regarder des brinborions qu'une marchande de modes étale*' A doc.249). Berch went on to describe the other three *Times of Day* subjects, which Boucher continued to discuss until 1750 (cf. Laing, pp.224, 226–7).

4 Laing, p. 228, supposes that this qualification was made because the agent, Rémy, knew that the original was in Sweden.

5 *Inventaire du Fonds français du Cabinet des Estampes*, IX, 1962, p.384.

6 P. Grate in *Boucher*, exh. cat., Manchester, 1984, p.18, and see References General.

7 That this replica should have been made by studio assistants seems reasonable when one recalls the number of prestigious commissions on which Boucher was working in 1746 – for the Dauphin's *appartement*, the *Cabinet des Médailles*, Choisy, the Opéra and others for Sweden (cf. Laing, pp. 25–6, 226).

8 Gaillard issued a pendant plate after Gravelot's *Le lecteur*, a painting owned by Boucher (cf. Laing, p.228).

9 I.e. the same size as P390 which, nevertheless, has been described as a reduced copy (e.g. *Inventaire*, see note 5, *loc. cit.*).

10 For whom, see Laing, pp. 227–8. Prousteau owned six Bouchers, all of which were engraved; three appeared in his sale, of which *L'enlèvement d'Europe*, lot 52, was described as '*peinte dans l'école de M. Boucher, que l'on croit retouchée par ce Maître. Cl. Duflos a gravé une estampe après ce tableau*' (it is now in the North Carolina Museum of Art, Raleigh; A350/20). Prousteau's sale also included several proofs of the engravings after P390 and *L'enlèvement d'Europe*. See also note 2 above for another Boucher in Prousteau's collection.

11 According to C. de Ris, *Gazette des Beaux-Arts*, 2e, x, 1874, p.496, Basan '*n'était qu'un prête-nom*', but cf. the provenance and note 13 under Greuze P442.

12 Lord Hertford bought several pictures at this sale (Berchem P186, Heyden P225, du Jardin P641, Watteau P389, P391) and the fact that P390 was in London (as opposed to Paris) in 1870 would indicate it had been acquired in London.

Studio of Boucher

P481 *Seated Nymph with flutes*

Reclining on blue drapery, a shepherdess's straw hat and crook to the left; the *putto* with the tambourine has yellow drapery, the other blue.

Canvas, relined 96 × 140 rounded top corners

The canvas was made up to 101 × 147 in the course of relining in the nineteenth century (cf. P490). There is a damage above the flowers on the right and scratches below the blue drapery and above the flowers. Retouchings appear in the sky to the right, on the nymph's left leg and right foot, and round the edges. The varnish is discoloured.

The subject is possibly Euterpe, muse of lyrical poetry, who is said to have invented the flute; it has also been associated with Erato, muse of amorous poetry, and Terpsichore, muse of dancing. Boucher maintained a somewhat cavalier attitude towards antiquity, and his intention here is ambiguous.[1]

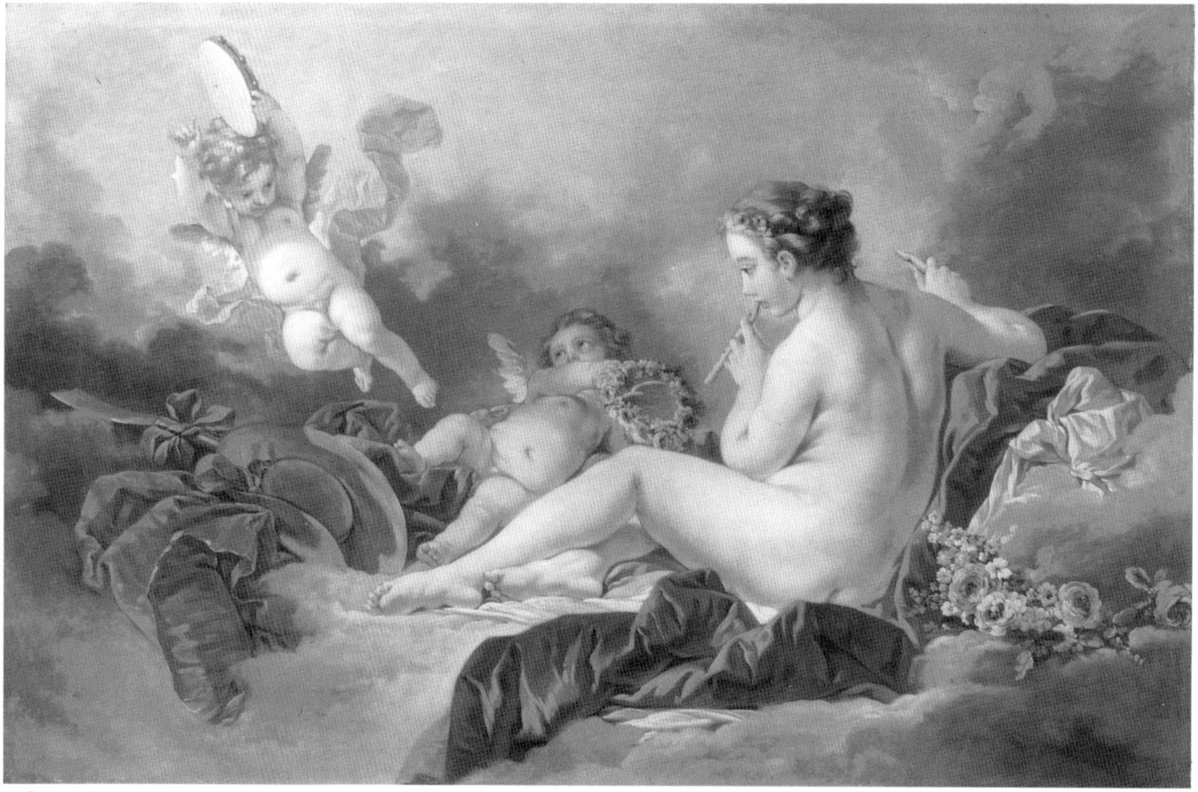

P481

The execution of P481 is hard and dry (the passage describing the hat and supporting drapery, for example, quite lacks Boucher's vigour), suggesting at best a studio production. A superior version (see below) is signed and dated 1752. From at least 1870 P481 hung as the pendant to P490, though they appear to be by different hands and at one stage were of different sizes, see P490.

Versions

LONDON Wallace Collection (M48); miniature by Charlier based on the New York version below, but without the *putto* with the tambourine.

NEW YORK private collection; 92 × 123, signed and dated 1752, the nymph with a plait down her back and more drapery; related drawings for the nymph and the *putto* with a tambourine are recorded (A389).

Provenance[2]

The 4th Marquess of Hertford; possibly Bagatelle inventory 1871 (927, as one of '*quatre panneaux de décoration*', with P385, P399 and P490); Hertford House inventory 1890.

References General

A390; cdA412 (as Boucher).

[1] For the subject, see G. Reynolds, *Wallace Collection, Catalogue of Miniatures,* 1980, no. 54 (M48). For Boucher's classical subjects cf. P484, P486 and P487 n. 1. The iconography of the muses became increasingly ill-defined; one has only to compare the figures by Raphael in the Stanze with those of Le Sueur and Stella in the Louvre (inv. no. 8057–61, 7969), for example. P481 is described as *Thalia/Euterpe* in *Boucher, his Circle and Influence,* exh. cat., Stair Sainty Matthiesen, New York, 1987, p.68.

[2] P481 has previously been associated with Mme. de Pompadour (see A390), but it seems of insufficient quality, cf. P490 Versions and note 3.

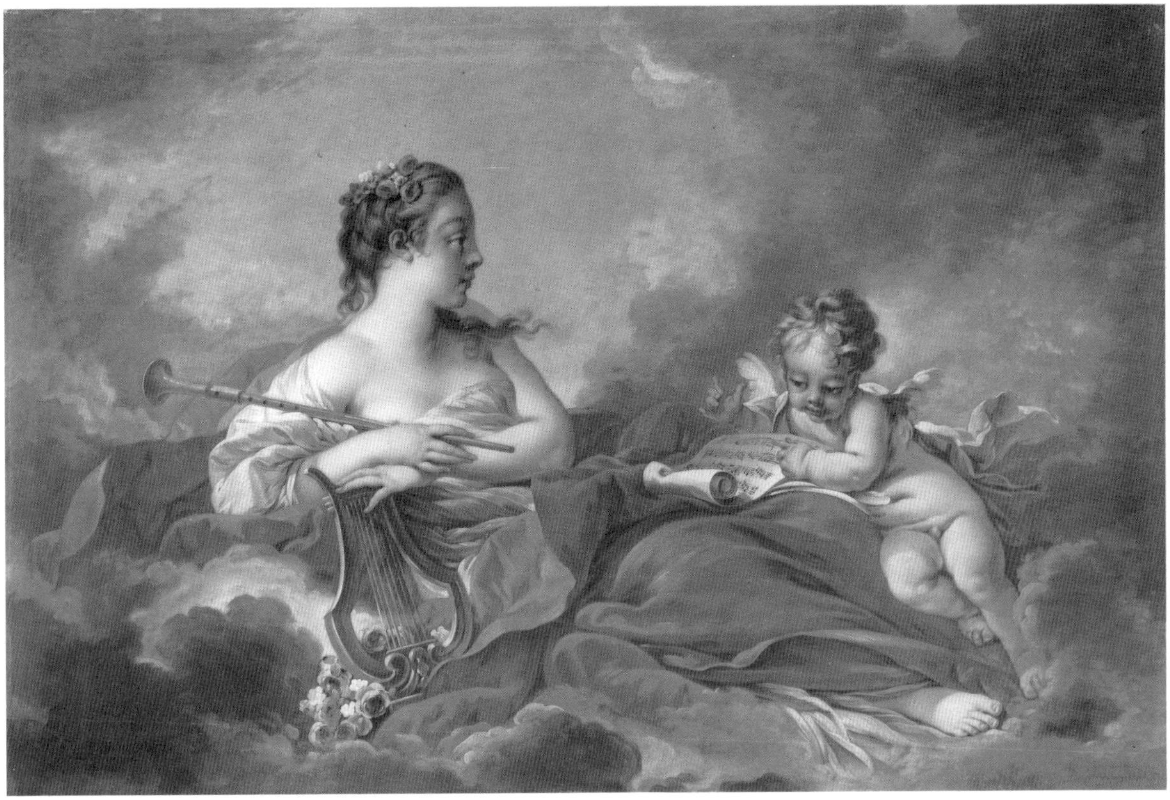

P490

P490 *The Muse Clio*

Wearing a red drape; the *putto* on the right has light blue drapery.

Canvas, relined 96 × 140 rounded top corners

The canvas was made up to 101 × 147 in the course of relining in the nineteenth century (cf. P481) but old fold marks indicate that at one stage it was reduced to 92 × 140. There are retouchings in the sky and the varnish is much discoloured.

The subject, Clio, muse of history, is identified from Daullé's engraving of 1756 (see Versions), although it has subsequently (but needlessly) been associated with Euterpe, muse of lyrical poetry (see Provenance), Polyhymnia, muse of singing and rhetoric,[1] and Erato, muse of amorous poetry.[2]

Although P490 has hitherto been identified with the Boucher of this subject which belonged to Mme. de Pompadour (see Versions), the execution is very bland, suggesting at best a studio production. It appears to have been sold in 1845 as an '*ancienne copie*' (see Provenance), and it shows several minor, but significant differences (principally in the drapery folds) from Daullé's 1756 engraving. Long regarded as the pendant to P481, it appears to be by a different hand and was at one stage a different size (see above).

Versions

The original belonged to Mme. de Pompadour; engr. J. Daullé 1756 as *Clio* (JR558); probably the '*Muse touchant une lyre, et à côté d'elle . . . un Amour tenant un livre de musique*', 94 × 137, in the Syncy sale, Paris, 29 April ff. 1789, lot 22.[3]

COPENHAGEN Wattrang sale, 21–3 April 1937 (49); 63 × 72.5, reversed and *chantourné*.
LONDON Christie's, 26 November 1976 (89); 93 × 128, with a wreath by the lyre instead of roses; ex Christie's, 29 March 1968 (91).
Wallace Collection (M67); miniature in the manner of Charlier, resembling P490 (see note 2 below).
PORTUGAL private collection; 81 × 127, signed and dated 1758, her right leg undraped and with a wreath by the lyre; exh. RA 1968 (58) (A489).

Ananoff records copies in the Caillard sale, Paris, 15–16 December 1881 (1), and the Magniac sale, Christie's, 2–4 July 1892 (119).

Provenance

Possibly the marquis de Cypierre sale, Paris, 10 March 1845 (15, '*Euterpe assise sur les nuages, appuyée sur une lyre, à ses pieds un Amour lit dans un cahier de musique. Pendant de* Terpsichore. *Ancienne copie*'), bt. Mosson, 257 fr.[4] The 4th Marquess of Hertford; possibly Bagatelle inventory 1871 (927, as one of '*quatre panneaux de décoration*', with P385, P399 and P481); Hertford House inventory 1890.

References General

A487; cdA514 (as Boucher).

1 Cf. A487; *Wallace Collection, Summary Illustrated Catalogue of Pictures*, 1978.

2 Cf. G. Reynolds, *Wallace Collection, Catalogue of Miniatures*, 1980, no.71 (M67).

3 It has been assumed that the Clio engraved by Daullé was one of the two Muses in the Pompadour sale (28 April ff. 1766, lot 18: '*Terpsichore et Polymnie . . . sur toile de forme contournée* [110 × 145]'; cf. JR558, A487 and previous editions of this catalogue, but this seems needlessly complicated. Pompadour had '*neuf tableaux représentants* les neuf Muses' in the Hôtel d'Evreux (J. Cordey, *Inventaire des biens de madame de Pompadour, rédigé après son décès*, 1939, p.29, no.259), of which Boucher may have painted several. I am grateful to Alastair Laing for emphasising this point to me. See also *Boucher, his Circle and Influence*, exh. cat., Stair Sainty Matthiesen, New York, 1987, pp.66–8.

4 Ananoff associated this sale with A489 (see Versions above), but Hertford probably also eventually acquired lots 14 and 175 from this sale (see Appendix III, nos. 19, 40). Cypierre was the grandson of J.-C.-F. Perrin de Cypierre who bought the Château d'Auvilliers from Mme. de Pompadour in 1760 (cf. *Boucher, his Circle and Influence*, 1987 [see note 3 above], p.68).

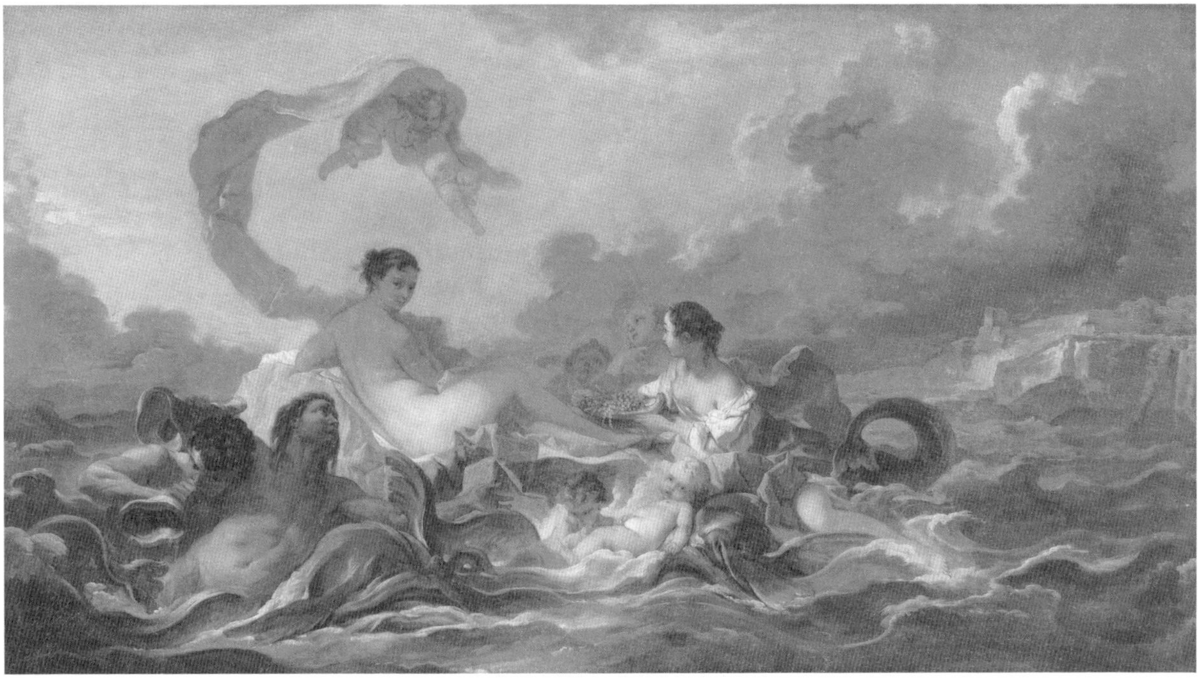

P433

After Boucher

P433 *The Birth of Venus*

Canvas, relined 67.3 × 119.2

There are retouchings in the sky, top right, and round the edges, and the varnish is greatly discoloured.

For the subject see Charlier P475.

P433 is a weak adaptation of Boucher's oval composition of 1743 (private collection, New York; A243); for another version, see P468 Ascribed to Charlier.

Provenance

S. Culley sale, Christie's, 22 June 1857 (90, Boucher, *Triumph of Amphitrite*),[1] bt. Nieuwenhuys, 20 gn.; probably bt. Sir Richard Wallace 1872; Hertford House inventory 1890.

Exhibition

Bethnal Green 1872–5 (379, as Boucher).

Reference General

A243/14 (as a studio piece).

[1] The canvas is inscribed in chalk, *verso*: *22 June/90*. Previous editions of this catalogue have also associated P433 with lot 4 in the Stacpoole sale, Paris, 1–3 March 1852 (*'Boucher, Le Triomphe d'Amphitrite . . . de la chambre de Louis XV'*, 375 fr.), but there seems to be no supporting evidence.

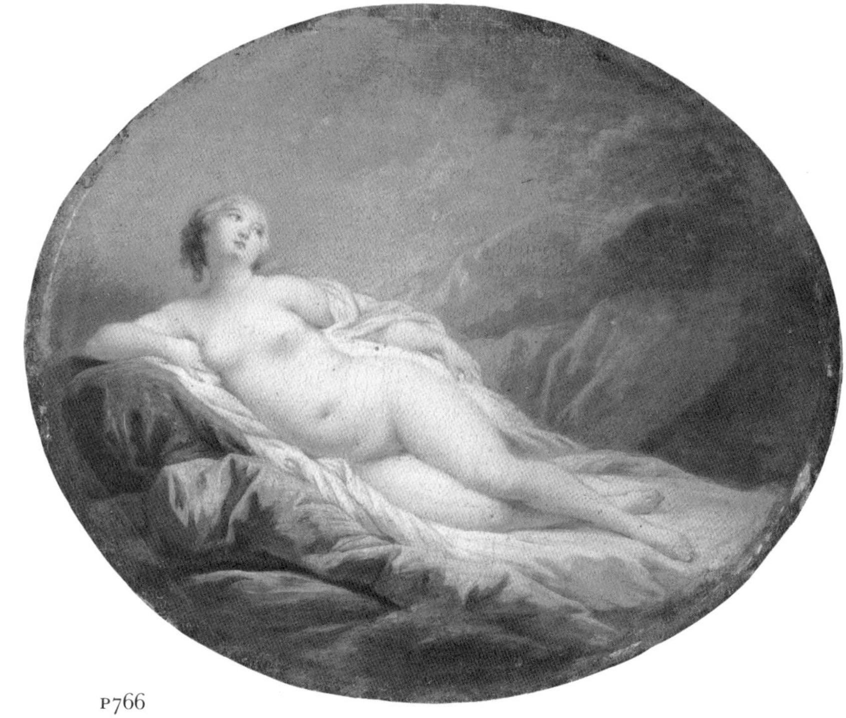

P766

P766 *Danaë*

Lying on white, blue green and pale lavender draperies.

Canvas 19.3 × 22 oval, laid down on panel[1]

There are small losses above her left hand, below her right knee and round the edges. The varnish is greatly discoloured.

The subject is taken from Ovid, *Metamorphoses* IV, 697–8: Jupiter, in the form of a shower of gold, seduces Danaë, daughter of Acrisius, King of Argos. See also P546 After Titian.

The composition relates directly to a drawing attributed to Boucher (Rodrigues sale, Paris, 28 November 1928, lot 25; A518/4, fig. 1434) and to a miniature in the manner of Charlier in the Wallace Collection (M139).[2] Doubtless all three works derived from a now lost Boucher painting.[3] P766 was previously attributed to A.F. Callet (1741–1823),[4] but the execution is very bland; it was first catalogued as part of the Wallace Collection in 1920 (the 14th edition of this catalogue).

Provenance

Probably acquired by Sir Richard Wallace c.1872–4; Hertford House inventory 1890 (as by an unknown artist).

[1] The panel is edged with an old French MS.

[2] Cf. G. Reynolds, *Wallace Collection, Catalogue of Miniatures*, 1980, no.73.

[3] Ananoff records four Danaës by Boucher in eighteenth-century sales (A, II, pp.317, 318, 322, 323).

[4] In the 1897 Hertford House inventory Claude Phillips pencilled *Callet* by P766 (Wallace Collection archives).

Philippe de Champaigne (1602–1674)

Born on 26th May 1602 in Brussels where he studied principally as a landscape painter under J. Fouquières. He came to Paris in 1621 and worked with the young Poussin on the decoration of the Luxembourg palace under the direction of N. Duchesne, whose daughter he married and whom he was to succeed as first painter to the Queen Mother, Marie de Médicis, in 1628. He became a naturalised Frenchman in 1629. For the Carmelite church, Faubourg Saint-Jacques, Paris, he painted six large Biblical subjects from 1628 (of which two are in the Louvre). He received commissions from the King in 1634–8, including the *Vow of Louis XIII* for Notre-Dame (now at Caen), and in 1635, amongst other portraits, Richelieu commissioned the *Louis XIII crowned by Victory* (Louvre). During the 1640s he came into contact with the Jansenists at Port-Royal whose spiritual rigour appealed to his serious nature and found strong expression in his work. He produced a number of portraits and altarpieces for Port-Royal, of which many are now in the Louvre including the remarkable *Ex-voto* of 1662, painted in thanksgiving for the miraculous cure of his elder daughter, a sister at the Convent. In 1656 he painted a series of large canvases (now distributed between the Louvre, Mainz and Tours) of hermit Saints in the desert for the *appartement* of Anne of Austria in the Val-de-Grâce, revealing his continuing ability as a painter of landscape. He was a founding member of the Académie Royale in 1648, his *morceau de réception* being the *Saint Philippe* of 1649 in the Louvre; he became *professeur* and *recteur*, lecturing on works by Titian, Poussin, Raphael and Reni. He died in Paris on 12 August 1674.

Abbreviation

D B. Dorival, *Philippe de Champaigne*, 1976

P119 *The Marriage of the Virgin*

Joseph in mauve with dull golden-yellow drapery, Mary in pinkish red with blue drapery, the High Priest in a white surplice and violet robes; from the left, the three foreground figures wear white and blue, green and red, bluish mauve and bright golden yellow. To the left of the right-hand column a woman offers a bunch of grapes to a child. The headband of the High Priest is inscribed, in Hebrew script: ADONAI (Lord), and that of a second figure to the left with simulated Hebrew script. Signed, bottom centre right: P. CHAMPAIGNE. F.

Oak panel 71.5 × 143.4 × 1.6 painted area 68.8 × 141.7

Nine vertical members, each imperfectly rectangular, tongued and grooved; measured on the front at the top edge their widths are (from the left) 8.5, 18.2, 17.9, 16.1, 18.5, 14.7, 17.8, 13.7, and 18 cm. Inscribed, *verso*, in a seventeenth-century hand, *cause* [?] *dela chambr*[*e*].[1] On the back, the edges are rebated to a depth and width of 1 and 1.5 cm., presumably to allow the panel to be jointed into a wooden framework; on the front there are unpainted margins 0.5 to 1.4 cm. wide. Cleaned by Allden in 1983. P119 is generally well preserved. There are six localised areas of

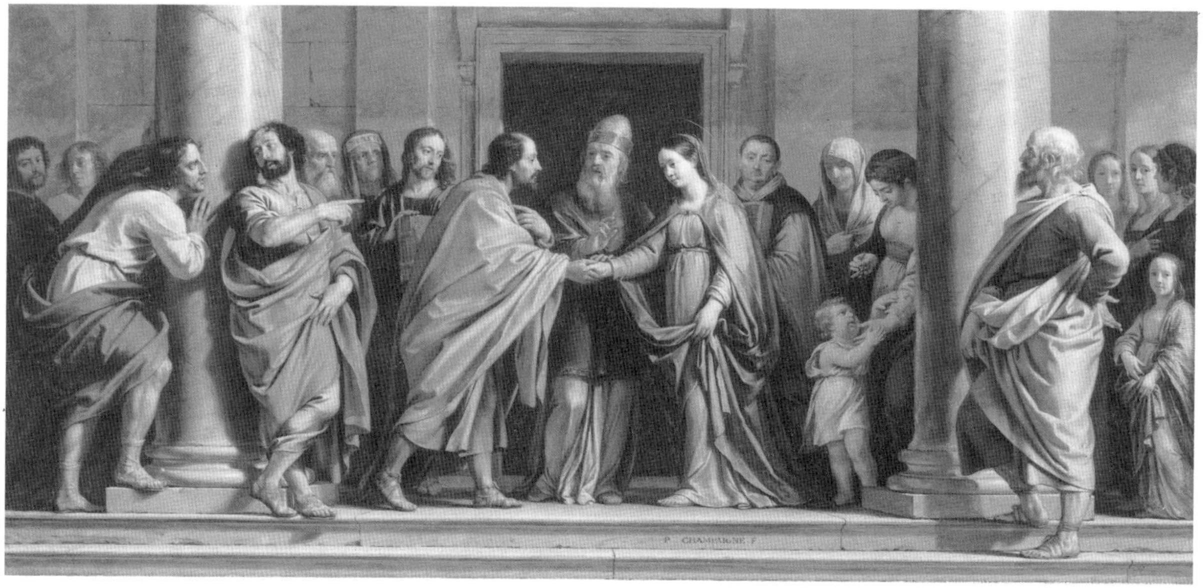

P119

losses, each of a circular formation: above the top step at the left edge, in the left-hand column above the knee of the figure in blue and white, between Joseph and the figure in green and red at the level of the latter's left hand and thigh, below Joseph's right elbow, behind Mary in the priest's left arm, and in the right-hand foreground figure's crooked left arm. In the background there are some minor losses and areas of wear particularly in the pilaster to the left of the door and in the top right-hand corner. At the right edge there are localised losses in vertical strips in the form of drips. There are numerous small *pentimenti,* notably in the shoulder of the man second from the left, in the blue drapery behind the left leg of the man third from the left and in his left hand, in the High Priest's head and right shoulder, the left arm of the woman offering grapes and the left hand of the child receiving them. P119 is painted on a grey ground.

The subject has no Biblical source, but the preceding events are described in the Golden Legend and the Apocryphal New Testament.[2] When, at the age of fourteen, Mary was to be married, suitors were called to the Temple and Joseph, by a sign from God, was chosen for her husband. The full story (see Murillo P14) was not accepted by Counter-Reformation writers,[3] and Champaigne accordingly omits the more colourful details commonly included by his contemporaries (Joseph's flowering staff, the descending dove and disappointed suitors breaking their staffs).[4] The marriage takes place on the steps of the Temple,[5] and is sealed by the linking of hands.[6] The three foreground figures and two on the extreme left may represent unsuccessful suitors; others appear to be priests, acolytes and virgins of the Temple, although the elderly man and woman in the background could be the Virgin's parents, Joachim and Anna. The grapes offered to a child foreshadow the Passion.

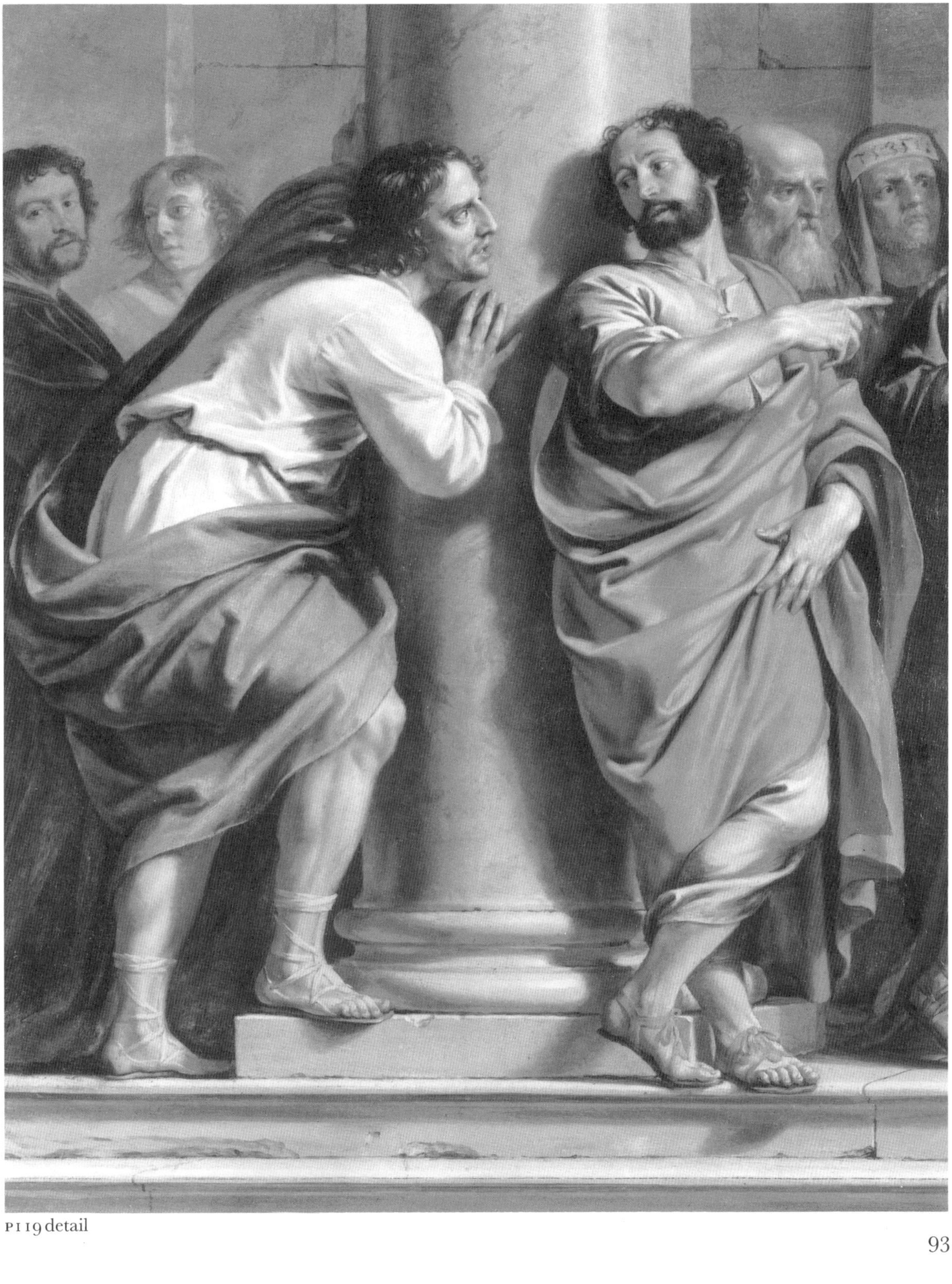

P119 detail

P119, which ranks among Champaigne's finest small-scale works, was almost certainly painted for the oratory of Anne of Austria (widow of Louis XIII) in the Palais Royal, Paris, probably c.1644. The commission is recorded by Sauval:

> *L'oratoire est environné de tableaux, où Champagne, Vouet, Bourdon, Stella, Lahire, Corneille, Dorigni & Paerson, ont peint en concurrence la vie & les attributs de la Vierge; travail où il se voit tant d'émulation, qu'il est assés difficile de juger laquelle de ces Histoires est la plus achevée; car enfin si ce ne sont pas leurs chefs-d'oeuvres, aussi ne sont-ce pas leurs coups d'essai.*[7]

The oratory must have been destroyed c.1752,[8] but five paintings recorded at the Palais Royal in 1788 were probably survivals from the scheme;[9] they include a *Marriage of the Virgin* by Champaigne which is reasonably identifiable with P119.[10] The commission is not documented, but an *Assumption* by Simon Vouet in Reims, apparently painted for the oratory, is dated 1644.[11] Although most decorative work in the Queen's *appartement* seems to have been undertaken from September 1645,[12] the oratory may have been completed earlier; it seems to be mentioned by Mme. de Motteville in the previous year.[13] The young girl on the extreme right of P119 seems to be Champaigne's daughter Catherine, whose likeness aged ten in 1647 is known in a drawing by Champaigne; her age in P119 could be consistent with a date of 1644.[14]

The Queen's oratory was a small private chapel; it connected with her bed-chamber[15] and had one window of '*cristal*' in a frame of silver.[16] It is probably seen, slightly altered, in a first-floor plan of the Palais Royal dating from 1745.[17] This shows, next to the third room of the Queen's *appartement* (presumably her *chambre*), a rectangular space leading to the east into a small oval room projecting over an inner courtyard. The altar was presumably placed in the projecting oval.[18] The Pourtalès sale catalogue (see Provenance) describes P119 as coming from the front of the altar, but this is probably an assumption based merely on its shape. It is also possible that P119 formed part of a frieze of paintings set into the panelling. A *Presentation in the Temple* by Sébastien Bourdon (Louvre) probably comes from the same scheme; it is also recorded in the 1788 inventory of the Palais Royal and is painted on a panel approximately the same height as P119.[19] Sauval also mentions a *Flight into Egypt* by Bourdon; this is perhaps the panel recently acquired by the Louvre which is the same size as the *Presentation*.[20] The *Annunciation* by Champaigne mentioned in the 1788 inventory has been associated with P134, but this is far from certain (see P134); more appropriate would be the lost *Annunciation* from the Duval sale of 1846 which is again on a panel approximately the same height as P119.[21]

The relief-like composition of P119 has suggested the influence of Poussin's *Marriage* from the first series of Sacraments (Belvoir Castle) and his *Marriage of the Virgin*, known in three drawings.[22] The latter is the closer (in the principal group, setting, and the man on the left who grasps a column),[23] but it is doubtful whether Champaigne could have known either work, unless he was able to study drawings by Poussin on the latter's visit to Paris in 1640–2.[24] The composition of P119 may also have been influenced by Veronese's *Supper at Emmaus* (Louvre) which then hung in the *grand cabinet* of the Queen's *appartement*, and by Champaigne's own study of antique bas-reliefs.[25] It certainly reflects a trend in Parisian painting of the 1640s towards an elegant classical style, tempered in Champaigne's case by a use of unclassical figure types. Besides Catherine de Champaigne (see above), the man on the extreme left may also be a portrait, but has not been identified; he also appears, appropriately several years younger, in Champaigne's *Presentation in the Temple* at Dijon (D46).[26] The foreground figure on the left in blue and white is perhaps taken from the same model as Judas in the *Last Supper* (D59, D61) and the High Priest and Joseph are types which recur inexactly in many of Champaigne's works.

Provenance

See above. Commissioned for the oratory of Anne of Austria in the Palais Royal, Paris, c.1644; recorded at the Palais Royal in 1788 among paintings intended for sale in England, but apparently never sent;[27] removed by 1796;[28] acquired by the comte de Pourtalès-Gorgier (1776–1855) by 1841;[29] his sale, Paris, 9th day, 31 March 1865 (140, '. . . *décorait autrefois le devant d'autel de la chapelle du Palais-Royal*'), bt. by the 4th Marquess of Hertford, 43,500 fr.;[30] rue Laffitte inventory 1871 (390); Hertford House inventory 1890.

Exhibition

Bethnal Green, 1872–5 (119).

Reference General

D19.

[1] '*cause*' possibly for *côté*. I am grateful to Maxime Préaud for checking the transcription.

[2] Jacobus de Voragine, *The Golden Legend*, trans. Caxton, 1900 ed., V, p.103, and M. R. James, *The Apocryphal New Testament*, 1953, pp.42, 73, 79–80 and 84.

[3] See E. Mâle, *L'Art religieux après le Concile de Trente*, 1932, p.355, citing among others Molanus. For a discussion of Champaigne's possible acquaintance with such texts, particularly Molanus, see D, I, pp.78–80.

[4] The staff and dove were included by Poussin (in the two series of Sacraments and drawings, see note 22 below), a suitor breaking his staff also by Jacques Stella (Musée des Augustins, Toulouse), and Michel I Corneille (exh. *Religious and Biblical themes in French Baroque Painting*, Heim, London, 1974, no.5).

[5] Dorival (D, I, p.76 and fig.iii) suggests Champaigne consulted the commentary on Ezekiel of Pradus and Villalpandus for details of the High Priest's robes and the Temple. Probably because of its small scale, these details are less pedantic in P119 than in others of his works (cf. D17, D45, D46).

[6] Joseph sometimes places a ring on Mary's finger, but some authors asserted that in Jewish custom, as in Roman law, the right hands were linked (for example, L. Richeome, *The Pilgrime of Loreto*, 1629, p.199, based on a misreading of Tobit VII, 24).

[7] H. Sauval, *Histoire et recherches des antiquités de la ville de Paris*, 1724, II, p.169. The other painters are: Simon Vouet (1590–1649), Sébastien Bourdon (1616–71), Jacques Stella (1596–1657), Laurent de La Hyre (1606–56), Michel I Corneille (1602–64), Michel Dorigny (1617–65), and Charles I Poërson (1609?–67). Jacques Sarrazin (1588/92–1660) may also have been involved (see note 9 below).

[8] To make way for Contant d'Ivry's transformation of the eastern part of the *appartement* (see V. Champier and G.-R. Sandoz, *Le Palais-Royal*, 1900, I, pp.360–5).

[9] Champier and Sandoz, *op. cit.*, I, p.521 (*Liste des tableaux destinés à la vente en Angleterre*, March 1788): an *Annunciation* and a *Marriage of the Virgin* by Champaigne, a *Presentation in the Temple* by Bourdon, a *Death of the Virgin* by Sarrazin and a *Visitation* by La Hyre. Besides P119, only Bourdon's *Presentation* can be identified (see note 19 below). Rosenberg and Thuillier have tentatively associated the La Hyre reference with a drawing in a New York private collection (P. Rosenberg and J. Thuillier, *Laurent de La Hyre, Cahiers du Dessin français*, I, 1985, no.50).

[10] As proposed by C. Stryienski, *La Galerie du Régent*, 1913, p.179, no.356, and Dorival. The identification seems also to be supported by the inscription on the *verso* of P119.

[11] Vouet's altarpiece was engraved by Michel Dorigny in 1647 with the inscription: HANC TABVLAM ANNA AVSTRIACA AVGVSTA GALLIARVM REGINA ET/RECTRIX IN PRECARIO SUO PIETATIS MONVMENTVM CONSECRAVIT.

[12] On 11 September 1645, the Queen received 20,000 *livres* from the Royal treasury for the '*ouvrages de menuiserie, peinture et dorure et autres qui sont a faire dans la gallerie et appartement de ladicte dame Reyne au pallais royal*' (Bibliothèque Nationale, ms. fr.10413, f.13v). For contracts passed with Simon Vouet in the same month, see R.-A. Weigert, BSHAF 1951, pp.101–5. The Queen's accounts for 1644 do not survive.

[13] *Mémoires de Mme. de Motteville*, ed. Petitot, 1824, II, p.74. Elsewhere (I, p.322) she records that the Queen's oratory '*est le lieu où elle* [the Queen] *se plaît le plus: elle y passe beaucoup d'heures du jour*'.

[14] Present whereabouts unknown (D326). Dorival regards her as slightly older in the drawing, the 1968 edition of this catalogue as 'at much the same age', and P. Hendy (*Apollo*, V, 1927, p.170) as the same age or a year younger.

[15] Vouet undertook decorations in the '*chambre attenant l'oratoire*' in 1645 (Weigert, *loc. cit.*).

[16] Sauval, *loc. cit.*

[17] Bibliothèque Nationale, Cabinet des Estampes, volume entitled *Logements des Officiers au Palais-Royal*, illustrated by Champier and Sandoz, *op. cit.*, I, p.364.

[18] In the seventeenth century the third room of an *appartement* would be the *chambre* (following the *salle* and *antichambre*) and, since it was considered improper to place rooms above an altar, chapels were commonly found in projecting rooms. On the 1745 plan the projecting oval is marked as a *cabinet* and has two window embrasures, so that some alterations, probably of the early-eighteenth century, must be assumed. In a reconstruction of Anne of Austria's *appartement*, which does not take account of the 1745 plan, T. Sauvel reached a similar conclusion for the position of the oratory (BSHAF 1968, pp.65–79).

[19] Louvre, inv.2802, 71 × 61, and see note 9 above. Dated c.1645 by G. E. Fowle, *The Biblical paintings of Sébastien Bourdon*, 1970, I, pp.106–7, no.34. The panel has a rebate on the back similar to that on P119 (I am most grateful to Pierre Rosenberg for information on both Bourdon panels here cited).

[20] Sauval, *loc. cit.*; Louvre, inv.RF 1983–73, 70 × 61. Dated c.1645 by P. Rosenberg, *Catalogue de la donation Othon Kaufmann et François Schlageter au Département des peintures*, 1984, p.36, no.2. The panel has been planed and cradled and it is thus impossible to say if it was once rebated (I am grateful to Othon Kaufmann for this information).

[21] See P134, note 16.

[22] W. Friedlaender and A. Blunt, *The Drawings of Nicolas Poussin*, I, 1939, nos.92–4. The last was later engraved by Gérard Audran (1640–1703); there is no evidence that a painting was ever executed.

[23] The connection is briefly discussed by Dorival, 'Poussin et Philippe de Champaigne', in *Nicolas Poussin*, ed. A. Chastel, 1960, pp.63–4. Dorival also suggests the influence of *Marriage* from the second series of Sacraments (Sutherland loan to the National Gallery of Scotland), but this seems impossible since it was not painted until 1647–8 (A. Blunt, *The Paintings of Nicolas Poussin, a critical catalogue*, 1966, p.79, no.118).

[24] Dorival (*loc. cit.*) suggests Champaigne would have known the engraving of the earlier *Marriage* published by Jean Dughet, but the engraving can be dated after 1657 (see Davies and Blunt, *Gazette des Beaux-Arts*, 6e, LX, 1962, p.212, nos.90–6).

[25] Champaigne's *inventaire après décès* includes '*deux bas-reliefs d'après l'anticque, ouvrage dudit deffunt*' (NAAF, 3e, VIII, 1892, p.184).

[26] He is conceivably Champaigne himself and, if so, the central woman in the group of three behind Catherine de Champaigne could be the artist's wife (as has been suggested to me by Anne Thackeray).

[27] See note 9 above.

[28] P119 does not appear among the paintings remaining at the Palais Royal, which were removed to the *dépôt* in the Hôtel de Nesle in 1795–6 (AAF, VI, 1912, pp.313–14).

[29] Cf. J. J. Dubois, *Description des tableaux . . . de M. le comte de Pourtalès-Gorgier*, 1841, pp.45–6, no.136.

[30] '*C'est un des prix les plus insensés de cette vente*' (*L'Artiste*, I, 1865, p.188).

P127 *An Echevin of Paris*

Brown eyes, grey hair; he wears a black skull cap and a gown half scarlet, half black, with black velvet trimmings, over a grey-black cassock with globular buttons. In the left background a framed panel probably of tooled and gilded leather with, above, the lower half of a column; behind the sitter, a pedestal apparently of marbled wood.

Canvas, relined 72.4 × 53 maximum, irregular

Relined in the nineteenth century,[1] when strips were added to both sides and the bottom bringing the stretcher size to 72.7 × 59.6. In the course of relining by Bobak and cleaning by Sanden in 1988, these additions were removed and the original, irregular, canvas was placed centrally on a new lining canvas and stretcher, measuring 73.7 × 55.5. The left and bottom edges were then made up to allow a sight size of 71 × 51. There are areas of wear particularly in the sitter's robes and at the edges, and small losses caused by flaking over most of the surface, particularly in the shadow to the left of the face, to the right of and below his left elbow, and in parts of the background architecture. The black patterning on the leather (?) panel continues faintly over the frame.

The sitter is dressed as a *greffier* or *échevin* of the Paris City Council;[2] a horizontal fold in his gown at the bottom suggests he is kneeling. P127 is certainly a fragment; the edges of the original canvas are roughly cut, the back of a second figure is visible on the left and the elbow of another on the right.[3] It almost certainly comes from one of the two lost group portraits of the Paris City Council painted by Champaigne in the 1650s.[4] In such group portraits the eight members of the Council were arranged with the *prévôt des marchands*, *procureur*, *greffier* and *receveur* on the left and the four *échevins* on the right.[5] P127 clearly comes from the right-hand side of a group and the sitter is, therefore, an *échevin*. Since the *échevins* appear to have been represented in order of seniority, the fact that figures are visible on both sides of him indicates that he was either the second or third *échevin*. The architectural background suggests he was near the centre of the group and he is thus more probably the second *échevin*.

Group portraits of the City Council were commissioned (together with individual portraits of each sitter) to commemorate each two-year term of the *prévôt des marchands*.[6] According to Guillet de Saint-Georges

> *Dans les années 1649, 1652 et 1656 il* [Champaigne] *fit pour la Maison de Ville de Paris, trois tableaux où sont les portraits des différents magistrats de la ville, élus sous trois diverses prévôtés; le premier sous la prévôté de M. le Féron,* [now in the Louvre][7] *le second sous celle de M. le Fébure, et le troisième sous celle de M. de Sève.*[8]

The two later portraits, both lost (D977 and D1146), may be associated with payments made to Champaigne on 30 June 1654[9] and 12 December 1657.[10] The first probably commemorated the first *prévôté* of Antoine Le Febvre (1650–2) showing the Council of 1651–2;[11] the commission (or the payment) may have been delayed by the Fronde.[12] The second may be associated with the first *prévôté* of Alexandre de Sève (1654–6) and would have shown the Council of 1655–6.[13] It is

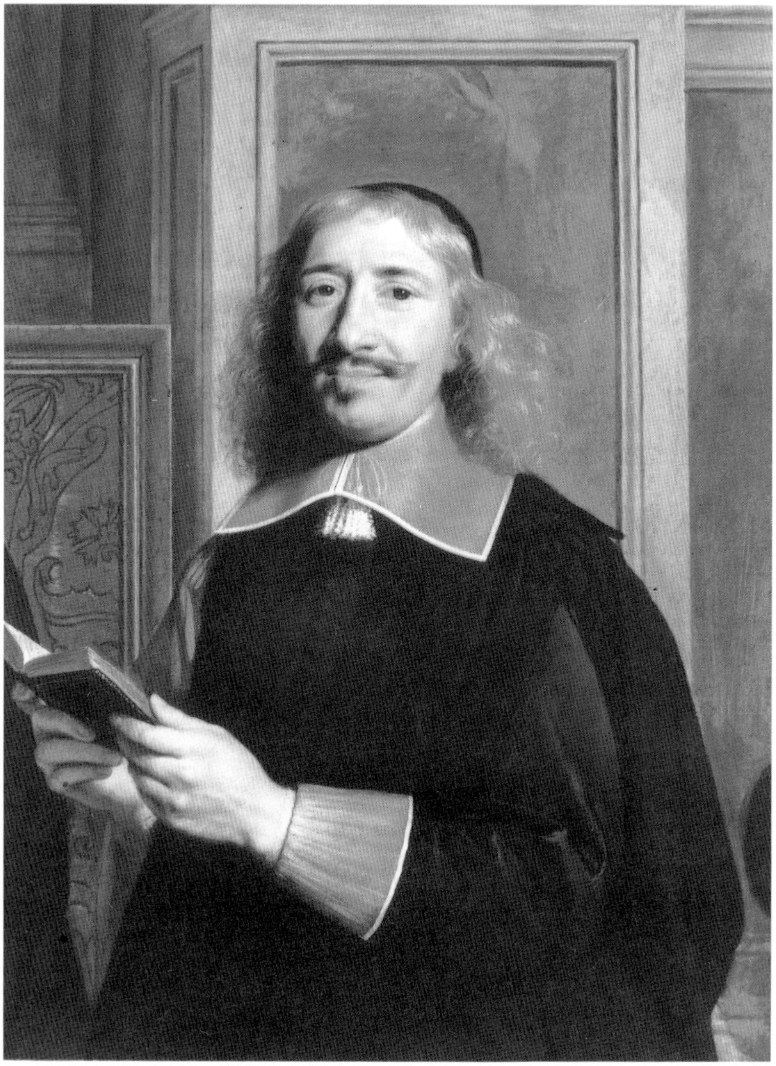

P127

impossible to distinguish fully the later history of these two groups. The earlier was installed in the *grande salle* of the Hôtel de Ville in 1654,[14] but seems to have been removed by the mid-eighteenth century.[15] One of the two groups was sent to the convent of the Récollets where it was confiscated at the Revolution and taken to the Dépôt des Petits-Augustins.[16] The other may have been one of the paintings in the Hôtel de Ville cut in pieces on 10 August 1792.[17]

Although there is evidence that the earlier of Champaigne's lost groups was cut in pieces,[18] P127 should probably be associated with the later group. The reasoning is intricate. A related fragment in Toledo, Ohio (see Related Works), would appear to have joined P127 on the right-hand side, according to the evidence of the architectural background and the position of the sitter's right elbow. Together,

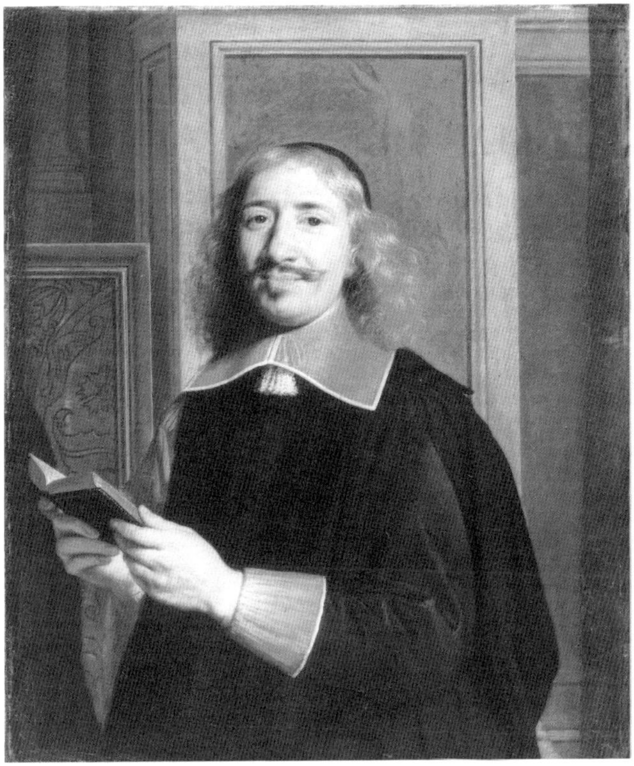

P127 before cleaning

P127 and the Toledo portrait must show either the second and third or the third and fourth *échevins*. But the features of the third *échevin* of the 1651–2 Council are known and do not agree with those seen in P127 or the Toledo portrait.[19] It follows that P127 and the Toledo fragment must come from the later group. The sitter in P127 is thus probably Jean Rousseau, second *échevin* of the 1655–6 Council (or possibly the third *échevin*, Antoine de la Porte).[20]

Related Works

BERLIN formerly Kaiser-Friedrich-Museum, no.1702 (destroyed 1945); 70.5 × 57, by Champaigne; portrait of André Le Vieux, probably one of the individual portraits painted at the same time as Champaigne's earlier lost group portrait of the City Council (D361).[21]

GENEVA private collection; 73 × 59 (including additions on both sides), by Champaigne; portrait of Germain Piettre; a fragment of Champaigne's earlier lost group portrait of the City Council (D202).[22]

TOLEDO Ohio, Museum of Arts (no.33.325); 80 × 65 (including additions at the top and on both sides), by Champaigne; *An Echevin*, a fragment from Champaigne's later lost group portrait of the City Council (D226, and see above).[23]

U.S.A. private collection; 54.6 × 43.2, by Champaigne; *An Echevin*, probably a fragment from a group portrait of the City Council, or one of the individual portraits painted at the same time (D376).[24]

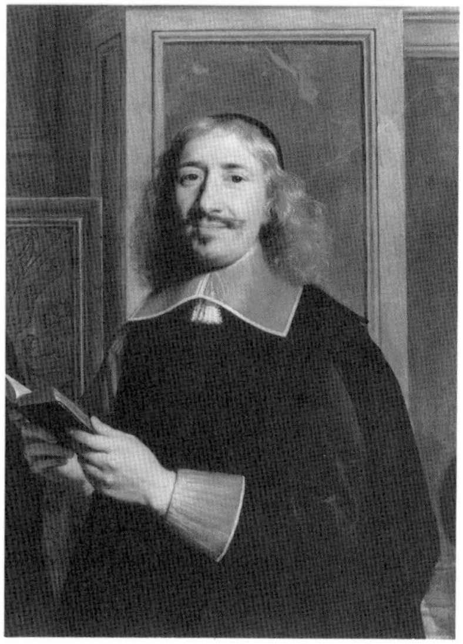

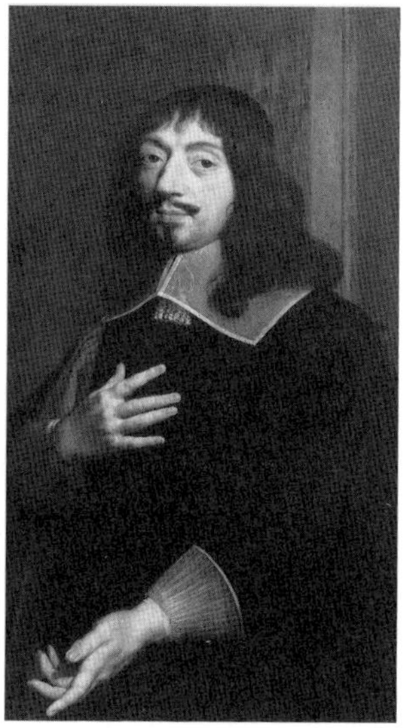

Above: P127

Right: Champaigne: *An Echevin of Paris*, excluding additions.
Museum of Arts, Toledo, Ohio

Showing their relative positions within the larger composition

Provenance

Acquired by the 4th Marquess of Hertford; rue Laffitte inventory 1871 (441, '*Champaigne, portrait d'homme*'); Hertford House inventory 1890 as '*Champaigne Man in black coat*'.

Exhibition

Bethnal Green 1872–5 (74, *A Portrait*).

References General

D174; A. Blunt, *The Burlington Magazine*, LXXXII, 1943, p.87.

[1] Several layers of French printed paper were applied to the stretcher; the lowest level included a title page '[*Ismén*]*ide et Hylas*/[*Nou*]*velle Grecq*[*ue*]' and in an upper layer were fragments of accounts with the dates 1831 and 1833.

[2] As first recognised by Hallays (*Journal des Débats*, 3 September 1909). For the costumes worn by the City Council, see D. Godefroy, *Le Cérémonial françois*, 1649, I, pp.978 and 988, and J. Tronçon, *L'Entrée triomphante de Leurs Maiestéz*. . ., 1662, part IV (*Marché à l'entrée de Leurs Maiestéz*), pp.7–8.

[3] Dorival's arguments for regarding P127 as an individual portrait may be discounted (cf. A. Blunt, *The Burlington Magazine*, CXIX, 1977, p.576).

[4] As first proposed by Blunt 1943, p.87.

[5] This was invariably the arrangement except that, where the King is present, the Council are sometimes arranged in a single group on one side. But neither of Champaigne's lost group portraits can have included the King (see note 13). The pattern only later became less rigid, when a narrative element was introduced.

[6] The *prévôt des marchands* was elected every two years and could be re-elected three times. Two *échevins* were elected every year and each served a two-year term. The other offices were permanent. Elections were held on 16 August (M. Dumolin, in G. Brière, M. Dumolin and P. Jarry, *Les tableaux de l'Hôtel de Ville de Paris*, 1937, pp.5–6).

[7] Commissioned on 8 October 1647, a payment of 1,200 *livres* recorded on 23 November 1648 '*pour avoir faict le tableau de la dernière prévôté et échevinage, fourni les petits portraits et fait dorer la bordure du grand*' (Dumolin, *op. cit.*, p.21).

[8] Guillet de Saint-Georges, in *Mémoires inédits sur la vie et les ouvrages des membres de l'académie royale de peinture et sculpture*, ed. L. Dussieux *et al.*, 1854, I, p.242.

[9] '*A Phles. Champagne paintre la somme de Quinze cens livres tz. a luy ordonné par mandem*^{t} *du xxvii*^{e} *juin mvi*^{c} *cinq*^{te} *quatre tant pour le grand tableau par luy faict dans leq*^{l} *lesdits s*^{rs} *prevost des marchans eschevins procureur du roy greffier & receveur sont rep.ntez que pour les huict petitz tableaulx quil a faictz fournis ausdictz s*^{rs} *ainsy quil est accoustumé*. . .', 30 June 1654 (Archives Nationales, Q^{1} 1099^{72}, t.II, f.287v, cited by Dumolin, *op. cit.*, p.22).

[10] '*Au S*^{r} *Champagne Peintre ordinaire du Roy la somme de quinze cens livres tournois a luy aussy ordonnée, par autre mandement desdictz sieurs Prevost des marchandz & eschevins signée de leurs mains en datte du sixiesme jour d'Octobre mil six cens cinquante sept pour un grand tableau pay luy peint auquel sieurs Prevost des march*^{ds} *et les eschevins precedens en charge procure. du Roy greffier et receveur de lad. ville sont representez, ensemble pour les huict petitz tableaux particulliers quil est obligé de fournir a chacun*. . .', 12 December 1657 (Archives Nationales, Q^{1} 1099^{74}, t.II, f.232v, cited by Dumolin, *op. cit.*, p.24).

[11] The 1654 payment was one of three made in that year to Champaigne, Le Brun and La Hyre, each for a group portrait of the Council (see Dumolin, *op. cit.*, pp.22–3). La Hyre's (known only in a study in the Albertina, Vienna, inv.11568, see P. Rosenberg and J. Thuillier, *Laurent de La Hyre, Cahiers du Dessin français*, I, 1985, no.54) commemorated Le Febvre's second *prévôté* showing the Council of 1653–4 (Guillet de Saint-Georges's description, *op.cit.*, I, p.112, names the *échevins*). On Guillet de Saint-Georges's evidence (see main text), Champaigne's must therefore have commemorated Le Febvre's first *prévôté* and would have shown the Council of 1651–2. But there is an element of doubt. A. de Champeaux (*L'Art décoratif dans le Vieux Paris*, 1898, p.206) states that Champaigne's group represented the Council '*réintegrés dans leurs charges par l'autorité royale*', i.e. at the outset of Le Febvre's second *prévôté* in October 1652 (see note 12 below), but there seems no evidence to confirm this statement for which no source is cited. Nothing is known of Le Brun's portrait.

[12] Le Febvre's first *prévôté* was cut short during the Fronde when, on 6 July 1652, he was replaced by Pierre Broussel. He was reinstated to serve a second term on 14 October following. At the same time all four *échevins* of the 1651–2 Council were reinstated and these *échevins* thus, exceptionally, served three-year terms (Dumolin, *op. cit.*, p.23).

[13] As implied by the 1657 payment which states that the *échevins* were the '*precedens en charge*' (see note 10). Dumolin associated this payment with a painting described by Thiéry in the Hôtel de Ville in 1787 as '*Louis XIV recevant l'hommage des Echevins en 1654*' but, since both Champaigne's payments were for the same sum, it seems inconceivable that one group included the King (see Dumolin, *op. cit.*, p.24 and L.-V. Thiéry, *Guide des Amateurs*, 1787, I, p.559). Thiéry may have wrongly described a portrait by Henri and Charles Beaubrun showing *The City Council paying homage to Louis XIV in 1660* (lost, engraved for Tronçon, *op. cit.*, see J. Wilhelm, *Revue de l'Art*, 1969, 5, p.30, fig.26), for which they received 2,500 *livres* in 1660 (see Dumolin, *op. cit.*, p.24).

[14] Cf. Dumolin, *op. cit.*, p.23.

[15] Cf. A. Babeau, 'L'Hôtel de Ville de Paris et l'inventaire de son mobilier en 1740', *Mémoires de la Société de l'histoire de Paris et de l'Ile-de-France*, XXVI, 1899, pp.241–2.

[16] Described as '*Huit portraits en pied de personnages du Parlement, représentés à genoux dans le même tableau*' (*Archives du Musée des Monuments français*, II, 1886, p.260, no.271) – possibly the painting by Champaigne from the Récollets recorded as requiring restoration in the 1790s, its size given as 12 × 5 *pieds* (NAAF, XVII, 1901, p.287). See D1146.

[17] Alexandre Lenoir records receiving from '*Le citoyen procureur de la Commune*' twelve fragments of paintings cut in pieces on 10 August 1792. According to Leroux de Lincy (in V. Calliat, *Hôtel de Ville de Paris*, 1844, part I, pp.20–1) the portraits in the Hôtel de Ville were cut up by Revolutionary officials removing the coats-of-arms.

[18] The fragment in Geneva shows Germain Piettre, *procureur* until 1654 (see Related Works).

[19] He was André Le Vieux, whose likeness is recorded in a portrait formerly at Berlin (see Related Works).

[20] He was identified by Dorival as the *greffier* Martin Lemaire, but is clearly an *échevin* (see above). Dumolin (*op. cit.*, p.22 n.2) noted the undeniable, but inexact, resemblance between P127 and the figure third from the right in the Louvre group (who is also shown in an individual portrait in the Musée Granet, Aix, D169), proposing P127 might be a replica of the Aix painting '*mais plus de face et plus flattée*'.

[21] The sitter was identified by Gaudibert (BSHAF 1955, p.44) through a convincing comparison with an engraving illustrated by G. Hartmann ('Les Anciens Merciers', *La Cité. Bulletin de la Société historique et archéologique du IVe arrondissement de Paris*, 1906–7, 18, p.141). If the portrait is a fragment (as suggested by Blunt 1943, p.87) then the corner of a table bottom left would suggest that Le Vieux was in the centre of the composition and thus the senior *échevin*. But this was only the case in the 1653–4 Council, whose group portrait was painted by La Hyre (see note 11). As Wilhelm suggests (BSHAF 1956, p.25), the Berlin painting is more probably one of the individual portraits associated with the group paid for in 1654, but probably representing the Council of 1651–2. The table may have been introduced for compositional reasons or to take account of Le Vieux's more senior position when the portrait was actually delivered. Dr. Irene Geismeier has kindly confirmed that no records exist which suggest the Berlin portrait showed signs of being cut from a larger painting; Friedlaender noted that it was 'of good quality and in excellent condition'.

[22] The sitter is identified by Gaudibert, *op. cit.*, pp.43–4, by the costume and comparison with Champaigne's 1647–8 group in the Louvre.

[23] If the above arguments relating to P127 are accepted, then the Toledo portrait would show Antoine de la Porte, third *échevin* of the 1655–6 Council, or possibly the fourth *échevin*, Claude de Santeuil.

[24] Cf. *French painting of the time of Louis XIII and Louis XIV*, exh. cat., Wildenstein, New York, 1946, no.9 (from which the measurements cited above are taken; Dorival gives 49.5 × 29.1). The sitter wears the costume of an *échevin* and cannot, therefore, be J.-A. de Mesmes whom he closely resembles (see Wilhelm, *op. cit.*, pp.25–6 and D195).

P129 *The Adoration of the Shepherds*

Set within a cave; Joseph in grey-blue with golden-yellow drapery, the Virgin in pink with blue drapery, the shepherd on the right in pale brick-red; the cherubs have pale mauve and blue draperies; behind the Virgin the ox and ass, the latter eating from a manger suspended from the wall; in the top left-hand corner, a cobweb. Inscribed on the banderole: [G]LORI[A.IN.]EXCELSIS.DEO.ET.IN.TERRA. PAX.HOMINIBVS[.BONAE.VOLUNTATIS.]LAUDA[MUS.TE . . .] (quoted from the Mass rather than Luke II, 14).

Canvas, relined 232.5 × 161.5 maximum

In the course of a double relining, probably in the nineteenth century, the size was made up to 234 × 163. A tear in the lining canvas was reinforced in 1977. P129 was strip lined by Bobak and cleaned by Lank in 1987–8, when an opaque grey layer of perished glue was removed from many areas and the vertical edges were made up to give a sight size of 231.7 × 160.7.[1] There are major losses in an area 4 cm. high along the bottom edge and in the right-hand shepherd's right arm, and areas of smaller losses along a horizontal seam 114.5 cm. from the bottom edge, along the vertical edges, in Joseph's yellow drapery and the lower part of the Virgin's dress; her blue drapery is also somewhat abraded. There are numerous small areas where the paint has been bleached by splashes of a corrosive material. A loss to the top layer in the Child's lip revealed a previous position for the mouth. P129 is painted on a double ground of red overlaid with grey. A reduced replica in Portland, Oregon (see Version) shows the composition extended on both sides, but since only the red ground is visible at the edges of P129, it has not been cut down.

The subject is taken from Luke II, 15–20. The main source of light radiates from the Christ Child,[2] 'the true sunne of our Night'.[3] Champaigne's respect for the text, in representing the Child in swaddling clothes, is unusual. The shepherds' gift of a lamb foreshadows the Pascal lamb and thus the Passion, and the group of three cherubs possibly refers to the Trinity. For the same subject, see Murillo P34.

The commission is first recorded in a sale catalogue of 1766 (see Provenance) which describes:

> *Un Tableau représentant l'Adoration des Bergers, peint par Philippe de Champagne: ce Tableau est d'une composition admirable & d'un clair obscur précieux: il n'y a que l'Enfant Jesus qui éclaire tout le Tableau; c'est M. le Cardinal de Richelieu qui l'a fait faire à Philippe de Champagne pour l'Abbaye de Quincy, qui a été réunie à l'Evêché d'Anvers: ce Tableau dont la beauté est parfaite, a été cause que Marie de Médicis, Reine de France, a fait ce Maître son premier Peintre, . . .*[4]

So specific a provenance seems unlikely to be a fabrication, although the sale catalogue is otherwise not wholly accurate. The assertion that P129 influenced the decision to appoint Champaigne first painter to Marie de Médicis is impossible and may be rejected as evidence for the date of the commission.[5] The abbey cannot be securely identified since no abbey of Quincy is recorded which had any connection with the diocese of Antwerp.[6] The catalogue may refer to one of two

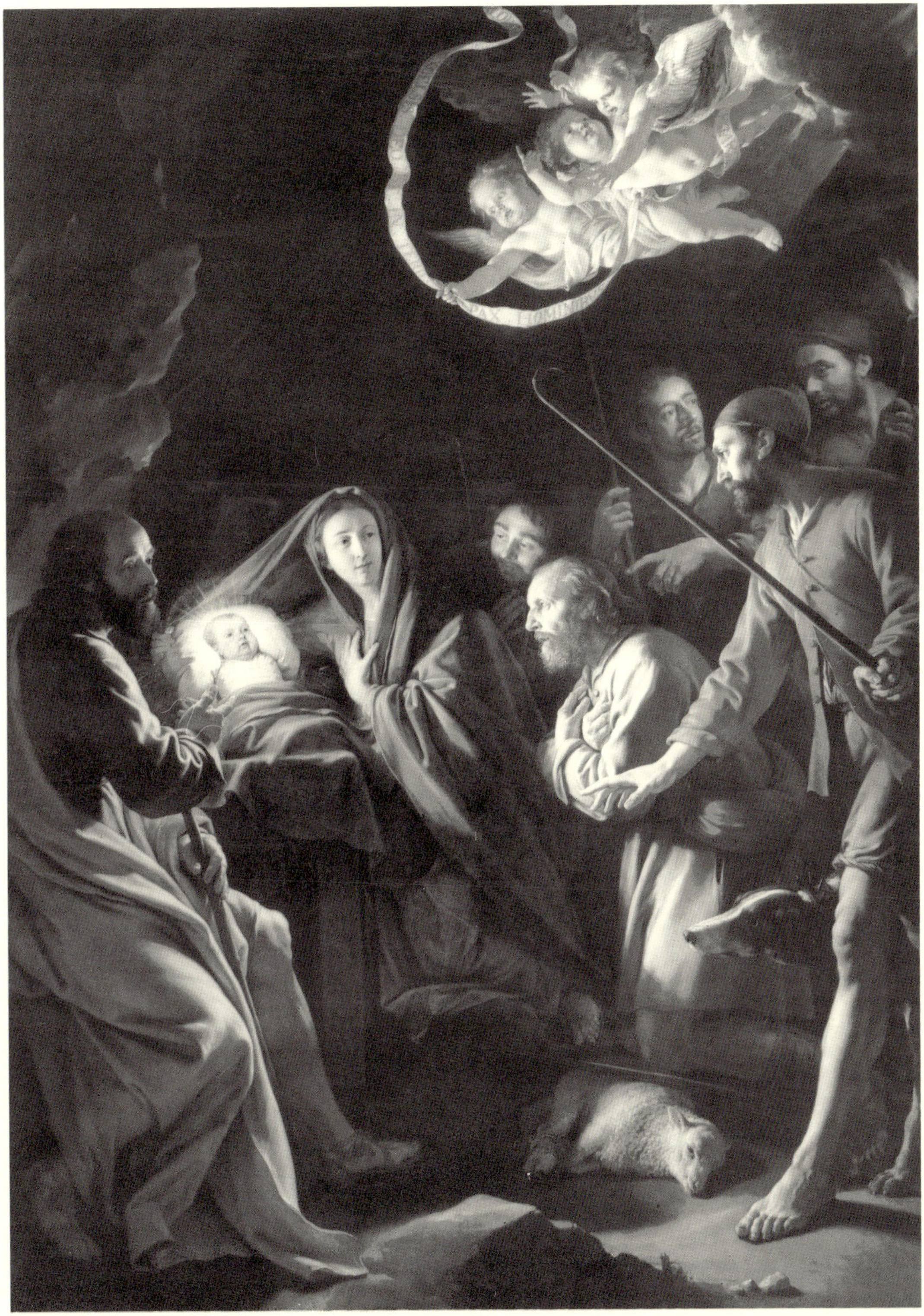

P129

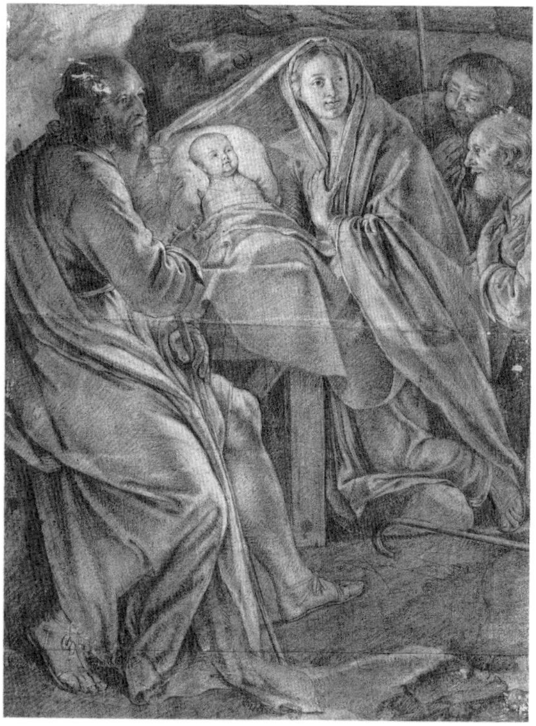

Attributed to Champaigne:
The Adoration of the Shepherds,
drawing.
Bibliothèque Nationale

French abbeys of Quincy: that of Saint-Benoît at Quinçay (Quincey or Quincy) near Poitiers, in the diocese of Poitiers,[7] or that of Notre-Dame at Quincy near Tanlay, in the diocese of Langres.[8] Dorival records that the former was suppressed in 1760, and this in one respect makes it the more likely candidate, since P129 appears in a Paris sale of 1765, while the abbey near Tanlay was not suppressed until the Revolution. However, the abbey near Poitiers was neglected in the early seventeenth century,[9] whereas that near Tanlay was the subject of extravagant expenditure by its abbot, Mathieu de Mesgrigny, who rebuilt the nave of the church from 1635/6.[10] A connection with the Quincy near Tanlay is also suggested by the presence of a copy of P129 in the *évêché* at Troyes (see Copies) and it should probably be regarded as the more likely location of P129. There are no obvious reasons why Richelieu should have commissioned an altarpiece for either abbey and, as suggested below, P129 may date from after his death; it is possible his name was included in the sale catalogue for commercial reasons.[11] The patron is thus unknown, but may have been Mesgrigny, or one of his successors.[12]

Generally regarded as an early work, P129 is dated c.1630 by Blunt,[13] and c.1628 by Dorival (on the apparently false evidence of the 1766 sale catalogue).[14] This early dating is perhaps suggested mainly by the strong chiaroscuro of P129 and its dependence on Rubens (see below); but the former is demanded by the subject and the latter need not imply an early date.[15] There are significant differences between the refined and highly resolved composition of P129 and the more

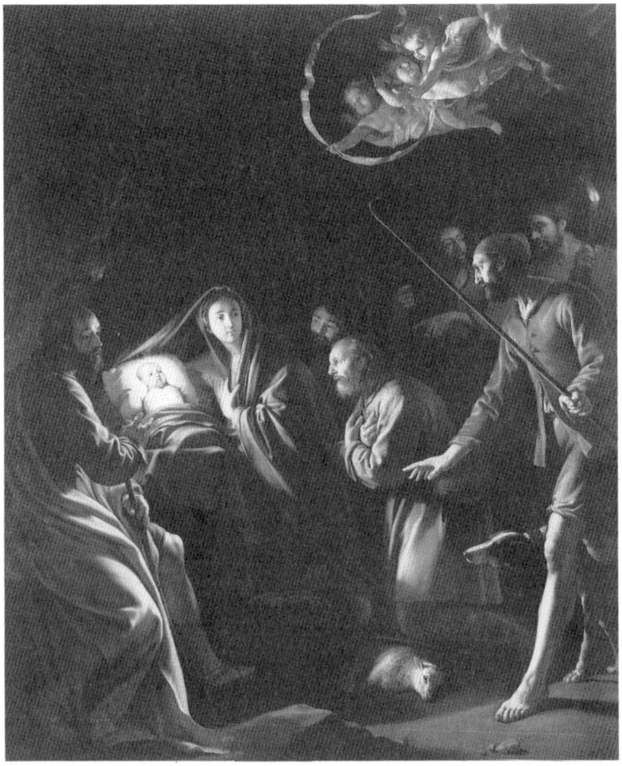

Champaigne:
The Adoration of the Shepherds.
Portland Art Museum, Portland, Oregon

turbulent and dramatic *Adoration of the Shepherds* in Lyon which certainly dates from 1628–9.[16] P129 seems closer to works of the 1640s, such as the *Nativity* at Lille (c.1643, D34) and the *Adoration of the Shepherds* in Rouen Cathedral (1644, D39) which employs some similar compositional devices.[17] The modelling of draperies and the colour suggest that P129 is somewhat later than the Rouen altarpiece; closer in both respects is the *Last Supper* of 1648 in the Louvre (D61) in which the figure of Judas is similar to Joseph in P129. The dating of P129 should probably, therefore, be revised to the mid-1640s, a proposal which is accepted by Rosenberg;[18] it could perhaps be placed as late as c.1648.

The composition of P129 bears a general resemblance to various *Adorations* by Rubens which could have been known to Champaigne through engravings. Those in Antwerp (St. Pauluskerk) and Fermo have been proposed as sources, but the Rubens *Adorations* in Munich, Rouen and Soissons Cathedral are closer.[19] As Dorival notes, Champaigne may also have known a lost *Adoration* by Rubens then in the church of SS. Michael and Gudule in Brussels. But in P129 the vigour of Rubens's compositions is replaced by a decorous equilibrium which reflects Italian influences, predominantly that of the Bolognese and perhaps particularly of Guido Reni. The shepherd and dog on the right may be a recollection of Raphael's *Adoration of the Shepherds* from the Scuola Nuova tapestry series.

Drawing

PARIS Bibliothèque Nationale, Cabinet des Estampes, *réserve*; fragment, attributed to Champaigne, showing the composition of P129 without the angels, the lamb or the three shepherds and dog on the right; *verso*, study of a head (D36, as a sketch).[20]

Version

PORTLAND Oregon, Art Museum (inv.66.83); 106.7 × 87.6, by Champaigne or his workshop; the edges are extended (see above) and the two shepherds, top right, more distant; probably a later reduced version or possibly a *modello* (D37, as possibly a sketch).

Copies

PARIS Louvre (inv.20813); 217 × 163, unfinished.
TROYES *Evêché*; 261 × 149 (see D35, as a copy or replica).

Provenance

Possibly painted for the abbey of Notre-Dame at Quincy, near Tanlay (see above). Possibly acquired by the dealer P. Le Brun (d.1771).[21] M. l'Abbé***. sale, Paris, 2 December 1765 (160, '*Un Tableau représentant l'Adoration des Bergers, de Philipe de Champagne*', [228.5 × 163]); M.***. sale, Paris, 15 December 1766 (113, [228.5 × 163], see above), 304 *livres* 3 *sous*; Pierre de Grand-Pré sale, Paris, 16 February ff. 1809 (31, '*composition de dix Figures* [sic] . . . *La Vierge placée à la droite* [sic] . . . *d'une belle conservation*' [228.5 × 163]), bt. Henry, 3,001 fr.; probably P. Panné sale, Christie's, 29 March 1819 (68),[22] bt. Féréol de Bonnemaison (d.1827), 101 gn.; Bonnemaison sale, Paris, 17 April ff. 1827 (52, '*de la collection . . . Grandpré*'), 4,900 fr.; Louis, marquis de Montcalm (1786–1862) by 1836;[23] his sale, Christie's, 2nd day, 5 May 1849 (128, as from the Bonnemaison collection), bt. by the 4th Marquess of Hertford, 350 gn.; seen in Hertford House 1854 by Waagen (IV, p.87: 'the painter's later time . . . happily composed . . . the effect . . . is crude and the colouring unusually cold'); Hertford House inventory 1870.

Exhibitions

Manchester, *Art Treasures*, 1857 (saloon H, no.37); Bethnal Green, 1872–5 (86).

References General

D35; M. Allden and R. Beresford, *The Burlington Magazine*, CXXXI, 1989, pp. 395-406.

1 For the restoration, see Allden and Beresford.

2 This idea, common in the seventeenth century and deriving ultimately from Correggio (*La Notte*, Dresden), had some textual authority; for example, in the *Revelations* of St. Bridget.

3 Louis Richeome, *The Pilgrime of Loreto*, 1629, p.232.

4 Before Dorival discovered this reference, P129 had been associated, incorrectly, with the Carmelite church in the Faubourg Saint-Jacques (A. Blunt, *Art and Architecture in France, 1500–1700*, 1953, p.216 n.148), and the series of tapestry cartoons of the Life of the Virgin painted for Michel Le Masle (A. Mabille de Poncheville, *Philippe de Champaigne*, n.d. [1953], p.43).

5 The decision was taken in 1627 when Champaigne was in Brussels; he was called back to Paris to take up the post, arriving on 10 January 1628 (A. Félibien, *Entretiens sur les vies et sur les ouvrages des plus excellens peintres*, 1725 ed., IV, p.316). There is no possibility that P129 was painted before Champaigne's return to Brussels in 1627.

6 See L.-H. Cottineau, *Répertoire topo-bibliographique des Abbayes et Prieurés*, 1935–70, II, col.2391–2. Besides the two abbeys mentioned below, there was also a priory at Quincy, near Vierzon, in the diocese of Bourges.

7 See D35, citing a manuscript history of the abbey by Dom Estiennot (Bibliothèque Nationale, ms. lat.12755), *Gallia Christiana*, II, col.1289–92 and E. Lecointre, 'Notice sur l'abbaye de St. Benoît de Quincey', *Mémoires de la Société des Antiquaires de l'Ouest*, 1851, pp.417–50. Dorival argues ingeniously that the reference to Antwerp derives from a misreading of Dom Estiennot's manuscript on the part of the sale catalogue's compiler; such diligent research would, of course, be unexpected in an eighteenth-century sale catalogue, and the use of the perfect tense remains unexplained.

8 *Gallia Christiana*, IV, col.830–3 and E. Lambert, 'Histoire de l'Abbaye de Quincy', *Annuaire historique du département de l'Yonne*, 1863, pp.189–224; 1864, pp.1–43.

9 In 1634 the altar had only a wooden crucifix and wooden candlesticks, the windows of the choir were largely walled up so that the monks could hardly see, the roof leaked, the chapter house was being used as a stable, there was no cloister, etc. (see Lecointre, *op. cit.*, p.22).

10 Lambert, *op. cit.*, 1864, pp.29, 32.

11 As suggested below (see note 21), it is probable that P129 belonged to the dealer Pierre Le Brun who, having failed to sell the painting in an anonymous sale of 1765, placed it in another anonymous sale in 1766, only then adding the details of its history – which, even if the claims regarding Marie de Médicis's opinion of the picture were not demonstrably false, would arouse suspicion.

12 A portrait probably of Mesgrigny's brother, François, in the Musée des Beaux-Arts, Troyes (inv.57.2.2; dated 1656), is perhaps attributable to Champaigne's workshop. Although Mesgrigny is recorded as abbot only until 1643, he was still acting, apparently as abbot, in 1648 (see Lambert, *op. cit.*, 1864, pp.30–2). He was succeeded, briefly, by Nicolas Mondin and, c.1650 (according to Lambert, *op. cit.*, 1864, p.34), by Pierre Balthasar Phélypeaux, son of the notable patron Louis Phélypeaux de La Vrillière. I am most grateful to Chantal Rouquet for information on the Mesgrigny family and portraits.

[13] A. Blunt, *op. cit.*, 1980 ed., p.253.

[14] Dorival's dating has been generally accepted; for example, by A. Sutherland Harris, *The Art Bulletin*, LXI, 1979, p.321; D. Lavalle in *La Peinture d'inspiration réligieuse à Rouen au temps de Pierre Corneille, 1606–1684*, exh. cat. Rouen, Eglise Saint-Ouen, 1984, pp.88–90, no.9, and A. Scottez in *Trésors des Musées du Nord de la France, La peinture français aux XVIIe et XVIIIe siècles*, exh. cat. Dunkerque, Valenciennes, Lille, 1980, pp.30–2, no.5.

[15] Dorival overstates the dependence of P129 on Rubens, linking it with the *Adoration* at Le Mans (D42 and see note 16 below). P129 does not appear any more Rubensian than the Lille and Rouen pictures of the 1640s (D34, D39), which may be compared with Rubens compositions engraved by Schelte a Bolswert and Paneels (C. G. Voorhelm Schneegvoogt, *Catalogue des estampes gravés d'après Rubens*, 1873, p.15, no.20, p.17, no.34).

[16] Félibien (*op. cit.*, p.317) dates the composition 1628–9; Dorival gives c.1629. P129 is also quite unlike an *Adoration of the Kings* at Le Mans (D42) which, although accepted by Blunt (*op. cit.*, p.431 n.105) and Dorival, is painted in an overtly Rubensian style quite unlike that employed by Champaigne in any other known work.

[17] The payment for the Rouen altarpiece in 1644 is recorded in Archives Départementales de Seine-Inférieure, G3559; see also Chanoine Jouen, *La Cathédrale de Rouen*, 1932, pp.109–10.

[18] Rosenberg regards the date of P129 as not far removed from the Rouen altarpiece of 1644 (letter on file dated 27 January 1988). A later date for P129 was also suggested by A. Thackeray, *Philippe de Champaigne's early commission of paintings for the Church of the Carmelite Convent of the Incarnation in the Faubourg Saint-Jacques in Paris*, unpub. thesis, Courtauld Institute, 1987.

[19] Champaigne could have known the first two in engravings by Schelte a Bolswert and Vosterman respectively (Voorhelm Schneegvoogt, *op. cit.*, p.15, no.23, p.17, no.35), the last possibly in the original since it may have been painted for Soissons (J. S. Held, *The Oil Sketches of Peter Paul Rubens*, 1980, I, p.449). The cobweb in the top left-hand corner of P129 may have been suggested by the Rouen composition.

[20] Catalogued by Lugt and Vallery-Radot as a copy (*Cabinet des Estampes, inventaire général des écoles du Nord*, 1936, no.244). Dorival argues from the absence of the lamb that the drawing is a sketch, but there are some weaknesses in draughtsmanship, particularly in Joseph's left calf, which suggest a copy. In the position of the left edge, the drawing is closer to the replica of P129 at Portland than to P129 itself, suggesting it is perhaps from Champaigne's workshop.

[21] Father of the more famous dealer J.-B.-P. Le Brun (1748–1813). The two anonymous sales of 1765 and 1766 were both organised by Pierre Le Brun and at least 13 paintings appeared in both sales. It seems quite possible that Le Brun was using the sales to dispose of stock.

[22] As a 'finished chef d'oeuvre, on canvas 7′ 10″ by 5′ 3″ [239 × 160], but the canvas has been enlarged by about 4½″ [11.5] on each side'. No such additions are visible on P129. Dorival regards this as a different painting, but did not know Bonnemaison was the buyer (D482).

[23] *Description des tableaux qui ornent le grand appartement de l'hôtel de Montcalm*, Montpellier, 1836, no.37 (cited by Dorival).

P134 *The Annunciation*

The Virgin in pinkish red with blue drapery and grey-green shawl, Gabriel in white with pale blue drapery; on the left a bed with green hangings, a chair *en suite* and a work-basket on the floor; in the background a *prie-dieu*, chimney-piece, firedog and shovel. The cherubs on the left have blue draperies, on the right blue and pink.

Canvas, relined 334.3 × 214.5 (maximum) including top section 50.5 × 168.8

In the course of relining before 1845,[1] the upper corners were made up with old canvas from another picture – on the left the foot and cloak of a classical figure, on the right a piece of furniture – and painted over in black. The original canvas was possibly slightly reduced in size during relining (the chair back on the left is almost invisible). Cleaned by Buttery in 1879 when a second lining canvas was added.[2] In 1985–6 both lining canvases were removed before a new lining by Bobak, and P134 was cleaned and restored by Lank.[3] Considerable areas of retouching in black-grey over old damages and losses were then removed mainly from the central area and infilled corners (as described above). There are major losses in the face of the cherub on the extreme right, in an area 10 cm. high along the bottom edge (where some old retouching remains) and along the top edge, but for its age and size P134 is generally well preserved. Smaller losses are mainly confined to the upper area, the edges, a vertical seam 98.5 cm. from the left-hand edge and

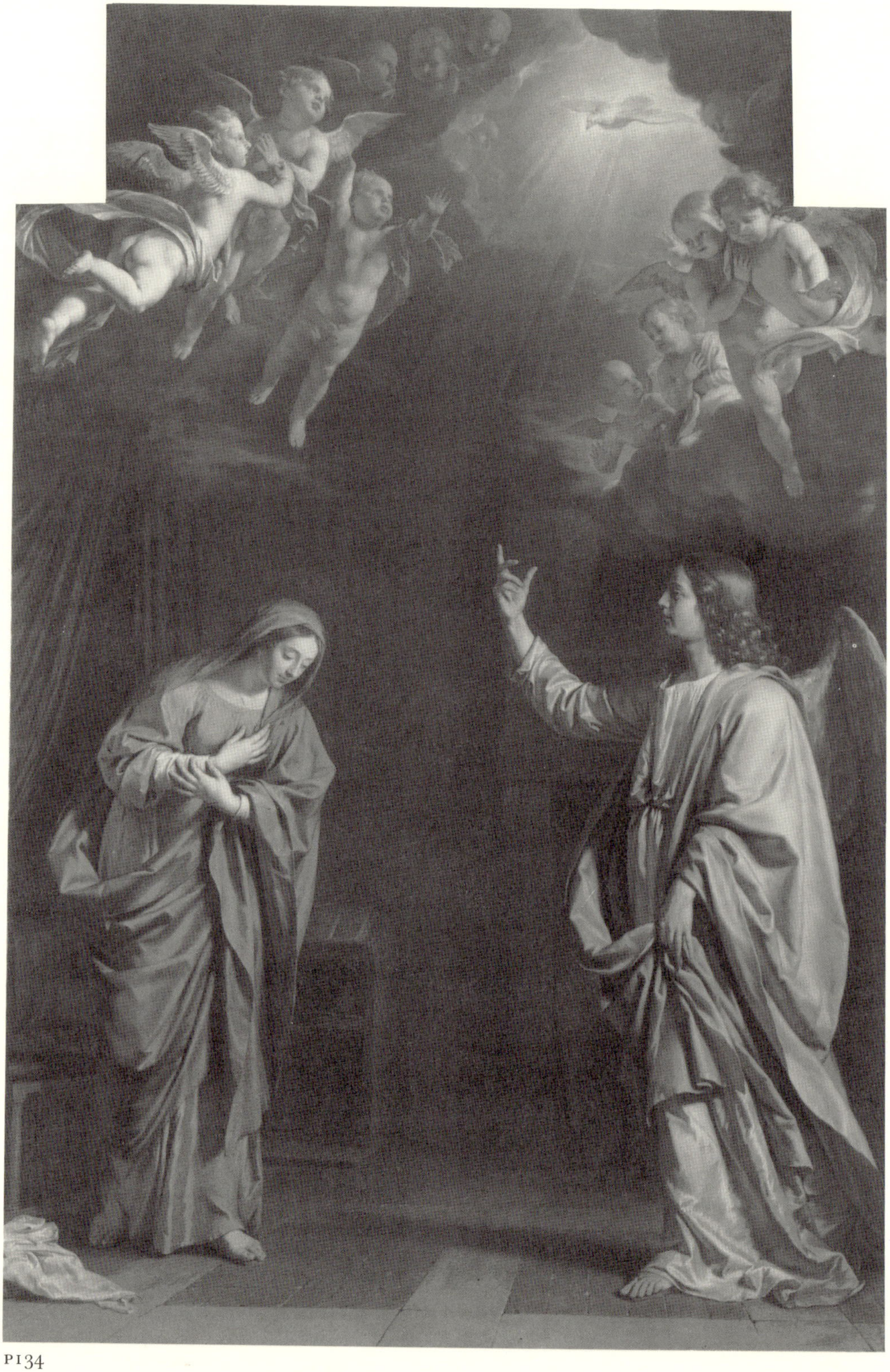

P134

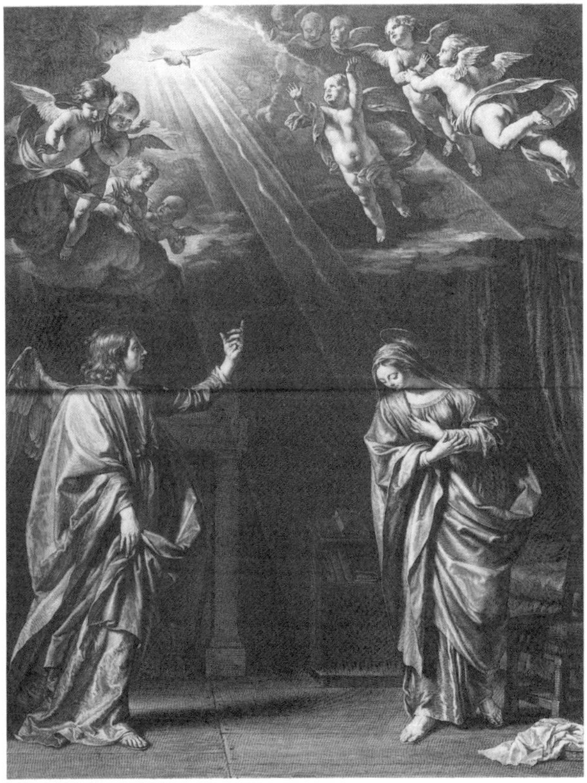

N. Pitau after Champaigne: *The Annunciation.*
Bibliothèque Nationale

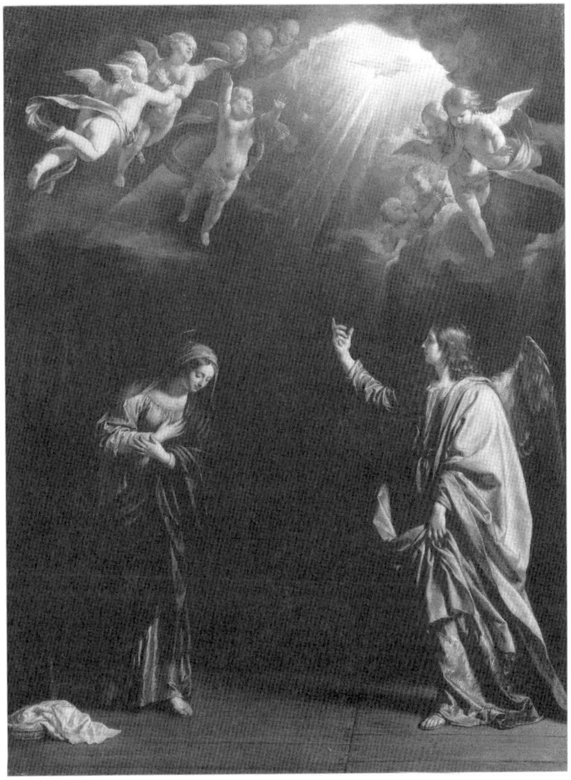

Champaigne: *The Annunciation.*
Ferens Art Gallery, Kingston-upon-Hull

horizontal tears across Mary's breast and legs. Other losses in significant areas are over Mary's left eye, in her right shoulder and drapery, in the angel's neck, the fingers of his left hand and his blue drapery. *Pentimenti* reveal that the group of cherubs on the left was originally placed lower and Mary's red dress was slightly shorter. P134 is painted on a double ground of terracotta red overlaid with grey.

The subject is taken from Luke I, 38: told by the archangel Gabriel that she will bear a son by the Holy Spirit, Mary submits to the divine will, 'Behold the handmaid of the Lord! Let it be unto me according to thy word'. This is the moment of the Incarnation. Gabriel indicates the dove of the Holy Spirit with his right index finger; it has been suggested, implausibly, that this gesture is symbolic of the Incarnation.[4] The work-basket and the book on a *prie-dieu* are traditional and refer to apocryphal accounts of Mary's previous activities.[5] Champaigne departs in some respects from the typical seventeenth-century pattern: Gabriel neither kneels on a cloud, nor holds a lily, and whilst one or both figures normally kneel, here they both stand.[6] For the same subject, see Murillo P68.

Although P134 is a major altarpiece of Champaigne's maturity, its early history is uncertain. It cannot be identified with any of the eight *Annunciations* by Champaigne seized from Paris churches and convents at the Revolution, of which seven

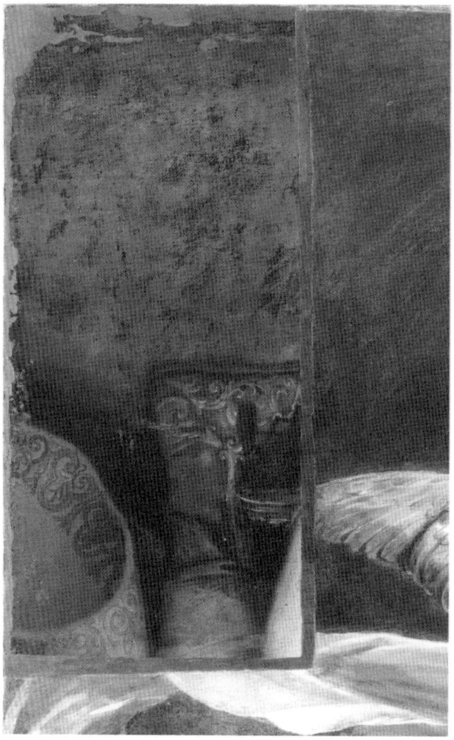

P134 detail, showing canvas infill in top left-hand corner

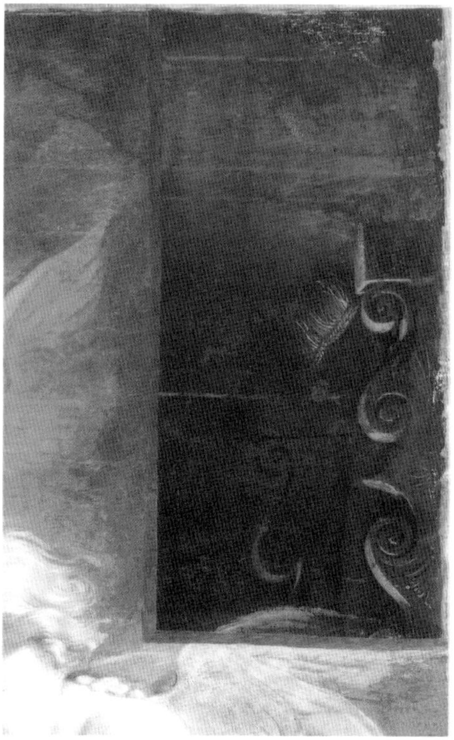

P134 detail, showing canvas infill in top right-hand corner

were smaller[7] and an eighth is now at Caen.[8] Three further *Annunciations* recorded in pre-revolutionary sources are possibilities,[9] but there is insufficient evidence to make a positive identification:

1 An *Annunciation* recorded by Guillet de Saint-Georges in the *chapelle de la congrégation* next to the church of the Jesuit Noviciate in Paris.[10] Guillet's text implies a date shortly after 1636, and the painting was described in the eighteenth century as '*toute retouchée*';[11] neither would be appropriate for P134. Nevertheless, Guillet's dating is not necessarily reliable,[12] and Dorival's identification of the reference with an altarpiece now at Montrésor (Indre-et-Loire) is not certain.[13]

2 An *Annunciation* recorded at the Palais Royal in 1788,[14] probably painted for Anne of Austria's oratory, c.1644 (see P119). Dorival associates P134 with this reference, arguing a date in the mid-1640s on stylistic grounds.[15] However, Anne of Austria's oratory was a small private chapel which already contained a sizeable altarpiece by Simon Vouet; it is highly improbable that it contained two major altarpieces.[16]

3 An *Annunciation* recorded by Guillet de Saint-Georges in the chapel of the Hôtel de Chavigny.[17] This altarpiece was commissioned by Léon Bouthillier, a pupil and friend of the Jansenist abbé de Saint-Cyran (see P645),[18] and was probably painted for the new chapel added to the Hôtel in 1642–3 by François Mansart.[19] Dorival's association of this reference with the *Annunciation* now in the church of

Notre-Dame-du-Port at Clermont-Ferrand is unconvincing,[20] and a tentative connection with P134 may be proposed.
It remains possible, however, that P134, like Champaigne's *Adoration of the Shepherds* P129, was not recorded in the early sources.

If P134 was painted for Mansart's chapel in the Hôtel de Chavigny then it would date from between 1643, when the chapel was completed, and 1648, when Léon Bouthillier was banished to his estates at Chavigny. The monumentality of P134 could suggest a somewhat later date; Mabille de Poncheville discussed the painting in the context of the Fronde (1648–53),[21] it was not engraved until c.1657, and there are certain parallels, particularly in the cherubs, with works of the mid-1650s.[22] However, as Dorival argues, P134 is similar in other respects to works of the mid-1640s: the treatment of draperies compares with the *Marriage of the Virgin* of c.1644 (see P119) and the statuesque figures with the *Presentation in the Temple* in Brussels of 1648.[23] A dating in the mid-1640s should, therefore, be regarded as possible. The unusual austerity of the composition[24] might be explained by the limitations of the subject and, perhaps, by the tastes of a patron with Jansenist sympathies.

Engraving

Nicolas Pitau c.1657,[25] reversed, based largely on the Kingston-upon-Hull version (see Versions), but the extended fingers of the angel's left hand and the central seraph at the top are as in P134.

Versions

KINGSTON-UPON-HULL Ferens Art Gallery; 74.3 × 54.6, by Champaigne or his workshop; differing in detail from P134;[26] probably a later adaptation or possibly a *modello*; ex colls. Vintimille and Vaudreuil[27] (D25).
NEW YORK, Historical Society; probably workshop; the Virgin, bust length with the dove.[28]

Copies

BRAY-SUR-SEINE (Seine-et-Marne) church; the Virgin alone, bust length.[29]
SABLONNIERES (Seine-et-Marne) church; 184 × 152; in reverse.
?VILLENEUVE-LES-AVIGNON Hospice.[30]
VILLESEQUE DES CORBIERES (Aude) church; 56 × 74; in reverse with the Virgin kneeling and the angels omitted.

Provenance

See above; purchased by Cardinal Fesch (1763–1839) from Gueilac, September/October 1800 (*vendémiaire an* IX);[31] Fesch sale, Rome, 17 March–15 May 1845 (36, '*Nous croyons que ce tableau appartenait à l'église Culture-Sainte-Catherine qui a été démolie . . .*', [337 × 215]), bt. by the 4th Marquess of Hertford, 560 *scudi* (2,800 fr.); rue Laffitte inventory 1871 (405); Hertford House inventory 1890.

References General

D24; B. Dorival, 'Les Oeuvres de Philippe de Champaigne sur le sujet de l'Annonciation', BSHAF 1970, pp.45–71 (pp.52 and 57–8); M. Allden and R. Beresford, *The Burlington Magazine*, CXXXI, 1989, pp. 395-406.

1 The stretcher closely resembles those of the Fesch Watteaus P391 and P416 and appears to be of early nineteenth-century manufacture.

2 '*Lining* [P134] *on same stretcher*' (transcript of Buttery Order Book in Wallace Collection archives).

3 For the restoration, see Allden and Beresford.

4 Dorival, *Revue de l'Art*, 11, 1971, pp.33–4.

5 That she was weaving, praying, or studying the prophecy of Isaiah, 'Behold, a Virgin shall conceive and bear a son' (M. R. James, *The Apocryphal New Testament*, 1953, pp.43 and 74, and Mrs. Jameson, *Legends of the Madonna*, 1857, p.181).

[6] The composition bears a probably coincidental resemblance to Santi di Tito's *Annunciation* of 1602/3 in S. Maria Novella, Florence (J. Spalding, *Santi di Tito*, 1982, pp.461–4, no.67, fig.99).

[7] Dorival, *op. cit.*, 1970, pp.51–6: altarpieces from the Ave-Maria [277.4 × 195.8], Sainte-Catherine-de-la-Culture [187.7 × 155], the convent of Port-Royal [163.2 × 97.9], and four paintings inventoried among '*Moyens tableaux*' (from the Oratoire, and the convents of the Cordeliers, the Dames Nouvelles Catholiques and the Dames de Ville l'Evêque).

[8] From the chapel of SS. Ferréol and Ferrutien, Notre-Dame. The abbé C.-P. Gueffier, *Description historique des curiosités de l'église de Paris*, 1763, p.233, states the chapel was decorated by Champaigne in 1654, a date which, among known *Annunciations* could only apply to P134. However, as Dorival shows, Gueffier's text is unreliable and the Caen painting, since it was deposited by the State in 1800/1, must have come from those seized at the Revolution, the Notre-Dame altarpiece being apparently the only possible candidate (Dorival, *op. cit.*, 1970, pp.53–4).

[9] Dorival, *op. cit.*, 1970, pp.57–9, also recording three further references to *Annunciations* which cannot apply to P134: a grisaille overdoor in the Carmelite convent of the Faubourg Saint-Jacques, another '*en deux tableaux séparés à demi-corps*' mentioned in Champaigne's Will, and a third in the Vaudreuil sale, 26 November 1787 (40, [73.4 × 51.7]) as from the Vintimille collection, also recorded in the *inventaire après décès* of Charles-Gaspard-Guillaume de Vintimille, archévêque de Paris, 24 March 1746.

[10] Guillet de Saint-Georges, in *Mémoires inédits sur la vie et les ouvrages des membres de l'académie royale de peinture et sculpture*, ed. L. Dussieux *et al.*, 1854, I, p.241.

[11] A.-N. Dezallier d'Argenville, *Voyage pittoresque de Paris*, 1757, p.375.

[12] The passage in question appears to be chronologically arranged, but is sometimes inaccurate; for example, the *Last Supper* painted for Port-Royal in 1648 is placed after works datable 1655–6 (Guillet de Saint-Georges, *op. cit.*, I, pp.241–2). According to Dezallier (*loc. cit.*), the walls of the chapel were painted with four scenes from the life of the Virgin by Jean-Baptiste de Champaigne (1631–81); if the attribution is correct, these cannot date from before the mid-1650s and it seems possible that they were commissioned at the same time as the altarpiece.

[13] Dorival's argument depends on the date implied by Guillet de Saint-Georges and on his own stylistic dating of the Montrésor canvas which, as Sutherland Harris notes (*The Art Bulletin*, LXI, 1979, p.321), may be later than he suggests. The fact that the Montrésor canvas appears in the Lenglier sale of 10 March 1788 (220) does not prove that it came from the Jesuit Noviciate, but establishes that it was not the *Annunciation* recorded in the Palais Royal in the same month (see note 14 below).

[14] See V. Champier and G.-R. Sandoz, *Le Palais Royal*, 1900, I, p.521 (*Liste des tableaux destinés à la vente en Angleterre*, March 1788).

[15] Dorival, *op. cit.*, 1970, p.57. The connection had also been made by C. Stryienski, *La Galerie du Régent*, 1913, p.179, no.357.

[16] For the Queen's oratory and Vouet's altarpiece, see P119 above. It is worth noting that an *Annunciation* by Champaigne, painted like P119 on panel and of similar scale, appeared in the Duval sale, London, 12 May 1846 (72, 27 × 28 *pouces* or inches [73.4 × 76.2 or 68.6 × 71.1], repr.), having possibly been acquired in Paris in 1793 (Le Bas sale, Paris, 26–7 April 1793, lot 33, as on canvas, [70.7 × 70.7]); see D255. It is impossible to judge the style from the engraving, but the simple classical pedestal which serves the Virgin as lectern and cupboard, would be consistent with a date in the mid-1640s.

[17] Guillet de Saint-Georges, *loc. cit.*

[18] See J. Orcibal, *Jean Duvergier de Hauranne, abbé de Saint-Cyran et son temps*, II, 1947, p.381.

[19] As suggested by A. Braham and P. Smith, *François Mansart*, 1973, I, p.219 (see also Sutherland Harris, *loc. cit.*). Dorival's suggestion (*op. cit.*, 1970, p.59) that the altarpiece was contemporary with alterations undertaken to the Hôtel by 1639 (not, as he states, in 1639) is less likely.

[20] The argument again depends on Guillet de Saint-Georges's text and a stylistic dating, which is disputable (the Clermont-Ferrand *Annunciation* appearing, if anything, earlier than that in Montrésor). If the Hôtel de Chavigny altarpiece was painted for Mansart's chapel (see note 19 above), then it cannot be identical with the Clermont-Ferrand painting, which is clearly earlier.

[21] A. Mabille de Poncheville, *Philippe de Champaigne*, n.d. [1953], pp.70–1 (P134 is discussed in Chapter IX, '*Au Temps de la Fronde*').

[22] There are close parallels for the cherubs of P134 in the lost *Vision of Dom Jean* of 1655 (D287) and the cherub on the right in the *Assumption* at Alençon of c.1656 (D86).

[23] Dorival in fact cites the small version of the *Presentation in the Temple* at Ponce (D47) on which a date of 1642 was once recorded. This date is apparently no longer visible and may have been incorrectly recorded, since the painting is a small version of the altarpiece in Brussels almost certainly painted in 1648 (see A. Sutherland Harris, *The Art Bulletin*, LXI, 1979, p.322).

[24] The severity of P134 approaches that of another *Annunciation* by Champaigne in Toulouse (D23), but Dorival's dating of this work to c.1641 (*op. cit.*, 1970, p.54) depends on his interpretation of the coat-of-arms which is surmounted by a ducal coronet rather than that of a marquis; this implies a date after 1663 when Armand Cambout de Coislin became a *duc et pair*.

[25] Pitau arrived in Paris c.1656 and the *Annunciation* was amongst his first works executed there (P. J. Mariette, *Abecedario*, IV, AAF, VIII, 1857–8, p.178 n.1). For the engraving, see also Dorival, *Gazette des Beaux-Arts*, 6e, LXXX, 1972, p.25, no.13.

[26] The differences may be summarized as follows:

a) The proportions are less vertical and the composition is consequently more open and expanded slightly at the edges.
b) The indented upper corners are absent.
c) In the cherub group on the left: the drapery held by the cherub on the extreme left is shorter and drapery appears behind the knee of the cherub on the right.
d) In the group of three seraphs the central seraph looks to the right.
e) The face of the cherub on the extreme right is thinner and his wing differently angled.
f) The small fingers of the angel's left hand are not extended.
g) The angel wears blue and mauve in place of white and blue.
h) The chimney-piece is slightly different.
i) The book on the *prie-dieu* is closed and the books on the shelf below differently arranged.
j) The floor is wooden.
k) The fall of the curtain behind the Virgin is more vertical.
l) The Virgin has a halo.

27 Dorival, *op. cit.*, 1970, pp.56–7, and see note 9. Also associated by Dorival with lot 58 in the d'Alberg sale, Paris, 21 March 1820, 73.4 × 54.4, but the catalogue describes the Virgin as placed on the right and dressed in white and blue.

28 *La peinture française du XVIIe siècle dans les collections américaines*, exh. cat. Paris, New York, Chicago, 1982, p.349, fig.3.

29 L. Houillon, 'L'Eglise de Bray-sur-Seine: restauration de tableaux', *Bulletin de la Société de l'Histoire et d'Archéologie de Provins*, 135, 1981, p.112.

30 According to a note by W. Gibson on file, but doubted by Dorival who suggests the painting may be an *Annunciation* by Gennari recorded at Villeneuve-lèz-Avignon in 1884 (*op. cit.*, 1970, p.57 n.1).

31 Abbé J.-B. Vanel, *Deux livres de Comptes du Cardinal Fesch, archévêque de Lyon*, 1923, p.53, one of two *Annunciations* by Champaigne which Fesch bought from Gueilac at this date; the other, lot 37 in the Fesch sale, is identifiable with the painting now at Montrésor. P134 appeared as no.67 in the 1841 Fesch catalogue.

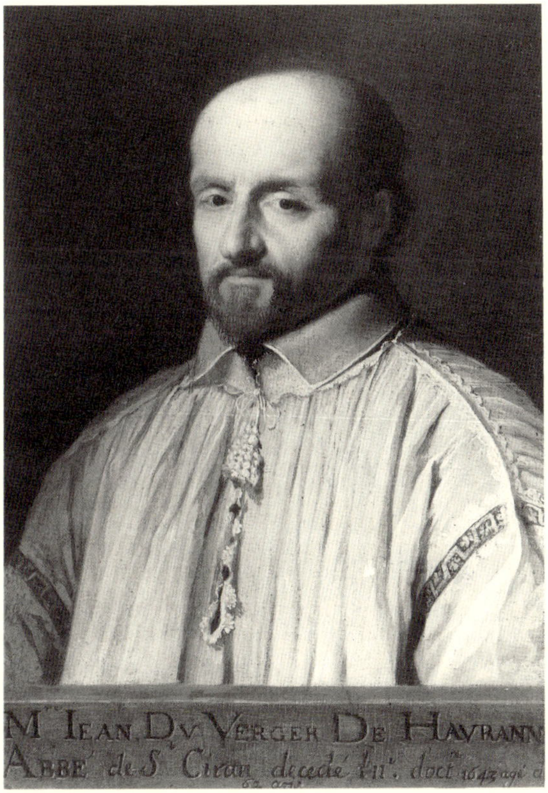

P645

After Champaigne

P645 *The abbé de Saint-Cyran*

Wearing a white surplice. Inscribed on the ledge: *M^{re}* IEAN DV VERGER DE HAVRANNE/ABBÉ *de St Ciran decedé l'11.e d'oct.^{re} 1643 agé de/62 ans.*

Panel 16.5 × 11.4[1]

Jean Duvergier de Hauranne, abbé de Saint-Cyran (1581–1643); at Louvain he met Cornelius Jansen (Jansenius) with whom he collaborated at Bayonne

1609–16 in theological studies; in 1636 he became spiritual director of the convent of Port-Royal, Paris, a centre of Jansenist beliefs; he was imprisoned by Richelieu at Vincennes 1638–42. He never permitted his portrait to be painted during his lifetime.[2]

P645 was catalogued as French school until 1920 and as After Champaigne in 1928 and 1968. It is one of several copies of the larger portrait painted by Champaigne from a death mask in 1647–8 and now in Grenoble (74 × 57; D215) which was engraved by J. Morin (d.1650);[3] this is one of the earliest known instances of Champaigne's association with the Jansenists. Blunt compared the format with that of a medieval *chef* reliquary, an appropriate association for a posthumous and venerated image.[4]

Versions

Dorival records the following known replicas of the Grenoble portrait besides P645:[5]
BUDAPEST, Szépmüvészeti Múzeum; 66.5 × 55; inscribed *Aetas 62 Ao 1645* [*sic*] (D1790).
MAGNY-LES-HAMEAUX (Yvelines) Musée National des Granges de Port-Royal; 70 × 54 (D1792).
NARBONNE Cathedral; 50 × 39 (D1792*bis*).
VERSAILLES Musée; 72 × 58 (D1793).

Provenance

Probably acquired by the 3rd Marquis of Hertford;[6] Hertford House inventory 1870 as '*Jean de Havrann*'; stolen from the Wallace Collection, 1982.

Reference General

D1791.

[1] There is no record of a detailed examination of the panel which is inscribed, *verso*, with an H and *13*[or B], separated by three small strokes above a *Bn* [?].

[2] See J. Orcibal, *Jean Duvergier de Hauranne, abbé de Saint-Cyran et son temps*, 1948, and A. Sedgwick, *Jansenism in Seventeenth-Century France*, 1977.

[3] Dorival, *Gazette des Beaux-Arts*, 6e, LXXV, 1970, pp.315–16.

[4] A. Blunt, *Art and Architecture in France, 1500–1700*, 1980 ed., p.256.

[5] For possible replicas recorded in sale and exhibition catalogues, see D1130–8. To these may be added an 'Abbé de St. Cyran' by Champaigne exh. BI 1863, lent Miss Caldwell.

[6] P645 was possibly the '*Terburg A Portrait of an Abbot*', listed at Dorchester House in 1842. In the 1870 inventory quoted above P645 was listed in a room otherwise containing only pictures acquired by the 2nd or 3rd Marquesses.

Jacques Charlier (c.1705–1790)

A miniaturist, primarily of erotic genre scenes, Charlier was born in the former province of Champagne (east of Paris) of a poor family. His work strongly suggests that he studied with Boucher, many of whose paintings he copied, but his early career is undocumented. From 1748 he received commissions from the *Menus Plaisirs*, including miniature portraits of Royalty for gold boxes and bracelets in 1749 and 1754, and he was styled *peintre en miniature du Roi* from 1753. Other patrons included Mme. de Pompadour, the duc de Caylus (who sold 50 Charliers, 19 April 1773, lots 55–8, and owned over 90 in all), the duc d'Aumont and the prince de Conti (for whom in 1772 he painted 12 large miniatures at 1,200 *livres* each[1]). Annuities were settled upon him by both the duc d'Orléans (1752) and Caylus (1771). In 1778 he offered 90 of his miniatures for sale, and on 10 March 1779 he offered 90 at an auction which he stopped, finding the bids too low. He died in Paris on 19 February 1790 '*à l'âge de quatre vingts et quelques années*'.[2] See also *Catalogue of Miniatures*, 1980, nos.51–84 (M46–68, 70, 72–4, 77–81, 139, 163).

[1] Cf. Conti sale, 8 April ff.1777 (910–15), where they fetched 4,107 *livres*.

[2] The principal sources for Charlier's biography are: A. Maze-Sencier, *Le Livre des Collectionneurs*, 1885, pp.499–500; P. Lespinasse, *La Miniature en France au XVIIIe siècle*, 1929, pp.44–9, and A. Blunt in *The James A. de Rothschild Collection at Waddesdon Manor, Gold Boxes and Miniatures of the eighteenth century*, 1975, pp.332–3.

P474 *Love offering the apple to Venus (after Boucher)*

Venus has a pink, pearl-studded girdle; one *putto* holds a bow and the apple, the other two doves on a blue leash; to the right a gold-striped blue drapery and a purple cushion.

Gouache on vellum 24 × 17.3 stretched over panel

There is some staining near the bottom edge and there are small losses in the sky. The upper left area appears to have been rubbed, and there are passages of oxydised lead white top left and top right.

The subject was described in 1781 as: '*L'Amour persuadant Vénus de quitter sa ceinture, pour obtenir la pomme d'or qu'il lui offre*'[1] (cf. Boucher P444).

P474 relates closely to another Charlier composition (see Version) which has been associated, probably correctly, with the now lost Boucher, *L'Amour offrant une pomme à Vénus*, from the prince de Conti's collection.[2] Conti commissioned a copy in miniature from Charlier in 1772 which may indicate the date of P474. See also the pendant P476.

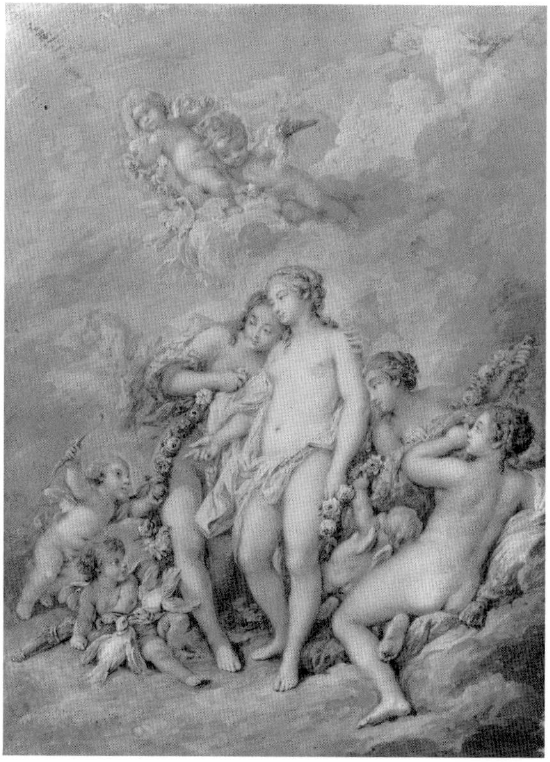

P274

Version

PARIS private collection; 41 × 32 oval, without the right-hand seated nymph; associated by Ananoff with the Conti commission of 1772 (see above), lot 910 in the Conti sale, Paris, 8 April ff. 1777[3] (A269/2, fig.802).

Provenance

Probably acquired by Sir Richard Wallace c.1872–4; Hertford House inventory 1890.

[1] Describing the Boucher painting from the Conti collection, Sireul sale catalogue, Paris, 3 December 1781 (25).

[2] A269, 107 × 69 oval. Ananoff dates it c.1744, but it was possibly later, judging by P474 and the version here described.

[3] Sold with the pendant Charlier miniature after Boucher's *Judgment of Paris* (cf.P476) as: '*Deux miniatures, de forme ovale, chacune . . .* [42.2 × 32.6]*; l'une représente Vénus remerciant Pâris de lui avoir adjugé la pomme d'or; l'autre représente la même Déesse, qui préside aux caresses que se font deux colombes dans les bras de l'amour . . . par M. Charlier, d'après F. Boucher . . .*'; they were bt. Dubois, 900 *livres* (see Charlier's biography above).

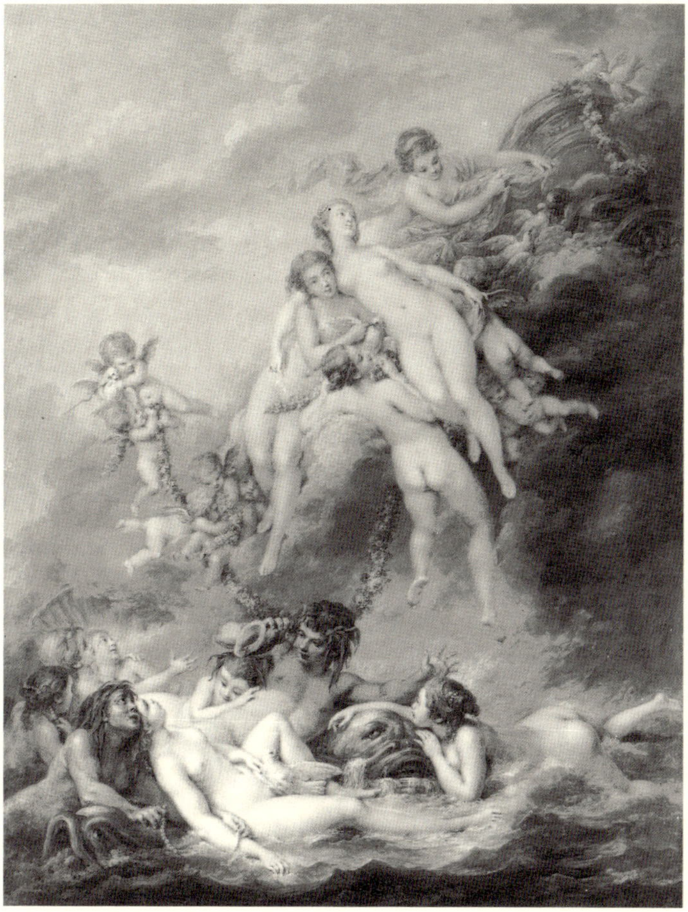

P475

P475 *The Birth of Venus (after Boucher)*

The uppermost nymph has pale lavender drapery and holds a turquoise-striped golden drape for Venus; the chariot, top right, upholstered in green.

Gouache on vellum 65.7 × 50.6 stretched over laminated board

Repaired and restretched by Wagstaff in 1978–9. There are several small losses in the head of the central dolphin, below the reclining nymph's right ankle, and round the edges.

Venus, goddess of love, rose naked from the sea and rode on a scallop shell to the isle of Paphos, where she was received by the nymphs of the Seasons and taken up to join the gods. See also P433 After Boucher and P468 Ascribed to Charlier.

P475 is copied from a Boucher composition otherwise known only through an oil sketch at Detroit (A619; see Boucher P444 note 1). P475 is of a squarer format, but the principal figures are similar; several derive from other Bouchers in the Wallace

Collection – the Venus recalls both the Venus and Juno in P444; the nymphs by her side the Venus in P429 and the Minerva (reversed) in P444, and the reclining sea nymphs resemble those in P486.

Provenance

The 4th Marquess of Hertford; rue Laffitte inventory 1871 (719); 105 Piccadilly 1874–5; Hertford House inventory 1890.

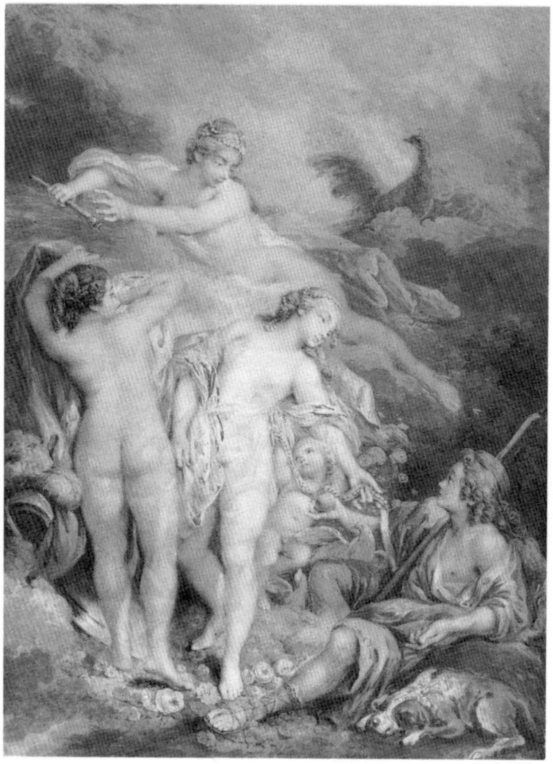

P476

P476 *The Judgment of Paris (after Boucher)*

Paris has red drapery; Minerva, on the right, a red-plumed helmet, black hair and blue drapery.

Gouache on vellum 23.6 × 17 stretched over panel

There are areas of oxydised lead white on Venus's drapery, Paris's shirt and on the dog.

For the subject, see Boucher P444; it was described in 1781 as: '*le Berger accordant la Pomme à Vénus qui lui remet sa ceinture*'.[1] See also the pendant P474.

P476 is copied from a Boucher now in a private collection in Paris (107 × 83; A524), apparently a later version of the Boucher formerly in the prince de Conti's collection (107 × 76 oval; A270), of which he commissioned a copy from Charlier in 1772 (see Version). As with the pendant P474, this may indicate the date of P476.

Version

PARIS private collection; 41 × 32 oval; showing Paris with a hat, without his crook and with his legs in a different position, and with Venus attended by different figures; associated by Ananoff with the Conti commission of 1772 (see above), lot 910 in the Conti sale, Paris, 8 April ff. 1777; cf. P474 note 3 (A270/3, fig.804).

Provenance

Probably acquired by Sir Richard Wallace c.1872–4; Hertford House inventory 1890.

[1] Describing the Boucher painting from the Conti collection, Sireul sale catalogue, Paris, 3 December 1781 (25).

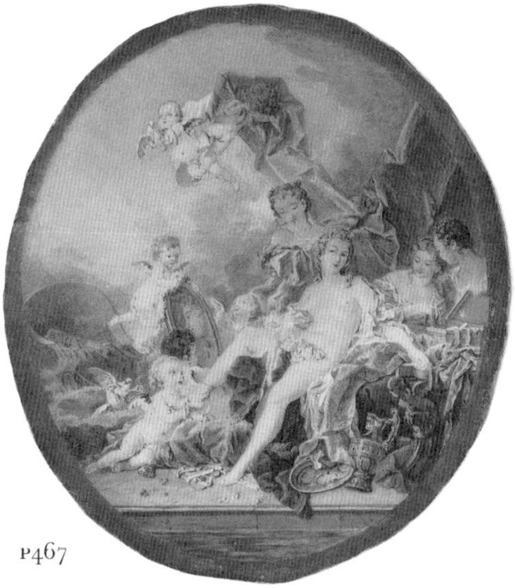

P467

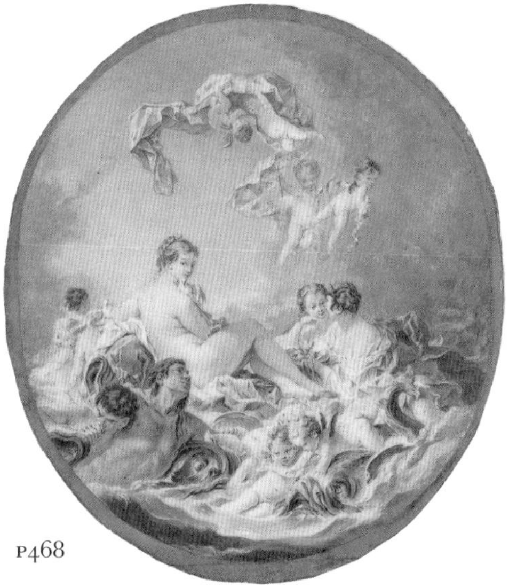

P468

Ascribed to Charlier

P467 *The Toilet of Venus (after Boucher)*

Venus reclines on a rich blue drapery, a plum-coloured canopy above.

Gouache on vellum 13.5 × 11.7 oval

A grey border gives an image size of 12.8 × 10.8. The colours appear to have faded.

See P468 below.

P468 *The Birth of Venus (after Boucher)*

Venus sits on a blue drapery, a grey-blue canopy above.

Gouache on vellum 13.5 × 11.6 oval

A grey border gives an image size of 12.6 × 11. The colours appear to have faded.

For the subject see Charlier P475 and P433 After Boucher.

P467 and P468 are copied from two Bouchers of 1743 now in a private collection in New York (each 102 × 88 oval; A243, A245), the colours agreeing with these originals. Both miniatures were described in the nineteenth century as by Charlier (see Provenance), although they are not in a style which is readily associated with him.

Provenance

W. Williams Hope (1802–55) of Rushton Hall, Northants., and Paris; his sale, Paris, 11 May 1858 (19, '*Charlier, Deux miniatures – La Toilette de Vénus et le Triomphe d'Amphitrite, dans leurs cadres de l'époque, en bois sculpté et doré*'[1]), 1,005 fr.; Allègre sale, Paris, 4th day, 16 May 1872 (281, '*Deux très-belles Miniatures sur vélin par Charlier . . . cadres en bois sculpté et doré, du temps de Louis XV. Collection Hope*'), bt. Mannheim for Sir Richard Wallace, 6,850 fr.; Hertford House inventory 1890.

Exhibition

Bethnal Green 1872–5 (1776, *The Triumph of Amphitrite* after Boucher by Charlier; 1777, *The Toilet of Venus* after Boucher, miniatures).

[1] These frames remain with P467 and P468.

Claude Gellée (1600–1682)

Called *Le Lorrain* and *Claude Lorraine*; born in 1600 in Chamagne, then in the duchy of Lorraine. His parents died in 1612 and probably in 1613 he went to Rome where it was said he was first a baker's assistant. He studied painting in Rome under the landscape painter A. Tassi and in Naples with Tassi's pupil, G. Wals (perhaps 1618–22). In 1625 he left Tassi's studio and returned to Lorraine where he worked with C. Deruet decorating the Carmelite church in Nancy. He returned the following year to Rome, and stayed for the rest of his life. His earlier landscapes were influenced by the Dutch painters then in Rome, Swanevelt and Breenbergh, but before 1635 he drew and painted in the Roman *campagna* and discovered the classical landscapes of Domenichino. In 1633 he was made a member of the Accademia di S. Luca and by the end of that decade his landscapes were being bought by Philip IV of Spain and Pope Urban VIII. At this time he began the *Liber Veritatis,* a collection of 195 drawings (now in the British Museum) recording each of his paintings, from 1637 until his death, before it left his studio. His later work achieved a fine serenity, particularly admired by Prince Colonna of Naples for whom Claude completed his last picture in 1682, the *Landscape with Ascanius shooting the Stag of Sylvia* (Ashmolean Museum, Oxford). He died in Rome on 23 November 1682.

Abbreviations

Kitson	M. Kitson, *Claude Lorrain: Liber Veritatis,* 1978
LV	*Liber Veritatis* (see biography above) with folio numbers (which are followed by Kitson and RP)
RD	M. Röthlisberger, *Claude Lorrain: The Drawings,* 2 vols. (text and plates), 1968
RP	M. Röthlisberger, *Claude Lorrain: The Paintings,* 2 vols. (text and plates), 1961
Smith	J. Smith, *A Catalogue raisonné of the Works of the most eminent Dutch, Flemish and French Painters,* VIII, 1837 (numbers refer to the catalogue of Claude's paintings, pp.194–384)

P114 *Landscape with Apollo and Mercury*

A morning scene; on the left Apollo as a shepherd with a white tunic and blue drape; behind him, in the mid-distance, Mercury in a silver-blue drape drives cattle over a bridge; in the foreground pale blue and yellow pelagonia flowers. Signed, to the left of Apollo: CLAUDE IV./ROMA/1660.

Canvas, relined 74.5 × 110.4

Relined by 1846 (see note 19), and probably between 1806 and 1814 when P114 was reframed;[1] the present surface suggests it was then heavily ironed and the glue unevenly applied. Cleaned by Lank in 1978. There is a double ground of white and deep pink covered by a dark red-brown *imprimatura.*[2] Craquelure is quite prominent in the central area, across the foreground and distance, and the darker green areas (the left foreground tree and beyond the pool on the right) have darkened further. The figure of Apollo was altered and the seated dog by his side

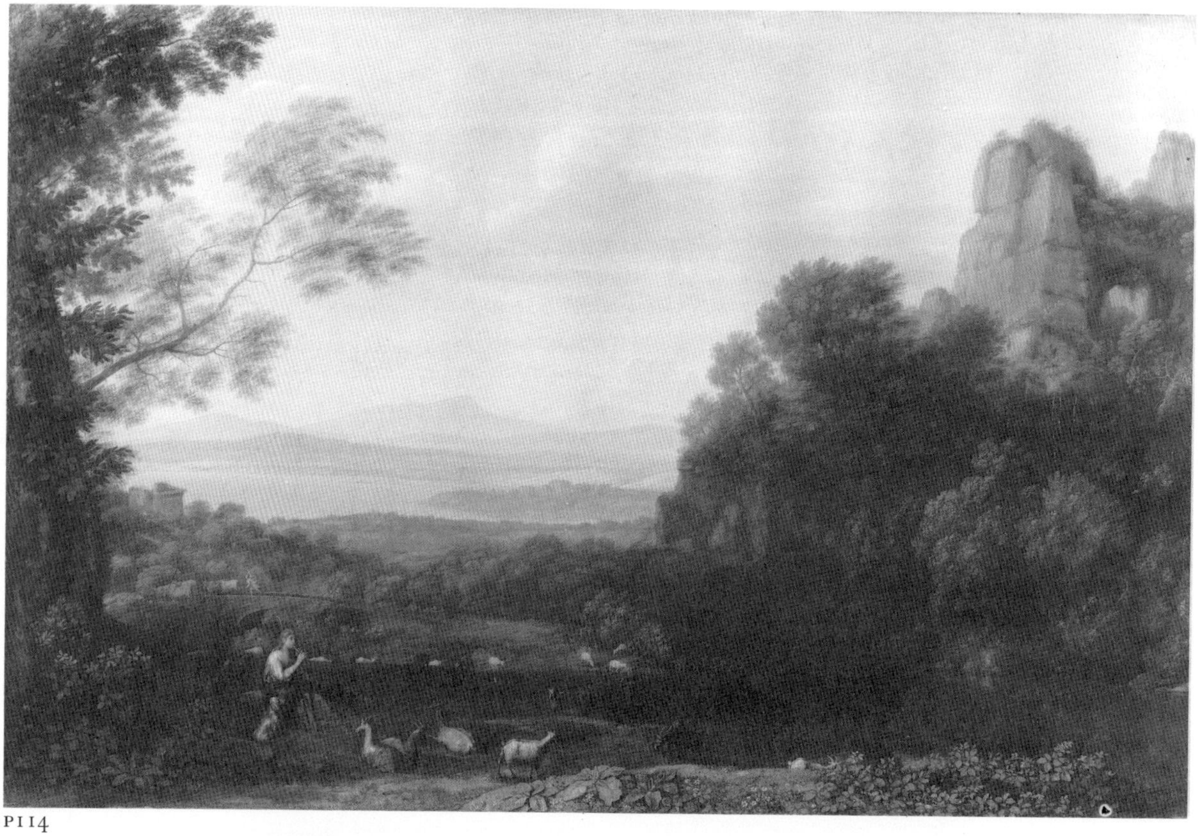

P114

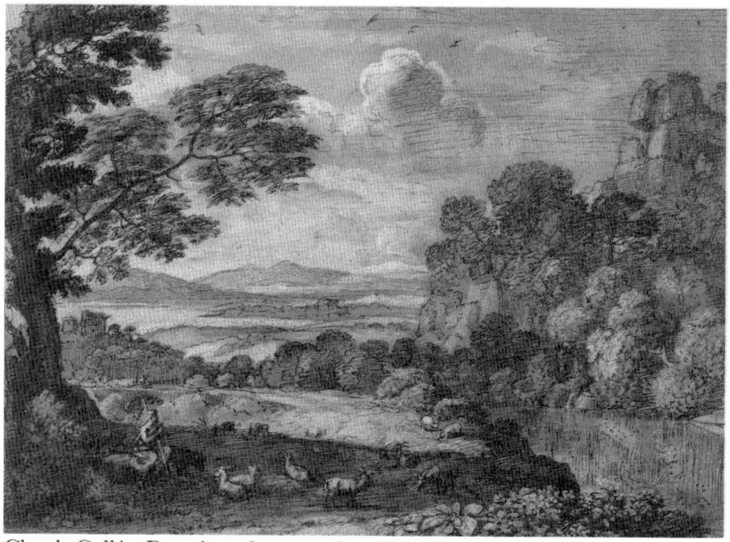

Claude Gellée: Drawing after P114 from the *Liber Veritatis*.
The British Museum

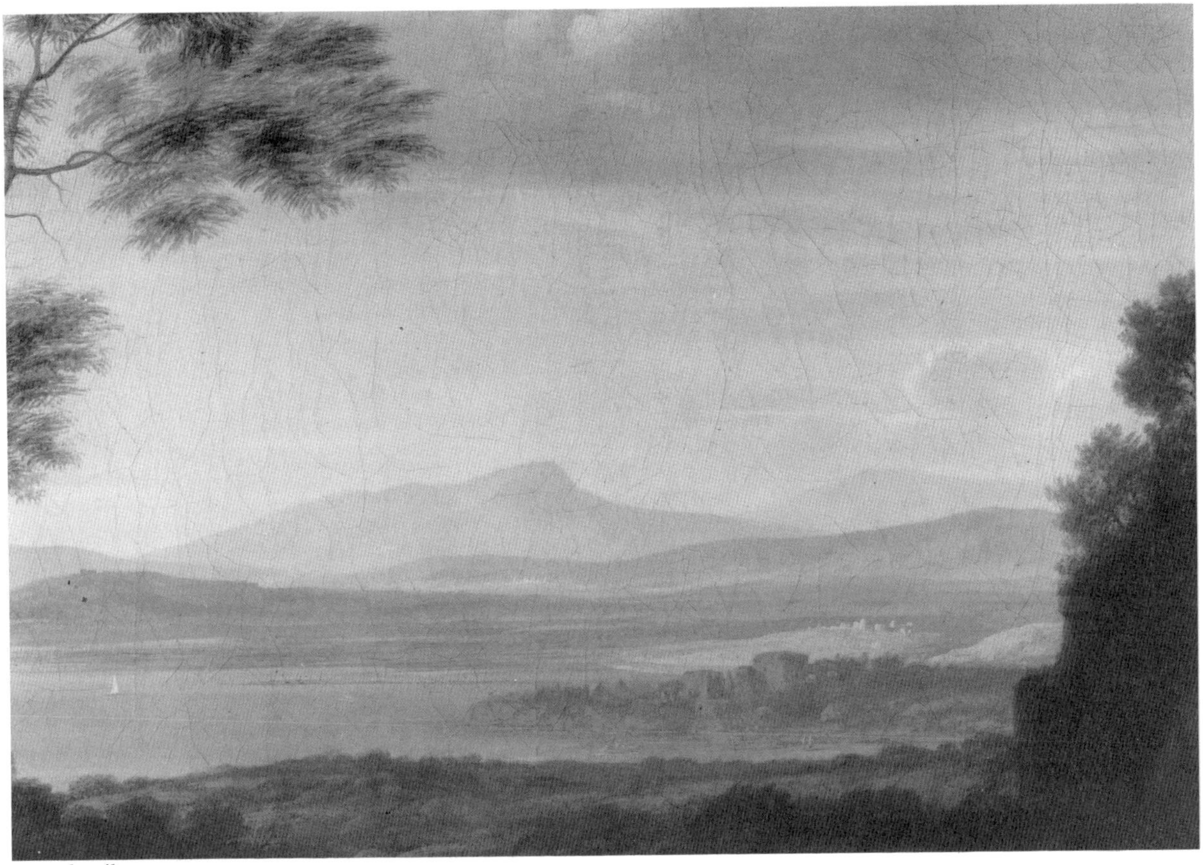

P114 detail

added by another hand.[3] Claude's original figure, which appears to have agreed closely with that seen in the *Liber Veritatis* drawing (LV152), remains partly and faintly visible: the left knee appears below the flute, the right leg and foot show through the dog's head and front leg, the original drapery extends behind Apollo's back, and the original staff may be detected beneath his left leg. The area containing the signature appears not to have been reworked. The consistent overall craquelure, and the recurrence of the present Apollo and his seated dog in an old copy (see below), suggest these alterations were made very soon after the original composition was completed.[4]

The subject, used several times by Claude between 1645 and 1666,[5] is most succinctly described in Ovid, *Metamorphoses* II, 679–86: Apollo, wearing a shepherd's cloak, carrying a staff in his left hand and a pipe of seven unequal reeds in his right, thought only of his love, the dead nymph Coronis, and neglected his cattle which were stolen by Mercury and hidden in the woods. The episode is further elaborated by other classical authors,[6] but Claude probably took Ovid as his source. Röthlisberger hinted that the contrasting foliage on the left (of a sturdy tree and a wispy willow) may deliberately echo the characters of Apollo and the mischievous Mercury.[7]

The modified Apollo in P114 is paralleled in the *Coast scene with Acis and Galatea* of 1657 (Dresden; LV141) which has figures repainted in the early eighteenth century by Louis or Bon de Boullongne.[8] P114 was painted for the Flemish dealer and painter Cornelis de Wael (1592–1667) who lived in Rome from 1656; Röthlisberger considers it likely that he commissioned P114 for an Antwerp client.[9] The *Landscape with Mercury and Battus* (Chatsworth; LV159) was very probably the pendant view; the *Liber Veritatis* drawing, dated 1663, is inscribed simply *pour Anvers*,[10] but the painting may also have been commissioned through de Wael.

Drawings

HAARLEM Teyler Museum (no.101); reversed, without Mercury and with a central pool; apparently a preliminary sketch for P114 and dated c.1659–60 by Röthlisberger (RD847).
LONDON British Museum (no.1957–12–14–158); 19.7 × 25.7, inscribed *quadro faict per il sigr/Deueal*, the *Liber Veritatis* drawing; the proportion is more square than P114 (RD849).
PARIS Louvre (RF4584); signed and dated 1660; deriving from the Haarlem drawing and without Mercury, but in the same sense, and more closely comparable to P114 (RD848).

Other drawings more loosely connected with P114 are in the Wildenstein Album (the figures of Apollo and Mercury, dated c.1660 by Röthlisberger, RD850) and in the Dumbarton Oaks Research Library, Washington (a finished landscape composition dated 1663, roughly combining the right half of P114 with the left half of the Chatsworth picture; exh. *Claude Lorrain*, Washington and Paris 1983, D55 (RD898 and cf. RP, p.358).

Engravings

After the *Liber Veritatis* drawing: R. Earlom 1777; L. Caracciolo 1815.

Copy

MONACO Sotheby's, 17 June 1989 (553); 120 × 160, see above.

Provenance

C. de Wael (1592–1667), Rome; possibly sent to Antwerp (see notes 9 and 10); baron Schönborn sale, Amsterdam, 16 April 1738 (2, '*Een Landschap door* Claudio Loroinese; *konstig en natuurlyk geschildert, Ao.1650*' [sic]; [79 × 117]), bt. Rutgers, 465 guilders, for Wilhelm VIII, Landgrave of Hesse-Cassel (1682–1760);[11] by descent to Wilhelm IX (d.1820); confiscated at Cassel, 1806, by général Lagrange for the Empress Joséphine (1763–1814);[12] listed in her *inventaire après décès* 1814, at Malmaison;[13] the prince de Talleyrand (1754–1838); listed in his sale, Paris, 7 July 1817 (17, '*Paysage, . . . un des principaux ornemens de la galerie des princes de Hesse-Cassel; depuis, dans celle de Malmaison. . .*'), but bt. immediately before the sale by W. Buchanan (1777–1864)[14] who, before 1824, sold it for 1,200 gn. to Edward Gray (d. before 1838) of Harringay House, Hornsea;[15] he sold it for 1,500 gn. to J. Bulkeley Owen;[16] for sale at Yates's Gallery, London, in 1837;[17] by 1842 with E. Higginson (*né* Barneby, 1802–71) of Saltmarsh Castle, Herefordshire;[18] his sale, Christie's, 3rd day, 6 June 1846 (205, 'Italian Landscape, from the Hesse Cassel, Malmaison, Talleyrand, Gray and Owen Collections'),[19] bt. by the 4th Marquess of Hertford, 1,400 gn.; Hertford House inventory 1870.

Exhibition

Bethnal Green 1872–5 (92, *Landscape*).

References General

LV152; RP152; Kitson, p.146; RD, pp.316–18; Smith, no.152; M. Röthlisberger and D. Cecchi, *L'opera completa di Claude Lorrain*, 1975, no. 222; J. Ingamells and K. Laing, *The Burlington Magazine*, CXXVI, 1984, pp.758–61.

[1] The frame round P114 when Lord Hertford acquired it (preserved in the Wallace Collection) is of the same pattern as that on the Mayer P348 (q.v. note 6, where identified as a Malmaison frame).

[2] Confirmed by paint analyses made by Pamela England at the Hamilton-Kerr Institute in 1978; samples were taken from a light and a dark area in the upper part of P114.

[3] This overpainting is discussed and illustrated by Laing in Ingamells and Laing 1984. Röthlisberger (RP, p.357) suggested that there were further overpaints in the framing trees on the left, the goats, and the rocks – but no trace of this was discovered during the subsequent cleaning.

[4] Röthlisberger (RP, p.357) stated that the dog had been added by 1738 but has since been unable to verify his source (letter on file dated 5 April 1978).

[5] See LV92, LV128, LV135, LV170 and RP230; a drawing of the same subject, dated 1673, is in Hamburg (RD1061). For further general discussion of the subject, see RP, p.250, Kitson, p.111, and *Claude Lorrain*, exh. cat., Agnew's, 1982, p.55. The subject of P114 was first identified by Röthlisberger (RP, p.356); in 1884 Mrs. Pattison, *Claude Lorrain*, p.234, listed P114 as an *étude pour Abraham chassant Agar et Ismael*' (LV173).

[6] E.g. Apollodorus and Diodorus Siculus tell how Coronis bore Aesculapius, the healer, by Apollo who killed her for her infidelity; Zeus slew Aesculapius with a thunderbolt, jealous of his healing powers, and Apollo then slew the Cyclops who had made the thunderbolts; for this Zeus condemned Apollo to serve a man for a year and he became a shepherd for Admetus, king of Pherae. Apollo and Mercury were eventually reconciled, Mercury giving Apollo the lyre and Apollo giving Mercury the *caduceus*, the messenger's wand.

[7] Cf. RP, p.25.

[8] Another instance of Claude's figures being modified is seen in the *Pastoral Landscape* of 1639 (Metropolitan Museum of Art; LV42) where a shepherdess has been painted out. Modifications to the figures in the *Pastoral Landscape* of 1642 in Berlin-Dahlem (LV64) are now thought to have been by Claude himself (cf. E. Schleier, *The Burlington Magazine*, CXX, 1978, pp.461–2).

[9] He had proposed (RP, p.357) that P114 and the Chatsworth picture were painted for H. van Halmale, dean of Antwerp, through de Wael's agency; he later (RD, pp.316–17) modified this view: 'that LV152 and LV159 were done as a pair for Antwerp is not entirely certain, but is most probable'. See also note 10 below. The Chatsworth picture may have been acquired by the 2nd Duke of Devonshire via the Netherlands (cf. RD, p.317).

[10] The subject illustrates the next episode in the story of Apollo and Mercury: Mercury's theft of the cattle had been observed by Battus whom Mercury then tried to bribe into secrecy. Claude had previously paired these subjects in 1654 (LV128 and LV131). Kitson (pp.151–2), while agreeing that the Chatsworth picture is probably the pendant of P114, points out that the horizon is higher in P114; he suggests the possibility that a second patron in Antwerp commissioned the Chatsworth picture, having seen P114 'at the house of a fellow citizen'.

[11] Rutgers wrote to Wilhelm VIII from Amsterdam on 18 April 1738 confirming his purchase (see *Oud-Holland*, VIII, 1890, p.198). P114 was catalogued in 1783 by Causid in the Landgrave's collection at Cassel: '*eine felsigte Landschaft, worinn ein Hirte eine Heerde Schaafe hütet; linker Hand eine perspectivische Aussicht. – Auf Leinwand* [72 × 117]' (*ibid.*, p.198 n.2).

[12] The confiscation was noted by Robert, a curator at Cassel, in 1816 (*Oud-Holland*, VIII, 1890, p.198 n.2). See also C. Gould, *The Trophy of Conquest*, 1965, pp.93–4.

[13] See S. Grandjean, *Inventaire après décès de l'Impératrice Joséphine à Malmaison*, 1964, p.144: '*Grande Galerie: Claude, un tableau représentant un Paysage site d'Italie, soleil levant, prisé huit mille francs*'.

[14] Cf. W. Buchanan, *Memoirs of Painting*, 1824, II, pp.305–8,325–7.

[15] *Ibid.*

[16] Smith, *loc. cit.*

[17] *Ibid.*

[18] Cf. H. Artaria, *The Gallery of Edmund Higginson*, 1842, p.250.

[19] The lining canvas is marked in chalk: *June 4/46/205*.

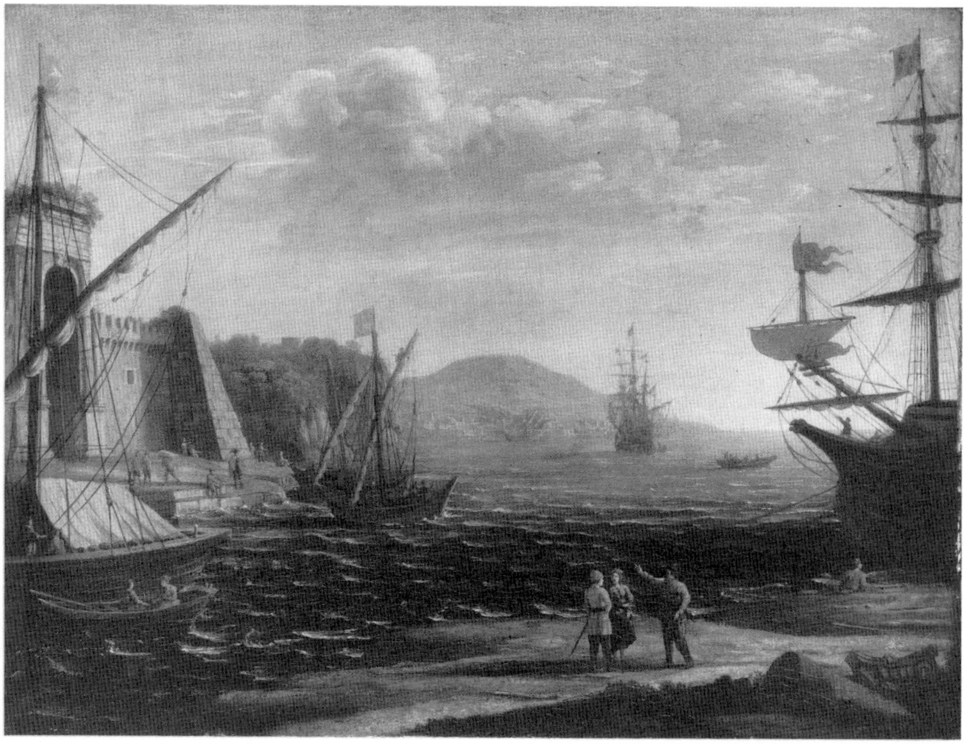

P125

After Claude Gellée

P125 *Harbour Scene*

An evening scene; the buildings on the left are adapted from the Arch of Titus and the Pyramid of Cestius; the right-hand ship flies the French blue flag with gold fleurs de lys.

Canvas, relined 41.5 × 54

Relined before 1857.[1] There are several small damages: in the sky centre left, by the prow and the centre yard arm of the right-hand boat, in the sea bottom left, and in the mid-distance to the right of the sailing boat. The varnish is much discoloured.

P125 is a reduced copy, probably of the eighteenth century, of the *Harbour Scene* of 1638 (LV31) which has been in the Bute collection since c.1800.[2] The Bute composition is slightly extended to the right, shows different figures and has the mid-distant sailing boat much closer. A full-size copy was in a Swiss private collection in 1960.[3]

Provenance

G.T. Braine sale, Christie's, 6 April 1857 (41, 'the subject of this . . . work is given in the "Liber Veritatis", No.31'), bt. Mawson for the 4th Marquess of Hertford, 500 gn.;[4] Hertford House inventory 1870, as Claude.

Exhibitions

Bethnal Green 1872–5 (127); RA 1889 (106), on both occasions as Claude.

Reference General

RP, p.154 (LV31 no.2).

[1] The lot number from the 1857 sale (see Provenance) appears in chalk on the lining canvas.

[2] 75 × 97, signed and dated 1638; RP31; Kitson, p.71.

[3] RP, p.154 (LV31 no.3).

[4] Lord Hertford had told Mawson before the sale, 'By your description of some of the paintings I must say I should like to have the Claude & the P. Potter if you are quite certain that they are without doubt originals & in a good state' (*Letters*, no.73, p.92; Paris, 3 April 1857).

François Clouet (active 1530, died 1572)

Son of the portrait painter Jean Clouet whose diminutive-name *Janet* passed to him as a patronym; two of his paintings bear the signature *Fr. Janetii opvs.* He succeeded his father as *peintre du Roi* in 1541, retaining the position under François Ier and Henri II, and he was favoured during the regency of Cathérine de Médicis. His portrait drawings in the Cabinet des Estampes and at Chantilly serve to identify many of his portraits in oil, and he also practised in miniature.[1] He died in Paris on 22 September 1572.[2]

[1] See G. Reynolds, *Wallace Collection, Catalogue of Miniatures*, 1980, pp.30–2, nos. 1 and 2 (M262–3).

[2] Concerning his biography see J. Adhémar, *Master Drawings*, XVIII, 1980, pp.155–68.

Abbreviation

Dimier L. Dimier, *Histoire de la peinture de portrait en France au XVIe siècle*, 3 vols., 1924–6 (vol.2 contains a numbered catalogue)

After François Clouet

P530 *Mary, Queen of Scots*

Auburn hair, brown eyes, wearing the white coif and wimple of French state mourning. Inscribed below: .MARIE.STVART.REYNE.DESCOSSE./VEVFE.DE.FRANCOIS. SECOND./ROY.DE.FRANCE.

Oak panel 29 × 25.3 × 0.2 made up to 34.2 × 25.3 with a horizontal member below

The lower section, bearing the crudely written inscription, is a later addition. A mahogany frame support glued to the *verso* (top and side strips 4.6 cm. wide, the bottom 5.5 cm. wide) has caused horizontal stress cracks, 4.3 cm. and 33 cm. from the top edge. Mahogany strips glued to the edges of the panel, making the overall size 39 × 30.2, were probably applied by Vallance who cleaned P530 in 1885. There are retouchings along the splits and in the face, dress and background. The varnish is discoloured.

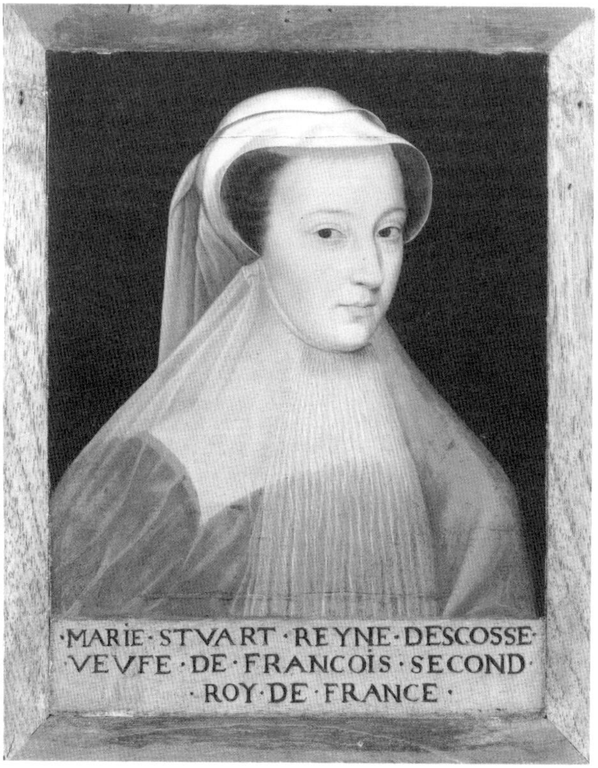

P530

Mary Stuart (1542–87), Queen of Scotland 1542–67 and of France 1558–60, daughter of James V of Scotland and Mary of Guise; sent to France 1548 and m. 1st in 1558 François II of France (d.1560); returned to Scotland 1561 and m. 2nd in 1565 Henry, Earl of Darnley (d.1567) and 3rd in 1567 James, Earl of Bothwell (m. diss. 1570); her Catholicism and claim to the English throne brought about her abdication 1567; fled to England where held captive before being executed in 1587; succeeded on the Scottish throne by James VI, her son by Darnley, later James I of England. The white mourning dress (*deuil blanc*) seen in P530 could have been occasioned by the death of either her father-in-law, Henri II, in July 1559, her mother in June 1560, or her husband, François II, in December 1560.

A label on the *verso* of P530, written in a late seventeenth- or early eighteenth-century French hand (*marie Stewart reyne d'escosse/veufve de François second/Roy de France/numero 451*) suggests the age and origin of the panel. It derives from a drawing of c.1559–60 by François Clouet in the Bibliothèque Nationale,[1] together with many other similar painted portraits (one of which belonged to the poet Ronsard).[2]

A second portrait of Mary Stuart, an early nineteenth-century miniature by William Bone copied from an anonymous posthumous portrait, is M25 in this

Collection; the likeness is dubious, as Cust first observed.[3] For a full discussion of Mary Stuart's iconography, see Cust, Foster and Strong (References General).

Provenance

Anon. sale, Christie's, 11 March 1815 (71, Zucchero, Mary Queen of Scots), bt. Yarmouth (later 3rd Marquess of Hertford), £8; Dorchester House inventory 1842 as Holbein; Hertford House inventory 1870 as Janet.

Exhibitions

Bethnal Green 1872–5 (420, as Unknown artist); RA 1880 (151, as School of Clouet).[4]

References General

Dimier, no.517, as after Clouet; L. Cust, *Notes on the authentic Portraits of Mary Queen of Scots*, 1903, p.54; J.J. Foster, *Concerning the true Portraits of Mary Queen of Scots*, 1904, p.34; R. Strong, *Tudor & Jacobean Portraits*, National Portrait Gallery, 1969, p.220.

1 Recueil Brisacier (Na 22 *rés.*), Dimier, no.465; J. Adhémar, *Gazette des Beaux-Arts*, 6e, LXXXII, 1973, p.173, no.404. A similar drawing is also in the Bibliothèque Nationale (Recueil Sainte-Geneviève, Na 22 *rés.*), Dimier, III, p.131, no.5; Adhémar, *op. cit.*, p.140, no.106. Another good version is in the Fogg Art Museum (Houghton Library 3.1968) and a copy is in the British Museum (1862–3–8–1; Dimier, no.488). For the dating of the drawing see also Adhémar, *Master Drawings*, XVIII, 1980, p.160.

2 Examples are at Windsor Castle and Hampton Court (each 28 × 23, ex coll. Charles I), the Scottish National Portrait Gallery (32.9 × 22.8, Dimier, no.518), the Musée Carnavalet (37.5 × 27, Dimier, no.519), the National Portrait Gallery, London (71 × 53) and ex coll. Mrs. A. Morrison (30.5 × 22.8, Dimier, no.520). Others in private collections are listed by Cust, pp.51–5; Foster, pp.32–5, and Strong, pp.219–20. For the Ronsard portrait, see *Oeuvres complètes de Ronsard*, Pléiade ed., 1950, II, p.294.

3 Cust, pp.143–4, writing of the Hatfield portrait and of the Bone copy, suggested the type 'shows little or no resemblance, except as regards the costume . . . and the Flemish *heuk* does not appear to have been worn at the Court of France'. Strong, p.221, implies the Hatfield portrait was painted in the first quarter of the seventeenth century. See also G. Reynolds, *Wallace Collection, Catalogue of Miniatures*, 1980, pp.320–1, no.314.

4 Reviewing this exhibition the *Athenaeum*, 10 January 1880, p.59, suggested, surprisingly, that P530 'can hardly be accepted as representing that unfortunate lady'.

Corneille de Lyon (active 1533, died 1575)

Born in The Hague, by 1533 he was established as a portrait painter in Lyon where he spent most of his life, known as *Corneille de la Haye*. In 1534 he was *painctre de la Royne Helienor* (Queen Eléanore) and in 1541 *peintre du Dauphin* (later Henri II). The French Court visited Lyon on four occasions in the 1530s, and in 1551 the Venetian Ambassador saw little portraits of all the French Court in his studio. Naturalised in 1547, he was received into the Catholic church in 1569 and was buried in Lyon on 8 November 1575.[1] His work has yet to be clearly defined; six portraits called Corneille in the Gaignière collection in the late seventeenth century are now in the Louvre, and eighteen associated with his name are in the Metropolitan Museum of Art, New York. Dimier's identification of a number of different hands within the corpus of 'Corneille' portraits has not found lasting favour.

1 For biographical details, see Dimier, I, pp.32–43, 100–1; S. Béguin and A. de Gröer, *La Revue du Louvre*, 1978, pp.28–42, and N.Z. Davis, *Revue de l'Art*, 47, 1980, pp.21–8.

Abbreviation

Dimier L. Dimier, *Histoire de la peinture de portrait en France au XVIe siècle*, 3 vols., 1924–6, (vol. 2 contains a numbered catalogue)

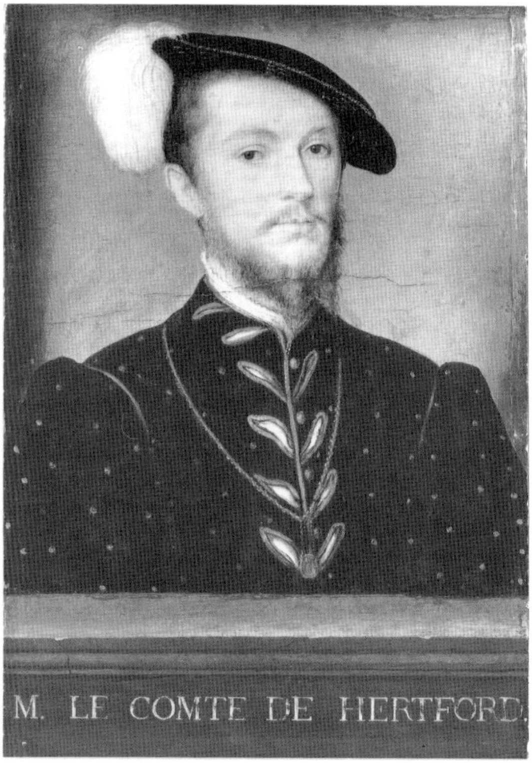

P532

P532 *Portrait of a young Man*

Light brown hair, blue eyes, wearing a black costume decorated with pearls and a locket hanging from a gold chain; green background. Inscribed below: M. LE COMTE DE HERTFORD.

Walnut panel 15.8 × 13.5 × 0.25 made up to 20.8 × 14.3 with oak capping strips and a horizontal oak member, 4.5 cm. high, along the bottom edge.

The lower section, bearing the inscription, is an addition. The original panel was severely attacked by worm, as is reflected in the disturbed and split area in the centre, and it was cradled with five horizontal battens and four vertical slats in 1878 by Vallance. Oak capping strips were then added on each edge and the painting made up to cover them. There are several small retouchings, most prominent in the flesh areas. The varnish is discoloured.

The identification of the sitter as Edward Seymour (1506?–52, cr. Earl of Hertford 1537 and Duke of Somerset 1547) cannot be sustained; the features do not sufficiently agree with those in his most authentic portrait.[1] Portraits identical with P532 (see Versions) have been variously named, and suggest that the sitter was French and of some eminence.

Painted probably c.1535, P532 is an elegant example of the portraiture associated with Corneille de Lyon. Dimier suggested it was by the Rieux-Châteauneuf Painter, a master he distinguished by his superior handling,[2] but several of the works he ascribed to this hand are now given to Corneille himself[3] and it would seem reasonable to include P532 among them.

Versions

PARIS Louvre (inv. no. 3258); panel 16 × 13.5, inscribed *François Ier roi de France*, the figure identical with that in P532; ex coll. Gaignière; currently attributed to the Workshop of Corneille de Lyon (Dimier, no. 298, as After the Rieux-Châteauneuf Painter).

A second similar portrait, 16 × 13, formerly identified as Jean de Bretagne, was in the de Kermaingant sale, New York, 27 November 1926, lot 133, as *A Man* (Dimier, no. 299, as After the Rieux-Châteauneuf Painter).

Provenance

William Beckford (1759–1844) of Fonthill; listed in his sale, Christie's, 18 September 1822 (11, 'A small portrait by Holbein on a green ground of Le Comte d'Hertford'), but not sold; J. Farquhar;[4] the 3rd Marquess of Hertford; Dorchester House inventory 1842 as Holbein; noted in 1854 in Hertford House by Waagen (IV, p.83) as F. Clouet; Hertford House inventory 1870 as Janet.

Exhibitions

Bethnal Green 1872–5 (12); RA 1880 (159),[5] on both occasions as F. Clouet.

Reference General

Dimier, no. 292.

1 For Somerset's iconography, see R. Strong, *Tudor & Jacobean Portraits*, National Portrait Gallery, 1969, pp.293–5; the most reliable image of him is the miniature by Hilliard painted in 1560 from an earlier portrait (Strong, fig. 576). Both Strong and the *Dictionary of National Biography* state that Somerset's portrait was painted by Holbein, but this is based on optimistic nineteenth-century attributions (cf. Provenance above and note 4 below). It may be observed that the inscription on P532 is curious; Somerset was Earl of Hertford for only ten years and is remembered as the Duke of Somerset or the Protector Somerset; the inscription on P532, however, was almost certainly added after his death – perhaps in the following century.

2 Dimier, I, pp.40–2; II, pp.73–6, and *Les Arts*, September 1905, p.24. He identified the master's '*couleur limpide et éclatante, le modelé vigoureux, la touche spirituelle*'.

3 E.g. Dimier, nos. 287 and 288 are attributed to Corneille de Lyon by A. de Groër, *La Revue du Louvre*, 1978, p.38. The portrait of Rieux-Châteauneuf, on which Dimier (no. 295) based his identification, is now considered to be one of several replicas of the portrait of Jean d'Albon Saint-André (cf. de Gröer, p.42 n.12; it is now in a private collection, Cleveland, Ohio).

4 Farquhar bought Fonthill and its contents before the Christie's sale took place; doubtless Hertford bought P532 from him soon after, for it did not appear in the second Fonthill sale which Farquhar entrusted to Phillips, 23 September ff., 1823. A second alleged Holbein of Somerset from Fonthill appeared in the Hamilton sale, Christie's, 17 June 1882 (8, 51 × 38); it is now in a private collection.

5 Reviewing the exhibition, the *Athenaeum*, 17 January 1880, p.94, remarked (following Waagen) that P532 'bears on unusually good grounds the name of Clouet', and admired its exquisite delicacy of touch, precision of modelling and great brilliancy. These were the qualities by which Dimier was to distinguish the Rieux-Châteauneuf Painter (see note 2 above).

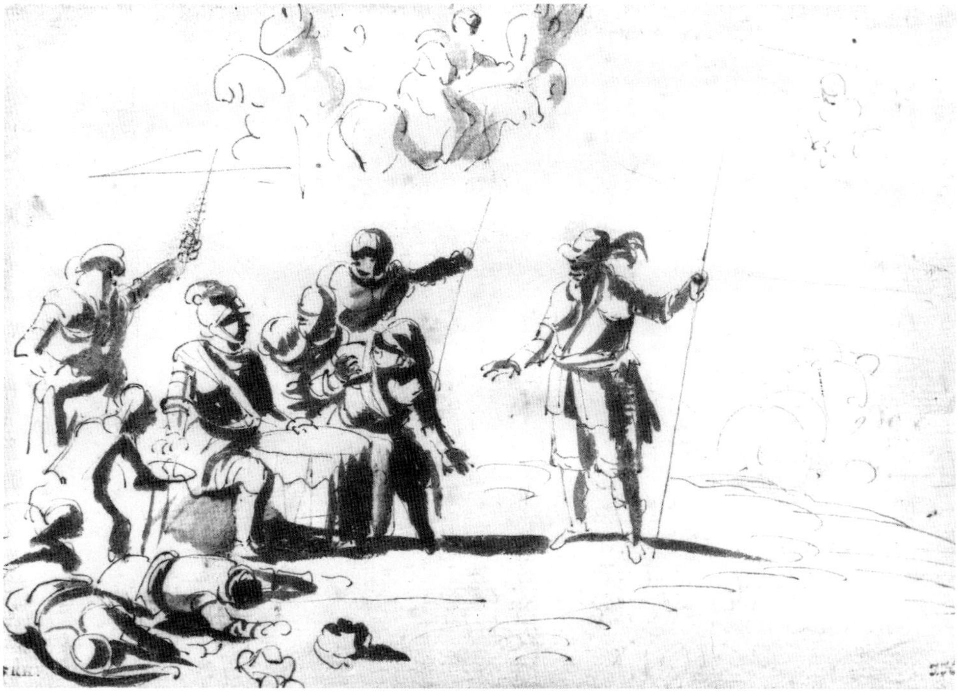

P769

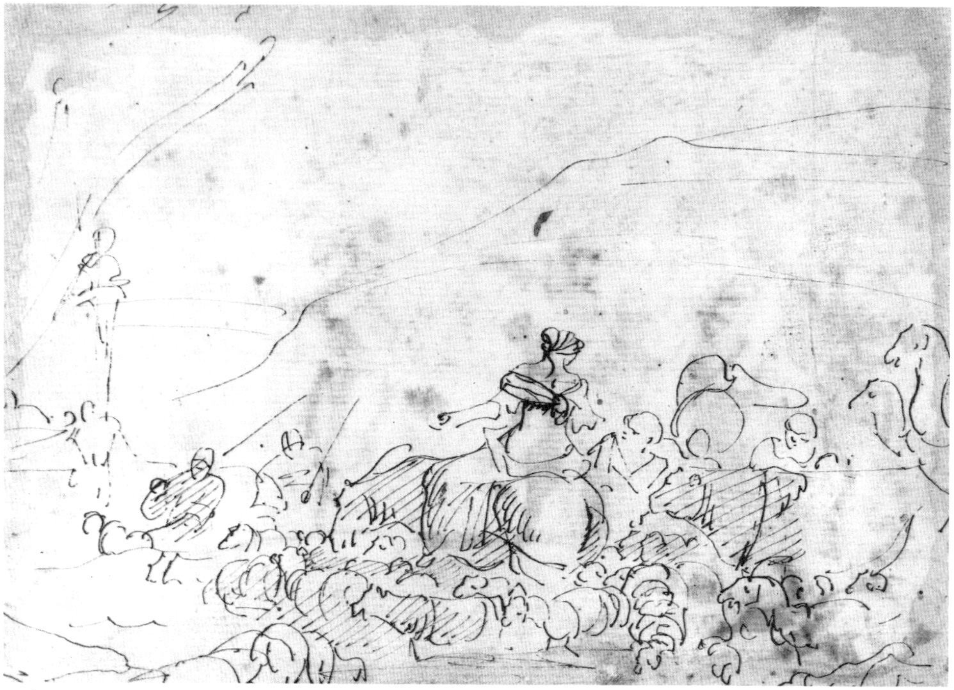

P769 *verso*

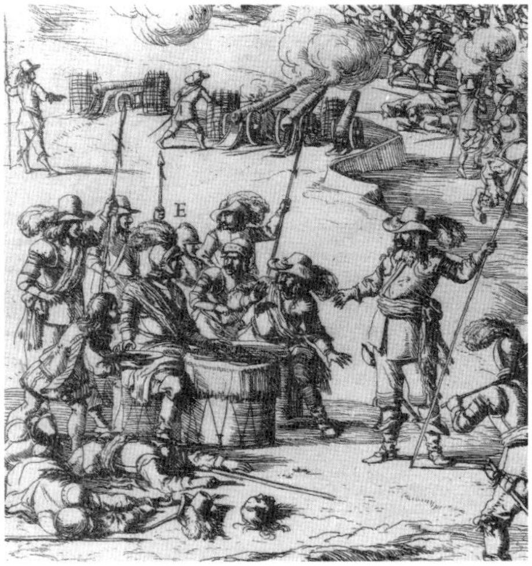

Courtois:
The Capture of Oudenarde 1587,
engraving, detail.

Jacques Courtois (1621–1676)

Called *Le Bourguignon, Il Borgognone, Giacomo Borgognone* and *Giacomo Cortese*; born on 12 February 1621 in Saint-Hippolyte (Franche-Comté), the son of J.-B. Courtois under whom he first studied. In 1636 he went to Italy. He followed the Spanish army in Milan 1636–9, and proceded to Bologna (where he met Reni and Albani), Florence and Siena, before reaching Rome c.1640. Although he painted landscapes (which had been admired by Reni) and some religious frescoes, he became known above all for his battle scenes, in which he introduced an element of involvement, then quite new. In Rome he knew Pietro da Cortona and the *bamboccianti*, P. van Laer and M. Cerquozzi, and his work compares in some respects with that of Salvator Rosa. In 1657, following the death of his wife (whom he was thought to have murdered) he became a Jesuit and there is a brooding *Self-portrait* in the Uffizi. He died in Rome on 14 November 1676.

Abbreviation

Holt E. Holt, 'The Jesuit Battle Painter: Jacques Courtois (le Bourguignon)', *Apollo*, LXXXIX, 1969, pp.212–23

P769 *The Duke of Parma dining on the Battlefield*

Brown ink and wash on paper 14.8 × 20.7

The paper bears part of a watermark (a five-pointed star is clear) comparable with Heawood 6.[1] The collectors' marks of Richard Houlditch (Lugt 2214) and Thomas Hudson (Lugt 2432) appear, respectively, bottom left and right.[2] The *verso* was revealed during cleaning and remounting by Harding in 1985.

P769 is a sketch for part of *The Capture of Oudenarde 1587*, a composition engraved in 1647 (see below). The engraving carries a key which described the subject of P769 (lettered E) as: *while the Duke of Parma dined an enemy cannon ball killed some and scattered others of his entourage, but he himself was unmoved* (trans.).[3] Alessandro Farnese, Duke of Parma (1545–92), commanded the Spanish forces of Philip II during the wars of Dutch independence.

P769 is on a slightly larger scale than the engraving and shows a simpler composition.[4] The engraving carries no signature, but an attribution to Courtois has long been accepted[5] and is largely confirmed by P769 which typifies his vigorous technique. It is one of his earliest known drawings.[6] The *verso* gives an interesting indication of a landscape composition and recalls Berchem.

Engraving

J. Courtois 1647, ALDENARDA CAPTA AN. 1587, 28.8 × 39, inscribed *168* in the top right-hand margin and with lettered key, see above (F. Strada, *De Bello Belgico*, II, 1647, book iv, f.p.168).

Provenance

Arthur Pond (1701–58) by whom given c.1747 to Richard Houlditch (d.1760) whose mark appears on P769;[7] possibly Houlditch sale, Langford's, 3rd night, 14 February 1760 (51, 'Two [drawings] by Borgognone and F. Bolognese'), bt. Hudson, £2.9s; Thomas Hudson (1701–79) whose mark appears on P769; fourteen drawings by Courtois appeared in Hudson's sales of 1779 and 1785 (L.2972 and L.3835); the vicomte Both de Tauzia (1823–88), from whom bt. by Sir Richard Wallace, 1872;[8] Hertford House inventory 1890, unattributed.

Reference General

Holt, pp.216–17, 220–1.

[1] E. Heawood, *Watermarks mainly of the 17th and 18th centuries*, 1950.

[2] Cf. F. Lugt, *Les Marques de Collections*, 1921 (and see note 7 below).

[3] *Convivante. Parmensi Princ. hostilis globus adstantium alios ferit, alios fugat, ipsum non terret.*

[4] The engraving reduces the drawing by 20%.

[5] See note 7, and cf. C.H. von Heinecken, *Dictionnaire des Artistes dont nous avons des Estampes*, IV, 1790, p.376 (*'on attribue* [*à Courtois*] *aussi les Batailles, qu'on trouve dans la première Edit. de F. Strada à Rome'*), and F.A. Salvagnini, *I Pittori Borgognoni Cortese (Courtois)*, 1937, p.43 (who attributes seven of the fourteen plates in the second volume of Strada to Courtois; three others are signed by J. Miel, two by G. Gimignani and two by F. Collignon).

[6] Cf. Holt, p.217: 'This is, as far as is known, the earliest drawing which can be connected with his works'.

[7] The mount formerly with P769 is inscribed in an eighteenth-century hand: *Borgognone*, and: [*pen*]*siero di Borgognone, per una stampa scolpita da lui con acqua forte, nell 'istoria di* [*Bello*] *Belgico – cioé, il Duca di Parma il pranzare intrepidamente sopra un tamburo in* [. . .]*i tutt' all' intorno da lui/Given me by Mr. Pond/*[signed] *R. Houlditch/about 1747*. For the connection between Pond and Houlditch, see L. Lippincott, *Selling Art in Georgian London, the Rise of Arthur Pond*, 1983, pp.26–9, 58, 60, 116, 122. Lugt (see note 2 above) conflated Richard Houlditch senior (d. 1737) with Richard Houlditch junior (d.1760).

[8] For Wallace's purchase of the Tauzia collection, see vol. I of this catalogue, 1985, pp.434–7.

Jean-Louis Demarne (de Marne) (1752–1829)

Born in 1752 in Brussels where he was baptised on 22 January 1754. In 1764 he came to Paris where he studied at the Académie 1769–77 under the history painter G. Briard. He first visited Switzerland and the Dauphiné in 1776 with N.-A. Taunay, and the sight of Karel Dujardin's works in the Randon de Boisset collection (sold in 1777) confirmed his inclination to paint picturesque scenes rather than history pieces. In 1779 he exhibited a landscape '*dans le goût de Carle Du Jardin*' at the exposition de la jeunesse. He was *agréé* in 1783 (*Paysage avec animaux*) and showed regularly at the Salon 1783–1827. His work, which also included village fairs and guard-room scenes, was profoundly influenced by seventeenth-century Dutch masters, such as Wouwermans, Potter, Palamedesz and Lingelbach. He never signed or dated his pictures and the titles of his exhibited works are repetitive. In 1806 he was commissioned to paint *Napoléon et Pie VII à Fontainebleau* (landscape by A. Dunouy; Versailles). He worked for the Sèvres porcelain factory 1809–13 and made a number of landscape and figure etchings. He was made *chevalier* of the Legion of Honour in 1828 and died at Batignolles, near Paris, on 24 January 1829.

Abbreviation

Watelin J. Watelin, *Le peintre J.-L. Demarne*, 1962 (with numbered list of works in sales)

P462 *Women and Soldiers revelling (Intérieur de corps-de-garde)*

The officer seated on the left has a yellow buff coat and a red sash; the lady behind him wears a white silk skirt; an open fire on the right.

Oak panel 49.4 × 56.8 × 1.3 two vertical members, the left 27.3 wide
painted area 48.7 × 55.5

The components are butt-jointed, the left 1.3 thick, the right 0.9. A vertical split 39 cm. from the left-hand edge reflects old worm damage. There are small losses above the dog's nose on the right, in the coat of the man standing on the right, and above the spear in the doorway on the right. A surface scratch runs down through the dancing lady's skirt. The varnish is much discoloured.

A seventeenth-century scene in the manner of Palamedesz. Both architecture and perspective are weak. Demarne showed *corps de garde* scenes at the Salons of 1783 and 1787 and P462 probably dates from that period. The 1832 sale catalogue (see note 1) said that he regarded P462 as his *chef d'oeuvre* in this genre, and that he had viewed it with satisfaction shortly before his death.

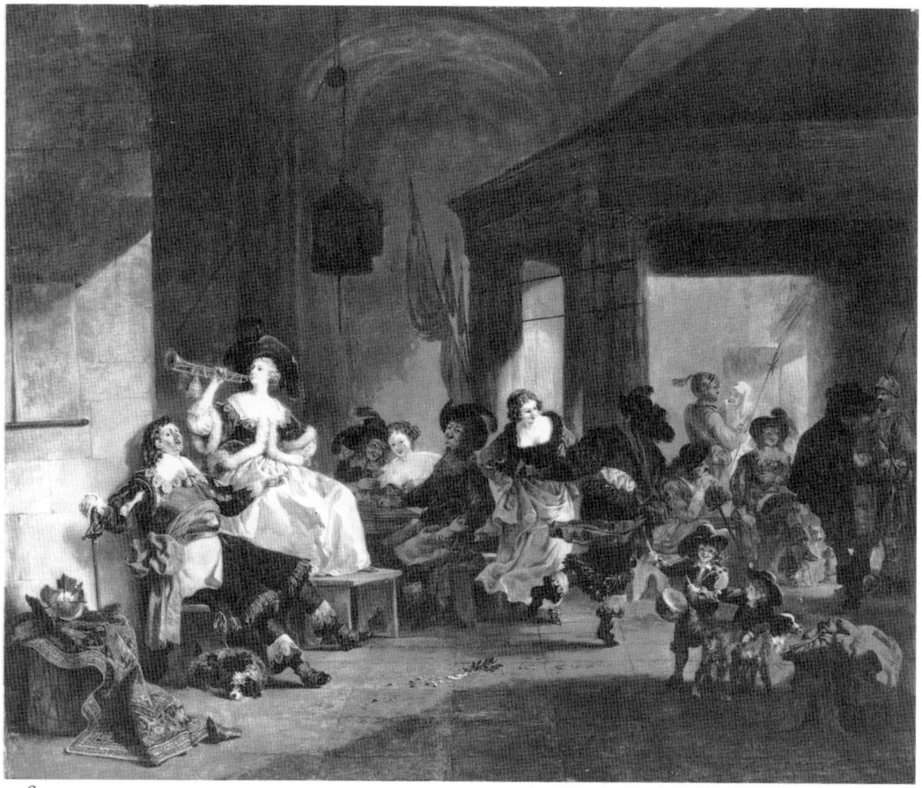

P462

Provenance

feu M. T., membre correspondant de l'Institut de France, sale, Paris, 2–3 April 1832 (13, *Intérieur de corps-de-garde* [with full description] *bois* [48.6 × 56.7]),[1] 2,200 fr.; the 4th Marquess of Hertford; reframed in Hertford House 1859;[2] Hertford House inventory 1870.

Exhibition

Bethnal Green 1872–5 (419).

Reference General

Watelin, no.844.

[1] The discursive description says that P462 *'n'a jamais été dans le commerce'*; *'le tableau . . . a toujours été regardé par Demarne comme étant son chef-d'oeuvre en ce genre. Quelque temps avant sa mort il fut chez le propriétaire demander à revoir ce tableau. Après l'avoir bien examiné, il dit ces paroles: "Hé bien! je suis vraiment content, et j'espère ne pas mourir tout entier"'*.

[2] Evans invoice.

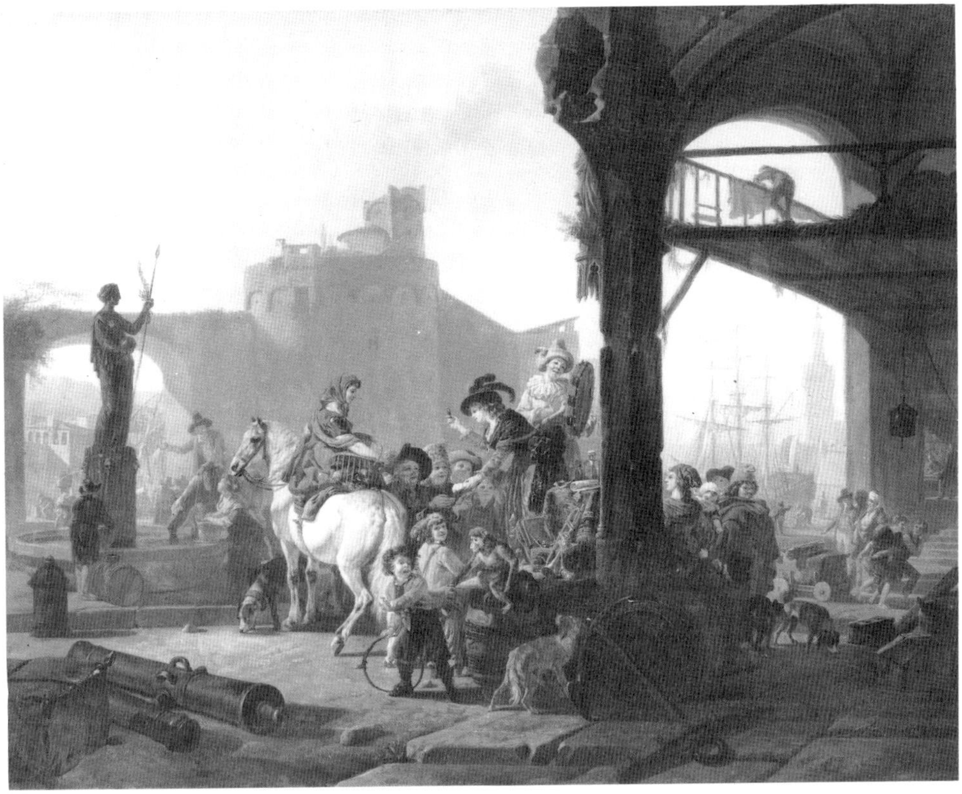

P469

P469 *The Elixir (La charlatane)*

On a raised platform a woman in a yellow dress with a black shawl sells potions, while a pierrot figure beats a drum behind her; the child in the centre foreground has a red coat.

Canvas, relined 49.3 × 60

There are small damages by the front leg of the white horse, below the chest in the bottom right-hand corner and on the right-hand edge. *Pentimenti* show that there was another horse on the left immediately behind the cannon, and that the edges of the fountain basin were redrawn. The varnish is much discoloured.

The setting recalls seventeenth-century Italianate port scenes by Lingelbach, but the pierrot and *charlatane* are late eighteenth-century French fairground figures. The architecture is weak and unconvincing. Demarne exhibited *Un charlatan de village* at the 1804 Salon and P469 may belong to that period.

Provenance

The comte de Nape, Paris, by 1817;[1] anon. sale, Paris, 5–7 December 1831 (3, *La charlatane* [with detailed description, canvas 48.6 x 62.1]), bt. Pérignon, 1,620 fr.; the 4th Marquess of Hertford; reframed in Hertford House 1859;[2] Hertford House inventory 1870.

Exhibition

Bethnal Green 1872–5 (415, *The Travelling Doctor: Port of Genoa*).

Reference General

Watelin, no. 207.

[1] The comte de Nape had begun to collect Demarnes by 1789 (cf. Watelin, no.206); in 1817 he published an *éloge* of the artist, together with detailed descriptions of those he owned (*Annales Encyclopédiques*, 1817, I, pp.36–78; P469 is described on pp.54–5). De Nape considered Demarne superior to Karel Dujardin and the Voltaire of painting; his views were modified by A. Wauters (*Biographie Nationale*, XIII, 1894–5, cols. 767–72) who wrote of '*cet artiste, aussi oublié aujourd'hui qu'il était autrefois célèbre*'.

[2] Evans invoice.

Alexandre-François Desportes (1661–1743)

Born on 24 February 1661 in Champigneulles (Champagne), he was sent as a boy to Paris where he studied from c.1674 with the ageing Flemish *animalier* Nicasius Bernaerts (d.1678), copying prints by Testa. He then attended the Académie and collaborated with other artists, including Rigaud, Parrocel and the decorator, Claude III Audran. In 1695–6 he worked as a portrait painter for King Jean III Sobieski in Warsaw. In 1699 he was *reçu* by the Académie, his *morceau de réception* being the *Autoportrait en chasseur* now in the Louvre. In 1700 he received his first commission from Louis XIV for whom he subsequently painted many hunt and animal pictures. He was made *conseiller* at the Académie in 1704 and exhibited regularly at the Salon from that year. In 1712–13 he spent six months in England. His Royal patronage continued after the death of the King in 1715 and amongst many other noble patrons he worked for the duc de Bourbon at Chantilly. He made designs for the Savonnerie factory and designed the *Nouvelles Indes* tapestries for the Gobelins 1737–41. His last Royal commission, from Louis XV in 1742, was for the decoration of Choisy (to which Oudry also contributed). He died in Paris on 20 April 1743. In 1784 his descendants sold the drawings and sketches left in his studio to Louis XVI and they were placed in the Manufacture de Sèvres.[1] They demonstrate a scrupulous observation of nature, witnessed by his son (Claude-François, 1695–1774, also a painter): '*aucune main étrangère ne touchoit à ses tableaux . . . ce qu'il n'avoit point encore fait, il apprenoit à le faire, à l'aide de la nature*'.[2]

[1] See *L'atelier de Desportes*, exh. cat., Louvre, 1982.

[2] C.-F. Desportes, 'La vie de M. Desportes', in L. Dussieux *et al.*, eds., *Mémoires inédits sur la vie et les ouvrages des membres de l'académie royale de peinture et sculpture*, 1854, II, p.105.

P594 *Dogs, Dead Game and Fruit*

Peaches, plums, figs and laurel on the stone ledge; a hound (left), spaniel and pointer (right); on the ground partridges and snipe, a mallard and hare by the beech tree. Signed on the pedestal, centre: *Desportes./1715*.

Canvas, relined 128.5 x 161.5

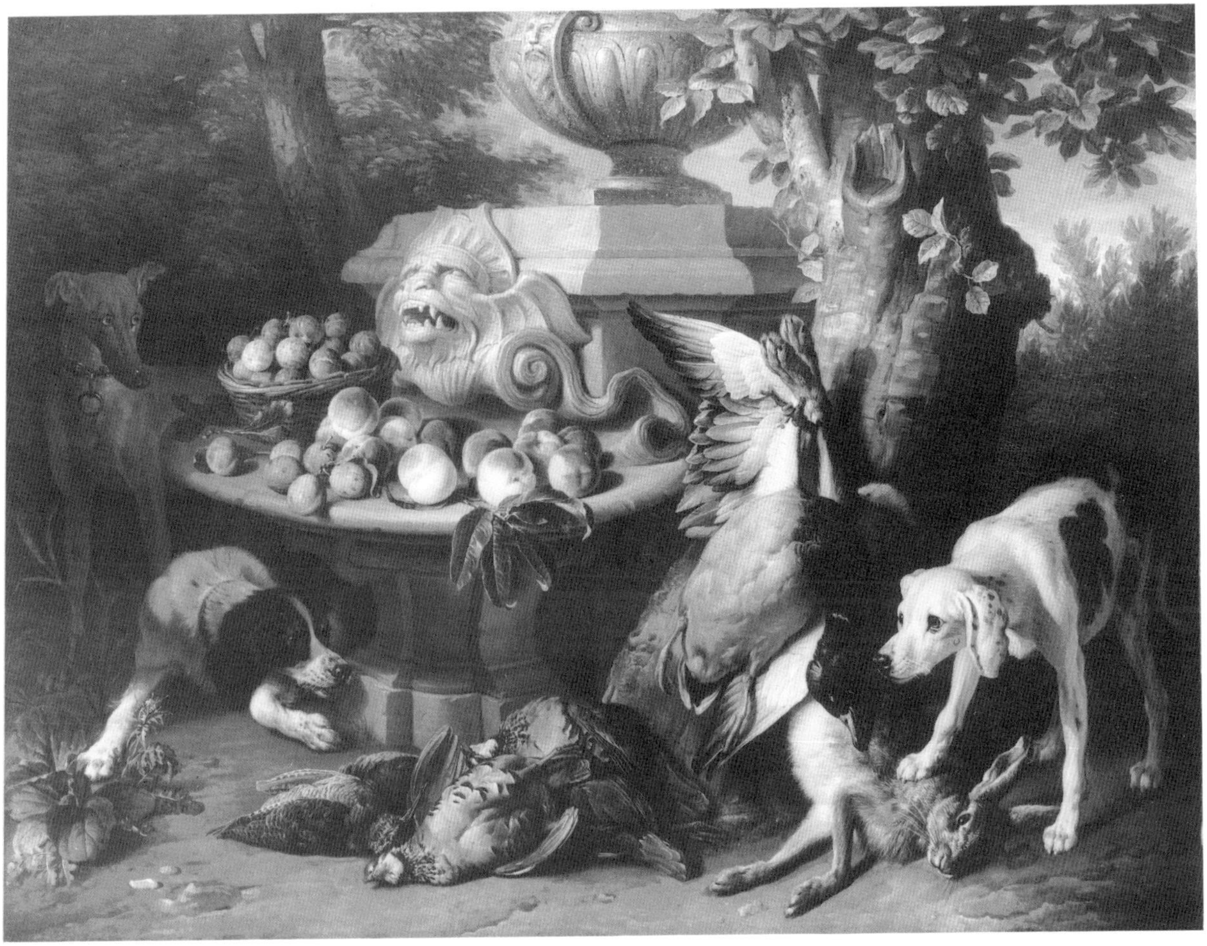

P594

The paint surface was transferred to a fine muslin supported by a double lining canvas c.1858.[1] The second lining canvas was replaced by Bobak in 1986 when the picture was cleaned by Lank. Seams in the canvas, 9.5cm. below the top edge, 7cm. from the left-hand side and 6cm. from the right, have been retouched. There are a number of very small losses, e.g. in the lower left foreground and in the sky. *Pentimenti* show the foliage upper right was modified.

P594 and the pendant *buffet* P628 were described in 1857 as '*incontestablement des meilleurs qui soient sortis du pinceau de Desportes*'.[2] Lord Hertford then described them as 'a little rubbish for the country . . . beautiful of the sort & perfect for my shooting place'.[3] The two pictures may be compared with the Oudrys P626 and P630, painted six years later, both for their subjects and grandeur, as well as for their somewhat whimsical architectural details; see Oudry P626.

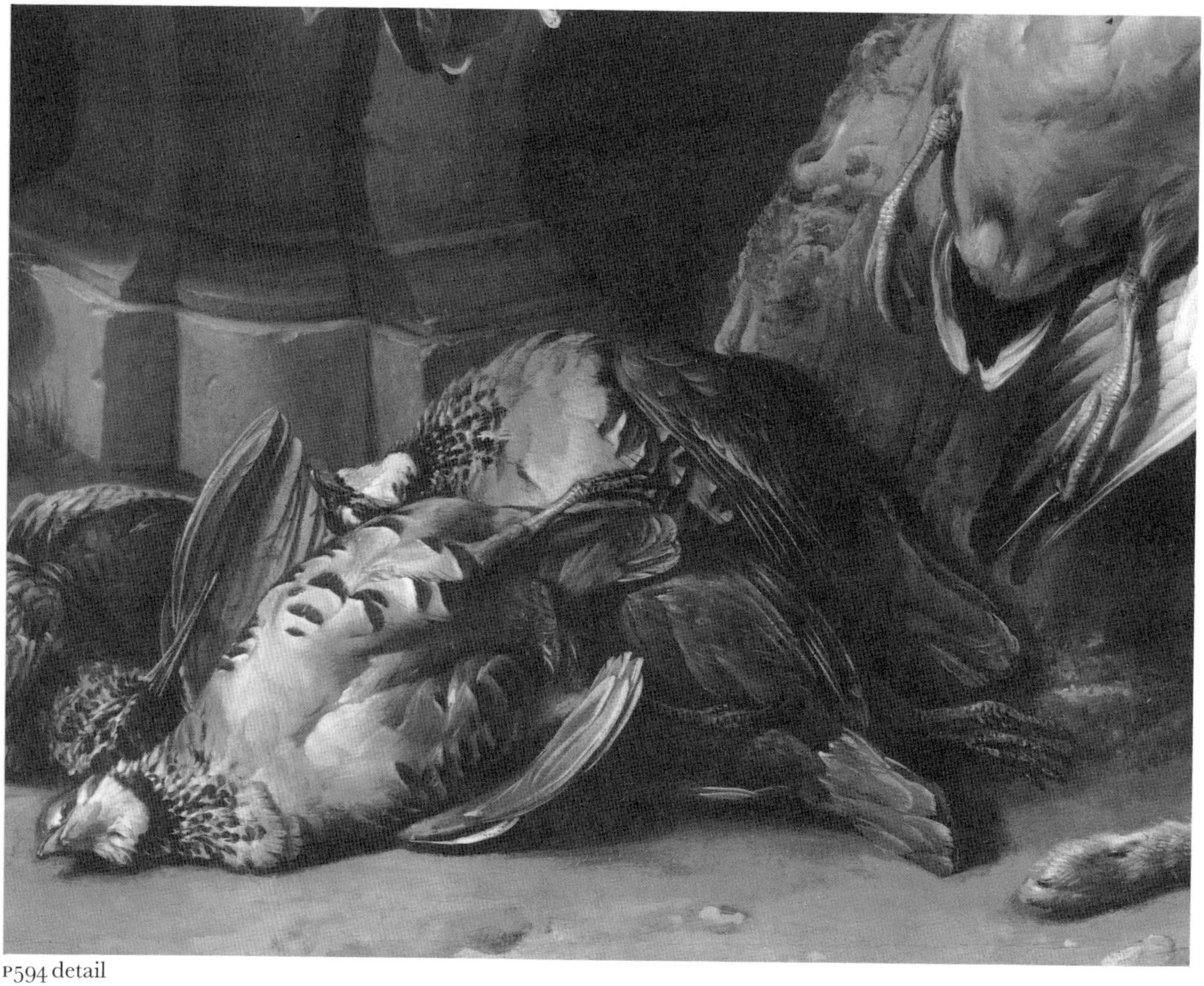

P594 detail

Version

TROYES Musée des Beaux-Arts (no.97); 105 × 130, a slightly reduced copy, without the porphyry vase, the hound and the pointer's hind legs.[4]

Provenance

With P628: bt. from Laneuville for 4,000 fr. by Théodore Patureau,[5] Brussels; his sale, Paris, 1st day, 20 April 1857 (65 [P628], 66 [P594]), bt. by the 4th Marquess of Hertford, 10,700 fr.;[6] rue Laffitte inventory 1871 (264 [P594], 263 [P628]); Hertford House inventory 1890.

Exhibitions

Boulevard des Italiens 1860 (124) lent Hertford; Bethnal Green 1872–5 (354).

[1] Scraps of a French newspaper dateable c.1858 were found between the original lining canvases.

[2] *Revue universelle des Arts*, V, 1857, p.189.

[3] *Letters*, no.77, p.98 (Hertford to Mawson, Paris, 28 April 1857).

[4] These omissions do not correspond with the additions made to the canvas of P594 described above.

[5] Cf. E. Le Roy, *Quelques notes sur la Collection de Tableaux de M. Théodore Patureau*, 1859, p.20, and see note 6 below.

[6] The *Revue universelle des Arts, loc. cit.*, commented on this price '*les tableaux de ce maître sont communs et on trouverait cent occasions d'acquérir des productions équivalentes à des prix bien inférieurs . . . Ils avaient coûté 4,000 fr.*'.

P623 *Two Dogs and Dead Game by a Fountain*

A brown-spotted pointer with a black and white spaniel resting; a partridge hangs by the fountain, a male and female pheasant in the foreground; an oak tree on the left with poppies.

Canvas, relined 195 × 129.5 including an addition 34.5 high to the top edge

The addition, made before 1855 and probably when the picture was relined, is crudely disguised by the overhanging branch. There are many retouchings, e.g. by the pointer's ear, on the fountain basin, on the partridge, down the right-hand edge and in the craquelure. Some blistering in the sky area in both the original and added canvases appears to be due to the relining. *Pentimenti* show the pointer's right hind leg and the spaniel's back were redrawn. The varnish is discoloured.

P623 was sold in 1855 as one of a set of three Oudrys, of which P624 Ascribed to Oudry, q.v., was another. The addition along the top edge of P623 was evidently made to make it conform with P624 and the third (now lost) 'Oudry'.[1] P623 was catalogued as Oudry until 1928 when it was first, and convincingly, given to Desportes.

Provenance

The baron de Commailles [Caumail], 25 rue du Faubourg Saint-Honoré; his sale, Paris, 2 August 1855 (39, Oudry, *Chiens gardant du gibier*, 195 × 129); the 4th Marquess of Hertford; rue Laffitte inventory 1871 (378, as Oudry); Hertford House inventory 1890, as Oudry.

References General

As Oudry (q.v. for abbreviations): Locquin, no. 193; Vergnet- Ruiz, no. 129.

[1] Commailles sale, lot 38: *Chiens surprenant un canard sauvage*, 195 × 129.

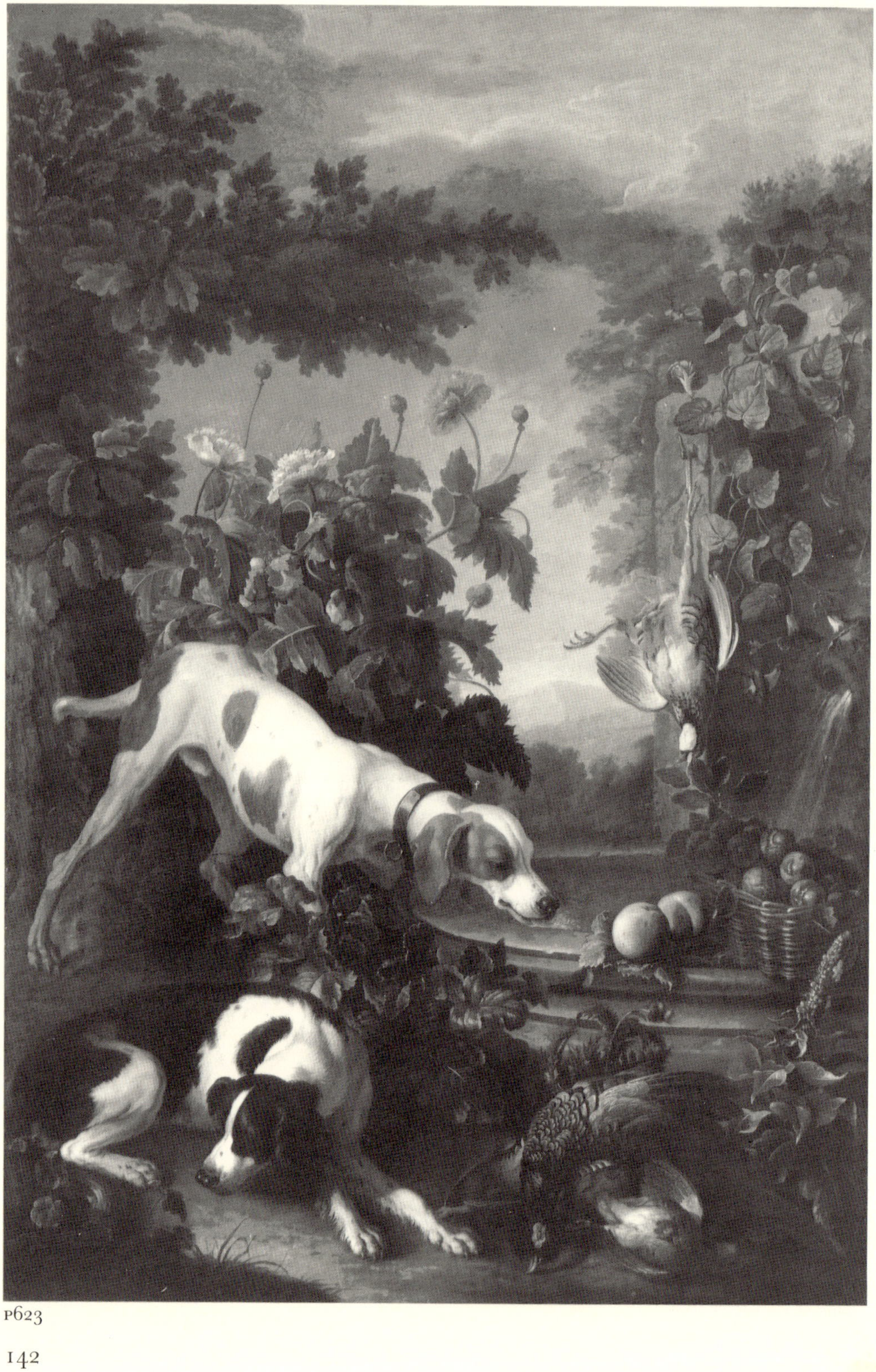

P623

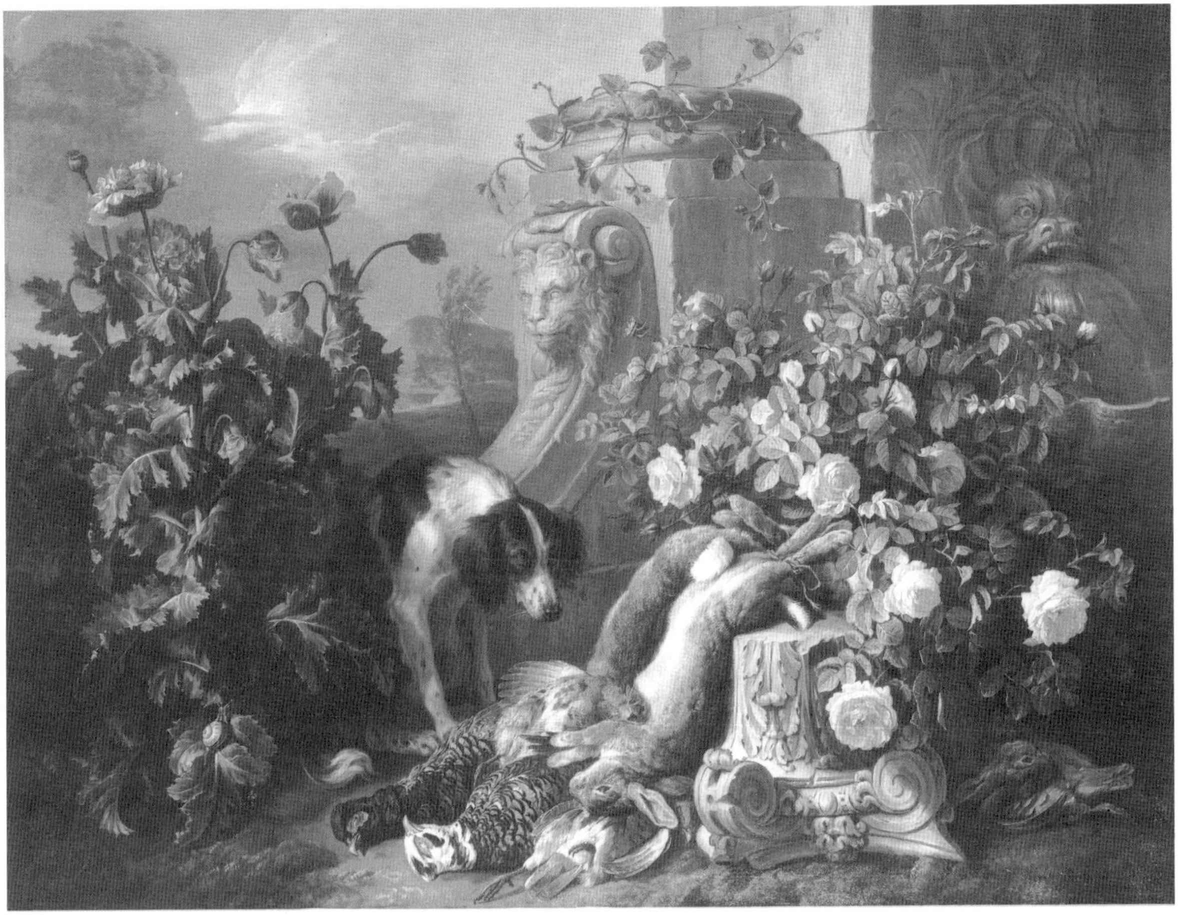

P628

P628 *Dog with Flowers and Dead Game*

A black-spotted spaniel with pheasants, partridges and hares; poppies on the left, white roses to the right and convolvulus over the plinth. Signed, upper right: *Desportes*.

Canvas, relined 128 × 160.5

The paint surface was transferred to a fine muslin supported by a double lining canvas c.1858 (see P594 note 1). The second lining canvas was replaced by Bobak in 1986 when the picture was cleaned by Lank. A horizontal seam 6 cm. below the top edge has been retouched. A *pentimento* shows that there was originally more foliage above the spaniel's back.

See the pendant P594. A related composition in Brunswick[1] which shows the upturned Roman capital seen in P628 with partridges, hares, a spaniel and poppies, is dated 1716; it helps to confirm that P628 is contemporary with the pendant P594 (which is dated 1715).

Provenance

See P594.

Exhibitions

Boulevard des Italiens 1860 (123)[2] lent Hertford; Bethnal Green 1872–5 (359).

[1] Herzog Anton Ulrich-Museum, no.530, 97 × 130 (*Verzeichnis der Gemälde vor 1800*, 1976, p.16).

[2] The exhibition catalogue associated P628 with an Oudry described in the Salon *livret* in 1740: '*deux faisans morts jetés contre un tronc d'arbre, auprès d'une plante de pavot, avec des perdrix rouges et grises, et derrière un chien couchant qui semble les garder*'. This evidently cannot apply to P628 which was, however, otherwise identified in the catalogue as '*vente Patureau*', 126 × 159, '*collection d'un Amateur*' (Lord Hertford's sobriquet).

Gaspard Dughet (1615–1675)

Called *Gaspard Poussin* and *Le Guaspre*; born on 4 June 1615 in Rome, the son of a French cook, Jacques Dughet, and his Italian wife. In 1630 his elder sister married Nicolas Poussin with whom he studied landscape painting 1631–4, their close relationship leading to his being called Gaspard Poussin. In 1635 he went to Milan and Perugia and sometime in 1641–6 he was in Florence and Naples, but his life was otherwise spent in and around Rome. His earliest biographers described him as fond of hunting and fishing, and from c.1635 he had lodgings at Frascati and Tivoli. Although he evidently studied the landscapes of Titian, Claude, Cortona, Domenichino and, above all, Poussin, his own were distinguished by a degree of naturalism and the comparative insignificance of his figures. His first major public commission was for a cycle of landscape frescoes in the church of S. Martino ai Monti, Rome, in 1647–51; he received several fresco commissions, the last for the Palazzo Colonna in 1667–8. His reputation as a landscape painter was rivalled in his lifetime only by those of Claude Gellée and Salvator Rosa, and he was received into the Accademia di S. Luca in 1657. He died in Rome, after a long illness, on 25 May 1675. His influence on subsequent landscape painting was profound, and nowhere more than in England in the eighteenth century.

Abbreviation

Boisclair M.-N. Boisclair, *Gaspard Dughet*, 1986 (with catalogue including rejected paintings [R] and engravings [G])

P139 *The Falls of Tivoli*

Canvas, relined 98.7 × 81.5[1]

The canvas has a herring-bone weave and was relined before 1850 (see note 14). Cleaned and restored by Hargrave in 1978. There are several small losses and some worn areas in the sky, and the impress of an old stretcher round the edges of the canvas has been retouched. The blue in the drapery of the left foreground figure has partially decomposed and the darker green areas have darkened. *Pentimenti* show a slight reduction to the foliage above and to the left of the waterfall and a standing figure beyond was erased. The varnish is somewhat uneven.

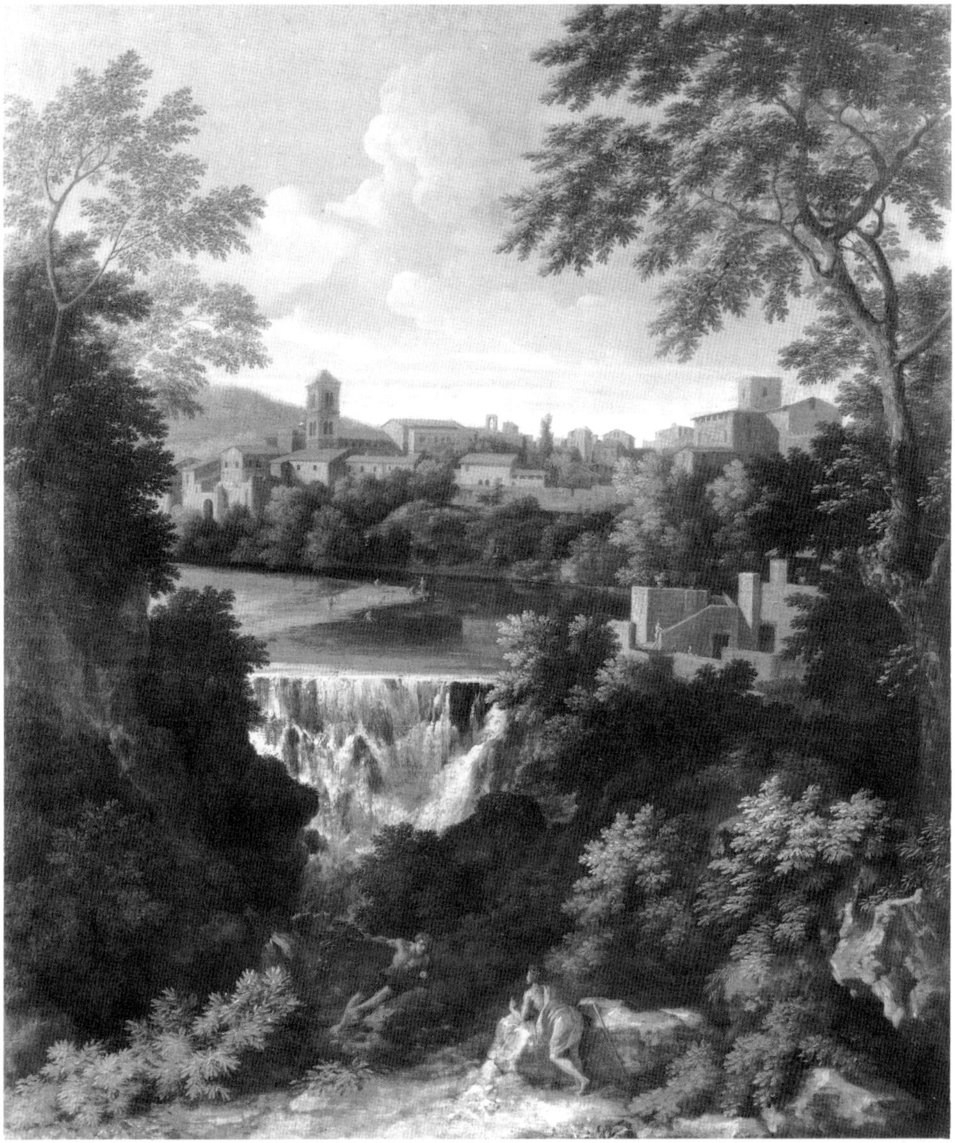

P139

Tivoli, eighteen miles north east of Rome on the edge of the Sabine mountains; P139 appears to show the first of the waterfalls of the river Teverone (now Aniene) on the north-east side (which disappeared when the river was rerouted in 1825–35); the church tower on the left is possibly that of S. Maria Maggiore.

P139 is one of the finest of Dughet's many views of Tivoli, where he frequently stayed throughout his life.[2] Boisclair has proposed a date of c.1661–3, while admitting that the chronology of his last years remains uncertain.[3] The carefully constructed, and probably reasonably accurate,[4] architecture recalls several Poussin compositions of c.1648–54;[5] the foreground and waterfall are vigorously painted, while in the mid-distance a rich warm brown ground frequently appears round the grey buildings. There is a pendant view, taken from a point further north and including the Temple of the Sibyl (Duke of Westminster's collection);[6] both were in Lord Waldegrave's collection by 1744 when they were engraved and published in Pond's series of *Italian Landscapes*.[7] The compositions were clearly recalled by British artists at Tivoli, such as Jonathan Skelton[8] and Thomas Jones who, in 1777, wrote in his *Memoirs*:[9]

> At Tivoli – the foaming Torrents rush down the Precipices into the deep Abyss with a fearful noise and Horrid Grandeur – The immense Masses of Stone rise abrupt – luxuriantly fringed with Shrubs, and crowned with antique towers and Temples . . . the Eye is charmed with the most beautiful variegated Tints – White, Grey, Red & Yellow – opposing, or blending their different Dyes together . . . In short – Gasper Poussin seems to have form'd his Style from this Country . . .

While a water-colour by Skelton of 1758 in the Victoria and Albert Museum[10] seems to have been a deliberate imitation of P139, other comparable views, by a follower of Orizzonte, Busiri and Pomardi, for example,[11] possibly owe as much to the topography of Tivoli as to the example of Dughet.

Engraving

J. Mason 1744, reversed, as in the collection of the Earl of Waldegrave; exh. *Gaspard Dughet*, Kenwood 1980, no.51 (Boisclair, G26).

Versions

CHATSWORTH; 48.2 diameter, including the Temple of the Sybil on the right, but otherwise resembling P139; probably painted after 1673; one of a set of four roundels by Dughet derived from earlier compositions listed at Chatsworth in 1761; exh. *Gaspard Dughet*, Kenwood 1980, no. 25 (Boisclair, no. 336).

MANCHESTER Whitworth Art Gallery (no. 01.1960); 36.8 × 48.2, an old copy of part of P139 without the tree on the right and reduced above and below; a version of this composition, 37 × 46, was in the Yarborough sale, Christie's, 12 July 1929, lot 69 (Boisclair, R57).

Provenance

James, 2nd Earl Waldegrave (1714–63) by 1744; his sale, Prestage's, 16 November 1763 (40, 'Gasper Poussin, A curious Landscape and Figures, with a Waterfall, 36 × 32 in.'), 100 gn.;[12] Gilbert Fane Flemming; his sale, Christie's, 2nd day, 22 March 1777 (46, 'G. Poussin, A landscape with a waterfall, uncommonly clear and perfect'), bt. by the 2nd Earl of Ashburnham (1724–1812), 210 gn.;[13] by descent to the 4th Earl (1797–1878); his sale, Christie's, 20 July 1850 (51, 'G. Poussin, View of Tivoli . . . from the collections of Lord Waldegrave and Mr. Fleming'), bt. Mawson for the 4th Marquess of Hertford, 480 gn.;[14] seen at Hertford House in 1851 by Waagen (II, p. 155: 'of the numerous pictures by Gaspar Poussin of this subject, this is decidedly one of the best'); Hertford House inventory 1870.

Exhibitions

Manchester, *Art Treasures*, 1857 (saloon H, no. 36); Bethnal Green 1872–5 (407).

References General

Boisclair, pp. 59, 108, 237; no. 207; A. French, *Gaspard Dughet*, exh. cat., Kenwood, 1980, under nos. 20, 51 and 69.

[1] Previous editions of this catalogue have recorded an undecipherable signature, but no trace of this can now be seen.

[2] Dughet rented a house at Tivoli, cf. Boisclair, pp. 22, 236–7 (under no. 204).

[3] See References General and Boisclair, p. 58. Earlier (*Revue de l'Art*, 34, 1976, p. 50), she had proposed c. 1665–6.

[4] The buildings in P139 compare closely with those seen in the later water-colour by Skelton which was probably executed *sur le motif* (see note 10 below), and a comparable roof-line may be adduced, for example, from G.F. Venturini's *Veduta della Cascata principale del fiume Aniene nella città di Tivoli* (pl. 27 in *Le Fontane* of c.1691), Richard Wilson's drawing of *Tivoli and the Great Cascade* of c.1753–6 (National Museum of Wales; exh. *Wilson*, Tate Gallery, 1982, no. 33) and from the related compositions listed in note 11 below.

[5] For example the *Landscape with Diogenes* and *Christ healing the Blind* of 1648 and 1650 (Louvre), the landscape of c.1651, no. 2310 in the Prado, and the *Exposition of Moses* of 1654 (Ashmolean Museum); D. Sutton, *Gazette des Beaux-Arts*, 6e, LX, 1962, pp. 298–9, emphasised Dughet's debt to Poussin and compared P139 with Poussin's *Funeral of Phocion* of 1648 (on loan to the National Museum of Wales), and see F. Arcangeli in *L'Ideale classico del seicento in Italia e la pittura di paesaggio*, exh. cat. Bologna, 1962, p. 261.

[6] Boisclair, no. 208; 99 x 81.3, exh. *Gaspard Dughet*, Kenwood 1980, no. 20; bt. by Earl Grosvenor at the Waldegrave sale 1763, lot 41. The fine eighteenth-century frame on this picture is similar to that on P139 which suggests both frames were made for Lord Waldegrave.

[7] For which see L. Lippincott, *Selling Art in Georgian London: the rise of Arthur Pond*, 1983, p. 138 (Mason's engraving after P139 illus. p. 136) and French 1980 (see References General), pp. 9–10.

[8] Skelton wrote to William Herring from Tivoli on 23 April 1758 saying that on the north-east side 'you would be surprized with all the most noble Romantic wildness of Gasper Poussin' (*Walpole Society*, XXXVI, 1956–8, pp. 42–3); at the same time Skelton was drawing the view of Tivoli which compares very closely with P139, see note 10 below.

[9] *Walpole Society*, XXXII, 1946–8, pp. 66–7.

[10] P12–1925; exh. *Gaspard Dughet*, Kenwood 1980, no. 69; the catalogue suggests that it was painted on the spot.

[11] Follower of Orizzonte, *Veduta di Tivoli con le cascate*, 11.2 x 19 (Pinacoteca, Macerata; illus. A. Busiri-Vici, *Orizzonte*, 1974, cat. R11); G.B. Busiri, *The Great Cascade at Tivoli*, c.1742, 98 x 137 (Felbrigg Hall; illus. *Gazette des Beaux-Arts*, 6e, LIII, 1959, p. 296), and S. Pomardi, *The Falls at Tivoli*, 1791 (water-colour, sold Christie's, 2 July 1983, lot 86).

[12] A. Graves, *Art Sales*, II, 1921, p. 343, gave this price with the buyer's name as *Lord Cunningham*, but since such a title is not recorded at this time, it was, presumably, an error.

[13] The Christie's copy of this sale catalogue has the buyer's name as *Dayroles* (perhaps Solomon Dayrolles) but another copy, in the library of the Courtauld Institute, London, has the buyer as Lord Ashburnham. In 1820 John Young, describing the pendant landscape in the Grosvenor collection, mistakenly said that P139 was sold at Lord Waldegrave's sale in 1763 to 'the late Lord Ashburnham, and is now in the possession of the present Earl' (*Catalogue of the Pictures at Grosvenor House*, 1820, p. 34, no.98).

[14] The chalk sale marks (*July 20/50//51*) remain faintly visible on the *verso* of the lining canvas which is also inscribed *463A* in black.

Jean-Honoré Fragonard (1732–1806)

Born on 5 April 1732 in Grasse (Provence), the son of a tradesman. He moved to Paris with his family c.1738. He studied briefly under Chardin c.1748 before becoming the pupil of Boucher c.1748–52. In 1752 he won the *prix de Rome* (*Jéroboam sacrifiant aux idoles*; Ecole des Beaux-Arts), and he attended the *Ecole royale des élèves protégés* under Carle van Loo, 1753–6. In 1756 he joined the Académie de France at Rome whose disciplines were irksome: Natoire told Marigny that Fragonard was very talented but impatient, careless in his copies and constantly changing his ideas.[1] In 1760 he met in Rome the abbé de Saint-Non with whom he toured in Italy before returning with him to Paris in 1761. In 1765 he was *agréé* by the Académie and his *Corésus se sacrifie pour sauver Callirhoé* (Louvre) was well received at the Salon. In 1766 he was commissioned to paint a ceiling canvas for the galerie d'Apollon in the Louvre, two overdoors for Bellevue and in 1770 two unspecified works for Versailles, but none was completed. At his second and last Salon in 1767 his exhibits were slight, and henceforth he turned for patronage to *fermiers-généraux*, content '*de briller dans les boudoirs et dans les garde-robes*'.[2] Later, in 1788, the Académie finally accepted that they would never receive a *morceau de réception* from him, because of his '*légèreté et insouciance*'.[3] He painted landscapes, portraits and genre scenes with equal assurance and the set of four panels, *The Progress of Love* (Frick Collection) rejected by Mme. du Barry in 1773, reveal an accomplished decorative talent. He visited the Netherlands, perhaps c.1763–4 and c.1772, and returned to Italy with the banker Bergeret in 1773–4. From 1778 he had his sister-in-law, Marguerite Gérard,[4] as his pupil and assistant, while his wife exhibited miniature portraits of children between 1779 and 1782. A number of his genre scenes became widely known in the 1780s through engravings, but the emergence of neo-classicism effectively ended his success. He drew illustrations for editions of La Fontaine, Cervantes and Ariosto in the late 1780s, and became a *conservateur* at the Muséum 1793–1800. His final years were spent comfortably but unproductively and he died in Paris on 22 August 1806. His son Evariste (1780–1850) was a successful pupil of David. Fragonard never fulfilled his early academic promise: '*il s'est détourné dans de petits sentiers inconnus, pour se faire un genre plus favorable au délire de l'imagination qu'à l'exacte vérité*'.[5]

[1] Cf. A. de Montaiglon and J. Guiffrey, *Correspondance des directeurs de l'Académie de France à Rome*, XI, 1901, pp.232, 317 (letters of 30 August 1758 and 24 October 1759).

[2] A. de Bachaumont, *Mémoires secrets*, XIII, 1780, p.35 (10 September 1769).

[3] Quoted in Rosenberg, p.430.

[4] A miniature portrait of her by F. Dumont is in the Wallace Collection, M101 (G. Reynolds, *Wallace Collection, Catalogue of Miniatures*, 1980, p.166, no.134, as *Madame Vigée Le Brun*).

[5] *Discours sur l'origine, les progrés et l'état actuel de la peinture en France*, 1785, pp.23–4 (quoted in Rosenberg, p.427).

Abbreviations

AF	A. Ananoff, *L'oeuvre dessiné de Jean-Honoré Fragonard*, vol.I (nos.1–588), 1961; vol.II (nos.589–1142), 1963; vol.III (nos.1143–1925), 1968; vol.IV (nos.1926–2726), 1971
Cuzin	J.-P. Cuzin, *Fragonard*, 1987 (catalogue including lost paintings [D])
Drawings 1978	E. Williams, *Drawings by Fragonard in North American Collections*, exhibition catalogue, Washington, New York, 1978–9
Goncourt	E. and J. de Goncourt, '*Fragonard*' in *L'art du XVIIIe siècle*, 1865 (reference is made to the French edition of 1883)
Mandel	G. Mandel and D. Wildenstein, *L'opera completa di Fragonard*, 1972
Portalis	R. Portalis, *Honoré Fragonard*, 1889
Réau	L. Réau, *Fragonard*, 1956
Rosenberg	P. Rosenberg *et al.*, *Fragonard*, exhibition catalogue, Paris, New York, 1987–8
WF	G. Wildenstein, *The Paintings of Fragonard*, 1960

P379 *Le petit parc*

With twelve figures, the seated foreground lady wearing a red skirt and the little gardener a red waistcoat and white shirt; the statue appears to be a Cybele between two lions.

Canvas, relined 36.6 × 45

There are small losses round the edges and in the bottom right-hand corner. Some of the craquelure has been retouched. There are matt areas bottom right, along the bottom edge and in the trees (upper right) and discoloured varnish has accumulated in the impasted passages.

The subject, etched by Fragonard as *Le petit parc* (see below), is, as Carlson seems first to have observed,[1] an imaginary *souvenir d'Italie*. In previous editions of this catalogue it was described as *Garden of the château de Fontainebleau* (1900), *Gardens of a Roman Villa* (1903) and *Gardens of the Villa d'Este, Tivoli* (1913) – whence the idea of a picturesque, overgrown Italianate garden certainly derived. Coffin suggested specifically that the subject was based on the Dragon Fountain at the Villa d'Este,[2] although there are fundamental differences.

The composition of P379 evolved through a drawing and an etching. The former has generally been grouped amongst those made by Fragonard when he stayed at the Villa d'Este with the abbé de Saint-Non in the summer of 1760,[3] but this is not certain. While it agrees closely in style with other drawings then made at Tivoli, it is not topographical and could as well have been made on Fragonard's return to Paris in 1761. From this drawing, or a version of it (see below), Fragonard made an etching c.1763 in which the lighting is more dramatic.[4] Saint-Non also etched this drawing, probably in 1764,[5] the second state of his plate introducing a pollard willow on the left and a bare tree on the right.[6] P379 further develops such picturesque qualities: a bright light is focussed on a group of colourful little figures, while the composition is framed with trees bearing slight autumnal foliage – hinting that Fragonard already knew landscapes by Ruisdael and Wijnants.[7] P379 is not painted on the coarse canvas Fragonard habitually used while in

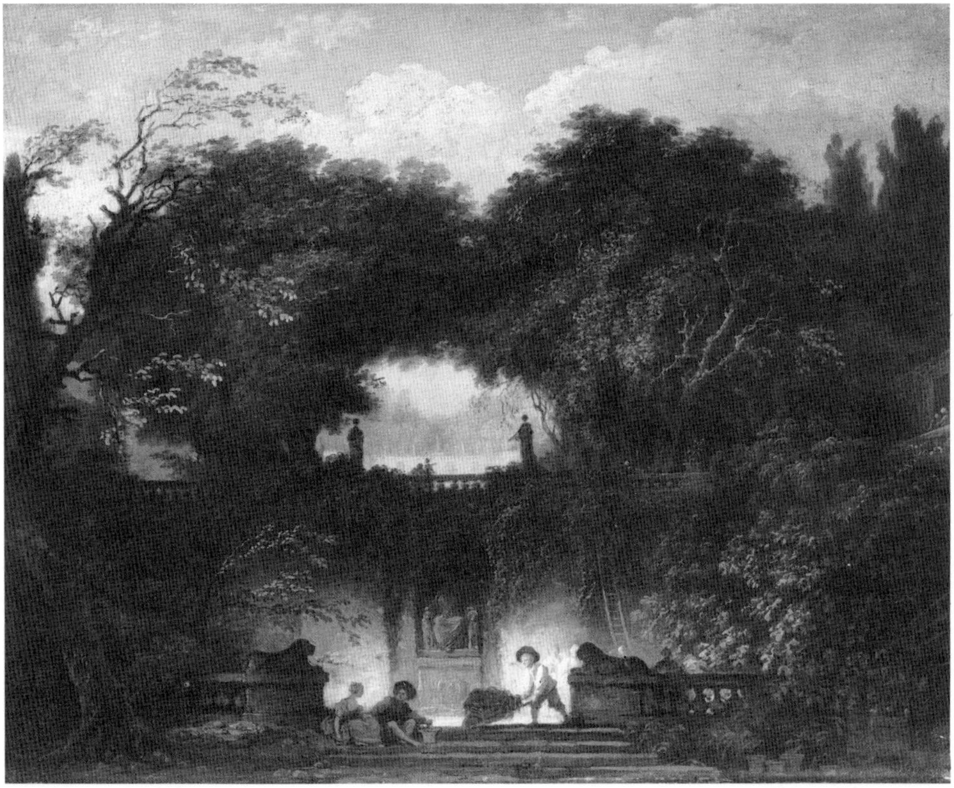

P379

Italy,[8] and the execution, with its rich textures and short calligraphic touches in the foliage, already anticipates that of *The Swing* in 1767 (see P430). Fragonard's continuing affection for Italianate parkscape is suggested by the exhibition of two of his Villa d'Este drawings in the 1765 Salon.[9] P379 probably dates from c.1764–5; Cuzin suggests c.1762–3.

Drawings

NEW YORK art market; sanguine compositional study, ex Doucet sale, 5 June 1912 (13) and coll. Decourcelle (AF351, fig.125).
Another composition study in sanguine, probably made after the New York drawing for the purpose of engraving, was in the Beurdeley sale, Paris, 13–15 March 1905, lot 66 (AF352, fig.126).
SACRAMENTO California, Crocker Art Gallery; a reversed version of the New York drawing, probably a counter-proof with added wash (AF2148, fig.578).

Etchings[10]

Fragonard c.1763 (see above and note 4); Saint-Non c.1764 (see above and note 5). The lower half of the composition was etched by F. E. Weirotter (1730–71; in Paris 1759–63 and 1765–6, Rome 1763–4, and Vienna 1767–71).

Version

NEW YORK private collection; 19.9 × 24.4, gouache on vellum, a reduced replica of P379, probably a later commission;[11] ex colls. de Bryas, Bowles (lent to the Portland Art Museum, Oregon); sold Sotheby's, New York, 14 January 1987, lot 181 (AF1575; illus. Rosenberg, p.154, fig.6).

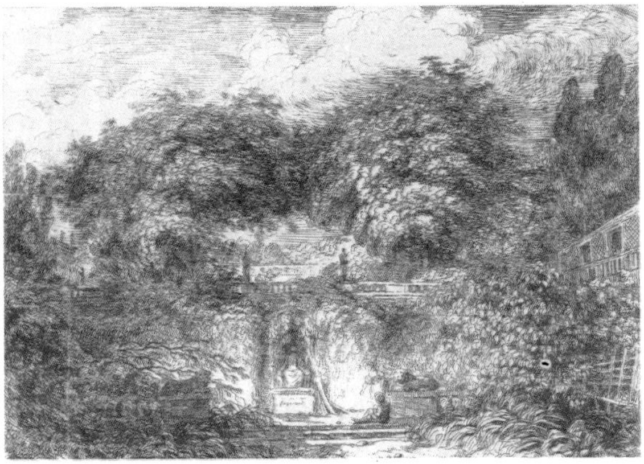

Fragonard: *Le petit parc*, etching. Bibliothèque Nationale

Provenance[12]

Probably anon. sale, Paris, 15 December 1777 (414, '*Terrace ombragée de grands arbres environs de Rome, toile* [37.8 × 45.9]'), 520 *livres*, and possibly Mercier sale, Paris, 1 October 1778 (17, '*Vue d'un jardin orné de plusieurs groupes de figures . . . parmi lesquelles on distingue sur le devant un paysan qui pousse une brouette*'); bt. from the comtesse Katherine Koucheleff, St. Petersburg, September 1867, by Richard Wallace;[13] the 4th Marquess of Hertford; rue Laffitte inventory 1871 (421, '*paysage avec figures*'); Hertford House inventory 1890.

Exhibition[14]

Bethnal Green 1872–5 (481, *Garden of the château de Fontainebleau*).

References General

Réau, p.185; WF106; Mandel, no.114; Rosenberg, pp.153–4; Cuzin, no.88.

[1] V. Carlson, *Regency to Empire: French Printmaking*, exh. cat., Baltimore, Boston, Minneapolis, 1984–5, p.150.

[2] D.R. Coffin, *The Villa d'Este at Tivoli*, 1960, p.131.

[3] For which, see A. de Montaiglon and J. Guiffrey, *Correspondance des directeurs de l'Académie de France à Rome*, XI, 1901, p.354, and Rosenberg, p.67; Fragonard and Saint-Non spent 'two or three months' at the Villa d'Este.

[4] See G. Wildenstein, *Fragonard aquafortiste*, 1956, no.II, where dated 1763–4, Carlson, *loc. cit.*, where dated c.1763, and Rosenberg, no.66.

[5] See Wildenstein 1956, no.II/1, Carlson, *loc. cit.*; Saint-Non's plate presumably followed Fragonard's and he etched three other subjects after Fragonard in 1764 (cf. L. Guimbaud, *Saint-Non et Fragonard*, 1928, p.193).

[6] The second state also omits the central statue in the niche, leaving that area white.

[7] His landscapes, so evidently indebted to these Dutch artists, are generally assumed to date from soon after his return from Italy in 1761 (cf. Rosenberg, pp.184–6; Cuzin, nos.106–14, dates the earliest c.1763–6). A drawing, *Terrace and Garden of an Italian Villa*, (National Gallery, Washington; AF313; *Drawings 1978*, no.8), shows Fragonard adding bare trees to frame a composition.

[8] For example, for *Le jeu de la palette* (Cuzin, no.81; Rosenberg, no.13), *L'enjeu perdu* (Cuzin, no.76; Rosenberg, no.18) and *Les apprêts du repas* (Cuzin, no.78; Rosenberg, no.17) were all painted on a broad-weave canvas in Italy. Rosenberg, pp.96, 153, suggests P379 is also on such a canvas, but this was due to a misunderstanding on our part.

[9] Cf. Rosenberg, nos.30 and 32 (AF894, fig.236; AF908).

[10] All three etchings (the Saint-Non in the second state) are illus. Rosenberg, p.153, and *Aspects de Fragonard*, exh. cat., galerie Cailleux, 1987, nos.39, 40, 40*bis*. The first state of the Saint-Non is illus. Carlson, *op. cit.*, p.151, fig.1.

[11] As M. Roland-Michel has suggested (*Aspects de Fragonard*, see note 10, under no.39).

[12] Réau, *loc. cit.*, gave the provenance of P379 as Nattier sale, 14 December 1778 (53), but this is Cuzin, no.82, *Vue prise à la Villa d'Este* (sold Sotheby's, Monaco, 28 June 1984, lot 86).

[13] See Boucher P399 notes 6 and 7.

[14] Wildenstein, *loc. cit.*, suggests P379 was exhibited in the Salon de la Correspondance, 1785: '*une vue de jardin, dans lequel de hauts arbres se joignent par les tiges . . . laissent apercevoir un château, différentes figures d'hommes . . .*', but this description seems inappropriate.

P382 *The Souvenir (Le chiffre d'amour)*

Auburn hair dressed with a pink ribbon, wearing a dull pink dress and white underskirt; a white shawl on the bench and an opened letter on the ground; she has inscribed the letter S on the tree. Signed, along the stone bench: *fragonard.*

Walnut panel 25.2 × 19 × 0.3

The panel is cradled with five vertical battens and five horizontal slats, and oak strips have been added to each edge, bringing the overall size to 26.5 × 20.5. There is a vertical split 3 cm. long running up from the bottom edge by the left of the skirt. There are minor losses above the dog's head and by his back, to the right of the girl's foot, in her sleeve, on her neck and above her ear. The later painting of the additional strips has spread over the edges of the original panel. The varnish is discoloured.

It appears that, having read her lover's letter, the girl carves his name on the tree, the dog emblematic of her fidelity. The motif, long familiar from Ariosto's *Orlando Furioso* IX (where Angelica carved Medoro's name on a tree),[1] was being used, for example, by Reynolds in a portrait contemporary with P382[2] and does not seem to warrant a specific literary source, although P382 was associated with both Ariosto and Rousseau's *Nouvelle Héloïse* in eighteenth-century sales (see Provenance).

Engraved in 1786 as *Le chiffre d'amour*, P382 is distinguished by its *sensibilité*, cool colour and neat finish. The same model and dog seem to recur in the drawing *S'il m'était aussi fidèle* (AF636, fig.198) which was engraved in 1776.[3] Wildenstein observed (p.25) that a number of similar subjects, showing ladies reading letters, were exhibited at the Salon 1777–9 (and cf. P455 below), and Cuzin has proposed c.1775–8 as the date of P382. Despite its evident quality, the Goncourts had found P382 '*de qualité très faible, et recuré et repeint*' in 1865;[4] Wildenstein had some reservations concerning the signature (which seem groundless), and it has frequently been proposed that P382 is a reduced replica of the engraved *Chiffre d'amour*.[5] The engraving shows the composition slightly extended on each side, and a painting similar to P382 but slightly larger (c.32 × 23) appeared in two eighteenth-century sales (see Provenance). The engraving could have been made from an intermediary drawing (cf. P430), or P382 may have been reduced in size. It is difficult to believe that it is a replica.

Engravings

See above. N. de Launay 1786, *Le chiffre d'amour*, the initials S.M. prominent on the tree and on the letter; dedicated to the vicomtesse de Polastron (illus. Rosenberg, p.428). M. de Gouy, circular; anon., oval (illus. *ibid.*, p.272); lithograph by Gilliaux c.1850.

Copies/Versions

A larger, freely-painted version of P382 was in a Danish private collection in 1980, ex coll. Kahn, New York. A small oil sketch, probably after P382, was in a Brussels private collection in 1965.

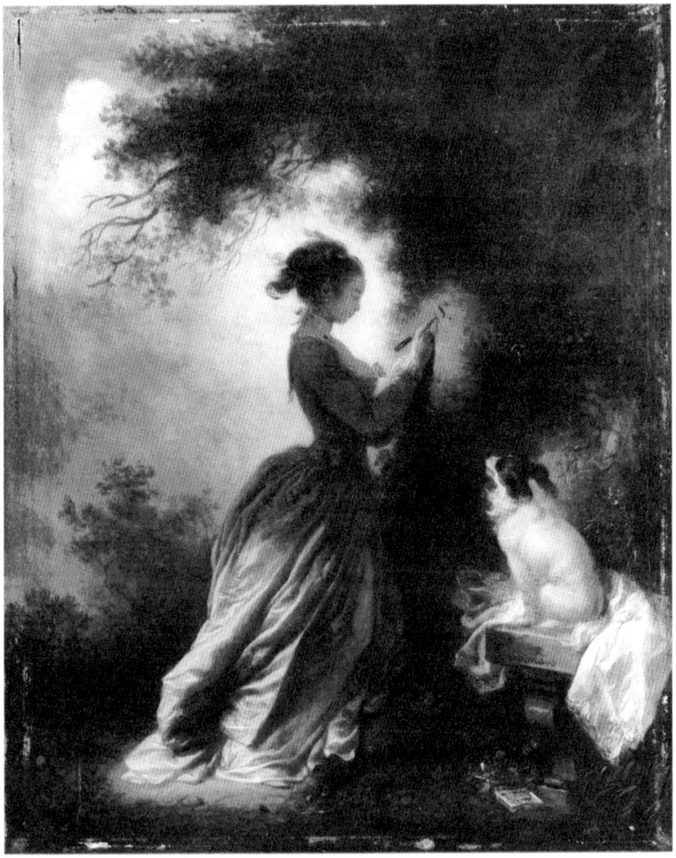

P382

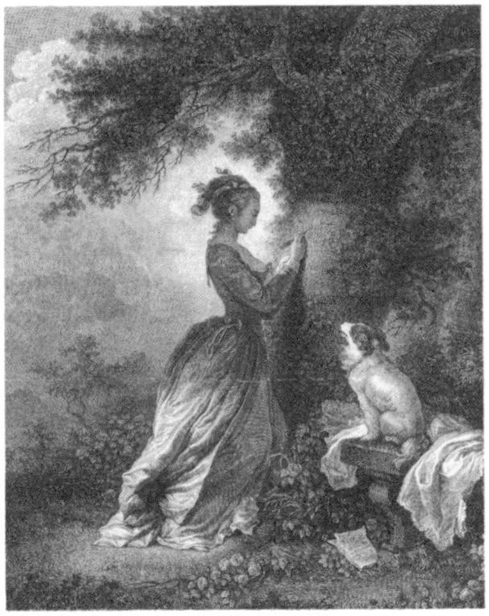

N. de Launay after Fragonard:
Le chiffre d'amour, 1786.
Bibliothèque Nationale

Provenance

Probably Calonne sale, Paris, 21 April 1788 (174, '*Angélique écrivant sur un arbre le nom de Médor . . . effet piquant et plein de charmes* [31 × 22.9]'), bt. Verrier, 720 *livres*; and Mme. Goman sale, Paris, 6 February ff. 1792 (99, '*une jeune femme près d'un arbre, occupée à écrire le nom de son amant; près d'elle un petit chien espagnol. Cette jolie composition est connue sous le nom de* La Belle Julie [from *La Nouvelle Héloïse*] [32.4 × 24.3]'); anon. sale, Paris, 11 April 1822 (11, '*Une jeune Demoiselle . . . est occupée à graver un chiffre sur un arbre; son chien a l'air de prendre part à l'action de sa maîtresse. Ce tableau est gravé. Bois* [21.6 × 16.2]'), 60 fr.; possibly anon. sale, Paris, 12–13 January 1834 (40, '*Jeune fille gravant un chiffre sur l'écorce d'un arbre*'); the duc de Morny (1811–65); his sale, Paris, 3rd day, 2 June 1865 (99, *le Souvenir*), bt. by the 4th Marquess of Hertford, 35,000 fr.; rue Laffitte inventory 1871 (199); Hertford House inventory 1890.

Exhibitions

Boulevard des Italiens 1860 (132) lent Morny; Bethnal Green 1872–5 (570, *A Lady carving her Name*); RA 1896 (83, *The Letter*).

References General

Goncourt, p.373; Portalis, p.273; Réau, pp.163, 228; WF390; Mandel, no.414; Cuzin, no.310 and D5.

[1] On this subject generally, see R. W. Lee, *Names on Trees, Ariosto into Art*, 1977; P382 is mentioned p.75.

[2] See *Reynolds*, exh. cat. RA 1986 (103) – *Mrs. Lloyd*, first exh. RA 1776.

[3] See also *Drawings 1978*, no.27, where its similarities to another drawing, which may also show the same model, *La résistance inutile* (*ibid.*, no.28), are emphasised, and Rosenberg, no.119.

[4] Goncourt, *loc. cit.*, made this observation at the Morny sale in 1865, cf. their comments on *The Swing* (P430) on the same occasion.

[5] Cf. previous editions of this catalogue; Portalis, p.273; WF389, and Mandel, no.415.

P394 *The Fountain of Love*

The lovers have pink roses in their fair hair; she wears a white drapery, he yellow; Signed, bottom right: *fragonard.*

Canvas, relined 63.5 × 50.7

The surface was heavily ironed in the course of relining. An overall craquelure has been extensively retouched and the paint surface is tending to lift in the upper left and right areas. There are losses round the edges and small damages in the trees (upper centre) and in the foreground (centre left). The varnish is discoloured.

Two lovers, driven on by their passion, seek the soothing waters of the fountain of love; '*affamés tous deux, l'oeil brûlant, ils tendent la soif et le désir de leurs lèvres à la coupe enchantée*'.[1]

P394 may be dated c.1784, immediately before the engraving by Regnault announced late in 1785. It is one of a group of four subjects painted in the 1780s in which Fragonard adopted a new style and approach to the description of love;[2] the profile heads, sculptural figures and melting chiaroscuro, besides the classicising imagery, anticipate Prud'hon. The models for the two lovers in P394 seem to recur in the drawing *La première leçon d'équitation* (Brooklyn Museum; AF12, fig.2), and the male model alone in the *Adoration des bergers* (Cuzin, no.300), the *Tête de jeune homme* (Le Havre; Cuzin, no.318) and in the drawing *Le retour au logis* (AF36, fig.11). P394 became one of Fragonard's best-known pictures; it is held by Marguerite Gérard in her self-portrait *L'élève intéressante* of 1786,[3] and was one of three paintings mentioned in Fragonard's obituary in the *Journal de Paris*;[4] for Portalis it was one of his most sensual subjects ('*l'ivresse de la jeunesse célébrant ses vingst ans*'), for Cuzin (p.212) it remains '*l'un des sommets de l'oeuvre*'.

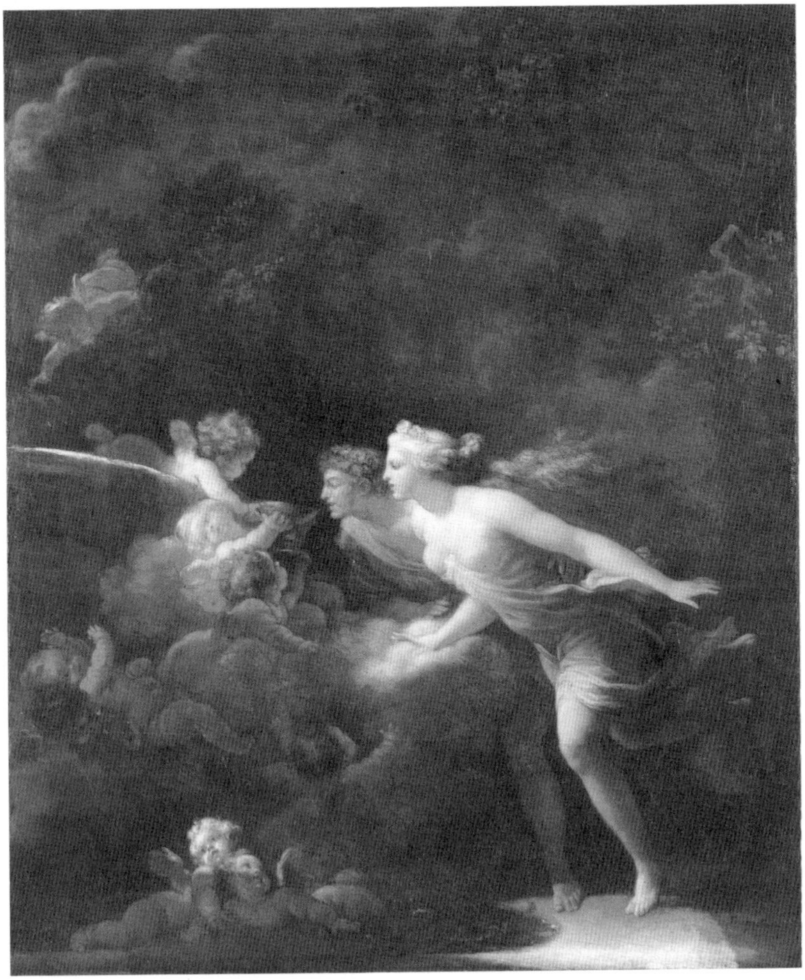

P394

Drawing

A sanguine study for the man's head was in the J.S. sale, Paris, 10 December 1930 (11), bt. Cotareanu (AF711, fig.202).

Engraving

N.-F. Regnault 1785, *La Fontaine d'Amour*, reversed (illus. Rosenberg, p.546).[5]

Versions

NEW YORK private collection; 47 × 37.5, sketch for P394, ex colls. Bernstein and Bartholini; Laughlin sale, Sotheby's, 10 June 1959, lot 22 (Cuzin, no.374).
PARIS private collection; 53 × 46, ex colls. Saint, Walferdin and Paillard; Lariboisière sale, Paris, 27 March 1936, lot 17 (Cuzin, no.375, with some reservations concerning the attribution).

Another version, 62 × 51, attributed to Fragonard, sold Christie's, 11 April 1913 (50), was with J. Willys, Toledo, Ohio (Cuzin, under no.373). A grisaille version, probably a copy, was in the More sale, Brussels, 12 April 1929 (100).

Provenance

C.-N. Duclos-Dufresnoy (1733/4–94), *notaire*; his sale, Paris, 3rd day, 20 August 1795 (28, '*. . . gravée par N.F. Regnault, sous le titre de la Fontaine d'Amour* [62.1 × 50.6]'), 37,600 fr. *en assignats*; Villeminot, *payeur général de la marine*; his sale, Paris, 25 May 1807 (21, '*le sujet agréable de la Fontaine d'Amour connu par la gravure*, [64 × 56]'), 601 fr.; Nicolas Demidoff (1773–1828); Anatole Demidoff (1813–70); his sale, Paris, 2nd day, 26 February 1870 (106, as from Nicolas Demidoff), bt. by the 4th Marquess of Hertford, 31,500 fr.; rue Laffitte inventory 1871 (422); Hertford House inventory 1890.

Exhibition

Bethnal Green 1872–5 (344, *The Fountain of Pleasure*).

References General

Goncourt, pp.329, 370–1; Portalis, pp.70–1, 277; Réau, p.163; WF488; Mandel, no.516; Cuzin, no.373.

[1] Goncourt, p.329.

[2] The others being *Le serment d'amour* (a version at Grasse; Cuzin, nos.363–4, as c.1780–2), *L'invocation à l'amour* (a version in the Louvre; Cuzin, nos.377–8, as c.1785; Rosenberg, nos.280–1) and *Le sacrifice de la rose* (a version at Buenos Aires; Cuzin, nos.385–9, as c.1788–90; Rosenberg, nos.284–5).

[3] Engr. by Vidal illus. Rosenberg, p.416, and see S. Wells Robertson, BSHAF 1977, pp.183–4. The image she holds is not reversed in Vidal's plate.

[4] Quoted by Rosenberg, p.595; the other works mentioned were *Corésus et Callirhoé* and *Le sacrifice de la rose* (see note 2 above).

[5] Announced in the *Mercure de France*, December 1785 (cf. Rosenberg, p.428). In 1791 Regnault's engraving of Fragonard's *Le songe d'amour du guerrier* (Louvre; Cuzin, no.253; Rosenberg, no.283) was announced as the pendant to his earlier plate of P394, but the two paintings are not obviously related. It may be observed, however, that the condition of *Le songe* is closely comparable with that of P394 (cf. Rosenberg, p.548, fig.3).

P404 *'Say Please' (Dites donc s'il vous plaît)*

The mother wears a white blouse and yellow skirt with a red drape; she holds a large loaf; a classical bust stands above the writing slab which is inscribed and signed: A.B.C.D.E.*Fragonard*/G.H.I.K.L.M.N.

Canvas 28.9 × 37.2[1]

The edges have been retouched. There is broad craquelure in the lighter areas and the surface is tending to lift in the lower left area. The varnish is discoloured and spotted.

Fragonard painted several pictures of peasant family life in a dilapidated Italian interior. The earliest (such as *Les apprêts du repas* in the Pushkin Museum and *L'enjeu perdu* in the Hermitage[2]) have been dated c.1759–60 during his first stay in Italy, but P404 belongs with those painted after his second visit in 1773–4, in which the contrast between the simplicity of the family's life and the decayed grandeur of their surroundings is more wittily stressed.[3] One of this series, *L'heureuse fécondité* (see note 3), was sold and engraved in 1777. Cuzin has dated P404 c.1780 when a version of the composition was engraved (see below). It has been supposed that the tiny boy in P404 was the artist's son, Evariste (b.1780),[4] and that the mother was his sister-in-law, Marguerite Gérard,[5] but the former is impossible (from the date of the first engraving) and the latter unproven. The tortoiseshell cat in P404 and a similarly undressed baby boy recur in *Le premier pas de l'enfance* (Fogg Art Museum) by Fragonard and Gérard which Cuzin (no.409) has dated c.1785.

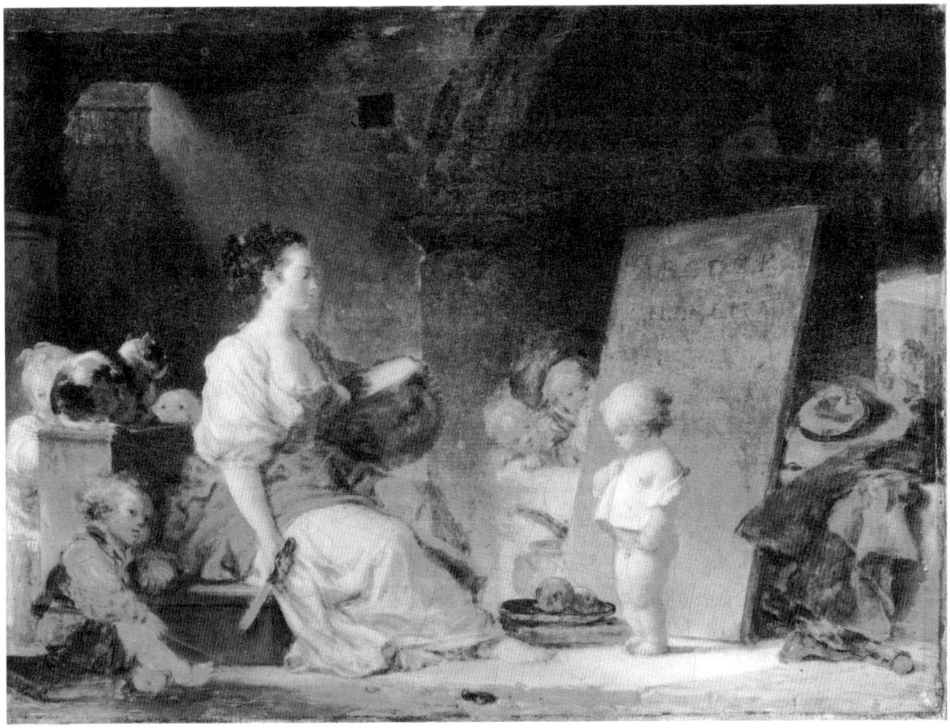

P404

Drawings

PARIS G. Menier (formerly); compositional study, showing the mother and little boy but with differing secondary figures and a low arch running across the background (AF600, fig. 190; illus. Rosenberg, p.417).
Private collection; compositional study, similar to the Menier drawing but with different setting, resembling the engravings by Gautier-Dagoty and de Launay, see Versions (AF599, fig. 191).

A third compositional study in the Bérard collection, Paris, is listed by Ananoff (AF601).

Engravings

See Versions.

Copy

A reduced copy, 12 × 18, was in an English private collection in 1980.

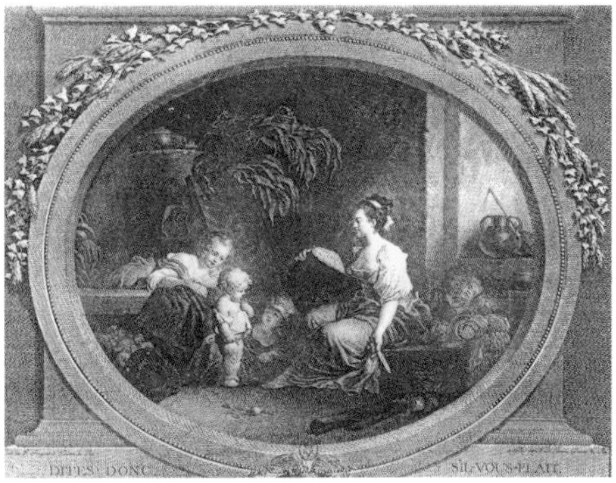

N. de Launay after Fragonard: *Dites donc s'il vous plaît*, 1783. Bibliothèque Nationale

Versions

PARIS private collection; oil on paper 28 × 36, similar to the second drawing described above (without the writing slab, bust and cat, different secondary figures and architecture); the composition engr. E. Gautier-Dagoty 1780 (illus. Rosenberg, p.425) and N. de Launay 1783 (illus. *ibid.*, p.458); possibly the picture in the Saubert and Desmarest sale, Paris, 17 March 1789 (94, '. . . *gravé sous le titre* Dîtes donc s'il vous plait [27 × 37.8]') and/or in the Duclos-Dufresnoy sale 1795 (see Provenance); anon. sale, Paris, 28 March 1979, lot 163 (Cuzin, no.350 and D11).
Seligmann 1941; 39 × 47 oval, composition as above; ex colls. Pillet-Will and Owen (Cuzin, no.349).
Sir Basil Zaharoff 1921; 28 × 37, copy or replica of P404; ex Muhlbacher sale, Paris, 13–15 May 1907 (25).

Provenance

Possibly C.-N. Duclos-Dufresnoy (1733/4–94) and his sale, Paris, 1st day, 18 August 1795 (28*bis*, '*Intérieur rustique . . . composition . . . connue par l'Estampe gravée par N.* Delaunay, *sous le titre, Dites donc s'il vous plait* [27 × 35.8]'), 4,466 fr. *en assignats*; the comte de Perregaux (1785–1841); his sale, Paris, 8–9 December 1841 (49, '*La maîtresse d'école. Munie d'un grand pain . . . entourée d'une demi-douzaine de marmots dont un, debout, et la tête baissée devant elle, reçoit une réprimande qu'il écoute d'un air piteux, mais non sans amuser deux espiègles à moitié cachés derrière un grand tableau destiné à écrire. Toile* [38 × 37[6]]'), bt. M. de l'Etoile, 385 fr.; the 4th Marquess of Hertford;[7] Hertford House inventory 1890.

Exhibition

Bethnal Green 1872–5 (445, *The Schoolmistress*).

References General

Goncourt, p.376; Portalis, p.282; Réau, p.167; WF468; Mandel, no.492; Cuzin, no.348.

[1] The stretcher is inscribed, *verso*, probably in a late eighteenth-century hand: *No 84* and *No:30*.

[2] Cf. Cuzin, nos.78, 77.

[3] Cf. Williams, *Drawings 1978*, p.118. Related compositions include: *L'heureuse fécondité* (versions in a private collection, New York, and National Gallery, Washington; Cuzin, nos.311–12, as c.1776–7); *L'éducation fait tout* (São Paolo; Cuzin, no.352, as c.1780), and *Le petit prédicateur* (Cuzin, no.351, as c.1780), and the drawings *Le déjeuner de l'âne* (Fogg Art Museum; AF3, fig.3; *Drawings 1978*, no.45, as second half of the 1770s) and *La lecture à la ferme* (AF640, fig.518).

[4] Cf. Lady Dilke, *French Painters of the XVIIIth century*, 1899, II, p.68, and Réau, p.82. The identification is denied, for example, by Cuzin, p.255 n.23

[5] Réau, p.82, and L. Dimier, *Histoire de la peinture française au XVIIIe siècle*, II, 1926, p.30.

[6] The English edition of the sale catalogue gave the size as $11\frac{1}{4} \times 14\frac{3}{4}$ ins., i.e. 28.6 × 37.5. The pendant in the Perregaux sale, lot 50, *L'heureuse famille*, was bt. by Polivanoff, 470 fr., and appeared in an anon. sale, Versailles, 24 May 1970, lot 27 (Cuzin, no.314, as c.1778).

[7] Portalis seems first to have published P404 as the Perregaux picture. Previous editions of this catalogue have said that it was bought at the sale by de l'Etoile for Lord Hertford.

P412 *A Boy as Pierrot*

Fair hair, blue eyes, wearing a white costume with blue trimming on the hat and cuffs, and holding pink roses.

Canvas, relined 59.8 × 49.7

Relined in London between 1844 and 1871;[1] cleaned in 1987 by Lank. There are minor losses in the top of the hat, in the forehead and his left cheek, and in the background upper left and bottom right.

It has been supposed that the sitter was the artist's son, Evariste (b.1780), but comparison with Fragonard's drawing of him c.1785 (Louvre; AF103, fig.48; Rosenberg, no.294) is not conclusive and both Wildenstein and Cuzin deny the supposition. The sitter recurs, it would seem, in the *Portrait de l'enfant blond* attributed to Fragonard (Cuzin, no.371).

Together with a pendant, *Jeune fille au collier de perles* (Los Angeles County Museum; Cuzin, no.380), P412 was listed in the collection of the marquis de Livois who died in 1790 (see Provenance). Although attributed to Boucher in 1872 and unattributed in 1890 (see Provenance), P412 shows Fragonard's hand in the vigorous execution of the sleeve, collar and flowers, and in its bright, delicate colour. Cuzin has suggested it may have been influenced by the memory of a Watteau *Pierrot*.[2] It may be compared in its ingenuousness with *L'enfant à la curiosité* (Portland, Oregon) which Cuzin (no.286) has dated c.1775, and it relates closely to a number of miniatures which have been attributed to Fragonard. The dating of P412 seems inseparable from a discussion of these miniatures.

Freely executed in water-colour on ivory, they appear to echo Fragonard's technique in oil and wash,[3] while having, as Schidlof observed, nothing to do with the technique of a professional miniaturist.[4] Fragonard's wife, Anne-Marie Gérard, practised as a miniature painter, exhibiting portraits of children 1779–82 (and eleven such miniatures were sold in 1782–5). He was also friendly with the Swedish miniaturist P. A. Hall who was in Paris 1766–91 and who owned eight oils by Fragonard (including '*une tête d'après moi, dans le temps qu'il faisait les portraits au premier coup pour un louis*') and eleven drawings in 1778.[5] The Geneva miniature listed below is accepted as Fragonard by Williams who has suggested a date of c.1770 (contemporary with his *têtes de fantaisie*).[6] Perhaps a slightly later date, coinciding with his wife's activity and contemporary with *L'enfant à la curiosité*, may be suggested. P412 not only reproduces the costumes, concealed hands and accessories of these miniatures, but imitates their simple compositions; hitherto dated c.1785 or later, it may well be somewhat earlier.

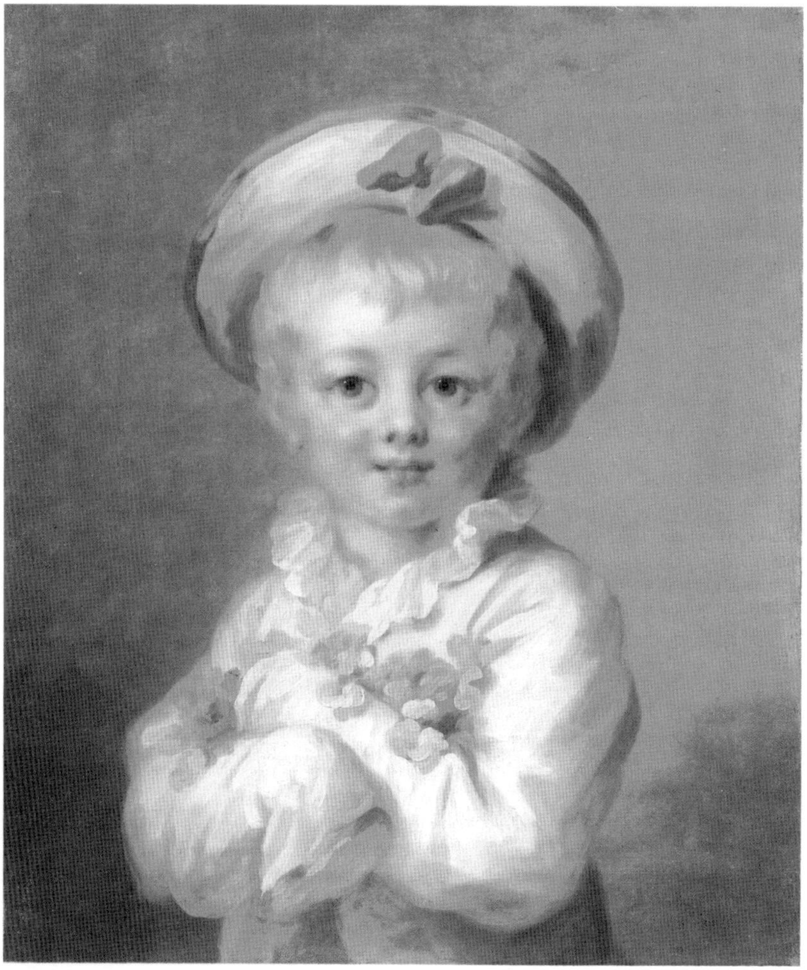

P412

Copy

Miniature, 15.2 × 11.4, oval; Pierpont Morgan sale, Christie's, 3rd day, 26 June 1935 (521) as Fragonard.[7]

Versions (miniatures)

GENEVA Sotheby Parke Bernet, 7 May 1982 (314); 8.2 high, rectangular; to right, similar costume with hanging cuff and flowers; with pendant of a boy with a sword (see note 6).[8]

LONDON Christie's, 8 December 1982 (192); 6.8 high, oval; to left with head turned to front.

PARIS Palais Galliera, 18 June 1963 (16); 7 high, oval; bust-length; ex Walferdin sale, 12 April 1880 (101).

In the Villot sale, Paris, 25 January 1864, lot 53 was: '*Petit garçon habillé en Pierrot. Tête de face, cheveux blonds, chapeau de feutre blanc bordé d'un velours bleu. Fraise au col. Habit blanc avec des rubans bleus. Il tient des roses sur son bras. Forme ovale 3.2 × 2.7*'. Portalis (p.318) noted this was described as a copy in an annotated sale catalogue.

Two miniatures *dans la manière de Fragonard*, each described as *jeune garçon en costume de Pierrot*, were in the Tondu sale, Paris, 3 April ff. 1865, lots 744 and 746.

Provenance

The marquis de Livois (1736–90); Livois catalogue, 1790, no.245, as '*Fragonard, le buste d'un jeune garçon de grandeur naturelle en habit de Pierrot avec un chapeau gris bordé d'un ruban bleu. Les 2 mains sont dans les manches de son habit tenant des roses. Toile* [59.5 × 48.6]'; the collection was dispersed in 1799, when P412 was valued at 30 fr.;[9] possibly Mantion and Wagner sale, Paris, 8 February 1841 (65, *enfant en pierrot*), 353 fr.; C. Cope sale, Christie's, 8 June 1872 (34, Boucher, *Portrait of a Boy as Pierrot*), bt. C. Davis for Sir Richard Wallace, 870 gn.; 105 Piccadilly 1874–5; Hertford House inventory 1890 as unknown artist.

References General

Réau, p.181; WF520; Mandel, no.543; Cuzin, no.379, pp.228–30.

[1] The stretcher bears, *verso*, the stamp: *F. Leedham*, who is recorded in London 1844–56 and 1866–71.

[2] F. Schmidt-Degener (*Onze Kunst*, XXI, 1917, pp.100–1) even suggested a Rembrandt influence.

[3] For Fragonard as a miniaturist, see Portalis, pp.129–32, 317–19; Mandel, nos.569–76; T. H. Colding, *Aspects of Miniature Painting*, 1953, pp.146–8, and L. R. Schidlof, *The Miniature in Europe*, 1964, I, p.266. For other miniatures associated with Fragonard, see G. Reynolds, *Wallace Collection, Catalogue of Miniatures*, 1980, nos.91–3, 277 (M 110–11, 136, 112).

[4] Schidlof, *loc. cit.*

[5] See F. Villot, *Hall*, 1867, pp.74–5, 77.

[6] E. Williams, 'A Pair of portraits in miniature by Jean-Honoré Fragonard', *Art at Auction, Sotheby's 1981–2*, 1982, pp.210–12.

[7] Cf. G. Williamson, *Catalogue of the Collection of Miniatures, the property of J. Pierpont Morgan*, III, 1907, no.539, illus.

[8] Illus. Williams, *loc. cit.*

[9] Information from R. Planchenault, letters on file dated 11 October and 19 November 1921; see also Planchenault, 'La collection du marquis de Livois', *Gazette des Beaux-Arts*, 6e, x, 1933, pp.14–22.

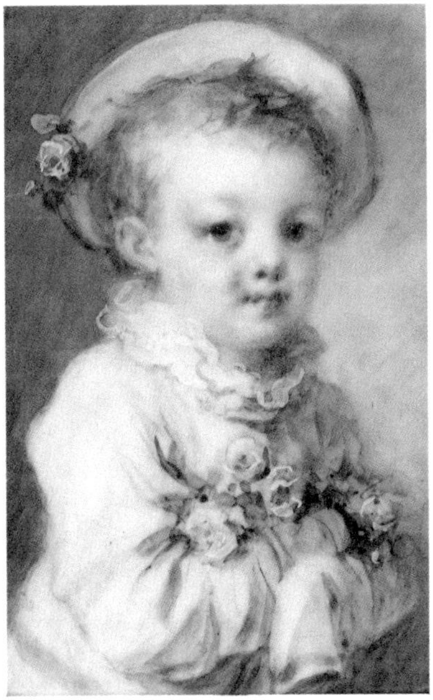

Attributed to Fragonard:
Boy as Pierrot, miniature.
Sotheby Parke Bernet, Geneva,
7 May 1982

P430 *The Swing (Les hazards heureux de l'escarpolette)*

The girl in coral pink, the reclining man in grey, the man pulling the swing in dark blue; a fountain in the left mid-distance. Signed indistinctly, below left: *fr . . . . . rd.*

Canvas, relined 81 × 64.2

Made up to 81.8 × 64.8 in the course of relining in the mid-nineteenth century, when the surface was also heavily ironed.[1] There are small losses in the foliage top left and upper centre (by the end of the swing rope). The thinner passages of the foliage appear to be worn. The varnish is slightly discoloured. In 1865 the Goncourts considered that P430 '*ou du moins ce qui restait de lui sous le récurage et le*

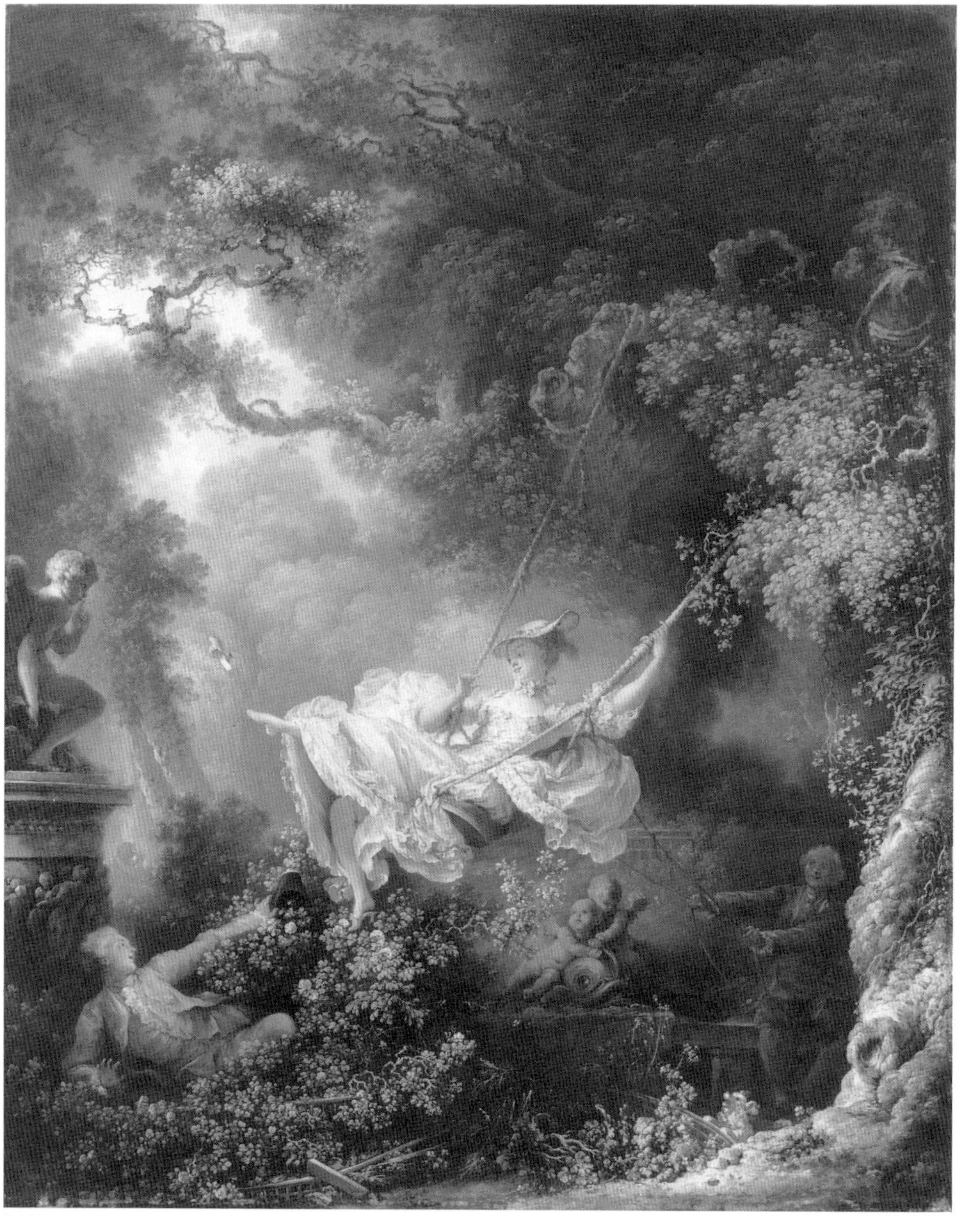

P430

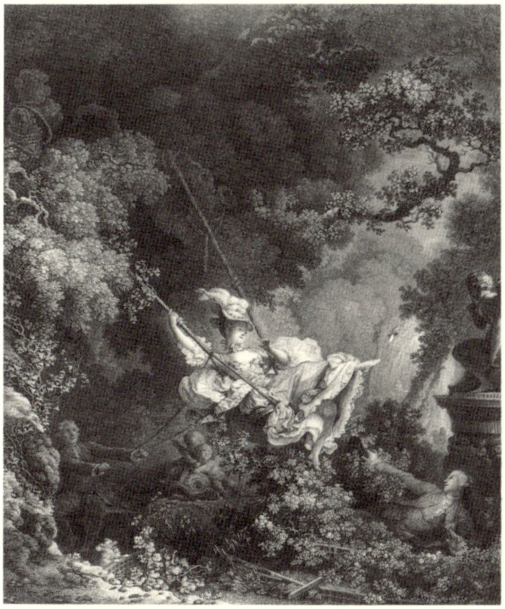

N. de Launay after Fragonard:
Les hazards heureux de l'escarpolette, 1782.
The British Museum

repeinturlage . . . avait l'air d'une vraie copie de passage',[2] but the harshness of this judgment is not borne out by its present condition.

The circumstances of the commissioning of P430 were recorded by Ch. Collé in October 1767:[3]

> *Croiroit-on, me disoit ce peintre* [G.-F. Doyen[4]], *que peu jours après l'exposition de mon tableau* [*Sainte Geneviève des Ardents*] *au Salon* [from 25 August 1767], *un homme de la Cour m'a envoyé chercher pour m'en commander un dans le genre que je vais vous dire? Ce seigneur étoit à sa petite maison avec sa maîtresse lorsque je me présentai à lui pour savoir ce qu'il me vouloit. Il m'accabla d'abord de politesses et d'éloges, et finit par m'avouer qu'il se mouroit d'envie d'avoir, de ma façon, le tableau dont il alloit me tracer l'idée.*
> *'Je désirerois, continua-t-il, que vous peignissiez madame (en me montrant sa maîtresse) sur une escarpolette qu'un évêque mettrait en branle. Vous me placerez de façon, moi, que je sois à portée de voir les jambes de cette belle enfant, et mieux si vous voulez égayer davantage votre tableau, etc.' – J'avoue, me dit M. Doyen, que cette proposition, à laquelle je n'aurois jamais dû m'attendre, vu la nature du tableau d'où il partoit pour me la faire, me confondit et me pétrifia d'abord. Je me remis portant assez pour lui dire presque sur-le-champ: 'Ah! monsieur, il faut ajouter au fond de l'idée de votre tableau, en faisant voler en l'air les pantoufles de madame, et que des amours les retiennent.' Mais comme j'étois bien éloigné de vouloir traiter un pareil sujet, si opposé au genre dans lequel je travaille, j'ai adressé ce seigneur à M. Fagonat* [sic], *qui l'a entrepris et qui fait actuellement cet ouvrage singulier.*

Instead of a Bishop, P430 shows the swing controlled by a cheerful elderly man, probably the husband inadvertently encouraging the lover.[5] The subject, including the iconography of the swing, the significance of the lover's raised hat and the narrative role of the sculpture, has been discussed at length by both Wentzel and Posner.[6] It is not known who the patron was. The Goncourts, who first associated P430 with Collé's account, made no attempt to identify him,[7] but

Portalis, doubtless influenced by the fact that P430 had been described when exhibited in 1860 (see Exhibition) and sold in 1865 (see Provenance) as from the baron de Saint-Julien sale, suggested:

> *C'est pour le baron de Saint-Julien que Fragonard avait exécuté* le Colin-Maillard[8] *et* la Balançoire [see below], *deux de ces tableaux décoratifs où il mettait en scène des enfants avec tant de verve et de couleur. C'est pour cet amateur, dit-on, que fut faite la fameuse* Escarpolette. *Elle figure du moins dans son catalogue, en 1788.*

But no Saint-Julien sale is recorded in 1788; his two sales of 21 June 1784 and 14 February 1785 contained five Fragonards, but not P430.[9] Portalis's identification has, however, been repeated ever since.[10] There were further confusions: Lachaise equated P430 with *La balançoire* from the Cypierre sale in 1845[11] (now National Gallery, Washington; Cuzin, no.339), and it would appear that Ph. Burty, who compiled the 1860 exhibition catalogue, had confused P430 with *La bascule*, formerly in the Saint-Julien sale of 1784 (see note 9; now in the Thyssen-Bornemisza collection, Lugano; Cuzin, no.43). The first certain owner of P430 was Ménage de Pressigny, who was guillotined in 1794.

From Collé's account P430 may be securely dated 1767. It presents a marked contrast with the *Corésus et Callirhoé* (Louvre) for which Fragonard had been acclaimed at the 1765 Salon. In 1765 he had been given a studio in the Louvre as a historical painter of the greatest promise, yet in 1767 he painted P430, aptly described by Nolhac as his '*tableau de réception dans l'art galant*'.[12] A description of his Louvre studio was published by Villot in 1859:

> *il y avait peint des espèces de décorations, on y voyait des guirlandes de fleurs, des arbustes, un jet d'eau, une balançoire et de riches draperies. Un jour fantastique l'aidait à reproduire les effets et les scènes qu'il affectionnait.*[13]

The seductive *mise en scène* of P430 might well have been contrived in this studio.[14] A drawing of before 1772, *Le dessinateur* (Metropolitan Museum of Art; AF650, fig.702), shows an artist sketching in an enclosed garden of comparable abundance. The slightly whimsical tree trunk on the right of P430 and the calligraphic touches in the foliage recur in *La bonne mère* (which also belonged to Ménage de Pressigny; Cuzin, no.261). The sculpture on the left, Falconet's *L'amour menaçant* of 1757,[15] recurs on the same carved plinth in *La main chaude* (National Gallery, Washington; Cuzin, no.341), and the plinth alone in *Le sacrifice de la rose* (see P394 note 2); it has been identified as a *cinerarium* formerly in the Museo Capitolino, Rome.[16] The cool blue-green tonality of P430 seems unmatched in Fragonard's work and further distinguishes his best-known painting in which, as Nolhac observed, '*la grace de l'exécution, le tact du peintre, ont sauvé la grivoiserie du sujet*'.[17]

Engraving

N. de Launay 1782, *Les hazards heureux de l'escarpolette,* reversed, showing the girl with plumes in her hat, the lover with his buttonhole on the other lapel; from a drawing by P.-P. Choffard.[18]

Copies/Versions

PARIS private collection 1980; 25.4 × 20.3, a version derived from the engraving but without the male figures; ex coll. Carnarvon.

'*Une toute petite esquisse des hazards de l'Escarpolette*' was in the collection of H. Walferdin (1795–1880).[19] A '*charmante répétition*', 82 × 65, reversed with the girl in blue, was with baron Edmond de Rothschild 1889.[20] A version was with Mrs. F. Sharon, New York, c.1900.[21]

Provenance

M.-F. Ménage de Pressigny (d.1794), *receveur général,* rue des Jeûneurs; seized by the *commission temporaire des Arts, 26 brumaire an* III [19 November 1794] ('*Le jeu de l'Escarpolette* [81 × 65] *sur toile, de Fragonard*') and valued at 400 *livres* by J.-B.-P. Lebrun, 17 *brumaire an* III;[22] possibly the marquis des Razins de Saint-Marc (1728–1818);[23] the duc de Morny (1811–65), who offered it to the Louvre, 10 April 1859;[24] his sale, Paris, 2nd day, 1 June 1865 (98, *l'Escarpolette*), bt. by the 4th Marquess of Hertford, 30,200 fr.;[25] rue Laffitte inventory 1871 (527); 105 Piccadilly 1874–5; Hertford House inventory 1890.

Exhibition

Boulevard des Italiens 1860 (131) lent Morny.

References General

Goncourt, pp.330–1, 372; Portalis, pp.58–9, 62, 276; Réau, pp.68–9, 157–8; WF237; Mandel, no.231; Cuzin, no.147.

1 The stretcher is stamped, *verso*: MOMPER A PARIS; he relined many of Morny's pictures (cf. Greuze P454, Pater P420, P424, Watteau P416) and see Lancret P422 and After Nattier P414.

2 Cf. his comments on the Fragonard P382 in the same sale.

3 Ch. Collé, *Journal et Mémoires,* 1868, III, pp.165–6. Collé had returned to Paris on 1 October 1767. Both Goncourt and Portalis gave the date of this account as 1766 (repeated in previous editions of this catalogue), and cf. P. Alfassa, *La Revue de l'Art ancien et moderne,* XXVII, 1910, p.292, where P430 is dated 1766.

4 Doyen (1726–1806) had been acclaimed at the 1767 Salon for his *Sainte Geneviève*; 'Doyen emporte la palme sans contre dit', wrote Bachaumont (*Mémoires secrets,* XIII, 1780, p.7; letter of 6 September 1767).

5 Cf., for example, Portalis, p.58; W. Bürger, *Gazette des Beaux-Arts,* 1ère, VII, 1860, p.349.

6 H. Wentzel, 'J.H. Fragonard *Schaukel*', *Wallraf-Richartz-Jahrbuch,* XXVI, 1964, pp.187–218; D. Posner, 'The Swinging Women of Watteau and Fragonard', *The Art Bulletin,* LXIV, 1982, pp.75–88.

7 Nor, for example, did F. Naquet, *Fragonard,* 1890, p.26.

8 See note 9.

9 In the 1784 sale, lot 75: *Colin-Maillard* and *La balançoire,* each 210 × 93 (Cuzin, nos.44, 43); in the 1785 sale, lot 108: *La résistance,* 44 × 38 (Cuzin, D106), lot 109: *Le verre d'eau,* 43 × 38 (Cuzin, D3); lot 110: *Le verre d'eau,* 73 × 92 (Cuzin, D56).

10 Two Saint-Juliens have been confounded: François-David Bollioud, seigneur de Saint-Julien (1713–c.1789), *receveur général du clergé,* who m. in 1748 Anne-Madeleine de la Tour du Pin; '*immensément riche, il forma une bibiothèque très importante par le nombre, mais médiocre par la qualité des ouvrages*' (Olivier, Hermal and Roton, *Reliures Armoriées françaises,* II, 1925, pl.130), and Louis-Guillaume Baillet, baron de Saint-Julien, who published minor works on the fine arts 1748–75 (*Biographie Universelle,* 1843 ed., XXXVII, p.340). Réau, Posner, Wentzel and Cuzin assumed the *receveur général du clergé* must have commissioned P430, stipulating a Bishop out of piquancy.

11 Dr. Lachaise, *Manuel pratique et raisonné de l'amateur de Tableaux,* 1866, p.336.

12 P. Nolhac, *Fragonard,* 1931, p.110.

13 F. Villot, *Notice des tableaux exposés dans les galeries du Musée du Louvre,* 1855, p.127. Other descriptions of Fragonard's Louvre studio published in the mid-nineteenth century by de Launay, Renouvier and Blanc are assembled by Rosenberg, *La Revue du Louvre,* 1987, pp.245–6, 248 n.19.

14 Cecil Beaton used the landscape from P430 as a background for portraits of Royalty 1938–45.

15 A familiar image in later eighteenth-century France; cf. in this Collection, the bronze and gilt-bronze candelabrum F140 and the Sèvres biscuit figures C492–3.

16 C. Vermeule, *European Art and the Classical Past,* 1964, p.129.

17 Nolhac, *op. cit.,* p.113. In 1903 R.H. Nevill reflected (*The Burlington Magazine,* III, 1903, p.56) that it was 'almost pathetic' that P430 'so thoroughly French in conception, should have found a permanent home in England . . . a public which by nature and training is unsympathetic towards irresponsible and unfettered frivolity'.

18 De Launay dedicated his plate to Fragonard, making no mention of the ownership of the painting; see also note 20 below.

19 Goncourt, p.372.

20 Described by Portalis, pp.58–9, 276, and Réau, p.157. Portalis thought this picture may have been the one engraved by de Launay, though it does not show plumes in the lady's hat.

21 Letter on file of 19 May 1922 refers.

22 Cf. Archives Nationales, F^{17}1268, no.175. The seizure was first published by Wildenstein.

23 Wildenstein cited this provenance.

24 *Ibid.*

25 Lachaise (see note 11 above) compared this price with that fetched by *La balançoire* at the Cypierre sale in 1845 (see main text above) – 751 fr. – to demonstrate Fragonard's rapidly rising critical fortune.

P455

P455 *A Young Scholar*

Auburn hair tied with a red and yellow ribbon, wearing a brown dress, leaning on a table. Signed, on the page of the open book: *fragon . . .*

Canvas, relined 45·3 × 37·7

There is a damage in the background by the right-hand edge, and the surface was heavily ironed during relining. There are many small retouchings, most noticeably by the nose, mouth and her left eye. A *pentimento* shows the front of the neck was moved slightly to the left. The varnish is discoloured and spotted.

One of a number of half-length figures of studious girls painted by Fragonard c.1763–c.1778,[1] recalling ter Borch or Metsu and comparable with some of the *têtes d'expression* by Greuze (cf. P427). P455 was probably painted c.1775–8 (contemporary with *The Souvenir,* P382), as Cuzin has suggested. A pendant, *Jeune fille à la croisée* or *La joie* (Cuzin, D146), was sold with it in 1789 and 1872 (see Provenance).

Provenance

Calonne-Angelot sale, Paris, 11 May 1789 (111, '*Deux jeunes filles vues à mi-corps* . . . [each 45.9 × 35]'); the comtesse de Montesquiou-Fezensac sale, Paris, 29–30 January 1872 (6, *L'Etude*), 3,700 fr.;[2] Sir Richard Wallace, 1872; Hertford House inventory 1890.

Exhibition

Bethnal Green 1872–5 (491, *A young Scholar*).

References General

Portalis, pp.276, 280; WF377; Mandel, no.401; Cuzin, no.309.

[1] *La lettre*, private collection, USA (Cuzin, no.91, as c.1763–5?); *La liseuse*, National Gallery, Washington (Cuzin, no.179, as c.1770–2; Rosenberg, no.136); *La lettre*, Cincinnati Art Museum (Cuzin, no.290, as c.1775?), and *La Lettre*, private collection, New York (Cuzin, no.306; as perhaps c.1775).

[2] The pendant, called *La joie*, was lot 7.

P471 *The Musical Contest (Conversation galante dans un parc L'amoureux couronné)*

The girl carries a yellow parasol and wears a white dress with a pink bodice and overskirt; the musette player has yellow breeches and a pink cape, the right-hand youth with a flute a yellow jacket and turquoise cape.

Canvas, relined 62 × 74

Until 1987 P471 showed additions of 24 cm. on the left, 10 cm. on the right, 5 cm. above and 3 cm. below, giving a size of 70 × 108. These additions, made before 1842 (see Provenance), are slightly darker and less accomplished than the original painting. X-radiography reveals that they are on four separate pieces of canvas, closely matching the original; it also shows distinctive cusping and nail holes on the original canvas. When P471 was cleaned by Lank in 1987 the additions were folded back over a new stretcher so that the picture is now seen in its original form. The paint surface is somewhat worn on the right above the urn and there are small losses on the girl's right arm and breast. A *pentimento* shows her right arm was originally placed a little higher.

P471 was acquired by Lord Hertford in 1842 as a Boucher and was described as such in earlier editions of this catalogue (1900–28).[1] An attribution to Fragonard was first proposed by Mathey (letter on file of 19 November 1947) and was subsequently published by Watson in 1961[2] and in the previous edition of this catalogue (1968). Now that the additions have been identified Fragonard's authorship seems beyond dispute, and Cuzin has proposed a date of c.1754–5, immediately after he left Boucher's studio. While subject and setting recall Boucher (cf. P482 and P489 of 1749), the execution and figures compare much more closely with those of early works by Fragonard. The figures resemble those of *La coquette fixée* (Cuzin, no.37, as c.1754?) and *Les amants heureux* (Norton Simon Museum; Cuzin, no.40, as c.1754–5); the curving tree and whimsical stone balustrade recur in *Le jardinier* (Detroit Institute of Art; Cuzin, no.13, as 1753?), and the still-life of fruit and flowers and the girl's head and right arm recall similar

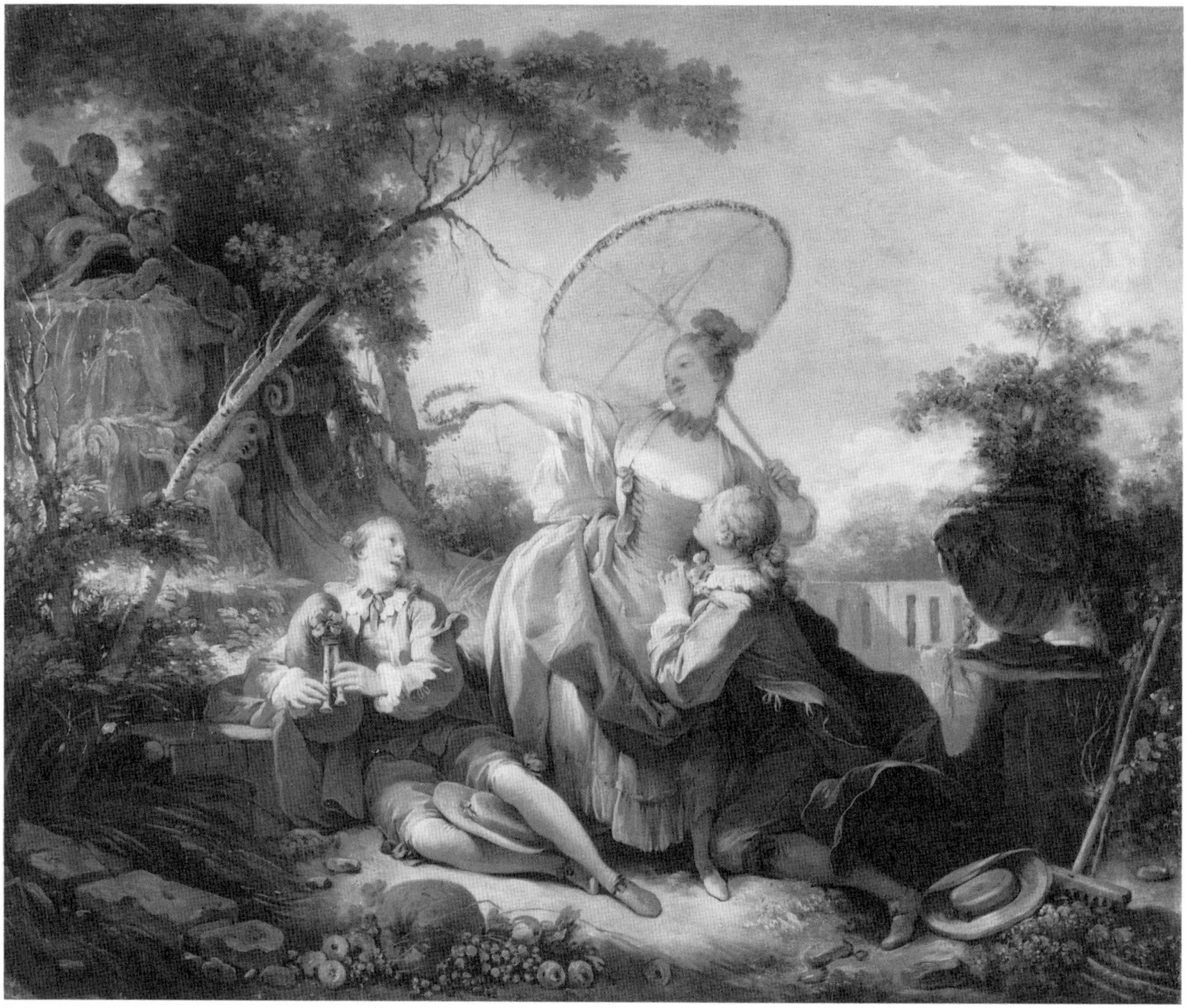

P471

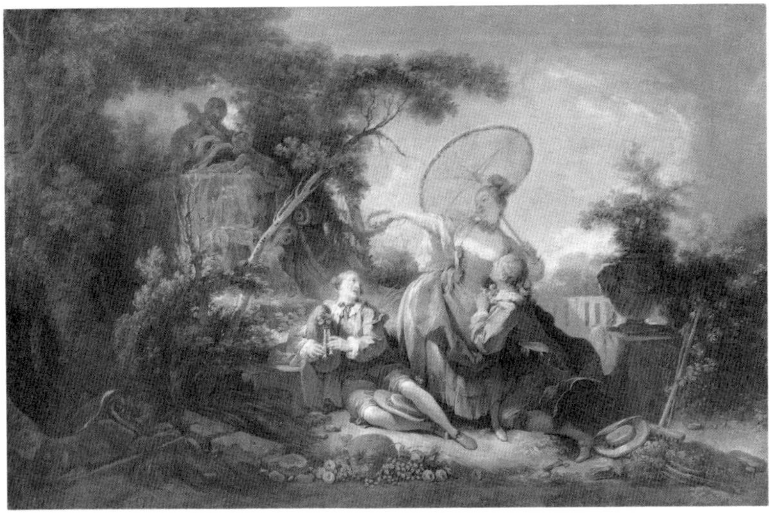

P471 before cleaning

passages in *La bascule* (Thyssen-Bornemisza collection, Lugano; Cuzin, no.43, as c.1755). The pose of the girl also recurs in the drawing *La basse-cour* (Musée de l'Ile-de-France, Cap Ferrat; AF2, fig.1) which was etched by Saint-Non in 1762.

Copy

LONDON Sotheby's 5 July 1989 (203); 70 × 90, showing additions, less part of the right-hand side; possibly by the same hand as the additions on P471; possibly anon. sale, 2 March 1839, see below; ex. coll. Boone, Baltimore.

Provenance

[?Anon. sale, Paris, 2 March 1839 (1, '*Boucher, au pied d'une fontaine, deux jeunes gens, ayant lutté sur leurs instruments en présence d'une jeune fille, sont dans l'attente du prix . . .*'), 520 fr.]; the vicomte d'Harcourt sale, Paris, 31 January 1842 (21, '*Boucher, Scène pastorale . . . deux jeunes bergers . . . l'un avec sa musette, l'autre avec son flageolet, attendent le prix du concours; une jeune et jolie fille debout entre eux et dont la délicieuse tête est garantie du soleil par une ombrelle jaunâtre . . . toile 71 × 109*'), 721 fr.;[3] the 4th Marquess of Hertford; reframed in Hertford House 1859;[4] Hertford House inventory 1870 as '*Boucher, pastoral*'.

Exhibition

Bethnal Green 1872–5 (408, Boucher, *Pastoral Group*).

References General

Mandel, no.584, as attributed; Cuzin, no.38.

[1] Where it said that the initials *f.B.* could doubtfully be read in the lower left corner (i.e. in an added section); I could find no trace of them.

[2] F.J.B. Watson, *The Connoisseur*, CXLVII, 1961, p.39: apropos of its omission from Wildenstein's 1960 catalogue: 'I personally would also assign the Boucher *Musical Contest* to Fragonard'.

[3] The Harcourt sale catalogue alleged that P471 had been in the Blondel de Gagny sale of 1776 and that of the comte de Merle in 1784, but it does not appear in those sale catalogues. It may, however, have been in the Blondel d'Azincourt sale, 18 April ff. 1770 (37, '*Une Pastorale composée de trois figures, dans un jardin*. . . [64.2 × 75.1]'), as Alastair Laing has suggested (letter on file, dated 1 May 1989).

[4] Evans invoice.

French School c. 1715–20

P122 *Madame de Ventadour with portraits of Louis XIV and his Heirs*

From the left: Mme. de Ventadour in black *grand habit*[1] attending the infant Louis XV (then the duc d'Anjou) in silver brocade; the Grand Dauphin in blue coat and black stockings, Louis XIV seated in a brown suit, and the duc de Bourgogne in red with a flowered waistcoat; they all wear the blue ribbon of the Saint-Esprit; in the background bronze busts of Henri IV (left) and Louis XIII.

Canvas, relined 127.6 × 161

The surface was heavily ironed during relining. There are small damages in Bourgogne's staff, Louis XIV's right calf and left shoe and ankle, in the Grand Dauphin's wig, and round the edges; horizontal lines of retouching at 13 and 32 cm. below the top edge suggest the original canvas may once have been rolled. Areas of craquelure have been retouched in the landscape, in Mme. de Ventadour's skirt, round her head and shoulders, and on the table behind her. *Pentimenti* show alterations to the left-hand edge of the table, the fruit upon it, the scarlet drape over the *tabouret* on the left, the bust of Louis XIII, and the right-hand dog's tail; carved swags hanging from the corners of the stucco frame on the back wall and beneath the table have been partly erased. The varnish is much discoloured.[2]

Charlotte-Eléanore de la Motte-Houdancourt (1651/2–1744)[3] m. in 1671 the duc de Ventadour by whom she had one daughter[4] and from whom she separated in 1679; she was sometime mistress of the maréchal duc de Villeroy (later *gouverneur* of Louis XV) and in 1684 was made *dame d'honneur* to the duchesse d'Orléans; in 1704 she was named *gouvernante des Enfants de France, en survivance* from her mother, the maréchale de la Motte-Houdancourt (1624–1709); on 7 March 1712, during a violent epidemic (probably of measles[5]), she was instructed by the King to have his two great-grandsons, the ducs de Bretagne (1707–12) and d'Anjou (1710–74, later Louis XV) baptised (and her sister, the duchesse de la Ferté, see note 9, then became Anjou's godmother); she then hid Anjou from the Royal doctors, whose prescriptions failed to save the lives of his brother and parents, and was credited with saving his life;[6] he was then the only surviving direct male heir of Louis XIV who, on his death bed, told her:

> *pour vous Madame, j'ai bien de remerciements à vous faire du soin avec lequel vous élevez cet enfant et de la tendre amitié que vous avez pour lui; je vous prie de la lui continuer, et je l'exhorte à vous donner toutes les marques possibles de sa reconnoissance;*[7]

in 1717 Louis XV once said to her: '*ah maman, je ne reconnois plus de raison quand il faut m'éloigner et me séparer de vous*'[8] and he continued to value her devotion and kindness; in 1722 Mme. de Ventadour's successor *en survivance* was named as her grand-daughter-in-law, the princesse de Soubise (d. 1724), and in 1729 as her grand-daughter, the duchesse de Tallard (1699–1754), who received the post *en titre* in 1732. Since her great-great-grandfather, the maréchal de Souvré, had been *gouverneur* to Louis XIII, her great-grandmother, Mme. de Lansac, *gouvernante* to Louis XIV, and her mother *gouvernante* to the children of Louis XIV, the Grand Dauphin and the duc de Bourgogne, Mme. de Ventadour's family had served all

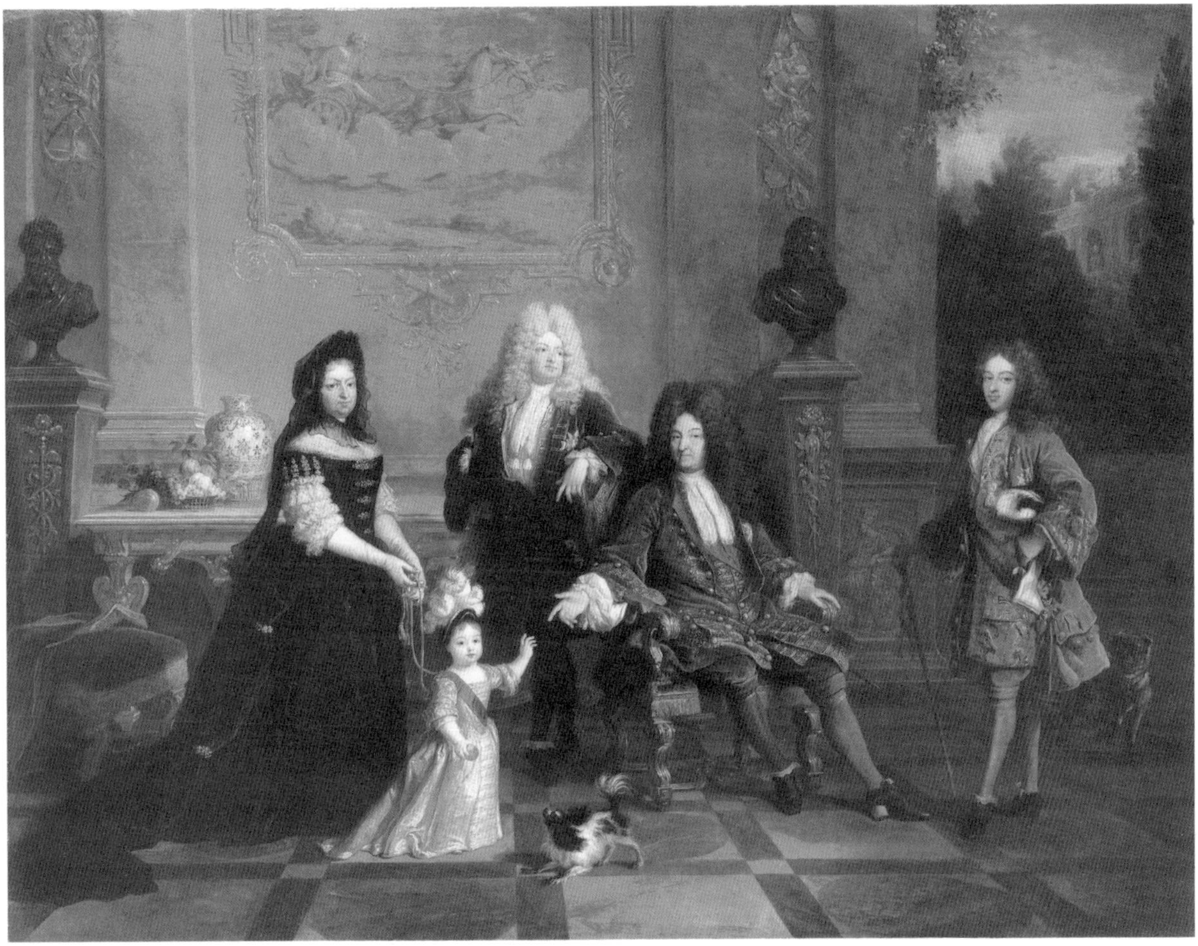

P122

the Bourbons shown in P122. This succession of *gouvernantes* was celebrated in a series of historical portraits formerly in the Hôtel de la Ferté,[9] belonging to Mme. de Ventadour's sister, the duchesse de la Ferté.

P122 evidently commemorates Mme. de Ventadour[10] as *gouvernante*. Her prominence indicates that it must have been commissioned by or for her, and that the Royal infant is the duc d'Anjou whose life she preserved and who, as Louis XV, held her in such high regard.[11] Her descent from a line of *gouvernantes* and her important part in the preservation of the Bourbon line are suggested by the surrounding Royal portraits, none of which is original. They are:

Henri IV (1553–1610), who acceded as the first Bourbon King in 1589, from his bust attributed to M. Jacquet (Louvre)

Louis XIII (1601–43), his son, from the posthumous statue by S. Guillain (Louvre)

Louis XIV (1638–1715), eldest son of Louis XIII, the head from Rigaud's whole-length portrait of 1701 (Louvre)

Louis, the Grand Dauphin (1661–1711), eldest son of Louis XIV, from his portrait *en famille* by Mignard of c.1686/7 (Versailles)

Louis, duc de Bourgogne (1682–1712), eldest son of the Grand Dauphin, his head from Rigaud's portrait of 1703 (Versailles), his pose from Rigaud's 1701 portrait of Louis XIV (see above)

The heads of Louis XIII, Louis XIV and Louis XV are carefully aligned and Louis XIV deliberately indicates his successor. The duc d'Anjou is probably meant to appear as he was when Mme. de Ventadour was nursing him in 1712, although this is inconsistent with the ages of his relatives (which are themselves inconsistent, as the above list demonstrates). The setting evokes, without illustrating, Versailles (cf. Exhibitions and note 22) and makes discreet reference to the power and wisdom of the Bourbons through the images of Apollo (derived, apparently, from La Fosse's ceiling in the Salon d'Apollon at Versailles[12]) and Athena (on the plinth to the right), and the presence of Mercury's caduceus and Hercules's club on the two sculpture stands. Although P122 could have been painted in 1712 to mark the survival of the duc d'Anjou through Mme. de Ventadour's agency,[13] such a celebration could have proved premature in those uncertain times; it was more probably painted after Louis XV's accession in 1715, when his survival had assumed still greater significance.[14]

The earliest assessment of P122 was made in 1755 by C.-N. Cochin, Louis Silvestre and Carle van Loo (see note 18); they attributed it to F. de Troy ('*Nous le croyons de M. De Troy le père*'), but noted that the principal heads were copied '*et qu'elles se sentent de la servitude qu'entraine après soy la nécessité d'imiter une ressemblance*'; they thought it may have been painted '*depuis la Mort de la plus part des personnes qui y sont représentées*' and therefore without regard to comparative ages. '*Dans ce câs*', they concluded, '*le jeune enfant pourroit être le Roy Louis quinze, ce qui augmenteroit l'interêt du tableau qui nous a parû plus important par ces motifs que par sa beauté réelle*'. Their judgment remains valid and it is perhaps significant that, so soon after the deaths of F. de Troy and Largillierre in 1742 and 1746, they should have hesitated over an attribution which, ever since, has wavered unsatisfactorily between the two (see Provenance and Exhibitions).[15] The compiler's proposal in 1983 that P122 was by neither[16] elicited a strong response from Lastic, insisting on an attribution to Largillierre (see References General). The derivative quality of P122 makes attribution difficult. It compares closely in content with a smaller group portrait (Paris, private collection) which shows similar dogs (a spaniel and a bull terrier), a comparable architectural setting and still-life, and the same slightly hestitant perspective; this is also attributed to Largillierre by Lastic.[17] P122 has some slight affinity with the unattributed portrait formerly in the Hôtel de la Ferté and now at Leeds, see note 9(e) – the setting, the figure of Louis XV and the trailing plant hanging over a pilaster; the other Royal group including Mme. de Ventadour from that same collection (now lost), see note 9(f), was attributed to P. Gobert in the eighteenth century.

Provenance

Probably painted for Mme. de Ventadour (d.1744) and possibly passed to her grand-daughter, the duchesse de Tallard (d.1754); C. Leclerc de Lesseville, *président au parlement*, by 1755 when he offered it to the Direction des Bâtiments as F. de Troy;[18] Ludwig (1721–78), prince de Salm-Salm, Paris and Senones (Lorraine),[19] by whom given to F.-I. de Mirbeck (1732–1818), *avocat au parlement*, who in 1783 exhibited it as Largillierre; he offered it to the *musées royaux* in 1817 as Largillierre;[20] his grand niece, Mme. Josset de Saint-Julien, who offered it to the *musées royaux* in 1820;[21] her daughter, Mme. Huper, by 1835 when it was examined by a number of artists and certified as Largillierre;[22] exhibited for sale by Mme. Huper in Paris and Boulogne-sur-Mer, 1836–7; the 4th Marquess of Hertford by 1867[23] (and probably acquired in Paris after 1851[24]); rue Laffitte inventory 1871 (228, '*Largilliere, Louis XIV et Mme de Maintenon*'); Hertford House inventory 1890.

Exhibitions

Salon de la Correspondance, 1783 (46, Largillierre, *Louis XIV, avec le Grand Dauphin, le Duc de Bourgogne et le Duc de Bretagne enfant amené par Mde. la Duchesse de Ventadour. On voit les bustes de Henri IV et de Louis XIII; la scène est dans la Galerie de Versailles*) lent Mirbeck;[25] Paris, rue du Doyenne, no.8, February 1836, and Boulogne-sur-Mer, Grande rue, *dans une des salles du Collège*, August 1837, on each occasion as Largillierre (the description as in 1783 except that the child was identified as Louis XV), lent Mme. Huper;[26] Bethnal Green 1872–5 (406, Largillière, *Louis XIV and his Family*).

References General

Journal des Débats, 11 February 1836 ('Tableau de Largillière représentant Louis XIV et quelques personnes de sa famille', signed D[27]); E. Dacier, BSHAF 1920, pp.52–5, BSHAF 1922, pp.116–21; W.G. Constable, *The Burlington Magazine*, XLI, 1922, p.122, and XLII, 1923, p.97; G. Pascal, *Largillierre*, 1928, pp.44, 64 no.84; Ch. Maumené and L. d'Harcourt, 'Iconographie des Rois de France', AAF, 4e, XVI, 1931, pp.138–9, no.189; J. Cailleux, *The Burlington Magazine*, April 1971, adv. supp., pp.xi–xiii; J. Ingamells, *ibid.*, CXXV, 1983, pp.92–5 (and reply from Lastic, pp.425–6); G. de Lastic, *L'Oeil*, 365, December 1985, pp.36–45.

1 Her dress, with the *fontange* and black veil, may suggest a *dévote* (Ventadour was much influenced by Mme. de Maintenon, cf. *Mémoires de Saint-Simon*, ed. A. de Boislisle, XII, 1896, p.43), rather than court mourning (which was suggested in the *Summary Illustrated Catalogue of Pictures*, 1979, p.247, and by Lastic 1985, p.44). D. de Marly, *Louis XIV & Versailles*, 1987, pl.6, describes Ventadour's dress as 'the black *grand habit*'.

2 P122 was described as '*beau et bien conservé*' in 1755 (see note 18); in 1836 the *Journal des Débats* indicated (and apparently exaggerated) some imperfections: P122 '*a encore souffert du défaut de soin et de conservation . . . tous les bords ont été retouchés. Trois ou quatre pouces de hauteur, sur toute la largeur, vers le haut du tableau, ont été ajoutés et repeints. L'un des chiens, placé à droite du spectateur, a été entièrement refait, comme l'attestent les restes peints du premier chien que l'on voit encore, et deux bustes en bronze placés sur deux gaînes, et représentant à gauche Henri IV, et à droite le grand Condé, sont évidemment d'une main très moderne et même peu habile*'. A review of the 1836–7 exhibitions (see note 26) insisted that P122, '*déjà vieux de plus de cent ans, est on ne peut pas mieux conservé*'.

3 Her biography is scattered through the pages of the *Mémoires de Saint-Simon*, the *Journal du marquis de Dangeau* and the *Mémoires du duc de Luynes*.

4 Anne-Geneviève (1673–1727) who m. 1st in 1691 L.-C. de la Tour (*dit* the prince de Turenne, d.1692), and 2nd in 1694 Hercule, prince de Rohan (d.1749), by whom she had two children, the duchesse de Tallard (1699–1754) and the prince de Soubise (d.1724).

5 The epidemic has also been called scarlet fever or *fleck-fieber*, a variety of typhus (cf. M. Kroll, *Letters from Liselotte*, 1970, p.154).

6 E.g. *Mémoires du duc de Luynes*, VI, 1861, pp.185–6: '*Deux circonstances de sa vie méritent de n'être pas oubliées; la première est d'avoir sauvé la vie du Roi . . . La seconde . . . est qu'elle est la seule femme particulière qui ait été assise sur les fleurs de lis* [the throne]. *L'âge du Roi dans le temps de son lit de justice ne permettoit pas qu'il fût sans sa gouvernante*'.

7 *Journal du marquis de Dangeau*, XVI, 1859, p.127.

8 *Ibid.*, XVII, 1859, p.23.

9 Described by Dacier 1920 (pp. 40–55), 1922 (pp.111–26) and BSHAF 1952, pp.154–7, and by W. Wells, *Leeds Arts Calendar*, V, 18, 1952, pp.22–9. There were five portraits, each 250 × 196, and a horizontal composition, as follows:
a) *Mme. de Lansac with the Children of Louis XIII*, 250 × 196 (Versailles, as French school 17th century)
b) *The maréchale de la Motte-Houdancourt with the six Children of Louis XIV*, now 140 × 120 and showing only three children (coll. the comte de la Motte-Houdancourt, Paris, 1922)
c) *The maréchale de la Motte-Houdancourt with the duc de Bretagne*, now 164 × 152 (Burdett-Coutts sale, Christie's, 4 May 1922, lot 100 as Largillierre, and later coll. P.-L. Weiller, Paris; attrib. to F. de Troy by Cailleux 1971, p.xiv)
d) *The maréchale de la Motte-Houdancourt* [?] *with the three Children of the Grand Dauphin* (lost)
e) *The duchesse de la Ferté* [?] *with the ducs de Bretagne and d'Anjou*, now 167.7 × 153 (Leeds City Art Galleries, no.23.50, as French school 18th century)
f) *The Baptism of the ducs de Bretagne and d'Anjou with Mme. de Ventadour and the duchesse de la Ferté*, horizontal composition (lost)
It appears that these pictures were collected (and some commissioned?) by the duchesse de la Ferté (1654–1725/6, youngest sister of Mme. de Ventadour and godmother to the duc d'Anjou). All six pictures were sketched by G. de Saint-Aubin in 1768 at the Hôtel de la Ferté (illus. Dacier 1920, f.p. 40; Wells, p.25); he described the portraits as *ancien*, attributing (a) to Mignard, (c) to Antoine Coypel and (f) to Gobert. In 1757 Dezallier d'Argenville (*Voyage pittoresque de Paris*, 3rd ed., p.105) had attributed all the portraits to

Mignard and (f) to Gobert. Another composition showing Mme. de Ventadour *'levant le Roi'* was amongst a set of eight Royal portraits listed in the *inventaire après décès* of L.-U. Lefèvre de Caumartin, 31 December 1720 (cf. *Gazette des Beaux-Arts*, 6e, XLVIII, 1956, p.144).

[10] She was identified as Mme. de Maintenon in the 1871 Inventory (see Provenance) and in the earliest editions of this catalogue (1900–08), and as the maréchale de la Motte-Houdancourt (her mother) by Constable 1922. Dacier 1920 rediscovered her proper identity, as cited in the descriptions of P122 given in 1755, 1783 and 1835–7 (see note 18 and Exhibitions). Comparable engraved portraits of Ventadour show her in 1715 seated in a carriage with Louis XV on his entry into Paris (illus. Kroll, *op. cit.*, f.p.209) and in 1715 holding Louis XV *en laisse* on the terrace at Vincennes (illus. *Louis XV*, exh. cat., Hôtel de la Monnaie, 1974, p.219). An engraving showing her much younger is illus. N. Mitford, *The Sun King*, 1966, p.231, and for two other Royal groups including Ventadour see note 9 above.

[11] When the commemorative character of P122 was not recognised, the child was often identified as the duc de Bretagne – who, as Dacier 1920 first explained, could have been painted while the other Bourbons depicted were alive, between 1709 (when Ventadour became his *gouvernante*) and 1711 (when the Grand Dauphin died), although he was not then the Dauphin. Bretagne was also proposed in 1783 (see Exhibitions), by Constable 1922 and 1923, in the 1928 and 1968 editions of this catalogue, by Maumené and d'Harcourt 1931, by Cailleux 1971, and in the 1979 *Summary Illustrated Catalogue of Pictures*. The child in P122 compares closely with the portrait of the unbreeched Anjou dated 1714 by Gobert (Prado, no.2262) and with the infant Anjou seen in the Hôtel de la Ferté portrait, see note 9(e) above; his dark eyes, so evident in P122, were described, for example, by the duchesse d'Orléans (*Correspondance complète*, ed. G. Brunet, 1891, I, pp.152–3, 284); he was identified as Anjou in P122 in 1755 (see note 18 below), 1835–7 (see Exhibitions), in the earlier editions of this catalogue (1900–20), by Ingamells 1983, and Lastic 1985.

[12] Maumené and d'Harcourt 1931, suggested that the stucco frame round the Apollo was *'d'un style assez étrange et semble d'époque Louis XVI'*, but their misgivings were groundless.

[13] As proposed by Lastic 1985, p.44.

[14] The possibility of a date as late as c.1720–5 was canvassed by Cailleux 1971, and a date in the 1720s was also adumbrated by Watson (*ibid.*).

[15] F. de Troy was proposed in 1755 (see note 18 below), by O. Kümmel (Thieme-Becker, XXII, 1928, p.383), H. Vollmer *ibid.*, XXXIII, 1939, p.440), E. Bénézit, *Dictionnaire des Peintres*, 1955 and 1976 (*ad vocem*, but P122 also appeared under Largillierre), Cailleux 1971, Ingamells (*Summary Illustrated Catalogue of Pictures*, 1979, pp.246–7) and M.N. Rosenfeld (*Largillierre*, exh. cat., Montreal, 1981, p.81). Largillierre was proposed in 1783, 1835–7 and in the 1871 and 1890 Inventories (see Provenance and Exhibitions), in all previous editions of this catalogue (though with qualification in 1928 and 1968), by Dacier 1920 and 1922, by Constable 1922 and 1923, and by Lastic – see References General and *Minneapolis Institute of Arts Bulletin*, LXIII, 1976–7, p.83 n.19 (suggesting the furniture in P122 might be identified in Largillierre's *déposition* for the sumptuary law of 1700, cf. NAAF, 1ère, III, 1874–5, p.224), *L'Oeil*, 323, June 1982, p.30, and *Revue de l'Art*, 61, 1983, p.74. An attribution to Largillierre was criticised by L. Réau, *Histoire de la peinture française au XVIIIe siècle*, I, 1925, p.56 n.2; Pascal 1928 (*'la technique sèche, dure et surtout la mollesse cotonneuse des figures ne permettent que bien difficilement – étant donnée l'importance des personnages - d'attribuer à Largillierre cette oeuvre de second plan'*), and Maumené and d'Harcourt 1931 (*'attribué sans preuves à N. de Largillierre . . . nous repoussons l'attribution . . . que rien n'autorise à maintenir'*).

[16] See References General; Rosenfeld (BSHAF, forthcoming) also accepts this negative view.

[17] 64 × 81, illus. and discussed by Lastic, *L'Oeil*, 323, June 1982, p.28, as *Inconnue et ses enfants*, c.1705–10, and *ibid.*, 365, December 1985, pp.39, 41, 44, as *La marquise de Noailles avec ses deux filles*, c.1699; see also Ingamells 1983, p.95 and fig.40. It is perhaps of better quality than P122.

[18] This episode was first mentioned by C. Mauricheau-Beaupré, BSHAF 1923, p.72. M. C. Michel generously provided me with transcripts of the relevant documents from the Archives Nationales (also published in part by Lastic 1985). On 27 August 1755 Lesseville offered P122 to Marigny describing it as having been in his possession *'depuis du tems'* and attributed by *'plusieurs peintres'* to F. de Troy [Arch. Nat. 0^1 1908(2), no.75]. On 20 October 1755 C.-N. Cochin, writing also on behalf of Silvestre and van Loo, reported on P122 to Marigny, *directeur des Bâtiments*: *'Nous le croyons de M. De Troy le père: il représente le Roy Louis quatorze, M. Le Dauphin son fils, et M. Le Duc de Bourgogne, père du Roy; on y voit aussy Mme de Ventadour et un jeune Prince enfant qui pourroit être le Roy regnant, quoique l'âge de trois à quatre ans qu'il paroist avoir, s'accorde mal avec les dattes de la mort de ces Princes. Ce tableau est beau et bien conservé, la couleur en est vigoureuse et les étoffes belles. Ce qui peut diminuer de son mérite, c'est que les principales testes sont copiées et qu'elles se sentent de la servitude qu'entraine après soy la nécessité d'imiter une ressemblance. Ce tableau peut interesser par la réunion de la famille Royale, dont cependant les portraits particuliers et originaux doivent être à Versailles. Nous croyons qu'il peut avoir été fait depuis la Mort de la plus part des personnes qui y sont représentées et qu'ainsy on a pû rassembler ces portraits sans observer exactement le rapport des Ages. Dans ce câs le jeune enfant pourroit être le Roy Louis quinze, ce qui augmenteroit l'interêt du tableau qui nous a parû plus important par ces motifs que par sa beauté réelle. Sy le Roy veut l'acquérir, nous croyons pouvoir l'estimer 2000 ou 2400 livres au plus'* [Arch. Nat. 0^1 1908(2), no.96]. Marigny wrote to Lesseville on 4 November 1755 declining his offer (*idem*, no.100).

[19] Cf. *Journal des Débats* 1836: *'On nous a dit que cette peinture appartenait au commencement de ce siècle, au prince de Salm-Salm, qui en fit cadeau à un jurisconsulte célèbre, dont les conseils et les soins lui avaient été utiles dans le gain d'un procès considérable. Ce jurisconsulte, M. de Mirbel* [sic], *conserva toute sa vie cette peinture qui par succession tomba en partage à l'une de ses petites nièces, à qui il appartient aujourd'hui'*. Lastic 1985, p.39, recounts that in 1772 Mirbeck had successfully negotiated for prince Salm-Salm the free passage of goods across the frontiers of Salm Salm, a tiny principality in Lorraine belonging to the Holy Roman Empire.

[20] As recounted by Lastic 1985, pp.39–40 (quoting Archives du Louvre, P5 and P30).

[21] *Ibid.*

[22] A copy of this euphoric certificate was printed with the *affiche* for the 1837 exhibition, examples of which, in French and English, were formerly affixed to the stretcher of P122:

> *Nous soussignés, certifions que* le tableau *que nous avons vu chez Mme Huper, née Josset de St. Julien, demeurant île St.-Louis, rue Poultier, No 14, et représentant* Louis XIV *en pied, dans la galerie de Versailles, entouré d'une partie de sa famille, est de la plus grande beauté, et que* Largillière *s'est placé par cette admirable production à côté de* Rubens *et de* Vandick; *que ce chef d'oeuvre est du plus grand prix et digne d'orner un musée . . . /* VIGÉE LE BRUN, *Baron* GROS, HORACE VERNET, KINSON, ALFRED JOHANNOT, ALEXANDRE LENOIR, *créateur du musee des monuments français.* HOUCHETOULE *et* HENRY, *experts du musée royal. / Paris, le 5 juin 1835.* (this date was incorrectly given as 25 June in previous editions of this catalogue).

Early in June 1835 (*'environ quinze jours avant* [*la*] *mort* [*du baron Gros*]', i.e. about 10 June), Mme. Vigée Le Brun told a dinner party *'qu' elle était allé voir, ce jour même, dans une maison de l'île Saint-Louis, un beau tableau de Largillière* [P122] *et elle exprimait, en peintre dont l'esprit égale le talent, son admiration pour cette oeuvre presque entièrement ignorée'* (quoted in J. Tripier-Le-Franc, *Baron Gros*, 1880, p.517, as indicated by Lastic 1985, pp.42, 45 n.5).

23 When listed in Lord Hertford's Paris collection by W. Bürger, 'Les Collections Particulières', *Paris Guide*, 1867, I, p.538 (*'Largillière'*).

24 Lord Hertford was in London 1848–51 and he then brought over those pictures previously acquired in Paris which, therefore, generally appear in the Hertford House inventory of 1870.

25 This exhibition was devised by Pahin de la Blancherie, 'a businessman of dubious character', and all the exhibits were, apparently, for sale (cf. Cailleux 1971, p.xiii; Lastic 1985, p.38). For Mirbeck, see also Dacier 1922.

26 A review of the Paris exhibition, signed A. Lenoir (cf. note 2) and headed *Variétés/Exposition du tableau de Largillière*, was pasted to the stretcher of P122: *'Ce chef-d'oeuvre d'art, et nous dirons presque ce monument historique, est maintenant en la possession de Mme Hupper de Saint-Julien, nièce de M. de Saint-Laurent, qui escorta Louis XVI à Varennes, et qui, à ce titre, fut guillotiné pendant la terreur. C'est le dernier débris de sa fortune et l'unique espoir de sa famille'*; the review ended by quoting another certificate (a variant of that quoted under note 22 above) by Henry, dated 25 September 1835 (quoted in full in previous editions of this catalogue). It is perhaps significant that the *Journal des Débats* 1836 concluded its review by expressing the hope that P122 would be acquired by the Crown or the State, *'et à ces voeux nous joignons l'espérance que ceux qui possèdent ce tableau ne tomberont pas dans la faute trop commune d'élever leurs prétentions si haut qu'il est assez ordinairement impossible de les satisfaire'*.

27 Lastic 1985, p.45 n.3, identifies the author as E.-J. Delécluze (*'sous cette initiale il est aisé de reconnaître l'ancien élève de David . . .'*).

French School early 19th century

P599 *Charles Joseph, prince de Ligne*

Powdered wig, wearing the uniform of a Marshal in the Austrian army; white coat with gold lapels, red trimming and gold buttons, and the cross of the Order of Maria Theresa.

Canvas, relined 19 × 15

A diagonal tear runs down to the left of the head and there is a damaged area above the head to the right. The edges are abraded and the varnish discoloured.

Charles Joseph, prince de Ligne (1735–1814); born in Brussels, a distinguished officer with the Austrian army (until 1790), courtier and wit of European renown, and author of numerous volumes of memoirs. His country seat was the Château of Beloeil, near Ath in Belgium; he was elected *chevalier* of the Order of the Golden Fleece in 1772 and *commandeur* of the Order of Maria Theresa in 1789.

P599, a vigorous sketch, appears to date from the earlier nineteenth century and probably derives from an unknown portrait of c.1795 (see below); in execution it may be compared with the copy of the Reynolds portrait of the duc d'Orléans by Roqueplan, P603 in this Collection. No other version of the portrait is known; it shows the sitter apparently a little older than in his portrait by Leclercq of c.1790 (Beloeil),[1] but without the Golden Fleece. The likeness compares closely with that of a plaque formerly in the collection of the duc de Clary,[2] and the uniform is similar to that in the Leclercq portrait. A mid-nineteenth century inscription, *verso*, reads: *le prince de Ligne,/esquisse peinte au château de Beloeil/par* [*Greuze*? erased] *Gainsborough* [added].

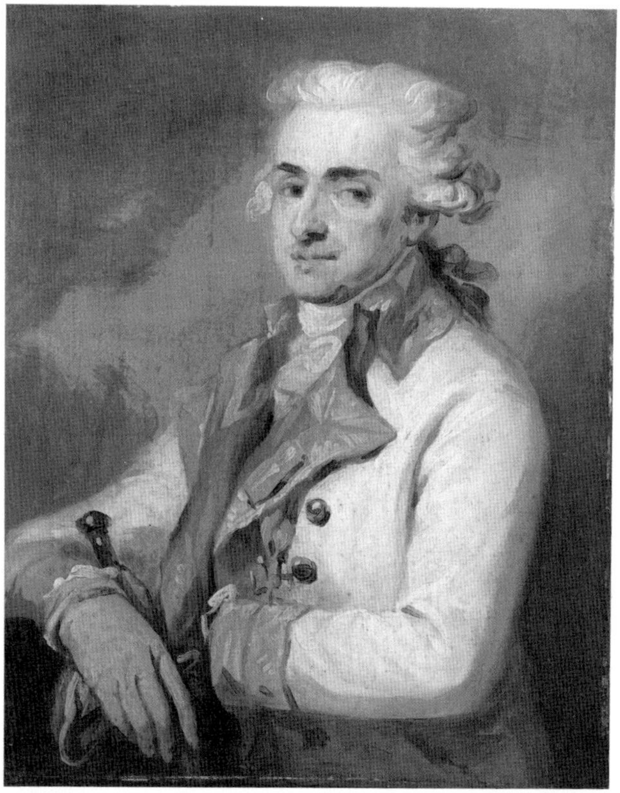

P599

Provenance

Acquired by the 4th Marquess of Hertford; rue Laffitte inventory 1871 (707, '*Gainsborough, Le prince de Ligne*'); Hertford House inventory 1890 as unknown artist.

Exhibition

Bethnal Green 1872–5 (16, unknown, *Prince de Ligne*).

[1] Exh. *La Toison d'Or*, Bruges, 1962, no.249; showing the Golden Fleece and the Cross of Maria Theresa.

[2] Illus. E. Benedikt, *Karl Josef fürst von Ligne, ein genie des Lebens*, 1936, f.p.96. Other portraits of de Ligne include a whole-length by Grassi of 1807 (illus. de Ligne, *Fragments de l'histoire de ma vie*, 1928 ed., I, front.), a bust by J.-B. Isabey of 1814 (illus. *ibid.*, II, front.), and a miniature showing him in old age (illus. Benedikt, *op. cit.*, f.p.272).

Jean-Baptiste Greuze (1725–1805)

Born on 21 August 1725 in Tournus (Saône-et-Loire), he studied under C. Grandon at Lyon before moving c.1750 to Paris. His studies at the Académie were desultory, but he was *agréé* in 1755 with *La lecture de la Bible* (Paris, private collection) which attracted attention in the Salon that year. In 1755–7 his patron Louis Gougenot, abbé de Chezal-Benoît, took him to Italy where Marigny also favoured him with two commissions from Mme. de Pompadour and where he painted *La paresseuse Italienne* (Hartford) and *Les oeufs cassés* (see Appendix III, no.78), both of which were praised at the 1757 Salon. In 1759 he married Anne-Gabrielle Babuti whose extravagance and infidelity were to cause him much hardship. His moral genre scenes, combining a topical *sensibilité* with the domesticity of seventeenth-century Dutch masters, attracted Diderot's praise at successive Salons: '*c'est la peinture morale ... le pinceau n'a-t-il pas été assez et trop longtemps consacré à la débauche et au vice? Ne devons-nous pas être satisfait de le voir concourir enfin avec la poésie dramatique à nous toucher, à nous instruire, à nous corriger et à nous inviter à la vertu?*'[1] By 1769 he had also shown some distinguished portraits and established a Russian clientele, but in that year his exhibited *morceau de réception* (eight years overdue), the ambitious *poussiniste* history *The Emperor Severus reprimanding his son Caracalla* (Louvre), was much criticised and he was *reçu* only as a *peintre de genre*. He consequently withdrew from the Salon for thirty years, exhibiting privately in his Louvre studio. In the 1770s he achieved a marked commercial success with engravings of his subject pictures, and by the end of the decade he was turning increasingly to painting languid *têtes d'expression* (of which the 4th Marquess of Hertford became an uncritical admirer). In 1792 he painted Napoleon as an artillery Captain (whole-length at Versailles), and in 1793 he joined the *Commune des Arts*, directed by Restout and David. He finally divorced his wife the same year. He exhibited again at the Salon in 1800, 1801 and 1804 and died in Paris on 21 March 1805. His career had been hampered both by his wife and by his inordinate vanity; '*c'est un excellent artiste*', wrote Diderot, '*mais une bien mauvaise tête*'.[2]

[1] *Salon de 1763* (Diderot *Salons*, ed. J. Seznec, I, 1975, p.233).
[2] Diderot to Falconet, 15 August 1767 (*Correspondance*, ed. G. Roth, VII, 1962, p.98).

Abbreviations

Brookner 1956	A. Brookner, 'Jean-Baptiste Greuze', *The Burlington Magazine*, XCVIII, 1956, pp.157–62 and 192–9
Brookner 1972	A. Brookner, *Greuze; the rise and fall of an eighteenth-century phenomenon*, 1972
MM	J. Martin and Ch. Masson, *Catalogue raisonné de l'oeuvre peint et dessiné de J.-B. Greuze*, 1908
Munhall	E. Munhall, *Jean-Baptiste Greuze*, exhibition catalogue, Hartford, San Francisco, Dijon, 1977
Smith	J. Smith, *Catalogue raisonné of the Works of the most eminent Dutch, Flemish and French Painters*, VIII, 1837 (numbers refer to the catalogue of Greuze's paintings, pp. 400–44)
Smith, *Supplement*	*Supplement* to the above catalogue, 1842 (numbers refer to the catalogue of Greuze's paintings, pp. 809–12)

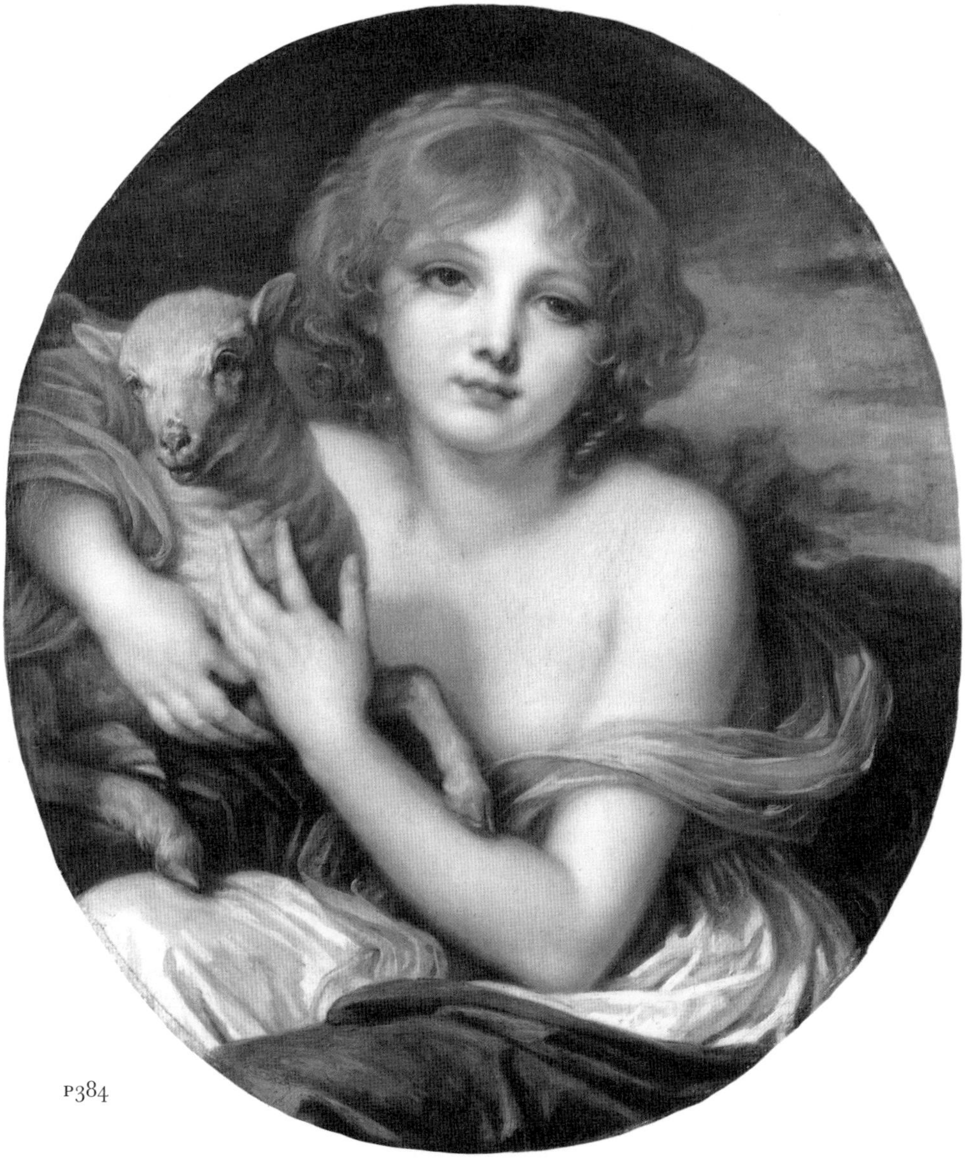

P384

P384 *Innocence*

Fair hair dressed with a pale red ribbon, blue eyes, wearing a white shift with a purple drape.

Mahogany panel 63 × 53 × 0.6 oval

Small losses have been retouched on her upper arm, left breast, chin and left cheek. There are traces of reticulated bitumen below her left wrist and arm, and a shrinkage craquelure by her left shoulder. The edges are knocked in places. *Pentimenti* suggest the hair spread further to the left above the lamb. The varnish is discoloured. The *verso* is covered with a rough canvas scrim.[1]

The subject was described by Mantz as combining '*la précoce coquetterie de la femme avec la naïveté de l'enfance*'.[2] At least two other Greuze compositions show a girl holding a lamb.[3]

Brookner (1972, p.128) suggested that P384 belonged in technique to the 1790s; the first owner died in 1794 (see Provenance). Despite the reservations expressed in previous editions of this catalogue, there is no doubt that P384 is the prime version of the subject from the Pourtalès collection (see notes 1 and 8). Lady Dilke's exaggeration of the price P384 fetched at that sale lent it an added attraction in the later nineteenth century.[4]

Drawings

Compositional studies in an anon. sale, Paris, 18 March 1857 (57), and formerly in the Hulot collection (photograph in the Bibliothèque Nationale listed by MM under 469).

Engravings

A. Louis 1852; D.-J. Ruyter; H. Garnier 1865 (for the *Gazette des Beaux-Arts*).

Copies/Versions

DOUAI Tesse sale, 10–15 February 1913 (8); 45 × 38, bust length.
HARTFORD Wadsworth Atheneum; pastel 67.3 × 47 oval; copy after Greuze, ex coll. B. Knower.
NEW YORK F. Mont 1949; 43 × 30.5, half-length version without the lamb, called Greuze; ex coll. von Weinberg, Frankfurt.
Sotheby's Arcade Auction, 9 December 1988 (82); panel 50.2 × 41, oval, half-length, without the lamb.
PARIS de Curel sale, 3 May 1918 (38); 65 × 54 oval, weak copy sold as ex colls. Pourtalès, Clery and Turenne d'Aynac;[5] probably the picture with J.-O. Leegenhoek, Paris, 1951.
RINGWOOD Hampshire, private collection; oval, a less finished version with the mouth more pursed and the elbow placed lower.[6]

A *Jeune fille tenant un agneau entre ses bras, esquisse avancée* was in the *veuve* Dupont sale, Paris, 28 December ff. 1807 (67); probably the same picture in the Didot sale, Paris, 28 March ff. 1814 (45, '*Etude de jeune fille tenant un chevreau dans ses bras. Figure à mi-corps. Elle a la gorge et les bras nus et est coiffée d'un petit bonnet. Il existe des Figures de Greuze plus terminées, mais il n'en est pas de plus séduisantes*').

A late-nineteenth-century Berlin porcelain plaque reproducing P384 was sold Sotheby's Belgravia, 27 July 1972 (276).

Provenance

C.-N. Duclos-Dufresnoy (1733/4–94), *notaire*; his sale, Paris, 2nd day, 19 August 1795 (13, '*Une jeune Fille assise & vue à mi-corps, tenant dans ses bras un Agneau, symbole de l'innocence . . . B* [*ois*]. *forme ovale* [62 × 50]'), 25,600 fr. *en assignats*; the comte de Pourtalès-Gorgier (1776–1855) by 1841;[7] his sale, Paris, 8th day, 27 March 1865 (264, '*. . . connue sous le nom de l'*Innocence, *Ovale, Toile* [60 × 51]'), bt. van Cuyck for the 4th Marquess of Hertford, 100,200 fr.;[8] rue Laffitte inventory 1871 (710, '*Petite fille à l'agneau*'); Hertford House inventory 1890.

Exhibition

Bethnal Green 1872–5 (447, *Innocence*).

References General

Smith, no.35; MM469.

[1] Doubtless the reason why P384 was described as on canvas in the Pourtalès catalogue (see note 7) and sale, see Provenance.

[2] P. Mantz, *Gazette des Beaux-Arts*, 1ère, XVIII, 1865, p.113.

[3] *L'Amitié* (illus. Ch. Normand, *Greuze*, 1892, p.101, an adaptation of the portrait of the comtesse Mollien at Baltimore, cf. Munhall, no.106), and *Girl with a Lamb* (National Gallery, London, no.1154).

[4] Lady Dilke (as 'E.F.S.P.', i.e. Mrs. Pattison), 'Greuze', *Encyclopaedia Britannica*, 9th ed., XI, 1880, p.189, stated that P384 fetched 1,000,200 fr. at the Pourtalès sale; the statement remained in the 11th edition, 1910. It so impressed Conan Doyle that in *The Valley of Fear* (part I, *Strand Magazine*, September 1914) he placed a Greuze in Moriarty's study as evidence of ill-gotten wealth, allowing Holmes to discourse on P384 at the Pourtalès sale.

[5] This provenance was the subject of a law suit in Paris in 1920.

[6] Cf. Waagen IV, p.369; illus. *The Burlington Magazine*, IV, 1904, p.21.

[7] Cf. J.-J. Dubois, *Description des tableaux . . . de M. le comte de Pourtalès-Gorgier*, 1841, p.59, no.183 (as *toile*, 60 × 50.5).

[8] The National Gallery, London, copy of the Pourtalès sale catalogue records van Cuyck buying for Hertford, and Lord Ward as the underbidder. The *Chronique des Arts*, 16 April 1865, p.142, corrected a previous statement that P384 had been bought by a Rothschild. That P384 was the Pourtalès picture is absolutely proved by comparing it with the photograph of the latter published by Goupil in 1863 (*Souvenirs de la Galerie Pourtalès*, pl.31); it is clear that the Pourtalès picture is on panel and the surfaces match exactly in condition.

P388 *Psyche*

Red hair dressed with a blue ribbon set with pearls, wearing a blue-grey drape trimmed with gold over a white dress. Signed, *verso*: *J. B. Greuze/1786.*

Mahogany panel 44.4 × 37.8 × 1.2[1]

The edges are abraded and the varnish is much discoloured. The *verso* is covered with a rough canvas scrim.

Psyche, deserted by her lover Cupid (Apuleius, *The Golden Ass* IV–VI); '*cette victime . . . incline tristement la tête . . . avec tous les signes d'une douleur muette*'.[2]

The Patureau sale catalogue of 1857 suggested that P388 showed Greuze '*élevé à la hauteur du Corrège*'; Brookner considers it belongs to his most mannered period.[3] Munhall (p.198) commented that P388 (and P440) probably derived from *L'innocence entraînée par les Amours* (Louvre; completed by 1786), where Martin and Masson (*loc. cit.*) and the Goncourts[4] had, unconvincingly, suggested the reverse. P388 originally had a pendant, *L'Amour* (see Provenance).[5]

Lithograph

W. Le Roy 1857 (for the Patureau sale catalogue).

Versions

BRUSSELS private collection 1961; pastel 51 × 30.5 oval, dated 176[?]6.
BULAWAYO private collection 1965; 40.6 × 33.
LONDON Wallace Collection, see P440.

Provenance

Painted for M. B.;[6] his sale, Paris, 3 December 1827 (19, *Psyche* with pendant *L'Amour*: '*ces deux précieux tableaux ont été faits par Greuze, pour le propriétaire de ce cabinet*'), 5,055 fr.; the comte de Perregaux (1785–1841); his sale, Paris, 8–9 December 1841 (53),[7] bt. Laneuville, 8,550 fr., for Théodore Patureau, Brussels; his sale, Paris, 2nd day, 21 April 1857 (52, '. . . *provenant des collections de M. B., Paris, 1827, et du feu M. le Comte Perregaux, 1841* . . .'), bt. by the 4th Marquess of Hertford, 27,700 fr.;[8] rue Laffitte inventory 1871 (665, '*La frayeur*'); Hertford House inventory 1890.

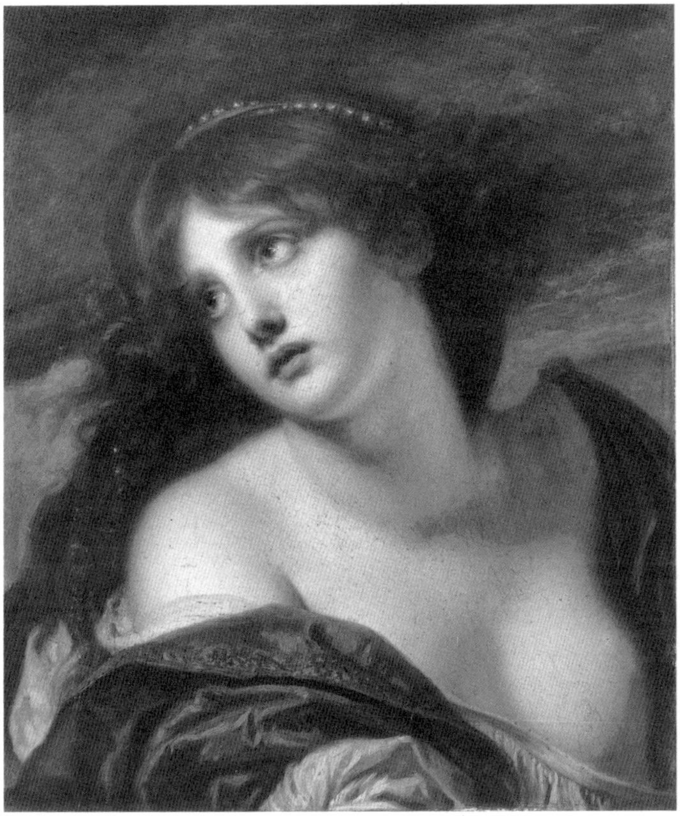

P388

Exhibition

Bethnal Green 1872–5 (?423, *A Magdalen*).

References General

Smith, no.72, and *Supplement*, no.8; MM513.

[1] The frame bears the label: CH. BOURDO [N?] /DOREUR/RUE DE MOSCOU 10B/PARIS.

[2] From the Perregaux sale catalogue 1841.

[3] Brookner 1956, p.196, and 1972, p.128: 'the Greuze girl . . . seems to have reached her peak in the late 1780s, for the three heads [P388, P398 and *La colombe retrouvée*, see P398] are more extreme than any other of this genre'.

[4] E. and J. de Goncourt, 'Greuze', *L'Art du dix-huitième siècle*, 1882–3 ed., p.348.

[5] MM413; M. B. sale, 1827, lot 19; Perregaux sale, 1841, lot 52, bt. for Napoleon III, 30,000 fr.; given by the Empress Eugénie to the Grand Duchess Maria of Russia. See also note 6.

[6] The catalogue of the B. sale stated that the collection had been formed in Paris some fifty years before, and that the owner had left the capital at the Revolution; he had commissioned four panels from Greuze, each the same size: *Amour* and *Psyche* (19), *Bacchante* (20), and *Head of a Girl* (21).

[7] P388 bears on the *verso* an inscription in red paint: T.P.*53*, which probably refers to the Perregaux sale, rather than to T. Patureau. Such an inscription does not recur on other paintings in the Wallace Collection from the Perregaux or Patureau collections.

[8] Lord Hertford told his agent Mawson he had acquired 'a pretty head of Greuze' at the Patureau sale, '& a esquisse by Do. [P407] – nothing wonderful but pretty' (*Letters*, no.77, p.98; Paris 28 April 1857).

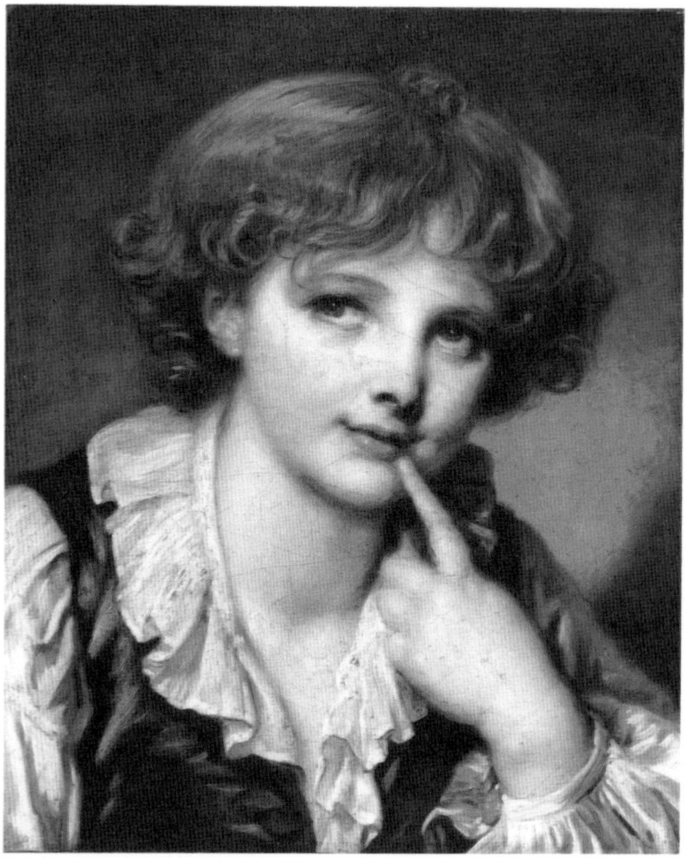

P396

P396 *Head of a Boy (Espièglerie)*

Chestnut hair, brown eyes, wearing a grey jacket over a white blouse.

Canvas, relined 39.5 × 31.2

There are small losses in the hair, above the head and in the bottom left corner, and retouched areas by his right ear, above the head to the left and on his right cheek. *Pentimenti* show changes to the left sleeve above the elbow, the left cuff and the bottom of the collar. The varnish is discoloured.

Dated c.1782 by Brookner (1972, p.126) and c.1775 by Burollet[1] together with portraits, apparently from the same model, in the Musée Cognacq-Jay[2] and at Montpellier.[3] The drawing of the hand is weak. P396 has been called the portrait of a girl (see Provenance and cf. P419). The title *Espièglerie* was invented by Phillips for the first edition of this catalogue in 1900.

Provenance
The prince de Beauvau sale, Paris, 21 April 1865 (5, '*Tête de jeune garçon . . . cette ravissante tête [a] autant de charme et de grâce que si c'était celle d'une jeune fille* . . ., 40 × 32'), bt. by the 4th Marquess of Hertford, 16,100 fr.; rue Laffitte inventory 1871 (369, '*L'Indécision*'); Hertford House inventory 1890.

Exhibition
Bethnal Green 1872–5 (either 384, 411, 442 or 443, each *Girl's Head*).

Reference General
MM975.

[1] H. Burollet, *Musée Cognacq-Jay, Peintures et dessins*, 1980, under no. 35.
[2] *Ibid.*; *Portrait d'un jeune garçon*, a copy in Glasgow Art Gallery (no. 433).
[3] *Le petit mathématicien*, illus. Brookner 1972, pl. 72.

P398 *The Souvenir (Fidelity)*

Fair hair dressed with a plum-coloured ribbon set with pearls, blue eyes, wearing a white dress with purple trimming and a golden yellow drapery; brown and white dog. Signed on the tree trunk, centre left: *Greuze*.

Canvas, relined 52.2 × 42.3

Craquelure around the mouth has been retouched. The varnish is discoloured.

P398 may be dated c.1787–9. It is one of a series of similar heads of which one in Berlin is dated 1787 and another in Moscow is dateable 1789 (see Versions).

Engraving
Benarth 1805.

Copy
PARIS private collection 1983; 55 × 46.5, copy by A. Vestier, the dog showing its tongue and with a central white patch.[1]

Versions
BERLIN Dahlem, Gemäldegalerie (no. 494C); 38 × 30, bust length, dated 16 July 1787.
LONDON Sotheby's, 28 March 1979 (45); panel 40 × 32.5 oval, a dove replacing the dog; ex Foxe sale, New York, 1 December 1942 (82).
MONTPELLIER Musée Fabre; 66 × 55, *La Prière du matin*, whole-length kneeling figure, the head similar to that of P398 (Brookner 1972, pl. 70).
MOSCOW Pushkin Museum; panel 46 × 37, *La colombe retrouvée*, as London version above and with stars around her head; painted for Prince Yussupov in 1789[2] (Brookner 1972, pl. 76).
PARIS Palais Galliera, 26 May 1972 (15); 40 × 32, bust length.
SIENA art market 1971; ex coll. Prince Paul of Yugoslavia.
UPTON HOUSE Warwickshire; 45 × 38, bust length.

Bust-length versions also appeared in the Demidoff sale, Paris, 21–2 February 1870 (123, *La Volupté*), 45 × 38, ex coll. Monville, and in the Schneider sale, Paris, 6–7 April 1876 (48), 40 × 32.

Provenance[3]
M. Saphorin, Vienna, 1805; a Polish nobleman, 1836, bt. Smith who sold it to Col. R.H. Fitzgibbon (1793–1864), later 3rd Earl of Clare; his sale, Christie's, 1st day, 17 June 1864 (32, *A young Girl caressing a Spaniel*), bt. Durlacher for the 4th Marquess of Hertford, 1,020 gn.; Hertford House inventory 1870.

Exhibitions
BI 1831 (92, *The Favourite*) lent Fitzgibbon; Bethnal Green 1872–5 (413, *Fidelity*).[4]

References General
Smith, no. 108; MM812.

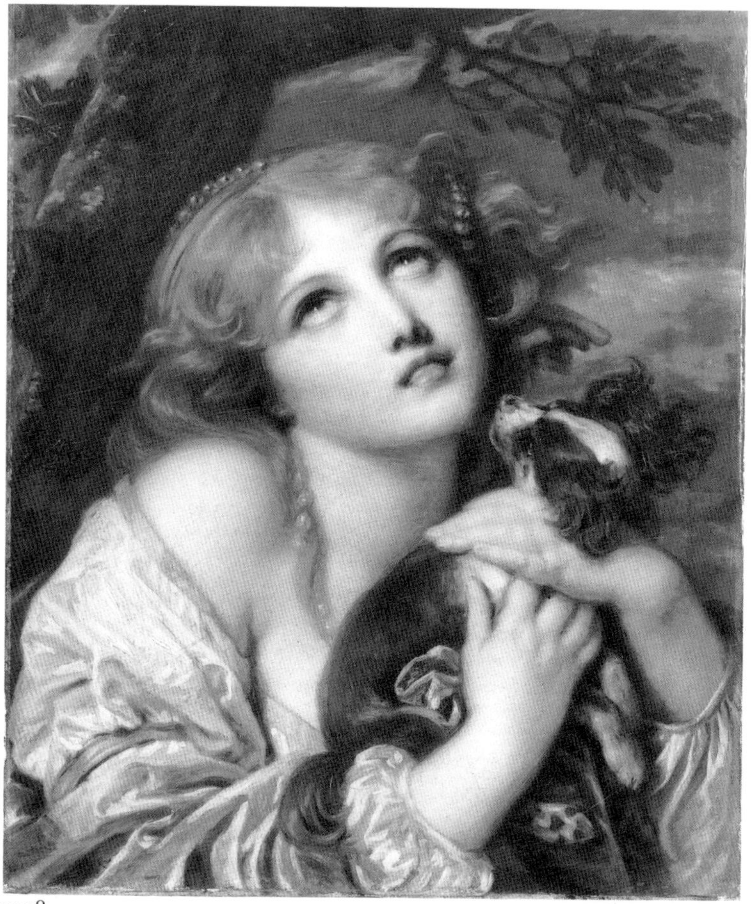

P398

[1] I am grateful to Mme. A.-M. Passez (letter on file dated 15 January 1983) for notice of Vestier's copy.

[2] Cf. Brookner 1956, p. 196; 1972, p. 126. It was the subject of a letter from Greuze to the Prince, dated Paris, 20 April 1790: '. . . *cette colombe, qu'elle presse contre son coeur si amoureusement, avec ses deux mains, n'est que l'image de son amant caché sous cet emblême; son âme est agitée d'un sentiment si doux et si pur que la femme la plus délicate la pourra regarder avec complaisance sans en être blessée. J'ai ajouté sur sa tête une couronne d'étoiles pour indiquer que le sentiment nous égale aux dieux pour un instant. C'est un grand tableau dans une petite toile*' (BSHAF 1922, p.398). See P421 for a similar coronet of stars.

[3] The pre-1837 provenance as recorded by Smith, *loc. cit.*

[4] At the close of the exhibition Alfred de Rothschild (letter of 31 March 1875, Wallace Collection archives) offered to exchange his Sèvres porcelain, for which he had paid £2,500, for P398, but Wallace (draft reply, *ibid.*) declined, explaining that he wished to keep his collection intact.

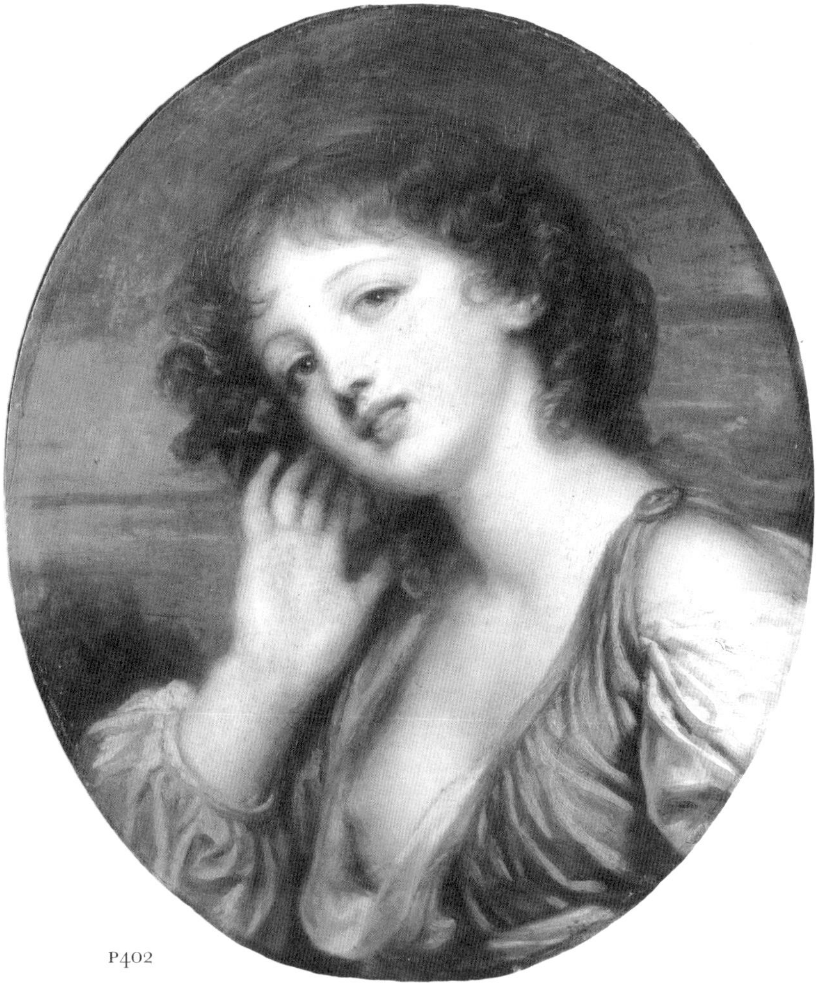

P402

P402 *The Listening Girl*

Auburn hair dressed with a red ribbon, wearing a gold-trimmed purple dress over a white chemise.

Mahogany panel 48.1 × 39.2 × 0.6 oval

There are some retouchings on the hand and patches of reticulated bitumen beneath the arm and in the hair. *Pentimenti* show the hand was further to the left and the hair spread higher and to the left. The edges are abraded. The varnish is much discoloured. The *verso* is covered with a rough canvas scrim.

Probably painted in the 1780s. The drawing of the fore-arm is particularly weak. The pose recalls Rembrandt's *Woman at her mirror* (Br. 387; Hermitage) and has been associated with Reynolds's *Self portrait as a deaf man* of c.1775 (Tate Gallery, no.4505).[1]

Provenance

J. Lafitte sale, Paris, 15 December 1834 (20, '*buste d'une jeune fille dont le regard paraît vague; elle porte la main pour recevoir sa tête légèrement inclinée; elle est coiffée en cheveux et négligement ajustée d'un vêtement qui laisse entrevoir une partie de sa poitrine*'), bt. Dubois, 6,709 fr.; the 4th Marquess of Hertford;[2] reframed in Hertford House 1859;[3] Hertford House inventory 1870.

Exhibition

Bethnal Green 1872–5 (see P396).

References General

Smith, no.83; MM828.

[1] Cf. E. Wind, *Journal of the Warburg and Courtauld Institutes*, II, 1939, p.185; he suggested P402 may have induced Reynolds to paint his self portrait, but if there is a connection it probably worked in reverse.

[2] A note by Murray Scott in the Wallace Collection archives alleges that Lord Hertford paid £600 (15,000 fr.) for P402, but he may have confused it with P396.

[3] Evans invoice.

P403 *Portrait of a Lady*

Brunette with brown eyes, dressed *à l'anglaise* with a black hat trimmed with blue, red and white plumes and a blue ribbon, a white dress with pink ribbons and a black shawl with lace trimming; her left elbow rests on a pale yellow cushion.

Canvas, relined 61 × 50.4

Cleaned by Byard in 1922 when the four corners, originally angled, were made up to right angles. It may once have been framed as an oval. The paint surface is worn and was heavily ironed in relining. There is a scratch behind the head, small losses on her right shoulder and left cheek, and a prominent shrinkage craquelure in the hair and shoulders. *Pentimenti* suggest the plumes were originally larger and that an alteration was made by her left arm. The varnish is discoloured.

P403 was exhibited in 1872 as a portrait of Sophie Arnould (1744–1802), and this title has been used in previous editions of this catalogue. It cannot, however, be retained. Costume and style indicate a date of c.1786,[1] yet it is unlikely that the sitter is aged forty. The most authentic portrait of Arnould, the marble bust by Houdon of 1775 now in the Louvre (which Lord Hertford had acquired seven weeks before P403, see P413 note 2), shows more gaunt features, incompatible with those seen in P403 ten years later. Lord Hertford kept P403 by his bed in the rue Laffitte,[2] which might indicate that he held it in some affection, but he called it simply a *portrait de jeune femme*; as such it had been sold in 1849 and 1858, described in 1867 (see note 2) and listed in 1871 (see Provenance).

For further discussion of Greuze portraits of Arnould, see P413.

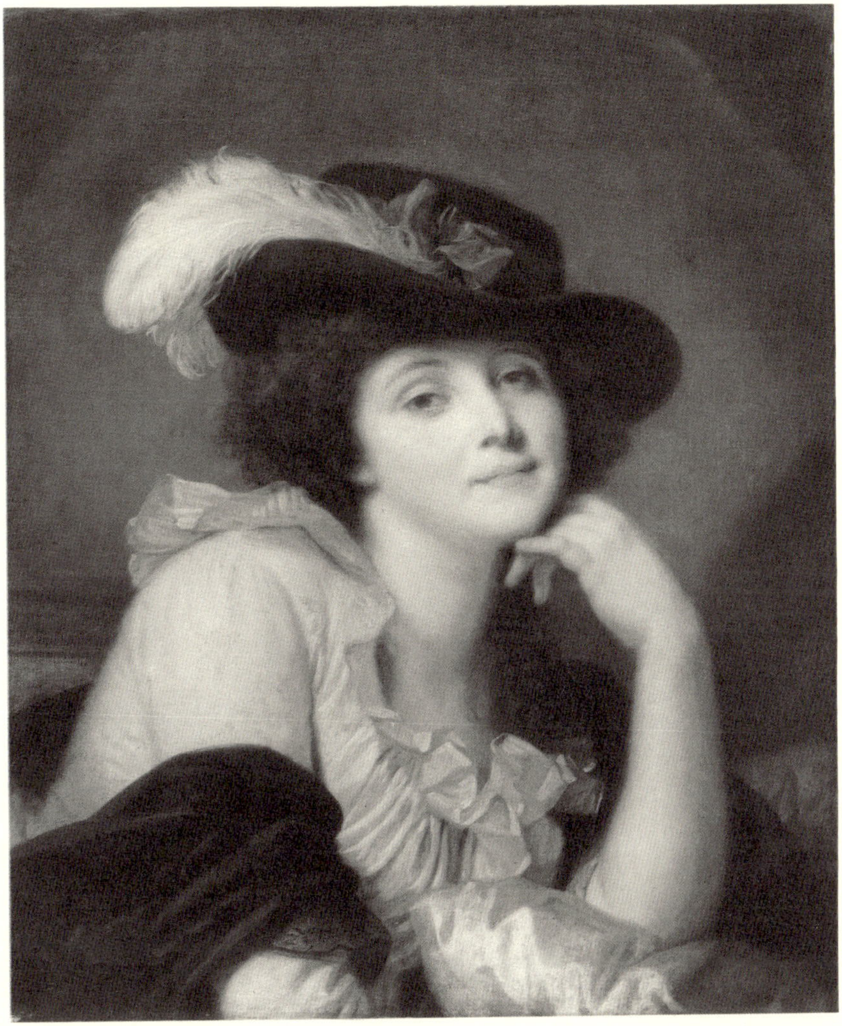

P403

Version

PARIS A. Rouart 1908; similar composition with different head, called a '*première idée*' for P403, but evidently not by Greuze.[3]

Provenance

W. Williams Hope (1802–55) of Rushton Hall, Northants., and Paris; his sale, Christie's, 3rd day, 16 June 1849 (100, *A Young Lady*), bt. in, 120 gn.; his sale, Paris, 11 May 1858 (17, *Portrait de jeune femme*), bt. by the 4th Marquess of Hertford, 5,600 fr.; rue Laffitte inventory 1871 (711, '*portrait de femme*'); Hertford House inventory 1890 as '*Portrait of a Lady*'.

Exhibition

Bethnal Green 1872–5 (410, *Sophie Arnould*).

Reference General

MM under 1054.

[1] Cf. Brookner 1956, p.196, 1972, p.127.

[2] W. Bürger, *Paris-Guide*, 1867, I, p.538, described a Reynolds portrait in Lord Hertford's bedroom (now identified as the Lawrence P41, see vol. I of this catalogue, p.119) '*ayant pour pendant, de l'autre côté d'un lit magnifique, une* Jeune Fille *de Greuze, accoudée sur un coussin; robe blanche et chapeau à plumes*'.

[3] Illus. *Les Arts*, 75, March 1908, p.12, and see p.10.

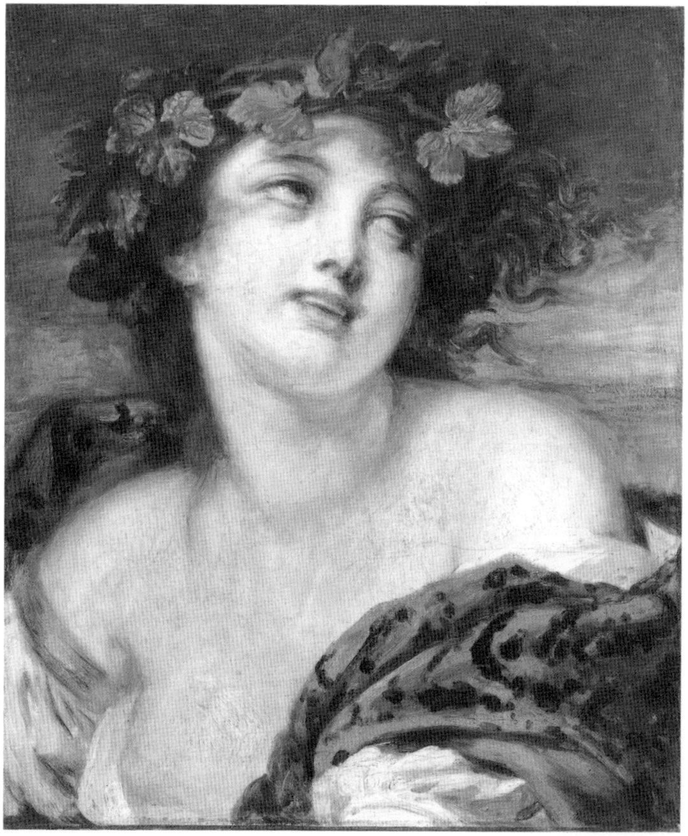

P407

P407 *Bacchante*

Vine leaves in her brown hair, brown eyes, wearing a leopard skin with purple and white drapes over her left arm.

Canvas, relined 45·7 × 37·3

There are retouchings on the shoulders, below the neck and to the right of the nose. The varnish is unevenly discoloured.

Bacchantes were the votaries of Bacchus, god of wine (cf. Boucher P487).

Probably painted in the late 1780s. The pose recurs in *L'Innocence entraînée par les Amours* (painted by 1786; Louvre) and *La réconciliation* (drawing of c. 1785; Phoenix Art Museum; Munhall, no.97).

Lithograph

W. Le Roy 1857 (for the Patureau sale catalogue).

Copies/Versions

BERLIN van Diemen sale, 13 October 1937 (125); 40 × 32, with different costume.
Lepke, 24–6 February 1925 (166); miniature oval copy, like the Waddesdon version below.
EAST LOTHIAN private collection; 41.3 × 32.3, looking to front, without leopard skin; exh. RA 1889 (109).[1]
LONDON Christie's, 30 October 1981 (146); 39.4 × 31.1, dated 17[63?]; with different costume; ex Christie's 12 December 1980 (42).
Knoedler c.1930; 46 × 36 oval, wearing white gauze dress with collar, pose as East Lothian version above; ex coll. Ongaria, Venice.
J. F. Minken 1949; as East Lothian version above, after Greuze; possibly the picture with Jourado, London, 1932.
Sabin 1938; 38 × 30.5, sketch resembling Waddesdon version below; exh. BI 1866 (13); ex coll. Salaman.
Wallace Collection (M14); miniature by Augustin 1799, resembling the East Lothian version above and probably after the *Bacchante* by Greuze in the Augustin sale, Paris, 19 December 1839 (1).
Wallace Collection (M304); miniature by Sicardi 1788, resembling the Waddesdon version below, once described as *Mme. Cail en Bacchante*.
PARIS Say sale, 30 November 1908 (10); 42 × 33, as East Lothian version above.
Schlichting collection, formerly; 38 × 32.5, with different costume.
RICHMOND Virginia, private collection 1968; pastel 51 × 46, copy.
TROYES Musée des Beaux-Arts; 44 × 41.5, as East Lothian version above; ex colls. Thomassin and Millard.
VIENNA Akademie (no.843); 46 × 36, as Waddesdon version below.
WADDESDON Manor; 45.7 × 38.1, looking slightly to right; ex coll. Demidoff; engr. Rajon.[2]

A *Bacchante*, panel 44 × 37, was in the M. B. sale Paris, 3 December 1827 (20), see P388 note 6.

Provenance

Dubois sale, Paris, 7 December ff. 1840 (122), 3,510 fr., bt. Théodore Patureau, Brussels; his sale, Paris, 1st day, 20 April 1857 (53, as '*collection de M. Du Bois, 1840*'), bt. du Blaisel for the 4th Marquess of Hertford, 17,100 fr.;[3] rue Laffitte inventory 1871 (664); Hertford House inventory 1890.

Exhibition

Bethnal Green 1872–5 (385).

References General

MM425.

[1] Illus. *The Burlington Magazine*, LXXIX, 1941, p.51.

[2] See E. K. Waterhouse, *The James A. de Rothschild Collection at Waddesdon Manor, The Paintings*, 1967, pp.236–7, no.106.

[3] See P388 note 9.

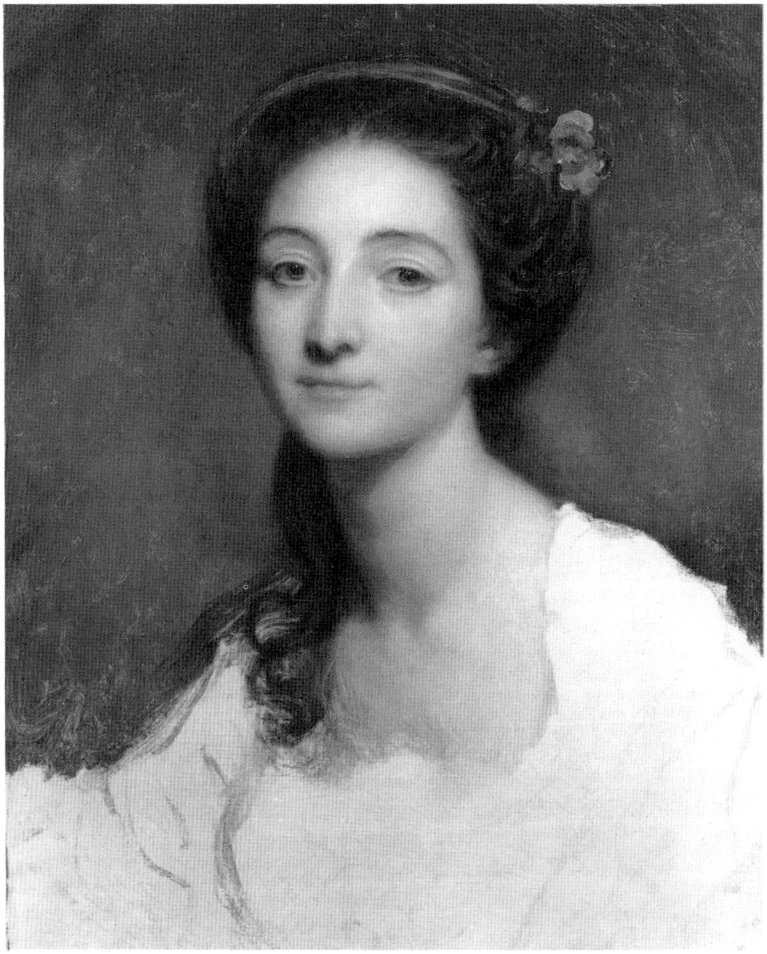

P413

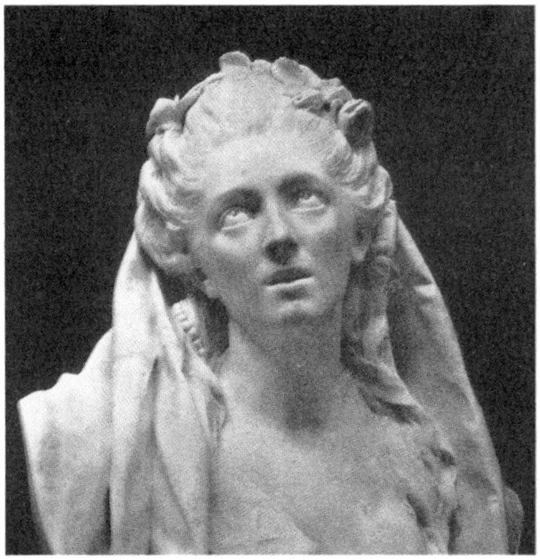

J.-A. Houdon: *Sophie Arnould as Iphigenia*, 1775, marble. Louvre.

P413 *Portrait of a Lady, called Sophie Arnould*

Chestnut hair dressed with a blue ribbon and white roses; blue-grey eyes; only the head is finished, the lower area showing the white ground.

Canvas, relined 49.6 × 39.3

Cleaned by Lank in 1988 when overpainting in the lower area (summarily indicating the folds of a dress) was removed. There are damages in the centre of the lower area, at the bottom of the neck, and to the left of the head. The top corners were originally angled and have been made up with separate pieces of canvas.

P413 was bought in 1843 as the portrait of the actress, singer and wit, Sophie Arnould (1744–1802), and it was exhibited as such in 1847 (see Exhibitions).[1] The head bears some resemblance to the marble bust of her as Iphigenia executed by Houdon in 1775 (also owned by Lord Hertford)[2] and to her portrait engraved by Bourgeois de la Richardière after Quentin de Latour,[3] but the identity was questioned during the 1843 sale.[4] In 1848 P413 was brought by Lord Hertford from Paris to Hertford House, where it was listed as *Head of a Young Girl* (see Provenance); perhaps it was a confusion of this history which led to P403 by Greuze (q.v.) being called Sophie Arnould in 1872.

There is no contemporary record of Greuze having painted Sophie Arnould, but in 1773, which would also appear to be a reasonable date for P413, he dedicated to her the engraving of *La cruche cassée*. In the course of the nineteenth century several Greuze pictures came to be called Sophie Arnould, as follows:

1 Didot sale, Paris, 6 April ff. 1825 (143, '*L'Heure du Rendez-vous, Portrait de mademoiselle Arnoult . . . représentée en peu plus qu'en buste, la tête nue, un fichu de gaze noire sur les épaules, et une lettre à la main . . .* [43 × 36]').
2 Portrait exhibited at the Hôtel Pillet-Will, Chaussée d'Antin, 1848.[5]
3 Portrait exhibited RA 1892 (61) lent by the Earl of Normanton; 68 × 54.6, three-quarter length standing, holding a wreath of flowers above a lamb.[6]
4 See P403.

Of these the first and second remain untraced, the third appears to be a typical Greuze fancy picture of the 1790s, and the fourth is certainly not of Arnould.

Provenance

Mainnemare sale, Paris, 21 February 1843 (16, '*Portrait de Sophie Arnould . . . dont le buste n'est qu'à peine ébauché*'), bt. by the 4th Marquess of Hertford, 7,500 fr.;[7] reframed in Hertford House 1859;[8] Hertford House inventory 1870 as '*Head of a Young Girl*'.

Exhibitions

Bazar Bonne-Nouvelle, 1847 (*Sophie Arnould*) lent Hertford, see note 1; Bethnal Green 1872–5 (499, *Female portrait*).

Reference General

MM under 1054.

[1] When C. de Ris (*L'Artiste*, VIII, 1847, p.157) commented: '*Portrait de Sophie Arnoult . . . Le cou démesurément long et mal emmanché sur les épaules offre un commencement de flexion qui rappelle par trop celui du canard. Mais la tête est bien modelée et n'est pas peinte dans cette manière sèche et cotonneuse qui fait la triste originalité de Greuze. Ce portrait est loin de valoir celui de Wille, exposé l'an dernier au Bazar Bonne-Nouvelle, et qui fait partie, je crois, comme celui-ci, de la galerie du marquis d'Herford*'. In fact the portrait of Wille had been lent by Delessert (cf. Munhall, no.39).

[2] Bt. by Lord Hertford at the Véron sale, Paris, 22–3 March 1858 (64), 13,800 fr.; by descent to Murray Scott; bequeathed to Lady Sackville, who sold it to Seligmann; acquired by Edgar Stern, who bequeathed it to the Louvre in 1947. See *The Burlington Magazine*, XCII, 1950, p.172, and p.172, fig.25.

[3] Illus. A. Besnard, *La Tour*, 1928, fig.245.

[4] Cf. *Cabinet de L'Amateur*, II, 1843, p.157: '*il est au moins douteux que ce soit la tête de cette danseuse*'. It was perhaps also significant that P413 was omitted from the iconography of Arnould compiled by the Goncourts in 1857 (*Sophie Arnould*, 1893 ed., pp.305–10), but see also note 5 below.

[5] Goncourt, *op. cit.*, p.305: '*un portrait à l'huile de Sophie Arnould aurait été peint par Greuze . . . Ce portrait a figuré, en 1848, dans une exposition au profit des Artistes à l'hôtel Pillet-Will, Chaussée d'Antin*'. Might the authors have confused exhibitions of 1847 and 1848? In the 1922 edition of *Sophie Arnould* (ed. E. Bergerat), p.263 n., P403 (*sic*) was identified with this reference and illus. as the frontispiece.

[6] Illus. *The Burlington Magazine*, IV, 1904, p.20.

[7] Hertford's copy of the Mainnemare sale catalogue is now in the Wallace Collection library. Several of the prices are pencilled in, but at the end is the calculation of the cost of his purchases with the 5% buyer's premium. Apart from P413, they include works by Bonington (P273), Delaroche (P276, P604) and Vernet (see vol. I of this catalogue, p.22, and vol. II. pp.99, 114, 305 no.235).

[8] Evans invoice.

P415 *Girl with a gauze scarf*

Fair hair dressed with white roses and a pink ribbon, blue eyes; wearing a white gauze scarf, and a grey bodice with pink ribbons on the sleeves.

Canvas, relined 56.3 × 45.4 oval[1]

The rough edges of the original canvas were made up to 57 × 46 in the course of relining. There are several small losses: on the edge of the scarf to the left, in the bodice, in the background by the chin, above her right shoulder and above her left arm. A broad craquelure has been retouched in the face. The varnish is much discoloured.

Dated c.1770 by Brookner (1956, p.192; 1972, p.116). Though it is framed as the pendant to P419, P415 appears to be later; the size is different and the image less elaborate.

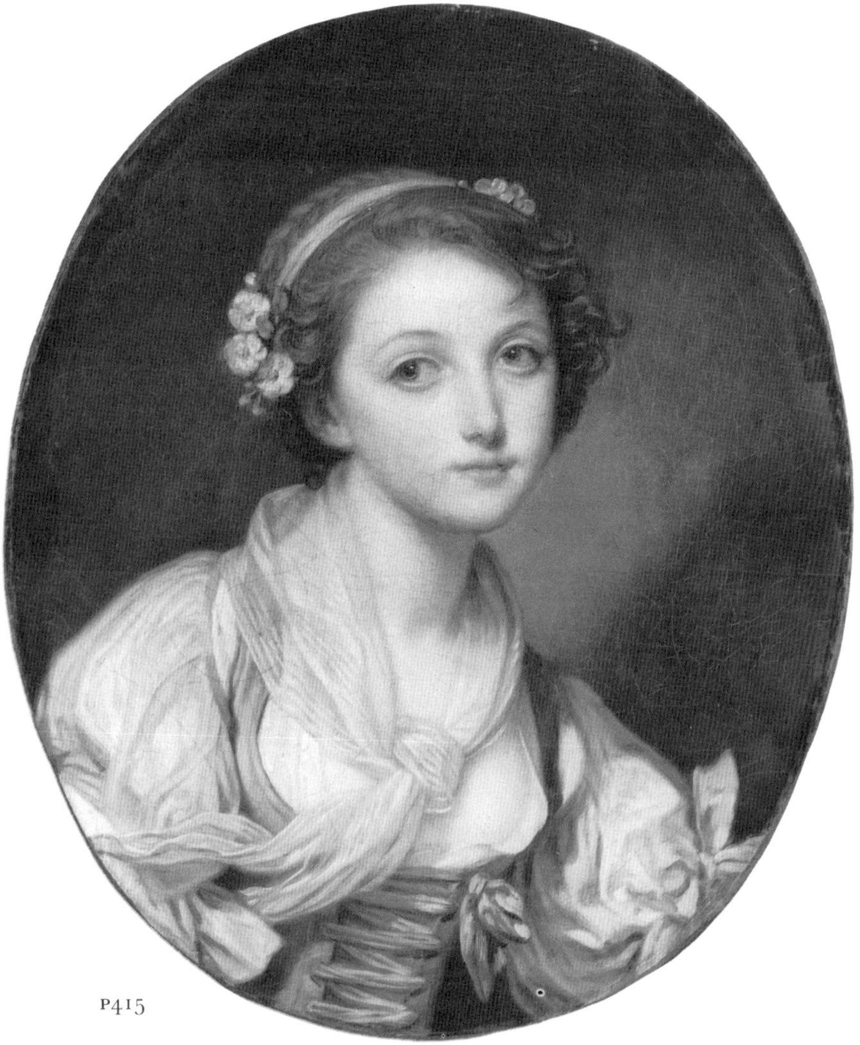

P415

Provenance

Acquired by the 4th Marquess of Hertford probably in Paris after 1851 together with P419;[2] rue Laffitte inventory 1871 (227); Hertford House inventory 1890.

Exhibition

Bethnal Green 1872–5 (see P396).

[1] The stretcher bears a label, *verso*: *ch[assis]* . . . *J. B. Greuze/* . . . *Jeune fille* (cf. P419).

[2] Since there is no evidence that Lord Hertford reframed P415 and P419, he probably acquired them in their present frames, as a pair.

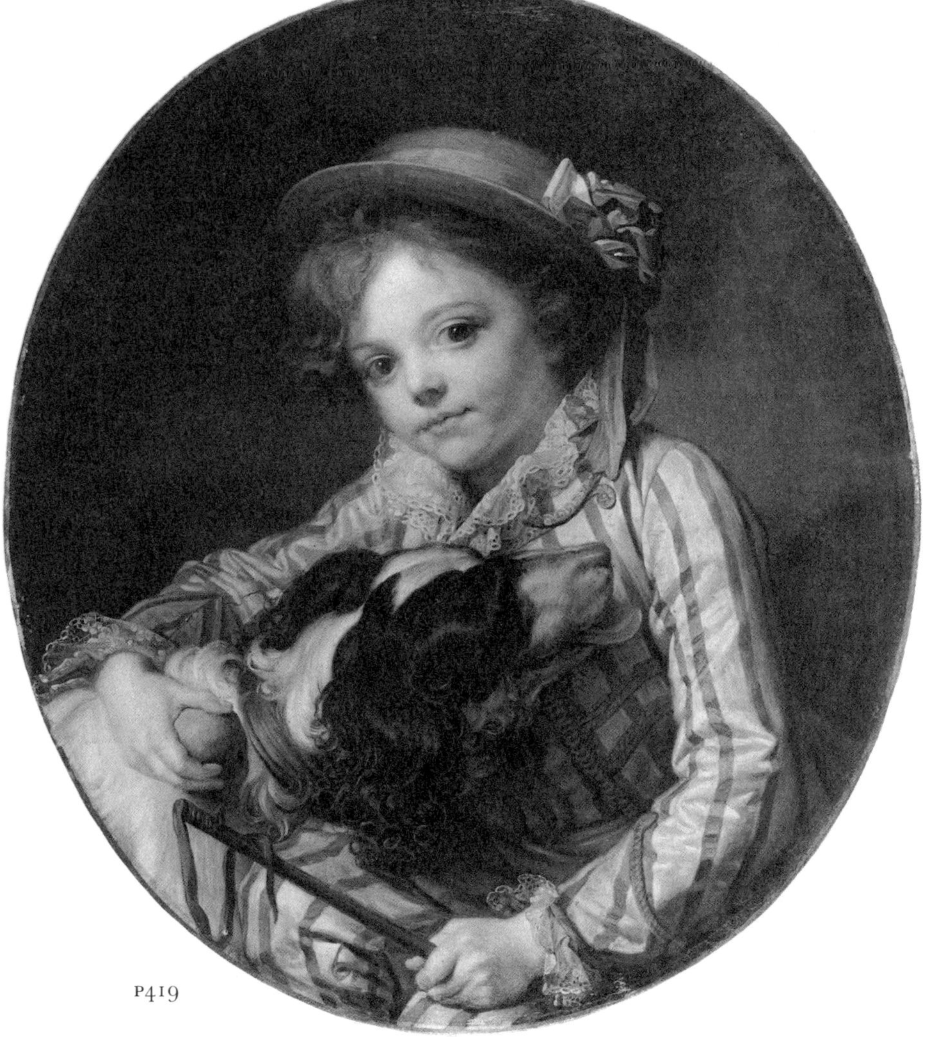

P419

P419 *Boy with a Dog*

Wearing a grey hat with a blue ribbon, a blue-striped golden-yellow suit with lace collar and cuffs and grey piping; holding a whip and a yellow ball; the dog is brown and white.

Canvas, relined 60 × 50.5 oval[1]

The edges of the original canvas are uneven and have been retouched. There are several greenish retouchings in the background area and small losses in, above, and to the left of the hat. Craquelure on his right hand has been retouched. There is a *pentimento* on the forearm of his left sleeve. The varnish is discoloured.

Dated c.1760 by Munhall.[2] P419 appears to be earlier than P415 which is framed as the pendant, although Brookner (1956, p.192; 1972, p.116) regarded them as companion pieces of c.1770. A version formerly with the baron de Castille was called a portrait of Edouard Froment de Castille, but P419 was engraved in 1779 as a genre scene (see Engraving).

Drawing

PARIS Charpentier, 21 March 1952 (40); compositional study within a painted oval frame; ex colls. Dupan, Walferdin, Courtois and Groult (MM317).

Engraving

C.-G. Schultz 1779, reversed.

Copies/Versions

LONDON Christie's, Pierpont Morgan sale, 3rd day, 26 June 1935 (539); miniature copy attributed to Greuze, called *A Boy;* catalogued in 1907 as *A Young Girl.*[3]
MOSCOW Arkangelskoye; 34 × 26, version with plain costume and without the left arm; ex coll. Yussupov (MM461).
PARIS Palais Galliera, 31 May 1972 (38); 49.5 × 39.5 rectangular, without left hand and part of right hand.
Petit, 22 November 1923 (47); 65 × 54 rectangular, a weak version extended below and right, called portrait of Edouard Froment de Castille; probably the picture ex colls. de Castille and Cazaigne (cf. MM under 460).
Mme. C. Lelong sale, 11–15 May 1903 (520); 64 × 52 as a portrait of Edouard Froment de Castille, but not the version sold in 1923, see above (MM1125).
WADDESDON Manor; 61 × 49.5, copy without the dog.[4]

Provenance

C.-N. Duclos-Dufresnoy (1733/4–94), *notaire;* his sale, Paris, 2nd day, 19 August 1795 (14, '*Un Enfant vû à mi-corps; coëffé d'un petit chapeau à rubans, vêtu d'un habit de Matelot, portant fraise & manchettes de dentelles, il tient d'une main un fouet & de l'autre une balle, & paroît jouer avec un épagneul appuyé sur ses genoux . . . T[oile] forme ovale* [59.4 × 53.3]'), 9,100 fr. *en assignats;* see P415 thereafter; rue Laffitte inventory 1871 (226).

Exhibition

Bethnal Green 1872–5 (448).

References General

Smith, no.36; MM under 460.

[1] The stretcher bears a label, *verso*: *chassis 3/No 5/ Greuze/L'Enfant au chien* (cf. P415).
[2] E. Munhall, *Baltimore Museum of Art News*, XXVI, 1962, p.21.
[3] G. Williamson, *Catalogue of Miniatures in the J. Pierpont Morgan Collection*, III, 1907, no.532.
[4] Cf. E.K. Waterhouse, *The James A. de Rothschild Collection at Waddesdon Manor, The Paintings*, 1967, p.238, no.108, as After Greuze.

P421 *Ariadne*

Auburn hair dressed with pearls, brown eyes, wearing a white shift with a plum-coloured drape.

Mahogany panel 49 × 42.8 × 1

The gesso preparation on the panel was unevenly applied, e.g. top right and in a semi-circular area bottom centre. The edges are abraded and show minor losses. *Pentimenti* show changes to the drapery at her breast (bottom centre) and her thumb. The varnish is much discoloured. The *verso* is covered with a rough canvas scrim.

The subject is taken from Ovid, *Metamorphoses* VIII, 169–82: Ariadne, daughter of King Minos, abandoned on the isle of Naxos by her lover Theseus after he had slain the Minotaur. The stars round her head refer, presumably, to the constellation Ariadne's Crown (and cf. P398 note 2).

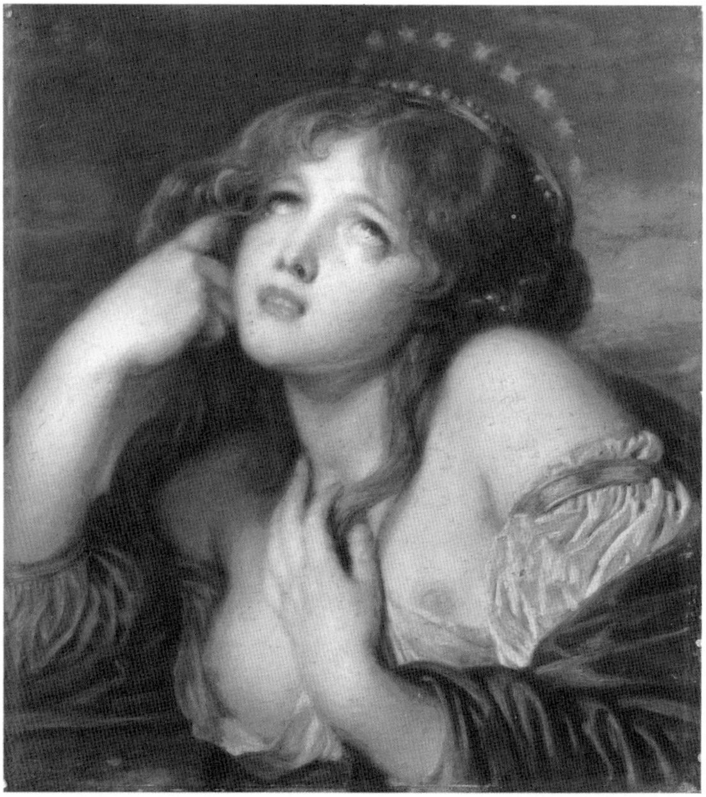

P421

One of Greuze's last works, P421 was probably the *Ariane dans l'île de Naxos* shown in the 1804 Salon.[1]

Version

PARIS Hulot sale, 9–10 May 1892 (153); pastel 40 × 34, a similar head but dressed as a bacchante.

Provenance

W. Williams Hope (1802–55) of Rushton Hall, Northants., and Paris; his sale, Christie's, 3rd day, 16 June 1849 (123), bt. Mawson for the 4th Marquess of Hertford, 530 gn.; reframed in Hertford House 1859;[2] Hertford House inventory 1870.

Exhibitions

Probably Salon 1804 (220), see above; Bethnal Green 1872–5 (374).

Reference General[3]

MM40.

1 Cf. Brookner 1972, p.87; Munhall, p.26.

2 Evans invoice.

3 Smith, no.112, described a similar picture, panel 58.4 × 43.2, as Erard collection 1832, 2,600 fr.; but there was no Greuze in the Erard sales of 1832 or 1833 (Lugt 12962, 13071 and 13350).

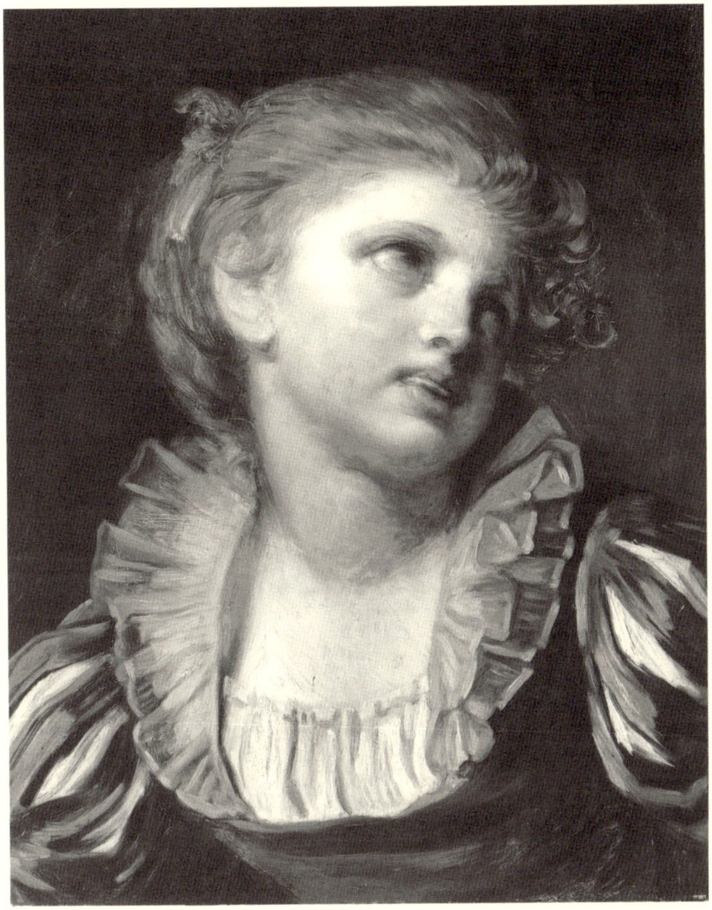

P425

P425 *Girl in a blue dress (L'espagnole)*

Fair hair dressed with a blue ribbon, grey eyes, wearing a blue dress with slashed sleeves.

Mahogany panel 40.5 × 31.8 × 0.3

Additional strips down each vertical edge bring the size to 40.5 × 33.5. The panel was treated in 1984/5 by Bobak who removed a cradle which had caused several vertical cracks to appear – principally at 7.5, 15 and 30 cm. from the left-hand edge. The panel now has a convex warp. Cleaned by Haines in 1903 and by Lank in 1985. There are small losses along the bottom edge, below her left sleeve and in the top left area. *Pentimenti* show changes to the collar and shoulders.

The costume is an imaginative evocation of historical Spanish dress, as had been proposed by Carle van Loo.[1]

A very late work, dated c.1804 by Brookner (1956, p.199; 1972, p.129); the execution is heavy and uninspired.

Replica

Demidoff sale, Paris, 3rd day, 26 February 1870 (124, *L'Espagnole*), 45 × 38, engr. Courtry (MM464).

Provenance

A.-J. Carrier (1800–75); his sale, Paris, 9–10 March 1846 (108, *Tête de jeune fille*), bt. by the 4th Marquess of Hertford, 2,800 fr.; reframed in Hertford House 1859;[2] Hertford House inventory 1870.

Exhibitions

Bazar Bonne-Nouvelle, 1846 (77, *Etude de jeune Fille*) lent Hertford; Bethnal Green 1872–5 (see P396).

Reference General

MM580.

[1] Cf. *Conversation espagnole* of 1754 by C. van Loo in the Hermitage (M.-C. Sahut, *Carle Vanloo*, 1977, no.147), and see G. Wildenstein, *Fragonard*, 1960, pp.14–15.
[2] Evans invoice.

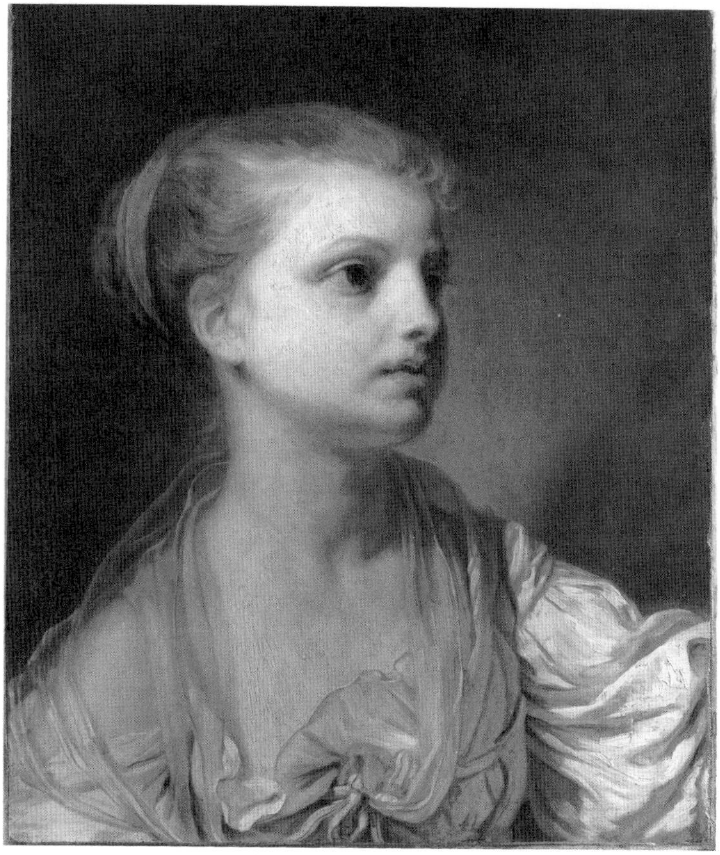

P427

P427 *Girl in a white dress (L'anxiété plaintive)*

A blue ribbon in her fair hair, grey eyes, with a white dress and scarf.

Canvas, relined 45.6 × 37.6

Cleaned by Haines in 1903. There are small damages to the right of her nose in the background and on the right-hand edge above the shoulder.

Dated c.1765 by Brookner,[1] P427 was sold as a *tête d'expression* in 1845 (see Provenance). A drawing of the same model in a comparable pose is in the Musée Fabre.

Provenance

E.W. Lake by 1837;[2] his sale, Christie's, 11–12 July 1845 (62, *L'anxiété plaintive*), bt. by the 4th Marquess of Hertford, 195 gn.; Hertford House inventory 1870.

Exhibition

Bethnal Green 1872–5 (?395, *A Portrait*).

References General

Smith, no.129; MM826.

[1] Brookner 1956, p.161; 1972, p.106, where she suggests P427 may have been amongst those heads exhibited by Greuze in the 1765 Salon – though the *livret* gave the sizes of both the *Tête de fille* and *Tête de petite fille* as 15 × 12 *pouces*, i.e. 40 × 32 cm., somewhat smaller than P427.

[2] Smith, *loc. cit.*

P428 *Girl with Doves (L'Innocence tenant deux pigeons)*

Fair hair with a grey ribbon, blue eyes, wearing a white dress with a blue-lined grey drape; one dove in the cage and two in her hands. Signed, bottom left: *J.B. Greuze.*

Mahogany panel 70 × 58.8 × 0.4

The panel is supported by a constricting cradle of nine horizontal battens and seven vertical slats, which has caused a number of cracks along the horizontal grain (below her right elbow, through her left shoulder and in the upper left and right areas) and an undulating surface. The edges are abraded with some small losses. The varnish is discoloured.

It has previously been assumed that the date on the receipt from Greuze (now pasted on the back of the panel, see note 5), 17 August 1802, indicates the date of the picture.[1] But it is the date of the sale, and there seems to be no reason why P428 should not have been *L'Innocence tenant deux pigeons* shown at the Salon in 1800.[2] Although Greuze also described the subject (on the receipt) as *une jeune fille tenant deux pigeons appuyée sur un cage*, it was later claimed that it was the portrait of Mme. Dupuy, the mother of Emile de Girardin, but this seems very unlikely.[3]

Engraving

Beauvarlet, oval; lithograph by Patout from a drawing by Dupuis, 1833.

Copies

BRUSSELS Marey-Monge sale, 26 April 1926 (9); 75 × 63, bearing signature and date 1797.
LONDON Dallas gallery 1984; 72.4 × 60.3, copy by John Constable 1831, made for Lady Cordelia Jackson; ex Christie's, 22 April 1983 (54).[4]
NEW YORK Parke Bernet, 16 April 1949 (60); 63 × 52.

Provenance

Bt. from the artist, 17 August 1802, for 4,800 *livres* by Jos. Wilkinson;[5] his sale, Christie's 20–1 May 1816 (78, *Girl with a pair of Doves*), bt. in, 124 gn.; his (posthumous) sale, Christie's, 25 April 1828 (111, *Girl with a basket of eggs in her lap*), bt. Nieuwenhuys, 245 gn.; W. Wells (c.1768–1847) of Redleaf by 1831; his sale, Christie's 12 May 1848 (121, 'from the collection of – Wilkinson'), bt. by the 4th Marquess of Hertford, 750 gn.; Hertford House inventory 1870.

Exhibitions

Salon 1800 (178), see above; BI 1831 (69) lent Wells; BI 1844 (97) lent Wells; Manchester, *Art Treasures*, 1857 (saloon H, no. 33); Bethnal Green 1872–5 (427).

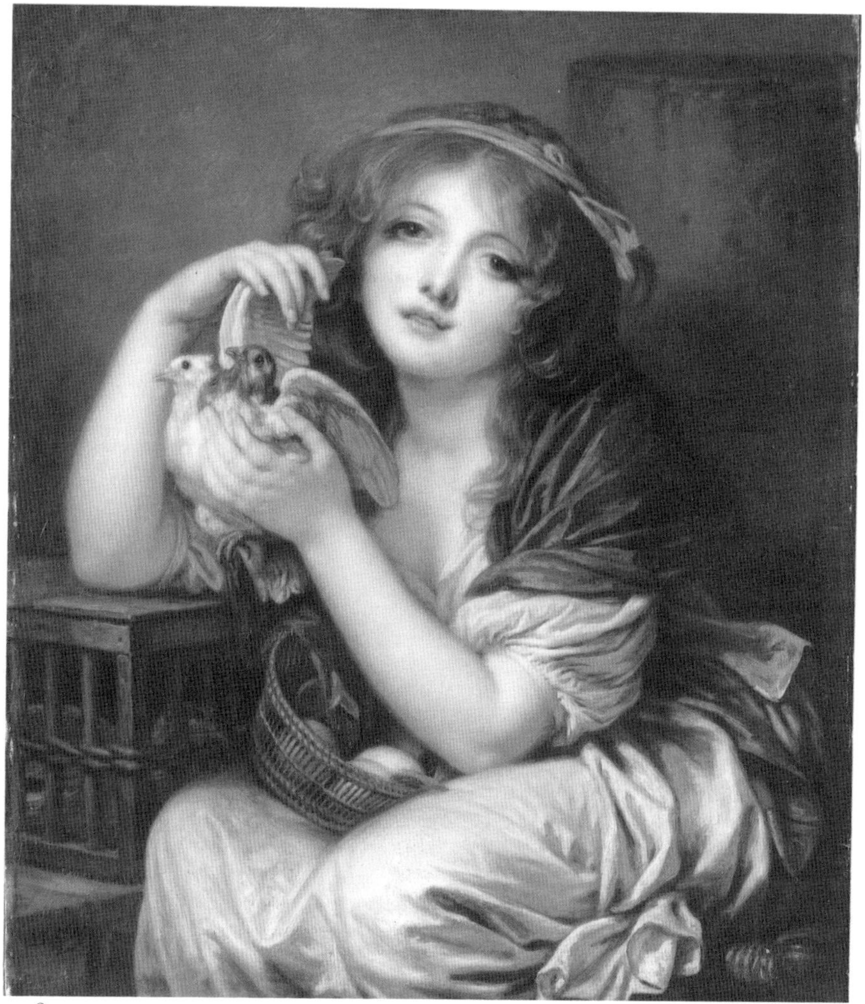

P428

References General

Smith, no. 75; MM785, 788, 1117.

[1] E.g. in previous editions of this catalogue and Brookner 1956, p. 199, and 1972, pp. 86, 132.

[2] Munhall, p. 26 n. 46, following earlier editions of this catalogue, suggested P428 was a version of the Salon picture; Brookner 1972, p. 132, classed it as a signed and dated copy.

[3] MM under 1117 quote a letter from Emile de Girardin to Arsène Houssaye: '. . . *et de ma mère l'admirable portrait connu sous le titre de:* La Jeune Fille à la colombe *chef d'oeuvre acheté, en 1848, 35,000 francs, par M. Herfort aux héritiers du baron Wilckenser* [Wilkinson]. *Actuellement collection Wallace*'. J. Richardson, *History Today*, December 1976, p. 811, describes P428 as the portrait of Mme. Dupuy, mother of Girardin; MM under 1117 call her Mlle. de Fagan, later Mme. Girardin. In the Fribourg sale, Christie's, 16 June 1963 (94), a Greuze *Jeune fille à l'oiseau* was described as a portrait of Mlle. Fagnon.

[4] Cf. G. Reynolds, *The later Paintings and Drawings of John Constable*, 1984, I, p. 230, no. 31.15, II, pl. 802; T. Boyd, *Country Life*, CLXIII, 1978, p. 1660. Lady Jackson commissioned the copy because the subject reminded her of her daughter who had left her; she would have seen the picture at the BI in 1831 (see Exhibitions).

[5] On the back of the panel and over the cradle is pasted Greuze's receipt: '*Je reconnois avoir reçu de Monsieur Wilkinson/la somme de quatre mille huit cent livres/pour un tableau représentant une jeune fille/tenant deux pigeons appuyés sur un cage/Fait à Paris le 17 aoust 1802/Greuze*'. This receipt was mentioned in the Wilkinson sale catalogue as being sold with the picture, so that it was stuck to the panel after 1828. As an Englishman, Wilkinson could not visit Paris before 25 March 1802 when the Peace of Amiens was agreed. Christie's copy of the 1816 sale catalogue has the seller's name inscribed as *Jos. Wilkinson*.

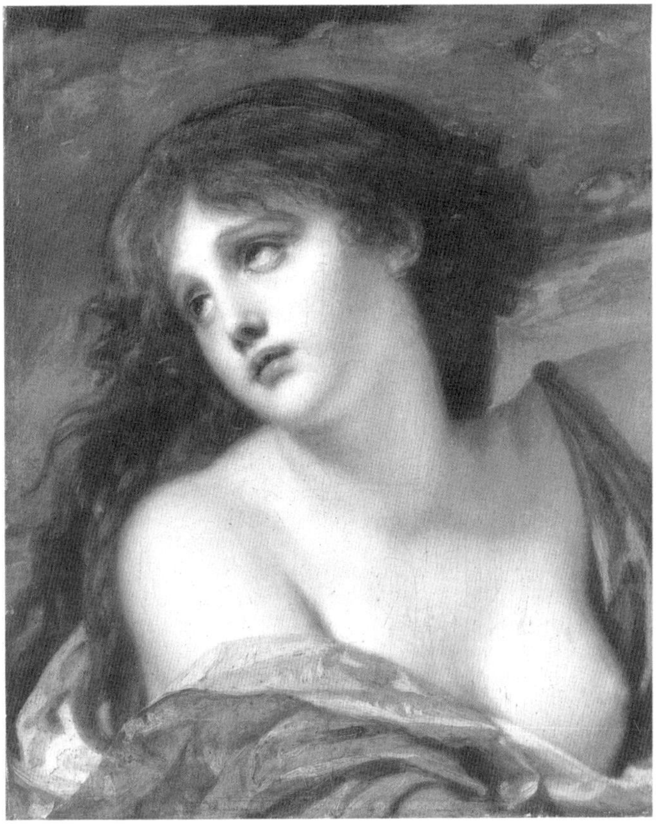

P440

P440 *Psyche*

Chestnut hair with a blue ribbon, wearing gold drapery over a white dress.

Mahogany panel 41 × 32 × 0.5

The panel is cradled with seven vertical battens and six horizontal slats; strips added to each side, bringing the overall size to 42.3 × 33, have been removed. There are small damages above the breast, in the hair to the left and on the left-hand edge. There is a general craquelure over the figure which has been retouched in the hair to the right. The varnish is much discoloured.

For the subject, see P388.

P440 may be dated c. 1786, the date inscribed on P388, the more finished version.

Version

See P388.

Provenance

Painted for J.-F. Boursault (c.1760–1842); his sale, Paris, 7 May 1832 (100),[1] bt. E. Higginson (*né* Barneby, 1802–71) of Saltmarsh Castle, Herefordshire; his sale, Christie's, 3rd day, 6 June 1846 (200), bt. Theobald for the 4th Marquess of Hertford, 1,000 gn.; reframed in Hertford House 1859;[2] Hertford House inventory 1870.

Exhibition

Bethnal Green 1872–5 (?465, *Sorrow*).

Reference General

Smith, *Supplement*, no.9.

[1] The sale catalogue, followed by H. Artaria (*Descriptive Catalogue of the Gallery of Edmund Higginson*, 1841, pp.253–4), said that P440 was shown by Vien to the Académie with the question, how long would they refuse the *cathedra* to one whose works they esteemed so highly?

[2] Evans invoice.

P441 *Votive offering to Cupid (L'offrande à l'amour Une jeune fille qui fait sa prière au pied de l'autel de l'amour)*

The girl has chestnut hair tied with a blue ribbon; she wears a white tunic with gold trimmings and blue sandals; bottom right pink and white roses on a blue drape and a silver-gilt antique ewer, and bottom left daisies; the altar bears a bas-relief of Pan and Syrinx.

Canvas, relined 145.5 × 113

Restored by Byard in 1922. The background is thinly painted. There is a V-shaped tear above Cupid and there are several retouchings: in the broad craquelure centre and upper left, in Cupid's body and below the crown he offers, in the girl's hair, in the trees upper right, and in the figure of Pan in the bas-relief on the altar. The canvas is buckled along the bottom edge. *Pentimenti* show minor changes to Cupid's wing and right ankle, on the right-hand side of the altar and on the base of the ewer bottom right. The varnish is discoloured.

P441 was one of several classical subjects painted by Greuze between 1765 and 1769,[1] and was shown in the 1769 Salon with *The Emperor Severus reprimanding his son Caracalla*, Greuze's contentious, neo-classical *morceau de réception*. It was completed by 1767,[2] the composition influenced by earlier renderings of the subject by Carle van Loo and Vien.[3] The statue of Cupid derives from an engraving in Mariette's *Traité des pierres gravées* of 1750.[4] Architecture, altar and ewer indicate an attentive study of the 'grecian' motifs then so much in fashion.[5] The bas-relief of Pan and Syrinx[6] on the altar is probably an original composition (see Drawings). Other parts of the picture are less erudite: the drawing of the girl, the hesitant perspective (e.g. the base of the altar, the parapet beyond and the size of the trees) and the solecism of the fleshy; rococo Cupid. Diderot was quick to seize upon such features in his review of the 1769 Salon; the girl's head, he wrote,[7]

> *est charmante, mais cette tête est d'un âge, et le reste de la figure est d'un autre. L'épaule est trop petite; la jambe droite est de mauvaise forme, le pié est trop gros; la figure est mal drapée. Le paysage est lourd et fatigué; les accessoires sont négligés; les pigeons sont si lisses qu'on ne sait s'ils ont de la plume. L'Amour est bien modelé et de bonne couleur, mais dans la crainte de le maniérer, on en a fait un petit Savoyard bien laid, un petit magot. Greuze connaît le beau idéal de son genre, mais il ne le connaît pas dans celui-ci. Si les mains de la jeune fille avaient été mieux coloriées, elles*

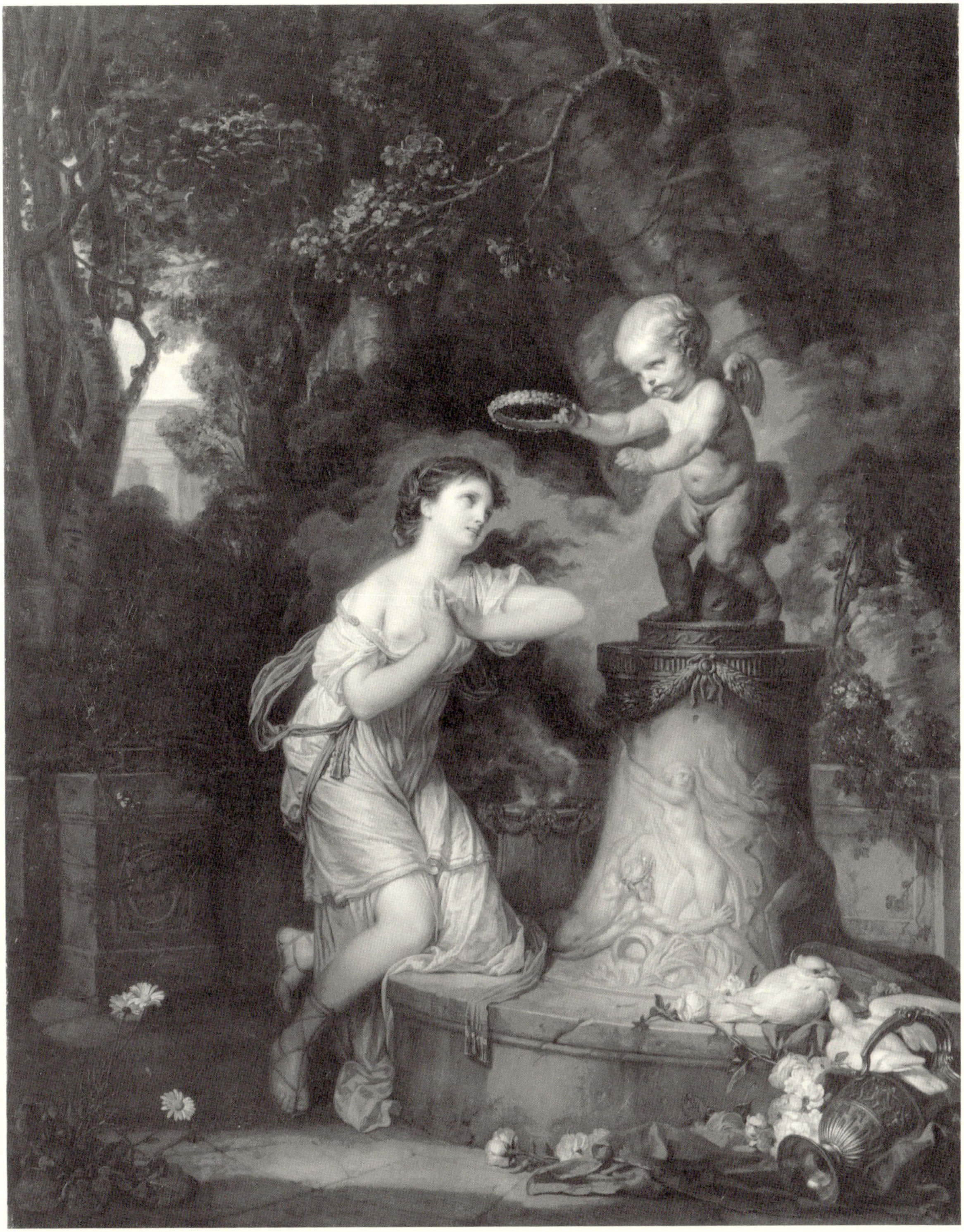

P441

se détacheraient davantage de dessus sa gorge. Si le paysage avait été moins fort, les figures paraîtraient moins mesquines, ces énormes troncs d'arbres auxquels on les rapporte les écrasent.

By 1769 P441 was in the collection of the duc de Choiseul (see Exhibitions) who hung it in the peacock-blue bedroom of his Paris hôtel on one side of a pier glass, balanced by another Greuze from the 1769 Salon, *Le baiser envoyé* (91 × 76; private collection); elsewhere in the room were Vien's *Femme grecque à la bain* of 1767 (Ponce) and J.-J. Caffiéri's marble *Innocence*.[8]

Drawings

NEW YORK Metropolitan Museum of Art (no.49.131.3); study for the Cupid's head, reversed, apparently from the life.[9]
(no.61.1.1); study for the river God on the bas-relief.[10]
PARIS Drouot, 20 March 1941 (12); signed compositional study, reversed, showing another figure outside the parapet; ex colls. Marquiset and Groult.
Palais Galliera, 27 March 1965 (4); study for the figure of the girl.
TOURNUS Musée Greuze (no.15); study for the Cupid's head, reversed, possibly from a sculpture.[11]
(no.6); study for the girl, reversed, probably from an engraving, and not by Greuze.

A study was in the Plinval sale, Paris, 15 April 1846 (MM under 66). Two studies of *Amour sur un piédestal* were in the Beurnonville sale, Paris, 16–19 February 1885 (330).
A nude study for the girl was in the M. de V. sale, Paris, 25–6 November 1907 (117).
A study of a girl's head leaning on her clasped hands, comparable with the girl's head in P441, was exh. RA 1968 (329).

Engravings

B.-A. Dunker and de Launay 1771, reversed (for the *Cabinet Choiseul*); C.-P.-A. Macret 1778.

Versions

AMIENS Musée de Picardie (no.605); 41 × 32, variant, possibly a compositional study , with a *putto* and two children and without trees; possibly the version, said to be signed and dated 1770, in the Van Os sale, Paris, 20–2 January 1851 (171).
PARIS Ader Picard Tajan, 15 June 1979 (22); 47 × 38, reduced replica painted for Mme. du Barry;[12] her sale 1777, 1,950 *livres*; Dulac sale 1778, 2,080 *livres*; de Cene sale 1778, 2,360 *livres*; Morel sale, 1778, 1,500 *livres*; de Calonne sales 1788, 1,463 *livres*, and 1793, 30 gn.; Cognacq sale, Paris, 11 June 1952, lot 74 (MM67).

A study of a girl's head relating to P441 is in the Musée Fabre, Montpellier (no.304). Another, 45 × 37, engr. P. P. Moles 1774, was in the Abbé de Gevigney sale, Paris, 1 December 1779, lot 59 (MM735), possibly the painting listed by Smith (no.48) as in the Duclos-Dufresnoy sale, 1795 (but not identifiable in that sale catalogue).

Provenance

By 1769 with the duc de Choiseul (1719–85); his sale, Paris, 6 April ff. 1772 (133), bt. Catelan, 5,650 *livres*, for the prince de Conti (1717–76); his sale, Paris, 8 April 1777 (742),[13] bt. Feuillet, 5000 *livres*; Dubois, *marchand*, sale, Paris, 5th day, 5 April 1784 (110 '. . . *connu par le Cabinet de M. le Duc de Choiseul, celui de Monseigneur le Prince de Conti, & par l'Estampe gravée par C. Macret*') bt. Seneville, 4,000 *livres*;[14] the comte d'Artois (1757–1836); seized by the *commission temporaire des Arts*, 19 *prairial an* II [7 June 1794] amongst works of art '*provenant de l'emigré d'Artois, trouvés dans la maison du Temple*';[15] valued at 3,600 *livres* by J.-B.-P. Lebrun, 15 *fructidor an* II [1 September 1794];[16] bt. by Cardinal Fesch (1763–1839) '*chez *** sur le quai: un Greuze l'Offrande à l'Amour, 2,000*', 1 *vendémiaire an* IX [22 September 1801];[17] his sale, Rome, 17 March–15 May 1845 (354), bt. by the 4th Marquess of Hertford, 6,160 *scudi* (34,797 fr.);[18] reframed in Hertford House 1857;[19] Hertford House inventory 1870.

Exhibitions

Salon 1769 (153, *Une jeune fille qui fait la prière au pied de l'autel de l'Amour*) lent Choiseul; Manchester, *Art Treasures*, 1857 (saloon H, no.34, *A Sylvan offering to Cupid*); Bethnal Green 1872–5 (380).

References General

Smith, no.19; MM66.

[1] *Jupiter and Aegina* (Metropolitan Museum of Art) and drawings of *Cimon and Pero*, *The Death of Cato*, *The Death of Patroclus* and *The Capture of Sabinus* (see Munhall, nos.59, 60, 65, 66, 66*bis* and fig.5).

[2] Diderot mentioned P441 in his *Salon de 1767* (*Salons*, ed. J. Seznec, III, 1983, p.225) and in a letter to Falconet, dated July 1767 ('*La jeune dévote est charmante. Pour moi, il me déplaira toujours . . . de voir une statue en scène avec une figure vivante . . .*'; Diderot, *Correspondance*, ed. G. Roth, VII, 1962, p.103).

[3] C. van Loo, *Le sacrifice à l'Amour* 1760 and *L'offrande à l'Amour* Salon 1761 (both unlocated; cf. M.-C. Sahut, *Carle van Loo*, 1977, nos.246, 247) show comparable landscape settings. Vien, *La vertueuse Athénienne* Salon 1763 (Strasbourg) shows a similar 'Greek' costume. In London Reynolds had also exploited the subject in his *Lady Sarah Bunbury* of 1763 (Chicago), see *Reynolds*, exh. cat. RA 1986, p.224. Greuze's borrowings are discussed by Brookner 1972, pp.112–13. He may also have known a drawing by Vien of 1753 (Musée Atger, Montpellier) for a fountain which incorporates a kneeling girl in 'grecian' costume, similar to the figure in P441 (illus. S. Eriksen, *Early Neo-Classicism in France*, 1974, pl.300).

[4] Pl.xx, *Vénus, Mars et l'Amour*, with the Cupid reversed; this derivation was first indicated by Brookner, *loc. cit.*

[5] Eriksen, *op. cit.*, p.50, quotes a Parisian jingle of 1764: '*La mode est pour le Grec; nos meubles, nos bijoux,/Etoffes, coëffure, équipage,/Tout est Grec, excepté nos âmes*', and for an account of the rise of this taste see pp.29–36, 48–50. Greuze would have known Le Lorrain's furniture *à la grecque* made for Lalive de Jully whose portrait he painted in 1759 and 1765 (*ibid.*, pp.195–7; Munhall, no.22).

[6] The chaste Syrinx, pursued by Pan, was turned into a reed on the banks of the river Ladon (Ovid, *Metamorphoses* I, 694–712).

[7] *Salon de 1769* (*Salons*, ed. J. Seznec, IV, 1967, p.107). Seznec (p.44) quotes similar criticism from Bachaumont, and Brookner (1972, p.67) from Raphaël.

[8] Cf. the interior view of the Hôtel de Choiseul painted by van Blarenberghe and set on a gold box by L. Roucel 1770–1 (Paris, private collection), published by F. J. B. Watson, 'Choiseul Boxes' in A. K. Snowman, *Eighteenth-century Gold Boxes of Europe*, 1966, p.148 and pl.378. See also Eriksen, *op. cit.*, pl.463.

[9] Cf. J. Bean, *Fifteenth to Eighteenth century French Drawings in the Metropolitan Museum of Art*, 1986, p.121, no.129.

[10] Cf. Bean, *op. cit.*, p.122, no.130; Munhall, no.56. Munhall records that Bean had associated this drawing with a design by Louis Boullongne in the Metropolitan Museum of Art (Bean, p.47, no.42), and that Dean Walker had remarked upon the similarity between Greuze's bas-relief and the painting of the same subject by Michel Dorigny (Louvre) engraved in 1666 (though some resemblance is, of course, inevitable).

[11] As observed by Munhall (letter on file dated 9 April 1964).

[12] Mme. du Barry owned this reduced version by 1774–5 (cf. C. Vatel, *Histoire de Madame du Barry d'après ses papiers personnels et les documents des archives publiques*, II, 1883, p.484).

[13] Lord Hertford's copy of the Conti sale catalogue (Wallace Collection library) is marked by lot 742: '*J'ai acheté ce tableau à Rome à la vente du Cardinal Fesch/Hertford*'.

[14] Three different prices are noted in the copy of the sale catalogue preserved in the Bibliothèque Nationale: *3,650*, *4,000* and *5,650*. The buyer's name, *Seneville*, appears opposite *4,000*.

[15] Archives Nationales, F^{17} 1269, no.20. I am grateful to Colin Bailey for this reference. Another *registre* gives the date of seizure as 3 *nivôse an* III [23 December 1795] (Arch. Nat. F^{17} 372, f.137; a similar text recurs in F^{17} 23, f.165).

[16] Archives Nationales F^{17} 1267, no.138. I am again grateful to Colin Bailey for this reference.

[17] Cf. Abbé J.-B. Vanel, *Deux livres de Comptes du Cardinal Fesch, archevêque de Lyon*, 1923, p.54.

[18] P441 had appeared as no.1835 in the 1841 Fesch catalogue. In the 1844 sale catalogue it was asterisked, indicating a picture taken from France (i.e. before 1815). Lord Hertford's copy (Wallace Collection library) has *8 avril* inscribed by lot 354, presumably indicating the day on which it was sold.

[19] Evans invoice.

P442 *The Broken Mirror (Le malheur imprévu)*

The girl has chestnut hair tied with a blue ribbon and wears a white satin dress; a black shawl hangs over the chair upholstered in pink and gold silk; black and white dog; blue curtain on the left.

Canvas, relined 56 × 45.6[1]

Heavily ironed in relining. A horizontal craquelure to the left of the girl's head suggests a reworking in that area. The varnish is unevenly discoloured.

An example of the sentimental genre scenes which were, perhaps, Greuze's most original achievement (see also P454). '*Voici votre peintre et le mien*', wrote Diderot; '*le premier qui se soit avisé, parmi nous, de donner des moeurs à l'art, et d'enchaîner les événements d'après lesquels il seroit facile de faire un roman*'.[2] In P442 the disorder of the room suggests the thoughtlessness of the girl, and the broken mirror, as Diderot indicated, her lost virginity.[3]

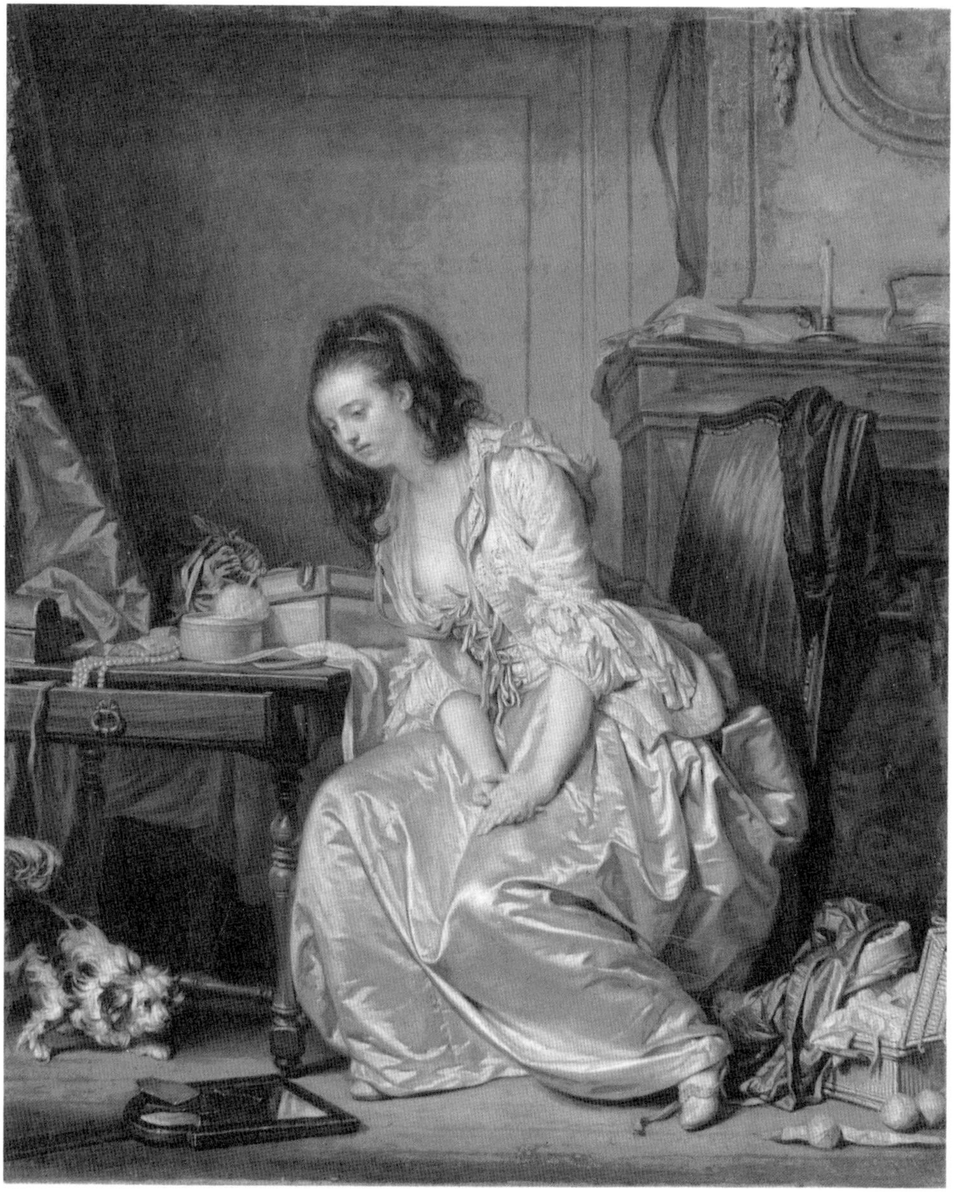

P442

Painted before 1763 and listed in the Salon *livret* that year, but not exhibited.[4] P442 reflects Greuze's growing affection for Rubens[5] with its free execution and rich draperies; the girl's pose relates, reversed, to Rubens's *Hagar in the desert* (Dulwich),[6] though he also made a study for the figure from a model (see Drawings). He may also have remembered Hogarth's prints of *Before* and *After* of 1736 in which a disordered dressing table with a half-open drawer, a broken mirror and an excited dog again described a maiden's downfall.[7]

Drawings

MONTPELLIER Musée Fabre; study of a girl in a mob cap, holding a ring in her lap, the pose almost identical to that of the girl in P442, signed and dated 1758. A counter-proof is in the Hermitage.[8]
TOURNUS Musée Greuze; compositional study, reversed, probably after the engraving of P442.[9]

Engraving[10]

R. de Launay *le jeune* 1779, *Le malheur imprévu*, reversed.

Versions

NEW YORK Parke Bernet, 12 November 1952 (86); 56 x 42, reversed copy; ex coll. Rosebery (Dalmeny) and Parke Bernet, 14 March 1951 (69).

A head *'qui semble avoir été la première idée de la figure du Miroir cassé'* was in the Ragu sale, Paris, 23 December 1849, lot 23 (MM866).

Provenance[11]

M. de Bossette 1763;[12] P.-L. Randon de Boisset (1710–76), *receveur général*; his sale, Paris, 27 February ff. 1777 (207, *'Une jeune fille desolée d'avoir laissé tomber son miroir de toilette qui est cassé & à terre, un chien le regarde'*), bt. Basan, 3,500 *livres*; Mme. B[asan] sale, Paris, 4 April 1791 (35), bt. in, 1,920 fr.;[13] Cardinal Fesch (1763–1839) by 1815; his sale, Rome 17 March–15 May 1845 (356),[14] bt. by the 4th Marquess of Hertford, 3,360 *scudi* (18,693 fr.); reframed in Hertford House 1859;[15] Hertford House inventory 1870.

Exhibitions

Listed in the Salon 1763 (139, *Une jeune fille qui a cassé son miroir, du Cabinet de M. de Bossette*) but not exhibited (see note 4); bazar Bonne-Nouvelle 1846 (78, *Le miroir cassé*) lent Hertford; Bethnal Green 1872–5 (425).

References General

Smith, no.30; MM168.

1 The stretcher bears, *verso*, the Roman customs stamp: RCA/DOG. DI/ROMA (in a circle) and the inscription: *No 636. du C.*, probably referring to a Fesch catalogue (see D. Thiébaut, *Ajaccio, musée Fesch, Les primitifs italiens*, 1987, p.26).

2 Diderot, *Salon de 1765* (*Salons*, ed. J. Seznec, II, 1979, p.144).

3 *Ibid.* (Seznec, p.147); writing of *La jeune fille qui pleure son oiseau mort* (Edinburgh) Diderot commented: *'Greuze a déjà peint une fois le même sujet; il a placé devant une glace fêlée une grande fille en satin blanc, pénétrée d'une profonde mélancolie. Ne pensez-vous pas qu'il y auroit autant de bêtise à attribuer les pleurs de la jeune fille de ce Salon à la perte d'un oiseau, que la mélancolie de la jeune fille du Salon précédent à son miroir cassé? Cette enfant pleure autre chose, vous dis-je'*.

4 Diderot, *Salon de 1763* (Seznec, I, 1975, p.237): *'Le petit livret du Salon nous promettait encore quelques autres morceaux de ce maître* [Greuze] . . . Une jeune fille qui a cassé son miroir*; le petit tableau qu'il appelle* Le tendre ressouvenir [P454]; *mais ces tableaux n'ont pas été exposés, parce que ceux à qui ils appartiennent n'ont pas jugé à propos d'y consentir'*.

5 Cf. Brookner 1972, p.104; Greuze was examining the Marie de Médicis cycle by Rubens in the Luxembourg in the summer of 1760; Brookner also suggests that the draperies of P442 'bear witness to the study of a master such as Terborch', but the touch is broad.

6 Cf. P. Murray, *Dulwich Picture Gallery Catalogue*, 1980, p.113, no.131; engraved in reverse by F. de Roy c.1750.

7 Illus. R. Paulson, *Hogarth's Graphic Works*, 1965, II, pls. 152–3; the pose of the girl in *After* recalls that of the widow in P454.

8 Cf. F. Monod and L. Hautecoeur, *Les dessins de Greuze conservés à l'Académie des Beaux-Arts de Saint-Petersbourg*, 1922, no.47, pl. xvii.

9 E. Munhall, letter on file dated 9 April 1964, considers this drawing not to be by Greuze.

10 P442 was not engraved by Dennel as stated in the Fesch sale catalogue and repeated by Smith, MM168 and previous editions of this catalogue; see note 11 below.

11 The Fesch sale catalogue stated that P442 had been in the Lalive de Jully collection where it was engraved by Dennel, but it was not in the de Jully sale. The error probably arose from a careless reading of the Boisset sale catalogue in which the provenance of lot 206, Greuze's *Père de famille lisant la Bible*, *'du Cabinet de M. de la Live de Jully'*, appeared in large type immediately above the description of lot 207 (P442) which was in a smaller face. Smith, MM168 and previous editions of this catalogue repeated the Lalive de Jully provenance.

12 Doubtless a mis-spelling of M. de Boisset (see Exhibitions).

13 The copy of the sale catalogue in the Bibliothèque Doucet gives the buyer as Basan *fils*, a prefatory note explaining: *'Les tabl. adjugés à Basan fils sont tirés po mémoire ne sont pas portés au p[rocès] v[erbal]'*. Cf. P390 Ascribed to Boucher, note 11.

14 P442 was no.1957 in the 1841 Fesch catalogue. In the sale catalogue printed in 1844 it was asterisked, indicating a picture taken by Fesch from France, i.e. before 1815. Lord Hertford wrote *27 mars* by lot 356 in his copy of the sale catalogue (Wallace Collection library), doubtless the day it was sold.

15 Evans invoice.

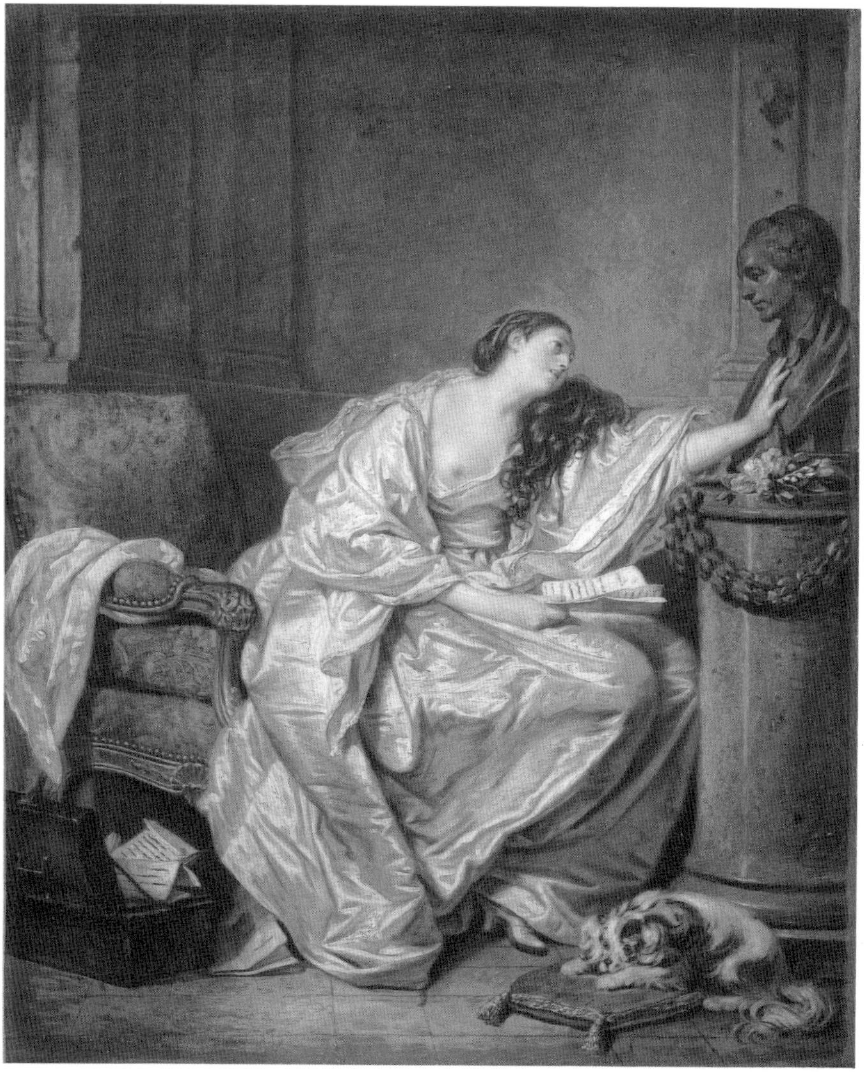

P454

P454 *The Inconsolable Widow (Le tendre ressouvenir)*

Chestnut hair tied with a blue ribbon, wearing a white satin dress; a white shawl with pink ribbons over the blue damask chair; red and white roses lie by the bronze bust; a brown and white dog on a blue cushion.

Canvas, relined 40 × 32

Heavily ironed during relining in the mid-nineteenth-century[1] when the edges were made up to 42 × 33.7. Some abrasion is apparent in the chair and dog; there is a damage to the right of the pedestal and there are retouchings above the bust, in the pedestal and in the floor. The varnish is somewhat discoloured.

The young widow rereads old letters before the bust of her husband, apparently vowing fidelity;[2] '*O Rousseau! ô Diderot! ô Marmontel! Le défunt, ou plutôt son buste, a un faux air d'encyclopédiste. Peut-on pleurer un encyclopédiste sans mettre un peu de drame dans sa douleur? La veuve en met donc, et beaucoup...*'.[3] In 1802 the subject was described as a woman regretting the absence of her lover (see Provenance), but the Salon title of 1763, *le tendre ressouvenir*,[4] would indicate she is a widow. For a general comment on Greuze's modern moral subjects, see P442.

Painted before 1763 and listed in the Salon *livret* that year, but not exhibited (see P442, note 4). The execution is less spirited than that of P442; the widow's head appears too small and her arms too long (as was noticed by Lagrange in 1863[5]). The fluted pilasters and draped pedestal hint at the neo-classical interest which Greuze had developed by the end of the decade (see P441). Bürger considered that the widow's figure was '*de la taille des femmelettes de Willem Mieris, à qui ça n'est pas loin de rassembler*'.[6] A drawing, probably contemporary with P454, *La lettre d'amour* (private collection; Munhall, no. 78), shows a comparable setting; a seated girl by a similar bust on a pedestal being urged by Cupid to write a letter.

Drawings

COPENHAGEN Royal Museum of Fine Arts (no. 13075); study for the widow's head.
LENINGRAD Hermitage; study for the dog.
NARBONNE Musée (no. 766 in 1923 catalogue); study for the seated widow.
PARIS Louvre (no. 4583); study possibly used for the widow's head (but also resembling the woman's head in *La paix du ménage*).

Provenance[7]

J.-J. Duché, *procureur général*, Montpellier; his sale, Montpellier, 2 September 1802 (51, '*Une femme assise sur un grand fauteuil lit des lettres de son Amant et addresse les regrets de son absence à son buste posé sur un socle de marbre*'), bt. Fontanel, 200 fr., for J.-J. Boussairolles (1741–1814), Montpellier; by descent to C.-J. Boussairolles who sold it, c.1850, to the duc de Morny (1811–65); his sale, Paris, 2nd day, 1 June 1865 (101, '*La veuve inconsolable . . . le désordre de la passion règne dans sa toilette*'), bt. by the 4th Marquess of Hertford, 8,100 fr.; rue Laffitte inventory 1871 (386, '*Les regrets*'); Hertford House inventory 1890.

Exhibitions

Listed in the Salon 1763 (138, *Le tendre ressouvenir*) but not exhibited (see P442 note 4); boulevard des Italiens 1860 (164, *La veuve inconsolable*) lent Morny; Bethnal Green 1872–5 (375, *Filial Piety*).

References General

MM221,[8] MM846.

[1] The stretcher is stamped, *verso*: MOMPER A PARIS, for whom, see Fragonard P430 note 1.

[2] As described by W. Bürger, *Gazette des Beaux-Arts*, 1ère, VII, 1860, pp.350–1. For discussion of the theme of the virtuous widow in late eighteenth-century art, see R. Rosenblum, *Transformations in late eighteenth-century Art*, 1970 ed., pp.40–4.

[3] L. Lagrange, *Gazette des Beaux-Arts*, 1ère, XIV, 1863, p.394.

[4] The identification of P454 with this title is accepted by Brookner (1972, p.63) and Munhall (pp.21–2); the Salon *livret* gave the size as *15 pouces sur 1 pied*, i.e. 40.8 × 32.6.

[5] Lagrange, *loc. cit.*

[6] Bürger, *loc. cit.*

[7] For this provenance I am grateful to M. A. Chevalier's *La collection de tableaux de J.-J. Boussairolles, mémoire de maîtrise*, Sorbonne, 1984 (and BSHAF forthcoming).

[8] MM221 identified P454 with a Magdalen by Greuze in the Wallace Collection, but see P388 under Exhibition.

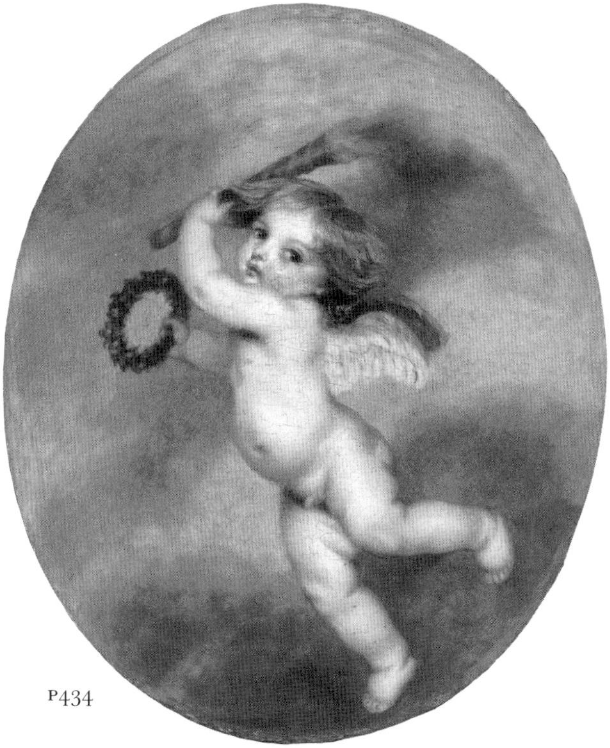

P434

Ascribed to Greuze

P434 *Flying Cupid with a torch*

Fair-haired, blue eyes, his wings with red edges, the torch with red bands. Signed, or inscribed, *verso*: *Greuze*.

Mahogany panel 27.2 × 22 × 0.6 oval

There is a small damage below his left foot and the panel is uneven in the upper left area. The edges are knocked and the varnish is discoloured.

The subject resembles a younger version of the Cupid seen in *L'innocence entraînée par les Amours* painted before 1786 (Louvre), and Munhall has suggested that P434 derives from it.[1] The execution is very weak, however, and the possibility of a pupil's work cannot be excluded.

Provenance

Anon. sale, Paris, 16–17 February 1844 (17), bt. in, 500 fr.; anon. sale, Paris, 7–8 March 1845 (100), bt. by the 4th Marquess of Hertford, 1,900 fr.;[2] reframed in Hertford House 1859;[3] Hertford House inventory 1870.

Exhibition

Bethnal Green 1872–5 (451).

Reference General

MM44.

[1] Munhall, under no. 100.

[2] Entry in the 4th Marquess's account book in the Wallace Collection archives: '*8 mars 1845 Un tableau de Greuze petit amour 1995*', i.e. 1,900 fr. plus 5% commission.

[3] Evans invoice.

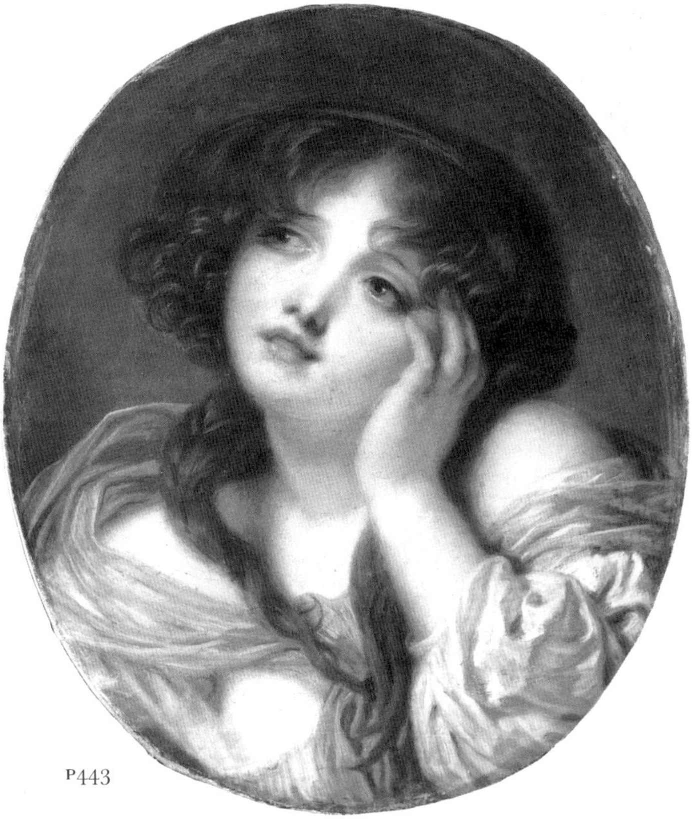

P443

P443 *Girl leaning on her hand*

Chestnut hair tied with a blue ribbon, grey eyes, wearing a white dress.

Canvas, relined 46 × 38 oval

Heavily ironed in relining. There is a *pentimento* in her left sleeve near the cuff. The varnish is greatly discoloured.

A very late Greuze composition related to P459 (also ascribed to Greuze). The drapery on her right shoulder is very weak and the nose is incorrectly aligned. As with P434 and P459, the possibility of a pupil's work cannot be excluded.

Provenance

Probably H. Broadwood, then W. Theobald sale, Christie's, 10 May 1851 (71, 'Head of a Girl, with light hair falling on her neck, in loose curls, in a white dress. Full of beautiful character. From the collection of H. Broadwood Esq.'), bt. Nieuwenhuys, 320 gn.; the 4th Marquess of Hertford before 1859 when it was reframed in Hertford House;[1] Hertford House inventory 1870.

Exhibitions

Possibly BI 1847 (12, *Head of a Female*) lent Broadwood; Bethnal Green 1872–5 (see P396).

[1] Evans invoice.

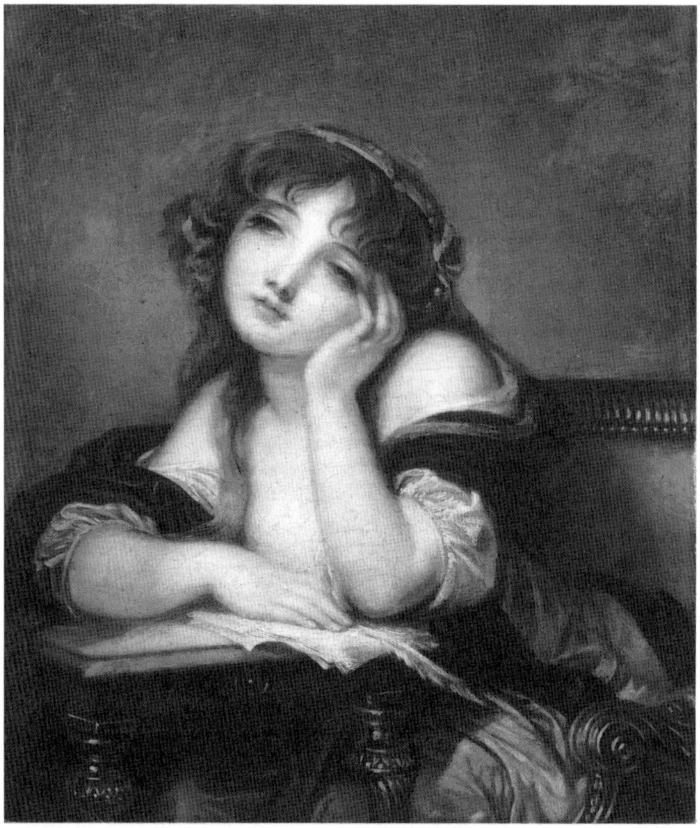

P459

P459 *The Letter Writer*

Chestnut hair dressed with pearls and a red ribbon, wearing a blue-grey shawl over a white dress. Signed, or inscribed, on edge of table to the left: *Greuze*.

Canvas 40.5 × 33.2

There are many small retouchings and minor losses in the skirt. The varnish is much discoloured.

P459 is a reduced and weak version of a late Greuze composition (see Versions). Although identified in previous editions of this catalogue as the *Jeune femme se disposant à écrire une lettre d'amour* shown in the 1800 Salon,[1] P459 is of poor quality and there is another late Greuze composition showing a girl preparing to write a letter.[2] P459 is perhaps the work of a pupil or imitator (cf. Provenance).

Version

LONDON Christie's, 25 March 1977 (16); panel 66.5 × 53, almost identical with P459, but the dress concealing more of the table leg; ex Christie's, 2 July 1976 (55).
See also P443, ascribed to Greuze.

Provenance

Possibly Redron sale, Paris, 24–5 October 1861 (33, *La lettre d'amour, d'après Greuze*), the 4th Baron Ashburton (1835–89), Christie's, 3 June 1871 (30), bt. in, and Christie's, 8 June 1872 (58, *La Méditation* . . . from the Redron collection), bt. Barre, 285 gn. Sir Richard Wallace, 1872; Hertford House inventory 1890.

Exhibition

Bethnal Green 1872–5 (373, *Girl reading a Letter*).

[1] And cf. Brookner 1972, p.86; but she qualifies this with a 'perhaps' on p.129, mentioning an alternative composition preserved in a drawing now in a private collection, New York (Munhall, no.78) – which, however, appears to be c.1763, see P454.

[2] Formerly Yerkes collection, New York; 61 × 50, half-length figure, her head on her left hand, a quill and paper on a table before her; ex colls. Daupais, Penthièvre and Montebello.

Antoine-Jean Gros (1771–1835)

Born on 16 March 1771 in Paris, he became a pupil of J.-L. David in 1785, entering the Académie in 1787. In 1793 he went to Italy, and he witnessed the battle of Arcole in 1796. In 1796–9 he lived in Milan where he first met Napoleon. He painted portraits and romantic literary subjects, but his reputation was made by his close association with Napoleon, whose deeds he celebrated in such large canvases as the *Pestiférés de Jaffa* (Salon 1804; Louvre) and the *Bataille des Pyramides* (Salon 1810; Versailles). He exhibited at the Salon 1798–1835 and was made *chevalier* of the Legion of Honour in 1808 and *officier* in 1829. He was elected to the Institut in 1815 and succeeded David as *professeur* at the Ecole des Beaux-Arts in 1816. He was made *baron* by Charles X in 1824. During his later years his *davidien* ideas were increasingly criticised and his unhappiness led him to take his own life, by drowning in the Seine, on 26 June 1835.

Abbreviation

Tripier-Le-Franc J. Tripier-Le-Franc, *Histoire de la vie et de la mort du baron Gros*, 1880

P303 *General Bonaparte reviewing Troops*

Napoleon, wearing the green coat with red piping of the *chasseurs à cheval*, on a white horse with a rich red saddle-cloth trimmed with gold; to the right a Staff Officer and two Hussars with red and gold shakos. Signed, bottom right: *Gros.fe.*

Canvas[1] 40 × 32.3

There is a small loss on the white horse's tail and finger-prints in the paint surface on the brown horse's tail on the extreme right. The varnish is discoloured.

Gros first painted Napoleon in 1796 (*General Bonaparte at Arcole*; Versailles); he painted a small equestrian portrait in 1797[2] and more portraits of him after he became First Consul in 1802 (and assumed the red uniform of that office), of which there is a standing whole-length of 1802–3 in the Musée de la Légion d'Honneur and an equestrian whole-length of 1802 at Malmaison. The heads in

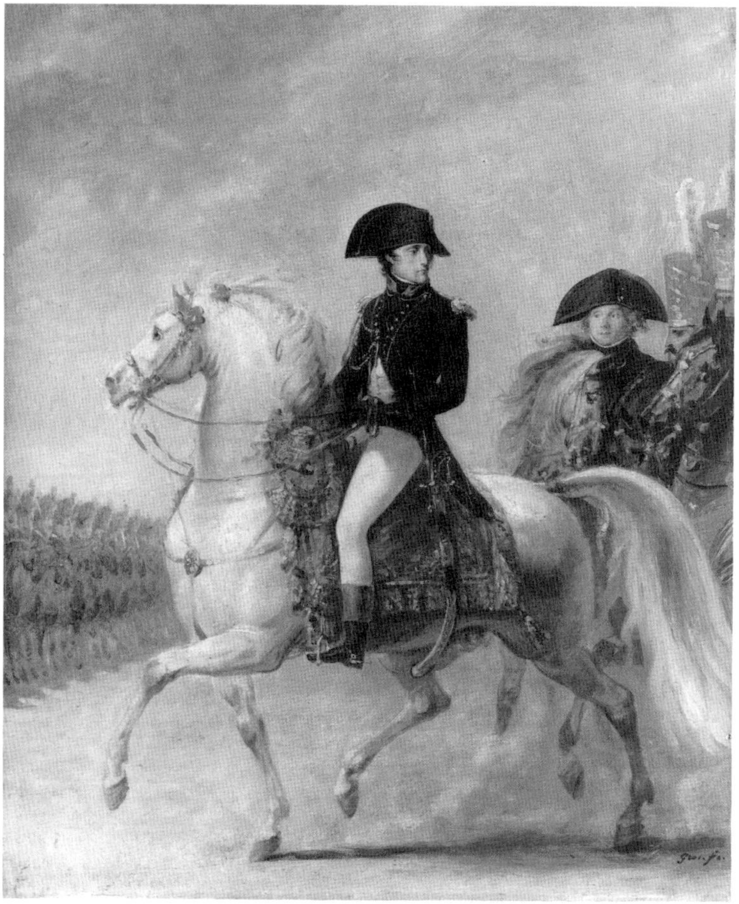

P303

all these portraits, and in P303, are similar and derived from sittings received at Milan in 1796. Whole-length portraits of the First Consul were painted in 1802–5 for the Cities of Lyon (seated) and Rouen (in a tent, with ships in the distance), and for the *tribunal d'appel* in Paris, and another equestrian portrait was painted for Milan in 1802.[3] A small whole-length was painted for Vivant-Denon in 1803.[4] P303 was presumably a first idea for one of the equestrian commissions, before the new uniform of the First Consul was seen.

Provenance

Anon. sale, '*Sujets de l'Empire*',[5] Paris, 5 February 1858 (2, '*Gros, signé, Le général Bonaparte passant une revue: il est suivi de son état-major. Nous signalons ce portrait comme une des oeuvres les plus remarquables de ce grand artiste.*'), 2,000 fr.; the 4th Marquess of Hertford; rue Laffitte inventory 1871 (221); Hertford House inventory 1890.

Exhibitions

Malmaison 1867 (140) lent Hertford; Bethnal Green 1872–5 (512).

[1] The canvas is inscribed in ink, *verso*: *No 11*, and bears an indistinct maker's mark. The frame bears the label of CROSET [*rue*] *Bergère no 22, successeur de Mr F . . . dain, Fabricant de Dorure sur Bois*.

[2] 80 × 70; exh. *Gros*, Petit Palais, 1936, no.17, lent baron de Courgaud; the uniform is similar to that of the Arcole portrait but with a plumed hat.

[3] For discussion of these Napoleonic portraits, see Tripier-Le-Franc, pp.183–202, and G. Lacambre in *French Painting 1770–1830*, exh. cat., Paris, Detroit, New York, 1975, under no.89.

[4] Panel 43 × 27; it was in the Denon sale 1826 and may have been the portrait offered in 1856 to the Louvre who declined it (cf. Tripier-Le-Franc, pp.665, 673).

[5] This sale contained only six paintings, all of First Empire subjects, cf. *Revue universelle des Arts*, VI, 1857, p.556. H. Mireur, *Dictionnaire des ventes d'art*, III, 1911, p.372, cited *Le Général Bonaparte passant une revue* in the Archinto sale, 18 May 1863, but there was no Gros in that sale.

Nicolas-René Jollain (1732–1804)

Born in Paris in 1732, he entered the Académie as the pupil of J.-M. Pierre, obtaining the second *prix de Rome* in 1754. *Agréé* in 1765, he was *reçu* in 1773, his *morceau de réception* being the *Good Samaritan* (formerly in S. Nicolas-du-Chardonnet, Paris). His exhibits at the Salon 1767–91 included decorative panels for the Petit Trianon (1786), the Carthusian Monastery in Paris (1771), the chapel at Fontainebleau (1781), Marly (see below) and designs for the Gobelins (1783). He was made *conservateur* of the Royal Collection in 1788, and in 1792 a member of the commission for the formation of a National Museum. He died in Paris in 1804.[1]

[1] Cf. P.-M. Gault de Saint-Germain, *Les trois siècles de la Peinture en France*, 1808, p.273 (*'né et mort à Paris'*); the date of death is taken from E. Bénézit, *Dictionnaire . . .*, 1976 ed.

P488 *Sleeping Child (Le sommeil)*

The left-hand *putto* under a golden-yellow drape with a brown curtain above; to the right a large gold vase.

Canvas, relined 95.7 × 142.7

There are small losses on the right-hand *putto's* right shoulder and retouchings round the edges (which have been made up to 96.8 × 144), in the curtain to the right and on the curtain tassels. *Pentimenti* show that where the curtain is draped round the two tree trunks there were originally garlands of flowers and that the curtain cords spread into the centre of the composition. The varnish is discoloured.

Previously catalogued as by Fragonard (see Taraval P483 note 1), the identification of the pendant P483 as the overdoor from Marly commissioned from Taraval in 1781 allows P488 to be identified as the original companion piece, commissioned from Jollain in 1781 by the Direction des Bâtiments for the Queen's Bed Chamber at Marly: '*4 pieds 3 pouces de large sur 3 pieds 8 pouces de haut environ* [c.120 × 139]. *Il représente par des enfans* le Sommeil'.[1] The edges of the original canvas appear to have been roughly cut in the course of the relining, and the original size perhaps agreed more closely with the approximate size given in the commission (but see also Taraval P483 note 3).

For further discussion, see Taraval P483.

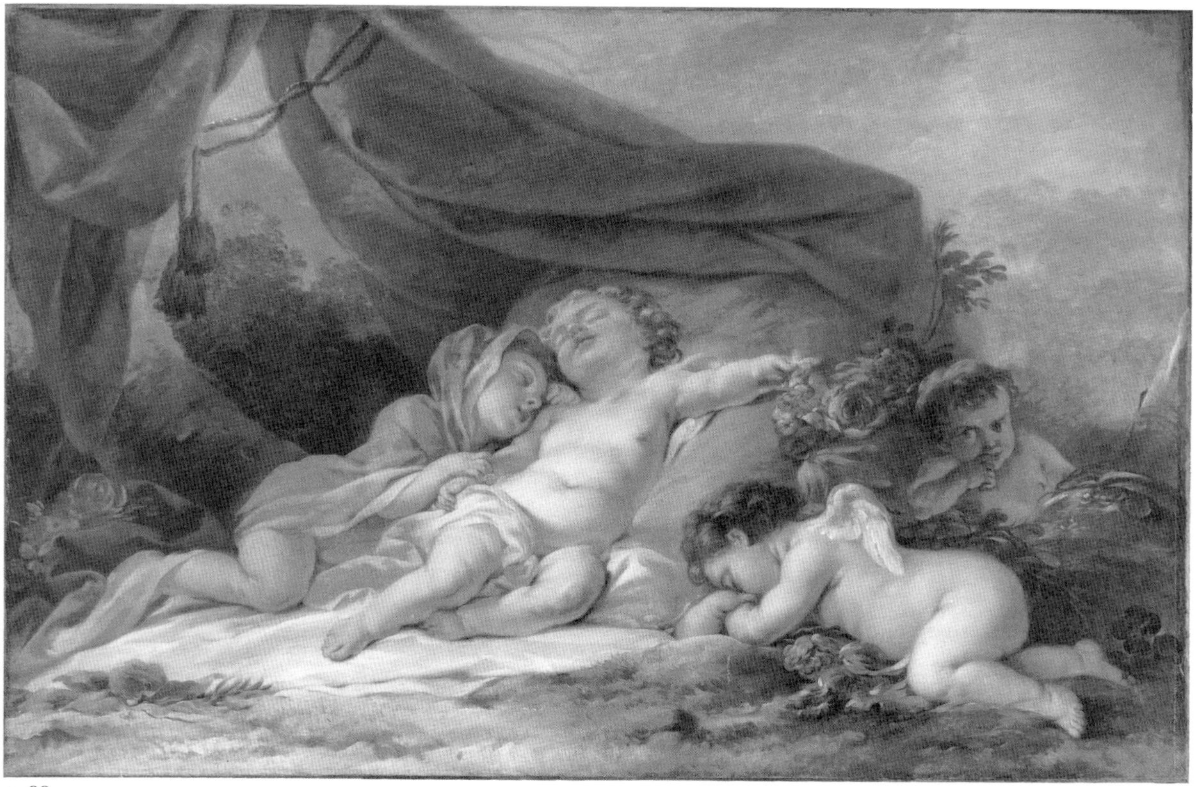

P488

Version

PARIS professeur Chauffard 1956; a reduced version.[2]

Provenance

Commissioned in 1781 through d'Angiviller by the Direction des Bâtiments du Roi for the *chambre à coucher de la Reine*, Château de Marly, 500 *livres*;[3] the contents of Marly were dispersed by 1796 (see Taraval P483 note 7); Ralph Bernal (c.1785–1854); his sale, Christie's, 6th day, 10 March 1855 (613, 'Boucher, Three nymphs and a cupid reclining in a landscape – the companion [to lot 612, see Taraval P483]'), bt., with lot 612, by the 4th Marquess of Hertford, 61 gn.; 5 rue Taitbout inventory 1871 as '*école de Boucher*' (see Taraval P483 note 8); Hertford House inventory 1890 as Boucher.

Exhibition

Palais Bourbon, *Ouvrages de Peinture exposés au profit de la colonisation de l'Algérie par les Alsaces-Lorrains*, 1874 (811 or 812, both Fragonard, *Amours endormis*) lent Wallace (see Taraval P483 note 9).

References General

J. Ingamells, *The Burlington Magazine*, CXXIX, 1987, pp.518–19. The following refer to P488 as Fragonard (q.v. for abbreviations): Portalis, pp.106, 270; Lady Dilke, *French Painters of the XVIIIth century*, 1899, p.65; Réau, p.145; WF64, as c.1748–52; Mandel, no.72.

[1] F. Engerand, *Inventaire des Tableaux commandés et achetés par la Direction des Bâtiments du Roi*, 1900, p.239.

[2] Réau, *loc. cit.*

[3] Jollain was paid on 21 January 1785 (Engerand, *loc. cit.*).

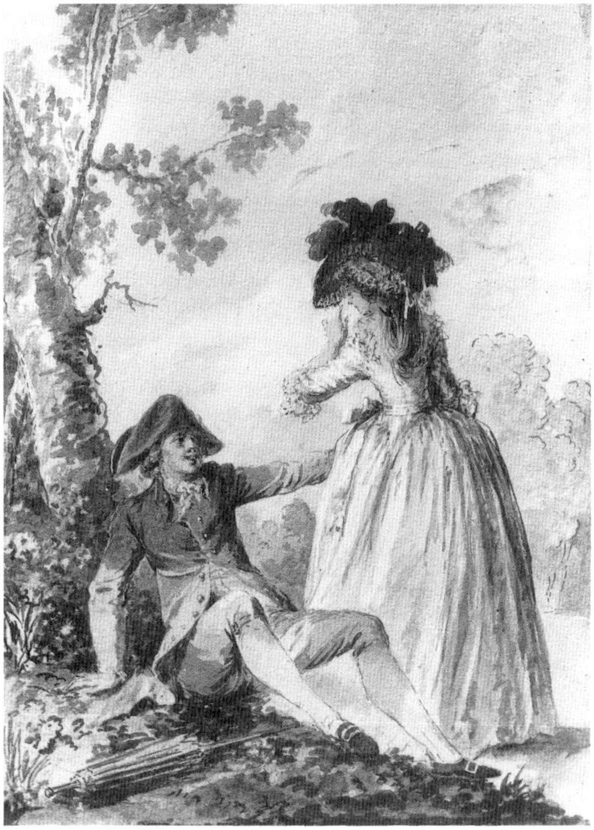

P772

Niclas Lafrensen (1737–1807)

Called *Nicolas Lavreince* or *Lawrence*; born on 30 October 1737 in Stockholm where he studied under his father, the miniaturist Niclas Lafrensen (1698–1756), and attended the Swedish Academy. He was in Paris 1762–9, probably practising as a miniaturist. He returned to Stockholm in 1769 to paint a number of miniature portraits for the Court, and was made *académicien* in 1773. In 1774 he returned to Paris to paint *galant* subjects in miniature (cf. M257–61 in this Collection) and gouache, many of which were engraved. He left Paris at the Revolution, returning in 1791 to Stockholm where he painted historical subjects in gouache and portraits in miniature, and where he died on 7 December 1807.

P772 *Conversation galante*

Grey wash, body- and water-colour on buff paper 16.9 × 11.9

Laid down on paper. Cleaned by Goodwin in 1988 when blackened lead white was treated. Originally backed with a printed sheet of 1775–7[1] inscribed, *verso*: *Lawrence/peintre suedois*.

P772 may be dated by costume in the mid-1780s.[2] The attribution was unnecessarily doubted in the 1928 edition of this catalogue.

Provenance

Probably bt. by Sir Richard Wallace from the vicomte Both de Tauzia (1823–88), 1872;[3] Hertford House inventory 1890.

[1] Printed on one side with a schedule of coaches from Paris with the dates 7 August 1775, 17 August 1776 and 23 January 1777.

[2] And cf. *Couples d'amour dans un parc*, gouache, dated 1784 (illus. P. Lespinasse, *Lavreince*, 1929, pl. xxxix), and *Le concert agréable* and *Scene in a Park*, both engraved in 1784 (illus. B.G. Wennberg, *Niclas Lafrensen*, 1947, figs. 27, 31).

[3] For Wallace's purchase of the Tauzia collection, see vol. I of this catalogue, 1985, pp.434–7. P772 was framed in France in the mid-nineteenth century, to judge by writing on the backboard which is also inscribed: *No 5*.

Nicolas Lancret (1690–1743)

Born on 22 January 1690 in Paris where in 1707 he began to study under Pierre Dulin, *professeur de l'Académie*. In 1711 he competed unsuccessfully against Lemoyne for the *prix de Rome*. He studied under Claude Gillot c.1712–13, a painter of theatrical subjects who had been Watteau's teacher. Later, probably c.1717, he was briefly the pupil of Watteau whose work he admired greatly. In 1719, two years after Watteau, he too was *reçu* as a painter of *fêtes galantes* (see P422). At the Expositions de jeunesse 1722–4 he showed principally *fêtes galantes*, but at the 1725 Salon his subjects also included a portrait, a bathing scene and a hunting piece. In 1725 he received his first commission from the Bâtiments du Roi, *L'accident de Montereau* (a scene from contemporary history, now lost). His subjects tended increasingly to illustration, genre and theatre pieces, and from 1728 he actively promoted the engraving of his paintings. He was made *conseiller* at the Académie in 1735 on submission of *La danse entre le pavillon et la fontaine* (Charlottenburg), and he exhibited regularly at the Salon from 1737. A further fourteen pictures were commissioned by the Bâtiments du Roi between 1735 and 1743. Lancret enjoyed a certain reputation as a connoisseur, and his collection of Italian and Dutch pictures was sold by his widow in 1782. He died in Paris on 14 September 1743. Though never as fanciful as Watteau, Lancret was his last pupil and with him passed the era of the *fête galante*. Frederick the Great subsequently acquired twenty-four of his paintings, of which twelve remain at Charlottenburg and four at Sans Souci (Potsdam).

Abbreviations

Bocher	E. Bocher, *Les Graveurs françaises du XVIIIe siècle, Nicolas Lancret*, 1877
Grasselli	M. Morgan Grasselli, 'Eleven new drawings by Lancret', *Master Drawings*, XXIII–XXIV, 1986, pp.377–88, pls.43–50
WL	G. Wildenstein, *Lancret*, 1924

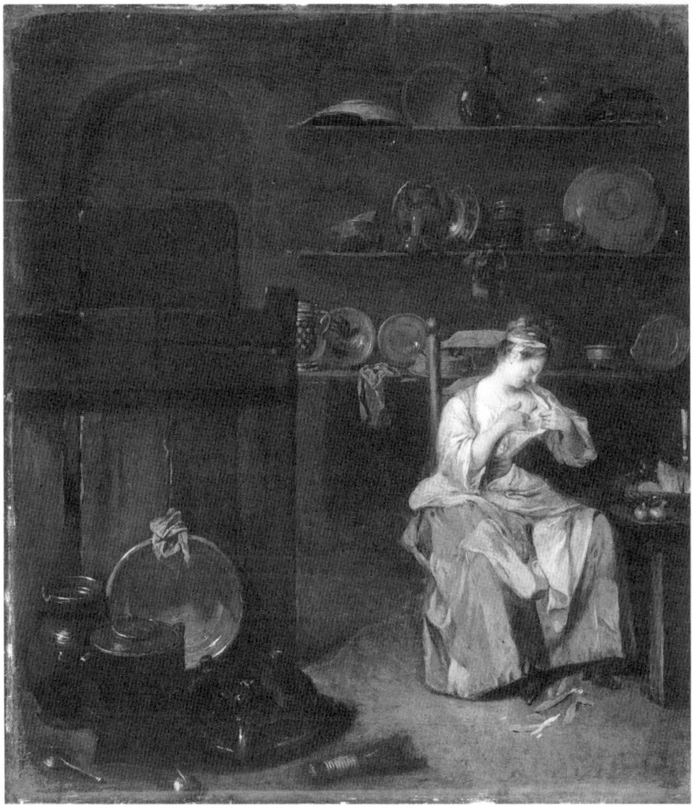

P378

P378 *A Girl in a Kitchen* (*La chercheuse de puce*)

Her skirt is striped in salmon pink, turquoise and pale green; a peeled orange and a knife lie in her lap.

Oak panel 29.7 × 25.5 × 0.8

The girl and the basket of fruit on the table are painted more thickly, and in brighter colours than the rest of the picture. There are two small losses behind the girl's head and another on the edge of the basket of fruit. A knot in the panel, top left, has disturbed the surface. *Pentimenti* show a dog to the left of the girl and another figure beneath her (there are traces round her head, by her right hip and by her left foot); her chair may originally have had arms, and the candle on the table to the right has been repainted. X-radiography has not helped to elucidate the earlier composition. The edges of the panel are abraded and the varnish is discoloured.

The girl's innocent activity, looking for fleas, was probably intended to arouse a mild erotic interest.[1] For the subject, see also P408.

Examination of the panel confirms that the girl and the still life on the table to the right were added to an older picture (which probably showed an older woman with the dog). The girl recurs, with only minor differences, in *Le nègre et la cuisinière* (WL 546) which, with P378, has traditionally been attributed to Lancret. Phillips (1908 catalogue) first suggested P378 might be the work of two artists; Batz (1946) attributed the earlier interior to Willem Kalf,[2] and his qualified attribution was retained in the 1968 catalogue. In 1974 Grisebach, while accepting that P378 had originally been a seventeenth-century Dutch interior, rejected the association with Kalf.[3] Lancret added figures to several such Dutch scenes: two by Kalf,[4] one described in 1745 as by Herman Saftleven,[5] and a further four, including P378, unattributed.[6]

Provenance

Robert de Saint-Victor, *président de la chambre des comptes*, Rouen; his sale, Paris, 26 November ff.1822 (625, '*Une servante dans sa cuisine, entr'ouvrant son corset, pour chercher une puce qui l'incommode. Ce joli tableau est meublé de buffet, casseroles et autres ustensiles de cuisine, b[ois* 27.2 × 24.5]'), 152 fr.; Morny and Belon sale, Paris, 25 November 1842 (23, '. . . *de la vente Saint-Victor*'), 400 fr.; the 4th Marquess of Hertford by 1859 when P378 was reframed in Hertford House;[7] Hertford House inventory 1890.

Exhibition

Bethnal Green 1872–5 (439).

Reference General

WL527.

1 The flea being envied as it explored the girl's body, cf. M. Françon, *Publications of the Modern Language Association of America*, LVI, 1941, pp.307–36, and J.F. Moffitt, *Gazette des Beaux-Arts*, 6e, CX, 1987, pp.99–103.

2 G. de Batz, *The Art Quarterly*, IX, 1946, p.309. Willem Kalf (1622–93) had worked in Paris 1642–6.

3 L. Grisebach, *Willem Kalf*, 1974, p.81 n.172.

4 *Ibid.*, pp.209, 231, nos. 2, 51; *Interior with Still Life*, signed by Kalf (private coll., Zurich) and *L'offre du nid* (St. Louis, City Art Museum) whose figures by Lancret were removed by cleaning in 1946, before it was acquired by the Museum (Batz, *loc. cit.*, and *Gazette des Beaux-Arts*, 6e, LXXXIV, 1974, *supp.*, *La Chronique des Arts*, Nov–Dec., p.29).

5 WL535: La Roque sale, Paris, April 1745, lot 55: '*un tableau original peint par Herman Zagtlieven . . . dans le goût de Kalf . . . une grange avec tous les instruments et batterie de cuisine, ornée de trois petites figures peintes par Lancret*'.

6 The other three being WL529–31, of which *La cuisine* and *Le valet galant* in the Hermitage were attributed to Kalf and Lancret in the eighteenth century, but Grisebach rejects the Kalf attribution (*op. cit.*, p.81 n.172).

7 Evans invoice.

P393 *Mademoiselle de Camargo Dancing*

Wearing a white muslin dress with a floral pattern and turquoise ribbons on the shoulders, she executes a *demi-pointe*, accompanied by fiddles, hautbois and bassoon, with pipe and tabor.

Canvas, relined 41.7 × 54.5

The edges have been made up, after relining, to 43.2 × 55. There are small retouchings in the trees on left and right, and in the centre of the sky. There is a marked craquelure round Camargo's head. *Pentimenti* show minor adjustments to the positions of her feet. The varnish is somewhat discoloured.[1]

Marie Anne de Cupis de Camargo (1710–70) was the first great virtuoso ballerina of the Paris Opera where she first performed in 1726 and, save for a period 1735–41 when she lived with the comte de Clermont at the Château de Berny, continued until her retirement in 1751. She released the ballet from the con-

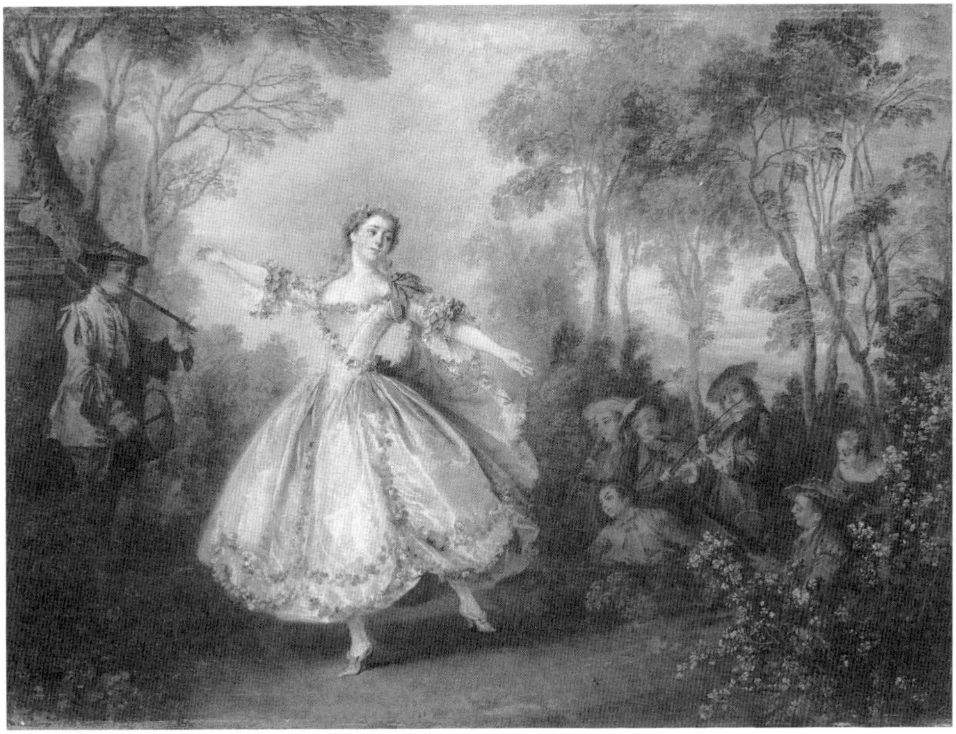

P393

straints of the seventeenth century, introducing a shorter skirt and the ballet slipper (though she still wears high heels in P393); she developed the *entrechat* and excelled in gavottes, tambourins, *marches* and *loures*. Mlle. Sallé, her great rival between 1727 and 1740, was the subject of a pendant portrait by Lancret.[2]

P393 was apparently painted by 6 August 1730 when Lancret was granted the copyright of engravings after a number of his pictures, including '*le portrait d'une danseuse*'.[3] It agrees exactly with the engraving by Cars (see Engravings) published in January 1731 and must be considered the prime version of a composition copied and engraved several times,[4] although it now seems impossible to disentangle the provenances of the autograph versions (see Versions). Despite such evidence of success, the picture was criticised anonymously in 1732 for Camargo's pose.[5] It has been suggested that the extreme left-hand figure is a self-portrait, though this seems unlikely.[6] The composition was used by Pater in 1731 for his portrait of Mlle. d'Angeville,[7] and by Pesne in 1745 for his portrait of Mlle. Cochois (Charlottenburg). Lancret's *Mlle. Camargo* (reclining in a garden) in the Forsyth Wickes collection, Boston, is perhaps wrongly named.

Drawings

Studies of dancers have been associated with P393, but relate to the dancer in *La ronde autour du mai* (WL139).[8]

Engravings

L. Cars 1731, reversed (Bocher, no. 17A), with verses below:[9]

Fidele aux lois de la cadence,
Je forme, au gré de l'art, les pas les plus hardis;
Originale dans ma danse,
Je puis le disputer aux Balons, aux Blondis.

The engraving (40.8 × 55.3) was described as being the same size as the painting then in the collection of Leriget de la Faye.[10]
Radigue 1731 (Bocher, no. 17B); anon. mid-eighteenth century;[11] J.F. Journet, the figure of Camargo alone; anon. mid-eighteenth century, without right-hand trees and with a single musician; E. Hédouin 1844 (for *L'Artiste*; Bocher, no. 17E);[12] W. Marks 1851 (Bocher, no.17C); Delauney 1872 (for the Pereire sale catalogue; Bocher, no.17D).

Versions

LENINGRAD Hermitage; 45 × 55, with minor differences, Camargo wearing a yellow dress with a red-lined cape dances on a paved terrace, the trees on the left in leaf, no pedestal on the left; possibly ex Cottin sale, Paris, 27 November 1752 (368, with a *Mlle. Sallé*, each 41 × 51); Catherine II by 1774 (WL584).[13]
NANTES Musée des Beaux-Arts; 45 × 54, differing only in the omission of the three figures immediately to the right of Camargo whose dress is light blue; acquired in 1810, ex coll. F. Cacault (WL583).
WASHINGTON National Gallery of Art (no.89); 76 × 107, only the figure of Camargo is the same; she is accompanied by a male dancer and surrounded by eighteen spectators; ex coll. Frederick the Great, given by Andrew Mellon, 1937; see note 4 (WL585). A drawing for one of the spectators is in the Pierpont Morgan Library (Grasselli, pp.383,385, pl.45).

Other copies/versions are recorded in the following sales:
COLOGNE anon. sale, 4 June 1912 (134); 34 × 27, with three musicians.
LONDON Naylor sale, Christie's, 22 July 1893 (52); 112 × 96.5.
Waterpark sale, Christie's, 12 June 1897 (112); 123 × 143, ex coll. comte de Bork, Paris.
Duncan-Sinclair sale, Lockhart's, 24 July 1922 (184).
A version was with Dowdeswell (c.1910?), photograph in Witt Library.
NEW YORK Fischer sale, 19–24 February 1912 (897); 96.5 × 114.5.
PARIS the prince de Carignan sale, 30 July 1742; '*un paysage avec la Camargo, par Lancré*', 43.4 × 54.2.[14]
Anon. sale, 2 May 1849 (12), and 8 May 1849 (27).
Soleirol sale, 29 April–2 May 1861 (83).
Anon. sale, 28 November 1861 (61), gouache on vellum.
Richard sale, 18 March 1872 (41), panel 47 × 58, after Lancret.
The marquis de Saint-Cloud sale, 12 February 1874 (20), after Lancret.
Mme. de R. sale, 4–6 April 1905 (288); 85 × 92.
Anon. sale, 22 May 1919 (111); 67 × 58, the dancer alone with a fountain behind (to judge from a photograph, not by Lancret, nor of Camargo).
VIENNA Dorotheum, 10 May 1977 (77), 48 × 58, attributed to Mercier.

The image was also used on a Liverpool transfer tile (*Connoisseur*, LXXVIII, 1927, p.30), and on a lacquer tray (*Apollo*, XXVI, 1937, p.87).

Provenance

J.-F. Leriget de La Faye (1674–1731), see Engravings; possibly Carignan sale, Paris, 1742, see Versions and note 14; anon. sale, Paris, 12 February 1864 (1), bt. Isaac Pereire (1806–80), 8,000 fr.;[15] Pereire sale, Paris, 2nd day, 7 March 1872 (65), bt. Delière for Sir Richard Wallace, 9,900 fr.; Hertford House inventory 1890.

Exhibition

Bethnal Green 1872–5 (433); RA 1889 (101).

References General

WL582; E. Dacier, 'A propos du portrait de la Camargo par Lancret', *Musées de France*, 1911, 3, pp.42–5.

1 Writing soon after the Pereire sale in 1872, J. Guiffrey (*Eloge de Lancret par Ballot de Sovot*, n.d., c.1875, p.44) described P393, with the pendant portrait of Mlle. Sallé, as having '*singulièrement souffert des retouches et des vernis*' (and see note 15 below).

2 See Wildenstein, p.109 and WL598–9; Bocher, no.71. The prime version was sold with P393 in 1864 and 1872 and last recorded in the Camondo sale, Paris, 1 February 1893 (10). A version was in the Cottin sale, Paris, 27 November 1752, probably with the Camargo now in the Hermitage.

[3] See Wildenstein, p.49; Guiffrey, *op. cit.*, pp.66–9.

[4] As proposed by Dacier, p.42, and Wildenstein. C. Sterling (*Musée de l'Ermitage: La peinture française de Poussin à nos jours*, 1957, p.42) suggested the Hermitage version may have preceded P393, but I.S. Nemilova (*The Hermitage, French Painting, eighteenth century*, 1986, pp.163–4) agreed with Dacier and Wildenstein. Grasselli (pp.383, 385) proposed the Washington version may have been the first; it resembles a *fête galante* rather than a portrait, and she notes that Lancret 'appears to have moved in general from complication to simplification'.

[5] Letter in the *Mercure de France*, April 1732, printed in Bocher, p.16; the writer maintained that Camargo's head was turned in the wrong direction, that her elbows should be on the same level, and that her left leg, slightly bent, would be incapable of holding the pose depicted, etc.

[6] Cf. E.M. Zafran, *The Rococo Age*, exh. cat., High Museum of Art, Atlanta, Georgia, 1983, no.43.

[7] Cf. F. Ingersoll-Smouse, *Pater*, 1928, figs. 201–4 (IS 549–50).

[8] Cf. *Les Arts du Théâtre de Watteau à Fragonard*, exh. cat., Bordeaux, 1980, no.140. The drawings are: Kunsthalle sale, Basle, 24 January 1970 (10); anon. sale, Sotheby's, 27 April 1977 (67), and in the Louvre (no.27.542).

[9] The verses attributed to Leriget de La Faye in 1770 ('Eloge de Mlle-Camargo', *Nécrologie des hommes célèbres de France*, printed in Bocher, pp.16–18), and to Voltaire (*L'Artiste*, I, 1864, p.142).

[10] In the *Mercure de France*, January 1731 (see *Inventaire du Fonds français du Cabinet des Estampes*, III, 1934, p.470; Wildenstein, p.109, gives this date incorrectly as July 1731). In June 1731 Lancret brought a successful action against the producer of some pirated plates (see Wildenstein, pp.50–2, 109; Guiffrey [see note 1 above], pp.70–6).

[11] Engravings here cited without Bocher references were described by E. Dacier, 'Les portraits gravés de la Camargo au XVIIIe siècle', *La Revue de l'Art ancien et moderne*, XXX, 1911, pp.143–8.

[12] Described, in error, as after the Nantes version by Guiffrey, *op. cit.*, p.40 (see note 1).

[13] Nemilova, *loc. cit.* (see note 4 above) gives the provenance of the Hermitage version as Carignan before 1742, Cottin 1742–52.

[14] See note 13 above. The Carignan picture has also been associated with the Washington version (Zafran, *loc. cit.*, see note 6 above), which is impossible as the sizes are different, but it could have been any of the other three versions (P393, Hermitage and Nantes).

[15] The Pereire sale catalogue gave the provenance of P393 and of the companion portrait of Mlle. Sallé as Frederick the Great, château de Rheinsberg: '*Lors de son avénement au trône, il donnait ce Château à son frère, le prince Henri de Prusse; ce prince étant mort en 1802, le Château, avec tout ce qu'il contenait, a passé par héritage à son troisième frère, le prince Auguste de Prusse, qui a laissé, en 1813, à mademoiselle de W... tout le mobilier, dont faisaient partie ces 2 tableaux, qui lui ont été achetés par le propriétaire actuel*' (reprinted in *L'Artiste*, I, 1864, p.142). W. Bürger, *Gazette des Beaux-Arts*, 1ère, XVI, 1864, p.201, repeated that P393 and its companion had belonged to Frederick the Great (whose picture of Camargo, however, is almost certainly that now in Washington, see Versions). Guiffrey (see note 1 above), rather curiously, doubted the authenticity of the Pereire Lancrets (p.44 n.1).

P401 *An Italian Comedy Scene (Arlequin et Polichinelle)*

Columbine in blue with flowers in her hair, wards off Harlequin who wears a costume of yellow, red and blue with a black mask, while Polichinelle in yellow with red and blue trimmings advances from the right.

Canvas 28.8 × 36.8

The edges are abraded and craquelure follows the impress marks of the stretcher. There is a *pentimento* on the wooden dagger in Harlequin's hand. The varnish is discoloured.

Probably painted in the 1730s. The subject may be compared with that of Watteau P387; Lancret separates the actors, leaving less ambiguity between the real and the theatrical. P401 had a pendant, *Joueur de flûte* (WL103, 113; see Provenance), last recorded in the Bolton sale, New York, 19 February 1912, lot 22.

Copy

STRASBOURG Musée des Beaux-Arts; 29 × 36 (WL324).[1]

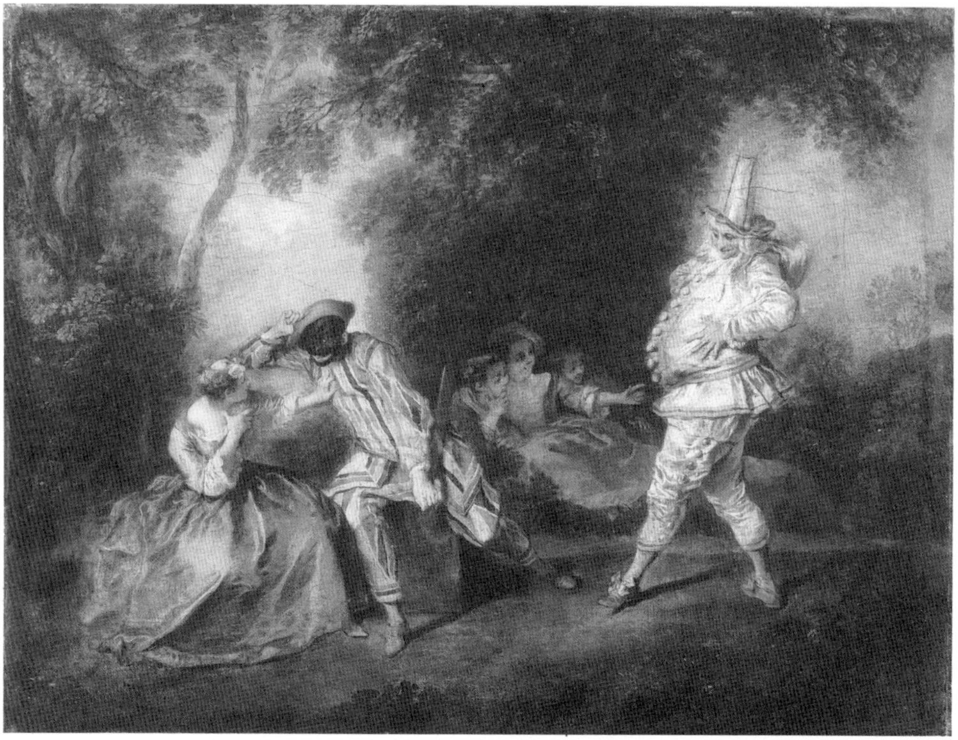

P401

Provenance

M. sale, Paris, 13 January 1778 (45, '*Deux tableaux . . . un sujet pastoral, composition de plusieurs personnages déguisés* [29.8 × 33.4]'); Trouard sale, Paris, 22 February 1779 (29, with pendant); anon. sale, Paris, 16 November 1780 (10, *Arlequin et Polichinelle*, with pendant [28.2 × 37.8]);[2] Prault sale, Paris, 27 November 1780 (10, '*deux paysages . . . une scène comique rendue par six personnages, dont l'un est sous un masque d'Arlequin, et l'autre sous un habit de polichinelle . . . un concert exécuté par un homme qui accompagne une femme avec sa flûte, en présence de quelques autres personnes* [28.5 × 37.9]'), 360 fr.; Samson sale, Paris, 27 October 1812 (56, '*Trois jeunes filles s'amusant des plaisantes contorsions d'un polichinel et d'un arlequin*'), 16 fr.; Brisebarre sale, Paris, 6 June 1814 (41, '*Deux personnages, l'un déguisé en Arlequin, et l'autre en Polichinelle, font rire plusieurs jeunes filles assises dans un jardin, à l'ombre des grands arbres* [29.8 × 37.9]'), 18 fr.; the 4th Marquess of Hertford; rue Laffitte inventory 1871 (260, '*Arlequin et Columbine*'); Hertford House inventory 1890.

Exhibitions

Bazar Bonne Nouvelle 1849 (22);[3] Bethnal Green 1872–5 (444, *Group of Masquers*); RA 1889 (111, *Harlequin and Punch*).

Reference General

WL323, 360.

[1] Exh. *Le Théâtre à Paris*, Musée Carnavalet, 1929, no.40; *Les Arts du Théâtre de Watteau à Fragonard*, Bordeaux, 1980, no.36.

[2] Cited under WL360.

[3] The stretcher is inscribed, *verso*: *ce tableau/a figuré/à l'exposition/des artistes/au Bazare/Bonnenouvelle/1849/sous le/No 22.*

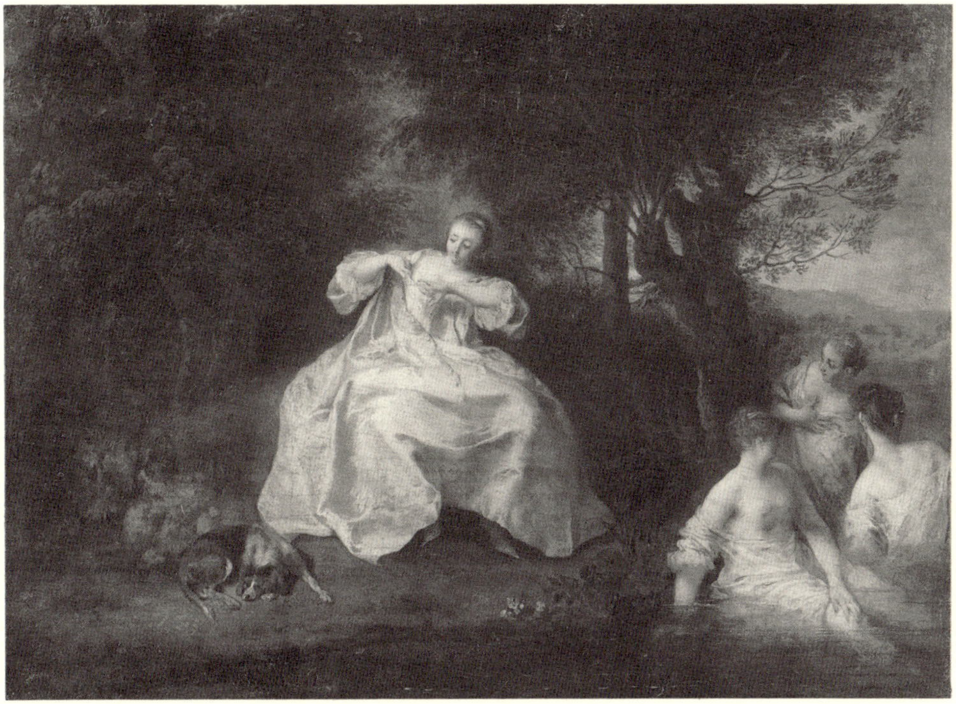

P408

P408 *Girls Bathing*

Canvas 24.5 × 30.7

There are small losses round the edges and on the foreground bather's left arm. There is a marked craquelure, and the varnish is discoloured.

For the motif of a girl looking for fleas (as the principal figure in P408), see P378 note 1. Lancret's bathers may be compared with those by Pater (see P426).

Lancret exhibited a *Bain des femmes* (130 × 97) in the 1725 Salon, but P408 may be somewhat later. The second bather from the right recurs in *L'été* (Hermitage; WL8) and *La soirée* (National Gallery, London; engraved in 1741; WL37); she also recurs, with the extreme right-hand bather, in *Les plaisirs du bain* (ex coll. Coote; WL433). The sleeping dog is taken from Watteau's *L'heureux loisir* (DV285), and recurs in Lancret's *Les amours du bocage* (engraved in 1736; WL455). The stolid figures and careful landscape recall the work of Cornelis van Poelenburgh.[1]

Copy

LONDON Wallace Collection (M128); oval miniature, probably French nineteenth century, adding a *voyeur* to the right of the main figure.

Provenance[2]

The comte de Pourtalès-Gorgier (1776–1855) by 1841;[3] his sale, Paris, 8th day, 27 March 1865 (276), bt. by the 4th Marquess of Hertford, 7,300 fr.;[4] rue Laffitte inventory 1871 (259, '*femme au bain*'); Hertford House inventory 1890.

Exhibitions

Bethnal Green 1872–5 (450); RA 1889 (104).

Reference General

WL428

[1] A comparable *Nymphes au bain* was one of five Poelenburghs in the Orléans collection (cf. C. Stryienski, *La Galerie du Régent*, 1913, pp.180–1). Lancret himself owned a small panel by Poelenburgh (23 × 30.5), '*Des rochers bordant une rivière, des baigneuses y sont au nombre de 8*' (Mme. Lancret sale, Paris, 5 April 1782, lot 121).

[2] Wildenstein associates P408 with the T. sale, Paris, 6 April 1829, lot 39: '*Sur le devant d'un paysage que traverse une rivière, on remarque plusieurs jeunes filles se baignant à l'ombre d'un massif d'arbres*', 75 fr.

[3] Cf. J.J. Dubois, *Description des tableaux . . . de M. le comte de Pourtalès-Gorgier*, 1841, pp.57–8, no. 180.

[4] At the time of this sale, P. Mantz described P408 as '*d'une parfaite délicatesse*' (*Gazette des Beaux-Arts*, 1ère, XVIII, 1865, p.112).

P409 *A Tale from La Fontaine (Le petit chien qui secoue de l'argent et des pierreries)*

Atis, dressed as a pilgrim with a black cape collar and staff, stands by the bed, a musette on the chair beside him; the foreground maid in a red skirt with blue overdress and white apron; a second maid threads pearls; the bed curtains are rust-red.

Copper 27.6 × 35.4

There are small retouchings behind Atis's head, in the bed curtains, at the foot of the bed and round the edges. The pilgrim's staff is abraded at the top. A heavy craquelure has been retouched at the foot of the bed. The uneven varnish is discoloured.

The subject is taken from the *Contes* of La Fontaine (III, xiii): Anselme, a magistrate of Mantua, goes on an embassy to Rome, leaving his wife, Argie; her lover, Atis, *en pèlerin jouant de la musette*, reaches her room with the help of the fairy, Manto, transformed into a spaniel which has only to shake itself to produce jewels and coins.

P409 is one of twelve illustrations painted by Lancret for the *Contes* of La Fontaine, of which ten (all on copper and the same size as P409) survive (cf. WL637–79).[1] Four were shown at the 1738 Salon. All twelve were engraved, the earliest in 1737, for the celebrated *Suite Larmessin* which eventually comprised thirty-eight illustrations to the *Contes*, first published singly between 1733 and c.1743.[2] The first eight subjects were furnished by Pater (cf. Pater P405) and engraved by Filloeul in 1733–6, and it seems that Lancret took up the series on Pater's death in 1736.

Drawing

CAMBRIDGE Mass., Fogg Art Museum (no.1974.168); study for the girl stringing beads (Grasselli, pp.386–7, pl.50).

Engravings

N. de Larmessin c.1738, reversed (Bocher, no.60A), with verses by Roy:

Que des pattes d'un chien il tombe des ducats,
C'est un vray tour de fée, un prodige incroyable.
Mais un coeur qui tiendroit contre un pareil appas,
Ce seroit un prodige aussi peu vraisemblable.

The print is the same size as P409.
Anon. eighteenth century with the same verses (Bocher, no.60B); anon. German copy of preceding (Bocher, no.60C).

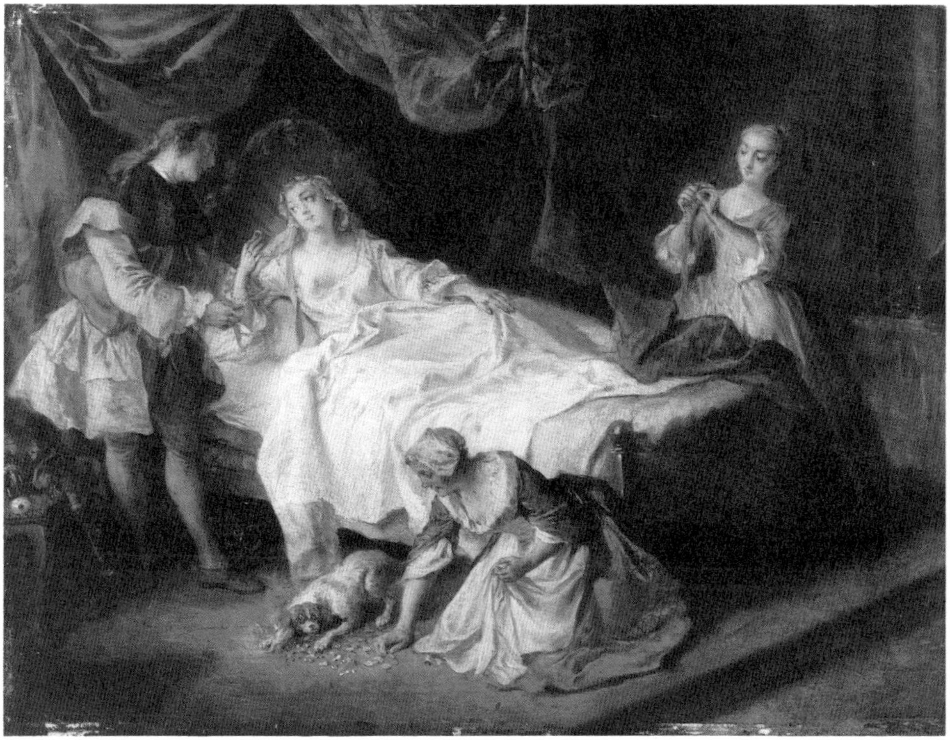

P409

Copies/Versions

HILDESHEIM private collection 1982; reversed.
LONDON Christie's, 28 March 1908 (107); 46 × 54.
Christie's, 28 February 1947 (151); 33 × 43, reversed; probably the picture with C.A. Heusch, Hillsborough, California, 1983.

Provenance[3]

Richard Wallace; his sale, Paris, 2 March 1857 (54), bt. Laneuville for the 4th Marquess of Hertford, 3,425 fr.; possibly rue Laffitte inventory 1871 (61, '*école française, scène galante*', or 91, '*école française, la surprise matinale*'); Hertford House inventory 1890.

Exhibitions

Bethnal Green 1872–5 (582, *The Broken Necklace*); RA 1889 (92, *The Broken Necklace*).

Reference General

WL666.

[1] Apart from P409, three are in public collections: *Le Gascon puni* (Louvre), *Les rémois* (Musée Nissim de Camondo, Paris), and *Les deux amis* (Clark Institute, Williamstown, Mass.).

[2] See P. Jean-Richard, *L'Oeuvre gravé de Boucher*, 1978, p.306; *Inventaire du Fonds français du Cabinet des Estampes*, IX, 1962, p.182, and XII, 1973, p.387. Lot 109 in the Lorangère sale, Paris, 2 March 1744, '*Les contes de la Fontaine*', contained 28 prints, including 8 after Pater, but only 11 after Lancret; this suggests that the *Suite* may not have been completed until c.1744.

[3] P409 might also be associated with the following sales: anon., Paris, 1 June 1787 (65, '*deux sujets de La Fontaine, cuivre* [29.8 × 32]'); M. de V.V., Paris, 18 February 1788 (110, '*deux sujets tirés des Contes de La Fontaine, cuivre* [27.1 × 35.2]'); anon., Paris, 4 December 1834 (40), and Mme. P., Paris, 4 May 1841 (63). See WL666, 676–7; Bocher, p.97.

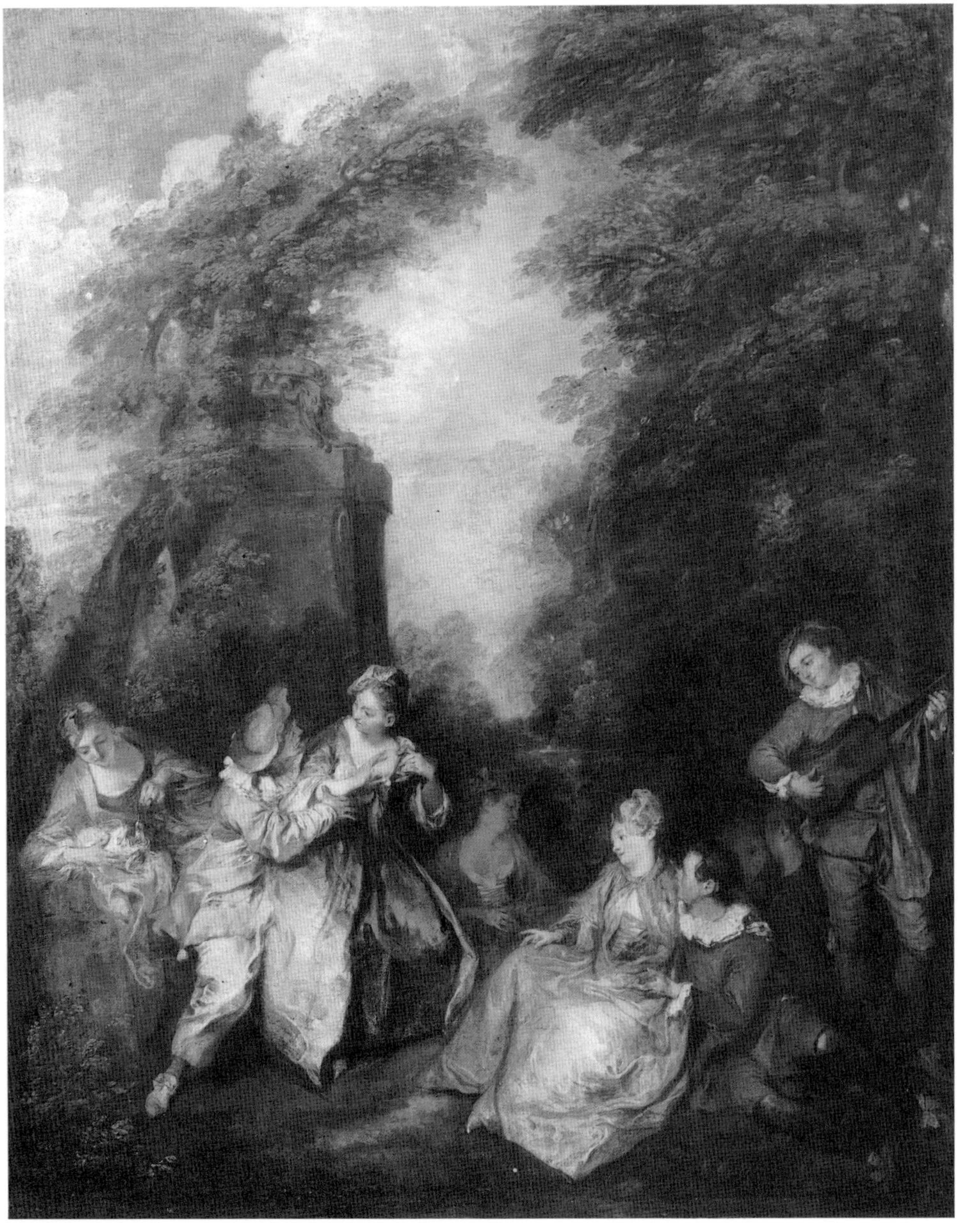

P422

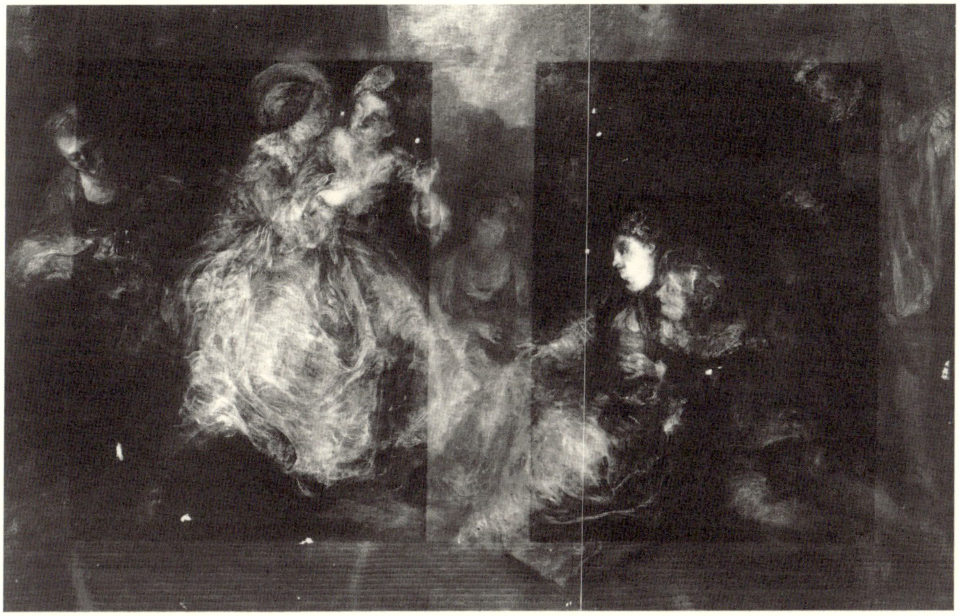

X-radiograph of P422, detail
(The Courtauld Institute)

P422 *Conversation galante*

On the left Pierrot, in pale blue-grey, embracing Columbine who wears a turquoise dress with a pale lavender overdress; on the right a reclining man in a red smock with a lady in a yellow skirt, blue bodice and pink cap, and a guitarist with a red cloak; on the far left a lady wearing yellow attends her dog.

Canvas, relined[1] 68.3 × 53.5

First relined in the mid-nineteenth century (see note 1), P422 was cleaned and relined again in 1984 by Lank, the edges made up to the old stretcher size, 73.7 × 58. There are several small losses: in the back of Pierrot's coat, by the guitarist's left leg, by the left upper arm of the reclining man, and in three places in the lower left area. The red-brown ground shows through the thinly painted passages in the sky, top left. *Pentimenti* and X-radiography reveal several changes within the composition. Pierrot and Columbine were more intimately grouped; his head was placed higher and much nearer to hers and he wore a smaller hat; she looked more to the front and her skirt covered Pierrot's right leg. To the right, the reclining man originally wore a cap, with his head alongside his partner's; his left hand was at her breast, and his left leg rested on his right. The trees to the right and in the central area were redrawn.

A scene from the *commedia dell'arte*, described in 1719 as '*une Feste galante*', see below.

In 1742 the Académie ordered Le Bas to engrave P422 for his *morceau de réception* (see Engraving),[2] revealing that the painting was already in their possession and allowing it to be identified with one of the two *fêtes galantes* which Lancret submitted on 24 March 1719 as his own *morceaux de réception*.[3] P422 is therefore the earliest dateable painting by Lancret; while the subject depends upon the example of Watteau, with whom he had so recently been studying, Lancret's figures are more substantial.[4] The changes in the composition (as described above) may have been made out of respect for the Académie. The group of Pierrot and Columbine recurs in a somewhat modified form in the *Declaration of Love* (Cleveland Museum of Art) which is probably a slightly later composition.[5]

Drawings

LILLE Musée des Beaux-Arts; study of a lady comparable with the figure of Columbine but in reverse.[6]
PARIS Ecole des Beaux-Arts; study for Pierrot and Columbine as they appear in P422, after the composition was altered.[7]

Engravings

J.-P. Le Bas 1743, reversed (Bocher, no. 20A), engraved as his *morceau de réception*,[8] showing minor variations in the shapes of the trees.
Carbonneau (for Blanc 1865).

Copies/Versions

BILBAO formerly C. N. Linker; 60 × 50, variant composition without the reclining man on the left.
DIJON Musée des Beaux-Arts; 33 × 30, variant composition with seven figures in a different landscape, attributed to Lancret.[9]
NEW YORK Ehrich sale, 24 March 1905 (21); 60 × 100, variant composition with the figure composition reversed and without Pierrot. Friedenberg sale, Parke Bernet, 4 May 1950 (106); 78 × 63, with different trees, ex Reid sale, New York, 14–18 May 1935 (1197).
PARIS anon. sale, 30 December 1936 (33); 36 × 28, reversed copy.

An old photograph of another copy is in the Witt Library.

Provenance

Received by the Académie, 14 March 1719; listed in the collections of the Académie Royale, 1792;[10] acquired by the 4th Marquess of Hertford; rue Laffitte inventory 1871 (253, '*Watteau, rendez-vous au parc*'); Hertford House inventory 1890 ('*Watteau, Pastoral Group with Musicians*').

Exhibition

Bethnal Green 1872–5 (?434, Watteau, *Loving Conversation*).

Reference General

WL284, 285.

[1] The stretcher is stamped, *verso*: MOMPER A PARIS (cf. Fragonard P430 note 1).

[2] There has previously been some doubt as to whether P422 was the picture engraved by Le Bas (cf. WL284–5, and previous editions of this catalogue), on the grounds that his engraving gave the size of the painting as *2p. 3 de hauteur sur 1p. 2 de largeur* [73.4 × 39.1]. But the proportions of his plate indicate that these sizes are incorrect (and perhaps should have read *2p. 3 × 1p. 8*, i.e. 73.4 × 54.4). Dezallier d'Argenville, (according to W. McAllister Johnson, *French Royal Academy of Painting and Sculpture; Engraved Reception Pieces 1672–1789*, exh. cat., Kingston, Canada, no.60, p.129) said that Le Bas's plate was made from the pendant to Lancret's *morceau de réception* (but he submitted two, see note 3 below). C. Blanc, *Les Peintres de Fêtes Galantes*, 1854, p.41 (and Blanc 1865, 'Lancret', p.5), followed by A. Fontaine, *Les Collections de l'Académie Royale de Peinture et de Sculpture*, 1910, pp.60–1, said the engraving was made from one of Lancret's *morceaux de réception*.

[3] On 24 March 1719 the Académie accepted from Lancret *'les tableaux qui luy avoient été ordonnez, représentant une Feste galante'* (A. de Montaiglon, *Procès-Verbaux de l'Académie Royale de Peinture et de Sculpture*, IV, 1881, p.280). Ballot de Sovot (*Eloge de Lancret*, 1743, ed. J. Guiffrey, n.d. [c.1875], p.21) and Blanc, *loc. cit.* (see note 2 above) stated that Lancret submitted two paintings (and cf. note 10 below).

[4] Ballot de Sovot, *loc. cit.*, described Lancret's *morceaux* as *'bien dans le genre de Watteau, mais dans une manière que M. Lancret s'étoit déjà faite à lui; et les vrais connoisseurs ne s'y méprennent pas'*.

[5] Cf. Cleveland Museum of Art, *Catalogue of Paintings*, III, 1982, no.34.

[6] Exh. *From Poussin to Puvis de Chavannes*, Heim Gallery, London, 1974 (61).

[7] Illus. P. Lavallée, *Dessins Français*, 1928, pl.7.

[8] Le Bas's initial submission to the Académie of two engraved portraits had been rejected on 5 January 1742 (A. de Montaiglon, *op. cit.*, V, 1883, p.312); on 27 January he was invited *'de graver pour sa réception un des tableaux de Lancret . . . représentant une conversation galante'* (*ibid.*, p.313), and he was duly *reçu* on 23 February 1743 (*ibid.*, p.337). See also W. McAllister Johnson, *loc. cit.* (see note 2 above).

[9] See J. Magnin, *La peinture au musée de Dijon*, 1918, p.52, no.101; photograph in Witt Library.

[10] *Inventaire des tableaux . . . dans les salles de la cidevant Académie de Peinture et de Sculpture, an II* [1793/4], nos.134, 135 (*'Lancret, Fêtes Galantes'*), quoted by Fontaine, *op. cit.*, p.154. Fontaine lists (pp.137–9) a number of *morceaux de réception* which were subsequently lost.

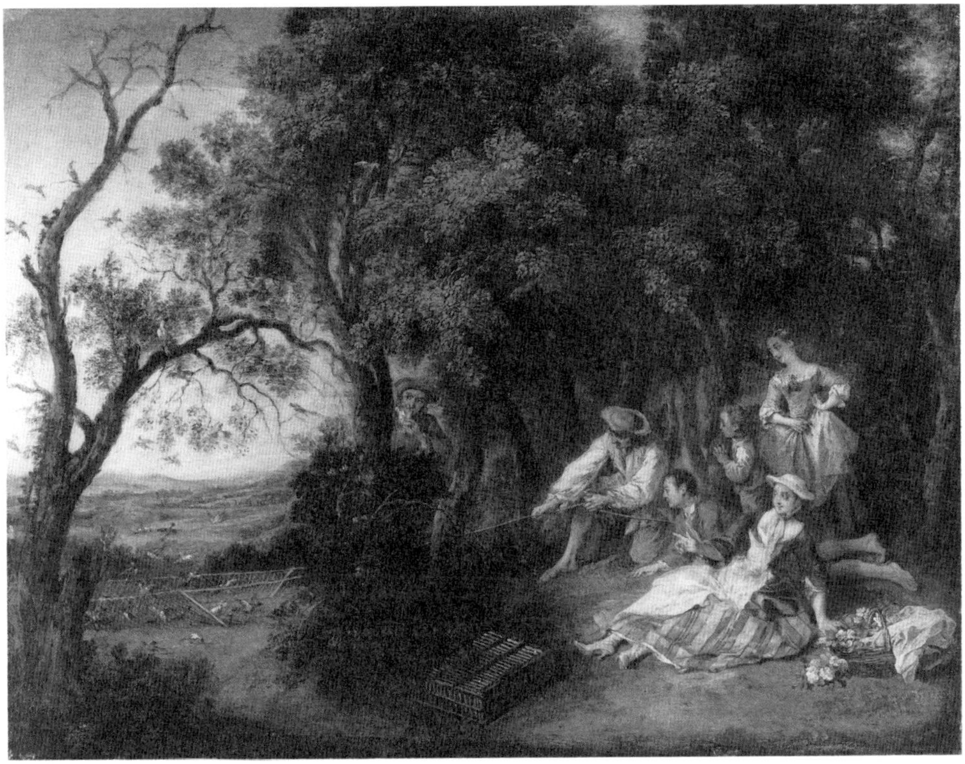

P436

P436 *The Bird Catchers (La chasse à la pipée)*

A man plays a flageolet while another pulls the bird trap closed; on the right the seated lady wears a red and white striped skirt, white apron, blue bodice and straw hat.

Copper, tinned on the *recto* 32.5 × 40.6

There are small losses and retouchings in the tree trunk by the pipe-player's head, the bird catcher's right arm, left leg and head, in the skirt of the seated lady, and round the edges. The paint is very thin in places, and the varnish is discoloured.

Probably painted in 1738, the date on the pendant P478 (q.v.). The subject[1] recurs in *Le printemps* (Louvre; WL11), one of the four seasons Lancret painted the same year for the *cabinet du Roi* at the Château de la Muette (cf. Wildenstein, pp.60, 71).

Drawings

LONDON British Museum (nos.1859–6–11–103 and 107); two studies for the bird catcher; exh. RA 1968 (401, 402).

Provenance

With P478: Fortier, *conseiller du Roi*; his sale, Paris, 2 April 1770 (36, '*Deux tableaux . . . une danse dans un jardin . . . treize figures . . . plusieurs en habit de caractère . . . dans l'autre . . . à l'entrée d'un bois à droite, un groupe de cinq figures, dont deux de femme, l'une assise & appuyée sur un panier de fleurs, & l'autre debout, regardent un paysan qui tire le filet, où les oiseaux sont prêts à se prendre, pendant qu'entre deux arbres, un autre paysan fait la pipée; cuivre* [32.6 × 39.4]'); César-Gabriel, duc de Praslin (1712–85); his grandson, Antoine-César, duc de Choiseul et de Praslin (1756–1808);[2] his sale, Paris, 18–25 February 1793 (162, '*Deux tableaux . . . une compagnie de personnages dont les uns s'amusent de conversation, d'autres à danser. Le pendant présente un sujet de la chasse à la pipée. Bois* (sic) [31.3 × 39.4]'); Paris, 1 October 1844, bt. by the 4th Marquess of Hertford, 2,060 fr. (*Lancret, deux tableaux*');[3] Hertford House 1859, when they were reframed;[4] Hertford House inventory 1870.

Exhibitions

Bethnal Green 1872–5 (443); RA 1889 (110).

Reference General

WL462.

[1] For a note on the bird-catchers theme in eighteenth-century French painting, see J.-L. Bordeaux, *J. Paul Getty Museum Journal*, III, 1976, pp.88–9.

[2] This inheritance, and the 1793 Choiseul-Praslin sale, are briefly discussed by Blanc, *Le Trésor de la Curiosité*, 1858, II, p.242.

[3] Entry in the 4th Marquess of Hertford's pocket book in the Wallace Collection archives. P436 and P478 were the only pair of Lancrets he owned, and they had been together in previous sales; it seems reasonable therefore to identify them with this entry. Wildenstein associated P436 with two nineteenth-century Paris sales: 25 March 1851 (77, '*La pipée, réunion des oiseaux, avec portraits de l'époque, attribué à Lancret*'), and 19 March 1857 (80, *La chasse au filet*) – but these descriptions are vague, and neither lot had a pendant.

[4] Evans invoice.

P448 *Fête in a Wood*

In the right foreground a cook(?) by a fire; a merry-go-round behind him; in the left distance a large coach and a lady handing flowers to its occupants. Indistinctly inscribed in red, bottom right: *23* or *93*.

Canvas, relined 64 × 90.8

The canvas is made up of four sections. Originally 60 × 79.2, 4 cm. was then added to the height, and vertical strips 8 cm. and 3.6 cm. wide added to the left and right respectively. The joins are marked by discoloured retouchings. These additions seem to have been made by the artist. There are many other retouchings, particularly apparent in the craquelure in the bottom left and central areas. The surface appears worn, e.g. around the figure of the cook in the right foreground and in the group around the coach. There is a damage in the trees in the centre of the composition. A *pentimento* shows an alteration to the right-hand tree trunk. The varnish is much discoloured.

Probably painted in the early 1720s, P448 particularly recalls two early Watteau compositions, *Les comédiens sur le champ de foire* and *La mariée de village*, which were acquired by Frederick the Great before 1763 and are now at Charlottenburg.[1] In the early nineteenth century the former, originally 61.7 × 81.3, was enlarged to 64.7 × 91.3 to make it a pendant to *La mariée de village*[2] – a curious parallel with the enlargement of P448 which seems, nevertheless, to have been contemporary. *La mariée de village* had been in the collection of Lancret's friend and patron, Leriget de La Faye (cf. P393). Some of the figures in P448 derive from other Watteau paintings: the central lady with her back turned recalls the lady in *L'enseigne de Gersaint* (Charlottenburg; CR212), and she recurs in Lancret's *Danse devant les chevaux d'Apollon* (Potsdam; WL136) and in a drawing (see below);[3] two of the

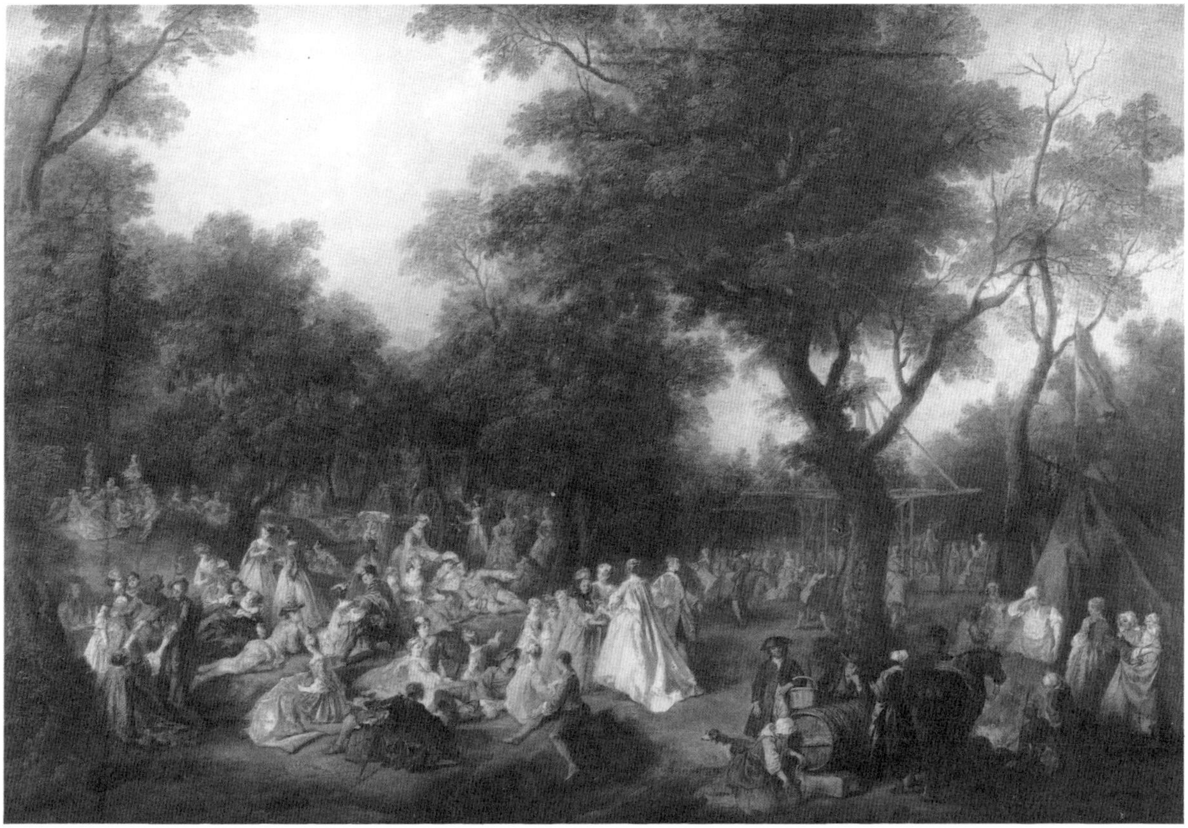

P448

couples on the left (a man handing up a lady, and a man embracing a reclining lady) recall groups in the Charlottenburg *Embarquement pour Cythère* (CR185); a lady seated in the centre-left foreground resembles a figure in *Les Champs Elisées* (see P389). The standing man facing right in the centre mid-distance resembles one of Watteau's *Figures de modes* (DV52). Lancret repeated the figure of the stooping maid in the right foreground in *Noces de village* (Waddesdon), and the youth seated to the left in the centre foreground in *La danse dans le bois* (Dresden; WL134).

Drawings

LILLE Musée des Beaux-Arts (inv. Pluchart, no.1494); study for the seated woman (left mid-distance) being embraced by a man (Grasselli, pp.381–2, fig.8; and see above).
PARIS Rodrigues sale, 28–9 November 1928 (188); study relating to the standing lady with her back turned in the centre of the composition, attributed to Pater (and see above).

Provenance

The inscribed number in the bottom right-hand corner (see description above) might possibly indicate that P448 came from the Koucheleff-Bezborodko collection (cf. C.-J. Vernet P135), in which case it may have been the unspecified painting called Watteau which Richard Wallace bt. from the comtesse Katherine Koucheleff, St. Petersburg, September 1867.[4] The 4th Marquess of Hertford; rue Laffitte inventory 1871 (355, '*Pater, Fête Champêtre*'); Hertford House inventory 1890 as Pater.

Exhibition[5]

Bethnal Green 1872–5 (376, Pater, *A Village Festival*).

Reference General

WL137.

[1] See P. Rosenberg, *Watteau*, exh. cat., Grand Palais, 1984, nos.P10, P11.

[2] Cf. Rosenberg, p.265, and H. Börsch-Supan, *La peinture française du XVIIIe siècle à la cour de Frédéric II*, exh. cat., Paris, 1963, no.31.

[3] This figure also recurs in the *Visite au camp*, once attributed to Pater (IS418), but given to Lancret when with Wildenstein in 1947 (photograph in Witt Library).

[4] See Boucher P399 notes 6 and 7. The supposition is also supported by the fact that the frame of P448 is of a similar pattern to that on the C.A. van Loo P451 which was certainly acquired from the comtesse Koucheleff in 1867.

[5] In the earliest editions of this catalogue Phillips proposed that P448 may have been the *Bal dans un bois* exhibited at the Place Dauphine (Exposition de jeunesse), cf. P. J. Mariette, *Abecedario*, III, AAF, VI, 1854–6, p.55: '*Il y a bien vingt quatre ans qu'il débute par deux tableaux: un Bal et une Danse dans un boccage, deux tableaux qui ont été à M. de Julienne et ensuite à M. le prince de Carignan, et je me souviens qu'ayant exposés à la Place Dauphine . . . ils lui attirent de grands éloges*'. Wildenstein, p.47, shows that the *danse dans un paysage* which Lancret exhibited at the Place Dauphine in 1724 was '*un assez grand tableau cintré*' (quoting Bellier de la Chavignerie, *Notes pour servir à l'histoire de l'Exposition de la jeunesse*, 1724, p.16).

P450 *La belle Grecque*

She wears a red toque and a red gown edged with black fur; her shoes are lime green with pink side panels.

Canvas, relined 68/69 × 56.7/51.1 irregular

Cleaned by Lee in 1986 when the original canvas was found to have been tilted to the right in the course of relining and a strip of canvas from another painting, 3 cm. wide, added to the right-hand side; the left-hand side was extended by 1 cm. at the same time. There are small losses round the edges, by her left arm, in the skirt and in the sky, top centre. *Pentimenti* show that her left upper arm was redrawn.

The title is taken from Schmidt's print of 1736 (see Engraving). It suggests (together with the related drawings, see below) that P450 is a fanciful subject, and not the portrait of an actress in character.[1] The costume doubtless alludes to the contemporary vogue for exotic tragedy in the French theatre; Schmidt's verses recall Zaïre, for example, as well as impromptu lines addressed by Voltaire to Mlle. Gaussin, his original Zaïre.[2] A pendant subject, *Le turc amoureux*, was also used by Lancret in one of the decorative panels he painted for Boullongne's hôtel in the place Vendôme (WL728), which would indicate that it was not a portrait.[3]

Probably painted c.1735, immediately before the engraving. P450 recalls Watteau's three portrayals of ladies in exotic costume, two *Polonaises* (CR166 and CR167; DV145) and *La rêveuse* (CR165; DV166).[4] Lancret made a number of drawings of a model wearing the same costume (see below), and she appears in *L'attache du patin* (Stockholm; WL19), *Le bal* (Potsdam; WL335), and *Music Party in a Landscape* (Fitzwilliam Museum, no.329).

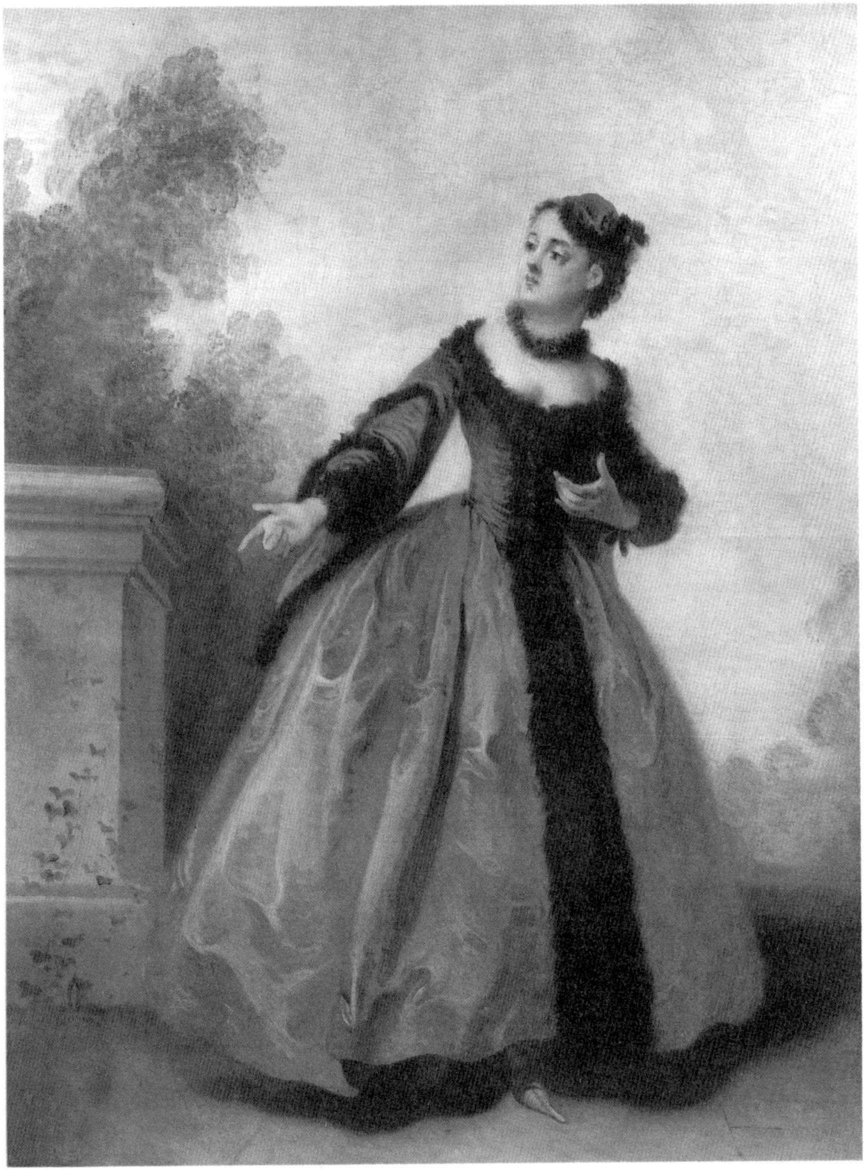

P450

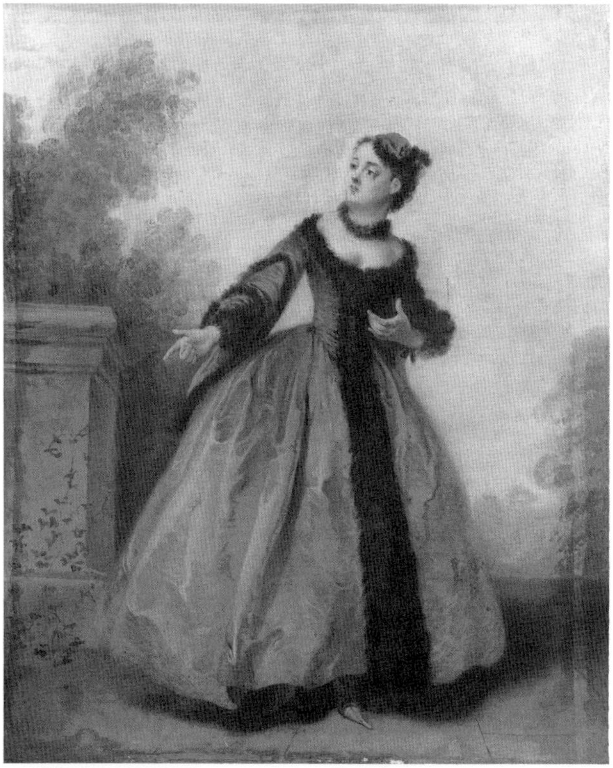

P450 before cleaning

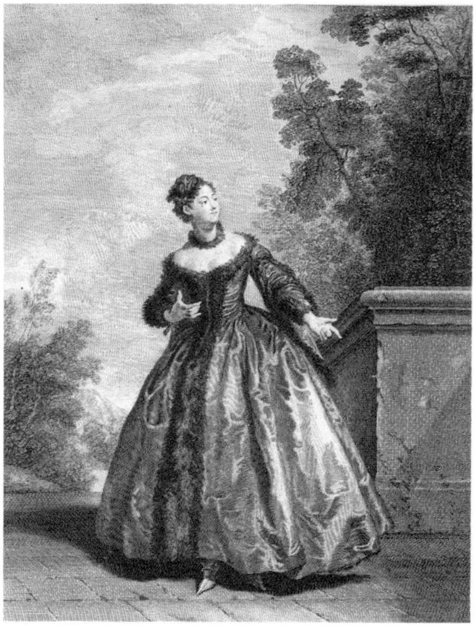

G. F. Schmidt after Lancret: *La belle Grecque*, 1736. The British Museum

Drawings

PARIS anon. sale, 16–17 May 1898 (218) as Pater; study for the figure.

A number of other drawings of the same model in the same costume are recorded: Strauss sale, Paris, 3–4 June 1929 (74), two studies on one sheet, ex coll. Goncourt; G. Dormeuil, Paris, exh. RA 1932 (729), two studies on one sheet (WL703); Camille Groult sale, Paris, 21 March 1952 (44, 45), two studies; anon. sale, Paris, 24 March 1955 (7); Stockholm, Nationalmuseum, exh. RA 1968 (397); Zurich, K. Meissner (exh. *Old Master Drawings from the* [*Meissner Collection*], Stanford University 1969, no. 12); another drawing, attributed to Pater, formerly in Berlin (photograph in Witt Library).

Engraving

G. F. Schmidt 1736, reversed (Bocher, no.15), with verses below:

Jeune Beauté, votre esclavage
Ne vous empesche pas de captiver les coeurs,
Les Sultans les plus fiers vous offrent leur hommage,
Et par le seul pouvoir de vos yeux enchanteurs,
Vous triomphez de vos vainqueurs.

The engraving shows a variant of P450: the trees are more clearly defined on the left, and the landscape more wooded on the right; the stone plinth is seen from a different angle and the terrace is flagged.

Versions

CHICAGO Art Institute (inv. C36415); 70 × 52.1, the composition extended all round with a paved terrace in the foreground and a stone staircase on the left (WL700).
LONDON Major sale, 1751 (35, *The Fair Grecian*).[5]
PARIS abbé de Gévigney sale, 1 December 1779 (539, '*une femme vêtue d'une robe rouge fourrée de marthe, le collier et la toque de même, sortant d'un bosquet où l'on voit un piédestal* [91.8 × 97.2]') (WL701), and lot 540 ('*Deux pendants, une jeune femme vêtue d'une robe cerise claire, fourrée de marthe . . . , un jeune homme dans le costume turc* [72.9 × 59.4]') (WL688–9).
Mme. Lancret sale, 3 April 1782 (8, '*deux tableaux sur toile* [99.3 × 40.8] . . . *un Turc* [and] *une femme turque se promenant dans un jardin; ces figures ont* [38.1] *de proportion*') (WL690–1).[6]
Beaujon sale, 25 April 1787 (119, '*un Turc dans un paysage . . . une femme turque aussi dans un paysage* [89.1 × 35.1]') (WL692–3).
Princesse de Poix 1924; 60 × 39, with pendant, *Le turc amoureux*; ex Béraudière sale, 18 May ff. 1885, lot 43 (WL686–7).

Provenance

Possibly Henri de Caisne (1799–1852); his sale, Paris, 6 April 1853 (154, *La belle Grecque*). Acquired by the 4th Marquess of Hertford in Paris; rue Laffitte inventory 1871 (426, '*Watteau, femme vêtue de rouge*'); Hertford House inventory 1890 as Lancret.

Exhibitions

Bethnal Green 1872–5 (462, Lancret, *Portrait of an Actress*); RA 1889 (124, Lancret, *Actress of the Comédie Française*).

Reference General

WL699.

[1] Lancret's portraits of Mlle. Sallé and Mlle. Camargo in character were both identified in the engravings (see P393 and Bocher, no.71).

[2] *Zaïre* was first performed in 1732; the heroine is there described as '*esclave d'un soudan*'. Voltaire wrote to La Gaussin: '*Le prophète de la Mecque/Dans son sérail n'a jamais eu/Si gentille Arabesque ou Grecque . . .*', and '*Ce sont tes yeux, ces yeux si pleins de charmes,/Qui du critique ont font tomber les armes*' (cf. F. Hawkins, *The French Stage in the Eighteenth Century*, 1888, I, pp.266, 282).

[3] See WL684, 694–8, and Provenance above. Versions were with Pardo, Paris, 1963 (WL698), and sold Sotheby's, 19 April 1967, lot 29 (WL686), and Christie's, 10 July 1987, lot 147 (WL697). The subject has been identified as the actor Le Kain (noted for his Orosmane in *Zaïre*), cf. *Le Théâtre à Paris*, exh. cat., Musée Carnavalet, 1929, no.41 (WL698).

[4] See P. Rosenberg, *Watteau*, exh. cat., Grand Palais, 1984, P26, who discusses the identification of Watteau's model with the actress Charlotte Desmares.

[5] See R. Raines, AAF, 4e, XXVI, 1984, p.179.

[6] M. Roland-Michel, *The Burlington Magazine*, October 1969, adv. supp., p.iii, suggests that these were the prime versions and therefore the subjects of Schmidt's engravings; if this was so, the measurements given in Mme. Lancret's sale catalogue are wrong.

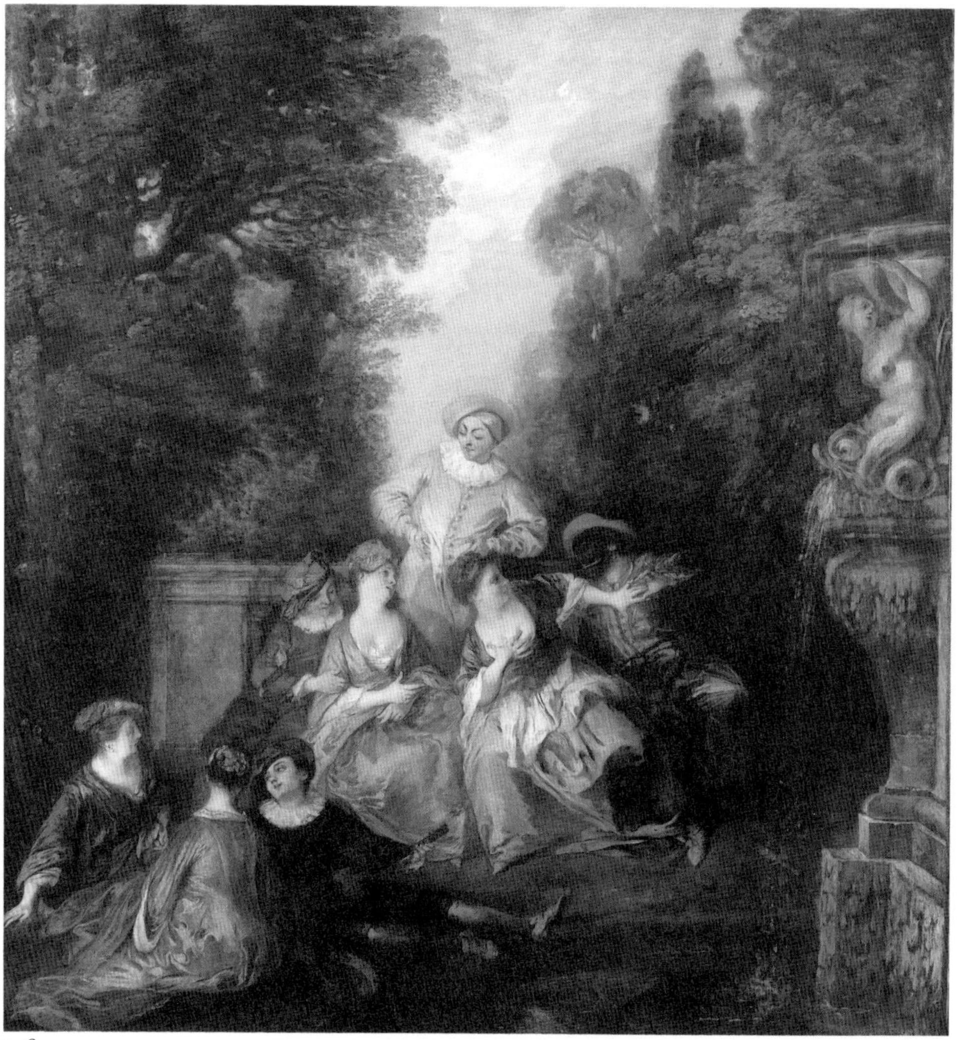

P465

P465 *Italian Comedians by a Fountain*

Harlequin's advances are rejected by a lady wearing a yellow skirt and scarlet bodice with turquoise sleeves; behind them stands Pierrot in pale grey; on the left, the seated lady with her back turned is in red.

Canvas 91 × 83

Cleaned in 1977 by Vallance. Three areas are damaged: in the trees on the left above the balustrade, in the red skirt of the seated lady on the left, and around the legs of the guitarist at her side. There are several minor retouchings; for example, by Harlequin's left foot, in the neck of the left-hand lady seated in front of the balustrade, and in Pierrot's right hip. *Pentimenti* and X-radiography reveal radical

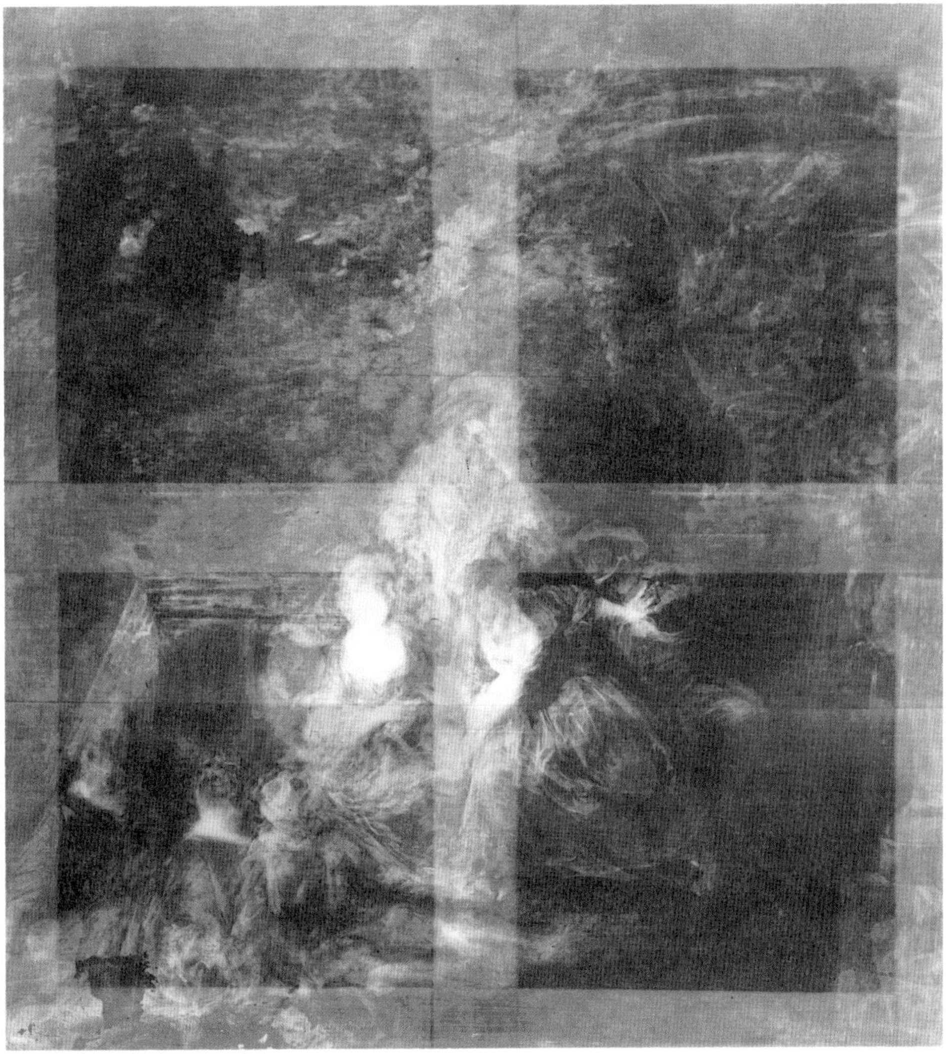

X-radiograph of P465
(The Courtauld Institute)

changes in the setting. There was a large classical urn on the right, the fountain was taller, and the balustrade turned away behind the extreme left-hand figure. The young man seated in front of the balustrade on the left was added after the balusters had been painted, and the standing figure of Pierrot was originally slightly taller.

The actors by the balustrade belong to the *commedia dell'arte* and appear to be (from the left): Mezetin, Flaminia, Pierrot, Silvia and Harlequin.[1]

P465 is an early work, comparable with P422 which is dateable 1719. The unsatisfactory figure in front of the balustrade on the left, the weak drawing of the guitarist, and the uncertain perspective of the fountain, might suggest that P465 is slightly earlier. The changes in the background, described above, were paralleled in *Les plaisirs du bal* (Dulwich Picture Gallery; CR164), painted by Watteau c.1716–17 when Lancret was probably his pupil. The strong central group of Lancret's substantial figures contrasts with his master's manner, and caused Phillips to question the attribution to Lancret in the earliest editions of this catalogue.

Copies/Versions

BERLIN Charlottenburg; copy, listed as Watteau in the eighteenth century.[2]
MOULINS H. Monceau 1923; 66 × 82 (WL291).
PARIS Menier sale, 24 November 1936 (28); 87 × 92, reduced in height and extended on the right.
Private collection 1984; 56 × 43.5, with overpainted architectural features on the right.
SAUGATUCK, Michigan; private collection; 53 × 39.

Provenance

Frank Hall Standish (1798–1839); bequeathed to Louis-Philippe of France; exhibited in the Louvre (Musée Standish), 1842–8, no.231 (Watteau, *Paysage*); Louis-Philippe/Standish sale, Christie's, 1st day, 28 May 1853 (31, Watteau, *Paysage*), bt. Mawson for the 4th Marquess of Hertford, 700 gn.;[3] Hertford House inventory 1870.

Exhibitions

Manchester, *Art Treasures*, 1857 (saloon H, no.28, as Lancret); Bethnal Green 1872–5 (449); RA 1889 (87).

Reference General

WL290.

[1] These identifications were tentatively made by L.K. Gallagher (letter on file dated 1 January 1983).

[2] See H. Börsch-Supan, 'Frédéric le Grand et Watteau', in *Watteau*, exh. cat., Grand Palais, 1984, p.553 n.23.

[3] Lord Hertford was aware that P465 was by Lancret, despite the sale catalogue description; he was particularly anxious to have it, see Introduction, p.15. In August 1853 P465 was seen in Hertford House by Waagen (IV, p.84, as Lancret) who remarked upon the unusually large figures.

P478 *Pastoral Revels (La danse dans un parc)*

The dancer wears a dull green suit, his partner a red skirt and charcoal bodice; the reclining man in the centre has a turquoise cloak. Inscribed, *verso*: *Peint par Lancret/1738.*

Copper 32.5 × 40.7

There are many small retouchings: in the skirt of the right-hand lady, round the piper's coat, in the reclining man's cloak, within an area of heavy craquelure above the right arm of the stooping man on the right, and along the bottom edge. There are *pentimenti* on both the piper's legs.

Pendant to P436. The garden architecture, which recurs in *La terre* (engraved by Cochin; WL4) and *Le jeu de colin maillard* (Potsdam; WL226), suggests the influence, or even the collaboration of Jacques de Lajoüe (c.1686–1761), whose *L'escalier*, for example, of before 1734–5 (galerie Cailleux 1984) shows a comparable setting.[1] The seated piper recurs in *Le feu* (engraved by Audran; WL5), the youth stooping over a girl in *Le jeu de colin maillard* and *La servante justifiée* (WL671, and cf. Pater IS452), and the dancers in *La danse* (WL147). All these pictures may be dated c.1732–8, which tends to confirm the inscription on the *verso* of P478 (see above).

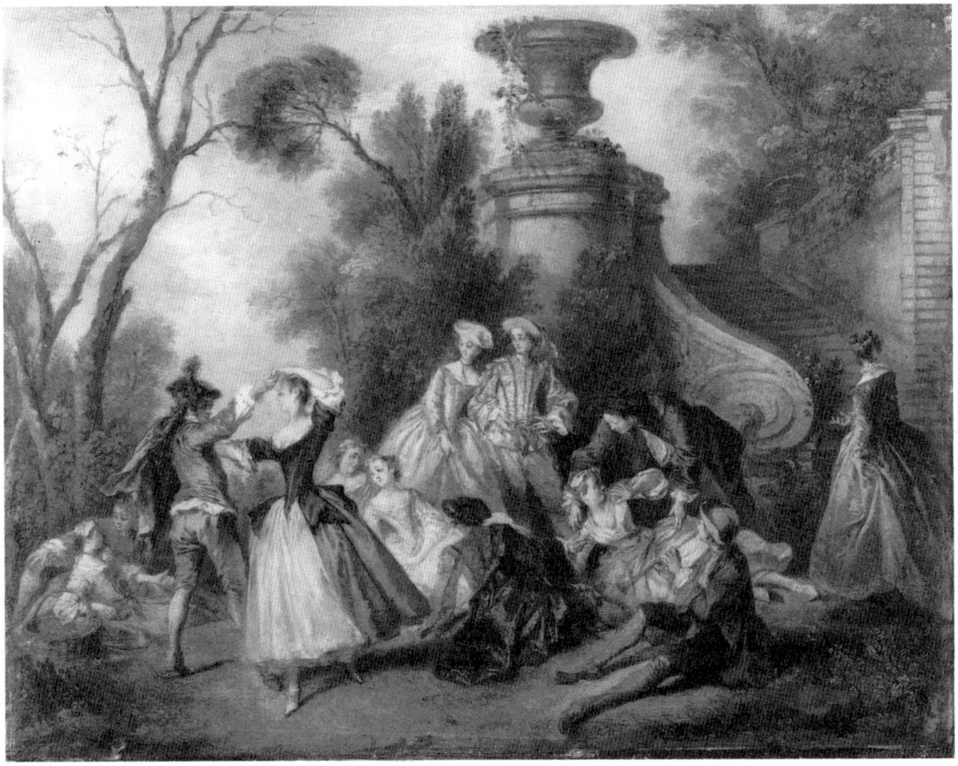

P478

Drawings

NEW YORK art market 1968; study for the standing man with his left hand on his hip, centre right.
PARIS Ecole des Beaux-Arts; study for the dancing couple.[2]

Provenance

See P436.[3]

Exhibitions

Bethnal Green 1872–5 (416); RA 1889 (105).

Reference General

WL138, 162.

[1] See M. Roland-Michel, *Lajoüe et l'art rocaille*, 1984, cat. P93, illus. pl. 3. She discusses the possibility of collaboration between Lancret and Lajoüe, without mentioning P478, on pp.75–8.

[2] Illus. P. Lavallée, *Dessins Français*, 1928, pl. 10, as Pater.

[3] Wildenstein associated P478 with lot 163 in the Viardot and Lavalard sale, Paris, 7 March 1856 (*Les plaisirs de la campagne*), but see P436 note 2.

François Lemoyne (1688–1737)

Born in Paris, son of a coachman in the Royal Household, he was taught briefly by his step-father, R. Tournières, before becoming the pupil of the *rubéniste* L. Galloche in 1701. He may also have studied briefly with P.-J. Cazes. In 1711 he won the *prix de Rome* at the Académie, but there were no funds for him to go to Rome. *Agréé* in 1716 (*Adoration of the Magi*[1]), he was *reçu* in 1718 (*Hercules slaying Cacus*; Ecole des Beaux-Arts). He produced nine paintings for the monastery of the Cordeliers in Amiens 1717–20 (five now in Sens Cathedral), and received thereafter regular commissions for religious subjects (e.g. Saint-Julien Chepteuil, Haute-Loire, 1718; Saint-Thomas d'Aquin, 1724, and Saint-Sulpice, 1731–2). By 1722 he had met François Berger (see P392, P417), who became his influential patron and with whom he visited Bologna, Rome, Naples and Venice in 1723–4. He then looked particularly at Michelangelo in the Sistine Chapel, Pietro da Cortona, Lanfranco and Parmigianino, although his own mature style suggests more the influences of Veronese, Sebastiano Ricci and Correggio. Boucher and Natoire were his pupils in the 1720s, as was D. Nonotte, his biographer, 1731–7; he also taught drawing to the engraver Laurent Cars. He had exhibited at the Place Dauphine in 1723 and showed an Italianate landscape and seven mythological subjects in the 1725 Salon. In 1727 he was adjudged joint winner, with J.-F. de Troy, of the *Concours* devised by the duc d'Antin, *directeur des Bâtiments* (*Continence of Scipio*; Nancy), and invited to prepare designs for the ceiling of the Salon d'Hercule at Versailles. Meanwhile in 1729 he painted *Louis XV according Peace to Europe* for the Salon de la Paix, and fourteen panels for the Hôtel Peyrenc de Moras 1729–30 (one survives at Nancy; the Hôtel is now the Musée Rodin). At the Académie he was made *adjoint à professeur* in 1727 and *professeur* in 1733. He finally painted the great ceiling at Versailles of the *Apotheosis of Hercules* 1733–6, a work universally admired, and was immediately made *premier peintre du Roi*. But he was already unstable, and acute paranoia led to his suicide in Paris on 4 June 1737 (see P392). An ambitious but conscientious artist, his suave fluency was achieved only by the greatest application.

[1] Probably the painting with the Heim Gallery, London, 1986, 100 × 81, whose composition relates closely to Rubens's *Adoration* in Antwerp, cf. P519 in the Wallace Collection and Bordeaux, D3, fig. 129.

Abbreviations

Bordeaux	J.-L. Bordeaux, *François Le Moyne*, 1984 (with catalogue of paintings [P] and drawings [D])
Caylus	the comte de Caylus, 'Vie de François Lemoine', read to the Académie, 6 July 1748, *Vies d'Artistes du XVIIIe siècle*, ed. A. Fontaine, 1910, pp.42–66
Nonotte	Donat Nonotte, 'Vie du peintre François Lemoyne', read to the Académie de Lyon, 15 November 1759, *Réunion des Sociétés des Beaux-Arts des Départements*, XXVI, 1902, pp.520–40
Saunier	C. Saunier, 'François Lemoine', in L. Dimier, ed., *Les peintres français du XVIIIe siècle*, I, 1928, pp.61–91

P392 *Time saving Truth from Falsehood and Envy*

The winged figure of Time has red drapery, Truth, whom he carries, white; Falsehood holding a mask in her left hand wears blue with a gold damask cloak.

Canvas, relined 149 × 113.5 enlarged to 180.5 × 148

The enlargements are in the form of four strips of canvas, of the same herring-bone weave as the original, 180.5 × 17.5 on the left, 180.5 × 17 on the right, 21.5 × 113.5 above and 10 × 113.5 below. For the dating of these additions, see below. All the joins are retouched and the additions are evidently painted on a different ground; that on the left is of a lighter tone, that on the right darker and showing many small losses. The edges of the extended canvas were roughly cut in relining. There is a damage by Truth's right calf, and there are small losses in Falsehood's right hand; a shrinkage craquelure below her right arm and by Time's left elbow has been heavily retouched. *Pentimenti* show alterations to the edges of the foliage above and to the right of Time and Truth; the stunted tree on the left (within the original canvas) was redrawn, and Time's right hand was slightly lowered. The varnish is much discoloured.

Truth is brought up from a dark well by her father, Time, who overcomes Falsehood, two-faced with her mask and alluring with her fine clothes, and Envy (identified in the 1797 sale, see Provenance) who recedes protesting. The subject ultimately derives from classical literary sources,[1] but the image first appears in a Venetian woodcut of 1536.[2] It recurs, for example, in Annibale Carracci's *Allegory of Truth and Time* of c.1584–5 (Hampton Court) and Poussin's *Time saving Truth from Envy and Discord,* painted for Richelieu in 1641 (Louvre). While P392 lacks the latter's political overtones, it perhaps embodies something of Lemoyne's obsession with fame; the well more resembles a pedestal on which Truth may stand secure (as Bordeaux, p.46, observes). Contemporary French versions of the subject include paintings by J.-F. de Troy (1733; National Gallery, London) and by Lemoyne's pupil, C.-J. Natoire (1740s; Waddesdon).

P392, commissioned by Berger (see below), was completed on 3 June 1737, the day before Lemoyne's suicide. Caylus (p.64) remembered:

> *la veille même de sa mort, il acheva un tableau commencé depuis longtemps qui représente le* Temps qui découvre la Vérité; *je n'ai point oublié la complaisance avec laquelle il me le montra après avoir donné devant moi les derniers coups à la terrasse.*

It is not clear how long Lemoyne had been working on P392, but the full composition and substantial figures suggest a late work. Berger's other Lemoyne commissions dated from 1722–4 (see below), but Lemoyne was '*fort long dans l'exécution de ses ouvrages*'[3] and the important commissions for Versailles, Saint-Sulpice and the Hôtel Peyrenc de Moras (1729–36) could have further delayed his progress. Berger came to Lemoyne's studio on 8 June 1737 to claim '*un grand tableau,* le Temps qui enlève la Vérité et terrasse le Mensonge, *d'environ 5 pieds de haut sur 3 et demy de large* [about 162 × 114], *qu'il a fait faire et payé*', together with the

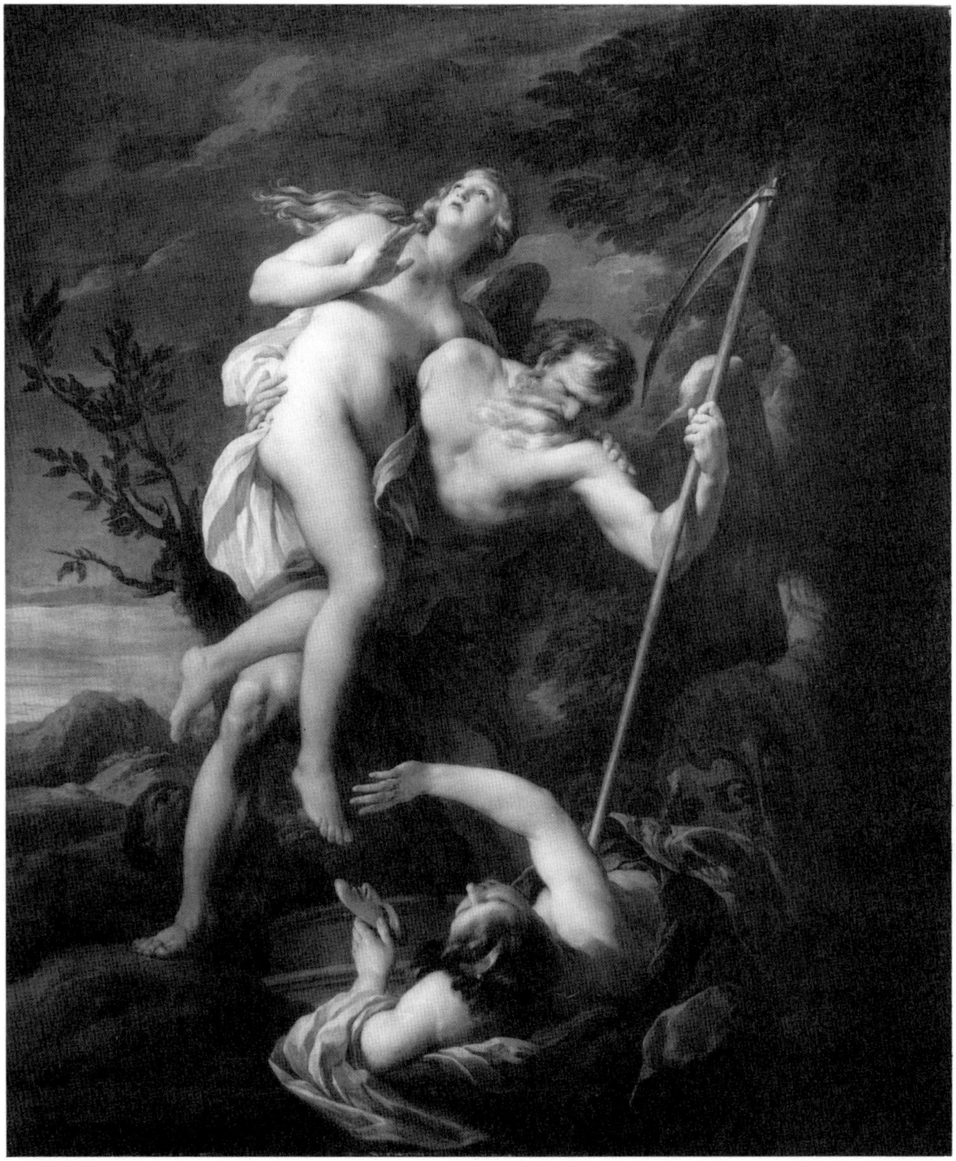

P392

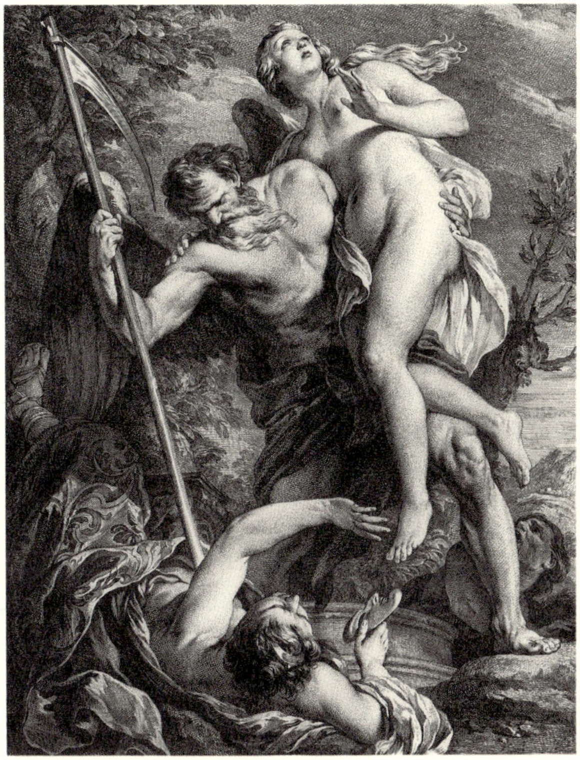

L. Cars after Lemoyne:
Time saving Truth from Falsehood and Envy, 1747.
The British Museum

frame which he had had delivered to the studio and which remained in its grey paper wrapping.[4] His claim was agreed on 9 August.[5] P392 was evidently without the additions we now see, as it was in 1747, on the evidence of the engraving by Cars (see Engraving); they had been made by 1793, according to the size given in the Lareynière sale catalogue (see Provenance), and they probably date from c.1757, according to the history of that remarkable collection of Lemoynes to which P392, with P417, once belonged.[6]

François Berger (1684–c.1747), *fermier général,* living in the rue des Quatre-fils in 1737 and an influential friend of the duc d'Antin (*directeur des Bâtiments*), had commissioned *Tancred and Clorinda* from Lemoyne in 1722 and, on receiving it, '*se proposa d'orner entièrement un cabinet des oeuvres de M. le Moine*'.[7] He bought P417 and commissioned *Hercules and Omphale, The Bather* and P392.[8] On his death his Lemoynes were acquired by Etienne Bouret (1710–77), *fermier général, 'qui en avoit encore réuni plusieurs autres du même maître, auquel cette collection rare a procuré une distinction unique dans ce genre'*.[9] Bouret's collection was described by Dezallier d'Argenville in 1757[10] in his new hôtel, rue Grange Batelière;[11] besides Berger's Lemoynes he had *The Continence of Scipio* (lent by the King), *Adam and Eve, Danish Knights rescuing Rinaldo from Armida's Castle, Pygmalion* and *Iphigenia*, and among his sculptures were '*les quatre bas-reliefs exécutés à la Fontaine de la rue de Grenelle, par M. Bouchardon*'.[12] In

1761 Bouret sold hôtel and contents to Jean-Joseph Delaborde (1724–94), *banquier de la Cour*,[13] but his *Iphigenia* went to Lalive de Jully[14] and the *Continence of Scipio* returned to the King.[15] Delaborde then had eight of the Berger-Bouret Lemoynes, as follows:

short title	size	date	Bordeaux no./present location
1 *Tancred and Clorinda*	162 × 289	1722	33/Besançon
2 *Perseus and Andromeda*	183 × 150	1723	44/Wallace Collection
3 *Hercules and Omphale*	183 × 150	1724	47/Louvre
4 *The Bather*	180 × 140	1724	48/–
5 *Time saving Truth*	150 × 113(?)	1737	97/Wallace Collection
6 *Adam and Eve*	230 × 155	1723–6	51/–
7 *Rinaldo and Armida*	122 × 183	1725	57/–
8 *Pygmalion*	212 × 168	1729	75/Tours

Of these *Perseus and Andromeda* and *Hercules and Omphale* had been shown as pendants in the 1725 Salon, but the eight large history pieces were otherwise unrelated and formed no overall scheme. Delaborde's collection was seen in December 1765 by Horace Walpole who recorded that 'in the second antechamber are four large tawdry pictures by Le Moine that cost £4,000, bas-reliefs in marble under them, hung on red damask',[16] strongly suggesting that Bouret's four Bouchardon reliefs were under four Lemoynes. Three Lemoynes were the same size (nos. 2–4 above) and it seems reasonable to suggest that P392 (no. 5) had been enlarged by Bouret, c.1757, to complete this display for his new hôtel. This suggestion is further supported by the existence of eighteenth-century copies of these four Lemoynes, that of P392 showing it extended, traditionally said to have been '*du Cabinet de Mr Bouret*' (see Copies below). Delaborde sold hôtel and contents to Grimod de Lareynière (1734–93), *fermier général*, in 1770, and in 1778 Lareynière transferred his collections to a new hôtel, rue Champs Elysées, where, in 1787, Thiéry noted '*une belle collection de tableaux de l'Ecole française et nommément de Lemoine*'.[17] Lareynière received an offer of 130,000 *livres* from Catherine II of Russia for his Lemoynes, which he considered inadequate,[18] but which in fact marked the turning point in Lemoyne's critical fortunes (see Provenance).

The composition of P392 relates to a drawing by Charles Le Brun of *Saturn abducting Cybele* (Louvre, inv. no. 29.851),[19] and to a marble group of the same title by Regnaudin which in Lemoyne's time was on the Parterre de l'Orangerie at Versailles.[20] The fair-haired figure of Truth and Falsehood's rich drapery suggest Venetian influences, while Bordeaux supposes Lemoyne may also have been influenced by Reni's *Nessus abducting Dejanira* (Louvre, then in the Royal Collection). The execution of P392 is noticeably tighter, and the colour somewhat stronger, than in P417; although completed in his last disturbed year, P392 hardly suggests Lemoyne's private anguish – as Caylus (p. 64) observed:

> *assurément il ne paraît aucune aliénation d'esprit dans cet ouvrage, il est même un de ses plus beaux morceaux de cabinet.*

Drawing

PARIS Louvre (inv. no. 30570); sheet with two studies for the head of Truth, one reversed (Bordeaux, D176, fig. 303).

Engraving

L. Cars 1747, reversed, without the additions, inscribed: *Dernier Tableau peint par F. le Moine . . . tiré du Cabinet de Mr Bouret . . .*, and dedicated to de Tournehem (Bordeaux, fig. 91a).[21]

Copies

ABBEVILLE Musée Boucher de Perthes; 182 × 153, with additions, ex coll. J.-A.-C. Boucher de Crèvecoeur, *fermier général*, in whose MS catalogue it was described as *'du Cabinet de M. Bouret, fermier général'*[22] (Bordeaux, pp. 91, 126, fig. 91b).
CLERMONT-FERRAND Musée Bargoin (no.68.37.1); Beauvais tapestry, 315 × 135, the composition reduced in width.
MAINZ Gemäldegalerie (no.515); 38.4 × 29.9, reversed.

A copy was in the Beauregard sale, Paris, 1 April 1868 (28).

The composition was also reproduced as an embossed plaque (Sotheby's 3 July 1980, lot 182) and on the cover of a Meissen gold box by G. Rémond and associates (Christie's, 19 February 1980, lot 134).

Provenance

See main text; commissioned by F. Berger; valued at 300 *livres* in Lemoyne's *inventaire après décès*, no. 22;[23] E. Bouret by 1747; J.-J. Delaborde, 1761; L. Grimod de Lareynière, 1770; his sale, Paris, 3 April 1793 (19, *'Le Temps découvrant la Vérité. Le Temps tient en l'air . . . la Vérité . . . tandis qu'il terrasse . . . le Mensonge et la Calomnie . . . Derrière, en demi-teinte et en plan coupé, on voit l'Envie qui va se cacher, 66 × 54 pouces* [178 × 137, the same size given for P417]'), bt. in (Le Brun), 12,000 *livres*; second Lareynière sale, Paris, 7 September ff. 1797 (6), 1,680 fr., bt. Radix de Sainte-Foix (d.1810); his sale, Paris, 16 January 1811 (40), bt. in;[24] P.-C. Prousteau de Montlouis (1763–1851); his sale, Paris, 5–6 May 1851 (102), bt. by the 4th Marquess of Hertford, with lot 103 (P417), 1,690 fr.; rue Laffitte inventory 1871 (703); Hertford House inventory 1890.

Exhibition

Bethnal Green 1872–5 (403).

References General

Caylus, p.66; Nonotte, p.539, no.58; Saunier, no.50; Bordeaux, P97 and p.91.

[1] E.g. Gellius, *Noctes Atticae*, XII, 11, 7; the subject has been fully discussed by F. Saxl, 'Veritas Filia Temporis' in *Philosophy and History, essays presented to Ernst Cassirer*, 1936, pp.197–222, and by G. de Tervarent, 'Veritas and Justitia triumphant', *Journal of the Warburg and Courtauld Institutes*, VII, 1944, pp.95–101.

[2] Illus., Saxl, *op.cit.*, f.p.64.

[3] Le chevalier de Valory, 'Jean François de Troy', c.1760, *Mémoires inédits sur la Vie et les ouvrages des membres de l'Académie Royale*, ed. L. Dussieux *et al.*, 1854, II, p.265.

[4] *'Procès-verbal d'apposition de scellés après le décès de* François Le Moyne, *Premier Peintre du roi'*, NAAF, 2e, IV, 1883, p.345.

[5] *Ibid.*, pp.351–2.

[6] In the account which follows C. Bailey (letter on file dated 16 June 1984) indicated the sales of the hôtel, rue Grange Batelière, and drew attention to Walpole's comments. His information is gratefully acknowledged.

[7] Nonotte, p.524. Berger's death date is suggested by the fact that Caylus spoke of him in the past tense in 1748 (p.53): *'c'était un de ces amateurs dont la France peut se vanter d'avoir produit un aussi grand nombre qu'aucun autre pays'*. Berger remains obscure; Nonotte (*loc. cit.*) called him *'ce généreux ami des arts et des artistes'*, and de Valory (op. cit., p.267, see note 3 above) considered that *'dans le petit nombre des amateurs qui existaient dans ce temps-là* [1727], *il étoit regardé comme un oracle dont le jugement sur les ouvrages de peinture devoit régler ceux du public; il n'étoit pas extraordinaire que le surintendant* [d'Antin], *fort peu au fait de cette partie de sa place, n'eût d'autres guides que lui'*. It was Berger who called for Lemoyne on the day of his suicide (cf. NAAF, V, 1877, pp.192–6, and 2e, IV, 1883, pp.339–41).

[8] Nonotte, p.524.

[9] Nonotte, p.525.

[10] A.-N. Dezallier d'Argenville, *Voyage pittoresque de Paris*, 1757, pp.185–6; see also *Almanach des Beaux-Arts*, 1762, pp.192–3. Nonotte's list of Lemoyne's paintings (pp.538–9) has *Perseus and Andromeda* and *Iphigenia* with Bouret, the others with Delaborde.

[11] Built by A.-M. Le Carpentier in the 1750s, cf. S. Eriksen, *Early Neo-classicism in France*, 1974, p.199.

[12] Cf. A. Roserot, *Bouchardon*, 1910, p.157. Bouret's bas-reliefs are considered to be those now in the Metropolitan Museum of Art, each 51.5 × 86, marble, reduced versions of the original bas-reliefs which remain *in situ* in the rue de Grenelle (see P. Remington, *Bulletin of the Metropolitan Museum of Art*, XXX, 1935, pp.232–6).

[13] In 1768 Delaborde was trying to regulate Bouret's finances: *'on sait que ce financier très opulent* [Bouret], *mais très dérangé dans ses affaires, avoit été réduit à la pension par M. de la Borde, qui s'étoit chargé de l'administration de ses biens'* (Bachaumont, *Mémoires secrets*, IV, 1777, p.70, 17 July 1768).

[14] Cf. Bordeaux, P71; Bouret's picture is thought to be that now in a private collection in Lisbon, 102 × 137.

[15] The painting with which Lemoyne was declared joint winner of the 1727 *Concours* (see Biography); 147 × 207, now at Nancy.

[16] H. Walpole, Paris Journals, 4 December 1765 (*Correspondence*, VII, 1939, p.280). In a chatty letter to Lady Suffolk, written the following day (*Correspondence*, XXXI, 1961, p.80), Walpole referred to his visit to Delaborde and commented that a grand Paris hôtel should have 'a grand cabinet, hung with red damask in gold frames, and covered with eight large and very bad pictures, that cost four thousand pounds . . . Under these, to give an air of lightness, must be hung bas-reliefs in marble'. This seems to be a conflation of different rooms in the rue Grange Batelière; there were only four bas-reliefs, see note 12 above.

[17] Quoted by L. Réau, '*La décoration de l'hôtel Grimod de la Reynière*', BSHAF 1937, p.12.

[18] Sainte-Foix sale catalogue, 1811 (and cf. BSHAF 1953, p.29). The decline of their value thereafter was spectacular; the average price of each Lemoyne in the Lareynière sales of 1793 and 1797 and the Sainte-Foix sale of 1811 was, respectively, 10,700 *livres*, 1,200 *livres*, and 450 fr. (and see Provenance). On 26 March 1793 the *Commission des Monuments* were advised of the forthcoming Lareynière sale and they noted that '*parmi ces tableaux, il s'en trouve huit de* Le Moine *qui passent pour être les plus beaux de cet artiste, et qu'il serait peut-être important de les acquérir pour la Nation*'. The secretary was asked to make enquiries (NAAF, 3e, XVII, 1901, p.203).

[19] Exh. *Charles Le Brun*, Versailles, 1963, no.152.

[20] Cf. Piganiol de la Force, *Nouvelle description . . . de Versailles*, 1751, II, pp.99–100, and F. Souchal, *French Sculptors of the 17th and 18th centuries; the reign of Louis XIV*, III, 1987, pp.250–1, who states that it was moved to the Tuileries Gardens in 1716; it is now in the Louvre. Souchal also lists (p.251) a *Temps qui découvre la Vérité, modèle* for the marble group at Versailles, shown at the 1699 Salon.

[21] Exh. Salon 1747. Laurent Cars (1699–1771) had studied drawing under Lemoyne and his engravings after his master's paintings were particularly prized: '*M.* Cars *semble être en possession de graver singulièrement les ouvrages de M.* Le Moyne, *dont il est élève et dont, conséquemment, il connoist mieux que personne la manière et les principes*' (Cochin to Marigny, 7 August 1763; cf. NAAF, 3e, XIX, 1903, p.274).

[22] One of four copies at Abbeville after Lemoynes in Bouret's collection, the others being of P417, *Hercules and Omphale* and *The Bather* (cf. Bordeaux, pp.91, 126); see main text above. All the copies are the same size, and they were probably made for Bouret when he sold the originals in 1761.

[23] Cf. NAAF, V, 1877, p.204.

[24] According to C. Blanc, *Le Trésor de la Curiosité*, 1858, II, p.279. Bordeaux has 'Augar (?)' as the buyer.

P417 *Perseus and Andromeda*

Andromeda has pink drapery and a gold-striped pale blue *cache-sexe*; Perseus wears a golden tunic and has a pale blue-green cloak. Signed, bottom centre: *f. Lemoyne./1723.*

Canvas, relined 183 × 149.7

Relined in 1905. A horizontal seam runs 63.5 cm. above the bottom edge, and the join has been retouched. There are also retouchings round the uneven edges, and small losses in the sky between Perseus and Andromeda, in the rock to the left of Andromeda, and in Perseus's cloak, below his head. *Pentimenti* show changes to Perseus's right arm and hand, to the outline of his billowing cloak, to Andromeda's right arm and hand (originally slightly higher) and the drapery behind them, and to her left arm and hand (originally slightly higher). The varnish is discoloured.

The subject is taken from Ovid, *Metamorphoses* IV, 663–752: Andromeda, daughter of Cassiopeia and Cepheus, King of Joppa, is offered, on the advice of Jupiter Ammon, as a sacrifice to a sea monster, sent by Neptune together with a flood to destroy Cepheus's kingdom; his attack was made to revenge Cassiopeia's boast that she and her daughter were more beautiful than the Nereids under Neptune's protection; Perseus, returning from his victory over the Gorgon Medusa (whose petrifying head he had attached to his shield) slays the monster and marries Andromeda. Andromeda's parents are seen lamenting their daughter's fate on the distant shore. See also Titian P11.

Painted before his visit to Italy,[1] P417 is much influenced by Veronese's *Perseus and Andromeda*, a version of which (now at Rennes) was in Louis XV's collection. Blanc

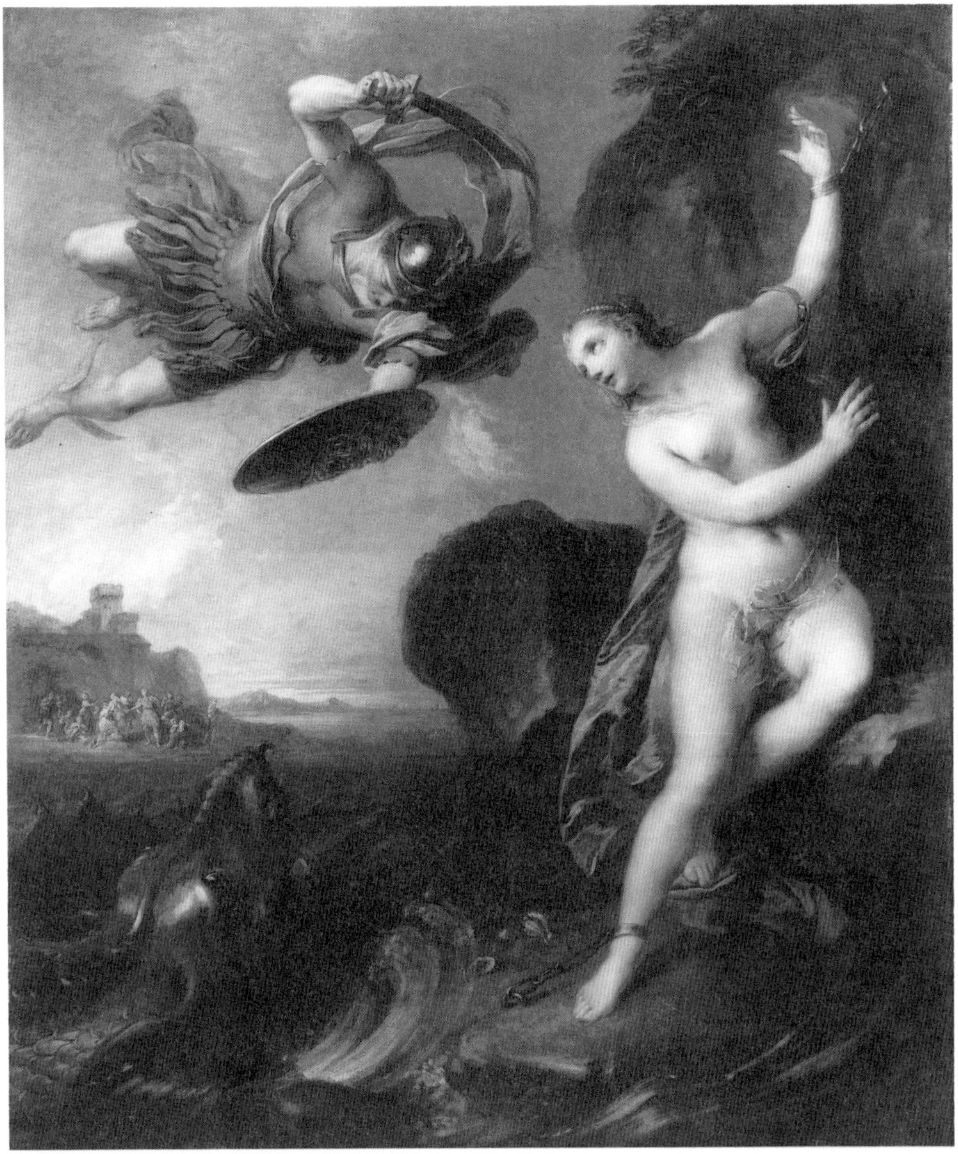

P417

indicated a comparison with Annibale Carracci's *Mercury delivering the Golden Apple* in the Farnese Gallery.[2] P417 achieved immediate success; it was bought by Berger from the 1723 Place Dauphine exhibition where it had received *'de grands éloges'*,[3] and was again exhibited at the 1725 Salon as the pendant to *Hercules and Omphale* (commissioned by Berger; now in the Louvre). P417 was the second Lemoyne to be acquired by Berger whose collection of his works is discussed under P392.

Drawing

A compositional study was in the Paignon-Dijonval collection (*Cabinet* . . ., 1810, no.3249) and anon. sale, Paris, 14 February 1914(81).

Engraving

L. Cars 1728, reversed (Bordeaux, fig.39a; see P392 note 21).

Copies/Versions

ABBEVILLE Musée Boucher de Perthes;. 182 × 153, ex coll. J.-A.-C. Boucher de Crèvecoeur, *fermier général,* in whose MS catalogue it was described as *'du Cabinet de M. Bouret, fermier général'*; see P392 note 22 (Bordeaux, p.91, fig.39b).
BRENTWOOD Essex, private collection 1969; 30.5 × 25.4, copy.
DUISBERG private collection 1961; copy.
LONDON N. Fischmann gallery c.1960; 95 × 80 oval, variant without group on distant shore. Spink 1925; 12.7 × 10.2, reversed copy.
VIENNA Dorotheum, 18–20 November 1954 (89); 66 × 55, variant with Perseus's head to the right, the dragon facing to front and no distant shore.

An *Andromède* on canvas was no.49 in Lemoyne's *inventaire après décès*;[4] Bordeaux suggests this may have been the reduced replica in the Martin sale, Paris, 13 December 1776 (166), and the Conti sale, Paris, 8 April 1777 (2070 [c.86.5 × 68.5]). Another reduced version was noted in the Villequier collection, hung as an over-door in 1793.[5]

The composition was also reproduced on a Vincennes wine-cooler (British Museum, Franks coll. no.506); on the cover of a Meissen gold box (Christie's, 29 March 1976, lot 205), and in a Fürstenberg porcelain group.[6]

Provenance

As P392; acquired from the artist by Berger, 1723; first Lareynière sale, 1793, lot 15, bt. in, 8,000 *livres*; second Lareynière sale, 1797, lot 4, bt. Sainte-Foix, 1,200 *livres*; Sainte-Foix sale, 1811, lot 43, 280 fr.;[7] Prousteau de Montlouis sale, 1851, lot 103.

Exhibitions

Place Dauphine 1723; Salon 1725 (n.n., see above); Bethnal Green 1872–5 (399).

References General

Caylus, p.65; Nonotte, p.538, no.17; Saunier, no.47; Bordeaux, P44.

1 Although, mistakenly, Dezallier d'Argenville, *Abrégé de la vie des plus fameux peintres*, 1745, II, p.426, said it was painted in Italy.

2 Blanc 1865, 'Lemoyne', p.2; he went on to say: *'c'est un de ces emprunts qu'il ne faut pas blâmer parce qu'ils sont toujours préférables à la bizarrerie du neuf'*. Bordeaux, p.91, also suggested the influence of this Carracci composition on P417.

3 Caylus, p.47, and cf. Nonotte, p.524. DV, I, p.42, say Lemoyne's *Andromeda* was bought by a private collector at the 1718 place Dauphine exhibition (repeated by T. Crow, *Painters and Public Life*, 1985, p.84), but P417 is dated 1723.

4 Cf. NAAF, V, 1877, p.206.

5 NAAF, 3e, XVII, 1901, p.323.

6 See *The Connoisseur*, XXXV, 1913, pp.14–16.

7 According to C. Blanc, *Le Trésor de la Curiosité*, 1858, II, p.149. Bordeaux had 'Augar (?)' as the buyer.

Nicolas-Bernard Lépicié (1735–1784)

Born on 16 June 1735 in Paris, the son of the engraver F.-B. Lépicié, *secrétaire perpétuel* at the Académie. He studied under Carle van Loo from c.1751 at the Académie where he was *agréé* in 1764 (*Guillaume le Conquérant*; Caen, Lycée Malherbe) and *reçu* in 1769 (*Achille et le centaure Chiron*; Troyes). Though he continued to paint ambitious histories, his talent was better expressed in the less vigorous genre scenes recalling Chardin and Greuze, as well as Teniers and ter Borch, which he began to paint in the late 1760s. He also painted portraits, including several studies of his young pupil, Carle Vernet (the son of Joseph, q.v.). He was made *adjoint à professeur* at the Académie in 1770 and *professeur* in 1777. In his last years he was overcome with religious scruples which led him to alter or destroy his works whose sensuality might offend the *Divine bonté*.[1] He died in Paris on 15 September 1784.

[1] Cf. P. Gaston-Dreyfus, '*Une dernière volonté de Lépicié*', BSHAF 1910, pp.25–32.

Abbreviations

GD	P. Gaston-Dreyfus, *Catalogue raisonné de l'oeuvre peint et dessiné de Nicolas-Bernard Lépicié*, 1923
Ingersoll-Smouse	F. Ingersoll-Smouse, 'Nicolas-Bernard Lépicié', *Revue de l'Art ancien et moderne*, XLVI, 1924, pp.122–30, 217–28; L, 1926, pp.293–6; LI, 1927, pp.179–86

P464 *Mother feeding her Child (Le devoir maternel)*

The mother has a white bonnet, pink shawl and a grey-blue dress. Signed above the bowl, below left: *Lépicié*.

Oak panel 13.8 × 10.2 × 1.5

The panel has been chipped top right, and there is a small loss bottom left. The varnish is discoloured.

The subject is a detail from the *Ménage de bonnes gens* of c.1774; a larger version of P464 is dated 1774 (see Versions). The model recurs in several Lépicié genre scenes between 1772 and 1777.[1]

Like the pendant P466, P464 appears to have been painted for the engraver J.-P. Le Bas; the two panels are doubtless contemporary and may be dated c.1774.

Engraving

J.-P. Le Bas, *Le Devoir Maternel*.[2]

Versions

LONDON Christie's 7 July 1971 (91); 43.8 × 36.9, signed and dated 1774, also known as *La bouillie*, identical with P464 (GD175).

The larger composition, *Ménage de bonnes gens*, 46 × 59, was in the Jourdan sale, Paris, 4 April 1803, lot 29 (GD174); engr. de Longueil 1788 (illus. Ingersoll-Smouse 1927, p.180).

Provenance

With P466: J.-P. Le Bas (1707–83); his sale, Paris, 15 April 1783 (14), 132 fr.; Robert de Saint-Victor, *président de la chambre des comptes*, Rouen;[3] his sale, Paris, 26 November ff. 1822 (568), 176 fr.; baron Vivant-Denon (1747–1825); his sale, Paris, 1 May ff. 1826 (166), 176 fr.;[4] J.-L. David (1792–1868); his sale, Paris, 18–19 March 1868 (33, *La leçon de lecture*; 34, *La jeune mère*); the 4th Marquess of Hertford; Bagatelle inventory 1871 (954); Hertford House inventory 1890.

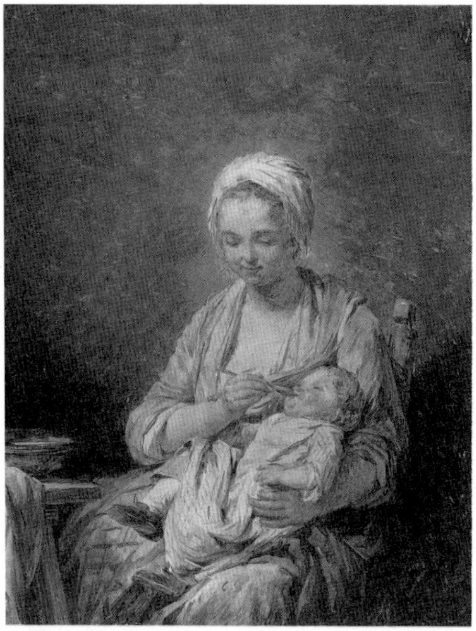

P464

Exhibition

Bethnal Green 1872–5 (580).

References General

GD176; Ingersoll-Smouse 1924, pp. 224–6.

[1] Cf. Ingersoll-Smouse 1924, p.130; a study of the same model, signed and dated 1772, looking appropriately younger and in the same pose as in P464, coll. Bardac 1924, illus. *ibid.*, p.129 (GD76, as a study for *Le lever de Fanchon* of 1773 at Saint-Omer).

[2] The plates after both P464 and P466 are inscribed *Le Bas direxit*. M. Bénard, *Cabinet de Paignon-Dijonval*, 1810, no.9334, described them as by C.-F. Le Tellier (1743–1800), but the *Inventaire du fonds français du Cabinet des Estampes*, XIII, 1974, pp.171–2, nos. 215–16, lists them under Le Bas.

[3] The seal of his office appears (damaged) on the *verso* of P464 and P466: a crown with three fleurs de lys, two and one, with inscription RIC . . . OTAIRE A ROUEN.

[4] The *verso* of P466 is inscribed: LEPICIE/*vente de Denon/1er May 1826/les deux/pendants/fr. 176.*

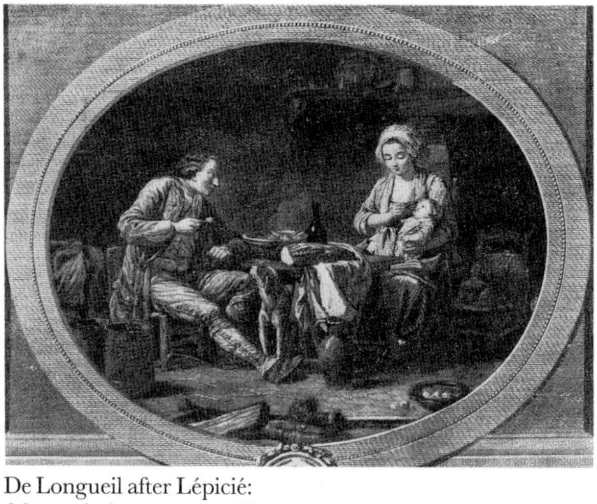

De Longueil after Lépicié:
Ménage des bonnes gens, 1788

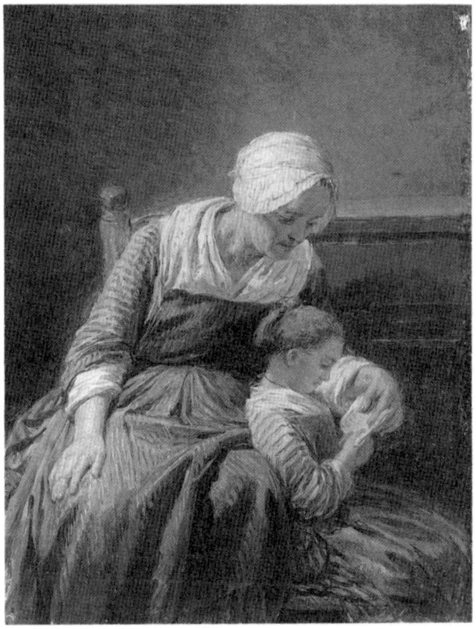

P466

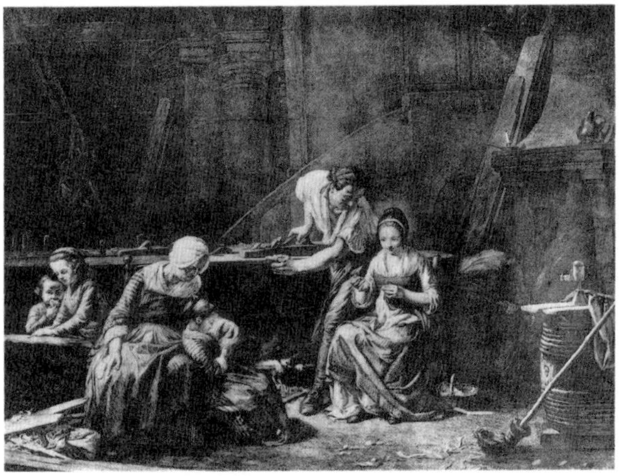

J.-P. Le Bas after Lépicié: *Atelier du menuisier*.

P466 *The Reading Lesson (L'éducation commencée)*

The mother has a white bonnet and a blue-grey dress, the child is in yellow. Signed above the child's skirt, below right: *Lépicié*.

Oak panel 13.7 × 10.2 × 1.5

A strip down the right-hand edge has been retouched and there is a small damage top right. The varnish is discoloured.

The subject is a detail from the *Atelier du menuisier* exhibited in 1775 (see Versions). Lépicié painted another figure from this composition on a small panel dated 1774.[1] For further commentary see P464.

Engraving

J.-P. Le Bas, *L'éducation commencée* (see P464 note 2).

Versions

The larger composition, *Atelier du menuisier*, 64 × 81, exh. Salon 1775 (21), was in the artist's sale, Paris, 10 February 1785, lot 1 (GD178);[2] engr. Le Bas (illus. GD, f.p. 76).[3]
A larger version, 90 × 130, coll. E. May 1923 (GD180).[4]
A reduced, modified version,[5] 49 × 62, showing the little girl reading in a bonnet, exh. *The Rococo Age*, High Museum, Atlanta, Georgia, 1983, no. 53 (GD179).
Three drawings survive for this composition: a study of the mother and child (in a bonnet) reading (Vienna, Albertina; illus. Ingersoll-Smouse 1924, p.226; GD405); a compositional study for the Salon picture (sold Drouot, 28 June 1938, lot 76) and another of the modified composition (Orléans, Musée des Beaux-Arts; illus. Ingersoll-Smouse 1927, p.181; BSHAF 1910, f.p. 26; GD408).

Provenance

See P464.

Exhibition

Bethnal Green 1872–5 (573).

References General

GD177; Ingersoll-Smouse 1924, pp. 224–6.

[1] Panel 21 × 18; the comte de D. sale, Marseille, 7 November 1916 (GD81).

[2] The *Atelier du menuisier* had a pendant, *Les accords* (or *La demande acceptée*), in which the same seven characters appear; considering the two together it seems clear that it is a mother who teaches her daughter to read (although Gautier described her as the grandmother, cf. BSHAF 1910, p.30).

[3] After he had turned *dévot* Lépicié asked Le Bas to modify this plate so that the carpenter's gaze was averted from the girl seated at his side; Le Bas refused and Lépicié then bought the plate and all the prints and destroyed them. Gaston-Dreyfus found a single example, inscribed *L'Heureuse Union . . . Peint par J.-B[te]. Greuze.*

[4] Photograph on file supplied by the Netherlands Gallery, London, in 1917.

[5] According to Lépicié's revised morality, cf. note 3 above, with the carpenter's gaze averted.

Carle Andrea van Loo (1705–1765)

Born on 15 February 1705 in Nice (then part of the Kingdom of Sardinia), son of the painter A.-L. van Loo (c.1641–1712). He first studied with his elder brother J.-B. van Loo (1684–1745) in Turin and Rome where he was also the pupil of B. Luti and the sculptor P. Legros. He came to Paris in 1720 and won the *prix de Rome* in 1724. In 1728, accompanied by Boucher and his nephews L.-M. (q.v.) and François (d.1732) van Loo, he went to Rome where he quickly gained recognition and was honoured by the Pope, Benedict XIII. In 1732 he went, via Florence, to Turin, entering the service of Charles-Emmanuel III of Sardinia; when war broke out with Piedmont in 1734 he returned to Paris. *Agréé* in 1734, he was *reçu* in 1735 (*Apollo and Marsyas*; Ecole des Beaux-Arts). An adaptable and fluent artist, his career went unimpeded: at the Académie he was made *professeur* 1737, *recteur* 1754 and *directeur* 1763. Having established his claim to *noblesse* he was made *chevalier* of the Order of Saint-Michel 1751. In 1749 he became the first *gouverneur* of the *Ecole royale des élèves protégés* and, in 1762, *premier peintre du Roi*. He briefly visited London in 1764 and died in Paris on 15 July 1765.

Abbreviation

Sahut M.-C. Sahut, *Carle Vanloo*, exh. cat., Nice, Clermont-Ferrand, Nancy, 1977

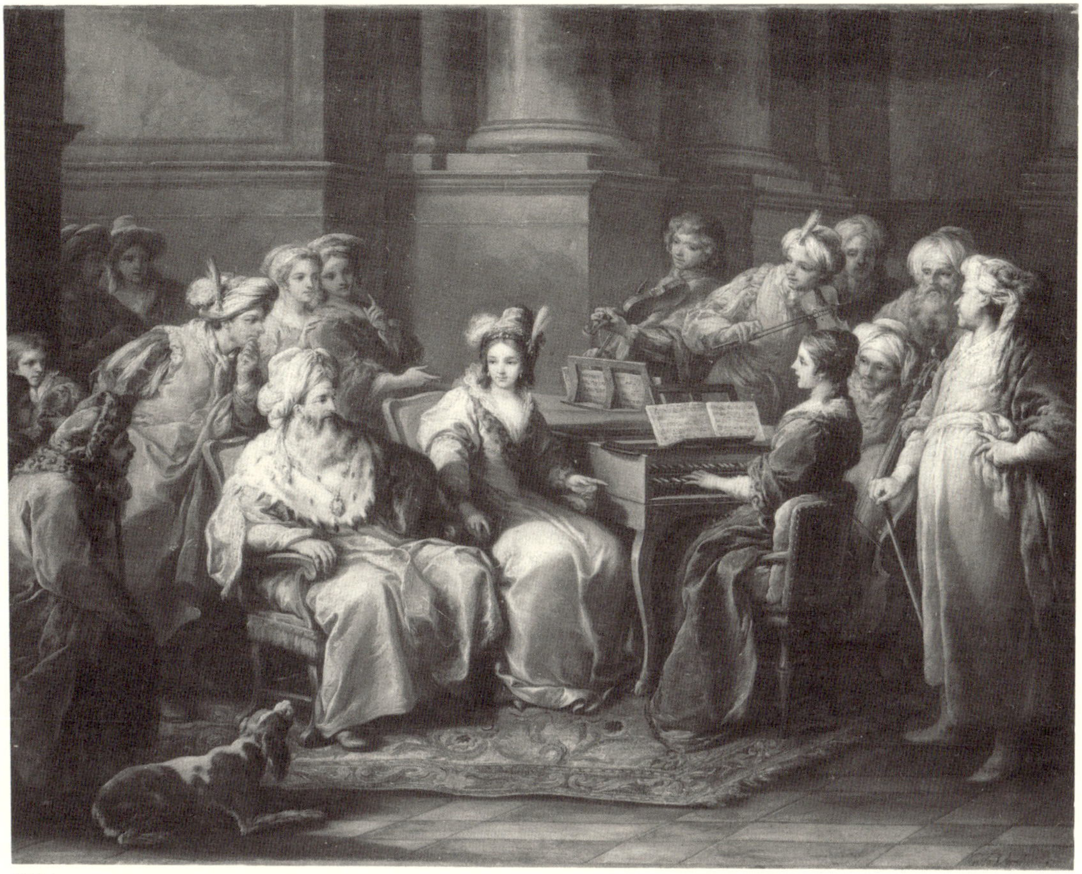

P451

P451 *The Grand Turk giving a Concert to his Mistress*

A lady in blue plays the harpsichord, her music inscribed: *aria del sig. handel/si ca . . . // si caro Car . . .*, accompanied by two violins and a cello. The Sultan and his mistress sit in red chairs, he in a gold robe and ermine cape, she in white satin; the foreground figure on the extreme left wears a red robe trimmed with leopard skin, and on the extreme right stands a man in gold robes with a blue cape and red boots. Inscribed, over a damaged signature: *Carle Vanloo. 1727 (sic)*.

Canvas, relined 72.5 × 91

The top 4 cm. has been repainted and was apparently once folded back over a smaller stretcher. There are two scratches in the upper right area and retouchings in the robes of the Sultan and of the figure immediately behind him. A surface stain runs down across the hem of the harpsichordist's skirt. The edges have been made up and the varnish is considerably discoloured.

Exhibited at the Salon in 1737 as *Le grand Seigneur donnant un Concert à sa Maîtresse* with a pendant, *Le Grand Seigneur qui fait peindre sa Maîtresse* (Museum of Fine Arts, Richmond, Virginia).[1] Both show the extravagant costume (a mixture of the oriental, French sixteenth century and Rubens[2]) which characterised the *turqueries* of the period (cf. Lancret P450 and Nattier P456),[3] and their subjects, music and painting, celebrate the then acclaimed talents of Carle van Loo and his wife, Christina Somis (1704–85), *'La Philomèle de Turin'*, whom he had married in 1733. She has been identified as the harpsichordist in P451,[4] and she was doubtless responsible for choosing the score of the aria *'Si caro, si'* from Handel's *Admeto* (first performed in 1727).[5]

Despite the present appearance of the signature (see above) the date must originally have read *1737*.

Drawings

Five studies from or for eight of the heads in P451 were engr. G. Demarteau: the turbanned violinist and the next figure on the right (reversed), the two ladies behind the Sultan (reversed), the man leaning on the Sultan's chair, the left foreground figure (reversed) and the two standing men on the extreme right (reversed) (Sahut, no.511, illus.).

Engraving

C.-A. Littret 1766, reversed, *Le concert du Grand Sultan*.

Copies

MONTRESOR (Indre-et-Loire) comte Stanislas Rey; 91 × 139, by J. Wall (1754?–98) before 1783, inscribed *637* (referring to the Polish Royal coll.); given by Stanislaus II to his sister, Ludwika Zamoyska, 1783, and at Montrésor since at least 1873 (illus. Ryszkiewicz, p.17).
POZNAN Musée National; 75 × 92, by F. Pinck, commissioned by Stanislaus II, 1791.
VERSAILLES anon. sale, 12 March 1962 (29); 75 × 80, reversed.

A *'copie faite dans l'école'* was in the Godefroy sale, Paris, 19 November 1785 (89), 73 × 97, probably the picture *'acheté à la vente de feu Carle Vanloo . . . pas entièrement terminé. L'acquéreur le fit depuis finir par Mr. Caresme'*, in the anon. sale, Paris, 6 December 1787 (42), 73 × 92. This, or another, was in the Béraudière sale, Paris, 18–30 May 1885 (49), 73 × 92. A later copy, 105 × 149, was with the comtesse de Talleyrand 1911.

A reversed oval copy on a Sèvres porcelain plaque of 1774 is set in a guéridon table, ex coll. Mme. du Barry, in the Louvre (OA.10.658).[6] A reversed oval copy in enamel, set in an eighteenth-century, probably Swiss, gold snuff-box, sold Christie's, Geneva, 25–6 April 1978 (337).

Provenance

Painted for Fagon;[7] Frederick II of Prussia (1712–86) by 1765;[8] the baronne Gartenberg-Sadogorska, by whom given to Stanislaus II of Poland (1732–98) before 1767;[9] kept at Warsaw, Lazienski and, from 1797, in St. Petersburg;[10] probably acquired by the comte Alexandre Bezborodko (1742–99), St. Petersburg;[11] by descent to the comtesse Katherine Koucheleff, from whom bt. in September 1867 by Richard Wallace;[12] rue Laffitte inventory 1871 (543); Hertford House inventory 1890.

Exhibitions

Exposition de tableaux à l'Académie, 6 July 1737;[13] Salon 1737 (see above); Bethnal Green 1872–5 (458, J.-B. Vanloo, *A Masquerade Party*).

References General

Sahut, no.52; L. Réau, 'Carle Vanloo', AAF, 4e, XIX, 1938, pp.22, 66–7; A. Ryszkiewicz, 'Sur quelques tableaux avec turqueries dans les collections polonaises', *Bulletin du Musée National de Varsovie*, XVI, 1975, pp.17–23; P.L. Near, *Arts in Virginia*, XXIII, 1983, pp.18–27.

[1] Sahut, no.53; now reduced to 66 × 76; painted for Jean de Jullienne; exh. Salon 1737; engr. B. Lépicié (showing full composition); copies with the comtesse de Talleyrand 1911 and sold Versailles, 12 March 1962, lot 29 (cf. Copies above).

[2] Cf., for example, P519 and P521 in this Collection.

[3] Cf. also A. Boppe, *Gazette des Beaux-Arts*, 3e, XXXIV, 1905, pp.54–5, repeated in the same author's *Les peintres du Bosphore au dix-huitième siècle*, 1911, pp.118–20. Van Loo's other *turqueries* were *Le contrat de mariage*, 1740, and *Une sultane prenant du café* and *Deux sultanes travaillant à la tapisserie*, 1754 (both portraits of Mme. de Pompadour), all in the Hermitage; a third *turquerie* for Mme. de Pompadour, *Une sultane jouant d'un instrument à cordes*, 1754, is now untraced (cf. Sahut, nos. 77 and 148–50).

[4] By Boppe, *loc. cit.*; Réau, p.67, and A.-P. de Mirimonde, *La Revue du Louvre*, 1969, p.246, and *L'iconographie musicale sous les rois Bourbons*, 1977, II, p.146. Comparison of the head with those in van Loo's portraits of his wife (Sahut, nos.76, 397–8) is not wholly convincing but, since it appears that the artist portrayed himself in the Richmond pendant, it probably was intended to show his wife.

[5] The music was recently identified by P. Wall (*Early Music*, XII, 1984, p.303). Christina Somis helped introduce Italian music to Paris (cf. Dandré-Bardon, *Carle Van Loo*, 1765, pp.23–4).

[6] Cf. S. Grandjean, *La Revue du Louvre*, 1979, pp.44–9.

[7] As stated by Dandré-Bardon, *op. cit.*, p.24; possibly Louis Fagon (1680–1744), *intendant des finances*, son of Louis XIV's doctor.

[8] Dandré-Bardon, *op. cit.*, p.58. The marquis d'Argens, Frederick II's chamberlain, described '*un tableau de figures grandes comme celles du Poussin, qui représente un concert turc*' in his collection (cf. Sahut, under no.52; text published in 1768, but probably earlier). Ryszkiewicz, pp.18–19, doubted that Frederick owned P451 – but he seems not to have known of d'Argens's comment.

[9] Baronne Gartenberg-Sadogorska's husband, Piotre Mikolaj, *directeur de la monnaie* in Warsaw, was ennobled in 1768.

[10] The King particularly admired P451; on 7 January 1767 he wrote to Mme. Geoffrin: '*Croirez-vous que j'ai trouvé ici un Carle Vanloo original admirable, mais si admirable qu'il enchante jusqu'aux gens qui n'ont pas témoigné dans toute leur vie le moindre goût pour la peinture? . . . selon moi, l'intention du peintre était de représenter un riche vieillard levantin-grec et chrétien qui donne à sa jeune femme un concert exécuté par des Européens, auquel assistent quelques Turcs. Ce tableau, qui a deux pieds dix pouces de largeur sur deux pieds trois pouces de haut* [73 × 92], *a, dit-on, un pendant dont le sujet est une peinture et dont je voudrais bien savoir des nouvelles. L'estampe de celui-ci devient insupportable à côté du tableau; entre autres le graveur a totalement manqué la jeune femme, qui, dans le tableau, est d'une beauté ravissante. On donnerait cette figure à Marianne, femme d'Hérode. On la voit regarder son mari avec douceur et attention, mais cela est joint à une mélancolie si majestueuse dans toute cette figure qu'on ne peut s'empêcher de lui porter respect et intérêt. Le vieillard est très-beau aussi dans son genre. Ce tableau, qui est du plus fini, n'est cependant rien moins que léché et il plaît également de loin et de près.*' *Correspondance inédite du roi Stanislas-Auguste Poniatowski et de Madame Geoffrin, 1764–77*, ed. Ch. de Mouÿ, 1875, pp.263–4). In 1795 Stanislaus directed that P451 should not be sold, but sent to St. Petersburg; in the *Catalogue des tableaux appartenant à sa majesté le roi de Pologne*, 1795, no.128, P451 was valued at '*300 à 400 ducats*' (quoted by Sahut, no.52).

[11] For whom see Boucher P399 note 6. Stanislaus gave at least two of his pictures (by Rubens and Giordano) to Alexandre Bezborodko who probably also made purchases at the Stanislaus sale in 1798 (of which no catalogue survives; cf. Ryszkiewicz, p.20).

[12] See Boucher P399 note 7.

[13] Identified by Sahut, no.52 (cf. *Mercure de France*, 1737, p.1620).

Louis-Michel van Loo (1707–71)

Born on 2 March 1707 in Toulon, the nephew of Carle van Loo (q.v.) and son of J.-B. van Loo (1684–1745) under whom he studied in Turin, Rome and Paris. He won the *prix de Rome* in 1725 (*Moïse enfant faisant tomber la couronne de Pharaon*; lost) and returned to Rome in 1728, accompanied by Boucher, his uncle and brother François. He returned to Paris in 1730 and was *reçu* by the Académie in 1733 (*Apollo and Daphne*; Ecole des Beaux-Arts). He was in Turin 1733–4 and worked in Madrid as Painter to Philip V of Spain 1738–52. He exhibited at the Salon 1753–69 and painted several portraits for Versailles between 1759 and 1770. He visited London in 1764 and succeeded his uncle as head of the *Ecole royale des élèves protégés* in 1765. Though principally a portrait painter, he also painted historical and mythological subjects. He died in Paris on 20 March 1771.[1]

[1] For his biography, see M.-C. Sahut in *Diderot & l'art de Boucher à David*, exh. cat., Hôtel de la Monnaie, 1984, pp.382–3.

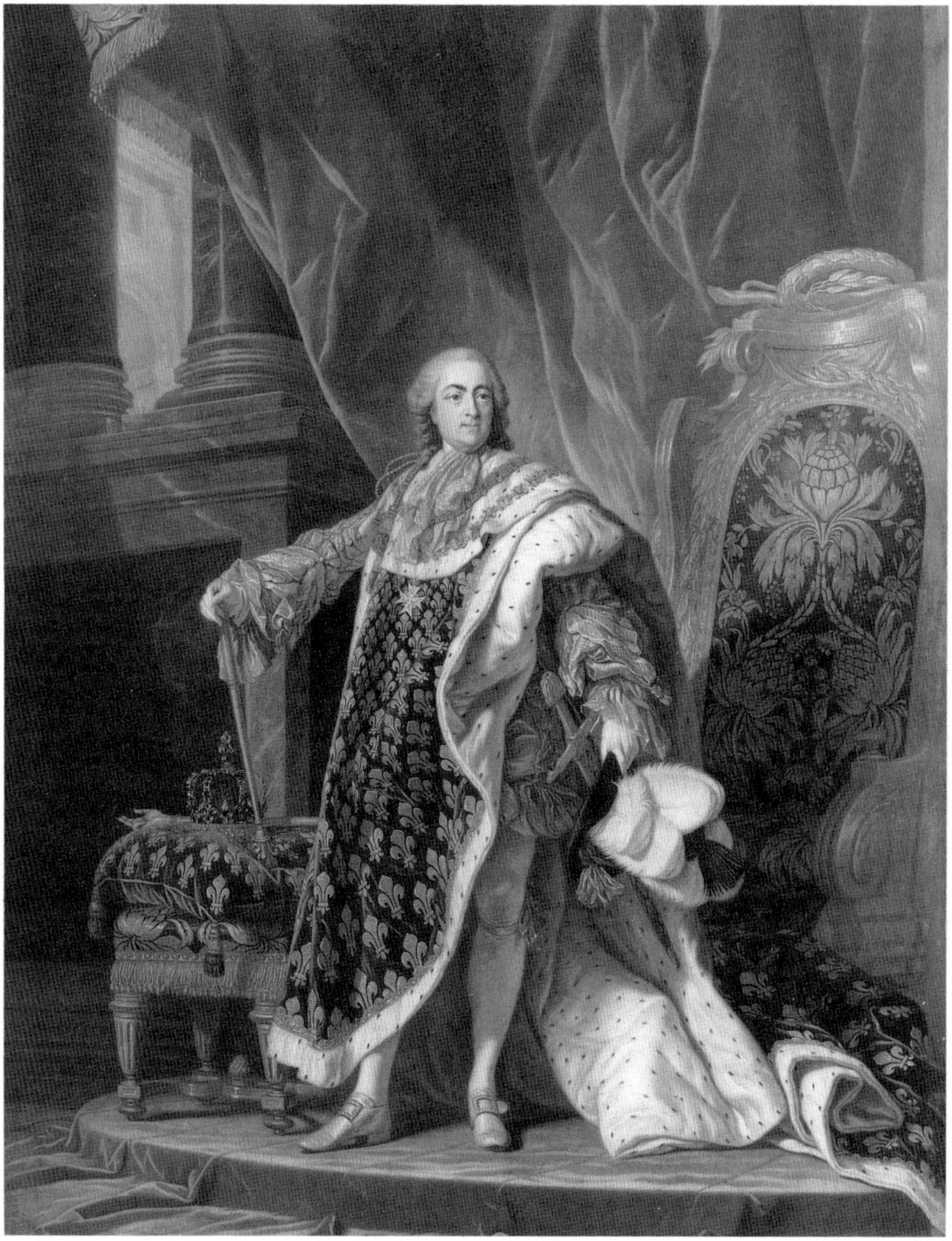

P477

Studio of L.-M. van Loo

P477 *Louis XV*

Powdered wig, grey eyes; in coronation robes, wearing a suit of white satin, an ermine-lined deep purple mantle with gold fleurs de lys, and the gold collars of the Golden Fleece and the Saint-Esprit; a black hat with white plumes in his left hand and in his right the reversed sceptre rests on a cushion matching the pattern of the mantle, on which also lie the crown and *main de justice*; red carpet and curtain, with blue marble columns; the throne is covered with blue damask ornamented with gold pomegranates.

Canvas, relined 136.6 × 104

Relined before 1836.[1] An overall craquelure has lifted in two places at the top of the throne. There are several old retouchings within the carpet and curtain. Each vertical edge has been (weakly) made up (by 3 cm. on the left and 4 cm. on the right, included in the measurements above) and the canvas was probably unfolded during relining. The varnish is discoloured.

Louis XV (1710–74), King of France 1715–74, m. in 1725 Marie Leczinska (see P437 After Nattier), by whom he had ten children.

P477 is a half life-sized, probably contemporary, copy of the portrait commissioned from van Loo in 1759.[2] He submitted a half life-sized version in 1760 and exhibited the finished life-sized portrait (260 × 194) at the 1761 Salon. It was placed in Versailles, but has since disappeared.[3] In 1761 he painted a replica to be used as a model by the copyists of the *surintendance*. Of the half life-sized copies then made, two were for Mme. de Pompadour and one for the duc de Choiseul;[4] others of similar size are now at Rennes and Abbeville.

Provenance

The duchesse de Berri (1798–1870); her sale, Paris, 22 February 1836 (190, Carle Vanloo, *Louis XV en pied* [135 × 103]); Ralph Bernal (c.1785–1854); his sale, Christie's, 6th day, 10 March 1855 (750, Rigaud, *Louis XV* [133 × 103]), bt. by the 4th Marquess of Hertford, 56 gn.; Hertford House inventory 1870 as '*Largilliere Louis XV*'.

Exhibition

Bethnal Green 1872–5 (393, as Callet, *Louis XV*).

Reference General

Ch. Maumené and L. d'Harcourt, 'Iconographie des Rois de France', AAF, XVI, 1931, p.342, no.147(i), as '*petite copie réduite*'.

[1] The relining canvas bears the stamp: *Galerie de S A Madame Duchesse de* BERRY with a crown, the number *117* painted in black, and *750/B* in white chalk (referring to the Bernal sale). The stretcher is inscribed *No 9* in black in an early nineteenth-century hand.

[2] The commission is discussed by Maumené and d'Harcourt, pp.339–43.

[3] Good life-sized copies are at Woburn (signed and dated 1762), in the Grand Trianon, and in the Royal Museum of Fine Arts, Copenhagen (signed). Another, signed *Frédou d'après M. Van Loo 1763*, is at Versailles.

[4] The Choiseul portrait is discussed by F. J. B. Watson in A. K. Snowman, *Eighteenth-century Gold Boxes of Europe*, 1966, p.153.

Marie-Françoise-Constance Mayer-Lamartinière (1775–1821)

Born in 1775 in Paris, the daughter of a successful government official, she first studied under J.-B. Suvée (who left Paris in 1801) and Greuze, whose work she imitated closely. She exhibited principally portraits at the Salon 1796–1801. In 1802 she became the pupil of Prud'hon (q.v.), to whom she dedicated the rest of her life, both as an artist and companion. She cared for his children (whose mother had become insane), while her work became inextricably involved with that of Prud'hon who would prepare compositions for her to paint (cf. P348 and Prud'hon P313) and exhibit at the Salon under her own name. In 1810 (presumably on the death of her father from whom she inherited some 80,000 fr.) she acquired a studio adjoining Prud'hon's in the Sorbonne. In 1821 the government requisitioned the Sorbonne and this threat to the *ménage*, combined with her highly-strung temperament, led her to take her own life in her studio on 26 May 1821. Prud'hon completed her last picture, *Une famille dans la désolation*, and showed it in the 1822 Salon under his name. When Prud'hon died in 1823 he was buried with her at Père-Lachaise.[1]

[1] Mayer's bibliography is partly inseparable from Prud'hon's, but separate accounts of her life include: Ch. Gueullette, *Gazette des Beaux-Arts*, 2e, XIX, 1879, pp.476–90, and XX, 1879, pp.337–57, 525–36; J. Doin, *Revue de l'Art ancien et moderne*, XXIX, 1911, pp.49–60, 139–50, and E. Pilon, *Constance Mayer*, 1927. Mayer's suicide was the subject of a lithograph by E. Devéria, published in *L'Artiste*, I, 1831, f.p.132.

Abbreviations

See under Prud'hon (p.314)

P348 *The Sleep of Venus and Cupid* *(Vénus et l'Amour endormis caressés et reveillés par les zéphyrs)*

Venus, with a golden drapery, reclines on a blue-grey cloth; a dull red canopy above. Said to have been signed by Mayer.[1]

Canvas, relined 96.5 × 144.5

Cleaned and relined by Buttery in 1879. Extensive shrinkage craquelure, particularly prominent in the golden drapery and the left background area, has been retouched. There are further retouchings on the neck of the foremost zephyr and on Cupid's left leg. *Pentimenti* show the trees continuing behind the red canopy, and the hands of the zephyr above Venus's head were altered. The varnish is much discoloured.

The French title quoted above is that given to P348 by Mayer in the 1806 Salon catalogue. It was listed at Malmaison in 1811 and 1814[2] as *Le sommeil de Vénus*, but in 1840 was sold as *Psyché*, a title retained (as *Le sommeil de Psyché*, see Provenance) by Blanc, Clément, Goncourt and in the earlier editions of this catalogue (1900–10). The resemblance of the Venus in P348 to the Psyche in Prud'hon's *L'enlèvement de Psyché* (Salon 1808; Louvre) may have induced this error.[3]

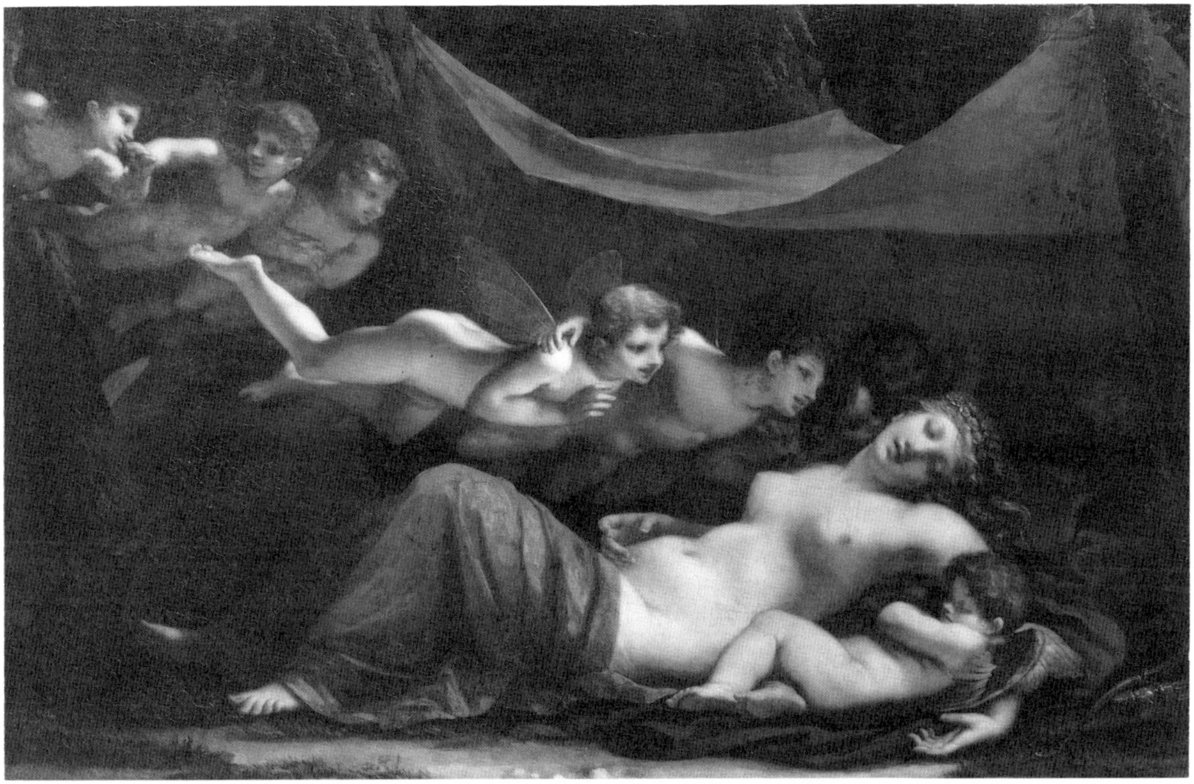

P348

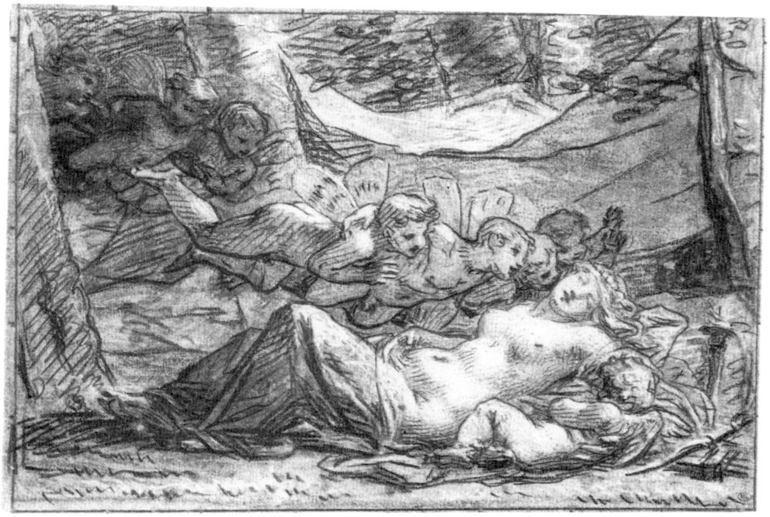

Prud'hon: Study for *The Sleep of Venus and Cupid*.
Louvre, Cabinet des Dessins (RF4632)

Similarly, although P348 was described at the Salon and at Malmaison (see note 2) as Mayer, it was sold in 1840 as Mayer and Prud'hon. The attribution is indeed debatable, since Prud'hon had first devised and sketched the composition (see below). In 1844 Blanc stated that P348 was entirely by Prud'hon (the zephyrs in particular being his *'chef d'oeuvre'*), and it was sold as such in 1860 and 1866. In 1872 Clément said it was painted by Mayer *'sous la direction et peut-être avec la collaboration du maître'*,[4] and in 1876 Goncourt thought it *'très retouché par Prud'hon'*. P348 was exhibited as Prud'hon in 1872 (see below) and was attributed to him in the earlier editions of this catalogue (1900–10). It is now impossible to distinguish between the hands of Mayer and Prud'hon; as Blanc observed, they became *'confondus comme leurs coeurs'*.[5] But it is clear from the earliest references to P348 that it was officially by Mayer, and it remains one of the more distinguished pictures attached to her name. The pendant, *Le flambeau de Vénus* (Salon 1808; Arenenberg, Napoleonmuseum), also bought by Joséphine,[6] shows a frieze-like composition, again devised by Prud'hon.[7]

Drawings

PARIS Louvre (RF4632); compositional study by Prud'hon, without the two zephyrs on the extreme right and with a rectangular quiver, lower right (Guiffrey, no.200).

Two further related drawings by Prud'hon are recorded: a compositional sketch (Boisfremont sale, Paris, 9 April 1870, lot 22; Guiffrey, no.199), and a study for Venus's hand (M. sale, Paris, 13 December 1866, lot 60; Guiffrey, no.201).

Versions

CHANTILLY Musée Condé (no.422); panel 23 × 34, compositional study by Prud'hon, with Venus's head slightly more raised, generally resembling the Louvre drawing (see above); engr. L. Flameng 1870, lith. Leroux (Guiffrey, no.197).
PARIS private collection; 54 × 91, unfinished study for the figure of Venus (Guiffrey, no.198).

Provenance

Bt. from the artist by the Empress Joséphine (1763–1814), Malmaison (see note 2);[8] the château passed to her son, Eugène, duc de Leuchtenberg (1781–1824), whose widow sold off the contents at Malmaison, 31 May–19 July 1829; P348 was then bt. Pourra, 1,010 fr.;[9] Lucien Bonaparte, prince de Canino (1775–1841);[10] his sale, Paris, 13–16 January 1840 (1, Mayer et Prud'hon, *'Psyché est endormie . . . les zéphirs . . . voltigent autour d'elle et viennent la caresser'*), bt. Dubois,[11] 4,400 fr.; Dubois sale, Paris, 16 February 1860 (28, Prud'hon, *Le sommeil de Psyché*), bt. in, 20,000 fr.; Dubois sale, Paris, 3 May 1866 (21, Prud'hon, *Le sommeil de Psyché*[12]), 14,550 fr.; the 4th Marquess of Hertford; rue Laffitte inventory 1871 (709, *'Mayer et Prud'hon nymphe endormie'*); Hertford House inventory 1890, as *'Prud'hon Sleeping Nymph and Cupids'*.

Exhibitions

Salon 1806 (375) see above; Bethnal Green 1872–5 (343, as Prud'hon, *Sleep of Psyche*).

References General

For abbreviations, see under Prud'hon: Blanc 1844, pp.469, 515, no.19; Clément, p.328; Goncourt, pp.313–14; Guiffrey, under no.199.

1 Goncourt, p.314: *'des amateurs assurent qu'il portait dans le principe la signature de Mlle Mayer, signature qu'il ne portait plus le jour où il est entré dans la collection de M. Richard Wallace'*.

2 *Catalogue des tableaux . . . dans la galerie et appartements . . . de Malmaison*, 1811, no.184 (reprinted in A.-M. de Lescure, *Le château de la Malmaison*, 1867, p.279), and *Inventaire après décès de l'Impératrice Joséphine à Malmaison*, 1814–15, no.1116 (published by S. Grandjean, 1964); P348 and the pendant by Mayer, *Le flambeau de Vénus*, were each valued at 400 fr., see note 8 below.

3 Clément, p.328, commented that P348, the pendant *Le flambeau de Vénus* and Prud'hon's *L'enlèvement de Psyché 'appartiennent à la même inspiration et doivent avoir été conçus à la même époque'*.

4 Elsewhere (p.302) Clément commented that Mayer *'ne voyait l'art que par les yeux de son maître et de son ami; elle s'efforçait uniquement de le suivre et de l'imiter, de se confondre avec lui en cela comme en toute autre chose'*.

5 Blanc 1844, p.469.

[6] See note 2 above. It can be seen hanging in the music room at Malmaison in a water-colour by A. Garneray (Malmaison; illus. Grandjean, *op. cit.*, pl.iii); it then had a frame similar to that now on P348 which may be assumed, therefore, to be the original, Malmaison, frame (and cf. Claude P114 note 1).

[7] See Guiffrey, nos.202–3.

[8] Blanc, Goncourt, and J. Doin (*Revue de l'Art ancien et moderne*, XXIX, 1911, p.141) said that P348 was commissioned by Joséphine, but she often made purchases at the Salon (cf. A.-P. de Mirimonde, 'Dépenses d'art des Impératrices Joséphine et Marie-Louise', *Gazette des Beaux-Arts*, 6e, L, 1957, pp.95, 100–1) and Grandjean (see note 2) makes no mention of a commission. Blanc, followed by Goncourt, gave the provenance of P348 as '*Collection de la Malmaison 1814, 800 fr.*' (as if it were a sale), but see note 2 above.

[9] The sale had no printed catalogue (and is not, therefore, listed in Lugt); P348 was no.649 in the *procès-verbal* by Casimir Noël (see Grandjean, *loc. cit.*, and in *La Revue des Arts*, 1959, p.196 n.8).

[10] Grandjean, *op. cit.* (see note 2), p.40, remarks that several Bonapartists made discreet purchases at the Malmaison sale. Lucien also owned a clock from Malmaison which he sold in Paris, 17–20 March 1834 (194), presumably also from the 1829 sale (cf. Grandjean, no.1530 n.).

[11] Dubois was described by Blanc (p.469 n.1) as '*un des amateurs les plus éclairés de Paris; il possède, dans sa maison rue de Lancry, des tableaux et des dessins des maîtres modernes, d'un prix inestimables*'.

[12] The copy of the sale catalogue in the Frick Art Reference Library is annotated: '*non pas de Prud'hon mais de Melle Mayer*'.

Jean-Marc Nattier (1685–1766)

Born on 17 March 1685 in Paris, son of the portrait painter and *académicien* Marc Nattier (1642–1703). He attended the Académie and made drawings from Le Brun's battles at Versailles and Rubens's Marie de Médicis cycle in the Luxembourg Palace. He declined a place at the *Académie de France* in Rome. In 1717 he painted portraits of the Russian Court, then in Holland. *Agréé* in 1715, he was *reçu* in 1718, his *morceau de réception* being the history piece *Persée et Phinée* (Tours). Although he completed the decoration, begun by Raoux, of the Hôtel du Temple for the *grand prieur*, Jean-Philippe, Chevalier d'Orléans, he soon specialised in portraiture. By the early 1730s he was known for the *portrait historique* in which his female sitters appeared with the attributes of nymphs or goddesses. Increasingly popular in Court circles, he was particularly favoured by the King's daughters, whom he painted both as the Seasons and the Elements. Of his many portraits at Versailles, those of the Queen (cf. P437) of 1748 and the whole-length of Madame Henriette of 1754 earned the highest praise. He exhibited at the Salon 1737–63, and in the Académie he was made *adjoint à professeur* in 1746 and *professeur* in 1752. His critical fortunes changed in the later 1750s and ill-health ended his career in 1762. He died in Paris on 7 September 1766. His brother Jean-Baptiste (1678–1717) had been a painter; his artist son was drowned in Rome in 1754.

Abbreviations

Huard G. Huard, 'Nattier' in L. Dimier, ed., *Les peintres français du XVIIIe siècle*, II, 1930, pp.119–32

Nolhac P. Nolhac, *Nattier*, 1925 ed. (first published 1904)

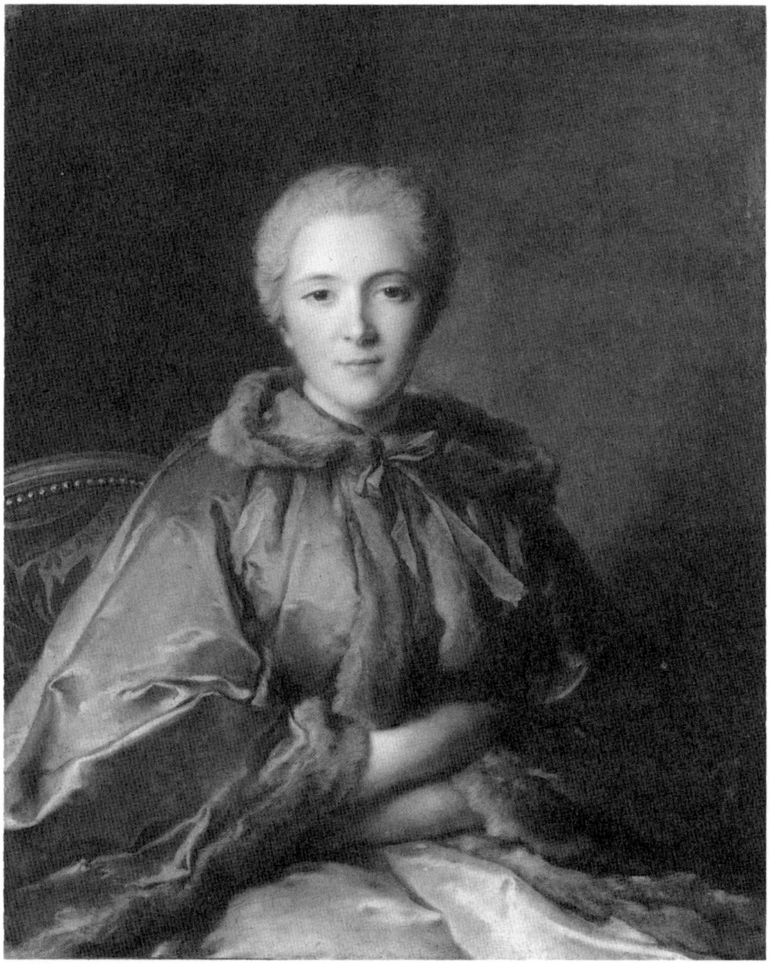

P453

P453 *The comtesse de Tillières*

Powdered hair, brown eyes, wearing a blue silk pelisse trimmed with squirrel fur;[1] the chair is covered with a yellow damask. Signed, below right: *Nattier P.x/1750.*

Canvas, relined 80 × 63

A vertical scratch in the upper left background has been retouched but there remain small losses either side. There are retouchings by the collar on the left, in the pelisse to the left and round the edges. The varnish is discoloured.

Michelle-Julie-Françoise-d'Esparbès de Lussard d'Aubetterre de Jonzac (c.1715–57), m. in 1730 the marquis de Tillières by whom she had two sons. The identity is given by a label, *verso*[2] (though the titles of P453 and P461, q.v., were confused in the earliest editions of this catalogue).

Provenance

The 4th Marquess of Hertford; either rue Laffitte inventory 1871 (440) or Bagatelle inventory 1871 (956), see P461; Hertford House inventory 1890 as '*Portrait of the Countess of de Dillieres*'.

Exhibition

Bethnal Green 1872–5 (480, *Portrait of the Countess de Dillieres*).

[1] See A. Ribeiro, *The Connoisseur*, CCII, 1979, p.231.

[2] '*Ce portrait par Nattier fameux peintre du règne de Louis XV est celui de Michelle Julie Françoise d'Esparbes de Lussard d'Aubetterre de Jonzac, Ctesse de Dillières morte le 2 Fevrier 1757 agée de près de 42 ans. après avoir vécu si saintement un grand nombre de ses dernières années. Que sa posterité a lieu d'espérer quelle intercède pour elle au ciel*'.

P456 *Mademoiselle de Clermont en sultane*

Dark hair, wearing a white shift and a red ermine-trimmed cloak; the bottom left attendant holding the pearls is in dull yellow; the maid on the right supporting the water butt wears red; the edge of the stone bath in the right foreground. Signed bottom centre: *Nattier.pinxit.1733*.

Canvas, relined 109 × 104.5

There are several retouched areas: the wall on the right, the chest of the bottom left attendant, the chin and hand of the man behind him, and the craquelure of the flesh areas. There are several *pentimenti*: the towel originally fell down to the floor on the right, there was a strong vertical fold in the red cloak (marked by mauled paint), the bottom left attendant's left shoulder was higher, and the maid holding the towel shows an altered neckline and left shoulder. The varnish is discoloured.

Marie-Anne de Bourbon (1697–1741), called Mlle. de Clermont, fifth and last child of Louis III duc de Bourbon, m. in 1724 Louis, duc de Joyeuse, who was killed within a few days when hunting;[1] *surintendante de la Maison de la Reine* 1725–41.

The pose relates to that of Nattier's earlier portrait *Mademoiselle de Clermont aux eaux minérales de Chantilly,* dateable 1729–30 (Chantilly),[2] but P456 is a more ambitious composition; it shows off the new fashion for *turquerie,*[3] and sensuously exploits Venetian colour and texture (see note 8) although the architecture (and particularly the *oeil-de-boeuf* window) is not above criticism. Mademoiselle de Clermont's portrait had previously been drawn in pastel by Rosalba Carriera in 1721,[4] and there are later portraits of her at Versailles.[5]

Copy

A nineteenth-century Limoges enamel plaque by R. Blanchet, sold Christie's, 24 September 1987 (97).

Version

A study for the head, 43 × 34, was with the marquis d'Estampes (Huard, no.40).[6]

Provenance

The duc de Saint-Aignan (1684–1776); his sale, Paris, 17 June 1776 (176, *Une Sultane au bain*), 171 *livres*;[7] Véron sale, Paris, 17 March 1858 (77, *Portrait de la duchesse de Châteauroux au bain . . . 1733*), bt. by the 4th Marquess of Hertford, 14,150 fr.;[8] rue Laffitte inventory 1871 (682, '*La toilette*'); Hertford House inventory 1890 as '*Unknown, Lady at her toilet with attendants*'.

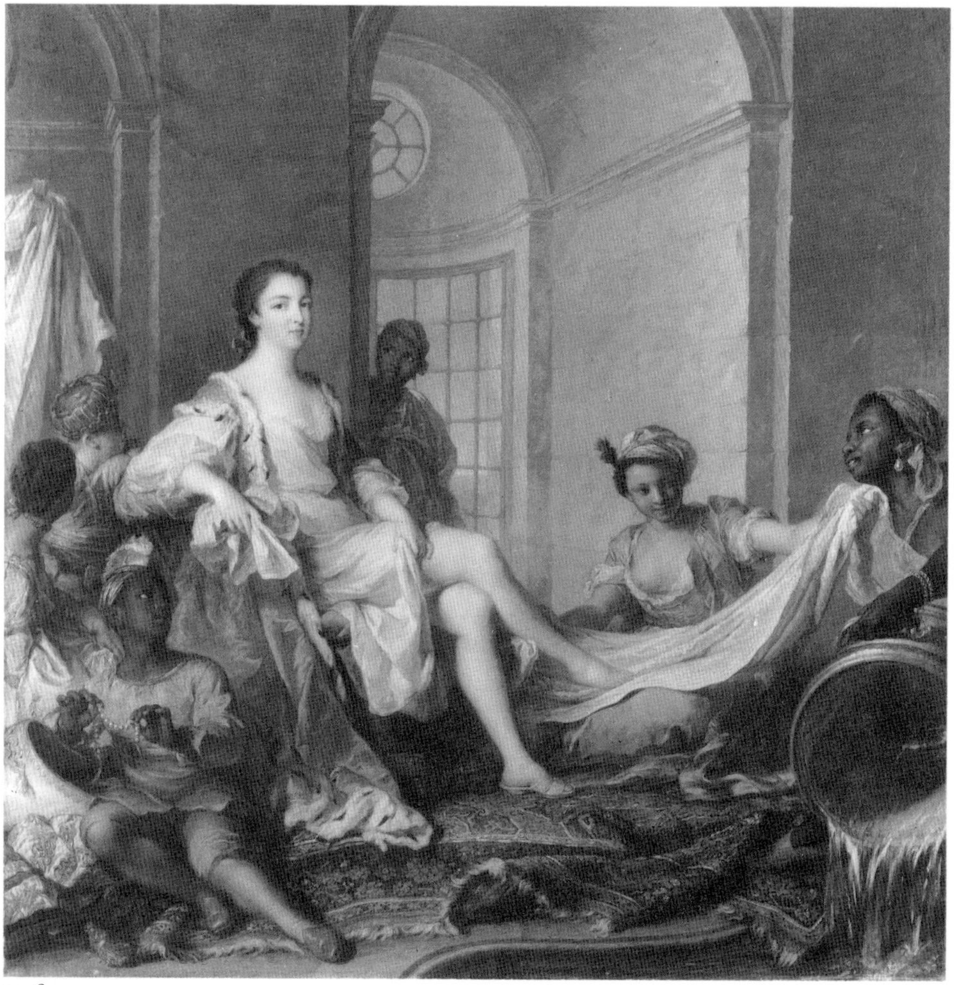

P456

Exhibitions

Salon 1742 (63, *feue Mademoiselle de Clermont, Princesse du Sang . . . en Sultane sortant du Bain, servie par des Esclaves*); Bethnal Green 1872–5 (389, *The Bath, a portrait of Madame de Châteauroux, a mistress of Louis XV*).

References General

Nolhac, pp.74, 76–7; Huard, no.38.

[1] This tragic romance provided the subject of *Mlle. de Clermont*, the novel by Mme. de Genlis published in 1802.

[2] 195 × 161, exh. Salon 1737, see F.-A. Gruyer, *La peinture au château de Chantilly, école française*, 1898, pp.279–86. Gruyer lists payments from the *maison de Mlle. de Clermont* in the *comptes de Chantilly* to Nattier between 1 May 1729 and 28 January 1731 totalling 3,121 *livres*, and associates them with the Chantilly picture (*'peint en 1729 et réglé définitivement à la fin de 1730'*). Nolhac (p.74) suggests these payments might cover both the Chantilly picture and P456, and since the heads are identical this seems probable. Huard, no.39, dated the Chantilly picture c.1737.

[3] On which see P. Hughes, *Eighteenth-century France and the East*, 1981, pp.12–14.

[4] Cf. *Journal de Rosalba Carriera*, ed. A. Sensier, 1865, pp.324, 356–7, 367, 512.

[5] Cf. C. Constans, *Versailles, Catalogue des Peintures*, 1980, no.667 (a variant by Brune of the Chantilly picture, commissioned in 1837), no.3926 (half-length by Rioult, commissioned in 1839), and nos.5629 and 5734 (anonymous French eighteenth-century half-lengths).

[6] This study could also have served for the Chantilly picture, see note 2 above.

[7] P456 was sketched by G. de Saint-Aubin in his annotated copy of the Saint-Aignan sale catalogue, see M. Le Moël and P. Rosenberg, *'La collection des tableaux du duc de Saint-Aignan et le catalogue de sa vente illustré par Gabriel de Saint-Aubin'*, *Revue de l'Art*, 6, 1969, pp.51–67 (P456 is discussed and illus. p.66).

[8] The purchase was described in *L'Artiste*, III, 1858, p.456: *'ce tableau . . . n'est pas encore le Nattier que nous connaissons tous, et dont Versailles nous révèle le maniérisme et le mensonge. Ici, l'ingénieux artiste est beaucoup plus près de la vérité: il est attentif au détail; il peint avec un soin merveilleux les draperies et les étoffes; il donne à ses colorations une intensité brillante et chaude qui manque souvent à ses portraits . . .'*.

P461 *The marquise de Belestat*

Powdered hair, grey eyes, wearing a white satin dress with an elaborate pleated bodice and a blue cape, ornamented with summer flowers. Signed, below left: *Nattier./p.x 1755*.

Canvas, relined 81 × 64

There are damages bottom centre and in the right background, and retouchings in the neck, cheeks, upper lip and round the edges. *Pentimenti* show the shoulders were redrawn. The varnish is discoloured.

Marie-Charlotte de Châteaurenaud m. in 1752 the marquis de Belestat (1725–1807) of Toulouse; she succeeded her mother as *dame de Mesdames* the same year and was in attendance at Versailles in 1754 and 1755;[1] her dispute with the comte de Lorge in 1754 over stealing at cards was judged, in verse, by Voltaire;[2] her husband was *mestre de camp de cavalerie* in 1755 and remarried in 1769. The identity is given by a label formerly on the *verso*.[3]

The titles of P453 and P461 were confused in the earliest editions of this catalogue until 1913. It was in fact P461 of which Nolhac wrote: *'ce buste assez médiocre . . . donne une idée des derniers ouvrages hâtifs du peintre'*. He also suggested that it may have been shown at the Salon in 1759 (15, Nattier, *Autres tableaux du même auteur*), but there is no other evidence for this.

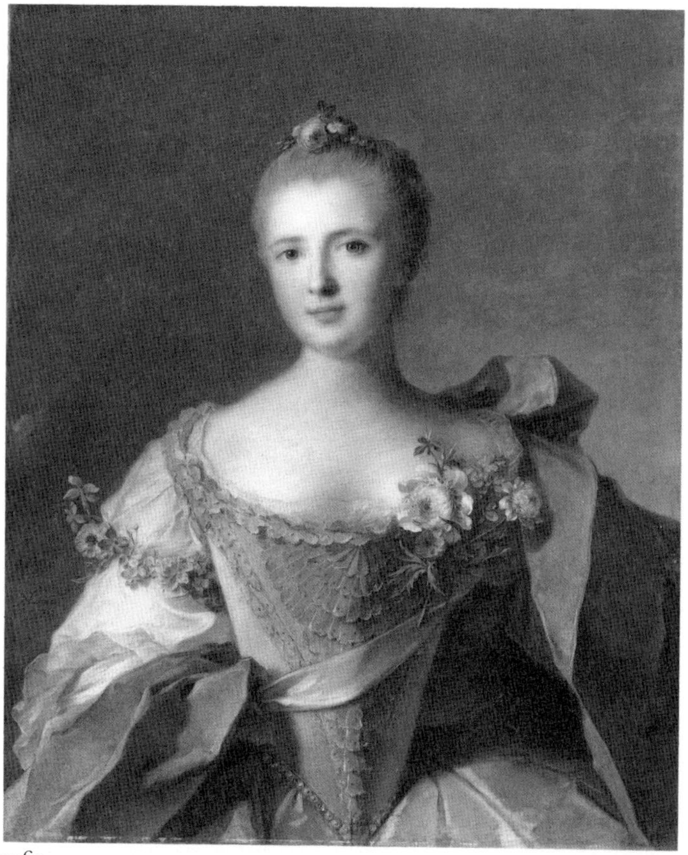

P461

Provenance

Vicomte de Gavarret-Rouaix, Toulouse; his sale, Paris, 6–7 February 1867 (83),[4] bt. by the 4th Marquess of Hertford, 5,200 fr.;[5] either rue Laffitte inventory 1871 (440) or Bagatelle inventory 1871 (956), both '*Nattier, portrait de femme*'; Hertford House inventory 1890 as '*Lady with bouquet and armlet of flowers*'.

Exhibitions

Toulouse, *Capitole*, 1756; Bethnal Green 1872–5 (476, *Portrait of a Lady*).

References General

Nolhac, p.228; Huard, no.73 (on both occasions as *La comtesse de Dillières*).

[1] See *Mémoires du duc de Luynes*, XII, 1863, pp.25–6, 33, 53, 141; XIII, 1863, p.129, and XIV, 1864, p.100.

[2] See *Voltaire's Correspondence*, ed. T. Besterman, XXV, 1957, pp.106–7. Her husband corresponded, and disputed, with Voltaire.

[3] '*Portrait à mi-corps de Mlle. de Châteaurenaud, première femme du marquis de Belesta, mestre de camp sous Louis XV. Chef d'oeuvre du maître exposé au salon Toulousain au capitol en 1756*'; this label was quoted in the 1867 sale catalogue.

[4] The sale catalogue described the frame as a '*très riche encadrement de bois sculpté*'; it remains with P461. See also note 3 above.

[5] As reported in *L'Artiste*, II, 1867, p.121.

After Nattier

P414 *Le maréchal duc de Richelieu*

Powdered wig, grey eyes, wearing the black and silver costume of a *chevalier* of the Order of the Saint Esprit; on the pale blue upholstered sofa lie his left glove, the *cordon* of the Order and the Mantle, richly embroidered with *flammes*, fleurs de lys, crowns, the H of Henri III (founder of the Order) and the Badge of the Order;[1] an arm harness and other pieces of armour lie beneath the sofa; the page wears a rich red livery.

Canvas, relined 81 × 60.5

Relined in Paris in the mid-nineteenth century.[2] There are several small losses: in and below his left leg, above his collar, in the upper left background, above his head, and round the edges. The paint surface is lifting in the right background area and the varnish is discoloured.

Louis-François-Armand Vignerot du Plessis, duc de Richelieu (1696–1788), *chevalier* of the Saint Esprit 1729, *maréchal de France* 1748, great-nephew of the Cardinal; courtier, diplomat and soldier, noted for his elegance, wit and self-esteem; he m. 1st in 1711 Mlle. de Noailles (d.1716), 2nd in 1734 Mlle. de Guise (d.1740) by whom he had a son and a daughter, and 3rd in 1780 Mme. de Rothe.

P414 has previously been described as showing the duc de Penthièvre (see Versions and Provenance)[3] or Louis, duc d'Orléans (see References General),[4] but Richelieu is identified by the similarity with his portrait engraved by J.-F. Mariage after (J.-B.?) van Loo,[5] the Richelieu provenance of the larger portrait by Nattier dated 1732 (see Versions) from which P414 was copied, and by the inclusion of the armour (a reference to his military achievements). The elegant pose conforms with Richelieu's well-attested vanity,[6] while the livery seen in P414 is similar to that worn by Richelieu's equipage on his entry into Vienna in 1725.[7]

P414, which appears to be a contemporary but pedantic copy, was in the nineteenth century attributed to Tocqué (see Provenance and References General) who is known to have copied Nattier's work.[8] The attribution of a second reduced copy (see Versions) to L.-M. van Loo was, possibly, based on the evidence of the engraving by Mariage (see above and note 5) which in any case suggests that Nattier had used van Loo as his source. The attribution (of the page?) to Lancret, proposed in 1851 (see Provenance) was fanciful.

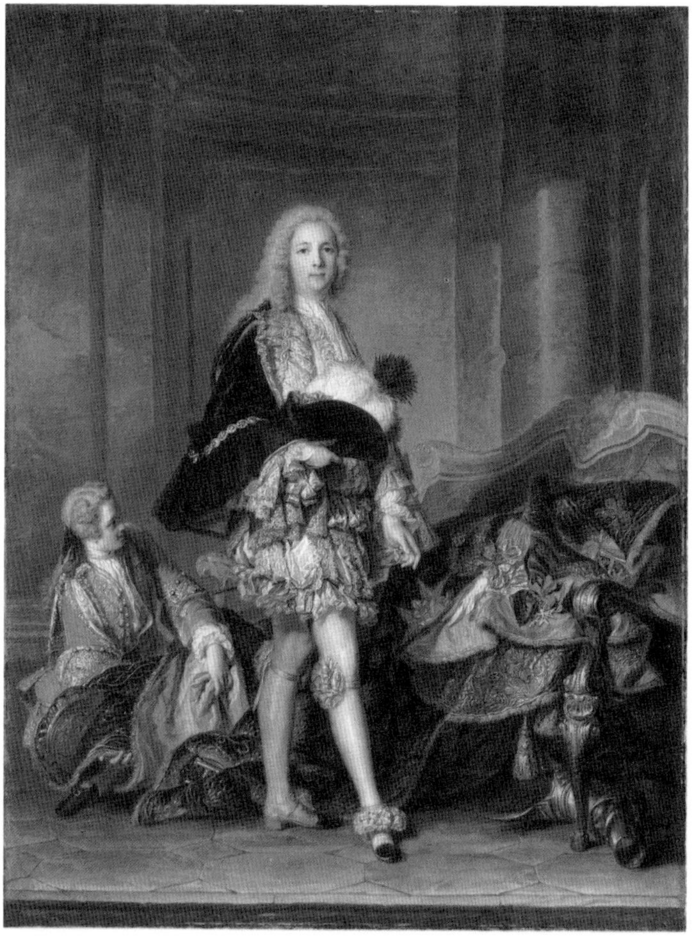

P414

Versions

LISBON Calouste Gulbenkian Foundation; 239 × 179.5, the original portrait, signed and dated *Nattier 1732*; ex coll. Richelieu (probably the *tableau de M. le Maréchal se revêtant des habits de l'ordre du Saint-Esprit* listed at the Château de Richelieu c.1750,[9] and probably Richelieu sale, Paris, 31 December 1846, lot 2, *Le Maréchal de Richelieu en grand costume*); Bischoffsheim sale, Christie's, 7 May 1926 (70, as ex coll. Richelieu and 'said to be the Duc de Penthièvre').
PARIS Palais Galliera, 2 December 1970 (152); 81 × 61, attributed to L.-M. van Loo and called *un personnage royal*; identical with P414, and possibly confused with it in the earlier sales cited in the Provenance below.
Banque de France; the *Galerie de l'Hôtel de Toulouse* by J.-F. Garneray, 35 × 26.5, exh. Salon 1812 (402), incorporates the composition of P414 in the foreground, evidently on the assumption that the *chevalier* was Penthièvre (see note 3).

Provenance[10]

Didot sale, Paris, 6 April 1825 (212, Tocqué, *duc de Penthièvre*, 81 × 62), bt. Leroi, 120 fr.; L.-D. Vèze sale, Paris, 10 December ff. 1846 (96, Tocqué, *Duc de Penthièvre, en costume de Grand-Amiral*, 82 × 65); P.-C. Prousteau de Montlouis (1763–1851); his sale, Paris, 5–6 May 1851 (175, Tocqué and Lancret, '*le duc de Penthièvre, grand amiral de France . . . Ce portrait est peint en 1742, le prince avait seize ans*'), 530 fr.; the 4th Marquess of Hertford;[11] rue Laffitte inventory 1871 (135, '*Tocqué, portrait du Régent*'); Hertford House inventory 1890 as unknown artist '*interior portrait of Louis XV, attendant with State Robes*'.

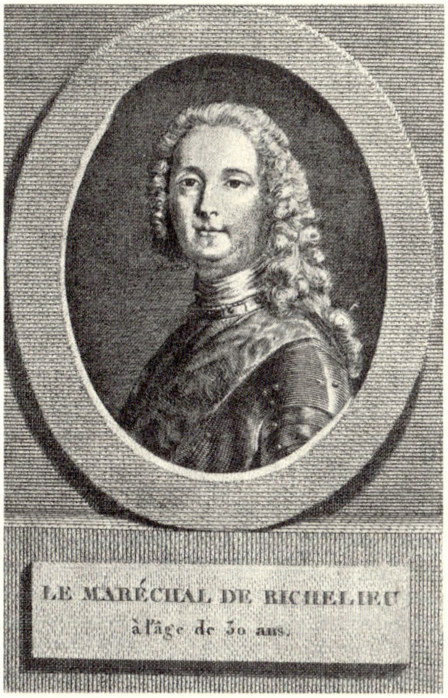

J.-F. Mariage after van Loo:
Le maréchal de Richelieu à l'age de 30 ans.

Exhibition

Bethnal Green 1872–5 (466, Nattier and Tocqué, *The Duke of Penthièvre*).

References General

Nolhac, pp.79–80; Huard, no.43; A. Doria, *Tocqué*, 1921, no.250, as attributed to Tocqué (on each occasion as of *Louis, duc d'Orléans*).

[1] The costume is described by A. Ribeiro, *Dress in eighteenth-century Europe 1715–89*, 1984, pp.134–5.

[2] The stretcher is stamped, *verso*: MOMPER A PARIS, for whom see Fragonard P430 note 1.

[3] The duc de Penthièvre (1725–93), son of the comte de Toulouse, was only seven in 1732, the date of Nattier's original portrait. This identification, however, seems to have been accepted from 1812 (see Versions above) to 1890 (see Provenance); it was exposed by Phillips in the first edition of this catalogue in 1900.

[4] Louis, duc d'Orléans (1703–53), was first proposed by Nolhac, *loc. cit.*, and his candidature has, until now, been tentatively accepted.

[5] *Le maréchal de Richelieu à l'âge de 30 ans/ /Vanloo pinx./L.-F. Mariage sculp.*, frontispiece for the *Mémoires du maréchal duc de Richelieu*, I, 1791 (illus. J. Levron, *Le maréchal de Richelieu*, 1971, f.p.225).

[6] Which is also demonstrated in the much later ceremonial whole-lengths by Roslin (Sorbonne) and Gault de Saint-Germain (copies by A. Couder of 1834 and 1835 at Versailles).

[7] Cf. *Mémoires du maréchal duc de Richelieu*, 1889, I, pp.215–17.

[8] Cf. Doria, *op. cit.*, p.13; Tocqué was Nattier's pupil and son-in-law. The stretcher of P414 is inscribed in pencil in a nineteenth-century hand: *Tocqué/Duc de Penthièvre*, doubtless referring to one of the nineteenth-century sales.

[9] Anon. mid-eighteenth-century, '*Description du Château de Richelieu*', NAAF, 2e, III, 1882, p.229.

[10] Previous editions of this catalogue, following Doria, no.250, have supposed that P414 may have been in the Cypierre sale, Paris, 10 March 1845, lot 97, *le duc de Penthièvre adolescent*, but that sale catalogue continued '*il porte la cuirasse; sa main gauche est appuyée sur sa hanche; fond de marine, avec quelques vaisseaux*'.

[11] Lord Hertford probably bought P414 at this sale, whence he bought other paintings, cf. Boucher P429, P432, P438 and P444, and Lemoyne P392 and P417.

P437 *Marie Leczinska, Queen of France*

Wearing a red gown trimmed with black fur; the open book is inscribed: LLE/ CHAP.IX.*233*.

Canvas, relined 54.5 × 45.5

The edges are uneven and were made up during relining. The craquelure has been extensively retouched and the varnish is much discoloured.

Marie Leczinska (1703–68), daughter of Stanislaus Leczinski, duc de Lorraine and former King of Poland, m. in 1725 Louis XV of France by whom she had ten children; from 1742 she led a homely and pious life at Versailles, as is reflected in Nattier's portrait (for which she had expressly asked to be painted *en habit de ville*).

P437 is a reduced copy, probably dating from the eighteenth century, of the Nattier portrait dated 1748 at Versailles, the last portrait to be taken of the Queen,[1] which was engraved (in the same sense) by Tardieu in 1755.[2] For a copy in miniature see M119 in this Collection, and for another portrait of the Queen after J.-B. van Loo, see M285.

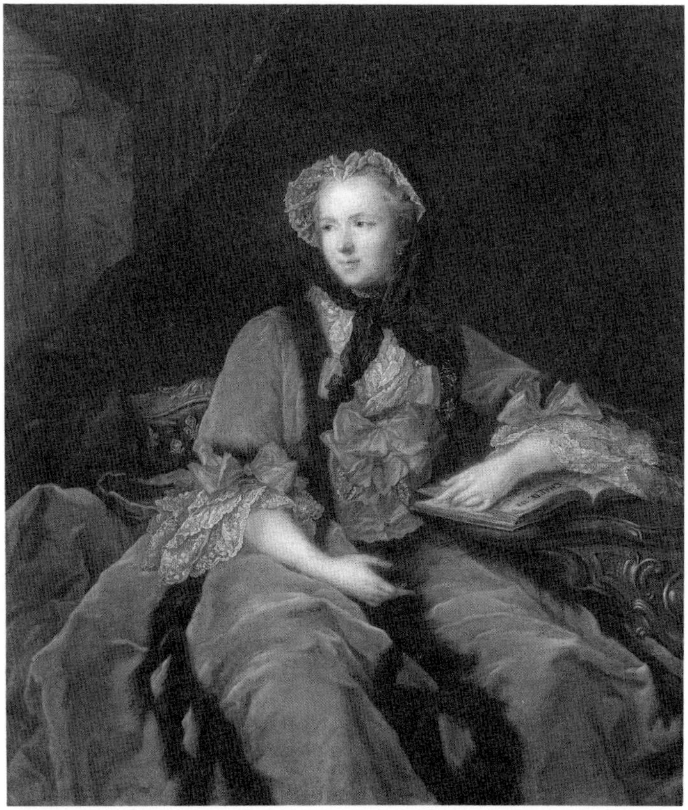

P437

Provenance

Possibly Dr. Gaudinot sale, Paris, 15–16 February 1869 (70, *Marie Leczinska*, 56 × 44), bt. by the duc de Mouchy. The 4th Marquess of Hertford; Bagatelle inventory 1871 (1001, '*Nattier, Portrait de femme*'); Hertford House inventory 1890.

Exhibition

Bethnal Green 1872–5 (412).

[1] 104 × 112, Huard no. 2; the Queen ordered two replicas, probably those in the Musée de Dijon, and formerly coll. Fezensac; see also Nolhac, pp. 139–46.

[2] Tardieu's engraving shows the book inscribed LLE/CHAP.IX.*233*//*Cette Reine adorée*/*de la France*.

Jean-Baptiste Oudry (1686–1755)

Born on 17 March 1686 in Paris, the son of a dealer and minor painter under whom he first studied. In 1704 he was briefly the pupil of M. Serre, and in 1706 he attended the Académie de Saint-Luc where he was received as a master painter in 1708. His real teacher, however, was Largillierre, with whom he studied 1707–12. He first practised mainly as a portrait painter, but from c.1719 he turned to animal and game subjects in the tradition of Hondecoeter and Weenix, composed in a somewhat theatrical manner (contrasting with that of his rival Desportes). *Agréé* in 1717, he was *reçu* in 1719, his *morceau de réception* being the allegorical *Abondance* (Versailles). He was a regular exhibitor at the *Salons de la jeunesse* 1722–5 and at the Salon from 1725. The first of many commissions from the Crown came in 1724 and he was soon favoured by the King of Sweden, the Margrave of Ansbach and the Grand Duke of Mecklenburg-Schwerin. Between 1728 and 1738 he concentrated on designs for tapestries, which included the celebrated *Chasses royales* for Louis XV; he became painter to the Beauvais factory in 1726 and director in 1734, and was appointed director of the Gobelins in 1748. At the Académie he was made *adjoint à professeur* in 1739 and *professeur* in 1743. Following the death of Desportes in 1743 he received many more commissions which he executed in more subdued tones and frequently with studio assistance. He died at Beauvais on 30 April 1755. Thirty-four of his paintings remain in the Museum at Schwerin. His son, Jacques-Charles (1722/3–78) painted less successfully in his father's manner.

Abbreviations

Locquin	J. Locquin, *Catalogue raisonné de l'oeuvre de Jean-Baptiste Oudry*, 1912
Opperman	H. Opperman, *Jean-Baptiste Oudry*, 1977 (with catalogue of paintings [P] and drawings [D])
Vergnet-Ruiz	J. Vergnet-Ruiz, 'Oudry', in L. Dimier, ed., *Les peintres français du XVIIIe siècle*, II, 1930, pp.154–92

P625 *Dog pointing Pheasants*

A brown-spotted pointer with male and female pheasants amongst wheat, poppies and cornflowers. Signed, bottom right: *J B Oudry 1748.*

Canvas, relined 118 × 153.5

There are some losses along the bottom and lower right-hand edges and the paint is tending to lift in the lower right area. There are *pentimenti* in the reeds lower left and foliage upper right. The varnish is much discoloured.

P625, P627, P629 and P631 form a set of four overdoors commissioned by Trudaine for his new château at Montigny-Lencoup (cf. Boucher P482 and P489) which became a *rendez-vous de chasse* for Louis XV.[1] They were shown together at the 1748 Salon as '*quatre tableaux d'environ 5 pieds de large sur 4 de hauteur* [c.130 × 162], *faits pour*

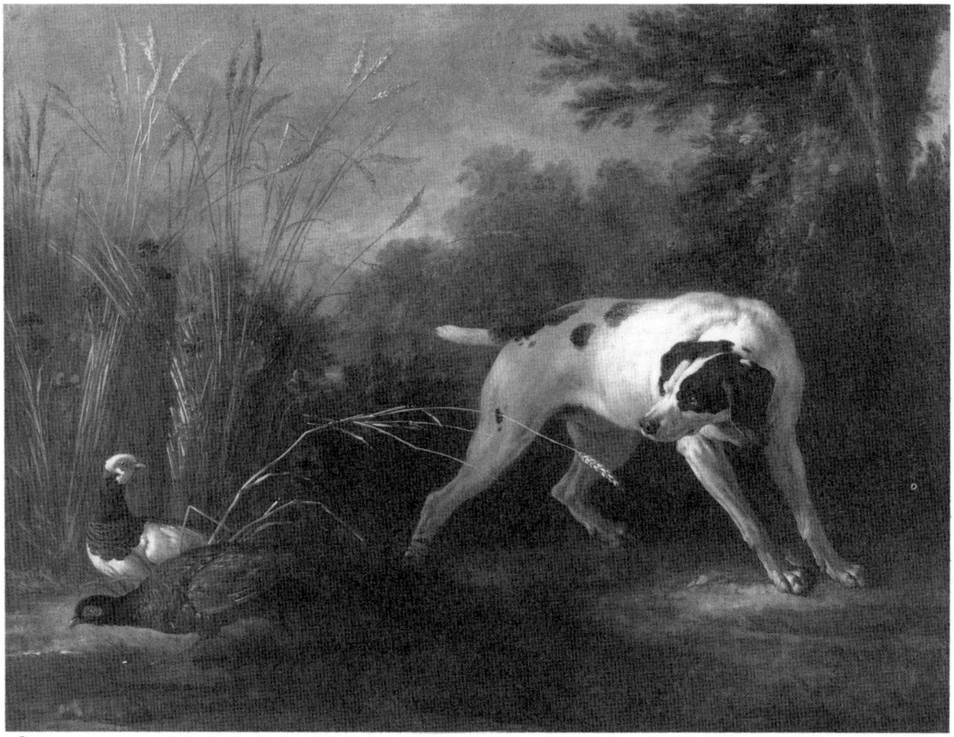

P625

M. de Trudaine pour être posez dans son Château de Montigny'.[2] The execution of the set is somewhat uneven, cf. P627 and P631, but they were to be seen, as Opperman expressed it, from a certain distance.

The two pheasants in P625 are based, in reverse, on those in Oudry's portrait of the King's pointer *Lise* of 1725–32 (Fontainebleau; Opperman P252); a related water-colour is in the Oudry Album in the Fogg Art Museum (Opperman, D902).

Provenance

With P627, P629 and P631: Daniel-Charles Trudaine (1703–69), *intendant des finances*, Château de Montigny-Lencoup (Seine-et-Marne); in 1818 the château was bt. by the comte George de Stacpoole (1736–1824) and passed to his son, Richard Stacpoole (1797–1848, cr. duc by Pope Gregory XV, 1831);[3] his sale, Paris, 1–3 March 1852 (6, '*Renard dans une basse-cour, Epervier emportant une perdix, Chien en arrêt devant un faisan, Chasse aux canards; ces quatre tableaux font pendants*'); the 4th Marquess of Hertford; rue Laffitte inventory 1871 (under nos.406, 407 and 437); Hertford House inventory 1890.

Exhibitions

Salon 1748 (22, *Un chien en arrêt sur des Faisans, dont un pintelé*); Bethnal Green 1872–5 (397).

References General

Locquin, nos.170, 194; Vergnet-Ruiz, no.96; Opperman, p.114 and P263.

1 See Boucher P482 note 2.

2 Salon *livret* 1748.

3 See Boucher P482 notes 3 and 4.

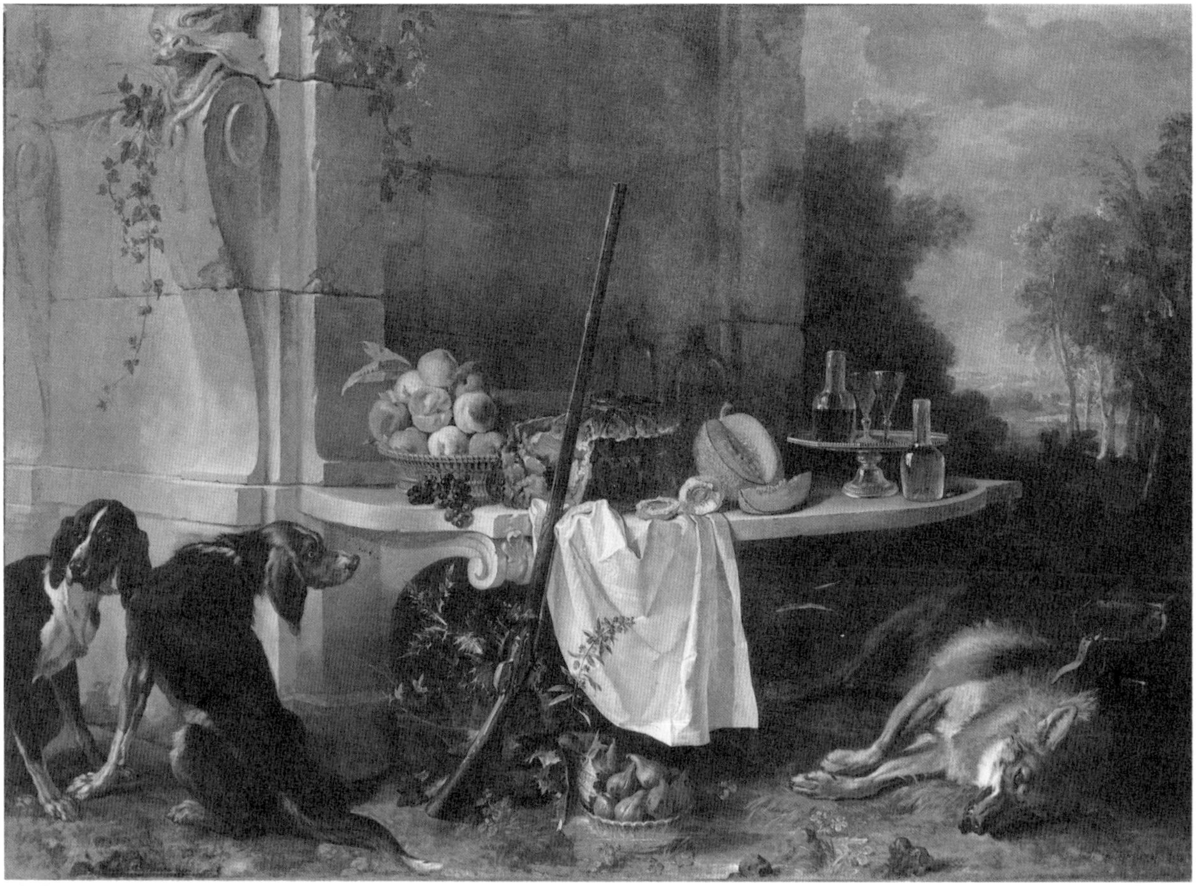

P626

P626 *The Dead Wolf*

Included on the stone ledge are peaches, grapes, a game pie decorated with fleurs de lys, a melon and a silver salver; in the foreground a bowl of figs stands in water by globe thistles and balsam; the gun is a single barrel flint-lock wild-fowling piece; a hunter's satchel on the extreme right. Signed, lower right: *peint par./J.B. Oudry. 1721.*

Canvas, relined 193 × 260

An old lining was replaced by Watkiss in 1979 when P626 was cleaned by Hargrave. A horizontal seam 97 cm. above the bottom edge and a vertical scratch by the left-hand glass bottle have been retouched. The darker passages in the wolf and dogs are worn. *Pentimenti* show two areas were reworked: on the left the bracket supporting the stone ledge originally sprang from the pilaster, the end mouldings of the ledge do not match, and to the right the trees were radically repainted, the sky reworked and ivy over the right-hand side of the stone niche erased.

P626 and the pendant P630 are *buffets* for a dining room and the fleurs de lys on the pastry in P626 and the elegance of the hunting equipment suggest a noble client. Each picture contains a number of *pentimenti* and some hesitancy in the handling of architectural detail and the articulation of the landscape backgrounds, but the compositions and the execution of the animal and still-life elements are of the highest quality. Opperman has emphasised their rococo qualities (asymmetry, cool colouring and fanciful light) which contrast, for example, with the compositions of the pendant *buffets* by Desportes (P594, P628) of only six years before; in 1858 the Oudrys were compared with these Desportes:

> *c'est en faire un pompeux éloge en déclarant qu'ils peuvent hautement rivaliser avec les magnifiques compositions de Desportes . . . à la vente de M. Patureau* [P594, P628][1]

With the *Dead Roe* of 1721 at Schwerin (which, like P630, shows a heron and somewhat whimsical architecture),[2] Opperman considers P626 and P630 to be Oudry's masterpieces. See also notes 4 and 5.

Copies/Versions

CONDE-EN-BRIE (Aisne), the comte de Sade; 254 × 254, a good studio replica of P626 with additions above and below; one of four Oudry panels in the grand salon (see also P630) installed by 1783 (Opperman, P420).[3] VERSAILLES anon. sale, 8 March 1964 (32); 230 × 290, as *atelier d'Oudry* (Opperman, p.940).

A *Repas de chasse royale – esquisse pour un tableau conservé à la Galerie Wallace à Londres*, exh. *La vigne et le vin dans l'art,* Musée des Arts Décoratifs, 1936, no.65, lent Mme *veuve* Doucet (Opperman, under P389).

Provenance

With P630: see note 3; the marquis d'Arbaud-Jouques (?1769–1849), *préfet des Bouches-du-Rhône*; his sale, Paris, 26 February 1858 (17, [P630], 18 [P626]), bt. Lebeuf de Montgermont, 14,000 fr.;[4] with Mme. Lebeuf in 1860; the 4th Marquess of Hertford; rue Laffitte inventory 1871 (374); Hertford House inventory 1890.

Exhibition

Boulevard des Italiens 1860 (297) lent Mme. Lebeuf.[5]

References General

Locquin, nos.131–2; Vergnet-Ruiz, nos.82, 84; Opperman, pp.57–60, 940 and P389.

[1] From the d'Arbaud-Jouques sale catalogue, 1858, lot 18.

[2] Opperman, P441; 163 × 129. See also note 3 below.

[3] The panels illus. *Connaissance des Arts,* January 1967, pp.42–3. They may have been installed by Leriget de La Faye (1674–1731, see Lancret P393), who bought and began to restore the château de Condé-en-Brie 1719–31. Opperman (under his P421, and letter on file dated 12 February 1973) points out that La Faye's mistress, the comtesse de Verrue, acquired her Paris hôtel, rue du Cherche-Midi, in 1719–20 and owned three Oudrys, two described as *Tableaux d'architecture* in her sale *après décès* in 1737. Opperman speculates whether these might not have been P626 and P630. Oudry's other masterpiece of 1721, the Schwerin *Dead Roe,* remained in his studio until his death.

[4] The sale catalogue described P626 and P630 as *'les chefs-d'oeuvres les plus admirables que nous connaissons de cet habile peintre'*. According to the *Revue universelle des Arts,* VI, 1857, pp.656–7, *'avant la vente un amateur avait refusé de les prendre pour 8,000 fr.'*.

[5] W. Bürger commented on P626 and P630 at this exhibition: *'Dans ces magnifiques pendants, Oudry, conseillé sans doute par son ami Largillière, a cherché les Flamands, comme composition et comme effet, Snyders surtout . . . Il a pourtant une touche ample et facile, de la lumière et de la couleur. En ce genre-là, l'ancienne école française n'a peut-être jamais fait mieux que ces deux grandes décorations d'Oudry'* (*Gazette des Beaux-Arts,* 1ère, VII, 1860, p.339).

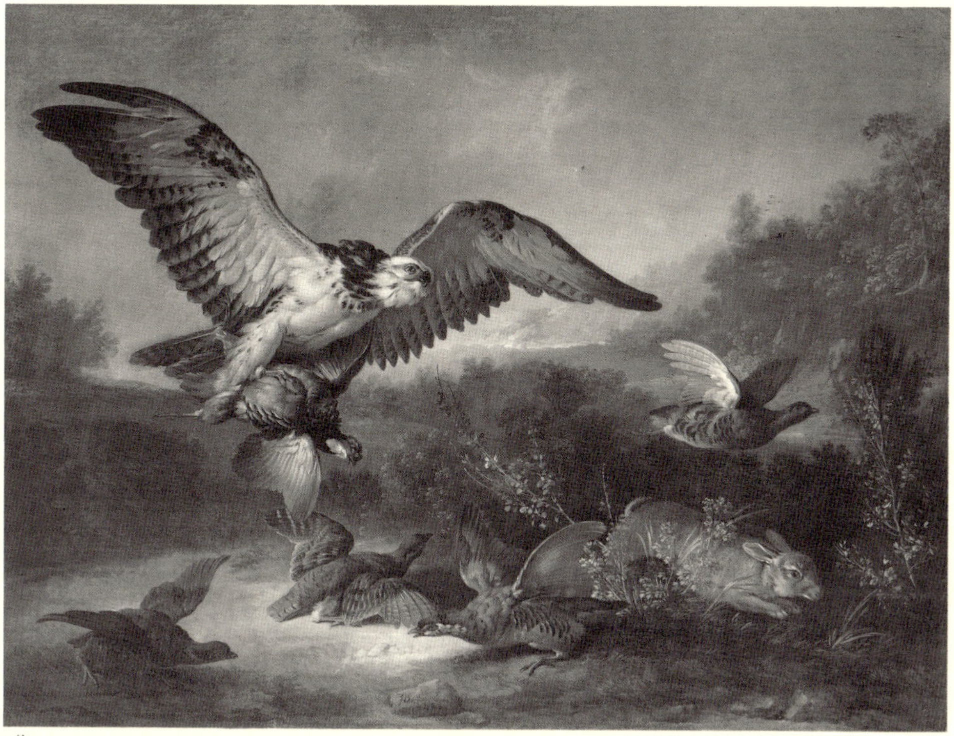

P627

P627 *Hawk attacking Partridges and a Rabbit*

The bird is probably a buzzard; the rabbit runs through broom. Signed, centre foreground: *J B. Oudry/1747.*

Canvas, relined 118 × 153

There are small losses in the hawk's left wing, in the captured partridge and along the bottom right-hand edge. All the edges have been retouched. There is a *pentimento* in the hawk's tail feathers.

P627 is the earliest of the set of four overdoors commissioned by Trudaine for Montigny-Lencoup, see P625. Opperman points out that the rabbit (and possibly the flying partridge?) is of inferior execution and probably by Oudry *fils*;[1] a drawing of 1746 (see below) confirms the basic composition is by Oudry himself.

Drawings

SCHWERIN Staatliches Museum (inv. 1175 Hz); study for the hawk (Opperman, D674, fig.338).

A preliminary study, showing the rabbit and the three foreground partridges, but including different hawks, signed and dated 1746, was in the Sayn-Wittgenstein sale, Munich, 26 November 1921, lot 439 (Opperman, D669A, fig.444).

Version

The group of the hawk with the dead partridge and the two centre foreground partridges was used in a Gobelins tapestry chair seat cover of uncertain date (cf. R. Wark, *French Decorative Art in the Huntington Collection*, 1961, pp.71–3, fig.28).

Provenance

See P625.

Exhibitions

Salon 1748 (24, *Un Oyseau de proye qui enleve une Perdrix, & d'autres épouvantées*); Bethnal Green 1872–5 (404).

References General

Locquin, nos.331, 356; Vergnet-Ruiz, no.59; Opperman, p.114 and P293.

[1] For Oudry *fils*, see J. Cailleux, *The Burlington Magazine*, July, 1982, adv. supp., pp.i-viii.

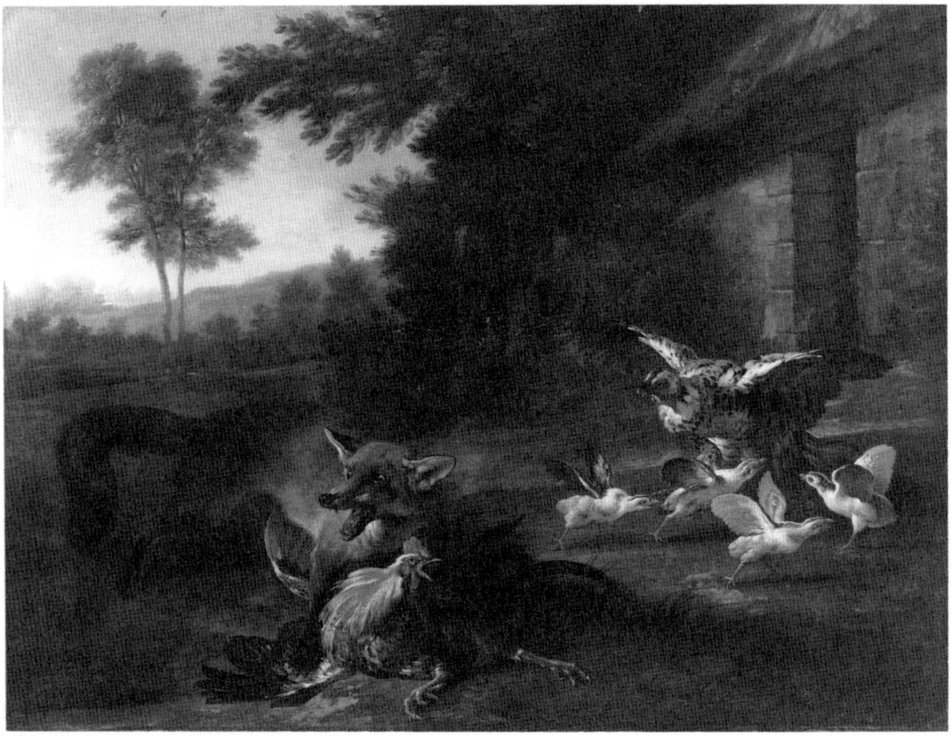

P629

P629 *Fox in the Poultry Yard*

The fox captures the cock while the hen looks on with her chicks. Signed, bottom left: *J B. Oudry/1748.*

Canvas, relined 118.4 × 153

There are losses round all the edges, some retouched, and a scratch near the upper left-hand edge. *Pentimenti* suggest the composition was altered in the area to the right of the fox (though this is not borne out by the drawing cited below). The varnish is much discoloured.

One of the set of four overdoors commissioned by Trudaine for Montigny-Lencoup, see P625.

Drawings
BERLIN Dahlem, Kupferstichkabinett (no.15025); preliminary compositional study, signed and dated 1746 (Opperman, D669, fig.340).
PARIS private collection; finished compositional study, signed and dated 1748 (Opperman, D671, fig.445).

Copy
WADDESDON Manor; 122 × 150, bearing signature, a weak replica (Opperman, P300).[1]

Provenance
See P625.

Exhibitions
Salon 1748 (25, *Un Renard qui tient un Coq, & une Poule qui veut défendre ses Poussins*); Bethnal Green 1872–5 (401).

References General
Locquin, nos.332, 358; Vergnet-Ruiz, no.50; Opperman, p.114 and P294.

[1] And see E. K. Waterhouse, *The James A. de Rothschild Collection at Waddesdon Manor: Paintings*, 1967, no.122.

P630 *The Dead Roe*

Two hounds on the left and a pointer on the right guarding a dead heron, partridge, plover and roe, while a pheasant flies off; a blue hunter's bag with a pink string pocket lies by hollyhock; viola and an ash plant on the right; the hunter's powder flask has blue straps; the gun is a breech-loading flint-lock wild-fowling piece. Signed on the stone ledge, lower right: *peint par J B. Oudry 1721.*

Canvas, relined 193 × 260

An old lining was replaced by Watkiss in 1979 when P630 was cleaned by Hargrave. A horizontal seam 95 cm. above the bottom edge has been retouched. The pheasant's tail is rubbed. There is a green reflected light on the left-hand side of the column at the foot of the balustrade. The signature was written over the first layer of varnish. *Pentimenti* show that a tree, centre left, was erased.

See P626. A similar hollyhock appears in the *Still Life with Monkey, Fruit and Flowers* dated 1724 (Chicago; Opperman, P447).

Copies
CONDE-EN-BRIE (Aisne), the comte de Sade; 254 × 254, a good studio replica, see P626 note 3 (Opperman, P419).
PARIS Petit Palais (inv. Dutuit, no.875); 80 × 122.5, bearing signature and date 1732, probably an eighteenth-century copy (Opperman, P397, as a studio replica partly retouched by Oudry).
Anon. sale, 21 December 1970 (1); 194 × 130, attributed to Oudry, a copy of the right-hand section (Opperman, p.940).
VERSAILLES anon. sale, 5 November 1967 (68); 150 × 169, a weak copy (Opperman, p.940).

Provenance
See P626.

Exhibition
Boulevard des Italiens 1860 (297) lent Mme. Lebeuf.

References General
Locquin, no.130; Vergnet-Ruiz, no.83; Opperman, pp.57–60, 940 and P388.

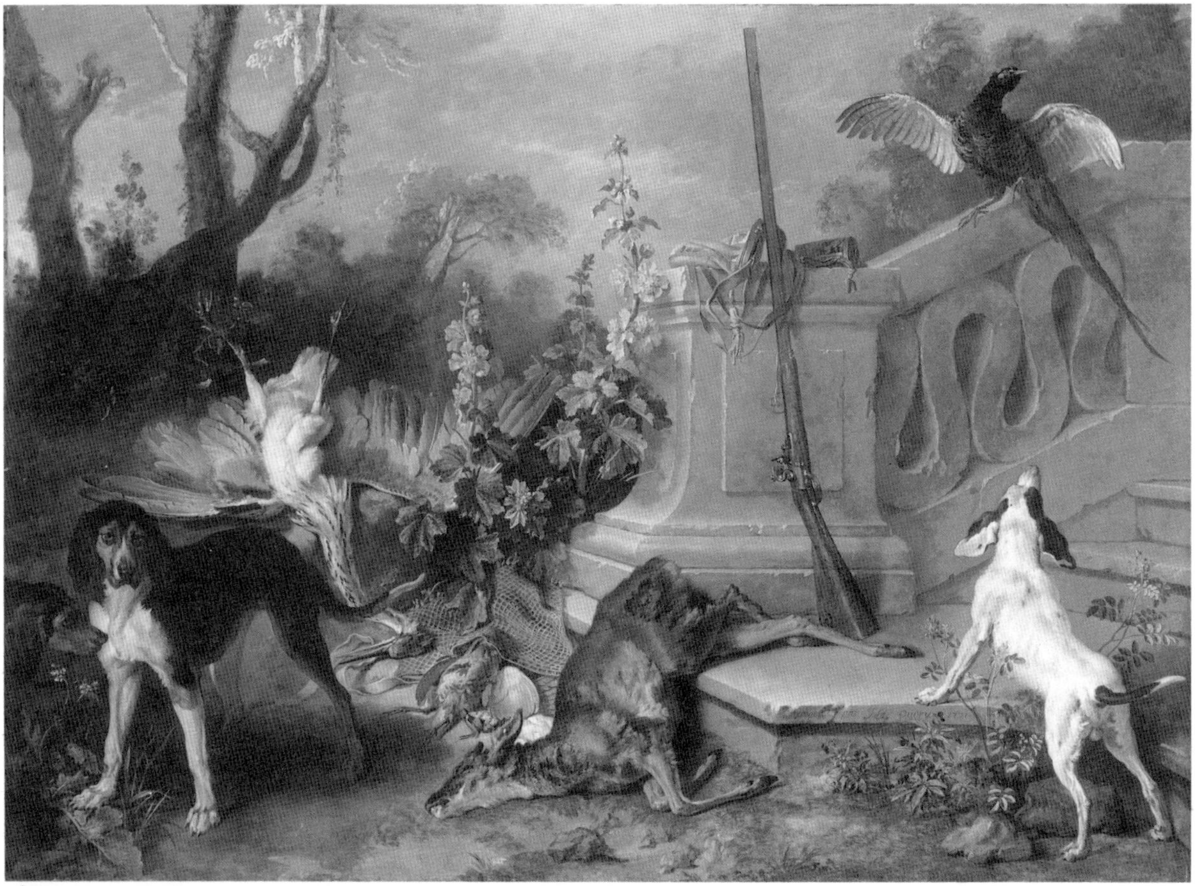
P630

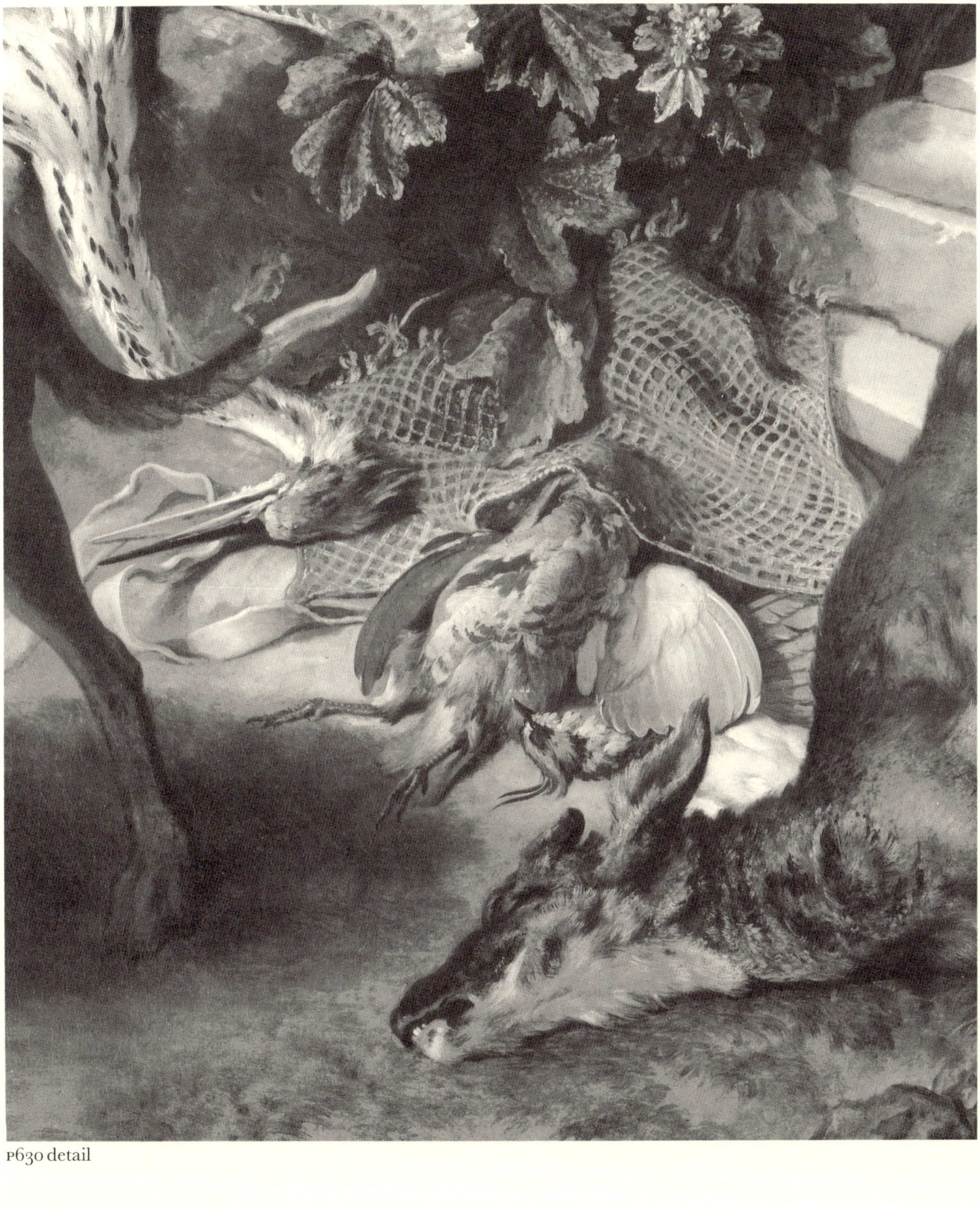

P630 detail

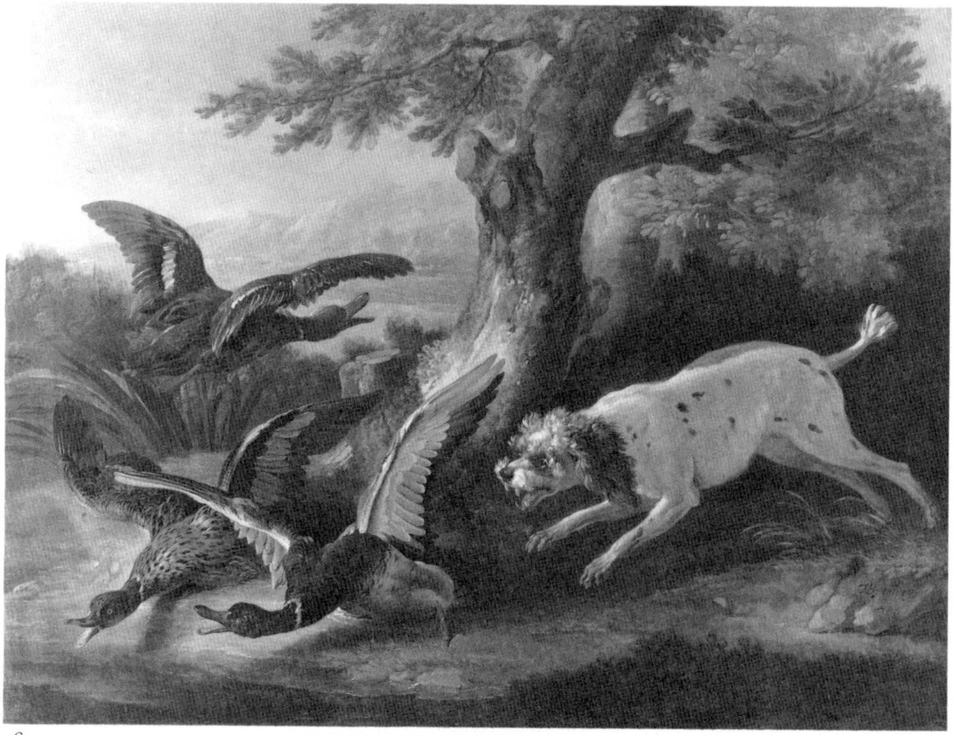

P631

P631 *Spaniel pursuing Ducks*

A barbet spaniel chasing three mallards, the drake in the foreground. Signed, lower right: *J B. Oudry/1748.*

Canvas, relined 118.5 × 153

Cleaned by Vallance in 1978. There are *pentimenti* on the flying duck's left wing and the bottom left duck's right wing, and it is now unclear whether the tree stump in the centre was meant to stand before or behind the central tree.

One of the set of four overdoors commissioned by Trudaine for Montigny-Lencoup, see P625. As with P627, Opperman suggests the collaboration of Oudry *fils*, the execution of the dog (and particularly the hind legs) being inferior. The Paris drawing listed below confirms that the basic composition is by Oudry himself.

Drawings

CAMBRIDGE Mass., Fogg Art Museum (Oudry Album, p.156);[1] sketch with a comparable dog amongst reeds (Opperman, D689, as 'ineptly drawn').

PARIS private collection; finished compositional study, signed and dated 1748 (Opperman, D620, fig.446).

Version

The subject recurs, reversed, within a Beauvais tapestry chair-back cover of c.1754–6, see F190 in this Collection.

Provenance

See P625.

Exhibitions

Salon 1748 (23, *Un Barbet qui surprend des Canards*); Bethnal Green 1872–5 (400).

References General

Locquin, nos.240, 357; Vergnet-Ruiz, no.53; Opperman, p.114 and P223.

[1] This Album, which includes work attributable to Oudry *fils*, is discussed by Opperman, pp.145–8.

Ascribed to Oudry

P624 *Hawk attacking Wild Duck*

A buzzard and two mallards. Inscribed on tree trunk, lower left: M.

Canvas, relined 194.5 × 129

The craquelure, which follows a regular pattern of lines and circles, has been retouched, as have the edges. There is a damage lower right, and blistering in the sky area appears to be due to relining.

P624 was sold in 1855 as one of a set of three Oudrys of which another (see P623) is now given to Desportes. One of several versions of a composition dating from c.1737 (see Versions), P624 is somewhat hard and slick in execution; Opperman, in 1982, described it as at best a studio replica and perhaps executed after Oudry's death.[1] The inscribed M (see above) remains unexplained.[2]

Versions

PARIS Musée des Arts Décoratifs; 81 × 90.5, signed and dated 1749(?); a version of the Schwerin picture, see below (Opperman, P297).
Anon. sale, 17 March 1943 (50); 37 × 48, signed and dated 1737 or 1739; probably a sketch for the Schwerin picture, see below (Opperman, P289).
Anon. sale, 6 June 1952 (76); 77 × 117, a version of the Schwerin picture, see below (Opperman, P299).
SCHWERIN Staatliches Museum (no.219); 129 × 162, signed and dated 1740; the birds are similar to those in P624, but the landscape is horizontal (Opperman, P290). A version also signed and dated 1740, was with Dr. K. Engel, Berlin, before 1939 (*ibid.*). A finished drawing for this composition is in the Philadelphia Museum of Art (Opperman, D673A, fig.443), and a study for the right-hand duck is also at Schwerin (Opperman, D929, fig.276). Water-colours of the hawk and of the ducks, attributed to Oudry *fils*, are in the Oudry Album in the Fogg Art Museum (pp.181, 185).[3]

Provenance[4]

The baron de Commailles [Caumail]; 25 rue du Faubourg Saint-Honoré; his sale, Paris, 2 August 1855 (40, *Oiseau de proie fondant sur des canards*, 195 × 129); the 4th Marquess of Hertford; rue Laffitte inventory 1871 (376); Hertford House inventory 1890.

References General

Locquin, no.355; Vergnet-Ruiz, no.57; Opperman, P298 (all as Oudry).

[1] Opperman, *J.B. Oudry*, exh. cat., Grand Palais, 1982–3, p.191. Earlier (Opperman, P298) he had suggested that P624 was from Oudry's studio, the birds possibly by Oudry himself.

[2] Could it refer to Medoro, whose initial Angelica carved on a tree (Ariosto, *Orlando Furioso*, IX; cf. R.W. Lee, *Names on Trees; Ariosto into Art*, 1977)?

[3] Cf. Opperman, pp.145–8, and 1982–3, *loc. cit.* (see note 1 above).

[4] Previous editions of this catalogue have suggested P624 may have been the picture sent by Oudry to Schwerin in 1734 ('a bird of prey falling upon ducks hidden in the reeds'; Opperman, P301), but this is now associated with an engraving by J.H. Tischbein of 1773 (*'gemahlt von Oudry 1733'*) which shows a different composition (see Opperman, *Oudry*, exh. cat., Kimbell Art Museum, Fort Worth, 1983, p.169, fig.91). In any case the execution of P624 is too weak for a prestigious commission.

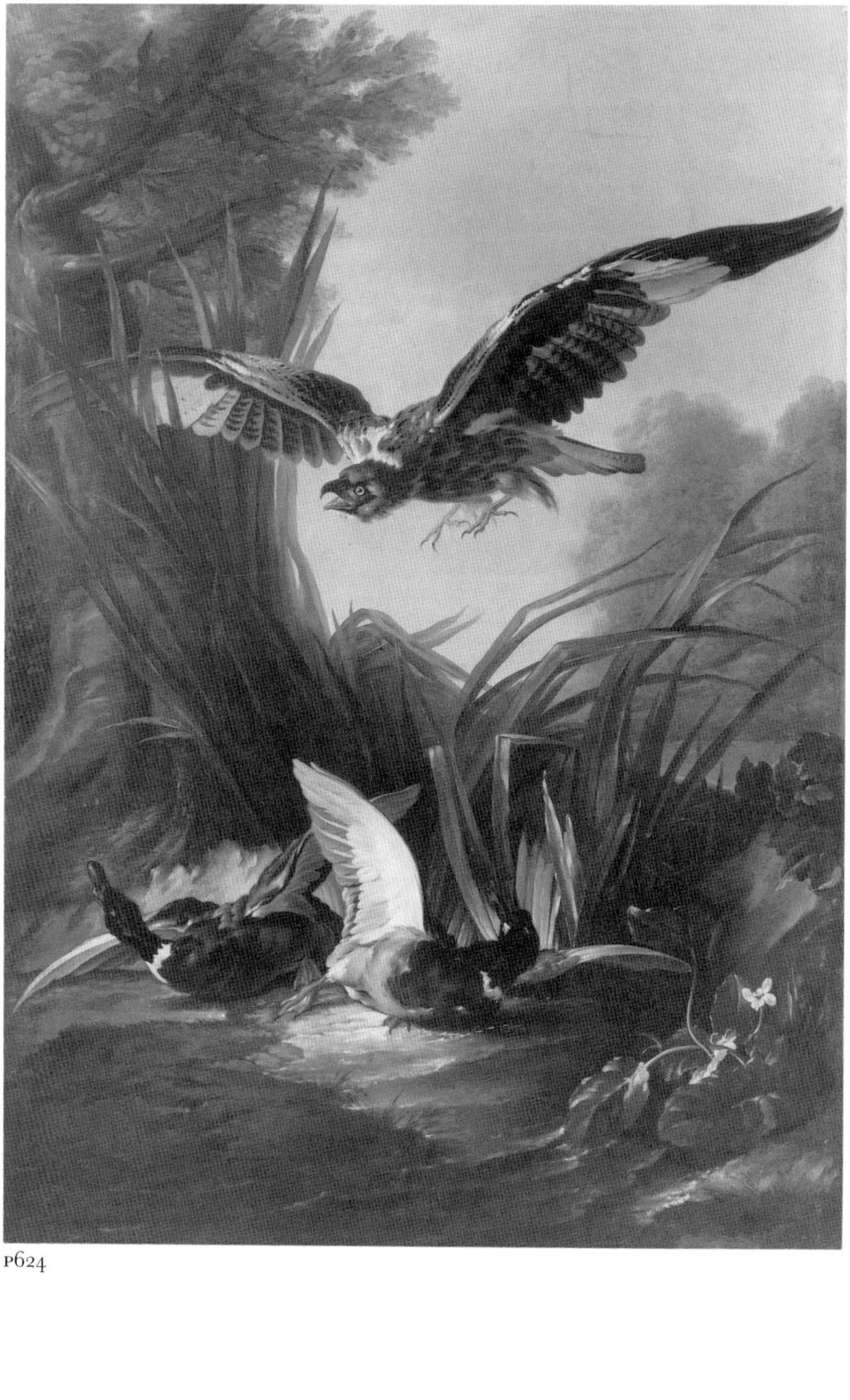

P624

Jean-Baptiste Pater (1695–1736)

Son of the sculptor Antoine Pater, he was born on 29 December 1695 in Valenciennes, where from 1706 he studied under J.-B. Guidé. Sometime after his master's death in 1711 he went to Paris where for a brief period his fellow townsman Watteau was his unco-operative teacher. Pater was back in Valenciennes 1716–18, in dispute with the local *Corporation de Saint-Luc* over his right to practise as a professional painter. He returned to Paris in 1718. For a month in 1721 he was again taught by Watteau, then fatally ill at Nogent-sur-Marne. *Agréé* in 1725, Pater was *reçu* as a painter of *fêtes galantes* in 1728 when he submitted the *Réjouissances de soldats* (Louvre) – which remains one of only three dated works. By 1729 he was living in the rue Quincampoix where he died on 25 July 1736. His work was almost wholly dependent upon Watteau, some of whose works he is said to have completed (cf. P460) and some he copied (cf. P420).[1] In the 1730s he seems to have broadened his repertoire to include illustrations (cf. P405), a series of *Baigneuses* (cf. P426), and some landscapes.[2] Though his colouring could be attractive, his drawing was often weak, and a relentless productivity (attested by Gersaint and Mariette) led to repetition and careless execution. He achieved, nonetheless, a certain reputation; of forty-one Paters acquired by Frederick the Great, twenty-six remain at Charlottenburg and five at Sans-Souci (Potsdam).

[1] For Watteaus completed by Pater, see IS589–92, and H. Adhémar, *Watteau*, 1950, p.128; for Pater's copies from Watteau, see IS594–609 and Adhémar, no.256.

[2] Adhémar, p.128, gives an alternative chronology with the *Baigneuses* before 1721.

Abbreviation

IS F. Ingersoll-Smouse, *Pater*, 1928

P380 *Watching the Dance*

The girl dancing wears a yellow skirt, pale blue bodice and pink sash, the man a green vest with yellow sash and a deep mulberry jacket; on the left a hurdy-gurdy player and a fiddler; a tambourine lies on the ground, centre.

Canvas, relined[1] 53.5 × 64.4

Cleaned and relined by Vallance in 1965–6. The paint is generally thin, noticeably in the dog on the left and the couple on the extreme right. There are small retouchings above the blue-striped skirt of the reclining lady on the right, and round the edges. The craquelure is marked in an area centre right, and has been touched in on the base of the stone urn.

Catalogued as *Conversation galante* until 1928. The men appear to wear costume, the ladies contemporary dress.

P380 possibly dates from the 1730s. The execution is somewhat skimped; the linked arms of the dancers and the legs of the reclining woman on the right being particularly weak. The dancers compare with those in P397 below and ultimately derive from Watteau's *Plaisir pastoral* and *Les bergers* (CR150, CR176). Many of the

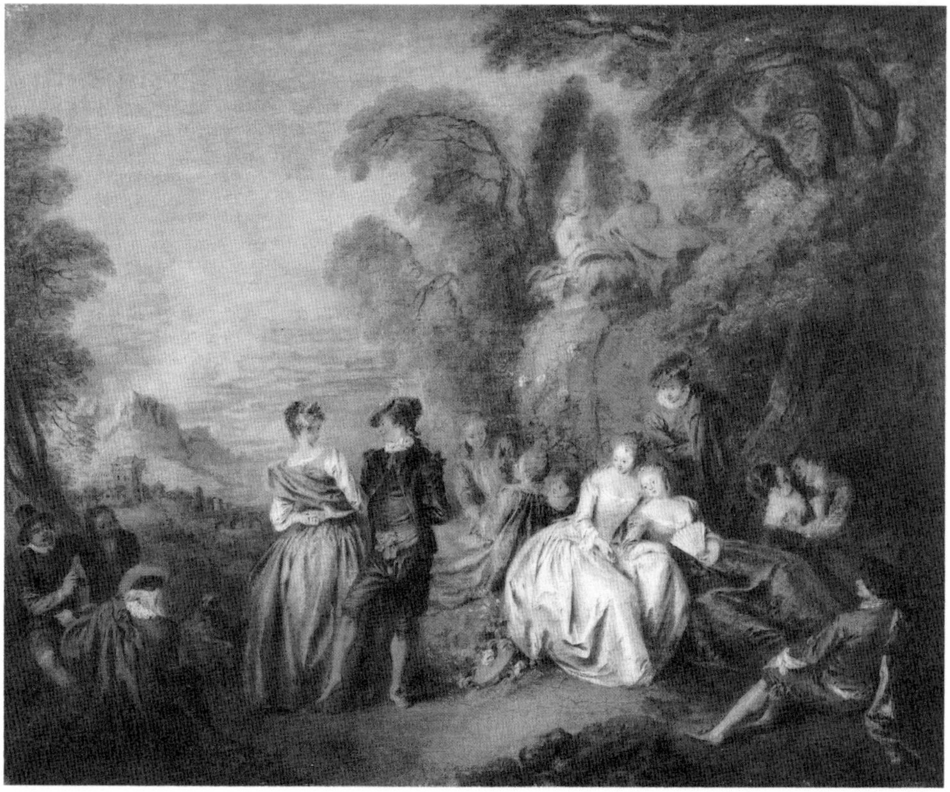

P380

figures recur in other *Danses* by Pater,[2] e.g. the dancers (in IS230, IS232, IS232*bis*), the fiddler (in IS239, IS240, IS243), the hurdy-gurdy player (in IS243), the seated lady in white alone (in IS55, IS230) and with her companion with a fan (in IS243 and, reversed, in IS280*bis*). The statue recurs in IS243, and see P458 below.

Version

LONDON Christie's, 11 July 1980 (20); 23.2 × 31.6, exh. RA 1968 (541).

Provenance

Charles Meigh of Grove House, Shelton; his sale, Christie's, 9 June 1855 (53, Watteau, *A Fête Champêtre from Boccaccio*[3]), bt. Caw for the 4th Marquess of Hertford, 65 gn.; Hertford House inventory 1870.

Exhibition

Bethnal Green 1872–5 (469 or 471, *Pastoral Landscape*).

Reference General

IS231.

[1] The original canvas inscribed, *verso*: *B B Micault N°6,* and the stretcher: *Benj. Hick.*

[2] The IS references quoted below are as follows: IS55 Metropolitan Museum of Art; IS230 Versailles, Petit Trianon; IS232 with Alfred de Rothschild 1884; IS232*bis* Louvre; IS239 Charlottenburg; IS240 with Alfred de Rothschild 1902; IS243 New Haven, Yale Art Gallery; IS280*bis* Frankfurt, Städelsches Kunstinstitut.

[3] Cf. *Garden of Boccaccio* by Stothard, engraved by F. Englehart 1829, which shows a *fête galante* à la Watteau.

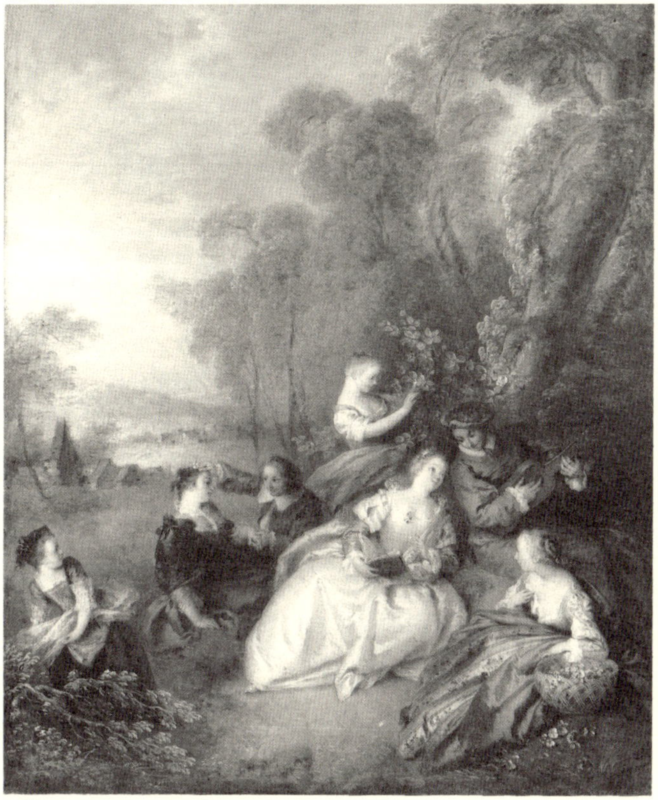

P383

P383 *A Concert (Le concert amoureux)*

The seated lady with the song book wears a white dress with turquoise sleeves and a lilac shawl; the seated girl in the right foreground has a striped yellow and white dress with a floral pattern and a blue overskirt.

Canvas, relined 57.1 × 46.2

There are minor losses round the edges, and the varnish is somewhat discoloured.

P383 is one of a set of four paintings (the others being P386, P397 and P400) engraved by Filloeul in 1739 as *'les plaisirs les plus ordinaires de la jeunesse'*.[1] Only the couples appear to be in costume; the others wear contemporary dress.

P383 and its companion pieces show Pater turning Watteau's delicately ambiguous subjects into genre scenes; they probably date from the 1730s. The guitarist in P383 ultimately derives from Watteau's figure in *La gamme d'amour* and *Récréation galante* (CR161, CR173). The seated girl with a basket of flowers is one of Pater's happiest creations and recurs in his *Fête champêtre* in Washington (IS30) with the seated lady in white, the girl picking flowers and the little girl on the left (reversed); in the *Délassements de la campagne* at Valenciennes (IS29) with the seated lady in white, and in the *Fête champêtre* in the Victoria and Albert Museum (IS28).

Engraving

P. Filloeul 1739, reversed, as *Le concert amoureux* in the président de Ségur's collection, with verses by C. Moraine:

Du luth et de la voix les sons mélodieux
Se dissipent dans l'air d'une extrême vitesse:
Les fleurs perdent bientôt leur eclat précieux.
De même, chers enfants, s'éclipse la jeunesse.

Pour vous en consoler, en l'honneur des Amours
Redoublez vos chansons, cueillez des fleurs nouvelles
S'ils ne vous donnent pas des faveurs éternelles,
Du moins ils vous feront jouir de vos beaux jours.

Copy

LONDON Christie's, 29 February 1926 (63); 44 × 28, reversed.

Version

BERLIN Charlottenburg; 55 × 44, replica, listed in 1744 (IS26).

Provenance

With P386, P397 and P400: the président de Ségur (?Henri-François, comte de Ségur, 1689–1751) in 1739 (see Engraving); acquired by the 4th Marquess of Hertford;[2] rue Laffitte inventory 1871 (704, 705); Hertford House inventory 1890.

Exhibition

Bethnal Green 1872–5 (382 or 432, *Pastoral Group*).

Reference General

IS25.

[1] Filloeul announced his set of plates in the *Mercure de France*, March 1739, p.537: '. . . *quatre estampes fort gracieuses, lesquelles représentent les plaisirs les plus ordinaires de la jeunesse. Elles ont* [49 × 36.7 *et*] *ont été copiées d'après les tableaux du sieur Pater qui sont au Cabinet de M. le Président de Ségur. La première représente* le Jeu de Colin-Maillard; *la seconde,* le Concert amoureux; *la troisième,* la Conversation intéressante, *et la quatrième,* la Danse. *Les vers qui sont au bas sont de la composition de M. Moraine*' (as quoted by IS, p.35).

[2] It is remotely possible that these were the four paintings described as four pastorals by Lancret in the Prousteau de Montlouis sale, Paris, 5–6 May 1851 (10), attached to a *paravent* with the four Bouchers P429, P432, P438 and P444, on the other side; see Boucher P429 note 2. P383 has previously been associated with lot 128 in the Choiseul sale, Paris, 6 April 1772: '*un Concert de personnes galamment vêtues; la scène se passe sur un péristile* . . . [51.6 × 59.7]', but the proportions are wrong; it is identified by Ingersoll-Smouse (IS209) with another composition, and it seems unlikely that P383, P386, P397 and P400 were ever separated. See also P386 note 1. P383, P386, P397 and P400 were indentically framed in 1900, but two of the frames were subsequently modified.

P386 *The Swing (La conversation intéressante)*

The right-hand seated lady wears a white bodice, yellow overskirt and a pale blue, pink and white striped underskirt; the left-hand lady has a blue hat with a primrose on it; the right-hand seated man has put down a tambourine, and his rival plays a hurdy-gurdy; smoke rises from the distant hill.

Canvas, relined 56.8 × 45.7

There are some minor losses, bottom right. *Pentimenti* show that the dog's forelegs were redrawn. The varnish is somewhat discoloured.

One of a set of four paintings, see P383. Apart from the child and the right-hand seated lady, all the figures appear to be in costume.

For possible dating, see P383. The legs of the kneeling youth on the right are hardly convincing, and the hands of the lady on the swing are weak. The motif of the swing was probably inspired by Watteau's *Plaisir pastoral* or *Les bergers* (CR150, CR176). The kneeling youth on the right recurs (reversed) in Pater's *Réunion en plein air* at Charlottenburg (IS58).

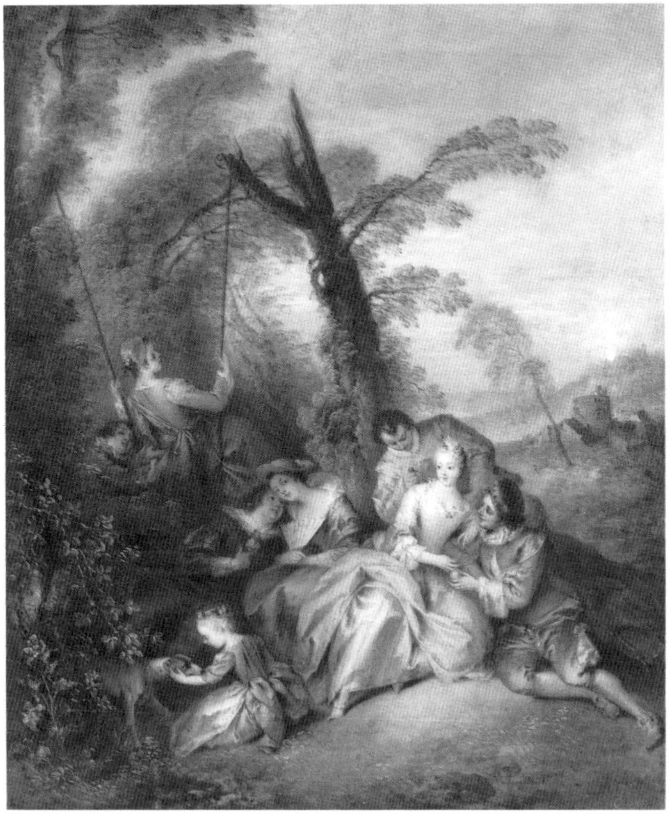

P386

Engraving

P.Filloeul 1739, reversed, as *La conversation intéressante* in the président de Ségur's collection (see P383 note 1), with verses by C. Moraine:

Assis sur un gazon, qu'on se plaît quand on s'aime,
A se communiquer les secrets de son coeur.
Un pareil entretient à certaine douceur
Qui paroist egaler la jouissance même.

Aminte néanmoins pense tout autrement:
A tout autre plaisir la folette est encline
Et suivant son humeur enjouée et badine.
Elle aime mieux en l'air trouver du mouvement.

Tamisier (for Blanc 1865).

Copy

LONDON Christie's, 29 February 1926 (63); 49 × 28, reversed.

Provenance[1]

See P383.

Exhibition

Bethnal Green 1872–5 (382 or 432, *Pastoral Group*).

Reference General

IS276.

[1] P386 has been associated with three sales: Choiseul, Paris, 6 April 1772, lot 129: '*une belle Compagnie vêtue galamment: le principal sujet est une Balançoire attachée à des arbres qui composent avec de beaux lointains le fonds du tableau: les étoffes sont d'une couleur agréable, les têtes très-gracieuses & d'une touche spirituelle . . .* [51.6 × 59.8]'; Conti, Paris, 8 April 1777, lot 673: '*Les amusements de la campagne. On y voit une dame sur une balançoire attachée à des arbres . . .* [51.6 × 59.8]'), and Wellesley, Paris, 15 June 1846, lot 3. The proportions of the first two are wrong for P386 and Ingersoll-Smouse identified all these references with the picture in the Patureau sale of 1857, bequeathed to the Louvre in 1926 (IS277*bis* and IS284); see also P383 note 2. This may explain why P386 was illus. *Apollo*, XCVII, 1973, p.47, as in the Louvre. Ingersoll-Smouse associated P386 with a fourth sale, Paris, 14–15 March 1842 (3, *L'escarpolette, tableau gravé*), but see, again, P383 note 2.

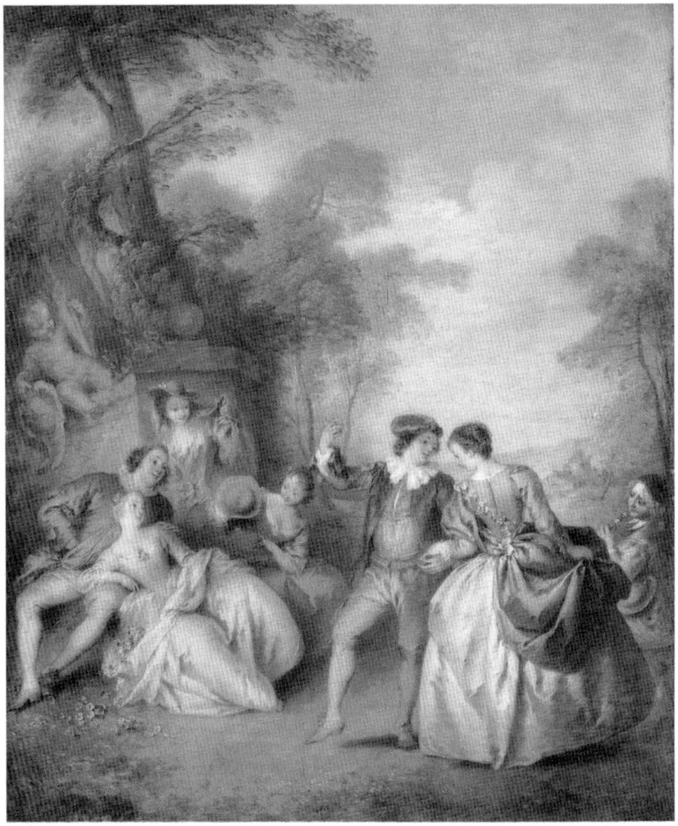

P397

P397 *The Dance*

The girl dancing wears a purple bodice, yellow skirt and a blue drape; her partner, who holds castanets in his right hand, has a purple coat over an orange-yellow suit; on the extreme right a bagpipe player; the statue shows a *putto* holding a shield and reeds.

Canvas, relined 56.7 × 45.7

There is a small damage above the wall on the left, and some minor losses round the edges. The varnish is somewhat discoloured.

One of a set of four paintings, see P383. The three men appear to be in costume, the others in contemporary dress.

For possible dating, see P383. The legs of the seated man on the left, and his partner's skirt, are weakly drawn. The dancers derive from Watteau's *Plaisir pastoral* or *Les bergers* (cf. P380 and P386). The seated man on the left recurs in Pater's *Fête galante* in the Victoria and Albert Museum (IS28); his partner in *Les loisirs champêtres* (IS43). The distinctive head of the bagpipe player reappears in *La fête du mai* (IS527).

Engraving

P. Filloeul 1739, reversed, as *La danse* in the président de Ségur's collection (see P383 note 1), with verses by C. Moraine:

Danse aimable, où la grace est jointe avec l'adresse;
Où dans tout son éclat triomphe la beauté,
Tu parois faite exprès par l'heureuse jeunesse
Et ton art par l'amour fût sans doute inventé.

A l'un et l'autre sexe il montra la cadence,
Il leur fit observer un juste mouvement;
Et sachant les tenir en bonne intelligence,
Leur union forma ton plus bel ornement.

The left-hand figure group alone engr. E. Vermorcken (Blanc, *Les Peintres des Fêtes Galantes*, 1854, and Blanc 1865).

Versions

BERLIN Charlottenburg; 55 × 45, with minor differences (IS229).
DALMENY; with a different musette player (illus. *Apollo*, CXIX, 1984, p.409).
LONDON Tooth's 1935; 74 × 60, extended on the right.
STOCKHOLM Bukowski's, 25 April 1956 (357); 58 × 50, similar to the Dalmeny version.

Provenance

See P383.

Exhibition

Bethnal Green 1872–5 (435).

Reference General

IS228.

P400 *Blind Man's Buff (Le colin-maillard)*

The blindfolded lady wears a gold and orange striped skirt; the seated lady on the right has a green skirt and a rich yellow bodice; on the left a seated man holds a musette.

Canvas, relined 57 × 45.6

There are some minor losses round the edges, and the paint is thin in the sky, upper left. The varnish is somewhat discoloured.

One of a set of four paintings, see P383. The man with a musette and the standing man, centre-left, appear to be in costume, the remainder in contemporary dress.

For possible dating, see P383. The stooping man, centre-right, derives from Watteau's *Colin-maillard* (CR10). The seated lady recurs in Pater's *Halte de troupes* at Charlottenburg (IS416).

Engravings

P. Filloeul 1739, reversed, as *Le colin-maillard* in the président de Ségur's collection (see P383 note 1), with verses by C. Moraine.[1]
E. Vermorcken (for Blanc 1865).

Copies/Versions

BRUSSELS H. D. Roussel sale, 23–4 May 1893 (16); 60 × 50 (IS296).
LENINGRAD ex Youssoupoff collection 1907; 46 × 37, reversed (IS298).
LONDON Lyons sale, Christie's, 8 July 1912 (73); 53 × 43 (IS under 295).
Tooth's 1935; 74 × 60.
PARIS the comte L. de L. sale, 21 April 1896; 69 × 55 (IS297).
Demonts sale, 23–5 May 1921 (67); copper 23.5 × 19.5 (IS under 300).
SWINTON Yorkshire 1971; 58 × 46, reversed.

Provenance

See P383.

Exhibition

Bethnal Green 1872–5 (437).

Reference General

IS295.

[1] Only a poor reproduction of this print is known to the compiler.

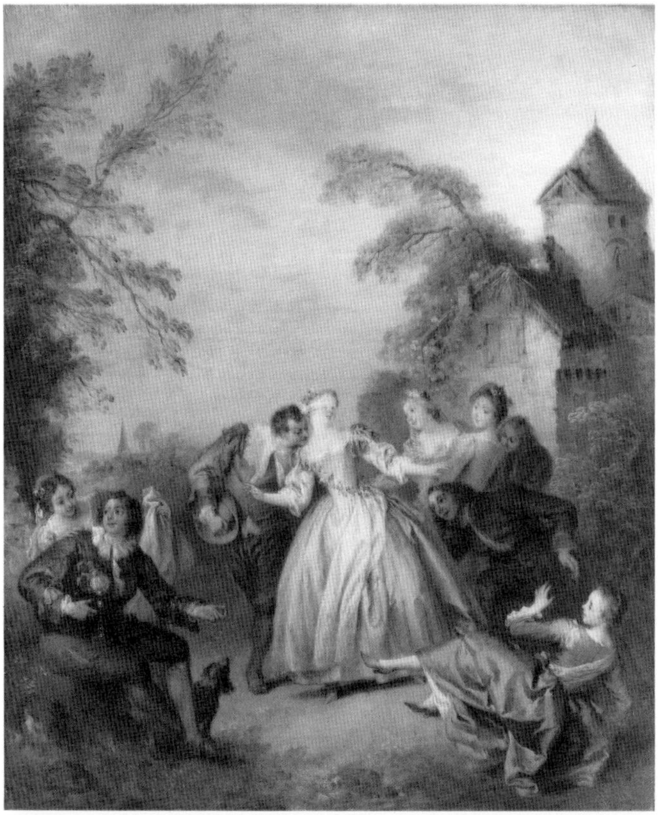

P400

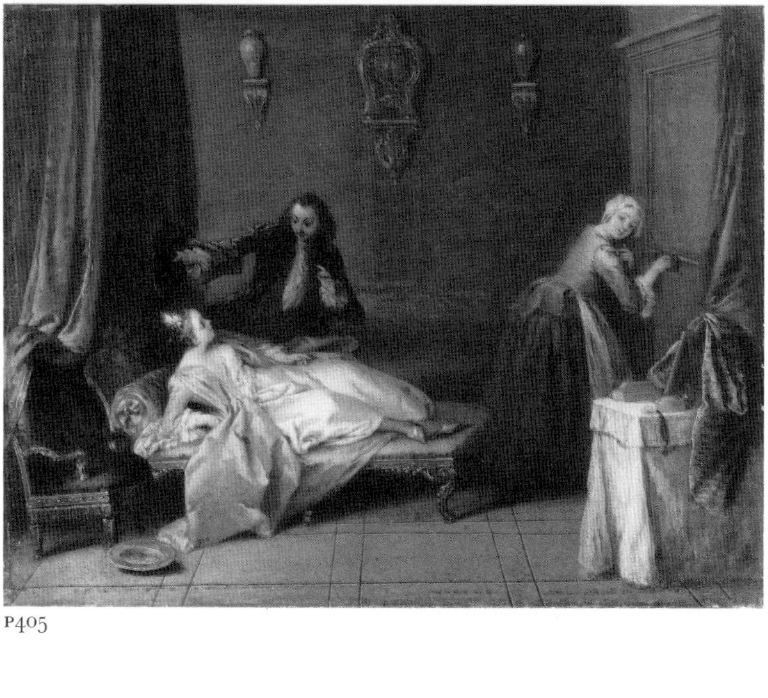

P405

P405 *The Boudoir (Sujet tiré des Contes de La Fontaine)*

The lady in white satin with a salmon pink gown and turquoise stockings; the day-bed has lavender upholstery; the man has a blue coat.

Canvas[1] 32 × 40

There are some minor losses, e.g. on the door, in the curtains by the door and on the left, behind the maid's back and in the bottom left corner. The surface is abraded top left and in the floor, below right. *Pentimenti* show adjustments to the upper part of the maid's figure, and the day-bed was originally a slightly shorter *duchesse* with a raised end. The varnish is somewhat discoloured.

The maid points over her shoulder to the man who seems to have emerged from behind the curtains. A variant composition (see Versions) suggests the narrative admitted some latitude. Ingersoll-Smouse identified P405 as an illustration to either *La confidente sans le savoir* or *Le remède* from La Fontaine's *Contes* (V, lix and lx), for which Pater otherwise made eight paintings, engraved by Filloeul 1733–6 (cf. IS470–88);[2] see also Lancret P409. Her suggestion seems entirely plausible.

P405 may be dated in the 1730s, contemporary with Pater's La Fontaine illustrations and with those he made for *Le roman comique* (Charlottenburg; IS489–502) which are the same size as P405. Both sets include comparable interiors (cf. IS476–7, IS497–8), and the male model recurs in IS497 and IS499. The *régence* furnishings are clumsily drawn; the lady's left leg appears curiously long, and the lock on the door is eccentrically placed. The figure of the reclining lady recurs, with minor variations, in P424, P426 and P458 below, in the *Repos dans un parc* (St Louis, City Art Museum; IS53) and in the *Halte de troupes* (with Agnew's 1986; IS412). The right-hand table with its furnishings recurs in P472.

Drawing

PARIS Musée Jacquemart-André (no.335); study for the reclining lady; the day-bed is shorter and the hands are slightly different.

Versions

LONDON art market 1962; slightly larger than P405, with a bare back wall, a shorter day-bed and a plain floor.
PARIS with D. Wildenstein 1928; panel 16.5 × 20.3, the man in costume, the maid on the left and a cat drinking from the saucer (IS482).

Provenance

Johann Anton de Peters (1725–95); his sale, Paris, 9 March 1779 (96, '. . . *une jeune femme sur son lit de repos; un homme qui semble lui parler, & dans le fond de la chambre, une femme de chambre qui ouvre la porte . . . toile* [32.6 × 44.9]');[3] [see note 1]; anon. ('Ch.') sale, Paris, 9 January 1868 (1, '*Manon Lescaut et le chevalier de Grieux*'), bt. by the 4th Marquess of Hertford, 2,190 fr.; possibly rue Laffitte inventory 1871 (61, '*école française, scène galante*', or 91, '*école française, la surprise matinale*'); Hertford House inventory 1890.

Exhibition

Bethnal Green 1872–5 (569, *The Visit*).

Reference General

IS481.

[1] An old ink inscription, *verso*, reads: *Pater hauteur 12 pouces largeur 15 p^ces 3 lignes*; fragments from an English sale catalogue of 1836 adhere to the stretcher; on the inside of the frame is written: *Mr. Hamon Pater.*

[2] Although Filloeul engraved eight illustrations for La Fontaine by Pater, in August 1739 he offered for sale ten paintings by Pater illustrating the *Contes* of La Fontaine (*Mercure de France*, August 1739, p.1834; quoted by IS, p.35).

[3] P405 is identified by a Saint-Aubin drawing in a copy of the sale catalogue, cf. E. Dacier, *Catalogues de ventes et livrets de Salons illustrés et annotés par Gabriel de Saint-Aubin*, IX, 1919; his sketch is cryptic and shows the back wall bare and the table on the right extended to the right.

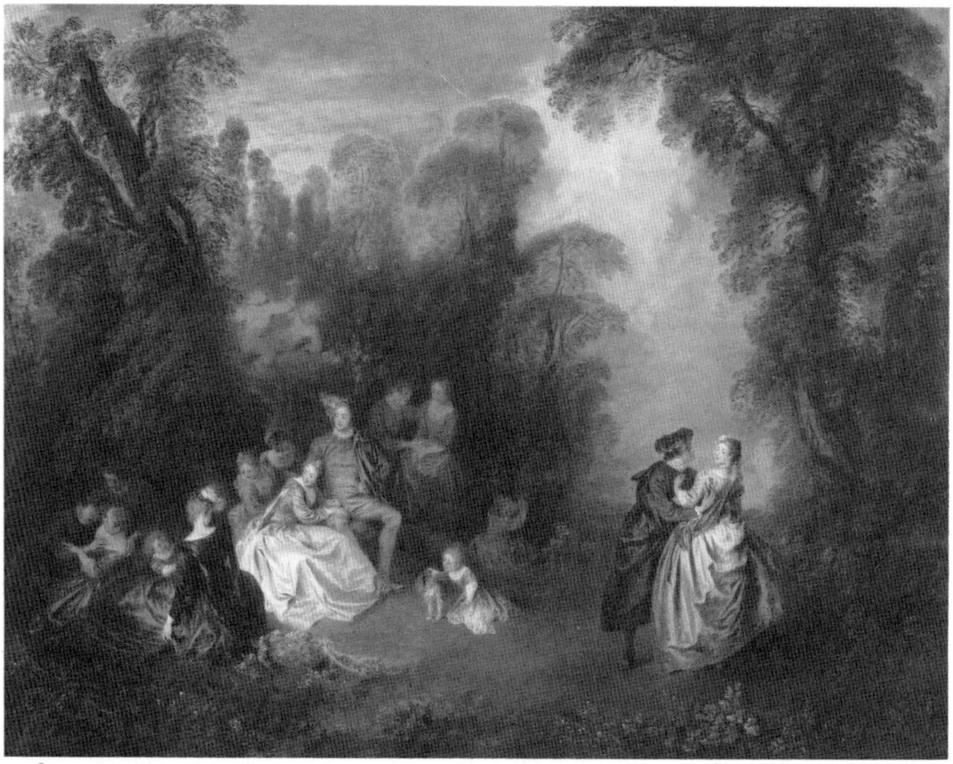

P406

P406 *Conversation galante by a Fountain*

The seated man, centre-left, wears an orange costume with a pink cape, his companion a white skirt with a lime-green bodice; in front of her the seated lady has a red skirt and black bodice; on the right the standing lady wears a purple skirt, yellow bodice and blue sash.

Canvas, relined 65 × 81.4

Cleaned by Vallance in 1966. There are small losses in the trees, upper right, to the right of the right-hand lady's skirt, and round the edges. *Pentimenti* seem to show a figure bending down to the distant seated girl with a dog by her side, and a second child beyond them; the trees around this group have also been altered.

The men are in costume, the others in contemporary dress.

The scale and distribution of the figures, and the character of the landscape, are particularly close to Watteau, and suggest a date in the 1720s. The standing lady on the right has a disproportionately small head and the drawing of her left arm is weak. The group of three figures on the extreme left (two men and a lady) with the girl to the right looking down at them, recurs in *La bergère couronnée* (Christie's, 20 March 1959, lot 46; IS355).

Provenance

Acquired by the 4th Marquess of Hertford; reframed in Hertford House 1859;[1] Hertford House inventory 1870 (*'Fête Champêtre, 15 figures'*).

Exhibition

Bethnal Green 1872–5 (469 or 471, *Pastoral Landscape*).

Reference General

IS50

[1] Evans invoice.

P420 *The Ball (after Watteau) (Les plaisirs du bal)*

The standing man on the extreme right is in red; the central female dancer wears a red hat, purple cape and a light, striped skirt; her partner a green suit and red hat.

Canvas, relined[1] 54.8 × 64.1

There are many small retouchings, particularly apparent in the architecture, the black skirt of the seated woman with a dog at her feet, and round the edges. *Pentimenti* show that the hat and legs of the central male dancer have been altered (see below).

P420 is one of several copies by Pater of Watteau's *Les plaisirs du bal* (52.6 × 65.4; Dulwich Picture Gallery; CR164).[2] Sold as by Watteau in 1865, P420 had been attributed to Pater by Bürger in 1860;[3] his attribution was challenged by Lagrange[4] and Zimmermann, but has been accepted by Goncourt, Dacier and Vuaflart, Réau, Ingersoll-Smouse, Adhémar and Rosenberg.[5] The architecture in P420 is somewhat clumsy: the banded column on the far right, supporting the balustrade, is not straight, and the right-hand column of the engaged pair, centre right, has been altered down the left-hand side. The figure of the central male dancer differs from Watteau's original in that the hat is smaller and the head and legs repositioned; *pentimenti* show that this figure was first accurately copied. Such modifications of the original composition characterised a number of Pater's copies;[6] he also used the composition for *Le sultan au jardin* (formerly Potsdam; IS561).

Provenance[7]

The duc de Morny (1811–65) by 1860; his sale, Paris, 3rd day, 2 June 1865 (113, as Watteau), bt. by the 4th Marquess of Hertford, 37,000 fr.; rue Laffitte inventory 1871 (526, *'Watteau, fête dans un parc'*); Hertford House inventory 1890.

Exhibitions

Boulevard des Italiens 1860 (268, as Watteau) lent Morny; Bethnal Green 1872–5 (424, as Pater).

References General

IS604; the following refer to monographs on Watteau, q.v., for abbreviations: Goncourt, p.139, as Pater; Zimmermann, p.188, as a copy groundlessly attributed to Pater; DV under 114, as Pater; Réau, no.113, as Pater; Adhémar, under no.196, as Pater; CR under 164, as attributed to Pater.

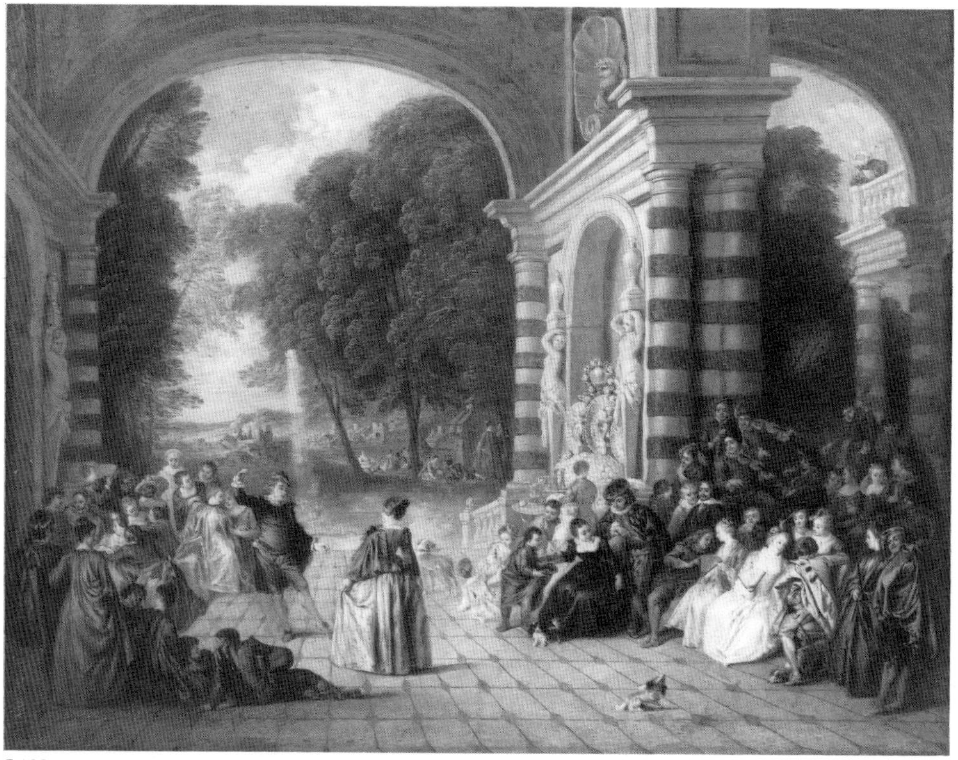

P420

[1] The stretcher is stamped, *verso*: MOMPER A PARIS, for whom, see Fragonard P430 note 1.

[2] Pater's copies are discussed by Ingersoll-Smouse, p.86 and IS600–9, and by Dacier and Vuaflart under DV114. The earliest references to them are: Pater's *inventaire après décès*, 1736; Selle sale, 19 February 1761 (37); Grammont sale, 16 January 1775 (61); Blondel de Gagny sale, 10 December 1776 (223), and the sales of Montullé (22 December 1783, lot 55) and Le Brun (11 April 1791, lot 197) which both mention '*deux ou trois imitations faites par Pater*'. See also C. G. E. Bunt, *The Connoisseur*, CXIX, 1947, pp.93–8 (where a tentative attribution to Quillard is proposed for P420).

[3] W. Bürger, *Gazette des Beaux-Arts*, 1ère, VII, p.271.

[4] L. Lagrange, *ibid.*, XIV, 1863, p.391; he considered an attribution to Pater impossible if P420 were compared with P424 (both were then in the Morny collection).

[5] P. Rosenberg, *Watteau*, exh. cat., Paris, 1984, p.370.

[6] One contained fewer figures (IS601), another altered the architecture and omitted a dog (IS606), another replaced the buffet on the right with a fountain (IS602). An entirely accurate copy by Pater, ex Wroxton Abbey, was sold Christie's, 8 July 1988, lot 61 (IS under 609).

[7] The association of P420 with earlier sales seems too tenuous to be useful (cf. the previous edition of this catalogue). Bürger, *loc. cit.*, see note 3 above, gave the provenance of P420 as the Grammont and Blondel de Gagny sales (see note 2 above), and Landegrave sale, 1 December 1784 (28, as *d'après Watteau*). Ingersoll-Smouse identifies the first and third of these sale references with her IS601, and the second with IS602. She also rejects the proposal made by Alfassa (BSHAF 1910, p.114 n.2) that Scotin's engraving of Watteau's *Les plaisirs du bal* (DV114) was made from a copy by Pater; Dacier and Vuaflart, *loc. cit.*, are less dismissive.

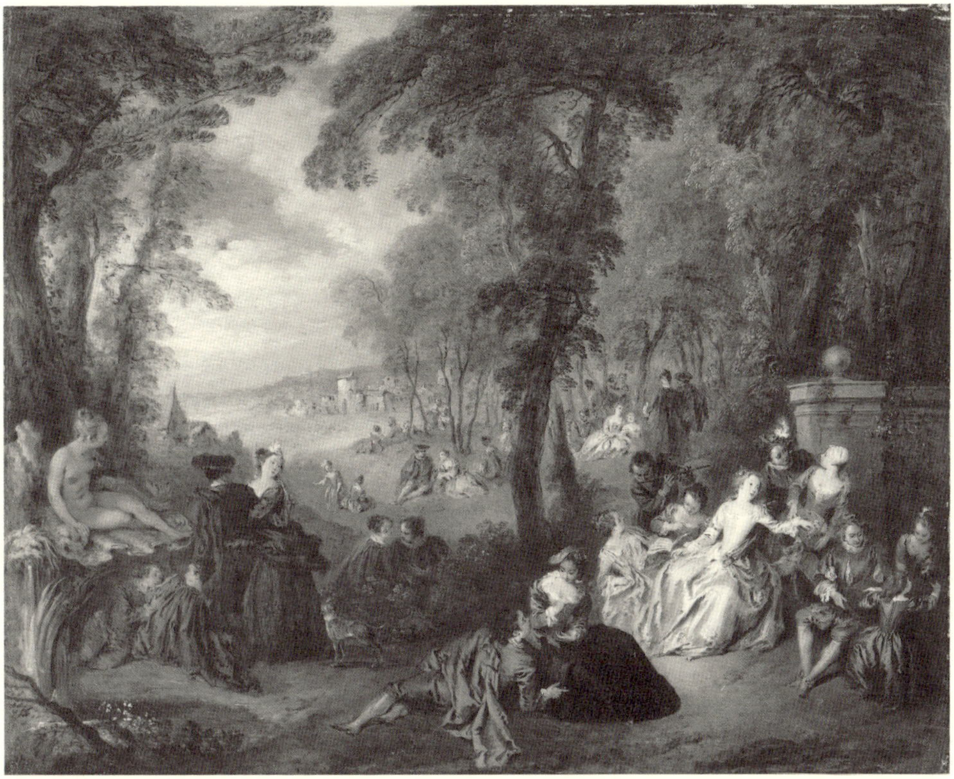

P424

P424 *Fête in a Park*

The reclining youth in the centre foreground wears a grey costume with a red drape, his companion a black skirt, yellow bodice and turquoise shawl; on the right two girls sing a duet with a flautist; the seated lady, centre-right, has a yellow and pale lavender striped skirt, white bodice and blue shawl; the statue on the left shows a nymph and a dolphin.

Canvas, relined[1] 52.7 × 64.4

There are retouchings in the sky, centre left, and the edges are somewhat abraded. *Pentimenti* show alterations to the trees on the left and the extreme right.

The men are in costume, the others in contemporary dress. The flautist is left-handed.

The lively execution and markedly Watteauesque character of the subject (cf. P391, for example), suggest a date in the 1720s (cf. P460). The departing couple on the left, who recall similar groups in Watteau's *Pèlerinage à l'isle de Cithère,* recur in Pater's *Fête champêtre* in the Metropolitan Museum of Art (IS24); the foreground couple, the centre-right seated lady and the group singing a duet recur in his *Fête galantes* at Kenwood and in the Dubernet-Douine sale, Paris, 11 April 1946, lot 27 (IS36*bis*, IS37). The reclining duettist recalls similar figures in P405, P426 and P458.

Provenance

The duc de Morny (1811–65); his sale, Paris, 2nd day, 1 June 1865 (107, *Amusements Champêtres*), bt. by the 4th Marquess of Hertford, 29,000 fr.; rue Laffitte inventory 1871 (524, *'le repos après la promenade'*); Hertford House inventory 1890.

Exhibitions

Boulevard des Italiens, 1860 (220, *Assemblée galante dans un parc*) lent Morny;[2] Bethnal Green 1872–5 (?428, *Landscape with Pastoral Groups*).

Reference General

IS36.

[1] The stretcher is stamped, *verso*: MOMPER A PARIS, and bears Momper's label, . . . *rentoileur des musées impériaux, 12 rue des Marais-St-Germain . . . Ateliers, 13, rue de la Sablière, Petit-Montrouge*. See also Fragonard P430 note 1.

[2] W. Bürger, *Gazette des Beaux-Arts*, 1ère, VII, 1860, p.275, considered P424 one of Pater's best; L. Lagrange, *ibid.*, XIV, 1863, pp.391–2, agreed.

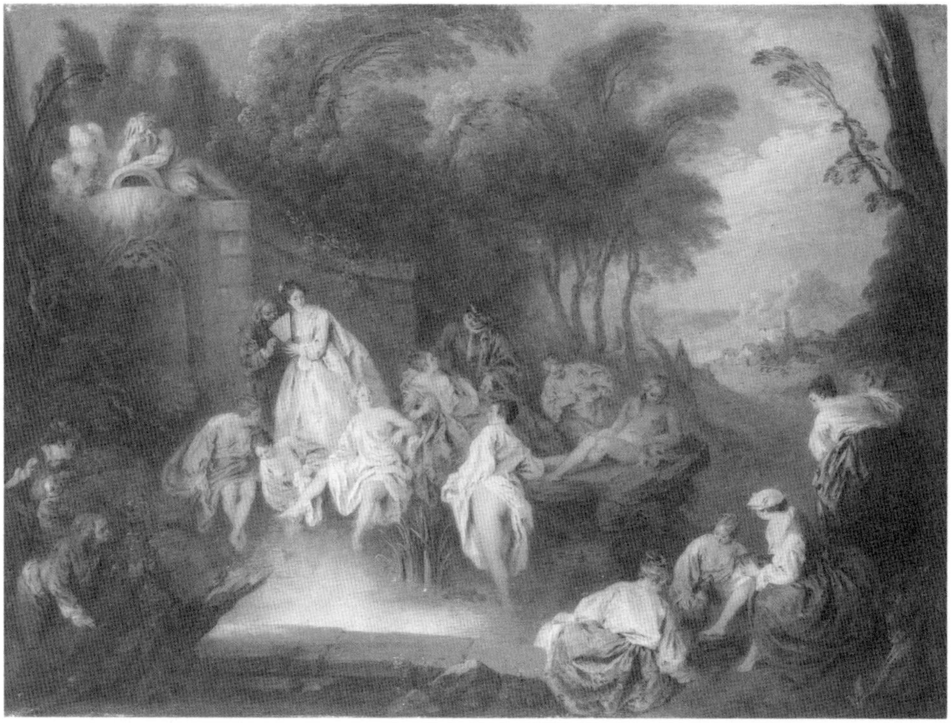

P426

P426 *Bathing Party in a Park*

Three voyeurs hide in the bushes, bottom left; the statue, centre right, shows a nymph with a dolphin.

Canvas, relined[1] 64.2 × 85

The edges are somewhat abraded. There is an overall craquelure, and some spotting in the discoloured varnish.

The subject does not derive directly from Watteau, and may belong to the later part of Pater's career in the 1730s.[2] Ingersoll-Smouse, who records eighteen comparable *Baigneuse* compositions (IS311, 313–28) suggests (p.14) that some may have been commissioned by members of the contemporary *cénacles galants*. The central pair in the mid-distance of P426 recall the composition of P405, and the girl alone recurs in P424 and P458 (and see entry for P405).

Versions

See above. The following compare most closely with P426:

GRENOBLE Musée (no.86); 65 × 83, unfinished, with minor differences in the central figure group (IS328).

INDIANAPOLIS Herron Museum of Art (no.64.1); 51 × 64, without the voyeurs and with other minor differences.[3]

Provenance

Acquired by the 4th Marquess of Hertford; reframed in Hertford House 1859;[4] Hertford House inventory 1870; 105 Piccadilly 1874–5; Hertford House inventory 1890.

Reference General

IS327*bis*.

[1] An old label, *verso*, reads: *Un bain de Femmes dans un lieu Champêtre, composi/tion capitale et gracieuse. L'on y compte seize Figures/tant femmes qu'Hommes.*

[2] Watteau's bathers, as seen for example in *La villageoise* (CR27), *Diane au bain* (CR113), and in the background of the portrait of La Roque (CR118), have none of Pater's wantonness,

[3] See Art Association of Indianapolis, *Bulletin*, June 1964, pp.24–5.

[4] Evans invoice.

P452 *The Vivandières of Brest*

In the centre foreground a reclining soldier in a red coat; behind him another smoking a pipe wears a blue coat, with alongside a standing lady in a tricolor hat; in the distance the smoke of battle.

Canvas 46.7 × 59.5

Cleaned by Buttery in 1879. There are several retouchings, e.g. in the centre foreground, in the tent awning on the left, and round the edges. The surface is slightly abraded in the lower right area. The varnish is much discoloured.

The title is taken from Le Bas's print of 1760; it probably refers to the repulse by the French of a British landing force at Brest in June 1694, but the scene is essentially fanciful, with love and war uncomfortably close.

The subject derives from military scenes by Watteau such as the *Camp volant* (CR44) and *Escorte d'équipage* (CR57). P452 may perhaps be dated in the 1720s when Watteau's influence was still fresh. Pater painted many similar *Haltes de troupes* (cf. IS397–419), in which several of the figures seen in P452 recur:[1] the

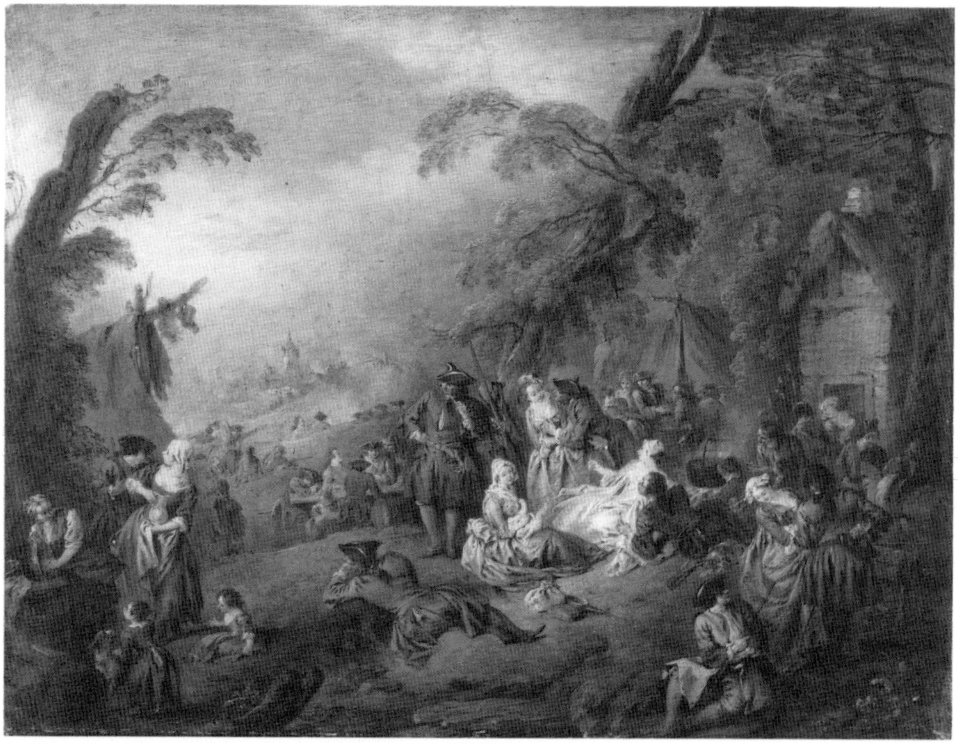

P452

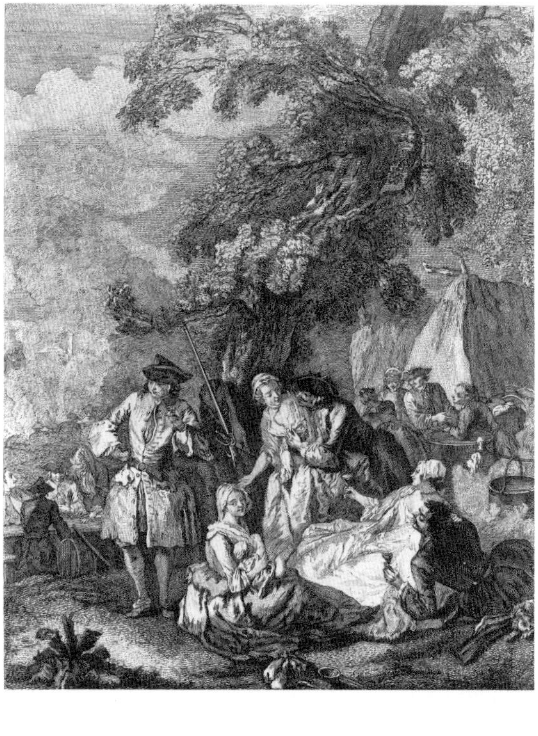

J.-P. Le Bas after Pater:
Vivandières de Brest, 1760.
Bibliothèque Nationale

reclining soldier in the foreground in IS412 (and he recalls a similar figure in Watteau's *Alte*, CR40, and *Détachement faisant alte*, CR55); the standing soldier with a pipe in IS406, IS408 and IS409; the girl with a pitcher in IS413, and the lady with a tricolor hat in IS417.

Drawing

LONDON Sotheby's, 4 December 1969 (52); study for the seated woman holding a child (exh. John Baskett, June 1968, no.42).

Engravings

J.-P. Le Bas 1760 (IS404, fig.200), as *Vivandières de Brest*, showing only the centre section of P452,[2] with verses by C. Moraine:

Hatez-vous, belles Vivandières
De servir du Dieu Mars les braves Nourissons.

Apres de longs travaux marmites et chaudrières
Doivent leur plaire mieux que mortiers et canons.

The engraving shows slight divergencies in the standing soldier's coat and the tent awning on the left.
Courtry 1872 (for the Pereire sale catalogue).

Provenance

Isaac Pereire (1806–80) by 1864;[3] Pereire sale, Paris, 2nd day, 7 March 1872 (71, *Les Vivandières de Brest*), bt. Delière for Sir Richard Wallace, 18,400 fr.; Hertford House inventory 1890.

Exhibitions

Champs-Elysées, *Tableaux de maîtres*, 1866 (131, *Marche des soldats*) lent Isaac Pereire; Bethnal Green 1872–5 (438, *Soldiers Halting*).

Reference General

IS405.

[1] The IS references quoted are as follows: IS406 sold Paris, 13–23 June 1917, lot 50; IS408 with baron Maurice de Rothschild, Paris, 1928; IS409, with Mme. Stern, Paris, 1928; IS412 with Agnew's 1986; IS413 Rheims sale, Paris, 9 June 1964; IS417 Metropolitan Museum of Art.

[2] Roughly equivalent to an area 33 × 24 in P452.

[3] W. Bürger, *Gazette des Beaux-Arts*, 1ère, XVI, 1864, p.201, described P452 in the Pereire collection as '*à peu près le pendant des* Loisirs champêtres, *achetés par Lord Hertford à la vente Demidoff*', i.e. P460.

P458 *Conversation galante*

The reclining lady wears a white skirt, lavender gown and grey-green bodice; behind her a man holding a staff decked with flowers.

Canvas, relined 46.5 × 39

A prominent craquelure has been filled to the right of the flowered staff; elsewhere the paint is very thin, e.g. the trees behind the distant building on the left, and the edges of the right-hand trees. There is some retouching in the sky and the edges are somewhat rubbed. The varnish is discoloured.

The seated man points out the embracing couple to his companion, while another lady picks flowers for her companion who also looks at the embracing couple; perhaps a progress of love is intended. The men wear costume, the women contemporary dress.

The foreground couple recur in Pater's *morceau de réception* of 1728, the *Réjouissance de soldats* (Louvre; IS397), possibly indicating a slightly later date for P458. The torso of the seated man seems a little exaggerated. The couple also recur, together with the embracing couple (reversed), in a *Conversation galante* formerly in baron Maurice de Rothschild's collection (IS32); the embracing couple recur in *The*

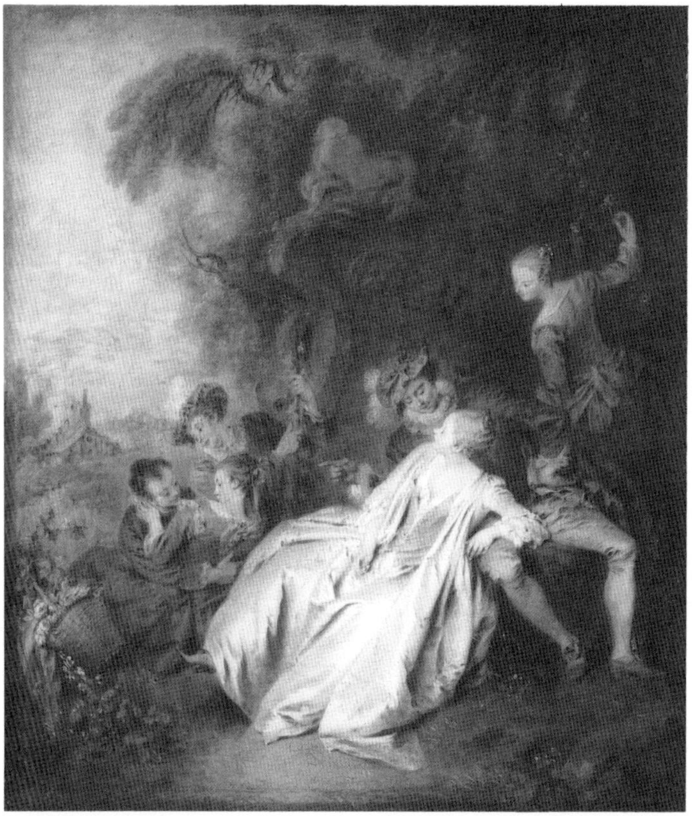

P458

Island of Cytherea engraved by Picart after Pater (IS315) and, reversed, in the *Baigneuses* formerly in the Kann collection (IS316), and in P460. The nymph shown on the statue recurs in P380, and the model for the reclining lady seems to recur, reversed, in P405, P424 and P426.

Provenance

Acquired by the 4th Marquess of Hertford; rue Laffitte inventory 1871 (?258, '*réunion galante*'); Hertford House inventory 1890.

Exhibition

Bethnal Green 1872–5 (?464, *Complimentary Conversation*).

Reference General

IS31.

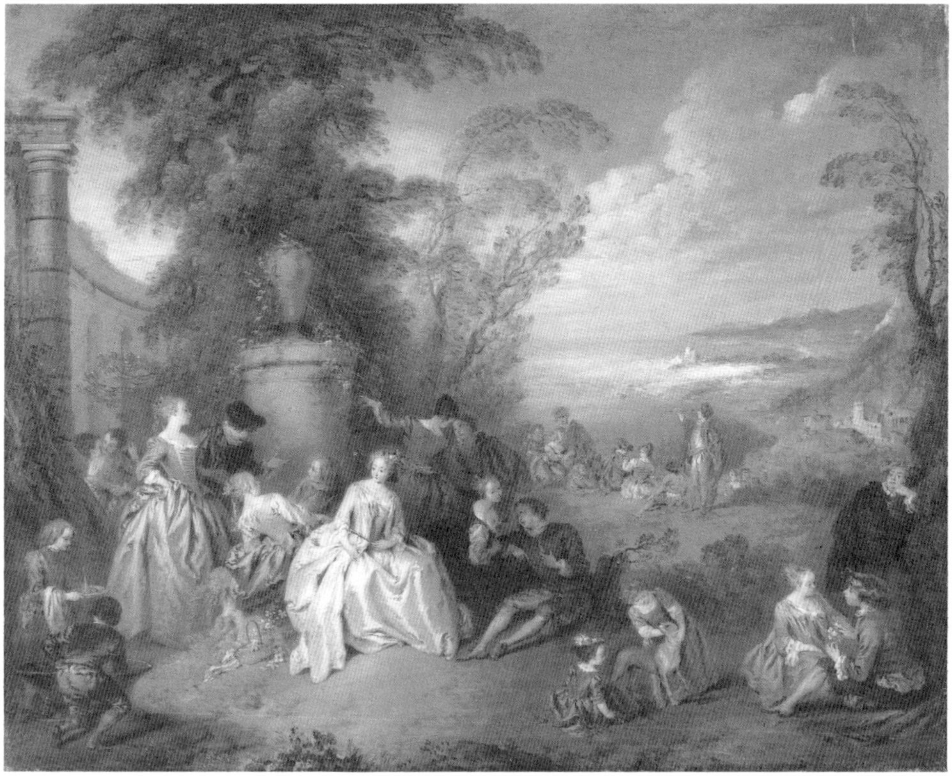

P460

P460 *Fête galante*

The seated lady, centre left, wears a white satin underskirt with a pale lavender gown; behind her, to the left, a standing lady with a yellow skirt and red bodice; on the extreme right stands a man in a red hat and black cape; in the mid-distance a man looks out to sea through a telescope.

Canvas, relined 53 × 64.2

There are some minor losses round the edges. *Pentimenti* show that a figure group in the right mid-distance was erased, and the trees in the centre distance were altered. The varnish is somewhat discoloured.

The men are in costume, the others in contemporary dress.

The detached observer on the extreme right derives from a similar figure in Watteau's *Récréation italienne* (CR129), and the couple in front of him and the children playing with a dog alongside are particularly Watteauesque, cf. P391. Ingersoll-Smouse (IS592), followed by Adhémar,[1] associated P460 with lot 530 in the Gévigney sale, Paris, 1 December 1779: '*Fête champêtre donnée dans un beau jardin . . . dont la plus grande partie des figures a été peinte par Watteau et le reste par Pater . . .*

[48 × 61]', but the extensive landscape and the wholly Pateresque character of the left of the composition might also suggest that P460 is contemporary with P424, and dates from the later 1720s. P460 is perhaps the most ambitious version of a composition which recurs with minor variations in the *Fêtes galantes* at Kenwood (IS39*bis*) and São Paolo (IS38). The girl leaning back and turning her head, centre left, recurs in another *Fête galante* at Kenwood (IS36*bis*); the right-hand foreground couple in a *Fête champêtre* on loan to the Pinakothek, Munich (IS45); the detached observer on the right, reversed, in *La balançoire* at Frankfurt (IS280*bis*), *Amour et badinage* (IS13–15), the *Fête galante* at Buckingham Palace (IS27), and elsewhere.

Versions

See above.

Provenance

See above. Anatole Demidoff (1813–70); his sale, Paris, 1st day, 13 January 1863 (10, *Les loisirs champêtres*), bt. by the 4th Marquess of Hertford, 17,800 fr.;[2] rue Laffitte inventory 1871 (?525, *'les bords de l'étang'*); Hertford House inventory 1890.

Exhibition

Bethnal Green 1872–5 (426, *Seaside View, with Figures*).

Reference General

IS39, 592

[1] H. Adhémar, *Watteau*, 1950, nos. 247 and 256, and p. 128 n. 3.

[2] A label, *verso*: *Tableaux/90*, probably refers to the Demidoff collection. See P452 note 3.

P472 *The Bath (Le plaisir de l'été)*

A voyeur peers through the window on the right; the maid seated on the left holding a slipper wears a blue skirt with a white apron; the maid in the right foreground is in red.

Canvas, relined 45.6 × 35.8

Cleaned in 1879 by Vallance. There are several small losses, most noticeable in the head and shoulder of the maid by the window and round the edges. A *pentimento* shows the bather's left thigh has been thickened. There is a general craquelure and the varnish is somewhat discoloured.

A pendant composition, *Le désir de plaire*, showing the lady at her dressing table surrounded by her maids, was engraved by Surugue in 1743 (IS520); the best version is in the Louvre (IS522).

P472 is a version of the composition engraved by Surugue (see Engraving). The table and its furnishings in the right foreground, the dish on the left and the patterned floor, compare with P405, suggesting that P472 may also date from the 1730s. Bürger thought the composition was by Watteau (see Versions, and notes 2 and 3), a curious aberration.

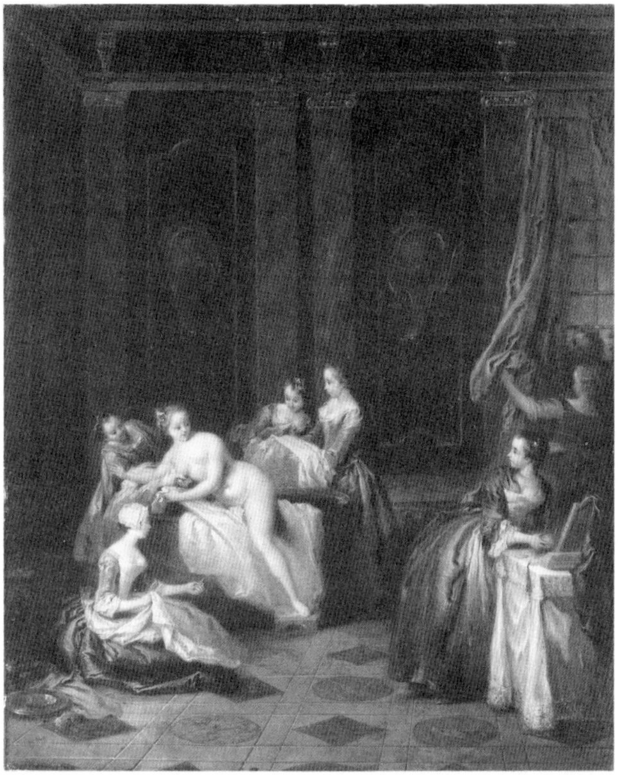

P472

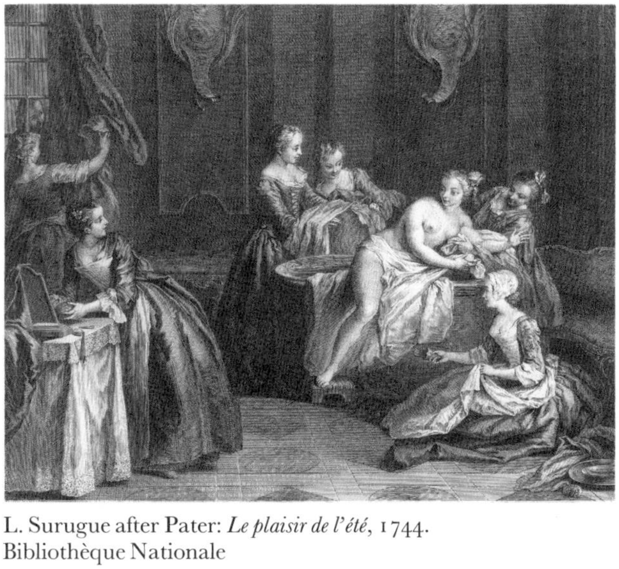

L. Surugue after Pater: *Le plaisir de l'été*, 1744.
Bibliothèque Nationale

Engraving

L. Surugue 1744, reversed (IS306, fig.198), as *Le plaisir de l'été*, in the collection of the abbé de Majinville, showing the composition reduced in height,[1] with verses by C. Moraine:

En sortant de ce bain dont la fraîcheur charmante
De Cupidon a su calmer les feux
Philis nous connaissons qu'au gré de votre atente
Ce petit Dieu s'est sauvé dans vos yeux.

Versions

BRUSSELS formerly with the duc d'Arenberg; 46 × 55, variant in a different setting, showing both the bather's legs; attributed to Watteau by Bürger[2] (IS310).
DETROIT Institute of Fine Arts (no.49.463); 43 × 34 (IS308).
LONDON Marquess H. de V. sale, Christie's, 5 June 1871, lot 215 (IS under 306).
Hamilton sale, Christie's, 6 November 1919 (39); 34 × 44, agreeing with Surugue's engraving (IS306).
Anon. sale, Sotheby's, 21 June 1950 (9); 44 × 36 (IS under 307).
Digby sale, Sotheby's, 20 June 1951 (32); 53 × 66.
Christie's, 28 November 1975 (40); 43 × 34.
PARIS anon. sale, 18 December 1920 (63); copper 28 × 36 (IS under 306).
POTSDAM Sans-Souci; 74 × 60, in a different architectural setting which, from a photograph, seems to have been altered (IS309).

Provenance

F. Laneuville, from whom bt. by the 4th Marquess of Hertford, 13 July 1852, 3,500 fr.; rue Laffitte inventory 1871 (252); Hertford House inventory 1890.

Exhibitions

Boulevard des Italiens 1860 (223) lent Hertford;[3] Bethnal Green 1872–5 (430).

Reference General

IS307.

[1] By the equivalent of 15 cm.

[2] W. Bürger, *Gazette des Beaux-Arts*, 1ère, VII, 1860, pp.276–7, quoting his catalogue, *Galerie d'Arenberg*, 1859, p.178.

[3] When noticed by Bürger, *loc. cit.*, as '*la composition n'appartient pas à Pater, bien que la peinture soit parfaitement de lui*'.

Nicolas Poussin (1594–1665)

Born in 1594 at Les Andelys (Normandy). After receiving his first training in Rouen with Noël Jouvenet, he came to Paris in 1612 where he worked briefly under Ferdinand Elle and Georges Lallemant and discovered antique sculpture, Italian paintings, and engravings after Raphael and Giulio Romano. In 1624, having spent some months in Venice, he arrived in Rome. His Ovidian mythologies and Bacchanals of the late 1620s and early 1630s reflect his admiration of Titian, but he also renewed his study of the antique and Raphael and admired the Carracci and Domenichino. In 1627 he received his first important commission from Cardinal Francesco Barberini (*The Death of Germanicus*, Minneapolis) and, through the same patron, he painted *The Martyrdom of S. Erasmus* for St. Peter's in 1628–9. From c.1630 he became involved with an intellectual circle around Barberini's secretary, Cassiano dal Pozzo, whose learned antiquarianism influenced him profoundly (*The Seven Sacraments*, Belvoir Castle and Washington, 1636–42). In 1640, on the summons of Louis XIII, he returned to Paris where the official commissions he received (for example the ceiling of the Grande Galerie of the Louvre) were unsuited to his temperament. He returned to Rome in 1642 and remained there for the rest of his life, working predominantly for a group of essentially middle-class patrons in France. He died in Rome on 19 November 1665.

Abbreviations

Blunt A. Blunt, *The Paintings of Nicolas Poussin: a critical catalogue*, 1966

FBD W. Friedlaender and A. Blunt, *The Drawings of Poussin: catalogue raisonné*, 1939–74 (5 vols.)

P108 *A Dance to the Music of Time (Il Ballo della Vita Humana)*

Early morning; three women and a man dance in a circle. Centre left, Poverty, a man barefoot in green with a wreath of brown leaves; on the right, Labour, barefoot in a pale brick-red dress and yellow headscarf; in the centre, Riches, in golden sandals and dress with white drapery, a jewelled band on her right arm, her hair decked with pearls; on the left, Pleasure, in white sandals, red dress and blue drapery, a garland of roses in her hair. To the left, a two-headed term hung with garlands of mixed flowers and a *putto* blowing bubbles; on the right, Time playing a lyre, with blue drapery over his right shoulder, and a *putto* holding an hourglass. In the sky, the chariot of Apollo is preceded by Aurora, in yellow and white scattering white and scarlet flowers, and followed by the Hours in yellow, pink and blue with insect wings. There is an illegible or simulated inscription on the band around the body of one of the horses.[1]

Canvas, relined 82.5 × 104[2]

Relined with a double canvas, probably in the early nineteenth century, when the canvas was made up on all sides to a stretcher size of 84.5 × 107.5. Surface cleaned by Vallance in 1946. Cleaned by Lank in 1975. Thumb prints, applied to the priming while still wet, texture the whole surface.[3] An L-shaped tear runs roughly

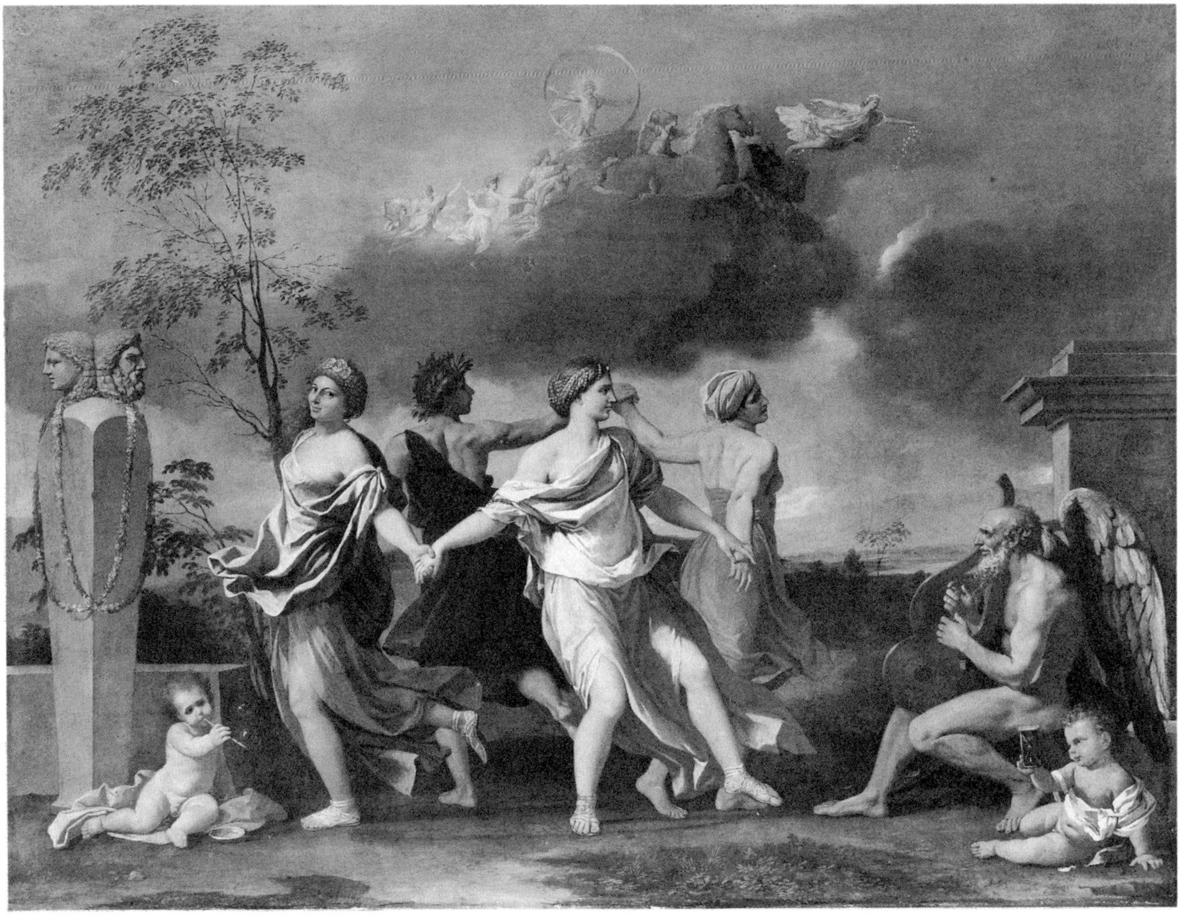

P108

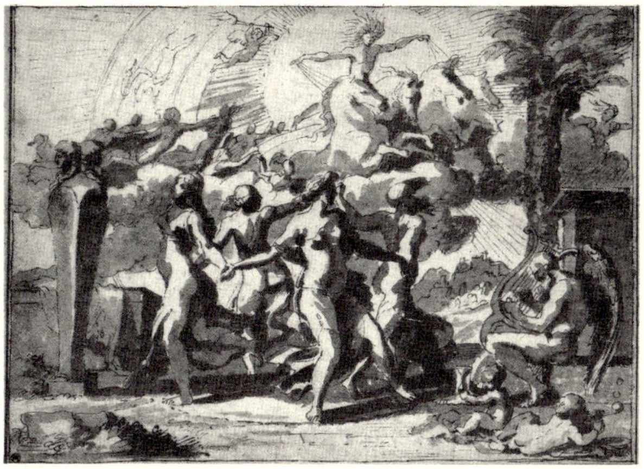

Poussin: Study for P108.
National Gallery of Scotland,
Edinburgh

vertically from the bottom through the left leg of Pleasure to the level of her breast, then horizontally through the shoulders of the other figures and into the sky, descending to the forehead of Time. The tear and parts of the blue and red draperies of Pleasure have been retouched. The surface is slightly abraded, as evident in the tree top left. In the landscape between Labour and Time a second, larger tree has been painted out and there are *pentimenti* in Pleasure's bare shoulder, Labour's left shoulder and the line of her dress below the arm of Riches, in Aurora's left arm and the term, which has been extended to the left. X-radiography reveals that, when the figures were blocked in, the draperies of Pleasure and Labour did not billow outwards and the draperies between Pleasure and Poverty at the level of the thigh were differently arranged.

According to Bellori, the '*morale poesia*' which forms the subject of P108 was dictated by the patron Giulio Rospigliosi (1600–69, later Pope Clement IX),[4] whose interest in allegory is reflected in other subjects he proposed to Poussin,[5] and in his own verse dramas.[6] The dancing group represents the perpetual cycle of the human condition: from Poverty, Labour leads to Riches and thus Pleasure which, indulged to excess, reverts to Poverty. P108 is described in these terms by Bellori[7] and Félibien[8] with one insignificant discrepancy: Bellori identifies the last figure as Luxury rather than Pleasure. Friedlaender suggested the idea was taken from the *Hypnerotomachia Polyphili*, but the correspondence is not close.[9] Bellori and Félibien explain the figures of Poverty, whose wreath of dry leaves signifies lost possessions ('*perduti beni*'), and Labour, whose bare shoulders and work-hardened, sunburned arms suggest hardship and suffering ('*lo stento del corpo e'l patimento*').[10] The attributes may have been drawn selectively and inexactly from Ripa's *Iconologia*: Poverty's wreath recalls the bed of dried branches on which Ripa's *Povertà dei Doni* reclines,[11] Labour's sleeveless dress corresponds to *Fatica Estiva*,[12] and jewels to *Richezza*.[13] If Ripa was the source, the fourth figure is not Luxury, but probably Pleasure, who wears a crown of roses.[14] In the drawing (see below) this figure has a peacock head-dress, which may have been intended to denote *Superbia* or

Prodigality.[15] It seems Poussin was not unduly concerned with the precise indentification of the figures. The dance is accompanied on the lyre by the figure of Saturn or Time. The bubbles and hourglass are symbols for the brevity of life.[16] The two-headed Janus term, with an old head looking back and a young head looking forward, refers to the passage of time. In the sky Apollo holds the ring of the Zodiac, his chariot preceded by the Dawn, Aurora, and accompanied by dancing figures representing eight of the Hours. The main figures are generally described as four women and are certainly shown as such in the drawing (see below) but, as Blunt argues, in the painting Poverty seems certainly male.[17] They were likened by Bellori to the Seasons, and by Félibien to the Seasons and the Ages of Man. By 1713, P108 was described as the *Dance of the Seasons*[18] and this mistaken identification led some eighteenth century commentators to criticise the aptness of Poussin's personifications.[19] The present title was first used in the 1913 edition of this catalogue.

P108 may be dated 1639–40 or perhaps slightly earlier. Friedlaender (1949)[20] gives 1638–40, having previously (1914) suggested 1643–4, Grautoff 1638–40, Mahon 1637–8,[21] Brigstocke possibly 1635–6 (see note 23), and both Blunt and Badt 1639–40. Sterling suggested P108 might be one of the *'trois ou quatre tableaux commensés . . . pour des personnes de considération'* mentioned by Poussin in a letter of 19 February 1639 to Jean Le Maire.[22] The spirited compositional study in the National Gallery of Scotland (dated by Badt c.1638) shows an earlier stage in the evolution of the composition. In the painting a palm tree behind the pedestal on the right has been omitted, the herm is more solid (see above), the *putto* blowing bubbles has been moved to the left, the landscape made more open and Apollo's chariot more distant. The strong shadows and rhythmic line of the drawing create a sense of sunlight and movement which are replaced in the painting by a cool dawn light and more statuesque figures. The composition perhaps derives from the group of Apollo (?) and the dancing Muses in Mantegna's *'Parnassus'* (Louvre),[23] the dancing figures from those in the Roman relief of the *Borghese Dancers* (see S155),[24] and the Apollo in his chariot led by Aurora recalls Reni's *Aurora* (Palazzo Pallavicini-Rospigliosi, Rome). Gombrich has suggested the influence of Giulio Romano's medallion of *Haedus* in the *sala dei Venti* in the Palazzo del Tè, Mantua.[25] In turn, Poussin's composition may have influenced Claude's *Dance of the Seasons* of 1662 (whose subject may also have been proposed by Rospigliosi).[26]

In the eighteenth century P108 was praised with certain reservations. Le François de Lalande described the colour as rather crude and the flesh tones too red.[27] Ramdohr praised the composition and the quality of execution, but found the head of Time meaningless and stupid-looking, the smile of Pleasure like a simpering grin, and the draperies stiff.[28] In 1803 Irvine informed Buchanan that the picture was 'rather dry' and thus 'such as I suspect would not do in England'.[29] But P108 was always admired as a moral conceit, for the beauty of its composition and correctness of drawing; Ramdohr saw in the dancing group 'an expression of Joy . . . which can leave neither the eye nor the spirit unmoved'.[30]

Drawing

EDINBURGH National Gallery of Scotland (D5127); pen and bistre wash, 14.9 × 19.7; exh. *Nicolas Poussin*, Louvre, 1960, no.159 (FBD, II, no.149 and V, p.100).

Engravings

J. Dughet/E. Baudet 1667–9, reversed;[31] M. Burghers 1694 (for the *Oxford Almanack*), reversed; B. Picart, reversed;[32] R. Morghen 1778–90;[33] T.-E. Lingée, reversed; A. Massard (for P. M. Gault de Saint Germain, *Vie de Nicolas Poussin*, 1806).

Copies

AMSTERDAM Cassirer 1948.
ARLES Musée Réattu (no. 868.1.152); 83 × 105, reversed.
LONDON private collection 1987; c. 83 × 104; ex coll. J. G. Frazer.
K. Preedy 1966; 74 × 101, the trees on the left fuller (illus. *Apollo*, LV, 1952, p.31).
Private collection, 1973; ex Christie's, 23 March 1934 (87), 83.5 × 103.7, as from the Palazzo Rospigliosi; possibly the copy of P108 recorded at the Rospigliosi Palace in 1713.[34]
T. G. Taylor sale, Christie's, 5 July 1935 (44); 78.4 × 103.7; ex coll. Carr.
Hampden sale, Christie's, 25 November 1938 (50); 98.7 × 124.
Sotheby's, 29 July 1964 (152); 96 × 132.
Sotheby's, 4 July 1984 (88); 77 × 109; ex Sotheby's, 22 February 1984 (36), ex coll. Earl of Darnley.
Sotheby's, 24 October 1984 (25); 78.5 × 103; probably ex Sotheby's, 30 November 1983 (247), and 24 February 1965 (42).
MILL VALLEY California, private collection 1967.
PARIS R. H. Ward 1938; the figure of Time alone.
Gallimard 1966 (illus. *Les Arts*, September 1908, p.5).
Drouot, 24 November 1975 (14); 79 × 107.
VENICE Manfrin 1856; 82 × 108.[35]

Copies recorded in early sales are, at Christie's: anon. sale, 2nd day, 27 May 1780 (101); R. Cosway sale, 2nd day, 3 March 1792 (71); anon. sale, 16 January 1800 (70); Otway sale, 3 May 1800 (39); anon. sale, 2 April 1801 (36), and in Paris: Coclers sale, 9 February 1789 (169), as an *ésquisse arrêté*, 43.5 × 54.4, ex Montullé sale, 22 December 1783 (38) and Godefroy sale, 25 April 1785 (40).

A copy in collage is at Stourhead. A copy on a Vienna porcelain plaque was in a private collection, Harpenden, 1969.

Exhibitions

Manchester, *Art Treasures*, 1857 (saloon H, no.35, *The Seasons dancing to the Music of Time*);[36] Bethnal Green 1872–5 (386, *Dance of the Seasons*).

Provenance

Painted for Giulio Rospigliosi (see above) and presumably hung in his Roman palace, the Palazzo Ludovisi in the Corso; thence to his nephew Giovanni Battista Rospigliosi and recorded in his inventory of 1713 in the Palazzo (Pallavicini-) Rospigliosi;[37] acquired by Cardinal Fesch (1763–1839) from the Rospigliosi Palace, 1806,[38] and taken to France;[39] Fesch sale, Rome, 17 March–15 May 1845 (397, '*La Danse des Saisons, ou l'Image de la vie humaine*'),[40] bt. by the 4th Marquess of Hertford, 5,970 *scudi* (29,850 fr.); Hertford House inventory 1870 ('*The 4 Seasons, dancing*').

References General

W. Friedlaender, *Nicolas Poussin, die Entwicklung seiner Kunst*, 1914, pp.80, 126; O. Grautoff, *Nicolas Poussin, sein werk und sein Leben*, 1914, I, pp.145–7, pp.120–1, no.73; E. Magne, *Nicolas Poussin*, 1914, pp.192, 215, no.278; Blunt, pp.81–2, no.121; K. Badt, *Die Kunst des Nicolas Poussin*, 1969, I, pp.201–2, 543–5; J. Thuillier, *L'Opera completa di Poussin*, 1974, no.123; A. Blunt, 'Poussin's "Dance to the Music of Time" Revealed', *The Burlington Magazine*, CXVIII, 1976, pp.844–8; D. Wild, *Nicolas Poussin*, 1980, II, p.90, no.95.

1 Possibly *P.N.* Grautoff records an illegible signature but, unless this is it, it cannot be found.

2 The stretcher bears, *verso*, the Roman customs stamp: RCA/DOG. DI/ROMA (in a circle) and the inscription: *No. 116. du C*, probably referring to a Fesch catalogue (see D. Thiébaut, *Ajaccio, musée Fesch, Les primitifs italiens*, 1987, p.26).

3 G. T. C. Lambourne of Scotland Yard established that the prints were made by a single, probably left, thumb (see Blunt, *op. cit.*, 1976, p.847).

4 On Rospigliosi, see F. Haskell, *Patrons and Painters*, 1980 ed., pp.57–8, and L. Freiherr von Pastor (tr. Ernest Graf), *The History of the Popes*, XXXI, 1957, pp.314ff.

5 *Time revealing Truth* (lost; Blunt, no.123), and *Et in Arcadia Ego* (Louvre; Blunt, no.120). The former, painted for Rospigliosi at about the same date as P108, has similar proportions and was possibly intended as a pendant.

6 These included '*La vita umana ovvero il trionfo della pietà*' performed in 1656 (*Dizionario Biografico degli Italiani*, 26, 1982, p.292, and see A. Blunt, *Nicolas Poussin*, 1958, pp.153–4).

[7] G. P. Bellori, *Le Vite de' Pittori Scultori et Architetti Moderni*, 1672, pp.447–8:

IL BALLO DELLA VITA HUMANA

Oltre le fauole esposte riferiremo alcuni concetti morali espressi in pittura, trà li quali bellissima è l'inuentione della vita humana nel ballo di quattro donne simile alle quattro stagioni. Figurò il Tempo à sedere con la lira, al cui suono quattro donne, la Pouertà, la Fatica, la Richezza, e'l Lusso scambieuolmente si danno le mani in giro, e danzano perpetuamente, variando la sorte de gli huomini. Ciascuna di loro esprime la sua propria forma: stanno auanti il Lusso, e la Richezza, questa coronata di perle, e d'oro, quella inghirlandata di rose e di fiori, pomposamente adorne. Dietro volgesi la Pouertà in habito mesto, cinta il capo di secche frondi, in contrasegno de' perduti beni. Viene ella accompagnata dalla Fatica, la quale scopre le spalle ignude, con le braccia indurate, e brune, e riguardando la sua compagna, mostra lo stento del corpo e'l patimento. A piedi il Tempo vedesi vn fanciullo, il quale tiene in mano, e contempla vn oriuolo a poluere numerando i momenti della vita. Dal contrario lato il compagno, come sogliono i fanciulli per giuoco, spira da un cannellino col fiato, globi di spuma, e d'aria, che si struggono in vn momento, in contrasegno della vanità, e brevità della vita medesima. Euui la statua di Giano in forma di Termine, e scorre in aria il Sole nel carro con le braccia aperte entro la fascia del Zodiaco, ad imitatione di Raffaelle, precedendo l'Alba, che sparge candidi fiori sù'l mattino, e dietro seguitano danzando le Hore à volo. Il soggetto di questa morale poesia fù dato al Pittore da Papa Clemente IX. in tempo che egli era Prelato. Preualse Nicolò nel concetto di si nobile, e peregrina inuentione, & ancorche le figure siano appena due palmi, potè corrispondere in esse felicamente alla sublimità dell'Autore, che aggiunse le due seguenti inventioni [*Time revealed by Truth* and *Et in Arcadia Ego*].

[8] A. Félibien, *Entretiens sur les vies et sur les ouvrages des plus excellens peintres*, 1685, ed. 1725, IV, pp.86–7. The description is clearly based on Bellori, but there are some differences (in Roman type below): '. . . *une Image de la vie humaine, representée par un bal de quatre femmes qui ont quelque rapport aux quatre saisons*, ou aux quatre âges de l'homme. *Le Tems sous la figure d'un vielliard, est assis, & jouë de la lire, au son de laquelle ces femmes, qui sont la Pauvreté, le Travail, la Richesse &* le Plaisir, *dansent en rond, &* semblent se donner les mains alternativement l'une à l'autre, *& marquer par là le changement continuel qui arrive dans la vie & dans la fortune des hommes. L'on connoit facilement ce que ce*[sic] *femmes representent. La Richesse & le Plaisir paroissent les premiers, l'une couronnée d'or & de perles, & l'autre parée de fleurs, & ayant une guirlande de rose sur la tête. Après eux est la Pauvreté vêtuë d'un miserable habit tout delabré, & la tête environnée de rameaux dont les feüilles sont seches, comme le simbole de la perte des biens. Elle est suivie du Travail qui a les épaules découvertes*, les bras décharnez & sans couleur. Cette femme regarde la Pauvreté, & semble lui montrer qu'elle a le corps las, & tout abbatu de misere. Proche le Tems & à ses pieds sont deux jeunes Enfants. *L'un tient une horloge de sable; & comme il l'a considere avec attention, il semble compter tous les momens de la vie qui s'écoulent. L'autre, en se joüant, soufle au travers d'un roseau, d'où sortent des boules d'eau & d'air qui se dissipent aussi tôt; ce qui marque la vanité & la briéveté de la vie. Dans le même Tableau est un Terme qui represente Janus. Le Soleil assis dans son char, paroit dans le ciel au milieu du Zodiaque. L'Aurore marche devant le char du Soleil, & répand des fleurs sur la terre: les Heures qui la suivent, semblent danser en volant*'.

[9] Friedlaender, p.80, and F. Colonna, *Hypnerotomachia Poliphili*, ed. G. Pozzi and L. A. Ciapponi, 1980, I, pp.25–6 (a circular dance of seven men and seven women each with two faces, one laughing, one crying). On this subject and for the literary tradition of the cycle of human life, see E. Panofsky, 'Et in Arcadia Ego'. *Philosophy and History. Essays presented to Ernest Cassirer*, 1936, pp.241–2.

[10] Félibien's description of Labour's arms ('*décharnez & sans couleur*') either contradicts or mistranslates Bellori ('*indurate, e brune*').

[11] C. Ripa, *Iconologia*, 1603, p.409, with three descriptions of simple *Povertà* none of which correspond to the figure in P108. Blunt (*op. cit.*, p.847 n.4) suggests that the use of a wreath apparently of laurel may be 'an allusion to the poverty which is often the lot of the poet or artist'.

[12] *Ibid.*, pp.145–6 (a robust young woman in a thin dress with her skirts tucked up and arms bare, in her right hand a scythe and in her left a flail, accompanied by a bull).

[13] *Ibid.*, p.434 (a woman in regal jewelled costume, in her right hand an imperial crown, in her left a sceptre or gold vase).

[14] *Ibid.*, pp.398–9 (a handsome youth of about sixteen in green, with a garland of roses in his hair, holding a line of hooks and a bunch of flowers; and two other similar descriptions).

[15] *Ibid.*, p.479 and J.-P. Valeriano, *Hiéroglyphiques*, 1615 ed., p.297. *Lusso* (with a peacock) is included only in the later editions of Ripa. Panofsky, *op. cit.*, p.241 n.2, associated this figure in the painting with Ripa's *Superbia*, but, as Blunt points out (*op. cit.*, 1976, p.847), there is really no correspondence.

[16] See note 7 above and, for the blowing of bubbles, Panofsky, *op. cit.*, p.241 n.1.

[17] Blunt, *op. cit.*, 1976, p.848 n.14.

[18] '*Un Quadro in tela di p.4 . . . rappresenta le 4 stagioni che ballano al suono del Tempo, opera di Nicolò Pusino*' (inventory of Giovanni Battista Rospigliosi, 26 June 1713, Federico Zeri, *La Galleria Pallavicini in Roma, Catalogo dei dipinti*, 1959, p.319, no.512).

[19] J.-J. Le François de Lalande, *Voyage d'un François en Italie, fait dans les années 1765 & 1766*, 1769, III, pp.451–2; J. J. Volkmann, *Historische-Kritische Nachrichten von Italien . . .*, Leipzig, 1770–1, II, pp.217–18.

[20] FBD, II, 1949, p.24, no.149.

[21] D. Mahon, 'Poussiniana. Afterthoughts arising from the exhibition', *Gazette des Beaux-Arts*, 6e, LX, 1962, pp.105–6.

[22] C. Sterling in *Nicolas Poussin*, exh. cat., Louvre, 1960, pp.235–6, and *Correspondance de Nicolas Poussin*, ed. Jouanny, AAF, V, 1911, p.13.

[23] Poussin had recently completed a series of Bacchanals which were to form part of the same scheme in the Château de Richelieu as the Mantegna and other works from the *studiolo* of Isabella d'Este (see Blunt, nos.136–8). Brigstocke (*Apollo*, CXVI, 1982, p.14 n.6) has suggested P108 possibly dates 'from as early as 1635–6, contemporary with or just after the Richelieu *Triumph of Pan*'.

[24] See F. Haskell and N. Penny, *Taste and the Antique*, 1981, pp.195–6, no.29, recording Poussin's admiration for the relief.

[25] E. Gombrich, 'The Sala dei Venti in the Palazzo del Tè', *Journal of the Warburg and Courtauld Institutes*, XIII, 1950, p.190 n.2.

[26] M. Röthlisberger, 'Claude Lorraine's "Dance of the Seasons"', *Pantheon*, XLV, 1987, pp.103–6. A related drawing probably belonged to Rospigliosi and remains in the Pallavicini (ex-Rospigliosi) collection.

[27] Le François de Lalande, *loc. cit.*

[28] F. W. B. von Ramdohr, *Ueber Mahlerei und Bildhauerarbeit in Rom für Liebhaber des Schönen in der Kunst*, 1787, III, p.62.

29 Letter of 20 September 1803, referring to 'The two Rospigliosi [Poussins] . . . engraved by Morghen' (W. Buchanan, *Memoirs of Painting*, 1824, II, p.145).

30 Ramdohr, *loc. cit.*

31 Dedicated to Rospigliosi as Pope; A. Andresen, *Nicolas Poussin, Verzeichnis der nach seinen Gemälden gefertigen Kupferstiche*, 1863, no.401 (Wildenstein, *Gazette des Beaux-Arts*, 6e, XLVI, 1955, p.292, no.161). According to Florent Le Comte, the print was by E. Baudet (*Cabinet des Singularitéz d'Architecture, Peinture, Sculpture et Graveure*, 1699, II, p.415).

32 Andresen, *op. cit.*, no.402a.

33 Made during Morghen's stay in Rome 1778–90; Andresen, *op. cit.*, no.400 (Wildenstein, *Gazette des Beaux-Arts*, 6e, LX, 1962, p.187).

34 Zeri, *op. cit.*, see note 18, p.320, no.522 ('*in tela di p.4 . . . e copia del Ballo del Pusino*').

35 Blunt (no.121, under copies nos. 2 and 11) associated this with a copy recorded by Burckhardt in the Accademia, but there is no copy there now (I am grateful to Giovanna Nepi Scire for this information).

36 Where described by C. Blanc, *Les Trésors de l'Art à Manchester*, 1857 ('*grave et touchante allégorie du Poussin: quatre femmes, caractérisant les diverses conditions de l'humanité, dansent au son de la lyre du Temps . . .*').

37 See note 18 above.

38 Suvée to Fesch, 31 December 1806, '*. . . Je vous fait bien mon compliment, Monseigneur, sur votre dernière acquisition des trois Poussin, surtout de celui du Repos en Egypte et de la Danse . . .*' (*Correspondance des Directeurs de l'Académie de France à Rome, nouvelle série*, II, *Directorat de Suvée, 1795–1807*, II, 1984, p.902; reference kindly supplied by F. Haskell), and see Blunt.

39 Asterisked in the Fesch sale catalogue, indicating a picture taken out of France (i.e. acquired before 1815, see note 2 above, and cf. Greuze P441 note 18 and P442 note 14). P108 was seen in Fesch's collection by Thomas Moore on 11 November 1819 (*Memoirs, Journal and Correspondence of Thomas Moore*, ed. Russell, II, 1853, p.69).

40 P108 had appeared as no.1056 ('*La danse des heures*') in the 1841 Fesch catalogue.

Pierre-Paul Prud'hon (1758–1823)

Born Pierre Prudon[1] on 4 April 1758 in Cluny, the son of a stone carver. He studied in Dijon 1774–8 and, after a period in Paris 1780–3, returned to win the Dijon *prix de Rome* in 1784. In Italy 1785–7/8 he produced little (save a large panel based on Cortona's Barberini ceiling, now at Dijon), but came to admire Leonardo da Vinci and Correggio.[2] He returned to Paris and produced vignettes, book illustrations and small anecdotal paintings. After a period at Rigny (Franche-Comté) his career blossomed under Napoleon. He made a series of decorative panels for Lanois, *fournisseur des armées*, 1796–9, and through the agency of his compatriot Frochot, *préfet de la Seine*, obtained a number of important commissions including two ceilings for the Louvre, 1801–3, state portraits and designs for state occasions (such as the Sacre in 1805, the celebration of Tilsit in 1807 and the arrival of Marie-Louise in 1810). He was made *chevalier* of the Legion of Honour in 1808 and in 1810 became drawing master to the Empress Marie-Louise. He exhibited at the Salon 1791–1824 (the last occasion posthumously), his best-known compositions being shown 1808–15. After the Restoration he was elected to the Institut in 1816 and commissioned to paint an altarpiece for the Tuileries (cf. P273), but his work had lost its impetus. In 1821 he was much affected by the suicide of his companion and pupil Constance Mayer (q.v.) and he died, in some misery, in Paris on 16 February 1823. A reflective artist, he had sought '*un ton doux et tranquille, mais vigoureux,* qui plaise au spectateur *sans l'éblouir et laisse l'âme jouir de tout ce qui l'affecte*';[3] for David he remained '*le Boucher, le Watteau de notre temps*'.[4]

1 After his marriage in 1778 he assumed the additional name of Paul and after 1780 he introduced the apostrophe in Prud'hon (cf. Clément, p.32).

2 Between 1808 and 1815 he painted in the missing head of Correggio's *Jupiter and Io* (Vienna) which had been cut out by Louis, duc d'Orléans, in the mid-eighteenth century (cf. Clément, p.412; Guiffrey, no.121).

3 Prud'hon to Desvoges, Rome, 1787 (Clément, pp.179–80).

4 Quoted by Clément, p.334.

Abbreviations

Blanc 1844	Ch. Blanc, 'Prud'hon', *Le Cabinet de l'Amateur*, III, 1844, pp.457–80 (with catalogue of prints, pp.486–509, and paintings, pp.510–19; reissued in Blanc 1865, 'Prud'hon')
Clément	Ch. Clément, *Prud'hon, sa vie, ses oeuvres et sa correspondance*, 1872 (first published in the *Gazette des Beaux-Arts*, 1869–70)
Goncourt	E. de Goncourt, *Catalogue raisonné de l'oeuvre peint, dessiné et gravé de P.-P. Prud'hon*, 1876
Guiffrey	J. Guiffrey, 'L'oeuvre de Pierre-Paul Prud'hon', AAF, XIII, 1924

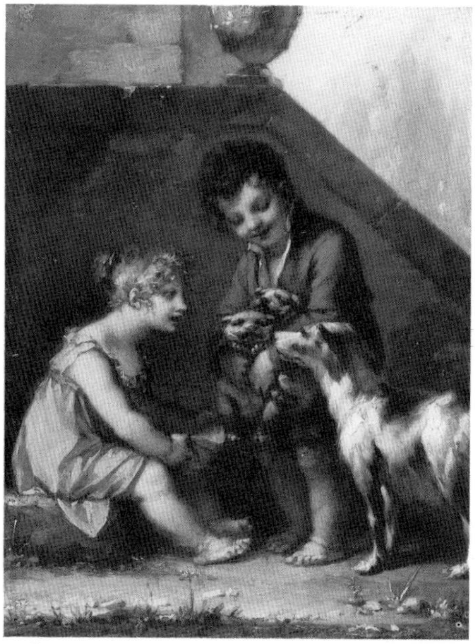

P264

P264 *Puppies (Oh! les jolis petits chiens)*

The little girl has a yellow dress, the boy a brown coat.

Fruitwood panel 21.8 × 16.1 × 0.9 painted area 21.5 × 16.1

Areas of wrinkled paint on the left suggest the panel was once subject to heat. There is a *pentimento* round the girl's right leg. The varnish is discoloured.

P264 probably dates from the later 1790s; comparable children and animals appear in the designs for the *Seasons* at the Hôtel de Lanois exhibited at the Salon in 1799.[1] A pendant, *Mange, mon petit, mange*, shows the children feeding a pet rabbit.[2]

Engravings

B.-J.-F. Roger;[3] J. Prud'hon (Prud'hon *fils*, 1778–1837); A. Colette, lithograph, in reverse.

Drawings

Guiffrey, no.753, records a compositional study in the B. sale, Paris, 4 April 1870 (44). Goncourt listed a dubious drawing coll. Clément c.1858. A related drawing by Mayer was with Bellanger c.1870.[4] It is possible that all these references describe the same drawing.

Versions

Guiffrey, no.752, lists a larger version, 65 × 54, in the A. sale, Paris, 29 January 1908 (44); for the pendant see note 2 below.

See also notes 3 and 5 below.

Provenance[5]

G. Constantin (d.1816);[6] Amédée Constantin (d.1836), from whom bt. for 3,000 fr., by Laperlier;[7] his sale, Paris, 1st day, 11 April 1867 (42, '. . . *gravé par Prud'hon fils*'), bt. by the 4th Marquess of Hertford, 6,300 fr.; rue Laffitte inventory 1871 (104); Hertford House inventory 1890.

Exhibitions

Boulevard des Italiens 1860 (412) lent Laperlier; Bethnal Green 1872–5 (553).

References General

Blanc 1844, p.517, no.33; Goncourt, under no.51; Guiffrey, no.751.

1 Cf. Guiffrey, nos. 848–51; the drawings are now in the Musée Condé, Chantilly.

2 A small version, 24 × 21, is in the Hermitage (no.5667), and a larger, 65 × 55, the pendant to the larger version of P264 described above, was in the Demidoff sale, 3 February 1868, lot 32 (Guiffrey, no.754). A drawing for the composition was in the Bryas sale, Paris, 5–6 April 1898, lot 142 (Guiffrey, no.755).

3 According to Blanc 1844, p.517, the subject of Roger's engraving was in the collection of M. Fischer, but Goncourt and Guiffrey assume it was P264.

4 Cf. Ch. Gueullette, *Gazette des Beaux-Arts*, 2e, XX, 1879, p.531.

5 P264 has previously been associated with the Thévenin sale, Paris, 27 January 1851 (59, '*Petits enfants jouant avec des chiens*'); according to Guiffrey (no.751) this was bt. Constantin, 2,000 fr., but the marked copy of the catalogue in the Wallace Collection library has the buyer's name as Fiché. Was this, perhaps, the picture from the Fischer collection, see note 3 above?

6 *G. Constantin* is inscribed on the stretcher of P264; Guillaume Constantin (d.1816) was Prud'hon's '*marchand attitré*' during the Revolution (cf. G. Hubert, *La Revue du Louvre*, 1980, p.257) and *garde des tableaux* at Malmaison from 1807. There is also an illegible seal on the stretcher.

7 According to Goncourt ('*M. Laperlier avait payé ce tableau 3,000 francs à Constantin fils*').

P272 *The Assumption of the Virgin*

A cluster of stars above her head, dressed in white with blue drapery; the left-hand angel in green with red drapery, the right-hand in deep red with umber drapery; a blue drapery above the little angels.

Canvas[1] 32.3 × 24.2 painted area 31.3 × 21

The unpainted canvas edges are hatched in pencil. There is a prominent general craquelure which particularly disfigures the sky and the umber drapery of the right-hand angel. *Pentimenti* show alterations to the lower central area where there appear to be a number of unrelated feet projecting from the drapery; the left leg of the second little angel from the right and the left arm of the right-hand angel were also altered. The varnish is discoloured. Squaring-up pencil lines are faintly visible in places.

The assumption of the Virgin has no Biblical source, but was described in the Golden Legend[2] (cf. P105 attributed to Gutiérrez; Meneses P7).

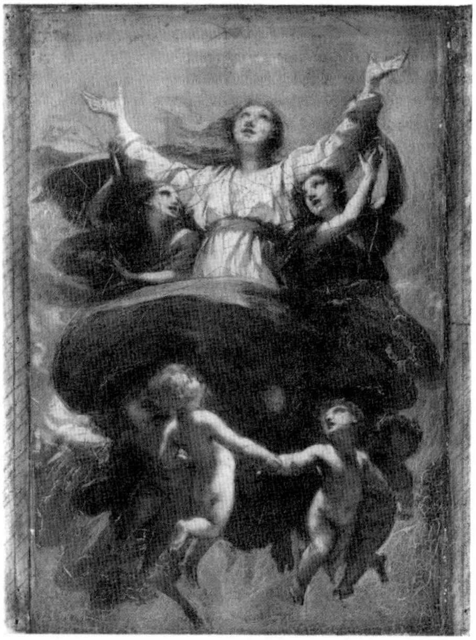

P272

An *Assumption of the Virgin* for the Tuileries chapel was commissioned from Prud'hon in 1816. He had completed an oil sketch by 17 August 1816,[3] probably P272, and the finished picture was shown at the Salon in 1819. According to drawings recorded by Guiffrey,[4] the composition underwent several changes: the Virgin was once on the left with her arms extended to Christ on the right (nos.318–19, 321); the composition seen in P272 previously showed the Virgin's arms crossed at her breast (nos.320, 322, 324); P272 and three other oil sketches (see Versions) show the little angels, resembling *amorini*, which were rejected by the Grande Aumônerie.[5] The final composition shows the Virgin supported by five archangels.

Versions

CHERBOURG Musée Henry (no.140); 32 × 24, sketch similar to P272 but with the right-hand archangel looking more to the centre (Guiffrey, no.317).

PARIS Louvre (no.7339); 216 × 149; see above, removed from the Tuileries in 1848 (Guiffrey, no.313).

Two further oil sketches are recorded, similar to P272: 21.5 × 14.5, ex coll. Marcille (illus. Clément, f.p. 406; Guiffrey, no.314), and 26 × 16, ex Feral sale, Paris, 22–4 April 1901, lot 60 (Guiffrey, no.316).[6]

Provenance

Prud'hon sale, Paris, 13 May 1823 (11), 1,500 fr.; Paul Périer (1809–49); his sale, Paris, 16–17 March 1843 (33), bt. by the 4th Marquess of Hertford, 12,000 fr.; rue Laffitte inventory 1871 (683); Hertford House inventory 1890.

Exhibition

Bethnal Green 1872–5 (341).

References General

Blanc 1844, p.475 n.1, p.512, no.4; Clément, pp.405–6; Goncourt, no.33; Guiffrey, no.315.

[1] Stamped, *verso*: BELOT/*rue de l'Arbre Sec/No.3*, and inscribed *Ca*[rdr?]*ier*. In 1890 P272 was in an elaborate frame, bearing the Seymour-Conway arms, which was subsequently used for the mirror F476.

[2] Cf. Jacobus de Voragine, *The Golden Legend*, trans. Caxton, 1900 ed., IV, pp.234–70.

[3] When Prud'hon wrote to Forbin, *directeur des musées*, saying that '*l'esquisse du tableau de l'*Assomption de la Vierge *pour la chapelle du roi est terminée*' (Clément, p.406).

[4] Nos. 318–33, of which no.318 is in the Metropolitan Museum of Art (no.37.165.105) and no.326, showing two angels supporting the Virgin, is in the Louvre (no.1283).

[5] Cf. Goncourt, p.90, and Guiffrey, no.314.

[6] Guiffrey lists a further five compositional sketches, attributed to Prud'hon, under no.317: Beurnonville sale, Paris, 30–1 January 1885, lot 181; coll. Tardieu 1826 (engr. Debucourt); coll. J. Gréau 1864; d'Espagnac sale, Paris, 2 May 1873, lot 188, and coll. W. Ritter 1923.

P295 *The Zephyr*
(Jeune zéphire se balançant au-dessus de l'eau)

Fair-haired, with wings and a dull blue drapery; a waterfall to the left.

Paper 20 × 15.5 on canvas[1] 21.4 × 16

The oil sketch on paper appears to have been stuck over an oil sketch on canvas; the zephyr's foot from the latter projects beyond the bottom edge of the paper, and the trees above the top left edge. Traces of reticulated bitumen show above his right thigh and along the bottom edge. The varnish is discoloured.

The subject is said to have occurred to Prud'hon on seeing the young son of one of his sitters, M. Lezay-Marnesia, playing on ropes hanging from the studio ceiling.[2] According to Landon, Zephyr, the west wind, son of Aeolus and Astraea, was often described in Greek mythology as a gentle youth with butterfly wings.[3]

P295 is one of a series of oil sketches for the larger painting shown at the Salon in 1814 (see Versions). Guiffrey also records four related drawings, one of which shows the leg positions reversed.[4] P295 was described by Mantz in 1847 as '*la perle des salons de M. d'Espagnac*',[5] and the composition was generally praised.[6]

Lithograph

P.-L. Grévedon ('*tiré du cabinet de M. le baron de Jassaud*').[7]

Versions

DES MOINES Iowa, Salisbury House Museum; 24 × 17.5, reversed, attributed to Diaz c.1848.[8]
MULHOUSE private collection 1962; 64 × 48; inscribed, *verso*: *A Mr de Joursanvault*.[9]
PARIS Louvre (RF2695); 130 × 98, see above; engr. Laugier; ex colls. Sommariva, Guénin, Valpinçon, Pereire and Mir (Guiffrey, no.207).
(RF2158); 128 × 97.5, grisaille sketch, without wings or drapery; engr. Lagrange 1863; ex colls. Constantin, Morny, Boisgelin, Bondy, Schlichting (Guiffrey, no.208).[10]

Three further versions are recorded:
S.-J. Rochard sale, Brussels, 13 December 1858 (44, '*suivant les renseignements transmis par le propriétaire, M. de Forbin ayant désiré posséder la première esquisse du tableau . . . Prudhon lui demanda trois jours avant de la lui livrer; il fit alors pour lui-même celle dont il s'agit ici, qui diffère par la grandeur et qui est faite sur panneau; la première, actuellement dans la galerie de M. le marquis d'Hertford, est sur papier*').
32 × 24, reversed (Margueritte sale, Paris, 2 April 1914, lot 61; Guiffrey, no.210).
80 × 64 (d'Espagnac sales, 1–3 March 1866, lot 255, and 2 May 1873, lot 186; Guiffrey, no.211).
A miniature version was in the collection of J. Murray Scott 1903.

Provenance

Given by the artist to the comte de Forbin (1779–1841), *directeur des musées*, 1818;[11] the baron de Jassaud;[12] the marquis Maison (1798–1869);[13] the comte d'Espagnac (1788–1873)[14] by 1844; his sale, Paris, 4 May 1847 (230, '. . . *cette réduction du grand tableau fut faite pour le comte de Forbin*');[15] général baron Servatius sale, Paris, 15 February 1854 (8), bt. in, 6,000 fr.; Faccioli sale, Paris, 5 March 1857 (70), 2,055 fr.; the 4th Marquess of Hertford by 1858;[16] rue Laffitte inventory 1871 (214); Hertford House inventory 1890.

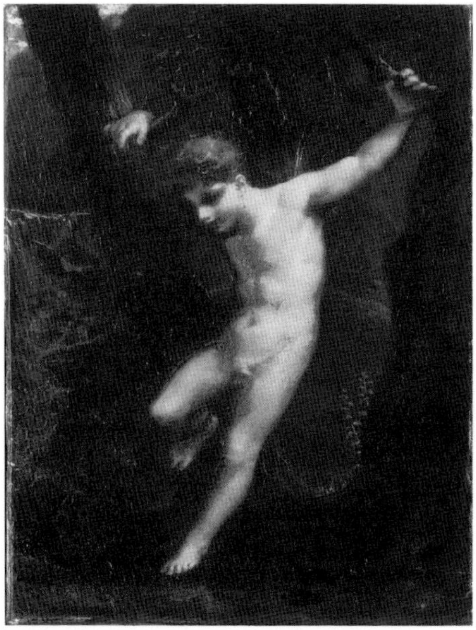

P295

Exhibitions[17]

Bethnal Green 1872–5 (563, *The Young Bather*); RA 1896 (85).

References General

Blanc 1844, p.516, no.23; Clément, pp.394–5; Goncourt, under no.44; Guiffrey, no.209.

[1] Stamped, *verso*: BELOT/*Rue de l'Arbre Sec.*

[2] Ph. Burty, *Gazette des Beaux-Arts*, 1ère, XVII, 1864, p.167, said that the boy posed for the picture, but Guiffrey (under nos.207, 560 and 562) suggests that Etienne Lezay-Marnesia, who was only five in 1814, was too young to have been the model.

[3] C.-P. Landon, *Annales du Musée, Salon de 1814*, note to pl.35.

[4] Chantilly, Musée Condé (Guiffrey, no.212). Other drawings are at Dijon, Musée des Beaux-Arts (Guiffrey, no.214); Power sale, Paris, 15–16 April 1864, lot 55 (Guiffrey, no.213), and a study for the head was in the Fleury Hébrard sale, Paris, 13 May 1861, lot 504*bis* (Guiffrey, no.215). A reversed compositional study, attributed to Prud'hon, was with H. Reitlinger, London.

[5] P. Mantz, *L'Artiste*, IX, 1847, p.100.

[6] Cf. W. Bürger, *Gazette des Beaux-Arts*, 1ère, VII, 1860, pp.353–4: '*une des oeuvres les plus populaires de Prud'hon, mais il s'en faut qu'elle soit des meilleures, – à notre avis. Drôle d'idée, pour un poëte, d'avoir fait du Zéphire un gros garçon, réel et charnu. Pourvu que la branche n'aille point casser sous son poids, et que ce Zéphire ne tombe pas lourdement dans le petit ruisseau!*' His comments were prompted by the sight of the full-scale grisaille, now in the Louvre, which had been lent by the duc de Morny to the boulevard des Italiens exhibition in 1860.

[7] Cf. Blanc 1844, p.491; he seems to identify the original as P295, see note 12 below.

[8] I am grateful to Marsha Tompkin for telling me of this picture (letter on file dated 2 November 1983).

[9] De Joursanvault (d.1792) had been Prud'hon's early patron; this inscription must refer to his only son.

[10] Exh. *French Painting 1774–1830*, Paris, Detroit, New York, 1975, no.143.

[11] Prud'hon wrote to Forbin, Paris, 5 August 1818, referring to the '*modeste don que vous avez bien voulu recevoir de moi (l'esquisse du* Zéphyre*)*' (Clément, p.395). According to *L'Artiste*, IX, 1847, p.100, Forbin sold P295 '*à la mort du peintre*', i.e. in 1823.

[12] Blanc 1844, p.516, said P295 had belonged to Forbin, Jassaud and Maison before entering the d'Espagnac collection, and he identified the lithograph by Grévedon (p.491) as after a picture in Jassaud's collection.

[13] *Ibid.*

[14] The cousin of the sitter in Vigée Le Brun's portrait P449.

[15] The copy of this sale catalogue in the Victoria and Albert Museum is annotated; '*tous les tableaux (sauf un, dit-on) ont été retirés par le propriétaire*'.

[16] P295 is recorded in Lord Hertford's possession in the Rochard sale catalogue, 13 December 1858, see Versions above.

[17] P295 was not exhibited at the bazar Bonne-Nouvelle in 1848, as stated by Guiffrey.

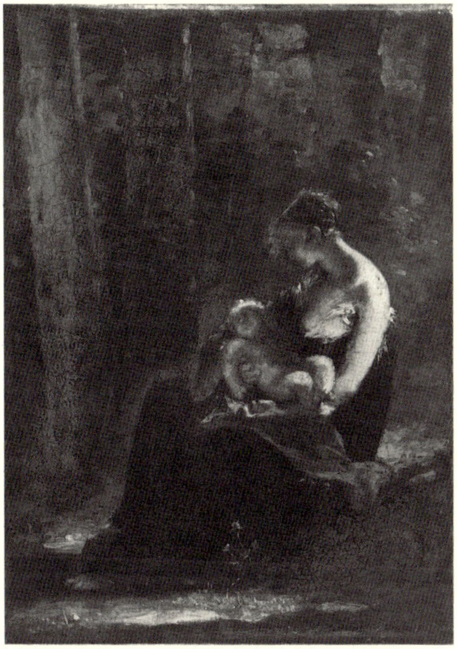

P313

P313 *The Happy Mother*

The mother has fair hair with a blue band; the baby lies on a red cloth.

Canvas 23.7 × 17

Restored in 1879 by Vallance. There is a general craquelure and mauled paint on the tree to the left of the mother and in the red cloth. The same tree and the mound on which the mother sits also show blanching.[1] The varnish is discoloured.

P313 is a sketch by Prud'hon for *L'heureuse mère* by Constance Mayer (194 × 147; Louvre) which she exhibited in the 1810 Salon (and again in 1814). A pendant, *La mère infortunée*, was similarly sketched by Prud'hon[2] for Mayer, whose picture (193 × 144; Louvre) was shown in the same Salons. For the collaboration of Prud'hon with Mayer, see Mayer P348.

Versions

PARIS Musée Jacquemart-André (no.243); 19.4 × 14.3; lith. G. Bellanger 1863, as *La joie* (Guiffrey, no.730).

Another oil sketch, 24 × 18, was in the Coutan-Hauguet sale, Paris, 16–17 December 1889, lot 24, as Mayer (Guiffrey, no.732).

Guiffrey also lists six drawings for this composition by Prud'hon, one in the Louvre (RF22; Guiffrey, no.733), one in the Power sale, Paris, 15–16 April 1864, lot 97 (Guiffrey, no.734), and four studies for the mother's head (Guiffrey, nos.735–8, private collections).

Provenance

D. Saint (1778–1847); his sale, Paris, 2nd day, 5 May 1846 (143), bt. by the 4th Marquess of Hertford, 1,350 fr.;[3] rue Laffitte inventory 1871 (90); Hertford House inventory 1890.

Exhibition

Bethnal Green 1872–5 (529).

References General

Blanc 1865, 'Prud'hon', no.35; Goncourt, pp.316, 350; Guiffrey, no.731.

1 Prud'hon's addiction to glazes was described by Clément (pp.380–1): *'lorsqu'il avait amené son tableau au ton voulu, il le terminait par de nombreux glacis, qui donnaient cette douceur, ce moelleux, ce vaporeux qu'il recherchait. Cette méthode a de graves inconvénients. Les dessous reparaissent fréquemment à travers les glacis: de là l'aspect blafard, crayeux de la plupart des tableaux de Prud'hon'.*

2 See Guiffrey, no.740; he also records a related drawing by Prud'hon (no.741). See also note 3 below.

3 Blanc, *loc. cit.*, gave the date of the Saint sale as 1833 and the price of P313 as 3,150 fr. Lot 144 in the Saint sale in 1846 was a sketch for the *Mère infortunée*, 24 × 17, attributed to Mayer, which fetched 421 fr. (a marked contrast to the price of P313). In the A. W. sale, Paris, 25 February 1863, were two sketches for the *Heureuse mère* and *Mère infortunée*, described as from the Saint collection (Guiffrey, under no.731, as copies).

P315 *The Empress Joséphine*

Dark hair, grey eyes, wearing a black dress with a high 'Elizabethan' collar.[1]

Canvas, relined 60 × 49.5

Relined in 1880 by Vallance. An unfinished sketch, the dress and collar lightly brushed in. The spandrels covered by the oval slip have a darker tone; there are some small losses round the edge of the oval. There is a *pentimento* on the right side of the neck. The varnish is discoloured.

Joséphine Tascher de la Pagerie (1763–1814) m. 1st in 1779 the vicomte de Beauharnais (d.1794) and 2nd in 1796 Napoléon (then General); she became his Empress in 1805; the marriage was dissolved in 1809 when she retired to Malmaison (an estate she had purchased in 1799) where she died. By her first marriage she bore Eugène (1781–1824) and Hortense (1783–1837), mother of Napoléon III. For other portraits of Joséphine in this Collection, see the miniatures by Aubry (M5), Isabey (M216), Quaglia (M288) and Saint (M295), and the later painting by Schopin (P568).

Following a commission from the Emperor, Prud'hon painted Joséphine's portrait in 1805, a languid whole-length, reclining to the left in, it is said, the grounds of Malmaison[2] (244 × 179, Louvre; Guiffrey, no.435). P315 probably relates to this commission[3] and may be associated with a drawing at Karlsruhe (Guiffrey, no.443)[4] which shows her whole-length standing to the right by a balustrade, her head at a similar angle. From the number of drawings he made of Joséphine it seems Prud'hon explored several poses: seated to the right (Louvre RF4105; Guiffrey, no.440), seated on a chaise-longue (Musée baron Martin, Gray; Guiffrey, no.444) and with her arms in different positions (Bayonne; Guiffrey, no.441).[5]

Another unfinished half-length portrait of Joséphine by Prud'hon at Malmaison (to the left with her left hand raised), for which there is a preliminary drawing at Gray, has been dated 1808–9.[6]

Provenance

Bequeathed by the artist to C.-B. de Boisfremont (1773–1838);[7] Mme. Power, *née* de Boisfremont; her sale, Paris, 15–16 April 1864 (1), bt. by the 4th Marquess of Hertford, 7,050 fr.; rue Laffitte inventory 1871 (684); Hertford House inventory 1890.

Exhibitions

Malmaison 1867 (141) lent Hertford; Bethnal Green 1872–5 (369, as *Portrait of a Young Lady* 1872, *Portrait of the Empress Josephine* 1874).

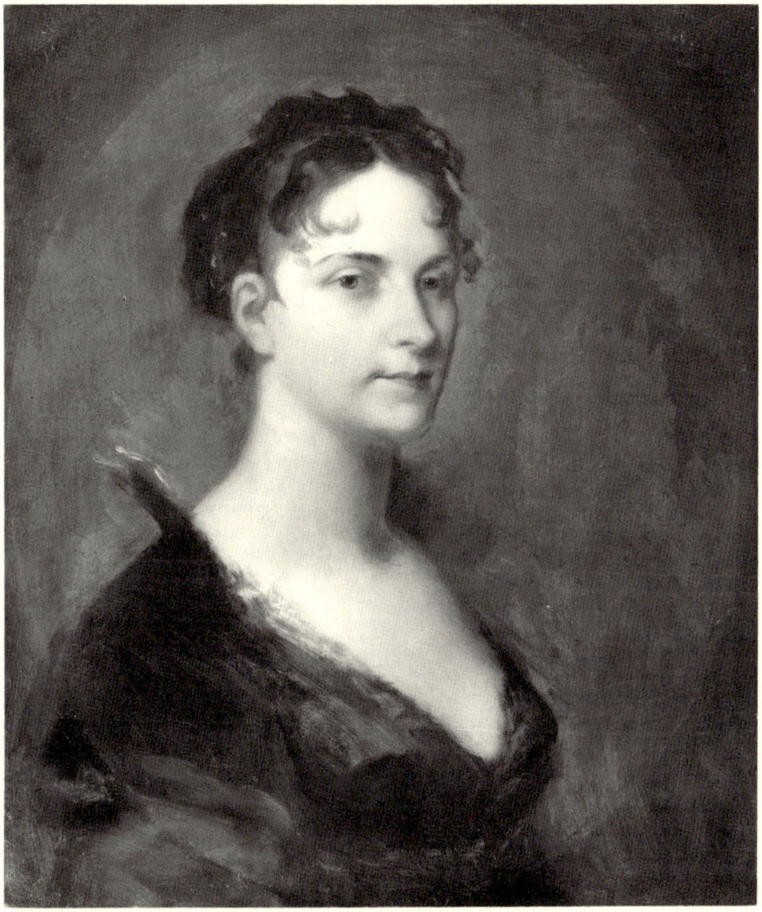

P315

References General

Goncourt, under no.13; Guiffrey, no.434 (both described the canvas as an oval).

[1] Such collars were worn in France at least between 1805 and 1817.

[2] Though the setting somewhat resembles that of P347.

[3] Although C. Baruteau (letter on file dated 30 October 1953) dated P315 *'1811 sans doute'*, without giving his reasons.

[4] Exh. *Die französischen Zeichnungen 1570–1930*, Karlsruhe, 1983, no.56, dated before 1805 and associated with the Emperor's commission.

[5] Other drawings of Joséphine by Prud'hon include two finished studies for the head seen in the Louvre portrait (coll. Weill; Guiffrey, nos.445–6), the second of which was listed by Goncourt (p.35) as if it were a study for P315.

[6] Cf. G. Hubert, *La Revue du Louvre*, 1980, pp.257–61; he states (p.260) that only the Louvre portrait was an official commission. Is it possible that this Malmaison portrait was also associated with the 1805 commission?

[7] Prud'hon left *'tous mes portefeuilles de dessins, études, etc. etc.'* to his friend Boisfremont, in whose arms he died (cf. Clément, pp.437, 438 n.2).

P347 *Venus and Adonis*

Both are fair haired; Venus reclines on a deep red cloth; Adonis wears a pelt and has a sword at his left side.

Canvas, relined 241 × 168

In poor condition. Cleaned by Haines in 1912. Severely reticulated bitumen disfigures all the darker areas[1] which have been extensively repainted. There are many discoloured retouchings in the flesh areas and the legs of the principal figures appear to have lost their glazes. The ruddy tone of the two heavily retouched *putti*[2] playing with a butterfly to the left and the obtrusive shadow on Adonis's forehead were doubtless also originally modified by glazes. There are *pentimenti* on Adonis's legs. An engraving of 1812 (see Engraving) indicated foliage in the lower left area, three *putti* chasing a dog(?) behind the trees in the left distance and two doves sitting on a branch over Venus's head, but these features are now scarcely legible.[3] The varnish is much discoloured.

The subject is described in Ovid, *Metamorphoses* x, 520–59 and 708–39: Venus fell in love with Adonis, the son of Myrrha's illicit union with her father Cinyras, and went hunting with him in wild country;[4] when he was killed by a boar she turned his blood into anemones. Prud'hon himself described the subject of P347:

> *au milieu d'une forêt ombreuse, Vénus, assise sur un tertre, retient Adonis près d'elle, par le charme de ses caresses; le jeune chasseur énivré paraît oublier qu'il veut partir. Au bord de l'eau, sur le devant, un Amour tient les chiens en laisse; plus loin, à l'écart, l'Amour livre au plaisir un papillon, symbole de l'âme; dans le lointain plusieurs autres Amours courent la chasse.*[5]

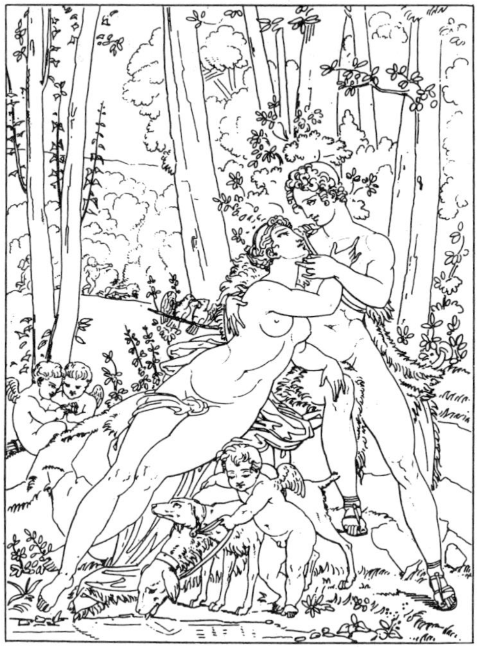

Normand *fils* after Prud'hon: *Venus and Adonis*, 1812

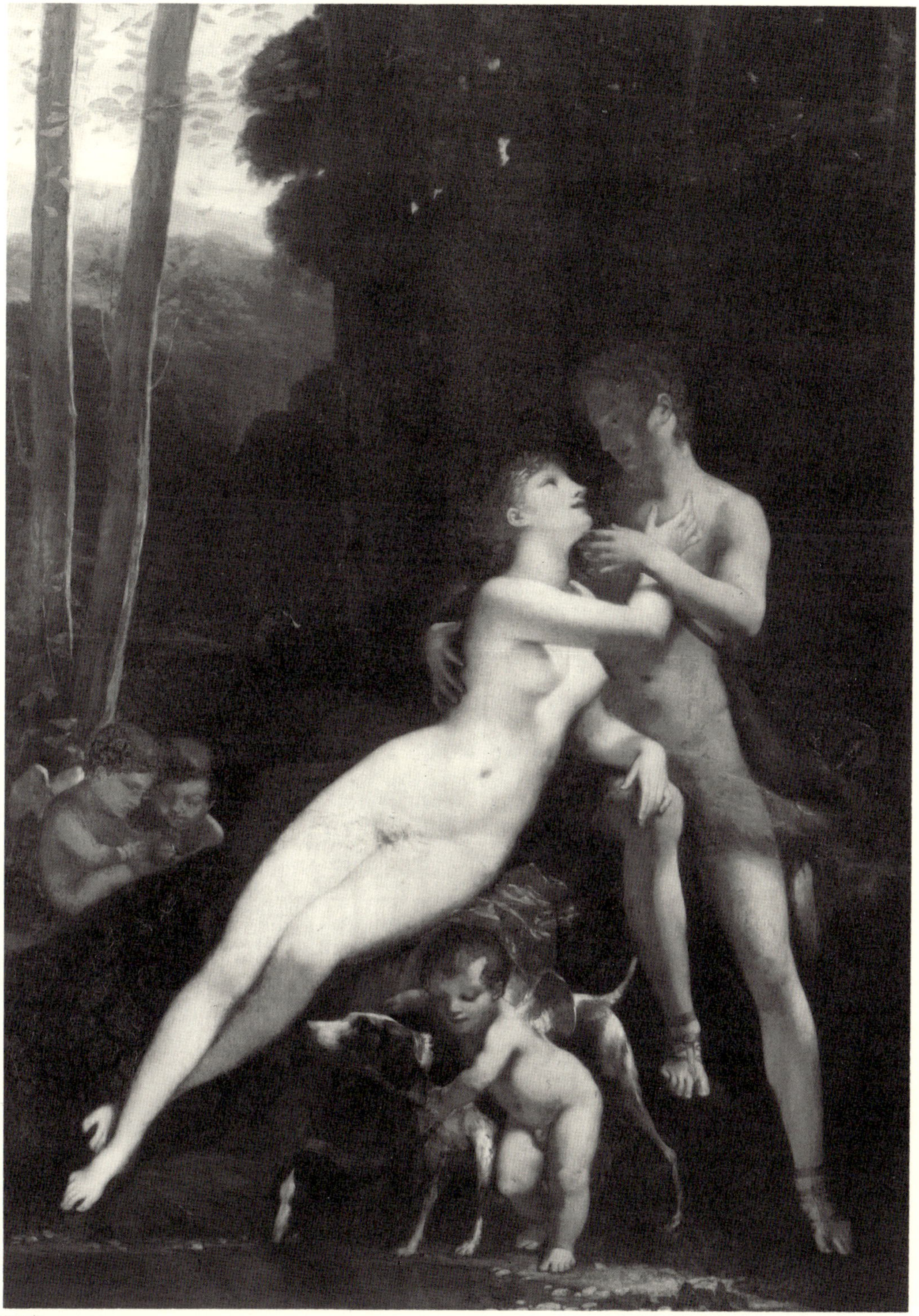

P347

According to Clément (p.382) P347 was commissioned by the Empress Marie-Louise in 1810 for the Tuileries, but the advent of the Russian war prevented payment and it remained in Prud'hon's studio until his death, valued at 12,000 fr.[6] It was shown at the 1812 Salon where it attracted some criticism; Adonis's right thigh does not support his torso, the foreground Cupid has a huge head and lacks a shoulder,[7] the main figures are both elongated and poorly posed, and the rose and violet tones (now scarcely legible) seem unconvincing.[8] Such criticism was *davidien* and did not prevent Clément, for example, counting P347 amongst Prud'hon's most accomplished works (although he too considered the figure of Adonis not to be above criticism). The composition evolved through a number of preliminary stages (see Drawings); Adonis's head was once more upright and there were several different groupings of the *putti* and dogs. The idea of the composition was perhaps derived from Correggio's *Jupiter and Antiope* which Prud'hon would have known in the Louvre.

Drawings

AMSTERDAM Rijksmuseum (no.78.1); compositional study with Adonis's head more upright, no foreground Cupid and three *putti* in the left mid-distance (Guiffrey, no.170).
BAYONNE Musée Bonnat; study of two *putti* playing with two dogs (Guiffrey, no.174).
CHANTILLY Musée Condé; study for the foreground Cupid (Guiffrey, no.173).
PARIS Louvre (RF29920); compositional study with Adonis's head more upright, the foreground *putti* and dogs as in P347 but with an additional flying *putto* on the left.
WASHINGTON National Gallery (nos.1972.48.2 and 3); separate studies for the figures of Venus and Adonis as seen in P347 (Guiffrey, nos.171–2).

Three other related drawings are recorded: a compositional study without the *putti* and with one dog (Lefèvre-Bougon sale, Paris, 1 April 1895, lot 104; Guiffrey, no.169); children playing with a dog (coll. C. Marcille 1924; Guiffrey, no.175), and a water-colour of the same subject (Couvreur sale, Paris, 1 December 1875, lot 196; Guiffrey, under no.175).

Engraving

Normand *fils* 1812 (for Landon, *Salon de 1812*, II).

Copies

Guiffrey (under no.162) records some paintings which he thought copies: 177 × 130 (Arosa sale, Paris, 31 March 1882, lot 43); 28 × 19 (comte de C. sale, Bordeaux, 25 November 1903, lot 251); 136 × 100, unfinished (anon. sale, Paris, 25 May 1866, lot 119), and 32.5 × 24.1 in the Musée de l'Avallonais, Avallon.

Versions

CHANTILLY Musée Condé (no.420); 72 × 57, Venus alone, half-length without right hand (Guiffrey, no.168).
CLUNY Musée Ochier; 64 × 49, Venus alone, carving her name on a tree (Guiffrey, no.167).
LONDON Sotheby's, 9 December 1936 (51); 20.5 × 14.5.
LYON private collection 1965; 61 × 51, with four *putti* behind Venus and two dogs in the foreground.
PARIS private collection; 37 × 26, with two *putti* and one dog in the foreground; lith. J. Boilly, and A. Lamy 1851; exh. bazar Bonne-Nouvelle 1846 (55); boulevard des Italiens 1860 (241); *The Romantic Movement*, Tate Gallery 1959, no.291 (Guiffrey, no.165).

Other versions are recorded: 77 × 56, with Venus embracing two doves (d'Espagnac sale, Paris, 2–3 May 1873, lot 185; Guiffrey, no.163); 46 × 39 (*ibid.*, lot 184; Guiffrey, no.164); oil sketch on paper (Duclos sale, Paris, 20 November 1878, lot 100; Guiffrey, no.166), and Venus alone with an urn by her feet (coll. Caron, Paris, c.1920).

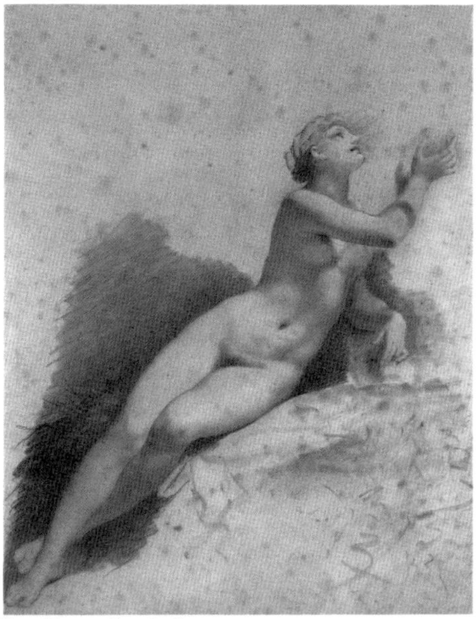

Prud'hon: Study for P347
National Gallery of Art, Washington

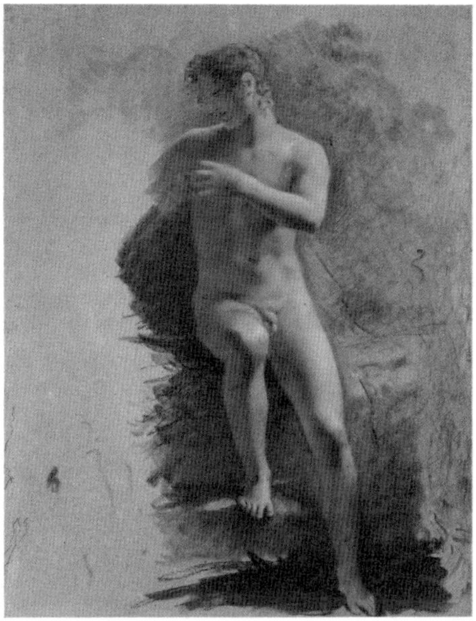

Prud'hon: Study for P347
National Gallery of Art, Washington

Provenance

Prud'hon sale, Paris, 13 May 1823 (3), 5,100 fr., bt. C.-B. de Boisfremont (1773–1838)[9] from whom acquired by L. Gouvion Saint-Cyr (1764–1830), *maréchal de France*, and sold by his son to Auguiot;[10] his sale, Paris, 1 March 1875 (56), bt. by Sir Richard Wallace, 6,700 fr.; Hertford House inventory 1890.

Exhibition

Salon 1812 (742, *Vénus et Adonis*).

References General

Blanc 1844, p.514, no.16; Clément, pp.382–90; Goncourt, no.38; Guiffrey, no.162.

[1] Clément (p.386) remarked of P347: '*l'exécution elle-même est mauvaise. Les ombres et les demi-teintes ont déplorablement noirci, et ici, comme dans tant d'autres peintures de Prud'hon, le bitume, la pommade, les glacis superposés se sont décomposés et ont fait leur oeuvre*'. Elsewhere (p.381) he observed: '*Prud'hon était un peu alchimiste, et il se préoccupait de procédés techniques beaucoup plus qu'il ne l'eût fallu . . . il s'employait beaucoup le bitume et, en outre, des pommades de sa façon, qui, dans les ombres surtout, ont noirci et craquelé sa peinture*'. Blanc 1844, p.479 n.1, quoted an account from J.-F.-L. Mérimée, *De la peinture à l'huile*, 1830, saying that if Prud'hon's pictures had been allowed to dry out thoroughly before the application of varnish the breaking up of their surfaces ('*les gerçures*') could have been avoided; Mérimée (and Clément, p.381 n.1) described Prud'hon's varnish as '*composé de mastic en larmes et de belle cire, fondus ensemble dans de l'huile siccative blanche*'. See also P313 note 1.

[2] Goncourt, p.99, remarked: '*il y a malheureusement des repeints très-maladroits dans les figures d'amours*'.

[3] The *cache-sexe* seen on Adonis (a continuation of Venus's drape?) does not appear on the engraving which is, however, *à trait* and perfunctory.

[4] The wild country in P347 somewhat resembles the background of Prud'hon's portrait of Joséphine at Malmaison, see P315 note 2.

[5] This description was used in the Prud'hon sale catalogue (see Provenance) with the explanation: '*cet article est extrait d'une note autographe laissée par feu M. Prud'hon*'. It is quoted, with minor variations, by Clément, p.383, and Guiffrey, p.59.

[6] As stated in the Prud'hon sale catalogue (see note 5 above). The subject was peculiarly appropriate for Marie-Louise who also lost her Adonis.

[7] M. Boutard, *Journal de l'Empire*, 23 November 1812, quoted by Clément, pp.388–9.

[8] Anon., *La vérité au Salon de 1812*, quoted by Clément, p.390.

[9] For de Boisfremont see P315 note 7. The price was very modest compared with Prud'hon's valuation of 12,000 fr.

[10] Cf. Clément, p.386: '[Saint-Cyr] *conserva* [P347] *pendant quelques années dans son château de Villiers, près de Neuilly, et son fils le vendit à M. Auguiot* . . .'.

Jean Raoux (1677–1734)

Born on 12 June 1677 in Montpellier where he first studied under J. Ranc. By 1704 he was in Paris, the pupil of L. de Boullongne, and he won the *prix de Rome* in 1704 (*David and Goliath*; unlocated). He was in Rome 1705–7, later visiting Florence and staying in Venice, where he met the *Grand Prieur de Vendôme* who gave him a pension and lodgings in the Temple in Paris. *Agréé* in 1716, he was *reçu* in 1717, his *morceau de réception* being the *Pygmalion* now in the Louvre. He painted genre scenes reminiscent of Schalcken (for which Voltaire compared him favourably with Rembrandt[1]), decorative panels for the Temple and he revived the *portrait mythologique*. He paid a brief visit to London in 1720 (at the same time as Watteau). He died in Paris on 10 February 1734.

[1]T. Besterman (*Voltaire on the Arts*, Zaharoff Lecture 1973, p.6) observed that this was because Rembrandt was then little valued, rather than Raoux overrated.

Abbreviation

Bataille G. Bataille, 'Raoux', in L. Dimier, ed., *Les peintres français du XVIIIe siècle*, II, 1930, pp.267–82

P128 *A Lady at her Mirror*

Fair hair, brown eyes, wearing a purple bodice with blue sleeves and an orange skirt.

Canvas, relined 79.7 × 64.2

The paint surface is lifting along her hairline, below her right hand and in the left background. There are damages in the skirt, across the nose, on her left shoulder, to the left of her head and above the mirror, and there is a surface scratch across her right shoulder. The blue on her right sleeve is worn and the varnish is discoloured.

Probably a late work; versions are dated 1723 and 1729 (see below). The model seems to recur in several comparable subjects.[1]

Versions

AIX Musée Granet (no.145); panel 20 × 18, similar to P128, wearing a yellow dress with blue sleeves (Bataille, no.43).
LONDON P. Larsen 1967; 66 × 54.5 oval, signed and dated 1729; without the bows on the shoulders.
Christie's, 2 December 1983 (46); 46 × 32.5, signed and dated 1723, showing two whole-length figures, one comparable with P128 (mistakenly described as from the Chavagnac sale).

Provenance

Mme. Gentil de Chavagnac sale, Paris, 20 June 1854 (52, *Jeune fille au Miroir*), bt. by the 4th Marquess of Hertford, 1,205 fr.;[2] rue Laffitte inventory 1871 (435); Hertford House inventory 1890.

Exhibition

Bethnal Green 1872–5 (475).

Reference General

Bataille, no.42.

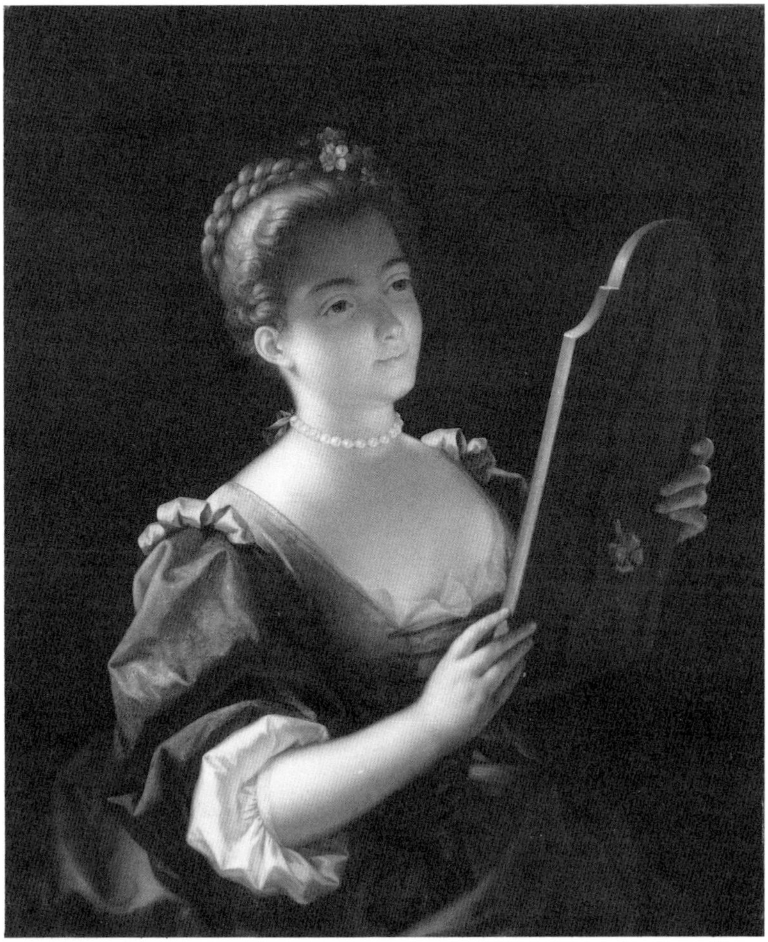

P128

[1] E.g. *Le duo*, Kraemer sale, 28–9 April 1913, lot 49 (Bataille, no.38) and *Two ladies with a mirror*, Sotheby's, 11 July 1979 (277); both these subjects were painted by Raoux for the Temple (cf. Bataille, p.270). The *Jeune fille lisant une lettre* (Louvre; Bataille, no.34) also shows a similar model.

[2] Lord Hertford described his purchase to Mawson (Paris, 3 July 1854) as 'a little insignificant 40£ head, pretty but of no importance' (*Letters*, no.47, p.59). The marked copy of that sale catalogue in the Wallace Collection library has '*beaucoup trop cher*' opposite lot 52.

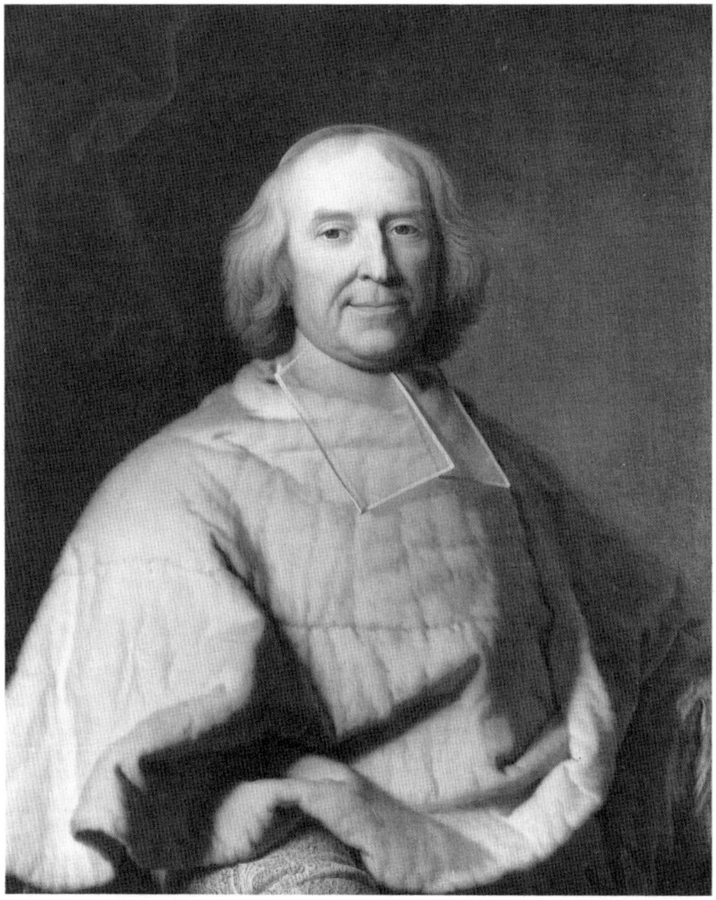

P130

Hyacinthe Rigaud (1659–1743)

Hyacinthe-François-Honoré-Mathias-Pierre Martyr-André-Jean Rigau y Ros, called Rigaud. Born on 20 July 1659 in Perpignan, he studied at Montpellier under P. Pezet and J. Ranc. Although awarded the *prix de Rome* in 1682 he did not go to Italy. *Agréé* in 1684, he was *reçu* in 1700 when he painted the fine whole-length of Louis XIV now at Versailles. Eminently successful thereafter, he became *directeur* of the Académie in 1733. He died in Paris on 27 December 1743.

Abbreviation

Roman J. Roman, *Livre de raison du peintre Hyacinthe Rigaud*, 1919

After Rigaud

P130 *Cardinal Fleury*

White hair, blue eyes, wearing a Cardinal's red-lined ermine cape; a brown curtain on the left.

Canvas, relined 80.5 × 64.5

The edges are uneven and were made up in the course of relining. There are damages below the nose, to the right of the head and along the bottom edge. There are minor losses in the head and the paint is lifting in the collar and cape (below right). The varnish is discoloured.

André-Hercule de Fleury (1653–1743), Bishop of Fréjus 1698, tutor to Louis XV 1715 when he became effectually *Premier ministre*; Cardinal 1726.

P130 is a copy derived from the three-quarter length portrait of 1728 by Rigaud.[1] His *Livre de raison*, which is not a complete record,[2] lists fourteen copies made between 1728 and 1735,[3] though it is open to doubt whether P130 was among such contemporary studio productions.

Provenance

Probably G.W. Taylor sale, Christie's, 13 June 1823 (26, Rigaud, *Portrait of Cardinal Fleury*), bt. Orchard, 10 gn. The 3rd Marquess of Hertford; Dorchester House inventory 1842; Hertford House inventory 1870 as *'A Cardinal'*, artist unknown.

[1] Previous editions of this catalogue supposed that P130 derived from Rigaud's 1706 portrait of Fleury as Bishop of Fréjus (Roman, p.126; now lost; engr. F. Cherau, the same head as in P130 but wearing a silk cape), but it relates, like all known versions, to the three-quarter length of 1728 showing Fleury as Cardinal. The best versions of this seem to be those at Goodwood and in the Nationalmuseum, Stockholm.

[2] Cf. M. Davies, National Gallery Catalogues, *French School*, 1957, p.200.

[3] Cf. Roman, pp.203, 204, 205, 211, 213. Examples are in the National Gallery, London; the Gemäldegalerie des Landesmuseums, Darmstadt; the Detroit Institute of Arts; the Musée H. Rigaud, Perpignan, and at Versailles; seven are recorded in London sales 1956–86.

Gabriel-Jacques de Saint-Aubin (1724–1780)

Born on 14 April 1724 in Paris, one of fourteen children of the *brodeur* and engraver G.-G. de Saint-Aubin under whom he first studied. He was later the pupil of J.-B. Sarrazin and studied at the Académie under Jeaurat and Boucher c.1750–4. Meanwhile from 1747 he taught drawing at J.-F. Blondel's *école des arts,* and his first etchings date from 1750. Having failed to win the *prix de Rome* (in 1752 he was placed behind Fragonard), he joined the Académie de Saint-Luc with whom he exhibited a number of paintings in 1774; he also exhibited paintings at the *Salon du Colisée* in 1776. An obsessive draughtsman and a close observer of elegant Parisian life, his biographer Dacier described him as '*singulier, bizarre, farouche et malpropre*'. He died in Paris on 9 February 1780. His brothers Charles-Gabriel (1721–86), Louis-Michel (1731–79) and Augustin (1736–1807) also practised as painters and engravers.

Abbreviation

Dacier E. Dacier, *Gabriel de Saint-Aubin*: I, 1929, *L'homme et L'oeuvre*; II, 1931, *Catalogue raisonné*

P780 *A Fête in the Colisée*

Inscribed round the top cornice: *les elements les saisons les points cardinaux les points de jour* and signed twice: on the left foreground pedestal: *colisée/dessiné sur le lieu par/Gabriel de St Aubin 1772,* and bottom left: *G. d S^t A 1772.*

Ink, water- and body-colour on paper 16.8 × 22.6[1]

The top edge of the paper has been reinforced on the *verso* with a horizontal strip of paper, 4 mm. wide. The paper bears the (cut off) watermark of a crown, comparable with Heawood 2747.[2] The water-colour is faded and the blue touches (on the capitals, for example) are now discordant.

The *Colisée,* which stood by the *Rond Point* in the Champs Elysées (between the rue du Colisée and the avenue Matignon) was designed by L.-D. Le Camus, in emulation of the Rotunda in Vauxhall Gardens, as a setting for *fêtes payantes.* It was opened, while still unfinished, in 1771, but proved both unsound and uneconomical and was demolished by 1785. P780 shows the central *grande salle de bal* which was screened with sixteen festooned corinthian columns and lit by an *oculus* in the roof. Above the columns were boxes, separated by caryatids representing, according to Saint-Aubin's annotations, the Elements, Seasons, Points of the Compass and Times of Day. The architecture was painted: the columns silver with gilt capitals and bases and plinths of red or green marbling; other features had white veined marbling; the upper boxes had green curtains and all other draperies were crimson.[3] Saint-Aubin made many drawings of the *Colisée* in 1772 (thirteen in one sketchbook), some dated May or July.[4] The occasion recorded in P780 has not been identified; Bachaumont described a disappointing *fête chinoise* on 11 July 1772 (see note 4) but by October the building was undergoing extensive repairs.[5]

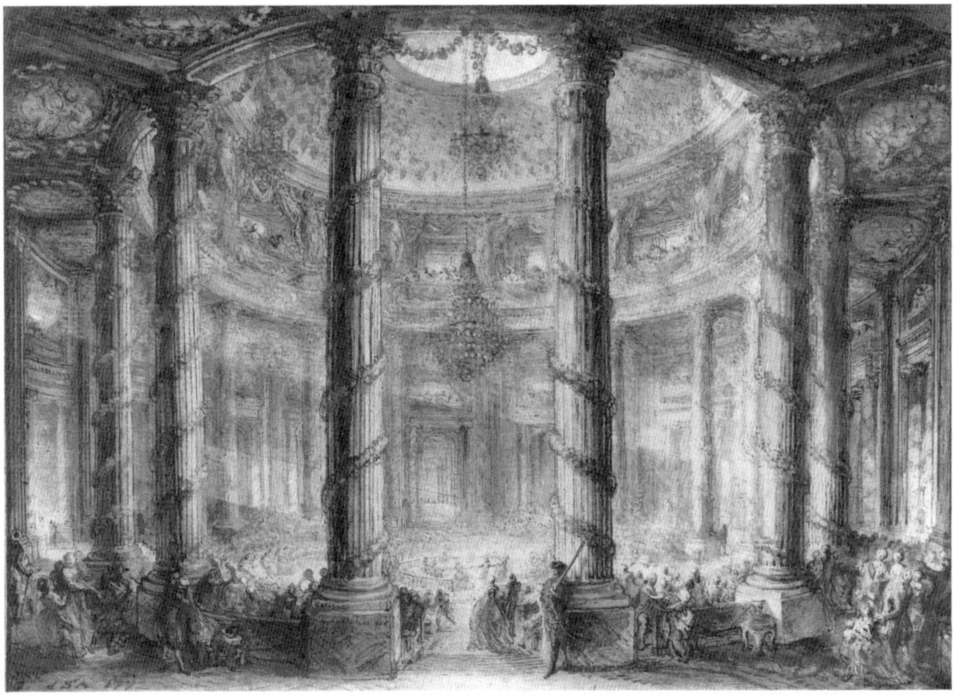

P780

Provenance

The 4th Marquess of Hertford; Hertford House inventory 1870, as '*The Pantheon Paris in 1772 miniature*'.[6]

Exhibition

Bethnal Green 1874–5 (1793, miniature, unknown artist. *Masqued Ball at the Pantheon, London*).

Reference General

Dacier, I, pp.46, 130; II, no.502.

[1] The silver frame of P780 contains packing of wood inscribed *Leferre*, whose name recurs on the frames of several miniatures in the Wallace Collection (see G. Reynolds, *Wallace Collection, Catalogue of Miniatures*, 1980, p.20, and nos.94–5, 101, 170, 182, 265 and 280); Leferre is recorded as a *bijoutier-garnisseur* in the rue Saint-Martin, Paris, 1806–60.

[2] E. Heawood, *Watermarks mainly of the 17th and 18th centuries*, 1950. The mark in P780 is cut off, but the end of the loop from which the hunting horn is suspended is visible; it differs from Heawood 2747 only in that the central jewel on the crown is round. P780 is also inscribed, *verso*, in pencil: *158*.

[3] For discussion of the *Colisée*, see A.-G. Gruber, 'Les "Vauxhalls" Parisiens au XVIIIe siècle', BSHAF 1971, pp.125–6, 129–34, from which the above description has been taken.

[4] See Dacier, nos.497–504; the sketchbook was in the David-Weill collection; Dacier, no.499 was with Terry-Engell in 1972. Dacier, no.501 (Louvre), is inscribed: *la Fête chinoise de juillet 1772 au Colisée*.

[5] Cf. A. de Bachaumont, *Mémoires secrets*, VI, 1777, pp.181–2, 244.

[6] In the 1890 Hertford House inventory P780 was listed as: '*Interior of a theatre with numerous figures and columns by D'Aubin 1772*'. P780 was previously catalogued as a miniature, M296, see *Wallace Collection, Catalogue of Miniatures*, 1935, p.116, where a mistaken provenance was cited (cf. Dacier, no.503).

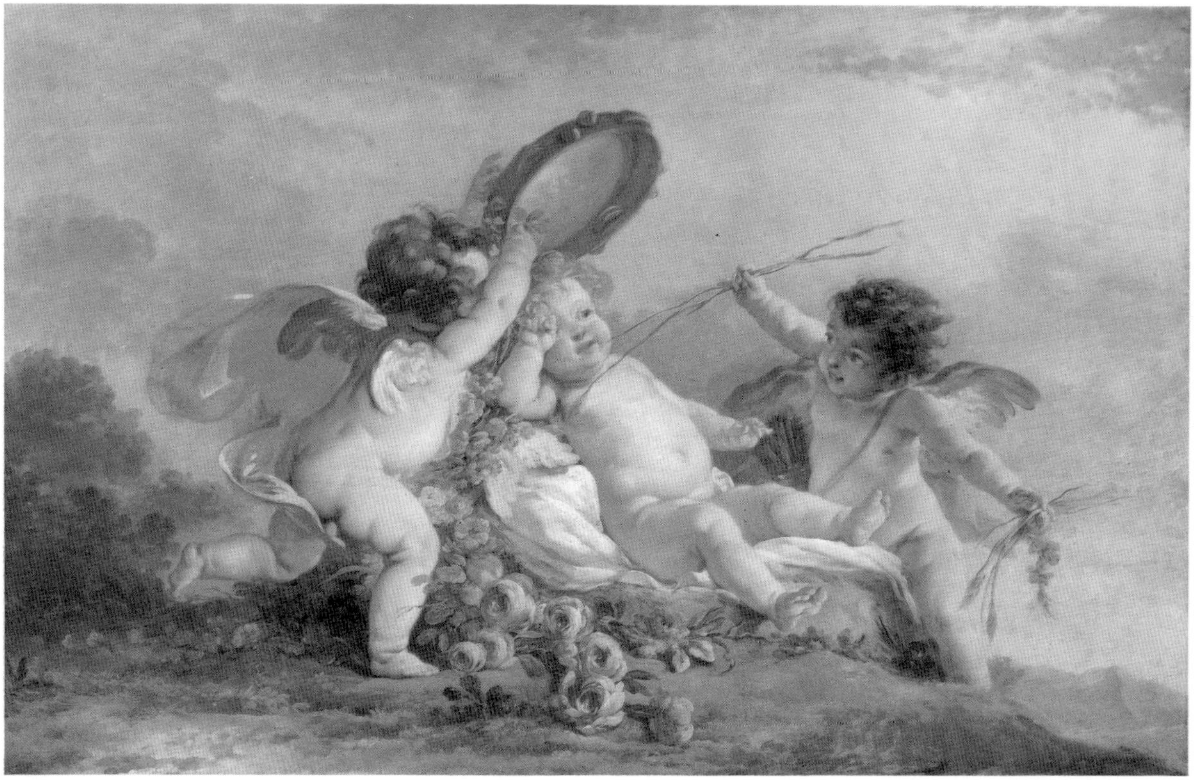

P483

Hughes Taraval (1729–1785)

Born on 27 February 1729 in Paris. From 1732 to 1750 he was in Stockholm where his father (and first teacher) Guillaume-Thomas Taraval (1701–50) was Court Painter to Frederick I of Sweden. He returned to Paris when his father died and entered the Académie as the pupil of J.-M. Pierre, winning the *prix de Rome* in 1756 (*Job reproached by his wife*; Marseille). He worked under Carle van Loo at the *école royale des Elèves protégés* 1756–9, before going to Rome where he was a diligent pupil under J. Natoire at the Académie de France 1759–63. *Agréé* in 1765, he was *reçu* in 1769, his *morceau de réception* being the ceiling painting for the Galerie d'Apollon in the Louvre, the *Triumph of Bacchus*. He achieved success as a decorative painter, his commissions including work for Bellevue (1767), the Ecole Militaire (1773), the Collège de France (1777), Versailles (1780), Marly (see below) and Fontainebleau (1781), as well as designs for the Gobelins (1777–85), of which he was made *surinspecteur* in 1783. He exhibited at the Salon 1765–85 (except 1771) and was made a member of the Royal Swedish Academy in 1775. He died in Paris on 19 October 1785.

Abbreviation

Sandoz M. Sandoz, 'Hughes Taraval', BSHAF 1972, pp. 195–255

P483 *The Waking of Cupid (Le réveil)*

The sun rises on the right; Cupid is fair-haired; the left-hand *putto* has pale lilac drapery, the right-hand pale blue. Signed, lower left: *Taraval 1781*.

Canvas, relined 95.5 × 142.7

There are several retouchings in the sky and round the edges (which have been made up to 96.5 × 143.8), and damages below the left-hand *putto's* left leg and drapery and in the sky to the left. *Pentimenti* show minor alterations to the right-hand *putto's* back, left leg, drapery and sash. The varnish is discoloured.

Previously catalogued with its pendant P488 (see Jollain) as by Fragonard,[1] the discovery of the signature and date on P483 allows it to be identified as the picture commissioned from Taraval in 1781 by the Direction des Bâtiments for the Queen's Bed Chamber at Marly: '*environ 4 pieds 3 pouces de large sur 3 pieds 8 pouces de haut* [c. 120 × 139]. *Il représente par des enfants,* le Réveil'.[2] The edges of the original canvas appear to have been roughly cut in the course of relining, and the original size perhaps agreed more closely with the approximate size given in the commission.[3]

Despite the general similarity of P483 to the pendant, Jollain P488, the former may be distinguished by its looser handling. The subjects of the commissions led both artists to emulate Boucher overdoors of 1759–64,[4] in marked contrast to the neo-classical subjects both were exhibiting at the Salon in the 1770s and 1780s.

Version

PARIS professeur Chauffard 1956; a reduced version.[5]

Provenance

Commissioned in 1781 through d'Angiviller by the Direction des Bâtiments du Roi for the *chambre à coucher de la Reine*, Château de Marly, 500 *livres*;[6] the contents of Marly were dispersed by 1796;[7] Ralph Bernal (c.1785–1854); his sale, Christie's, 6th day, 10 March 1855 (612, 'Boucher, Two nymphs with Cupid, reclining in a landscape – a sopraporta, about 4ft. 6in. wide'), bt., with lot 613 (see Jollain P488) by the 4th Marquess of Hertford, 61gn.; 5 rue Taitbout inventory 1871 as '*école de Boucher*';[8] Hertford House inventory 1890 as Boucher.

Exhibition

Palais Bourbon, *Ouvrages de Peinture exposés au profit de la colonisation de l'Algérie par les Alsaces-Lorrains*, 1874 (811 or 812, both Fragonard, *Amours endormis*) lent Wallace (see Jollain P488).[9]

References General

Sandoz, pp.203, 236, no.116 (as unlocated); J. Ingamells, *The Burlington Magazine*, CXXIX, 1987, pp.518–19. The following refer to P483 as Fragonard (q.v. for abbreviations): Portalis, pp.106, 270; Lady Dilke, *French Painters of the XVIIIth century*, 1899, p.65; Réau, p.145; WF65, as c.1748–52; Mandel, no.73.

[1] See References General and Exhibition. An attribution to Boucher was tentatively suggested by MacColl in the 13th and 14th editions of this catalogue (1913 and 1920) and accepted by Hendy in the 15th (1928); the 16th edition (1968) reverted, confidently, to Fragonard. Rosenberg (letter on file dated 30 January 1986), before the discovery of the signature on P483, tentatively but wisely proposed an attribution to Taraval.

[2] F. Engerand, *Inventaire des Tableaux commandés et achetés par la Direction des Bâtiments du Roi*, 1900, p.451.

[3] But the present sizes of P483 and P488 compare with those of overdoors by Jollain for the Petit Trianon (Versailles, nos.2548–9; 85 × 137 and 95 × 130), and cf. in this catalogue Boucher P399, P411, P423, P445, P447 and Studio of Boucher P481 and P490 (together these average 94 × 140).

[4] Cf. Ananoff, *Boucher*, 1976, nos.516–17, 566–7, 589–91.

[5] Réau, *loc. cit.*

[6] Taraval was paid on 7 March 1783 (Engerand, *loc. cit.*).

[7] Cf. E. Magne, *Le Château de Marly*, 1934, pp.224–5, and A. Marie, *Connaissance des Arts*, August 1972, p.65; the pictures had been removed by the sculptor Boizot in 1793, though P483 and P488, as overdoors, would probably have been left as fixtures. Marly was finally sold in 1796.

[8] Lord Hertford also placed in 5 rue Taitbout the Sèvres vases he bought at the Bernal sale (cf. S. Eriksen, *The James A. de Rothschild Collection at Waddesdon Manor, Sèvres Porcelain*, 1968, p.266).

[9] It was, presumably, a reference to this exhibition which led Hendy to cite 'Palais Bourbon' as the provenance for P483 and P488 in the 15th edition of this catalogue (1928).

Jean-François de Troy (1679–1752)

Baptised on 27 January 1679 in Paris, son of the portrait painter François de Troy (1645–1730) under whom he first studied, and at whose expense he went to Italy 1699–1706, staying in Rome, but also visiting many north Italian cities. In 1708 he was both *agréé* and *reçu* by the Académie, his *morceau de réception* being the *Niobe* now at Montpellier. He was made *adjoint à professeur* in 1716 and *professeur* in 1719. In 1727 he was declared joint winner, with Lemoyne, of the *Concours* devised by the duc d'Antin, *directeur des Bâtiments* (*Diane au bain*; Nancy). A versatile artist, he painted *tableaux de modes*, histories and mythologies in a colourful and fluent manner which owed something to both Veronese and Rubens. He undertook commissions for Versailles and Fontainebleau (see below) between 1724 and 1737, and designed two sets of tapestries for the Gobelins, each of seven subjects, the *Histoire d'Esther* (1737–40) and the *Histoire de Jason* (1743–6). He exhibited at the Salon 1737–50. In 1738 he succeeded Vleughels as Director of the Académie de France at Rome, where he died on 24 January 1752.

Abbreviation

Brière G. Brière, 'J.-F. de Troy', in L. Dimier, ed., *Les peintres français du XVIIIe siècle*, II, 1930, pp. 1–48

P463 *A Hunt Breakfast*

The man in the left foreground wears a blue coat over a red jacket; the seated lady on the right wears a golden yellow dress, and her companions are in white and pink; the man carving the pie wears red. Signed, bottom right: DETROY/*1737*.

Canvas, relined 54.7 × 44.8

The paint surface was heavily ironed in relining. There are prominent retouchings on the roof and upper wall of the house on the right, on the raised right hand of the man standing behind the carver, and small damages top centre, in the white napkin on the extreme right and down the right-hand edge. *Pentimenti* show the right leg of the man in blue in the left foreground was repositioned. The varnish is discoloured.

P463 and P470 are sketches for *un Déjeuner près d'une ferme* and *les abois d'un cerf* commissioned for the King's dining room at Fontainebleau and completed in 1737 (see Versions).[1] In that year de Troy also painted for the Queen's *cabinet* at Fontainebleau portraits of her father (the King of Poland) and son, the Dauphin.[2] These four paintings formed part of a major scheme of redecoration to which eight artists contributed twenty-three paintings.[3] P463 and P470, spirited sketches demonstrating de Troy's facility, were probably submitted for the King's approval; both are framed with rounded top corners, as specified by the Fontainebleau commission (see note 1), and it is possible that the frames are original.

In P463 the seated man in the left foreground (deleted in the final version) bears some resemblance to the seated man in the left foreground of the *Déjeuner d'huîtres* de Troy painted for Versailles in 1735 and now at Chantilly.

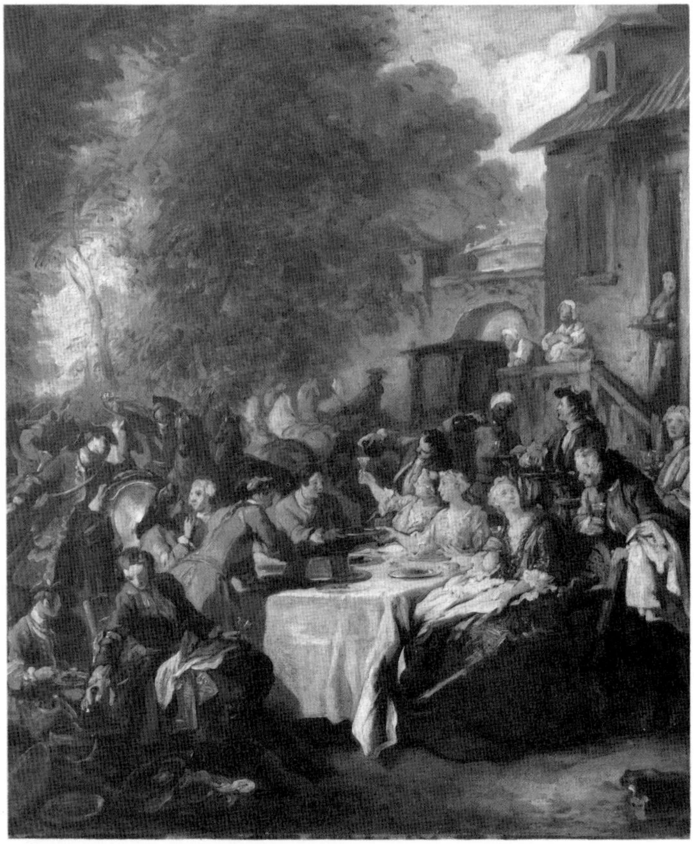

P463

Version

SWITZERLAND private collection; 240 × 169, signed and dated 1737, the finished painting from Fontainebleau, exh. Salon 1737. The composition shows some differences from P463: on the left the huntsman in blue and the standing figure behind him are replaced by two servants and a man seen from behind; the farm house differs in detail and there are two dogs in the foreground; the main group round the table remains the same; exh. RA 1932 (222).

Provenance

Bt. by Sir Richard Wallace from A. Beurdeley, 5 March 1872 ('*2 tableaux de de Troy, sujets déjeuner de Chasse*');[4] Hertford House inventory 1890.

Exhibition

Bethnal Green 1872–5 (455).

Reference General

Brière, p.17, and no.82.

[1] The commission, as cited in F. Engerand, *Inventaire des Tableaux commandés et achetés par la Direction des Bâtiments du Roi,* 1900, p.463, specified: 'un Déjeuner près d'une ferme, *plusieurs chasseurs s'empressent de servir des dames, on descend une chaise par l'escalier; ayant 7 pieds 7 pouces de haut sur 5 pieds de large* [246 × 162]; *sur un fond de paysage; cintré par en haut.* Les abois d'un cerf *mêmes forme et dimensions que le précédent*'.

[2] Now unlocated, cf. Brière, no.23.

[3] The artists (and number of works) were: Boucher (four pastoral subjects; unlocated), Domenchin de Chavanne (two landscapes; Fontainebleau), Galloche (two landscapes; Petit Trianon), Lancret (three pastoral scenes; unlocated), Natoire (six hunting and fishing scenes; unlocated), Parrocel (*Halte de grenadiers;* Louvre) and C.-A. van Loo (*Halte de chasse;* Louvre).

[4] The invoice (Wallace Collection archives) listed many other items and amounted to 160,000 fr.

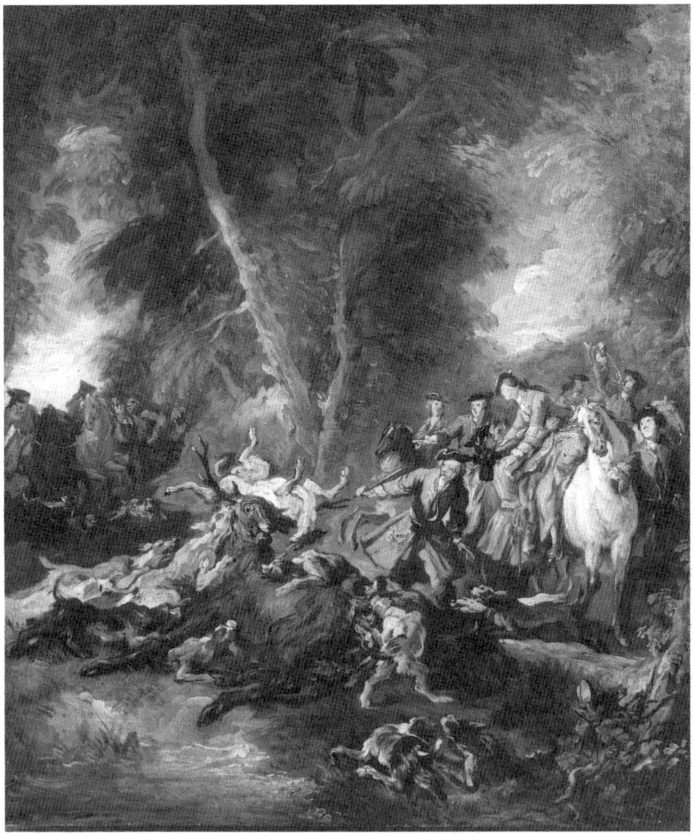

P470

P470 *The Death of a Stag*

A huntsman in red approaches the stag with a knife in his hand; on the right the mounted lady wears a lavender coat and pale blue skirt. Signed, bottom right: DETROY/*1737*.

Canvas, relined 54.5 × 45

The paint surface was heavily ironed in relining. There are small damages bottom left and right and an area in the trees, upper left, has been retouched. The varnish is discoloured.

For discussion, see P463.

Version
The finished picture, 246 × 162, exh. Salon 1737, is unlocated (see P463 note 1).

Provenance
See P463.

Exhibition
Bethnal Green 1872–5 (463).

Reference General
Brière, p.17, and no.83.

Claude-Joseph Vernet (1714–1789)

Born on 14 August 1714 in Avignon, where he first studied under his father, Antoine Vernet (1689–1753). He later studied with J. Viali and P. Sauvan in Aix. In 1734 he went to Rome, initially to make drawings from the antique for the marquis de Coumont, his patron in Avignon, but he stayed for eighteen years, receiving further tuition from the landscape painter A. Manglard and meeting Panini, van Bloemen and Locatelli. By 1739 he had acquired a reputation as a landscape and marine painter, his subjects reflecting Claudean calm or the agreeable terror of a shipwreck or storm. He was particularly popular with English patrons and in 1750 he received his first commission from the French Crown. He returned to Paris in 1753, when he was *reçu* by the Académie and was commissioned by Marigny, *directeur des Bâtiments* to paint the *Ports de France*. In 1763, after travelling round the French coast, he completed the series of fifteen (they are now in the Louvre and the Musée de la Marine).[1] His later work became somewhat repetitive, but his reputation remained considerable, Diderot preferring him to Claude. He died in Paris on 3 December 1789. His son Carle Vernet (1758–1836) and grandson Horace Vernet (1789–1863) were also painters, the latter greatly admired by the 4th Marquess of Hertford.

[1] Cf. P. Conisbee, *Joseph Vernet*, exh. cat., London, Paris, 1976, nos.36–50.

Abbreviations

Ingersoll-Smouse	F. Ingersoll-Smouse, *Joseph Vernet*, 1926
Lagrange	L. Lagrange, *Joseph Vernet*, 1864 (pp.322–450 contain extracts from his *Livre de raison* [MS now in the Musée Calvet, Avignon], *Journal 1745–86* and *Adresses 1735–6*)

P135 *A Storm with a Shipwreck*

A crowd come down the sloping path from the castle to watch; of the survivors, a swooning lady is in the right foreground, and two are in the rescue boat on the left. Inscribed, in pale yellow, bottom left: *217* (see note 3). Signed on rocky ledge, below centre right: *J. Vernet.f. 1754.*

Canvas, relined[1] 87 × 137

There are a number of discoloured retouchings in the sky upper right and the edges have been retouched.

P135 was commissioned by the marquis de Marigny, *directeur des Bâtiments*, with a pendant *Landscape with Fishermen and Washer-women* (London art market 1971).[2] P135 was painted in Marseille where Vernet resided between October 1753 and September 1754, and where he received payment of 150 *écus romains* from Marigny.

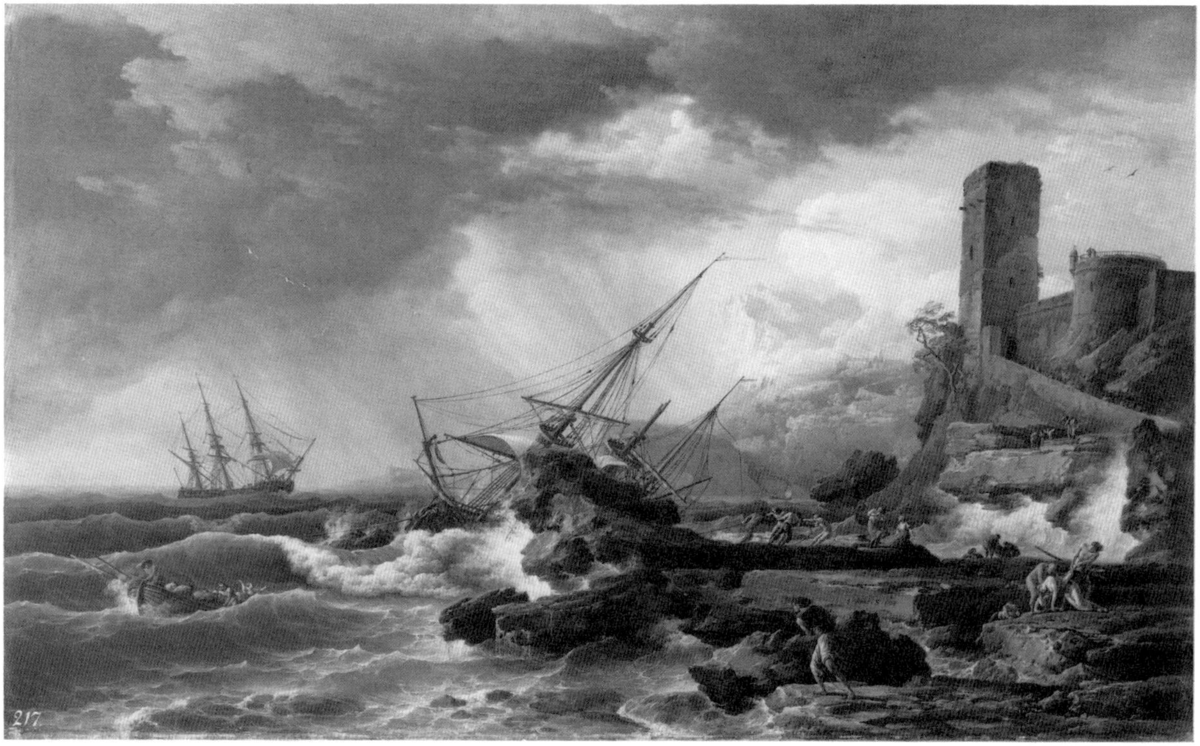

P135

Provenance

The marquis de Marigny (1727–81), see above; his sale, Paris, 18 March–6 April 1782 (137, with pendant), bt. Gros, 6,621 *livres*; the comte de Vaudreuil (1740–1817); his sale, Paris, 26 November ff. 1787 (88, with pendant), bt. Saubert, 9,600 *livres*; the comte Alexandre Bezborodko (1742–99), St. Petersburg;[3] by descent to his great-grand-nephew, Grigory Koucheleff; his sale, Paris, 5 June 1869 (39), bt. by the 4th Marquess of Hertford, 3,600 fr.; rue Laffitte inventory 1871 (97); Hertford House inventory 1890.

Exhibitions

Salon 1755 (102, *Tempête & Naufrage d'un Vaisseau . . . Tiré du Cabinet de M. le Marquis de Marigny*); Bethnal Green 1872–5 (368).

References General

Lagrange, pp.75, 341 (no.177), 362 (no.67); Ingersoll-Smouse, no.596.

[1] The stretcher is stamped, *verso*: E. GOUPIL and bears a torn, apparently eighteenth-century, label: *peint par . . .*

[2] 87.6 × 113.5, signed and dated 1757; exh. Salon 1757 (61); Lagrange, pp.341 (no.177), 363 (no.88); Ingersoll-Smouse, no.689. Marigny paid Vernet 1,000 *livres* for this picture; it was separated from P135 by 1793 when it was in a Lebrun sale, Paris, 11 January, lot 8.

[3] The Bezborodko-Koucheleff seal remains legible on the stretcher, *verso*. The *217* inscribed on P135 refers to the Bezborodko collection (cf. Vernet's *Port of Naples*, Louvre, inscribed *210*; illus. *French Painting 1710–74*, exh. cat. Toledo, Chicago, Montreal, 1975, no.110, pl.76). For the Koucheleff-Bezborodko collection see also Boucher P399 note 6.

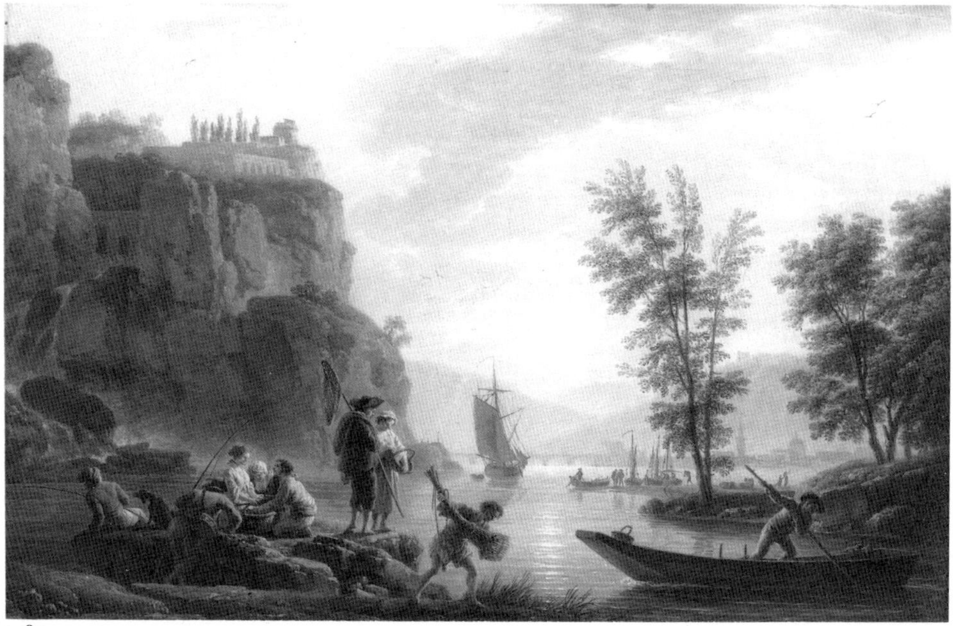

P480

P480 *A River Scene*

An early morning scene; in the centre a man with a lobster basket; to the left a fisherman with a red coat; the standing man, left of centre, is in blue, and the fisherwoman in the boat on the right has a red coat. Signed, bottom right: *J. Vernet.*

Canvas, relined 63.8 × 96.5

There is a small vertical tear by the lower right-hand edge, and a horizontal tear in the top right-hand corner. There are small retouchings in the lower left area, in the tree centre right, and round the edges. Isolated areas of craquelure appear upper right and centre foreground, and mark the impress of the central vertical stretcher member. The varnish is pitted and discoloured.

A late work, dated c.1781 by Ingersoll-Smouse, the handling of P480 is noticeably looser than that of P135, and the colour softer.

Provenance

Thomas Farrant sale, Christie's, 2 June 1855 (52, *Italian River scene*), bt. Caw for the 4th Marquess of Hertford, 111 gn.; Hertford House inventory 1870.

Exhibitions

RA 1872 (368); Bethnal Green 1872–5 (364).

Reference General

Ingersoll-Smouse, no. 1075.

Elisabeth-Louise Vigée Le Brun (1755–1842)

Born on 16 April 1755 in Paris, daughter of the portrait painter Louis Vigée (1715–67), under whom she first studied. By 1770 she was practising on her own account as a portrait painter, and copying Greuze, Rubens and van Dyck. A visit to the Netherlands in 1781 further increased her admiration for these Flemish masters. In 1776 she married the dealer J.-B.-P. Le Brun (1748–1813), by whom she had one daughter. Their Paris hôtel became a centre of fashionable society, amongst whom her beauty and style aided her professional success. She first painted Marie-Antoinette in 1778 (Vienna), and it was partly due to the Queen that she was *reçue* by the Académie in 1783, her *morceau de réception* being *La paix ramenant l'abondance* of 1780 (Louvre). She exhibited at the Salon 1783–91, 1798, 1802, 1817 and 1824. Her work attracted envious criticism before the Revolution, and in 1789 she quickly left Paris to practise with eminent success in Italy 1789–92, Vienna 1792–5 and St. Petersburg 1795–1801. She was able to return to Paris in 1801. She visited London in 1803–4 (staying briefly in Portman Square) and the Netherlands in 1805. Her later years were passed in Paris and Louveciennes. She composed her somewhat anodyne *Souvenirs* in 1834–5, and died in Paris on 29 May 1842.

Abbreviations

Baillio J. Baillio, *Elisabeth Louise Vigée Le Brun*, exhibition catalogue, Fort Worth, 1982

Souvenirs [E.-L. Vigée Le Brun] *Souvenirs de Mme. Vigée Le Brun*, 1869 ed., 2 vols. (vol. 2 containing the *Conseils pour la peinture des portraits*, pp.345–52, and her list of her works, pp.353–76)

P449 *The comte d'Espagnac*

Auburn hair, blue eyes, wearing a red coat; the chair and table top are green.

Canvas, relined 64.7 × 54 oval

There are minor retouchings in his left cheek, neck and nose and in the background area. *Pentimenti* suggest that the chair was originally different (with a finial?) and minor alterations were made to the neck, ear and edge of the scarf.

Joseph-François-Pierre-Guillaume de Sahuget d'Amarzit d'Espagnac (1776–1820) was the only son of J.-F.-P.-C. d'Espagnac (1750–1817), a *sous-lieutenant* of the King's household troops and a collector of repute, and his wife Charlotte, *née* His. He doubtless accompanied his father to Italy in 1791 and lived with him at Sassuolo, near Modena. He died without issue and the d'Espagnac collection and Italian property were claimed in 1824 by the sitter's cousin, A.-J.-J.-C. d'Espagnac (1788–1873),[1] cf. Prud'hon P295.

Vigée Le Brun listed '*le petit d'Espagnac*' amongst her portraits for 1786, and P449 was shown at the 1787 Salon. The sitter's lively expression recalls studies of children by Hals.

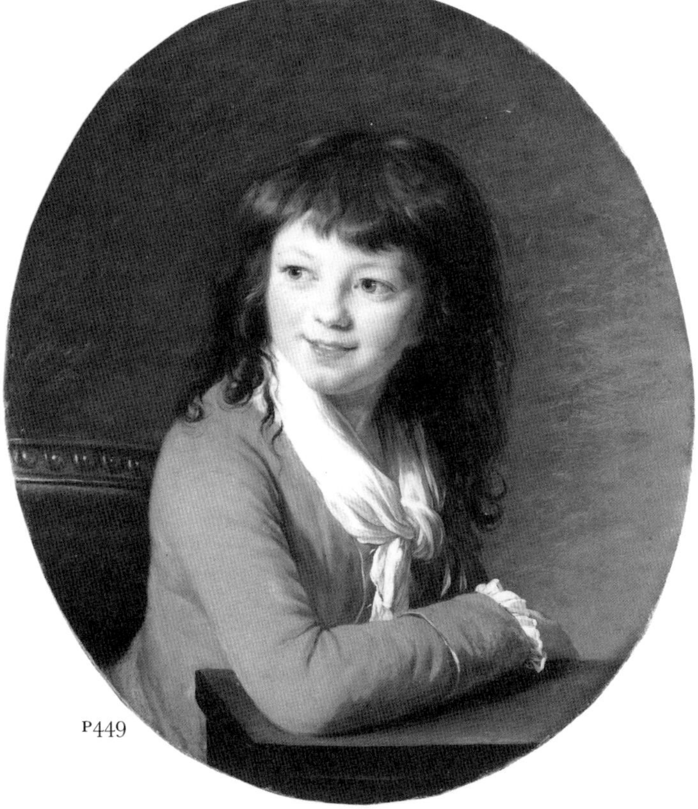

P449

Copy

A copy in miniature was in a French private collection in 1976.

Provenance

The d'Espagnac family, by descent; d'Espagnac sale, Paris, 2–3 March 1866 (262, *jeune comte d'Espagnac*), bt. in, 5,350 fr.; second d'Espagnac sale, Paris, 8 May 1868 (43), bt. by the 4th Marquess of Hertford, 5,050 fr.;[2] rue Laffitte inventory 1871 (433, *'Petite fille en costume de l'empire*); Hertford House inventory 1890 as *'young nobleman in red coat'*.

Exhibitions

Salon 1787 (100, *'M. le Baron d'Espagnac le fils'*); Champs-Elysées, *Tableaux de maîtres*, 1866;[3] Bethnal Green 1872–5 (417, *A Young Nobleman*).[4]

References General

Souvenirs, II, p.363; Baillio, p.70.[5]

[1] For the d'Espagnac family, see *Dictionnaire de biographie française*, XII, 1970, pp.1478–9.

[2] A cutting from this sale catalogue was recently removed from the frame of P449.

[3] *'Le* Portrait du jeune garçon, *de Mme Lebrun, revient de la galerie d'Espagnac, par les mains de M. Dugied, aussi souriant, aussi solide de dessin et de couleur'* (*Gazette des Beaux-Arts*, 1ère, XX, 1866, p.577). A.-L. Blum, *Vigée Le Brun*, 1920, pp.52, 98, suggested Dugied then owned P449, but the known provenance indicates otherwise.

[4] The d'Espagnac identity was restored by MacColl in 1923 (*The Burlington Magazine*, XLII, 1923, pp.182, 187).

[5] Baillio points out that the green table seen in P449 recurs in Vigée Le Brun's portrait of Mlle. Foucquet, also of 1786 (French private coll.; Baillio, no.23).

P457 *Madame Perregaux*

Powdered hair, brown eyes, wearing a black velvet costume with red bows and piping, and a black velvet hat with red plumes; green curtain with gold edging. Signed on the balustrade, lower left: *Vigée Le Brun.f.1789.*

Oak panel 99.6 × 78.5 × 0.6 four vertical members, the joins at 13.8, 33.6 and 55.5 from the left-hand edge
painted area 98.5 × 77

The panel has a cradle, probably dating from the late nineteenth century, of five vertical battens and five horizontal slats. It has a slight concave warp. There is a vertical split, 5 cm. long, on the top edge above the left-hand plume of the hat. Some filling has been lost from the bottom of the right-hand join. Two knots disturb the surface of the panel: above the hat to the left and in the lower right area, the latter treated by Cobbe in 1980. There are some minor losses round the edges. There are retouchings down the joins, round the knots, and on her left cheek, chin and collar. *Pentimenti* show changes to the waist, chin and neck (in each case flattering the sitter) and the balustrade was slightly lowered. The varnish is discoloured.

Adélaïde de Praël (1758–94), daughter of Bernardin, comte de Praël, m. in 1779 the banker J.-F. Perregaux (1744–1808) by whom she had a daughter (Hortense, 1779–1857, duchesse de Raguse) and a son (Alphonse, 1785–1841, comte de Perregaux, see Fragonard P404 and Greuze P388). Her husband was banker for the Le Bruns; he particularly cultivated his English clients (who included the 3rd Marquess of Hertford) and was a collector of some standing.[1] Mme. Perregaux's portrait was also drawn by C. Bornet c.1780 (pastel; private collection).[2]

Vigée Le Brun appears to have been pleased with the likeness in P457 (see note 10) which is also a fine example of her approach to female sitters. '*Je tâchais autant qu'il m'était possible de donner aux femmes que je peignais l'attitude et l'expression de leur physionomie*', she wrote,[3] and stressed the importance of selecting a sitter's pose '*qui convient à son âge et à son caractère, ce qui peut ajouter à la ressemblance*';[4] her dissatisfaction with contemporary female dress led her to make '*tous mes efforts pour le rendre un peu plus pittoresque*',[5] and to devise, possibly, the alluring out-door costume seen in P457.[6] Nolhac described *Mme. Perregaux* as '*fixée dans une attitude imprévue; elle semble prêter l'oreille, et ses yeux malicieux répondent déjà à des paroles lointaines*'.[7] Mme. Perregaux's *attitude* also makes sophisticated reference to Titian and van Dyck,[8] while the creamy flesh tones further indicate a Flemish influence.

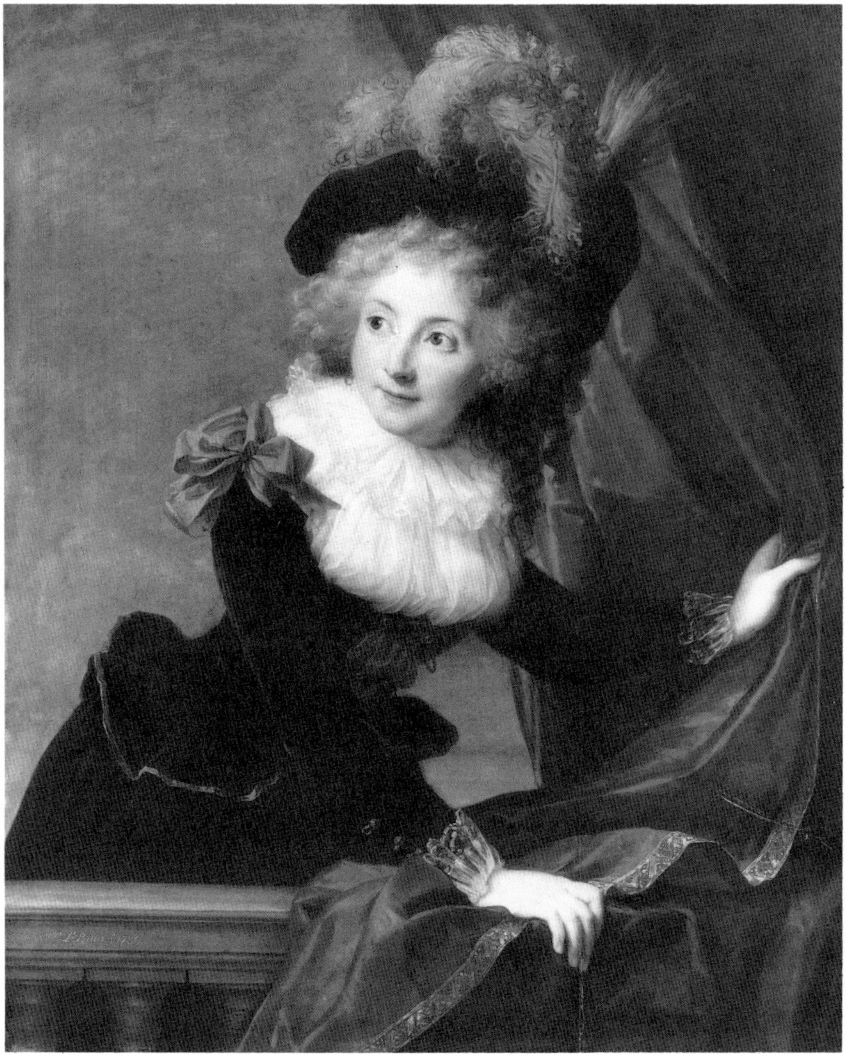

P457

Copies

GENEVA Sotheby's, 17 May 1984 (191); miniature, 9.6 high, attributed to G. Capet (1761–1818).

LONDON Sotheby's, 4 December 1985 (226); miniature, 8.2 high, in the manner of Capet.

Provenance

The Perregaux family (see above); anon. sale Paris, 24 April 1862 [*Portrait de jeune femme tirant un rideau*, 3,720 fr.];[9] the 4th Marquess of Hertford; Bagatelle inventory 1871 (928, '*Portrait de femme*'); Hertford House inventory 1890 as '*Unknown, woman in fancy costume*'.

Exhibitions

Possibly Salon 1791 (738, *Une jeune Dame Espagnole*);[10] Bethnal Green 1872–5 (394).

References General

Souvenirs, II, p.365 ('*Madame Péregaux*'); Baillio, pp.19, 128, 134.

[1] See P. de Pury, 'J.-F. Perregaux', *Musée Neuchâtelois*, January–February 1919 (off-print on file, pp.1–8), and G. de Bellaigue, 'J.-F. Perregaux', *Antologia di Belle Arti*, 29–30, 1986, pp.80–90.

[2] Illus. Pury, *op. cit.*, f.p.6.

[3] *Souvenirs*, I, p.37.

[4] *Ibid.*, II, p.346.

[5] *Ibid.*, I, pp.36–7.

[6] Baillio has associated P457 with the *Jeune dame espagnole* shown in the 1791 Salon (see note 10 below); the costume is not historically Spanish but its loose resemblance to seventeenth-century fashion was perhaps sufficient for it to be called *espagnol*.

[7] P. Nolhac, *Vigée Le Brun*, 1912, p.144.

[8] Titian's *Jacopo Spada* (Vienna), engraved by Teniers in 1660, shows a similar pose, and in van Dyck's *Strafford with his Secretary* (cf. O. Millar, *Van Dyck in England*, exh. cat., London, 1982, no.57) Mainwaring's head and gaze closely resemble Mme. Perregaux's attitude. Baillio (letter on file dated September 1987) further suggests the influence of Rubens's portrait of the Infanta Isabella (Brussels).

[9] The description and price are taken from Mireur (*Dictionnaire des ventes d'art*, VII, 1912, p.370); the sale was identified by A. Jouby (letter on file dated 20 November 1922); only the *affiche* now survives (cf. Lugt 26735), mentioning: '*un très beau portrait de jeune Femme de Mme. Vigée-Lebrun (1789)*'.

[10] Cf. Baillio, pp.19, 134. He also quotes, p.134, a letter from the artist to Mme. Perregaux, dated simply Paris, 30 July, asking her to lend P457 to the Salon:

> *Mde Le Brun envoÿe Savoir des nouvelles de Madame perregaux elle La prie de vouloir bien avoir La Bonté de lui envoyer son portrait ou de donner des ordres dans le Cas où elle L'enverroit chercher. Mde Le Brun ayant recu L avertiSement que tous Les artistes de L'aCademie ayent a envoyer Leurs tableaux pour avoir La grandeur de chacune afin de pourvoir a L'ordre des places au plus tot. Comme Le portrait de madame perregaux est le plus charmant de tous a Cause de Sa reSemblance mde Le Brun la mise a La tête de sa Collection et prie Le Bien aimable original de ne point L'oublier Et de recevoir L'assurance de Ses tendres sentimens Ce 30 juillet/a Madame ou monsieur perregaux/rue du Sentier/a paris*

It would appear that P457 was not exhibited at the Salon in 1789, the year it was painted; as Baillio has maintained (letter on file, see note 8 above), it would surely have attracted attention, but no mention of it survives amongst contemporary Salon notices. In 1791, on the other hand, M. Le Brun submitted two of his wife's three Salon exhibits from Paris (the third she sent herself from Italy), and it would have been diplomatic then to disguise the identity of P457, and to use the somewhat exotic costume as a pretext for the title *jeune Dame Espagnole* (see also note 6 above). However Mme. Vigée Le Brun was in Italy in 1791 and could not have written the letter quoted above in Paris, though she could have forwarded it to her husband. It remains a possibility that P457 was requested for the 1789 Salon, but refused by the owner.

Jean-Antoine Watteau (1684–1721)

Baptised on 10 October 1684 in Valenciennes (a Flemish town ceded to the French in 1678) where he first studied, perhaps under J.-A. Gérin. In 1702 he went to Paris, undertaking hackwork for *entrepreneurs* before studying under Claude Gillot, a painter of theatrical subjects, perhaps c.1704–7. He left Gillot to join Claude III Audran, a decorative artist and *concierge* of the Luxembourg Palace (then the home of the Marie de Médicis cycle by Rubens, which Watteau came to admire greatly). In 1709 he came second in the *prix de Rome* and, having sold a military subject to Pierre Sirois (see P381), he returned briefly to Valenciennes. In 1709–10 he published seven fashion plates (*Figures de modes*). *Agréé* in 1712, the subject of his *morceau de réception* was left, exceptionally, '*à sa volonté*'; eventually, in 1717, he submitted *Le pèlerinage à l'isle de Cithère* (Louvre), perhaps his finest work, and was *reçu* as a painter of *fêtes galantes*. Such elegant and amorous outdoor companies in rich costumes, ranging from the historical and theatrical (often from the *commedia dell'arte*) to the contemporary, ultimately derived from the Venetian pastorals of Giorgione and Titian, and seventeenth-century Dutch and Flemish merry companies. Watteau's study of sixteenth and seventeenth-century painting and drawing was greatly facilitated by Pierre Crozat who, after 1715, gave him the opportunity to see his fine collection in the rue de Richelieu. Twelve etchings from Watteau's figure drawings were published in 1715 (*Figures françoises et comiques*), and the first engravings after his paintings had appeared by 1719 (cf. P377). Pater (within the period 1713–16, and briefly in 1721) and Lancret (c.1717) were for a while his pupils, but he was not an easy master. In 1719–20 he visited London, but he returned to Paris in failing health. He stayed briefly with his friend, the dealer Edme-François Gersaint (Sirois's son-in-law), for whom he painted the celebrated *Enseigne de Gersaint* (Charlottenburg), and died at Nogent-sur-Marne, on the outskirts of Paris, on 18 July 1721.

Watteau's poor health (he died of tuberculosis) was, doubtless, largely responsible for his listless temperament – which seems reflected in his often slipshod practice as a painter. The finest expression of his talent is to be found in his figure drawings, which he used as a constant source for quotation. Such repetition aggravates the problem of chronology; very few of Watteau's works may be dated with certainty. Shortly after his death, his friend and patron Jean de Jullienne commissioned a corpus of engravings after his paintings and drawings (see FDDC and *Recueil* below) which quickly spread Watteau's influence and remains a guide to his authentic works.

Abbreviations

Adhémar	H. Adhémar, *Watteau, sa vie, son oeuvre*, prefaced by R. Huyghe, 1950
Brookner	A. Brookner, *Watteau*, 1967
CR	E. Camesasca and P. Rosenberg, *Tout l'oeuvre peint de Watteau*, 1983
DV	E. Dacier, J. Hérold and A. Vuaflart, *Jean de Jullienne et les graveurs de Watteau*, 4 vols., 1921–9; I Hérold and Vuaflart, *Notices et documents biographiques*, 1929; II Dacier and Vuaflart, *Historique*, 1922; III Dacier and Vuaflart, *Catalogue*, 1922; IV *Planches*, 1921 (numbers refer to the *Catalogue*)
FDDC	*Figures de différents caractères de Paysages et d'Etudes dessinées d'après Nature par Antoine Watteau*, 2 vols., 1726, 1728 (351 engravings commissioned by Jullienne; 1–132 in vol. I, 133–351 in vol. II)
Ferré	J. Ferré *et al.*, *Watteau*, 4 vols., 1972 (numbers refer to the catalogue in vol. 3)
Goncourt	E. de Goncourt, *Catalogue raisonné de l'Oeuvre peint, dessiné et gravé d'Antoine Watteau*, 1875
Hédouin	P. Hédouin, 'Watteau, catalogue de son oeuvre', *L'Artiste*, 30 November 1845, pp.78–80
Mathey	J. Mathey, *Antoine Watteau, peintures réapparues*, 1959
PM	K. T. Parker and J. Mathey, *Antoine Watteau, Catalogue complet de son oeuvre dessiné*, 2 vols., 1957
Réau	L. Réau, 'Watteau', in L. Dimier, ed., *Les Peintres français du XVIIIe siècle*, I, 1928, pp.1–56
Recueil	*Recueil Jullienne*, 4 vols., 1735; vols. 1 and 2 the FDDC (see above), vols. 3 and 4 containing engravings, commissioned by Jullienne, of 214 paintings and 73 drawings by Watteau (first published singly 1719–34)
Watteau 1980	P. Hulton, *Watteau, Drawings in the British Museum*, exhibition catalogue, 1980
Watteau 1984	P. Rosenberg, M. Morgan Grasselli, *et al.*, *Watteau*, exhibition catalogue, Paris, Washington, Berlin, 1984–5 (paintings [P] catalogued by Rosenberg, drawings [D] by Morgan Grasselli) (French ed.)
Zimmermann	E. H. Zimmermann, *Watteau, Klassiker der Kunst*, 1912

P381 *Gilles and his Family (Sous un habit de Mezetin)*

Six figures, including a little child (beneath the guitar); the instrumentalist, with a ten-stringed guitar, in a white satin costume with silver-blue stripes; the youth on the right in red, with a brown cap; the seated girl on the left in white with a pink rose in her hair.

Walnut panel 27.1 × 19 × 0.5 made up to 27.7 × 21 with additions 0.8 wide on the left, 1.2 wide on the right, and 0.3 wide at the top and bottom (the bottom strip broken).

The panel was cradled with four vertical battens and four horizontal slats in 1878 by Vallance; the slats were loosened in 1977. The edging strips appear to be later additions (see Engraving). There are faint diagonal scratches within the arch on the left. *Pentimenti* show alterations to the guitarist's right thumb, and the profile head of a man looking down behind the seated girl on the left has been erased. X-radiography suggests that the upper right area was reworked, the impost

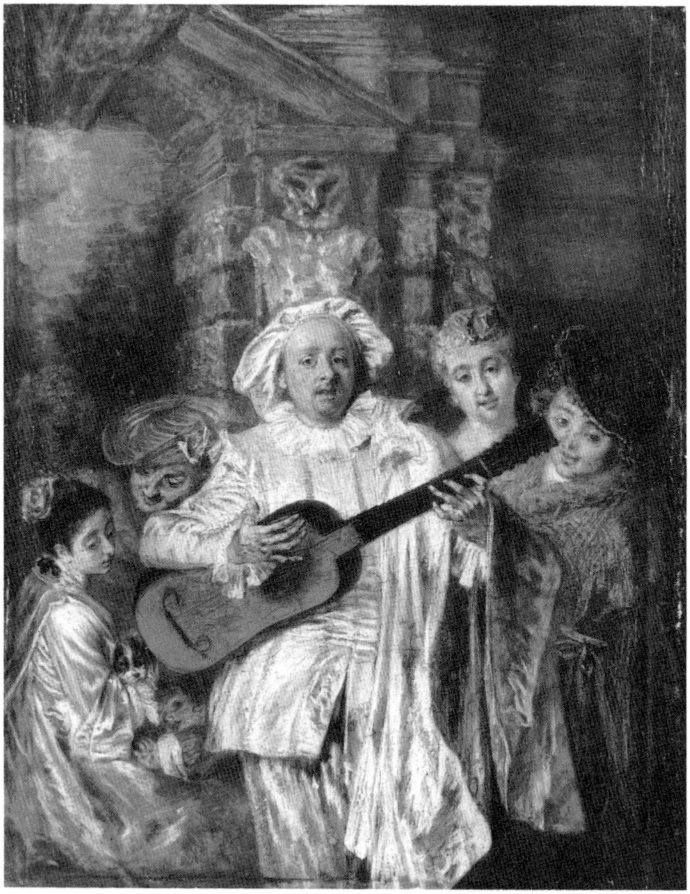

P381

moulding to the right of the arch was altered, and the right-hand youth originally held his right hand at his waist (holding a locket?). The paint is thin in the background areas, and the varnish is discoloured.

The French title given above is taken from the verses which accompanied Thomassin's print of c.1729 (see Engravings). P381 was described by Mariette as '*sieur Sirois, amy de Wateau, représenté au milieu de sa famille, sous la figure de Mezetin jouant de la guittare*'.[1] In the *commedia dell'arte* Mezzetin was Harlequin's rival, a rascally valet and musician (whose character is echoed in the faun seen immediately above).[2] Mariette's identification of Sirois seems confirmed by Watteau's inscribed study (see Drawings), but it is less certain that the supporting cast represent his family. Pierre Sirois (1665–1726), *marchand-vitrier,* an early patron and faithful friend of Watteau, had seven children, aged between about twenty-six and eleven when P381 was painted (see dating below).[3] The presence of a small child,[4] and the erasure of a male figure (described above), argue against a family portrait. All four of the supporting adult cast recur in Watteau's drawings, and

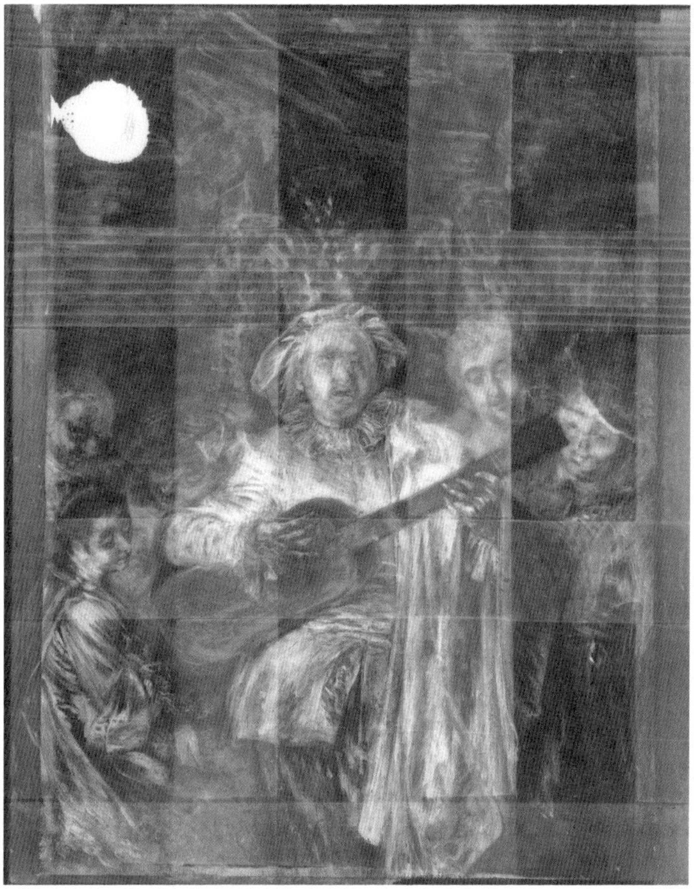

X-radiograph of P381
(The Courtauld Institute)

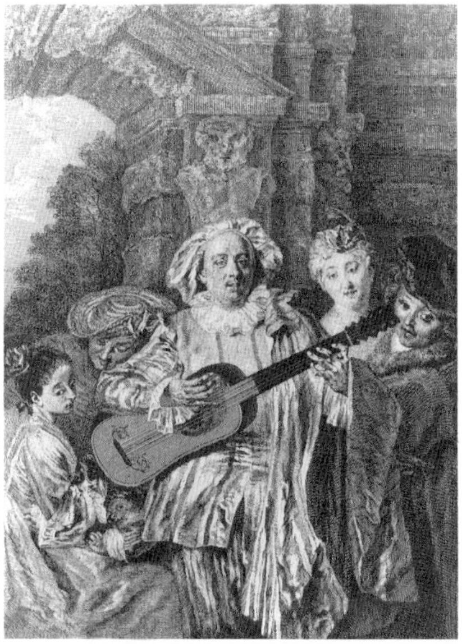

H.-S. Thomassin *fils* after Watteau:
Sous un habit de Mezetin, 1729.

some in his paintings;[5] the man in the straw hat repeats the figure in *L'indiscret* (CR140) of c.1715 (and see note 13). Portraiture was incidental to the *galant* subject, and in this respect P381 may be compared with *La famille* (CR114).[6] Apart from the seated lady on the left, all the adult figures appear to be in costume.

The influence of Rubens is apparent in the colour, handling and content (the arch echoes that of *The Garden of Love*); together with the somewhat uncertain spatial sense (due, apparently, to the casual quotation of separate drawings, see below), this could suggest a date of c.1716. Recent scholarship has generally favoured c.1716–18 (see References General): Posner considers P381 'late',[7] Nemilova 'from his maturity',[8] and Rosenberg c.1717.[9] Adhémar, alone, placed it 1712–15. The later date of c.1718–19, calculated according to the ages of the Sirois family, proposed by Hérold and Vuaflart (DV, I, p.39), and accepted by Mathey (see note 12), Morgan Grasselli,[10] and Watson (1968 catalogue), seems too late stylistically and the identifications of the Sirois family are problematical, as argued above.

Drawings

LONDON British Museum (no.1895–9–15–942); studies for the heads of the two ladies (PM925; *Watteau 1980*, no.24; *Watteau 1984*, D109, as c.1718–19[11]).
PARIS P. Bordeaux-Groult 1957; study for head of the guitarist, inscribed *Syroie*; dated 1718 by Mathey[12] (PM931).
ROUEN Musée des Beaux-Arts (no.822–1–76); sheet with studies for the heads of the left-hand man in a straw hat and the erased head on the extreme left (PM775; *Watteau 1984*, D80, as c.1716[13]). A copy of the head of a man with a straw hat was sold Drouot, 17 June 1966, lot 72 (illus. *Watteau 1984*, p.318).
STOCKHOLM Nationalmuseum (no.2836–1863); sheet with studies of the head of the model used for the right-hand lady (PM787; *Watteau 1984*, D125, as c.1720[14]).

A counter-proof sheet with studies of a child's head has been associated with P381 (PM708, and see P377 Ascribed to Watteau).

Engravings

H.-S. Thomassin *fils*, before 1729 (DV131), with verses by Gacon:

Sous un habit de Mezetin
Ce gros brun au riant Visage
Sur la guitarre avec sa main
Fait un aimable badinage.

Par les doux accents de sa voix
Enfants dune bouche vermeille
Du beau sexe tout a la fois
Il charme les yeux et Loreille.

The engraving omits the additions to P381 (as described above). It appeared in the *Recueil* on the same sheet as *Les habits sont italiens* (DV130; CR204), a closely related composition, but probably not conceived as a pendant.[15]
C.P. Lindemann (1700–54), reversed (DV 131C); A. Schmidt, reversed (DV131D); two anonymous plates (DV131A, B).

Copies

BIARRITZ N. Pendaries 1973; 121 × 94.
DOUAI Tesse sale, 10–15 February 1913 (10); 35 × 28.
LONDON G. Summers 1951.
NEW YORK Christie's, 5 June 1980 (144); 101.6 × 78.1, ex-Metropolitan Museum of Art (no.53.61.2).

Provenance[16]

Anon. sale, Paris, 9 April 1793 (79, *Concert dans un parc, six figures dans des habillements de caractère, formant un concert dans un paysage, bois* [27.2 × 19]'), 65 *livres*; Papillon de La Ferté (d.1794); his sale, Paris, 20 February 1797 (75, '. . . *six figures, dont un Scapin vu jusqu'aux genoux debout et jouant de la guitarre; le fond offre un portique d'architecture et fond de paysage, bois* [28.5 × 23.1]'), bt. Le Brun. Possibly Bouchardon sale, Paris, 13 September 1808 (51 '*Un petit tableau offrant un concert de famille*'). Anon. sale, Paris, 19 December 1825 (37,'*Scaramouche entouré de plusieurs personnes, hommes et femmes, qui l'écoutent jouer de la guitare*'); F. Duval, Geneva;[17] his sale Phillips, 1st day, 12 May 1846 (47, 'A composition of six figures, in theatrical costume . . . engaged in the service of Thalia; they were probably actors celebrated at the time . . .'),[18] bt. Farrer for the 4th Marquess of Hertford, 200 gn.; rue Laffitte inventory 1871 (667); Hertford House inventory 1890.

Exhibitions

Bethnal Green 1872–5 (452); RA 1889 (95).

References General

Goncourt, no.178; Zimmermann, no.63, as c.1716–18; DV131; Réau, no.193; Adhémar, no.92, as 1712–15; Mathey, p.69, as 1717–18; Brookner, pl.15, as perhaps 1716–18; Ferré, A9; CR181, as c.1717.

[1] Quoted under DV131, from P.-J. Mariette, *Notes manuscrites sur les peintres et graveurs*, c.1731, IX, f.191, no.7 (Bibliothèque Nationale, see DV, II, pp.114–16).

[2] As suggested by F. Souchal, AHAA, IX, 1987, p.177. For Mezzetin see, for example, F. Moureau in *Watteau 1984*, pp.510–12.

[3] For Sirois and his family see Hérold and Vuaflart, DV, I, pp.34–9. By his first wife (who d.1694) he had a daughter, Anne-Elisabeth (1692/3–after 1726); by his second (from whom he separated in 1705, and who d.1709), three daughters and three sons: Marie-Louise (1696/7–1725, who m. Gersaint in 1718); Marie-Anne-Elisabeth (1697/8–after 1726, who m. De Cuisy after 1718 and before 1726); Marie-Anne (b.1706); Pierre-Henri (1702–after 1736); François (1704–after 1726), and Gabriel-Henri (1705–81). Hérold and Vuaflart identified the figures in P381 as (from left to right): Marie-Anne-Elisabeth with Marie-Anne on her lap; François; Sirois himself; Anne-Elisabeth, and Pierre-Henri. See also notes 11 and 14 below.

[4] J. Mathey, BSHAF 1939, pp.157–8, considered the child a caprice: *'on peut pourtant accepter que la fantaisie de Watteau ait placé là un enfant qui n'était pas de Sirois'*.

[5] See Drawings. In addition: the left-hand seated woman in PM533 (cf. *Watteau 1984*, D25), PM579, PM665 (with the model for the left-hand man), and PM768; the left-hand man in the straw hat could be the same model as the lutanists in P410 and P377, and recurs frequently (cf. PM, pp. xii–xiii and 322; *Watteau 1984*, pp.154, 317); the right-hand woman in PM677, and in the *Retour de chasse* (DV19); the right-hand youth in PM740 and *Les entretiens badins* (DV95; cf. Adhémar, p.76). The left-hand seated woman seems also to recur in paintings by Pater, e.g. *La feste italienne* in the Louvre (IS4) and *Le déjeuner sur l'herbe* at Dulwich (IS199).

[6] *La famille* has been said to show the Le Bouc-Santussan family, but cf. *Watteau 1984*, p.380. D. Posner, *Antoine Watteau*, 1984, pp.208, 256–7, discusses Watteau's original use of portraiture in such costume pieces. PM, pp.xii-xiii, stress the difficulties of identifying portraits in Watteau's work; L. Gillet, *Watteau*, 1921, p.89, thought the two women in P381 were the same model, which rather proves the point. See also P410 note 16.

[7] Posner, *loc. cit.* He emphasises the apparent spontaneity of the composition and indicates the disproportionate size of the head of the man with a straw hat (p.290 n.51).

[8] I.S. Nemilova, *Watteau et ses oeuvres à l'Ermitage*, 1964, p.80.

[9] Cf. *Watteau 1984*, p.317.

[10] *Ibid.*, D109.

[11] Morgan Grasselli, proposed the identifications of Marie-Louise for the right-hand woman in P381 and in *L'enseigne de Gersaint* (as Gersaint's wife), and Marie-Anne-Elisabeth for the left-hand seated woman in P381.

[12] Mathey, BSHAF 1939, pp.157–8. Mathey, PM and N. Parmantier (*Watteau 1984*, p.49) consider the inscription to be by Watteau; Morgan Grasselli calls it *'ancienne'* (*Watteau 1984*, D109).

[13] Morgan Grasselli notes that the model for the man in the straw hat appears to be too old for the oldest Sirois boy, Pierre-Henri; *'ce fait nous empêche de nous fier entièrement au témoignage de Mariette'*. See also note 5 above.

[14] Morgan Grasselli proposed the identification of Marie-Louise Sirois (see also note 11 above).

[15] Cf. Posner, *op. cit.*, p.256.

[16] P381 has been associated, with insufficient evidence, with the following sales: Lollier, Paris, 6 April 1789 (55, *'cinque figures vêtues de differents habillements de caractère, vus jusqu'au genoux . . . bois* [25.6 × 18.9]'), and Grand-Pré, Paris, 16 February ff.1809 (40, *'un petit tableau représentant cinq personnages occupés à faire de la musique, dans le genre de Titien'*).

[17] Whose stamp remains on the *verso* of P381 (FD monogram within a wreath of oak leaves and acorns); it also appears on the *verso* of the van der Heyden P225.

[18] The *Times*, 13 May 1846, gave the size as 11 × $8\frac{1}{2}$ in., i.e. 27.9 × 21.6.

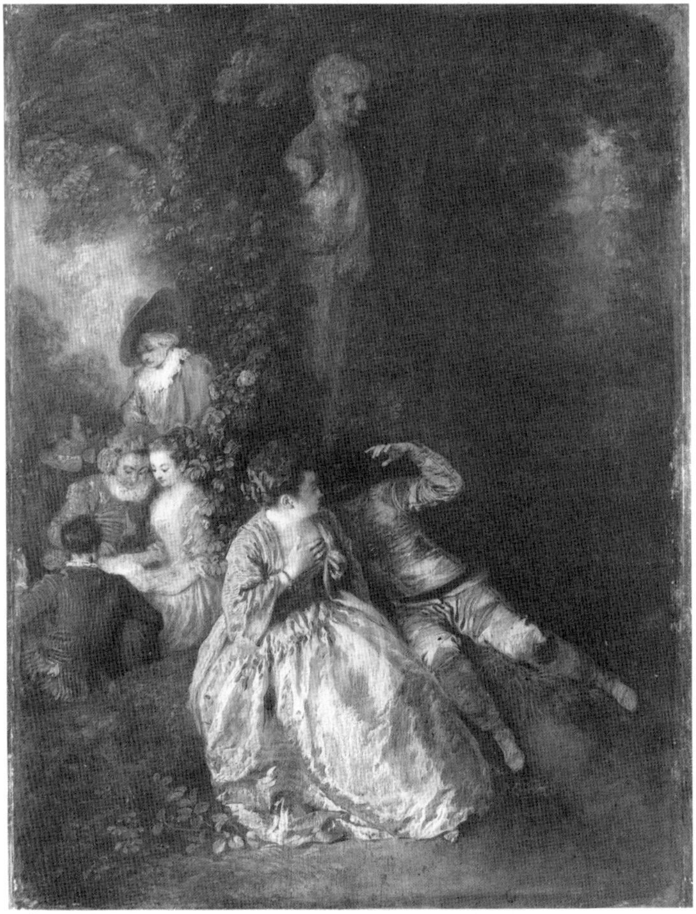

P387

P387 *Harlequin and Columbine (Voulez-vous triompher des Belles?)*

Columbine wears an apricot silk dress with a blue-lined hem, a red hat with blue trimmings and a blue flower on her wrist band; Harlequin's costume has red, blue and gold patches; in the mid-distance the seated couple have roses in their hair; beyond them Crispin (the *commedia dell'arte* valet) seen in profile.

Oak panel 36 × 24.9 × 0.3 of two sections, the left 11 wide, made up to 36 × 25.9 with oak strips down each vertical edge.

The panel is cradled with six vertical battens and five horizontal slats. The edging strips are evidently additions (see Engraving), very thinly painted. There are minor paint losses round the edges of the original panel. The paint on the herm is mauled, the darker areas of the wood on the right are indistinct, and the sky is very thin on the left. The varnish is slightly discoloured.[1]

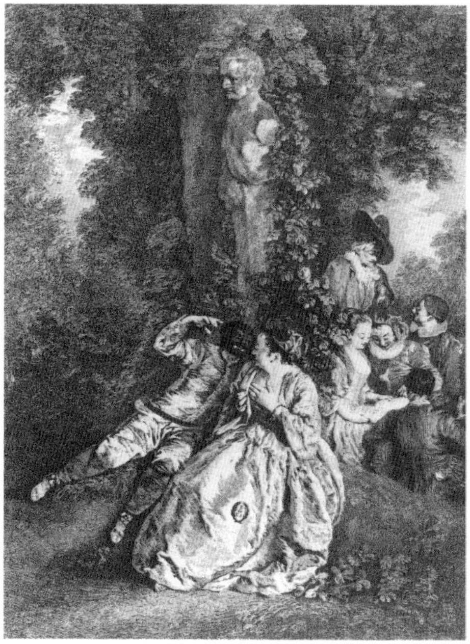

H.-S. Thomassin *fils* after Watteau:
Voulez vous triompher des Belles?, 1725.

The French title given above is taken from the verses which accompanied Thomassin's print of 1725 (see Engraving). P387 was described by Mariette as '*Arlequin contant fleurette à une belle; il est assis auprès d'elle, au pied d'un terme, & dans le fonds est une compagnie qui forme un concert*'.[2] It has been plausibly suggested that the subject derived from *Arlequin misanthrope*, a play by Louis Brancolelli and Brugière de Barante first performed in 1696,[3] although Harlequin proposing Columbine was a stock *commedia dell'arte* scene.[4] Mirimonde suggests that the roses growing over the herm (whose pointed ear indicates a faun) portend happiness.[5] The ladies wear contemporary costume, while the men are in theatrical dress.

As Brookner indicates, P387 seems later than P381, being more assured in handling and spatial construction. It is generally placed c.1716–18, though Adhémar and Mathey preferred an earlier date (see References General); Posner proposed c.1717,[6] and Nemilova placed P387 in Watteau's maturity.[7]

Drawings

ROUEN Musée des Beaux-Arts (no.822–1–76); sheet containing studies for the heads of the seated man in the left mid-distance and of Crispin behind him (PM775; *Watteau 1984*, D80, as c.1716).

STOCKHOLM Nationalmuseum (no.448); counter-proof sheet with a study for Harlequin's right arm and hand (PM48).

A related compositional counter-proof is also at Stockholm (no.485; PM132), and two sheets of studies of a woman's head, resembling that of the seated lady in the left mid-distance in P387, were in private collections in Paris in 1957 (PM756, one head engr. B. Lépicié, FDDC, no.221, and PM783, engr. J. Audran, FDDC, nos.98, 191, 217, 244).

Engraving

H.-S. Thomassin *fils* 1725, reversed (DV84), dedicated to Caylus, with verses by C. Moraine:

Voulez vous triompher des Belles?
Debitez leur des bagatelles;
Parlez d'un ton facetieux;
Et gardez vous bien au pres d'elles
De prendre un masque serieux.

L'Amour demande qu'on l'amuse:
Il est enfant: toute la ruse,
Pour luy plaire, est d'estre badin;
Et souvent au Sage il refuse
Tout ce qu'obtient un Arlequin.

The engraving differs from P387 in that the hat of the standing man in the left mid-distance has a lower crown and lacks the plume, and it omits the additions to P387 (as described above).

Copies/Versions

ANTWERP anon. sale, 12 December 1859 (133); panel 19 × 15.
BRUSSELS L. Thielens sale, 24 May ff. 1842 (179); '*Arlequin et Colombine. A gauche autres personnages faisant de la musique dans un bosquet. Tableau gravé. T[oile]* 39 × 32'.
DRESDEN Gemäldegalerie; eighteenth-century copy, adapted as an overdoor, from the Château d'Oberlichtenau.[8]
LONDON Wallace Collection (M142); miniature, late eighteenth-century.
Holford sale, Christie's, 17–18 May 1928 (131), reversed copy, 35 × 28.6.

A copy by H. Joseph set in a Meissen box of c.1750 was on the Berlin art market 1905.

Provenance

Johann Anton de Peters (1725–95); his sale, Paris, 9 March 1779 (95, '*Sept figures de caractère dans un jardin: sur le premier plan, Arlequin et Colombine sont assis* . . . [35.4 × 25.8]'); Mme. de Peters sale, Paris, 5 November ff. 1787 (129, as above);[9] Sir Thomas Baring, 2nd Bt. (1772–1848); his sale, Christie's, 2 June 1848 (115, 'A man in masquerade sitting at the base of a terminal figure; other figures reposing near him'), bt. Mawson, 150 gn.; Lord Henry Seymour (1805–59, brother of the 4th Marquess of Hertford), who bequeathed P387 to Richard Wallace;[10] rue Laffitte inventory 1871 (425); Hertford House inventory 1890.

Exhibitions

Boulevard des Italiens 1860 (272, as *L'indiscret* and *L'amour badin*)[11] lent Wallace; Bethnal Green 1872–5 (472); RA 1889 (99).

References General

Goncourt, no.179; Zimmermann, no.62, as c.1716–18; DV84; Réau, no.64; Adhémar, no.94, as c.1712–15; Mathey, p.69, as c.1714; Brookner, pl.21, as late 1716; Ferré, A14; CR152, as c.1716.

[1] CR refer to a recent cleaning of P387, but this is mistaken; they regret the loss of colour on the right. Adhémar found P387 '*beau, mais très noir; paysage disparu*'. An X-radiograph taken in 1961 revealed nothing.

[2] Quoted under DV84 from P.-J. Mariette, *Notes manuscrites sur les peintres et graveurs*, c.1731, IX, f. 192, no.32 (Bibliothèque Nationale; see DV, II, pp.114–16).

[3] J. A. Plax, *Watteau's* Voulez-vous: *an Interpretation and Inquiry into the Theme of Love*, unpub. MA thesis, University of Missouri, 1979 (quoted in T. E. Crow, *Painters and Public Life*, 1985, pp.69–70).

[4] Cf. P.-L. Duchartre, *The Italian Comedy*, 1966 (reprint), pp.279–81 (D. Posner, *Antoine Watteau*, 1984, p.281 n.38, suggests the engravings there shown might have derived from P387). S. S. Taylor, 'Le geste chez les maîtres italiens de Molière', *XVIIe Siècle*, 1981, p.290, also emphasises the traditional character of Harlequin's gesture in P381.

[5] A.-P. de Mirimonde, *Gazette des Beaux-Arts*, 6e, LVIII, 1961, p.269. F. Souchal, AHAA, IX, 1987, p.177, sees the faun as emblematic of love and pleasure.

[6] Posner, *op. cit.*, p.57: 'close in time to the Pilgrimage to Cythera'.

[7] I. S. Nemilova, *Watteau et ses oeuvres à l'Ermitage*, 1964, p.78.

[8] Cf. H. Marx in *Antoine Watteau*, ed. F. Moreau and M. Morgan Grasselli, 1987, p.297 n.34.

[9] In both Peters sales P387 was described, incorrectly, as engraved by Lépicié, but the identification is confirmed by a marginal drawing by Saint-Aubin in a copy of the 1779 catalogue (see DV84; illus. E. Dacier, *Catalogues de ventes et livrets de Salons illustrés et annotés par Gabriel de Saint-Aubin*, V, 1919); DV did not identify P387 in the 1787 sale.

[10] As *Arlequin* by Watteau (copy of his Will in the Wallace Collection archives).

[11] The different titles appearing, respectively, in the first and second editions of the catalogue. W. Bürger, *Gazette des Beaux-Arts*, 1ère, VII, 1860, pp.273–4, reviewing the exhibition, commented: 'L'Indiscret *est le titre que porte le tableau dans le catalogue, mais je crois qu'il a été gravé sous le titre*: l'Amour badin'.

P389 *Les Champs Elisées*

The seated girl in the left foreground wears a golden yellow dress with pale blue stripes; the standing man on the far right wears a deep red hat and a blue-lined black cloak over a golden yellow costume; in the centre foreground a girl holds a basket of pink and white roses; the trees show summer and autumn tints.

Mahogany panel 31.2 × 41 × 1 made up to 33.1 × 42.6 with pine edging strips

The paint on the edging strips is clearly not original. There are small losses by the statue and down the right-hand edge, and the paint is lifting in the bottom right area, along the back of the reclining man and in the figure of the standing man. X-radiography shows this area had previously been painted out with lead white (the uneven edge may be read just to the right of the standing man). The reclining female statue was then painted in. The rocaille shell on the right of the fountain and the dolphin below belong to the original composition. The area immediately to the left of the fountain is not entirely resolved (cf. Engraving). Craquelure in the upper right area reveals the brown-red ground. The varnish is discoloured and uneven.[1]

The title is taken from Tardieu's print of 1727 (see Engraving); it refers more to the character of the Champs Elysées than their topography.[2] Posner suggests that the subject may be the progress of love; the innocent dalliance of the foreground child and adult groups and the impassive man standing below the sleeping statue, contrast with the loving couples and energetic dancers in the mid-distance.[3] The women and children appear to wear contemporary dress, but the men are in costume. The subject compares closely with that of P391.

The extent of the landscape, the distribution of the figures and the subtle lighting, indicate a work of Watteau's maturity. P389 has been dated c.1716–17 by Posner[4] and Roland-Michel[5] (and see References General), but it might be a little later, as Mathey, Brookner, Watson (1968 catalogue) and Nemilova[6] have suggested. The fresh observation of the distant sunlit landscape contrasts with the summary hatching of the foreground grass and the *staccato* appearance of some of the foreground figures. P389 (with P391) is a particularly revealing example of Watteau's compositional technique. Thirteen of his known drawings were used for the figures (see Drawings). The right-hand child of the left-foreground group, together with the pose of the man standing by the fountain, was quoted from *L'accordée de village* of c.1711 (CR127 as c.1715) and she appears in *Récréation galante* of c.1717–18 (CR173); the statue of the sleeping nymph derives from the *Nymphe et satyre* of c.1715 (CR104); the seated woman pinning her corsage recurs in *Les deux cousines* of c.1716 (CR151); the seated woman to her right holding a fan appears as a background figure in *Plaisirs d'amour* of c.1717 (CR178), and the reclining man, seen between two trees in the mid-distance, recurs (reversed) in the background of *Réunion en plein air* of c.1717–18 (CR182). The vigorously dancing couple in the centre mid-distance recall Rubens's *Peasant Dance* in the Prado,[7] while the idea of the man standing by the fountain and the seated girl looking directly at the spectator could have been taken from Rubens's *Garden of Love* (Prado).

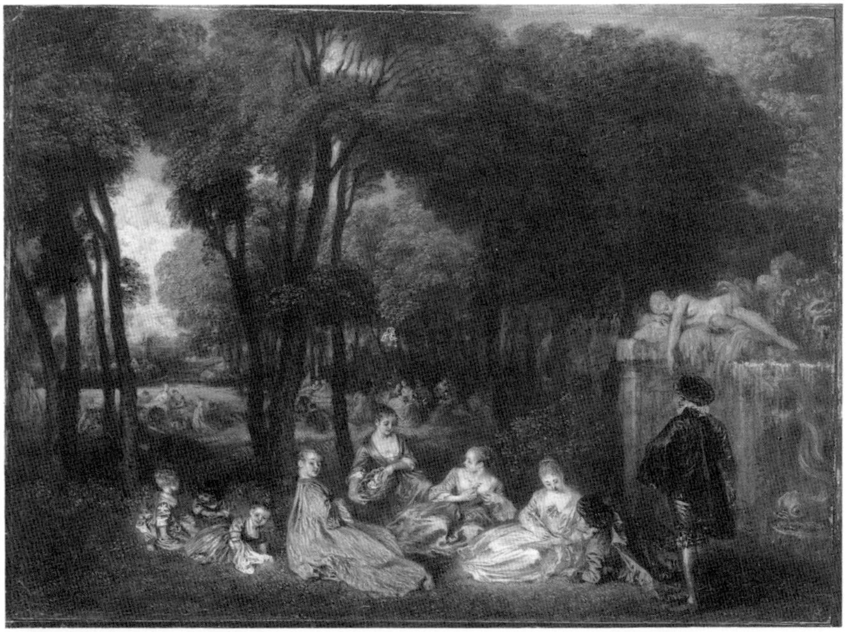

P389

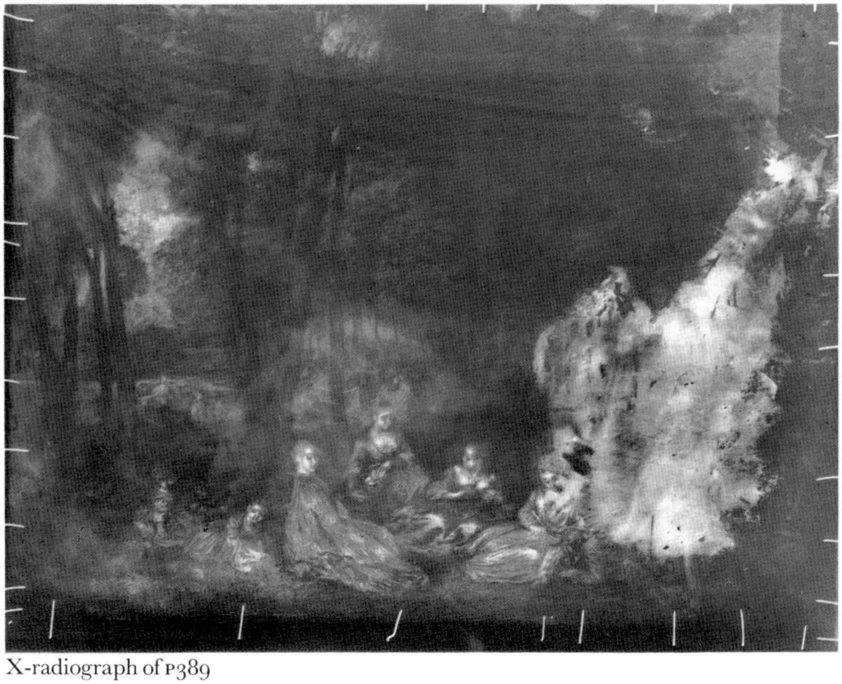

X-radiograph of P389
(The Courtauld Institute)

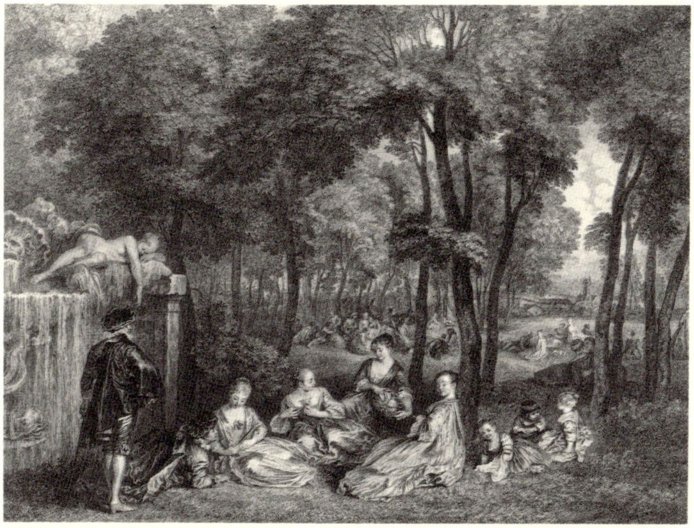

N.-H. Tardieu after Watteau: *Les Champs Elisées*, 1727. Bibliothèque Nationale

Drawings

Those marked * were also used for P391.

CHANTILLY Musée Condé; sheet with a study for the seated woman in the left foreground (PM614).

GERMANY private collection 1957; sheet with a study for the child on the left of the left foreground group (PM961; engr. J. Audran, FDDC, no.194).

LONDON British Museum (no.1846–11–14–25); sheet with a study for the woman pinning her corsage in the foreground (PM602; *Watteau 1980*, no.32).*
(no.1869–6–12–297); study for the man with a hurdy-gurdy in the centre mid-distance, and for the hands of the woman holding a basket in the foreground (reversed) (PM721; *Watteau 1980*, no.51).*
Princes Gate Collection, Courtauld Institute Galleries (no.222); sheet with a study for the seated woman in the mid-distance (PM638; engr. J. Audran, FDDC, no.294).*

MUNICH Staatliche Graphische Sammlung (no.13421); sheet with a reversed study for the reclining man seen between two trees in the mid-distance (PM651).*

NEW YORK H. Arnhold 1957; study for the man standing by the fountain (PM680).*

PARIS P. Bordeaux-Groult 1957; study for the seated woman holding a fan in the foreground (PM549; engr. J. Audran, FDDC, no.138; see also PM585 below).*
— sheet with a study for the child in the middle of the left-hand foreground group (PM691).
— sheet with a study for the hands of the seated woman holding a fan, and for the right hand of the man standing by the fountain (PM829).
A. Strölin 1957; sheet with a study for the reclining man in the right foreground (PM687).*
Private collection 1957; study for the seated woman seen between two trees in the left mid-distance (PM600).

SEVRES private collection 1957; study for the seated woman holding a fan (PM585; see also PM549 above).*

Three studies of a fountain, comparable with that in P389, are in the Nationalmuseum, Stockholm (PM203, PM206 and PM226).[8]

Engraving

N.-H. Tardieu 1727, reversed (DV133), as *Les Champs Elisées, Gravées d'Apres le Tableau Original peint par Watteau de mesme grandeur* [31.4 × 40.6] *du Cabinet de Mr. de Jullienne*, omitting the additions described above and showing more trees immediately to the left of the statue. A copy in pen and ink by Ingres is in the Musée Ingres, Montauban (no.531).

Copies

CAMPSBAY South Africa, private collection 1971; 147 × 118, ex coll. Lord de Saumerez.

NICE private collection 1953; 91 × 123.

TRIESTE private collection 1961; copy by R. Ranft.

A version in the collection of A. Maskin was engraved by William Blake in 1782 as *Evening Amusement* (DV133A). A painting attributed to Watteau, *Les Champs Elysées*, was in the Beckett Denison sale, Christie's, 20 June 1885 (1062), 34.3 × 44.5.

Provenance

Jean de Jullienne (1686–1766) by 1727 (see Engraving); by 1752 with A. Blondel de Gagny (1695–1776);[9] his sale, Paris, 10 December 1776 (222, *Les Champs Elisées, bois* [32.6 × 40.8]), bt. by his son, B.-A. Blondel d'Azincourt (1719–94), 6,505 *livres*; his sale, Paris, 10 February 1783 (34), when inspected with a view to purchase by Louis XVI,[10] bt. by the comte de Vaudreuil (1740–1817), 8,000 *livres*; the duc de Chabot (1733–1807);[11] his sale, Paris, 10 December 1787 (62, identified as from the Blondel de Gagny and d'Azincourt collections, *bois* [32.6 × 40.8]), bt. Dulac, 4,850 *livres*;[12] the duc de Morny (1811–65) by 1845;[13] his sale, Phillips, 2nd day, 21 June 1848 (77, '*Les Champs Elysées*, the smaller picture, panel [31.7 × 41.9]'), bt. by the 4th Marquess of Hertford, 900 gn.;[14] seen in Hertford House 1854 by Waagen (IV, p.83); Hertford House inventory 1870.

Exhibitions

Bethnal Green 1872–5 (446); RA 1889 (93).

References General

Hédouin, p.78, no.23; Goncourt, no.116; Zimmermann, no.77, as c.1716–18; DV133; Réau, no.158; Adhémar, no.184, as late 1716; Mathey, p.69, as 1718; Brookner, pls.38–9, as c.1718–19; Ferré, A25; CR156, as c.1717?.

1 When P389 was exhibited at the RA in 1889 the *Athenaeum*, 23 February 1889, p.249, commented: 'if it were possible to clean a Watteau (but we believe it is not) this example would benefit more than most'. There is no record of P389 being cleaned subsequently. See also note 10.

2 In 1716 the Champs Elysées were described as '*un grand terrein rempli d'allées, d'arbre & de verdure, où les Dimanches & Fêtes une partie du peuple de Paris vient se délasser du travail de la semaine*' (*Les Curiositez de Paris*, 1716, 1883 ed., p.43).

3 D. Posner, *Antoine Watteau*, 1984, p.174. F. Souchal, AHAA, IX, 1987, pp.181, 183–4, emphasises the erotic presence of the statue.

4 *Ibid.*, p.196, as c.1717.

5 M. Roland-Michel, *Watteau*, 1984, p.229, as c.1716–17.

6 I. S. Nemilova, *Watteau et ses oeuvres à l'Ermitage*, 1964, p.138.

7 In a drawing in the Musée des Arts Décoratifs, Paris (PM279), Watteau copied another energetically dancing couple from Rubens's *Kermesse* (Louvre; acquired by Louis XIV).

8 These drawings have been attributed to G. M. Oppenort (cf. M. Eidelberg, *The Burlington Magazine*, CX, 1968, pp.447–56, but see also K. T. Parker, *ibid.*, CXI, 1969, p.223).

9 Cf. Dezallier d'Argenville, *Voyage pittoresque de Paris*, 1752, p.232.

10 NAAF, 2e, I, 1879, p.430: J.-B.-M. Pierre to d'Angiviller, 6 February 1783, '*no.34 Les champs Elisées, par Wateau, ont une grande réputation, mais sont bien noirs*'.

11 Identified by Watson (1968 catalogue); previously thought to have been the duc de Choiseul. The sale was advertised as that of *le duc de Ch.*

12 P389 bears, *verso*, the initials *C: de B*, possibly in a late eighteenth-century hand. They may belong to an owner between the ducs de Chabot and Morny.

13 Cf. Hédouin, *loc. cit.*

14 See Introduction, p.13.

P391 *Fête in a Park (Divertissements champêtres)*

The seated youth in the centre foreground wears a deep purple cloak over a silver blue costume; the children on the left are in pink (left) and silver-blue; the standing man on the far right wears a deep red hat and a black cloak over a golden yellow costume; at his feet lies a youth in a gold-lined red cloak; the trees show summer and autumn tints.

Canvas, relined 127.2 × 191.7

Relined in the mid-nineteenth century (cf. P416 which is on an identical stretcher). Cleaned by Vallance in 1976. The lighter areas (e.g. the children on the left and the statue on the right) contrast strongly with the unworked brown ground in the lower left area and beneath and to the left of the statue; this imbalance was already noted in 1889.[1] A horizontal seam runs 10 cm. above the

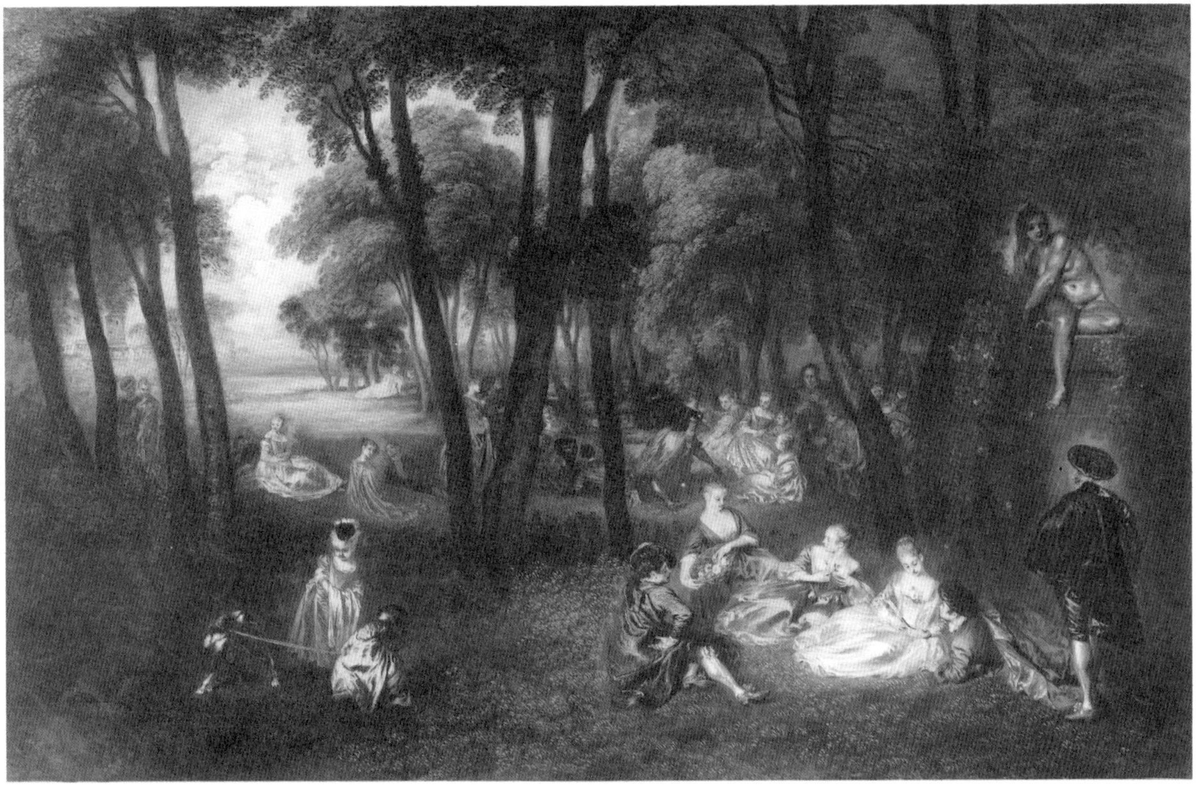

P391

bottom edge, but the addition appears to have been made by Watteau himself. There is a damage in a tree trunk, centre left (between the children and the seated youth), and there are minor retouchings along the left-hand edge. *Pentimenti* and X-radiography show a second female figure seated by the seated woman in the centre-left mid-distance, and the man at her side moved; the right-hand foreground tree has replaced two more distant trees.

P391 was not engraved for the *Recueil* (doubtless because of its similarity to P389, which was); the French title given above was first used by Zimmermann in 1912. From 1802 until the 1928 catalogue P391 was called *Amusements champêtres*, a title given to a quite different picture (CR189) in the *Recueil*. The subject relates closely to that of P389 but, as Posner has emphasised,[2] the mood is livelier. The distant figure groups have been brought closer and contrast more strongly with the foreground group who, however, are more flirtatious. There are now three couples, and the man by the fountain on the right is more engaged, his interest echoed by the curiously sensual statue.[3] As in P389, only the men seem to be in costume; the women and children wear contemporary dress.

Although closely allied with P389, P391 appears to be later. The addition to the bottom edge (described above), which originally came immediately below the foreground figures, as in P389, provides a higher view-point, and the larger scale makes it a more ambitious picture. It has generally been dated c.1718–20; Nemilova proposed 1718,[4] Posner c.1719–20,[5] Roland-Michel 1718–20,[6] and see References General. Adhémar, exceptionally, proposed 1716 for both P389 and P391, which seems too early. Watteau painted four other *fêtes galantes* on this scale (including P416), all generally dated 1717–20,[7] of which Camesasca compares P391 particularly with the *Embarquement pour Cythère* (Charlottenburg; CR185). Posner has suggested that P391 betrays evidence of Watteau's waning enthusiasm for the *fête galante*,[8] and his suggestion is supported by the somewhat tired execution (the flecks of grass, which worked in P389, here seem merely repetitive), the *staccato* quotation of figure drawings, and the unfocussed composition (which was more successful on the smaller scale). The statue recurs, reversed, in *La leçon d'amour* (CR153) and *Le bosquet de Bacchus* (CR141); the child holding the dog's leash in *L'amour paisible* (CR197), and other quotations are described under P389.

Drawings

Nine drawings used for P391 are listed with an asterisk under P389.

BAYONNE Musée Bonnat (no.1713); study for the seated woman seen in profile in the centre-right mid-distance (PM612).
LONDON British Museum (no.1895–9–15–934); study for the seated woman turning to the left with her hands crossed in the centre-right mid-distance (PM601; *Watteau 1980*, no.23; engr. F. Boucher, FddC, no.266).
(no.1859–6–11–98); study for the child holding a dog's lead (PM695; *Watteau 1980*, no.49).
(no.1875–6–12–558, *recto*); sheet with a study for the right hand of the seated youth in the centre foreground (PM827; *Watteau 1980*, no.46).
(no.1895–9–15–936); study probably used for the reclining woman in the centre-left distance (PM610; *Watteau 1980*, no.33; engr. F. Boucher, FddC, no.161).
PARIS Musée Cognacq-Jay; sheet with a study for the standing woman seen behind a tree in the mid-distance, centre-left (PM648).
ex Groult collection; life study used for the statue (PM529).

A drawing for the standing child in the left foreground was engraved by F. Boucher, FddC, no.85.[9] The distant Italianate buildings resemble parts of a *View of Bassano* which Watteau copied (PM390).

Provenance

For provenance before 1848, see P416. Thereafter: Morny sale, Phillips, 2nd day, 21 June 1848 (101), bt. by the 4th Marquess of Hertford, 1,050 gn.;[10] seen in Hertford House 1851 by Waagen (II, p.156; IV, p.83); rue Laffitte inventory (418, with P416, *'Fêtes champêtres, les deux tableaux prisés trente mille francs'*[11]); Hertford House inventory 1890.

Exhibitions

Manchester, *Art Treasures*, 1857 (saloon H, no.27, *Fête Champêtre*);[12] Bethnal Green 1872–5 (402); RA 1889 (91).

References General

Hédouin, pp.79–80, no.90; Goncourt, p.171; Zimmermann, no.98, as c.1719–21; DV, under 126; Réau, no.159; Adhémar, no.183 [printed 182], as late 1716; Mathey, p.69, as 1718; Brookner, pl.40, as 1720–1; Ferré, B48; CR183, as 1718?.

[1] When P391 was exhibited at the RA in 1889 the *Athenaeum*, 23 February 1889, p.249, commented that it seemed a little rubbed, somewhat sunken in the shadows, and slightly darkened. M. Roland-Michel, *Watteau*, 1984, p.210, suggested that P391, with P416, was 'perhaps very slightly over-cleaned'. See also J. Ingamells, AHAA, IX, 1987, pp.170, 172.

[2] D. Posner, *Antoine Watteau*, 1984, p.174.

[3] A.-P. de Mirimonde, *Gazette des Beaux-Arts*, 6e, LVIII, 1961, p.268, and *La Revue du Louvre*, 1962, p.16, suggested that the statue might represent Opportunity. F. Souchal, AHAA, IX, 1987, pp.181, 183, sees it more as a sensual Venus figure, with its life-like quality and colouring.

[4] I. S. Nemilova, *Watteau et ses oeuvres à l'Ermitage*, 1964, p.138.

[5] Posner, *loc. cit.*

[6] Roland-Michel, *op. cit.*, p.221.

[7] *Le pèlerinage à l'isle de Cithère*, 1717, 129 × 194 (Louvre; CR168); *L'embarquement pour Cythère*, 1718–19, 129 × 194 (Charlottenburg; CR185); *Récréation galante*, 1717–18, 111 × 163 (Berlin-Dahlem; CR173)

[8] Posner, *op. cit.*, p.196.

[9] This figure recurs in B. Picart's engraving *La bénédiction du lit nuptial* (published in his *Cérémonies et coutumes de tous les peuples du monde*, 1723–43); Roland-Michel, *op. cit.*, p.230, suggests Watteau took the figure from Picart (but the reverse is possible).

[10] Cf. *Art Journal*, 1 August 1848, p.257.

[11] The high valuation confirms the identification.

[12] Lord Hertford is supposed to have refused an offer of over 2,000 gn. for P391 during the Manchester exhibition (cf. W. Bürger, *Gazette des Beaux-Arts*, 1ère, VII, 1860, p.269).

P410 *The Music Party (Les charmes de la vie)*

The lutanist wears a costume of clover pink with silver stripes and blue and gold trimmings; the man standing on the extreme left has a deep red cloak and hat; the guitarist has a blue and silver striped bodice, white skirt and pink drape; the standing child is in pink.

Canvas 67.3 × 92.5 stretcher size 68.8 × 94.8

Described as 'much injured' in 1895,[1] and cleaned by Lank in 1980[2] when several areas of retouching were uncovered: the head of the seated woman with crossed hands on the left, a small area in the central part of the sky, the right-hand mid-distance, and the wine cooler in the right foreground. The head of the seated woman was retouched again by Lank in 1987. There are areas of abrasion beneath the stool and in the sky and mid-distance, and there are small losses in the paved terrace, along the edges, and in the sky (above and to the right of the lutanist). The head and left hand of the man standing on the extreme left show heavily mauled paint. There are a number of radical *pentimenti*: a seated woman looking at the guitarist was erased within the left-hand group and replaced by the profile head of a youth and another seated woman placed further to the right; behind her, in the mid-distance, a reclining couple beneath slender trees was erased; the lute was altered from a theorbo (cf.P377) to a chitarrone;[3] to the right of the lutanist, immediately beyond the paved terrace, a group of three couples with a small dog was erased, presumably when the negro servant and the sleeping dog were introduced in the foreground; the right-hand banded column was moved slightly to the left.

The French title given above is taken from Aveline's print of 1730 (see Engraving). The subject, which relates closely to that of P377, has been interpreted by Mirimonde as showing a lutanist vainly trying to tune his instrument in order to accompany the fair guitarist who, meanwhile, has already been accompanied on the bass viol by the man standing nonchalantly behind her; he is the successful suitor.[4] P410 elaborates the theme seen in P377; the chitarrone is still more cumbersome than the theorbo, and the rival suitor is here more obviously confident of his success. Posner has identified some possible seventeenth-century prototypes for the subject.[5] In 1784 the landscape view was identified as the Champs Elysées seen from the Tuileries (see Provenance, and P389 note 2); Josz and Adhémar accepted this as possible.[6]

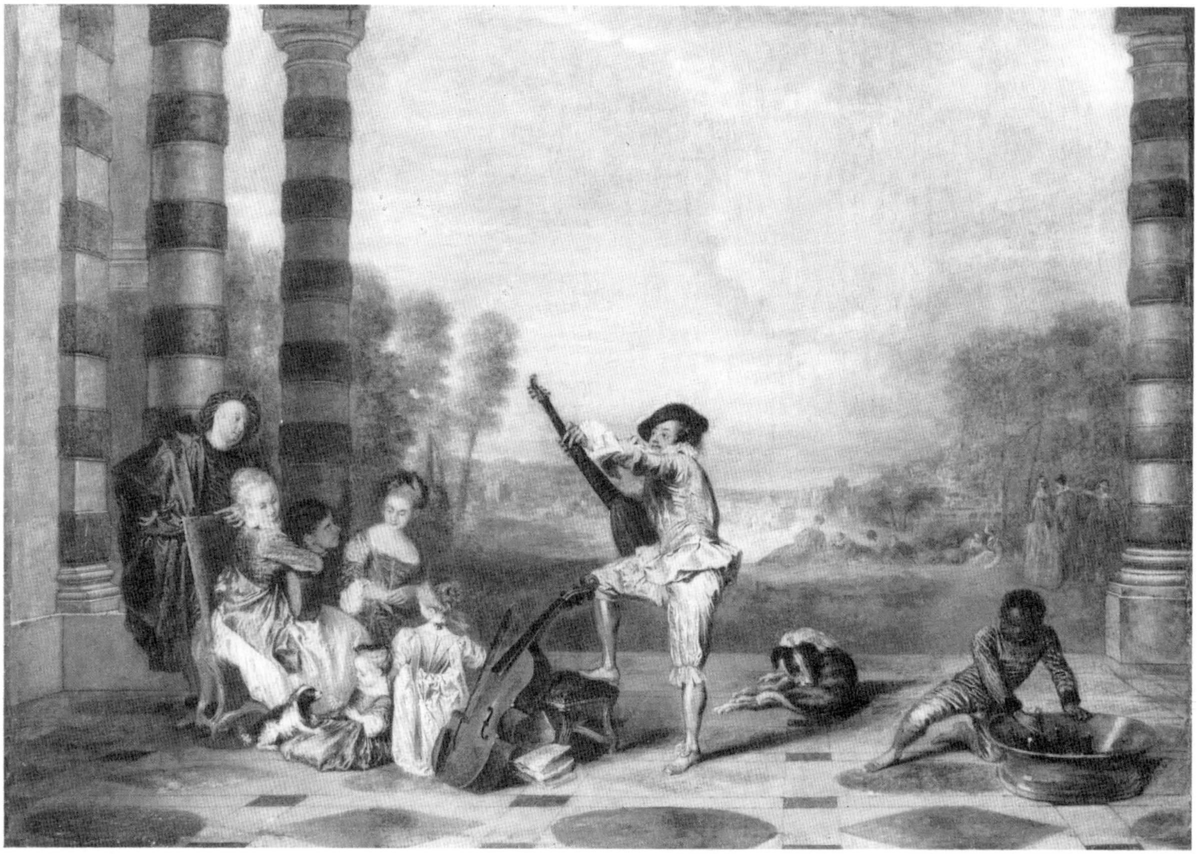

P410

P410 is the most elaborate, and probably the latest, version of a subject which may be traced from *L'enchanteur* of c.1712–14 (CR88), through *La leçon d'amour* of c.1716–17 (Stockholm; CR153), *Pour nous prouver que cette belle* (see P377), and *Le concert* of c.1716–17 (Charlottenburg; CR179), all of which show an isolated male instrumentalist standing before an elegant mixed company. P410 relates particularly closely to *Le concert*; the lutanist, the stool and bass viol, the two children and the idea of the paved terrace, are all taken directly from it – as were the two figure groups erased from the mid-distance. The removal of these groups, and the introduction of an elaborate (through not altogether convincing) architectural setting,[7] improves the spatial definition and enhances the drama. P410 has generally been placed a year or two later than *Le concert*; Nordenfalk suggested c.1718–19,[8] Posner[9] and Rosenberg[10] c.1717–18, Roland-Michel 1717–19,[11] and see References General. The model for the standing man on the left was Watteau's friend Nicolas Vleughels (with whom he was lodging in 1718–19);[12] he recurs in *Le concert*.[13] The model for the lutanist recurs in many of Watteau's paintings and drawings.[14] The dog is quoted from J. Audran's reversed engraving of the *Corona-*

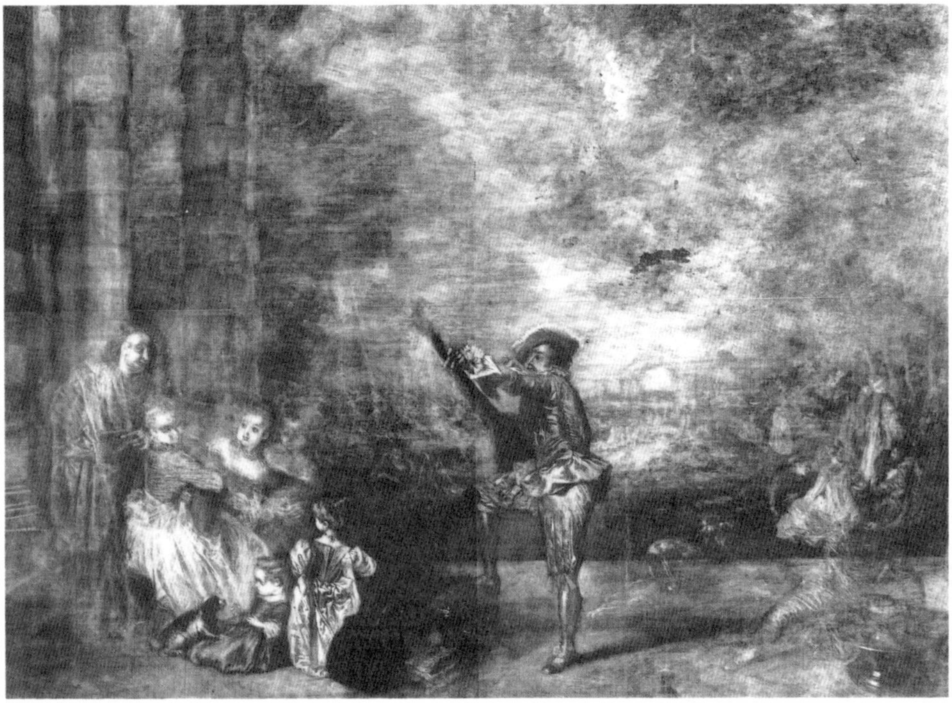

X-radiograph of P410
(The Courtauld Institute)

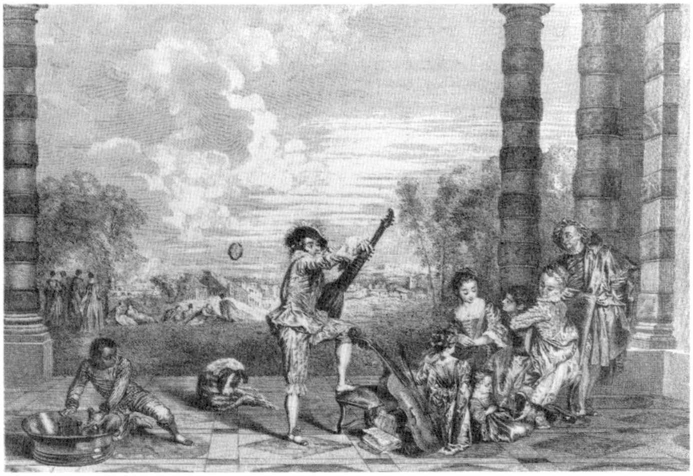

P. Aveline after Watteau: *Les charmes de la vie*, 1730

tion of Marie de Médicis by Rubens.[15] The scale of the dog and the negro page is too large, and so is that of the profile head in the left-hand group; these were all later modifications and quoted from drawings. The dog recurs in *L'enseigne de Gersaint* (CR212), and the little girl seen from the back in *L'occupation selon l'âge* (CR186).

Drawings

FRANKFURT Städelsches Kunstinstitut (no.1040); study for the standing man on the extreme left; according to Parker and Mathey the drawing bore an old inscription identifying Vleughels (PM917; *Watteau 1984*, D112, as mid-1719).[16]
The drawing of a similar head from a different angle, at Chantilly (PM619) was engr. L. Cars (FdDC, no.128); Mariette identified this engraving as of Vleughels (see under PM619).
KARLSRUHE Staatliche Kunsthalle (no.1977–33); sheet with a study for the seated woman in the right distance (PM592).
LONDON British Museum (no.1900–6–13–3); study for the profile head in the left-hand group (PM734; *Watteau 1980*, no.17).
(no.1895–9–15–934); study for the seated woman on the right of the left-hand group (PM601; *Watteau 1980*, no.23; engraved by F. Boucher, FdDC, no.226).
(no.1895–9–15–939); study for the reclining woman in the distance immediately to the right of the lutanist (PM628; *Watteau 1980*, no.38).
L. Burchard 1947; study for the head of the seated guitarist (not in PM; *trois crayons*, 11.4 × 9.6).[17]
PARIS Louvre (RF774); sheet with studies for the seated guitarist and the woman originally seated in the left-hand group but subsequently erased (PM825; *Watteau 1984*, D105, as 1717–18); the guitarist engr. B. Audran (FdDC, no.117), the seated woman engr. J. Audran (FdDC, no.284).
(no.33366); sheet with a study for the left-hand child (PM692).
(RF28721); sheet with a study for the head of the negro page (PM730; *Watteau 1984*, D81, as c.1716).
Musée des Arts Décoratifs; copy from Rubens's *Kermesse* (Louvre) used for one of the couples in the right mid-distance, subsequently erased (PM279).

A drawing for the negro page with the wine cooler was engraved in reverse by F. Boucher, FdDC, no.24. Another for the lutanist was engraved in reverse by B. Audran, a plate rejected for FdDC.[18]

Engravings

P. Aveline 1730, reversed (DV183), inscribed: *Les Charmes de la Vie, Gravées d'Apres le Tableau original peint par Watteau* [65.3 × 84.3], *du Cabinet de Mr. Glucq*, showing some minor variations in the distant buildings, the composition reduced very slightly all round.
A. Lalauze 1890 (for the *Gazette des Beaux-Arts*).

Copies/Versions

BERLIN Dahlem, Gemäldegalerie; 66 × 91.
CLEVELAND K.N. Weil 1957; copy on a fan (illus. *Apollo*, LXV, 1957, p.10).

A version of P410 listed by Adhémar (no.158) in fact relates more closely to *La perspective* (CR117).[19]

Provenance[20]

Glucq in 1730 (see Engravings), either J.-B. Glucq (1674–1748) or Claude Glucq (after 1674–1742);[21] anon. sale, Paris, 11 November 1784 (35, describing a negro page offering refreshments, a young man tuning an instrument, the engraving by Aveline, and the setting as '*vue des anciens Champs Elysées, de la galerie des Tuileries*' [64.3 × 97.9]); Pierre de Grand-Pré; his sale, Paris, 16 February ff. 1809 (35, '*Sujet agréable de divers Personnages, Hommes, Femmes et Enfans, rassemblés sous un grand Vestibule d'architecture, pour faire de la musique et prendre une collation . . . dans le milieu . . . un Homme de la plus belle figure, dans un habillement espagnol, qui est dans le mouvement d'accorder sa Guitare . . . gravé sous le titre du Concert champêtre* [92.4 × 65.3]'), bt. Chervin(?), 172 fr.; Simon-Jacques Rochard (1788–1872),[22] from whom bt. by the 4th Marquess of Hertford before 1854, when P410 was seen in Hertford House by Waagen (IV, p.83);[23] Hertford House inventory 1870.

Exhibitions

Bethnal Green 1872–5 (467, *Palace Garden with Figures*); RA 1889 (97).

References General

Hédouin, p.79, no.104; Goncourt, no.117; Zimmermann, no.52, as c.1716–18; DV183; Réau, no.157; Adhémar, no.157, as 1716; Brookner, pl.31, as 1718(?); Ferré, A24; CR184, as 1718(?); H. Lank and J. Ingamells, *The Burlington Magazine*, CXXV, 1983, pp.733–8.

1 C. Phillips, *Antoine Watteau*, 1895, p.67. In 1889 the *Athenaeum* (23 February, p.249) said P410 had lost some of its brilliance and the sky was described as dull. Zimmermann, *loc. cit.*, commented that it had lost a lot of its freshness.

2 For the cleaning of P410, see Lank and Ingamells, and J. Ingamells, AHAA, IX, 1987, pp.168–70.

3 As identified by Mirimonde, BSHAF 1962, p.48, but F. Gétreau in *Antoine Watteau*, ed. F. Moreau and M. Morgan Grasselli, 1987, p.242, emphasises that no instrument of precisely this type is known (see also P377 note 10).

4 *Gazette des Beaux-Arts*, 6e, LVIII, 1961, pp.264–5.

5 D. Posner, *Antoine Watteau*, 1984, pp.157–8, 248, 250, instancing a *Gallant Company* by H. Janssens and a *Self-portrait with Family* by Teniers the Younger. U. Moussalli, *Revue belge d'archéologie et d'histoire de l'art*, XXIV, 1955, p.80, and *Jardin des Arts*, XLVI, 1958, p.650, had suggested the influence of another painting by Janssens, *The Ball*, which Posner compares more particularly with *Les plaisirs du bal* (*op. cit.*, p.167), following K.T. Parker, *Old Master Drawings*, VII, 1932, p.7 n.5. Mirimonde, *loc. cit.* (see note 3 above) remarked that the subject of P410 was '*textuellement emprunté aux Hollandais*'; O. Banks, *Watteau and the North*, 1977, p.188, compared it with Steen's *Music making on a Terrace* (National Gallery, London, no.1421).

6 V. Josz, *Watteau*, 1903, p.309, (he further identified the chaussée d'Antin), and Adhémar, *op. cit.*, pp.189–90, 196. The banded columns in P410 compare with those formerly on the gallery of the Tuileries Palace which overlooked the Champs Elysées and the Tuileries gardens. Adhémar, *op. cit.*, p.196, suggested Watteau was recalling paintings by Lajoue, but it was, if anything, the reverse (cf. M. Roland-Michel, *Lajoüe et l'art rocaille*, 1984, p.168). Watteau might also have recalled the banded columns used by Salomon de Brosse at the Luxembourg Palace.

7 See Lank and Ingamells, p.734.

8 C. Nordenfalk, *Antoine Watteau och andra franska sjuttonhundratalsmästare*, 1953, pp.99, 154, and *Nationalmuseum Bulletin*, 1979, 3, p.116.

9 Posner, *op. cit.*, p.200.

10 *Watteau 1984*, p.358.

11 M. Roland-Michel, *Watteau*, 1984, p.271 ('a year or two later' than the Berlin *Concert* which she dates c.1716–17).

12 But the drawing could be earlier, cf. *Watteau 1984*, p.358. B. Hercenberg, *Nicolas Vleughels*, 1975, p.11, remarks on Vleughels's fondness of music. For Vleughels, see also N. Parmantier in *Watteau 1984*, pp.51–2.

13 *Watteau 1984*, p.358.

14 See P381 note 5.

15 First pointed out by P. Hendy, *The Burlington Magazine*, XLIX, 1926, p.137.

16 This drawing seems also to have served for the central viola player in *Le concert champêtre* (DV72; CR160), although this figure was identified by Mariette as M. Bougi (who was also the original owner of the picture). See also P381 note 6.

17 Illus. D. Sutton, *Antoine Watteau: Les Charmes de la Vie*, n.d. [1946], p.19.

18 Illus. *Ibid.*, p.9, and see DV, I, p.131.

19 Illus. *Gazette des Beaux-Arts*, 6e, LXIX, 1967, p.248 (it appears in the background of a photograph of Helleu).

20 P410 has also been associated with the Quentin de Lorangère sale, Paris, 2 March 1744 (34, *Un concert* [93.8 × 65.3]); Adhémar mistakenly said P410 had been in the Louis-Philippe/Standish sale of 1853, and Sutton, *op. cit.*, p.12, that it had been in the Paul Périer sale of 1846.

21 Dacier and Vuaflart preferred Claude Glucq (DV183 and see DV, I, p.209). N. Parmantier in *Watteau 1984*, p.40, remained uncertain.

22 Rochard was a *marchand-amateur* as well as a miniaturist, see C. Ephrussi, *Gazette des Beaux-Arts*, 3e, VII, 1892, pp.51–2; '*il semble . . . [que Rochard] cédait assez souvent ces précieuses trouvailles. Nous le voyons en relations suivies avec les grands amateurs tels que lord Hertford . . .*'. See also D. Robertson, *Sir Charles Eastlake*, 1978, pp.84–6, and S. Whittingham in *Pantheon*, XLIII, 1984, p.347 n.76; *Turner Studies*, 5, 1985, 2, p.46 n.2, and *Antoine Watteau*, 1987 (see note 3 above), p.276. According to B. Rochard (letter on file dated 31 August 1976), P410 was not listed in a catalogue of his collection printed privately in Brussels, 1847. Rochard had lent a *Musical Party* by Watteau to the BI 1837 (164) described as 'somewhat damaged' (*Blackwood's Magazine*, October 1837, p.500). In his sale, Christie's, 10–11 May 1844, were four Watteaus: lot 78 'A gentleman in a Spanish dress playing the guitar, a gentleman & lady seated beneath a bank with a child, two figures walking towards the distance, in which a river is seen' (bt. in 250 gn.), lot 105 'A party champêtre at a fountain of Neptune' (5 gn.), lot 133 'Two ladies and two gentlemen on a terrace in a garden; engraved' (9½ gn.), and lot 168 'A pastoral party, a lady feeding birds in a nest, oval' (bt. in 62 gn.).

23 When Mawson described P377 to Lord Hertford in 1856, he called it 'a very small composition part like Your Lordship's splendid picture bought of Rochard . . .' (*Letters*, no.62, p.75; London, 22 April 1856).

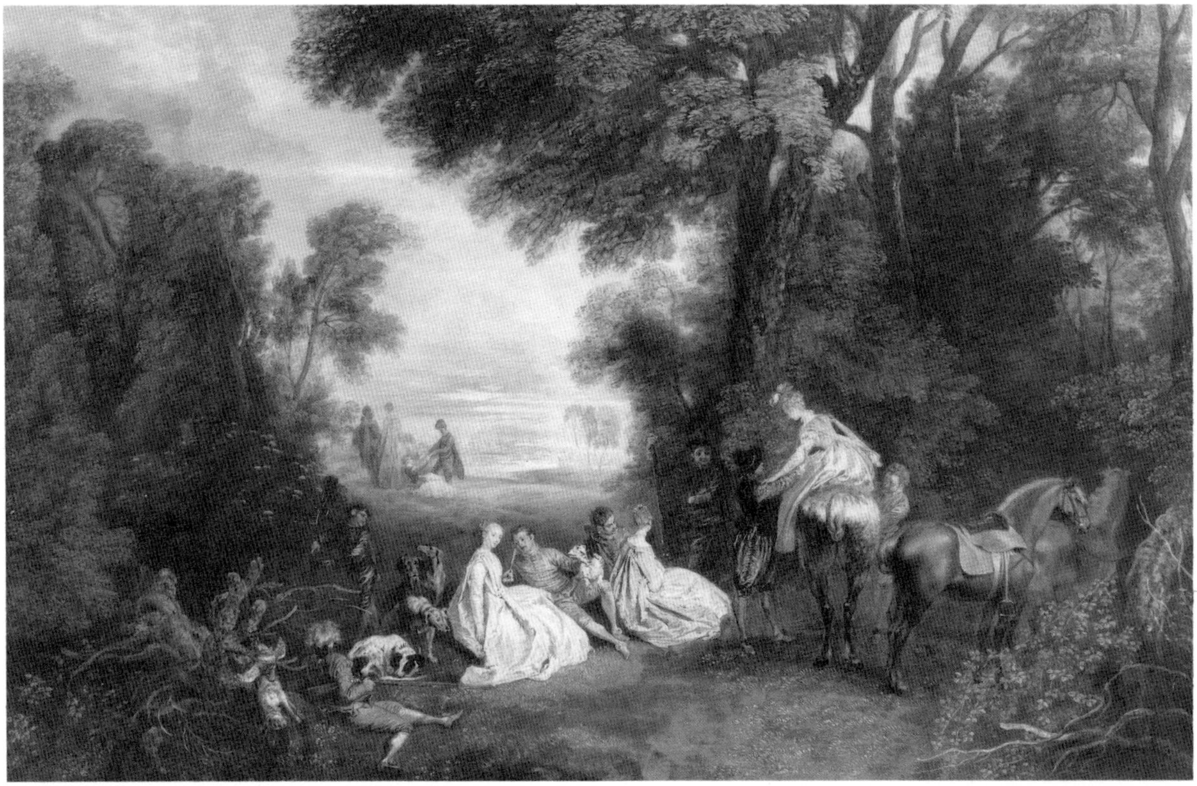

P416

P416 *The Halt during the Chase (Rendez-vous de chasse)*

The seated lady, centre left, wears pink and white; the seated lady in the centre pale blue and white; on the right a lady in yellow is handed down from a dapple-grey horse; in the left foreground a dead hare and two partridges.

Canvas, relined 124.5 × 189 including an added vertical strip 31 wide on the left[1]

Relined with a double canvas in the mid-nineteenth century (see note 1). Although the paint surface has a uniform appearance, the left-hand addition does not appear in Aubert's print of 1731 and is first documented in 1787 (see Engraving and Provenance). The trees on the left, which are less well observed than those on the right, must have been added by another hand to make P416 the pendant to P391 with which it had been paired since at least the mid-eighteenth century. Cleaned by Vallance in 1975, when one lining canvas was removed and the paint surface secured with wax impregnation. Reticulation has, however, recurred.[2] X-radiography reveals two major alterations. In the centre-left mid-distance there was a single-storey building (not unlike the Grand Trianon), now replaced by a distant figure group and trees, and where the man now hands a lady down from her horse there was a seated woman looking left, completing the foreground figure group.

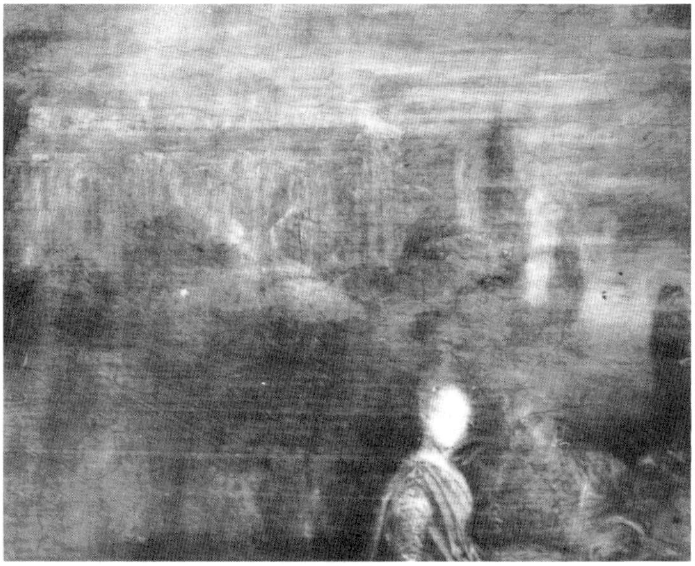

X-radiograph of P416, detail showing traces of the building in the centre left mid-distance, later erased
(The Courtauld Institute)

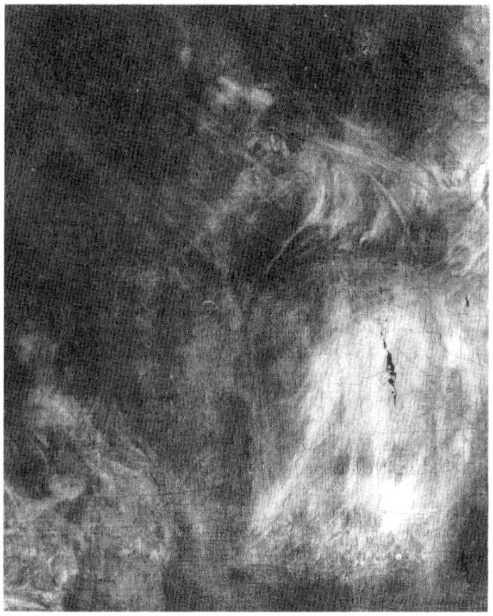

X-radiograph of P416, detail showing seated woman, later erased, immediately to the left of the woman alighting from her horse
(The Courtauld Institute)

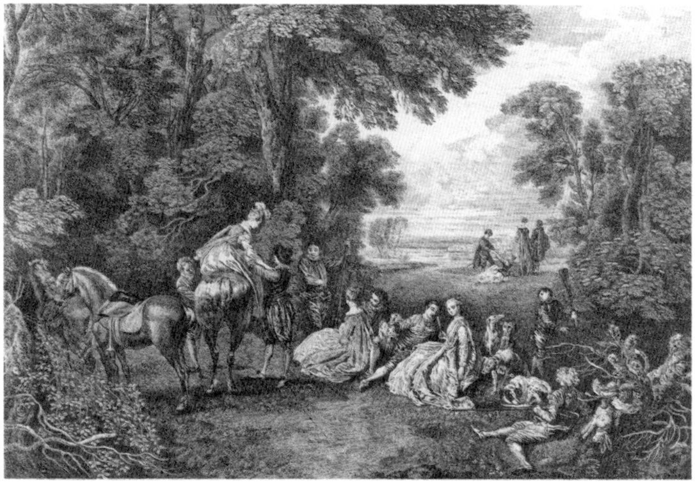

M. Aubert after Watteau: *Rendez-vous de chasse*, 1731

One of five large *fêtes galantes* by Watteau, generally dated 1717–20 (see P391). Compared with P391, P416 suggests a more confident approach to a large-scale composition (the addition on the left must be discounted); the broad diagonal sweep of the figures within the landscape with a distant view recall *Le pèlerinage à l'isle de Cithère* of 1717 (Louvre; CR168),[3] whose poetry, however, is lacking. The comparatively lame execution of P416 suggests a date of c.1718–20 when Watteau appears to have been tiring of the *fête galante* (see P391). The subject was not, apparently, an easy one; the changes described above suggest P416 may have begun as a *fête galante* before being changed into a *rendez-vous de chasse*, and the sporting elements are not entirely convincing.[4] They have been variously assigned to the influence of Wouwermans,[5] British sporting art seen in London in 1719–20,[6] and to earlier Flemish paintings.[7] In fact a print by Testa supplied both the boy on the left (with an uncomfortably long gun) and the four dogs by his side.[8] The group with the man handing the lady down from her horse is taken from a print by Callot, the seventeenth-century costumes almost unchanged.[9] The dead hare and partridges were taken from a much earlier drawing (see below), and two of the horses were quoted from the *Départ de garnison* of c.1710 (CR59; DV276).

P416 has often been dated 1720 on the basis of a letter allegedly written by Watteau to Jullienne on 3 September 1720, describing a large hunting scene he was then painting which he thought would appeal to Mme. de Jullienne; the canvas needed extending on the right '*où j'ai ajousté les chevaux dessous les arbres*'. This letter was published in 1852;[10] in 1890 Mantz associated it with P416,[11] and in 1910 Alfassa suggested P416 was painted as a wedding present for Jullienne (who had married on 22 July 1720).[12] Although accepted by Dacier and Vuaflart, the authenticity of this letter has been doubted by Parker,[13] Posner,[14] and Rosenberg,[15] and it has not been seen since publication. It may also be observed that P416 had left Jullienne's collection by 1731, which is curious if it had been a wedding gift, and that the present canvas has been enlarged on the left, while the horses are on the right.

Drawings

BALTIMORE private collection; sheet with a study of a soldier used for the standing man holding a gun, centre right (not in PM; *Watteau 1984*, D24, as c.1712–13).

ENGLAND private collection 1957; sheet with a study for the reclining sportsman in the left foreground (PM686).

LONDON L. Burchard 1957; drawing after Callot (see note 9) of the man handing the lady down from her horse (PM332).

PARIS Musée Cognacq-Jay (no.191); sheet with a study for the dog on the lap of the man seated in the centre foreground (PM898; *Watteau 1984*, D124).[16]

PROVIDENCE Rhode Island School of Design, Museum of Art; sheet with a study for the head of the seated woman in the foreground, centre left (PM778).

ROTTERDAM Boymans-van Beuningen Museum (FI17); a compositional study which includes the dead partridges and hare seen in P416 (PM908; *Watteau 1984*, D39, as after 1714).

STOCKHOLM Nationalmuseum (no.2824); sheet with studies for the seated woman in the centre-right foreground, and for the standing woman in the left mid-distance (PM637, noting a counter-proof in the Städelsches Kunstinstitut, Frankfurt).

Engraving

M. Aubert 1731, reversed (DV213), inscribed: *Rendez-vous de chasse Gravé d'Après le Tableau original peint par Watteau* [130.5 × 195.8]/*Ce tableau est dans le Cabinet de Mr. Racine de Jonqnoy* [sic], omitting the addition on the left-hand side, although the size of the painting given includes it. A copy in pen and ink by Ingres is in the Musée Ingres, Montauban (no.531).

Copies/Versions

A version in the collection of A. Maskin was engraved by William Blake in 1782 as *Morning Amusement* (DV213A). A painting attributed to Watteau, *Halte de chasseurs*, was in an anon. sale, Douai, 7 July 1772 (36), 57.1 × 78.9. Pater's *Le déjeuner sur l'herbe* (Dulwich Picture Gallery; IS199) shows a variation on the theme of P416.

Provenance

Jean-Baptiste Racine de Jonquoy (d. after 1745), *receveur général*, by 1731 (see Engraving); he owned the Château de Plaisance, Nogent-sur-Marne, between 1720 and November 1721;[17] since P416 was sold with P391 in the five following sales between 1787 and 1848, it is possible that Jonquoy owned both; the comte de Vaudreuil (1740–1817); his sale, Paris, 26 November ff. 1787 (59, *'un repos de chasse . . .* [and] *dans l'intérieur d'un parc, pres de 40 figures . . .* [each 130.5 × 195.8]'), 4,800 *livres*;[18] Le Brun sale, Paris, 11 April 1791 (196, same description as above: *'ils viennent de M.***, . . . 26 novembre 1787, no.59; vendus 4,800 livres. Nous les avons achetés ci-devant 10,000 livres sans bordure'*), bt. in, 2,400 *livres*; Montalot sale, Paris, 19 July 1802 (172, *'deux tableaux offrant des compositions capitales . . . L'un est gravé sous le titre des Amusemens champêtres, l'autre sous celui du Retour de chasse . . .* [116 × 195]'), 2,400 fr.; Emler sale, Paris, 27 December 1809 (37, *'Deux beaux paysages . . . gravés* [titles as above, 130.6 × 193.1], *cabinet de M. Vaudreuil et celui de M. Montaleau en dernier lieu . . .'*), bt. Simont, 1,250 fr.; Cardinal Fesch (1763–1839) by 1815;[19] his sale, Rome, 17 March–15 May 1845 (452, *Le Repos de Chasse*; 453, *Les Amusements Champêtres*, [each 131 × 196]),[20] bt. Horsin-Déon, 5,000 *scudi* (29,300 fr.), and sold by him to the duc de Morny (1811–65) in 1845 for 60,000 fr.[21]

P416 alone: Morny sale, Phillips, 2nd day, 21 June 1848 (102, *Le Repos de Chasse* [190.5 × 129.5] from the Fesch collection), bt. in, 730 gn.; Morny sale, Paris, 24 May 1852 (30, *Le Repos de chasse)*, bt. in, 25,000 fr.;[22] Morny sale, Paris, 2nd day, 1 June 1865 (112, *Rendez-vous de Chasse*, 125 × 190), bt. by the 4th Marquess of Hertford, 31,000 fr.; rue Laffitte inventory 1871 (418, see P391); Hertford House inventory 1890.

Exhibitions

Boulevard des Italiens 1860 (265) lent Morny; Bethnal Green 1872–5 (398); RA 1889 (102).

References General

Hédouin, pp.79–80, no.82; Goncourt, no.164; Zimmermann, no.103, as c.1719–21; DV213; Réau, no.163; Adhémar, no.198, as 1719; Mathey, p.69, as 1720; Brookner, pl.41, as 1720; Ferré, B48; CR207, as c.1720.

1 The stretcher is stamped, *verso*: MOMPER A PARIS and bears the label: *Momper, rentoileur des Musées Impériaux, 11 rue des Marais-St-Germain, Paris.* For Momper, see Fragonard P430 note 1.

2 M. Roland-Michel, *Watteau*, 1984, p.210, suggested that P416, like P391, had perhaps been 'very slightly overcleaned recently'. In 1890 P. Mantz, *Gazette des Beaux-Arts*, 3e, III, p.23, had remarked: *'Bien que la peinture ne soit pas dans un état parfait, le* Rendez-vous de chasse *. . . a vraiment grande allure'.* The reticulation was first noted in 1933 (note on file). For further discussion of this condition, see J. Ingamells, AHAA, IX, 1987, pp.171–3.

3 Also noted by Adhémar, p.198, and D. Posner, *Antoine Watteau*, 1984, p.199.

4 W. Bürger, *Gazette des Beaux-Arts*, 1ère, VII, 1860, p.270, thought the horses on the right the feeblest part of the picture; L. Lagrange, *ibid.*, 1ère, XIV, 1863, p.390, commented: *'Allons donc! chasser en ce déshabillé de boudoir . . . Il s'agit d'une autre chasse'.* Posner, *op. cit.*, pp.199–200, suggests, quite justifiably, that Watteau didn't seem to enjoy painting either P416 or P391.

5 Réau, *loc. cit.*

6 Adhémar, *loc. cit.*, but she also suggested (p.198) that Watteau added the horses in 1720, *'mais l'oeuvre avait été peinre bien avant . . .'.*

7 Posner, *op. cit.*, p.288 n.4.

8 *Venus and Adonis* by Pietro Testa (Bartsch 25), first associated with P416 by K.T. Parker, *Old Master Drawings*, VIII, 1933, pp.37–40; Parker also pointed out that the print contained two dead boars (see letter quoted in note 10 below) and was also used for three *putti* in *L'embarquement pour Cythère* (CR185).

9 *La foire de l'Impruneta* by Jacques Callot, see Drawings (PM332, where first associated with P416). According to Roland-Michel, *op. cit.*, p.231, Crozat owned some of Callot's drawings for this print.

10 AAF, II, 1852–3, pp.211–12. One of four letters allegedly written by Watteau, published by the baron Ch. de Vêze who said they were given to the marquise de Grollier by the abbé Campion de Tersan in 1812, and that he had made faithful copies of them in the presence of Mme. de Grollier and Tersan. The text he gave was:

> *'Monsieur! Par le retour de Marin qui m'a apporté la venaison qu'il vous a pleu m'envoier des le matin, je vous adresse la Toile où j'ai peinte la teste du sanglier et la teste du renard noir, et vous pourrez les dépêcher vers Mr de Losmesnil, car j'en ai fini pour le*

moment. Je ne puis m'en cacher mais cette grande toile me resjouist et j'en attends quelque retour de satisfaction de vostre part et de celle de madame de Julienne qui aime aussi infiniment ce sujet de la chasse, comme moi-mesme. Il a fallu que Gersaint m'ammenat le bon homme La Serre pour agrandir la toile du costé droit, où j'ai ajousté les chevaux dessous les arbres, car j'y éprouvois de la gesne depuys que j'y ay ajousté tout ce qui a esté décidé ainsi. Je pense reprendre ce costé là des lundi à midi passé, parce que des le matin je m'occupe des pensées à la sanguine. Je vous prie ne pas m'oublier anvers madame de Julienne à qui je baise les mains. A. Watteau'.

Of the four letters published, Hérold and Vuaflart (DV, I, pp.112–13) doubted two (but not the above) in 1929.

[11] P. Mantz, *Gazette des Beaux-Arts*, 3e, III, 1890, pp.22–3.

[12] P. Alfassa, BSHAF 1910, pp.132–4.

[13] Parker, 1933 (see note 8 above), p.40.

[14] Posner, *op. cit.*, pp.199, 288 n.4.

[15] Cf. *Watteau 1984*, p.17.

[16] A comparable dog's head appears in a much earlier drawing (PM12).

[17] Cf. DV, *loc. cit.*

[18] Both Goncourt, *loc. cit.*, and V. Josz, *Watteau*, 1903, pp.450–1, give 800 *livres*.

[19] In the Fesch sale catalogue lots 452 and 453 are asterisked, indicating the pictures had been acquired before the Cardinal settled in Rome. This implies that P391 and P416 cannot be identified with the sale of Mmes. Dumont de Frainays, Paris, 20 August 1833 (172), cf. DV126 and 1968 catalogue. P391 and P416 had appeared as nos.1827–8 in the 1841 Fesch catalogue.

[20] The annotated copy of the Fesch sale catalogue in the National Gallery, London, has '*Riunito al No 452*' inscribed by lot 453. Another copy in the Wallace Collection library, annotated by Lord Hertford, has '*le plus beau*' by lot 453 (P391).

[21] Hédouin, *loc. cit.* Bürger, p.269 (see note 4 above), gave the price as 45,000 fr.

[22] The *avant-propos* of the sale catalogue described the *Repos de chasse* as an '*oeuvre capitale colorée comme un Véronèse et qui n'a d'égale que celle qui lui fait pendant, et que le marquis d'Hertford a payé mille livres sterling . . .*', i.e. P391.

P439 *A Lady at her Toilet (La toilette)*

Deep red curtains; the papillon dog on blue silk, the maid holding a golden-yellow gown.

Canvas, relined 45.2 × 37.8 oval, made up to a rectangle with four canvas insets

Surface cleaned by Vallance in 1976. There is some abrasion in the flesh areas and in the right-hand curtain, and an old damage on the thigh. X-radiography shows that the oval canvas has been roughly trimmed and the added corner pieces (which appear to be of a similar canvas) do not marry up exactly. P439 was framed as an oval from at least 1869 to 1904; as a rectangle 1904–28,[1] and as an oval thereafter.

It would seem that the lady is removing her shift before putting on the gown proferred by her maid.[2] The erotic mood, established by her direct glance, is complemented by the carved cupid on the bed-head (whose shell device may suggest the birth of Venus).

According to Caylus, Watteau burned a number of 'indelicate' pictures just before his death.[3] P439 is one of three surviving oils (each relating to drawings) showing ladies in states of undress on a bed, the others being *La toilette intime* (private collection; CR157) and the *Remède* (Norton Simon Collection; CR135), which have been dated c.1714–15.[4] P439, with its fluent execution and rich colours, might be later, and has generally been dated 1716–19; Fourcaud proposed c.1718–19,[5] Parker and Mathey c.1717,[6] Roland-Michel[7] and Posner c.1716–17,[8] and see References General. Adhémar proposed that the model for the maid might have been English, encountered on Watteau's London visit in 1719–20.[9] Posner identified a close parallel with the composition in a Russian tapestry from a seventeenth-century Flemish design showing the *Toilet of Bathsheba*,[10] and several other influences have been suggested: Veronese,[11] Rubens,[12] engravings by van der Bruggen,[13] and a copy of Titian's *Danaë with Nursemaid* then in Crozat's collection.[14] Watteau's preparatory drawing, it may be observed, was from the life.

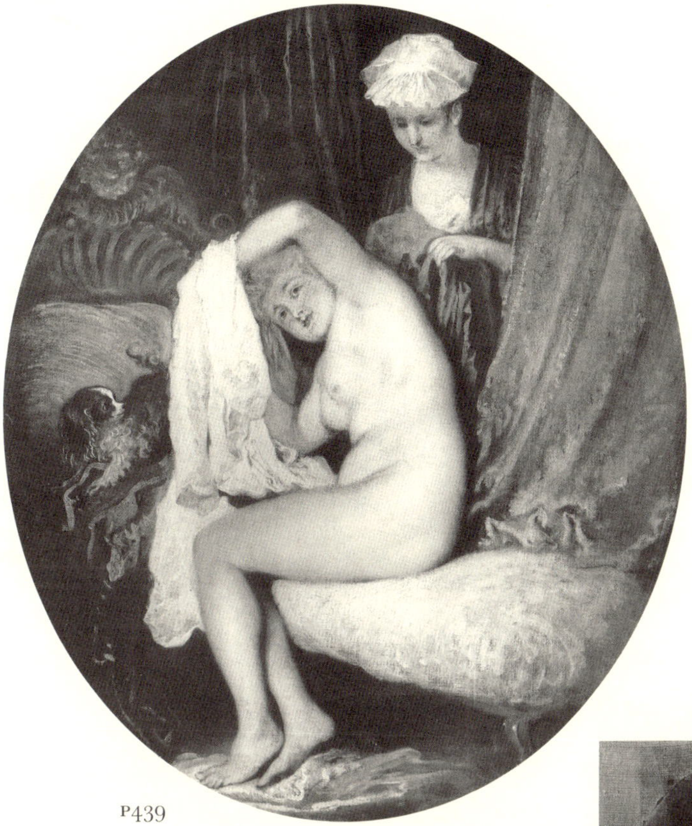

P439

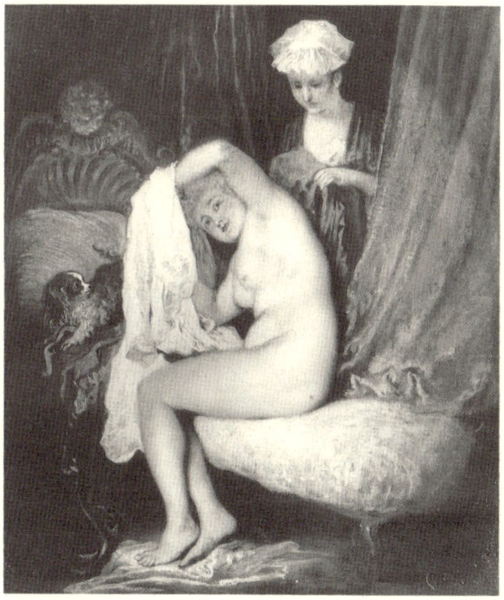

P439 with additions

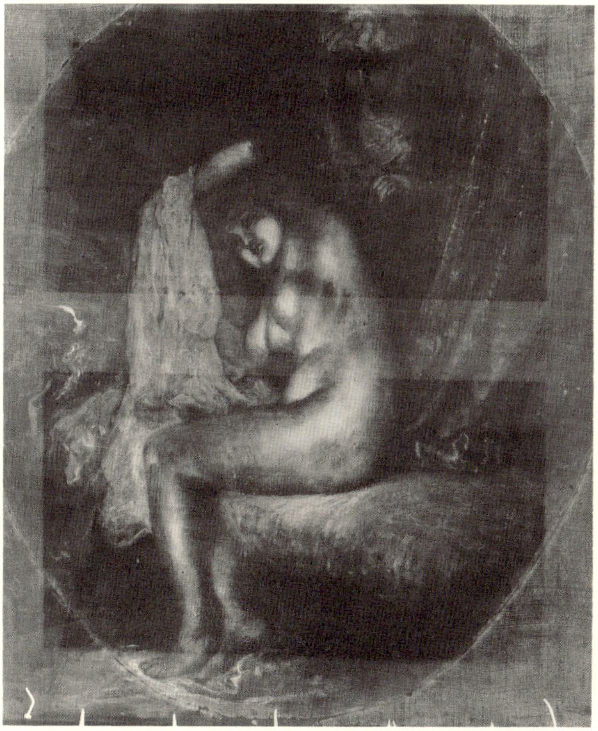

X-radiograph of P439 (trimmed along the top and sides)
(The Courtauld Institute)

Drawings

LONDON British Museum (no.1910–2–12–99); study for the nude figure and the curtains directly behind her, the bed replaced by a *chaise longue* (PM523; *Watteau 1980*, no.53).

A sheet with three studies of the same model was in the James sale, Christie's, 2nd day, 23 June 1891 (328).[15] A sheet with studies of a papillon dog which may have served for P439 was in the collection of the vicomte de Noailles in 1957 (PM897).

Engraving

A. Dézarrois 1910, rectangular (for the *Revue de l'Art ancien et moderne*).

Copy

VALENCIENNES Musée des Beaux-Arts (no.46–1–57); 94 × 76 rectangular, nineteenth-century copy, formerly attributed to Vleughels.[16]

Provenance[17]

Possibly Mme. Benech sale, Paris, 7 March 1828 (22, *Intérieur; jeune femme sortant du bain*, or 23, *La toilette*). The marquis Maison (1798–1869); his sale, Paris, 10 June 1869 (8, '*La Toilette. Forme ovale*', 46 × 38), bt. by the 4th Marquess of Hertford, 13,000 fr.; Bagatelle inventory 1871 (938, '*Le lever*'); Hertford House inventory 1890 ('*Lady seated on a couch dressing*').

Exhibitions

Bethnal Green 1872–5 (429); RA 1889 (108).

References General

Goncourt, pp.171–2; Zimmermann, no.50, as c.1716–18; DV, under 306; Réau, no.173; Adhémar, no.200, as 1719; Mathey, p.69, as c.1717; Brookner, pl.42, as 1720; Ferré, B82; CR175, as c.1717; D. Posner, *Watteau: A Lady at her Toilet*, 1973.

1 Illus. as such, for example, A.L. Baldry, *The Wallace Collection*, 1904, p.42, and Réau, f.p.16. The present frame bears the label of Grundy & Smith, 9 Exchange Street, Manchester.

2 As proposed, for example, by L. de Fourcaud, *Revue de l'Art ancien et moderne*, XXVII, 1910, p.36, and Adhémar, p.104.

3 The comte de Caylus, 'Vie de Watteau' (read to the Académie on 3 February 1748), quoted in Adhémar, p.182.

4 See *Watteau 1984*, P37.

5 Fourcaud, *loc. cit.*, p.38: '*un peu postérieur à* l'Embarquement pour Cythère *et, probablement, de l'époque où ce grand peintre habitait, avec Wleughels, rue des Fossés-de-la-Doctrine-Chrétienne*'.

6 Under PM772, a sheet containing studies used for *Le pèlerinage à l'isle de Cithère* and for a maid seen in the *Remède* and *La toilette intime*, they suggest that Watteau's '*série d'intimités d'un érotisme délicat*', including P439, were contemporary with *Le pèlerinage*. Their reasoning is criticised by Posner, pp.99–100 n.40.

7 M. Roland-Michel, *Watteau*, 1984, p.221.

8 Posner, p.29, and *Antoine Watteau*, 1984, p.106.

9 H. Adhémar, *l'Oeil*, 14, February 1956, p.22; she associates the maid seen in P439 with one in a drawing bearing an English water-mark (PM785) and therefore likely to have been executed in London 1719–20. Her inference is doubted, for example, by Posner, p.96 n.5.

10 Posner, *op. cit.*, 1984, p.99 (illus. p.101).

11 Goncourt, p.172.

12 CR175: '*La figure principale dérive de Rubens, peut-être à travers un dessin ayant appartenu à Crozat*'.

13 Adhémar, p.104.

14 Posner, p.27, and cf. p.103 n.74, where he suggests Watteau may also have known Rembrandt's *Danaë* (Bredius 474; in Crozat's collection after 1740).

15 Described by Fourcaud, *loc. cit.* (see note 2), p.37.

16 See Posner, pp.95–6 n.4, and B. Hercenberg, *Nicolas Vleughels*, 1975, p.186, no.2. A pendant copy at Valenciennes shows *La toilette intime*, reversed as in Mercier's engraving (DV306).

17 P439 has also been associated with the Conti sale, Paris, 8 April ff.1777, lot 667, '*Une femme assise, & sortant du bain; du paysage, des fabriques, & un jet d'eau servent de fond . . . toile* [54.4 × 43.5]', but this description is clearly not applicable to P439 (cf. Posner, p.95 n.3). Adhémar, no.200, also associated P439 with a *Toilette* attributed to Watteau, lent by Henry Broadwood to the BI 1835 (128), but this is not conclusive (cf. Posner, *loc. cit.*).

Ascribed to Watteau

P377 *The Music Lesson (Pour nous prouver que cette belle)*

The left-hand youth in dark grey; the lady in white with pink hair-ribbon and corsage; the left-hand child in grey with a grey-blue hat, the other in an olive-green dress; the lutanist wears a costume of clover-pink with silver stripes, silver stockings and a black hat.

Pine panel 16.1 × 19.9 × 1.1 made up to 18.6 × 23.7 with walnut strips along each edge; the additions are supported, *verso*, by mahogany strips down each vertical edge.

Cleaned by Mawson in 1856[1] and Lee in 1984 when it became apparent that the paint on the edging strips was not original[2] and extended in places over the main panel, most obviously on the woman's skirt. There is evidence of abrasion on the woman's hair-ribbon and the left-hand child's hat. X-radiography shows that the lutanist's head was first seen more in profile with a larger hat, his left hand was redrawn and the lute had a straighter neck. There appear to have been three positions for the lady's right hand: the end of a second hand remains visible within the edge of the open music book; a preparatory study in Oxford (see Drawings) clearly shows the present hand alone.

The subject has been variously interpreted. The French title given above is taken from the verses which accompanied Surugue's print of 1719 (see Engravings); they describe a mother singing accompanied by her husband, and anticipate the young man behind her becoming her lover. Mariette listed '*une femme tenant un livre de musique, accompagnée d'un homme qui accorde un guitare*'.[3] Mantz (1890) saw a music master and his pupil,[4] Josz (1903) an elder sister with her brother, two younger sisters and music master,[5] and Fourcaud (1905) a lady listening to a gallant's proposals while the lutanist tunes up.[6] Most recently Mirimonde elaborated Fourcaud's reading, suggesting that, while the lutanist struggles to tune his instrument and the children look on knowingly, the rival suitor is pressing his claim;[7] his interpretation is accepted by Posner[8] and Rosenberg.[9] The lute is a ten-stringed theorbo;[10] the fifth key is clear in the engraving, though hardly visible in P377. While the lady and right-hand child appear to wear contemporary dress, the other figures are in costumes suggestive of the seventeenth century.

Pour nous prouver que cette belle has previously been dated c.1716–17 (see References General). Mantz,[11] Fourcaud,[12] and Mathey (1939)[13] preferred c.1718. Surugue's engraving provides a *terminus ante quem* of 1719. The composition relates closely to that of P410, where the dating and subject is further discussed; the seated woman recurs in *Le concert* (CR179, see under P410). Although P377 has hitherto generally been accepted as the original Watteau composition engraved by Surugue (see References General), the clumsy draperies and the uncertain drawing of the singer's right hand (for which, however, there is a Watteau drawing, see below) suggest that, like the pendant *Arlequin, Crispin et Scapin* at Waddesdon

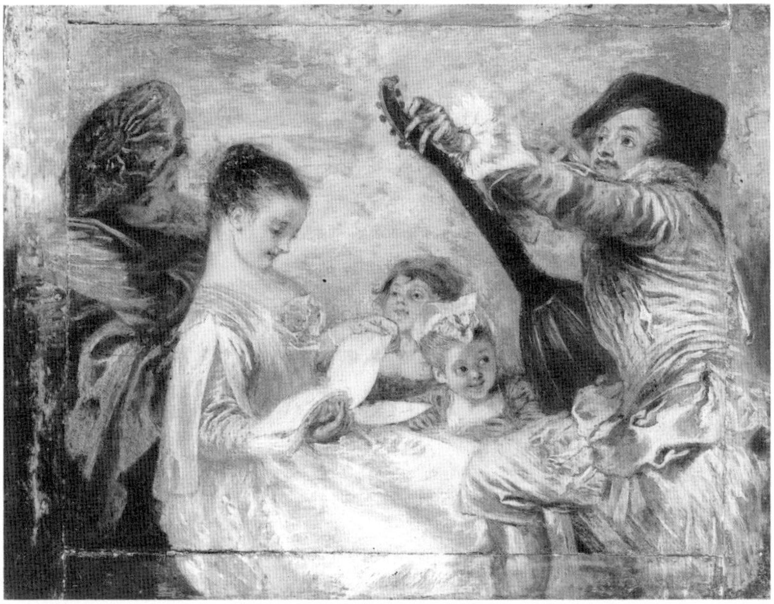

P377 showing additions

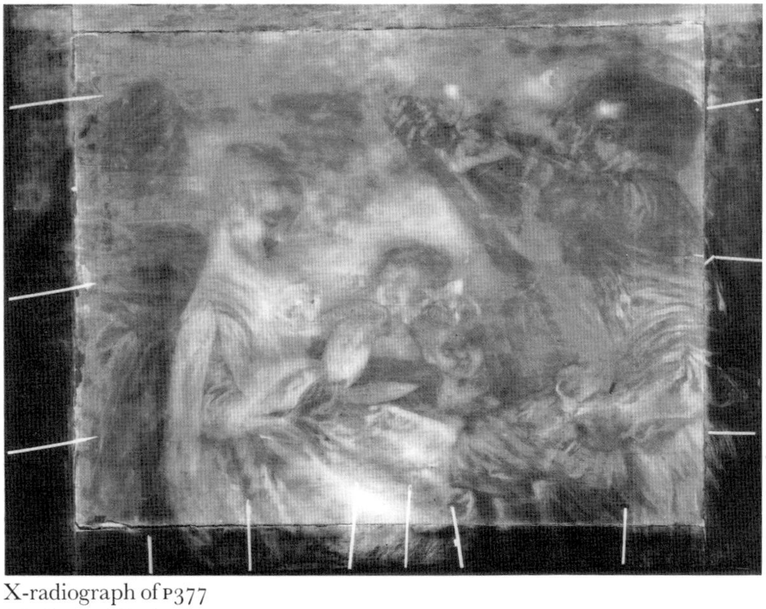

X-radiograph of P377
(The Courtauld Institute)

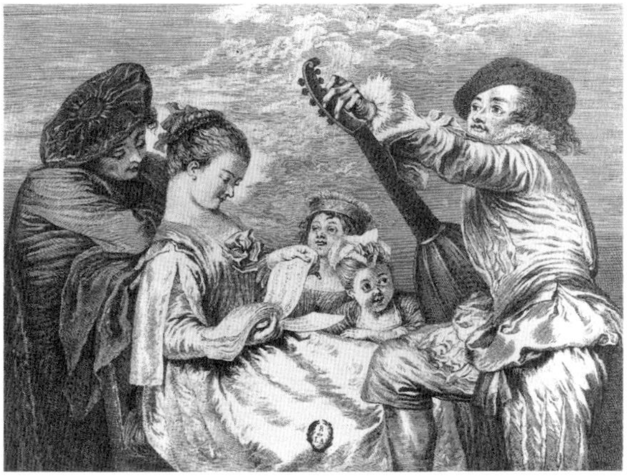

L. Surugue after Watteau:
Pour nous prouver que cette belle, 1719

(CR155), P377 may be an old copy.[14] The panels show a closely comparable construction (additions allowing the compositions to confirm with Surugue's engravings) and the X-radiographs suggest a similar facture;[15] the pair were together from at least 1790 to 1856 and they remain the best of the known versions.

Related Drawings

LONDON private collection; study for the left-hand child, showing the fur(?) decoration of the hat[16] as in Surugue's engraving (PM696).
NEW YORK Pierpont Morgan Library (no.I.278b); study for the right-hand child (PM709; *Watteau 1984*, D89, as c.1716–17).
A counter-proof sheet also in the Pierpont Morgan Library shows three different studies of the same head (PM708).
ORLEANS Musée des Beaux-Arts (no.1145); study for the right-hand child (PM711; *Watteau 1984*, D108, as c.1716–17).
OXFORD Ashmolean Museum; study for the seated lady (PM552; engr. B. Audran, FddC, rejected plate[17]).

A drawing of the lutanist's head from a slightly different angle was in a private collection, Amsterdam, 1957 (PM725). Another for the figure of the lutanist was engr. B. Audran (FddC, rejected plate, see P410).

Related Engravings

L. Surugue 1719 (DV96), with verses below:

Pour nous prouver que cette belle
Trouve l'hymen un noeud fort doux,
Le peintre nous la peint fidelle,
à Suivre le ton d'un Epoux.

Ces Enfants qui sont autour d'elle
Sont les fruits de son tendre amour,
Dont ce beau joueur de prunelle,
Pouroit bien gouter quel que jour.

The engraving shows some differences: the composition is slightly extended all round coinciding with the additions to P377; the left-hand child's hat has a more evident fur lining (as is shown on the drawing PM696); the right-hand child's left arm lies across the lady's lap; the lute has five stops on the left-hand side and the lutanist's hair is longer.
C. P. Lindemann (1700–54), reversed (DV96E); A. Schmidt, reversed octagonal (DV96F); Lyne, reversed (DV96G); two anonymous plates, one octagonal, reversed (DV96B,C); anonymous octagonal plate (DV96D); A. Lalauze 1890 (for the *Gazette des Beaux-Arts*).

Related Copies[18]

ALTHORP; 24.1 × 27.3, acquired before 1802, agreeing more closely with Surugue's engraving.[19]
BONN private collection, 1987; c. 25 × 40, extended to include a drapery on the left and trees on the right.
FARMINGTON Connecticut, Lewis-Walpole Library; water-colour copy by Horace Walpole, signed and dated 1736, apparently from the engraving.[20]
ITALY private collection; 80 × 160, with trees to left and right and distant figures on the right.
LONDON Phillips, 11 December 1987 (101); 92 × 110.
PARIS M. Roussel 1885; 61 × 83, reversed.
G. Hemerdinger 1909; 80 × 97, variant with balustrade in background.
J. Barville 1977.

Provenance

Sir Joshua Reynolds (1723–92); his sale, Christie's 1st day, 13 March 1795 (83, *Musical Conversation*, with pendant *A Masquerade*), bt. Bryan, 19 gn.; Bryan sale, 27 April 1795 (44, a pair, *Masquerade* and *Musical Conversation*); Edward Coxe sale, Coxe's, 3rd day, 25 April 1807 (7, *A Concert*), 7½ gn., (the companion *Masquerade* was lot 8, 9 gn.); the 1st Earl of Carysfort (1751–1828); his sale, Christie's 14 June 1828 (a Pair, small, a *Masquerade* and *Conversation*), bt. Samuel Rogers (1763–1853), 60 gn.; his sale, Christie's 5th day, 2 May 1856 (567, 'A Concert. From the Earl of Carysfort's collection'), bt. Mawson for the 4th Marquess of Hertford, 175 gn.;[21] (the *Masquerade* from the Carysfort collection was lot 566, bt. Bentley, 155 gn.); Hertford House inventory 1870.

Exhibitions

London, 28 Haymarket, 1791 (anti-room, no.30) lent Reynolds; BI 1829 (35) lent Rogers; Bethnal Green 1872–5 (377); RA 1889 (98).

References General

Hédouin, p.78, no.32; Goncourt, no.177; Zimmermann, no.56, as c.1716–18; DV96; Réau, no.61; Adhémar, no.162, as 1716; Mathey, p.69, as 1717–18; Ferré, A22; CR154, the original as c.1716, but the execution of P377 *'peut laisser quelques doutes sur l'attribution'*.

1 Hertford to Mawson, Paris, 5 May 1856: 'I accept with gratitude your offer of cleaning . . . the Watteau' (*Letters*, no.67, p.81).

2 Mawson in 1856 (letter to Hertford, London, 22 April 1856; *Letters*, no.62, p.75) had described P377 as 'much damaged & has been added all round'. Adhémar thought the additions may have been made by the artist. For further discussion of the cleaning see J. Ingamells, AHAA, IX, 1987, pp.165–8.

3 Quoted under DV96, from P.-J. Mariette, *Notes manuscrites sur les peintres et graveurs*, c.1731, IX, f.192, no.16 (Bibliothèque Nationale; see DV, II, pp.114–16).

4 P. Mantz, *Gazette des Beaux-Arts*, 3e, III, 1890, p.14.

5 V. Josz, *Watteau*, 1903, p.288.

6 L. de Fourcaud, *Revue de l'Art ancien et moderne*, XVII, 1905, p.116.

7 A.-P. de Mirimonde, *Gazette des Beaux-Arts*, 6e, LVIII, 1961, pp.265–6.

8 D. Posner, *Antoine Watteau*, 1984, p.160; Posner also suggests (p.258) that the subject may derive from seventeenth-century tavern scenes, such as those by Valentin.

9 Cf. *Watteau 1984*, pp.359–61.

10 F. Gétreau in *Antoine Watteau*, ed. F. Moreau and M. Morgan Grasselli, 1987, p.242, remarks that, though Watteau had *'un sens très ferme de la réalité instrumentale'*, no such instrument *'à caisse de luth, à cinq choeurs doubles de cordes et simple cheviller recourbé en arrière'* is otherwise known. Cf. P410 note 3, and Mirimonde, BSHAF 1962, p.48.

11 Mantz, *loc. cit.*, p.15, as 1718–19.

12 Fourcaud, *loc. cit.*, p.117

13 J. Mathey, BSHAF 1939, p.158.

14 For the Waddesdon picture, see E.K. Waterhouse, *The James A. de Rothschild Collection at Waddesdon Manor, Paintings*, 1967, no.135 ('the X-rays confirm that it is original'); Posner, *op. cit.*, p.290 n.54, rejects the attribution, and see Ingamells, AHAA, IX, 1987, pp.165–7. P377 and the Waddesdon picture are cited as pendants in DV96–7 and Adhémar, nos.162–3 (where the provenances of the Waddesdon picture and of a copy at Althorp are confused; for the latter, see K. Garlick, *The Walpole Society*, XLV, 1976, no.683).

15 I am grateful to Rosamund Griffin for permission to see this X-radiograph.

16 J.L. Nevinson, letter on file dated 2 February 1961, suggested this hat might be fur-lined, with a stiffened galloon braid.

17 Proof copy in the FDDC in the Bibliothèque de l'Arsenal, placed between nos.100 and 101.

18 DV96 lists two related compositions attributed to Watteau: anon. sale, Paris, 13 February 1832 (125, *Concert*), and Parisez sale, Paris, 25 January 1868 (58, *le Prélude . . . gravé*).

19 Illus. Fourcaud, *loc. cit.*, p.115; Zimmermann, no.138. See Garlick, *loc. cit.* (note 14), no.684. Waterhouse, *loc. cit.* (note 14), identified the Althorp picture with one of *'A Drunken Feast by Watteau: Ditto, Its companion'* in a MS Althorp inventory of 1750, but these were different pictures, cf. Garlick, pp.106, 117.

20 Illus. W.S. Lewis, *Horace Walpole*, 1961, p.17, pl.5.

21 For correspondence concerning this purchase, see *Letters*, nos.62, 64, 65, 67, pp.75, 78, 79, 81.

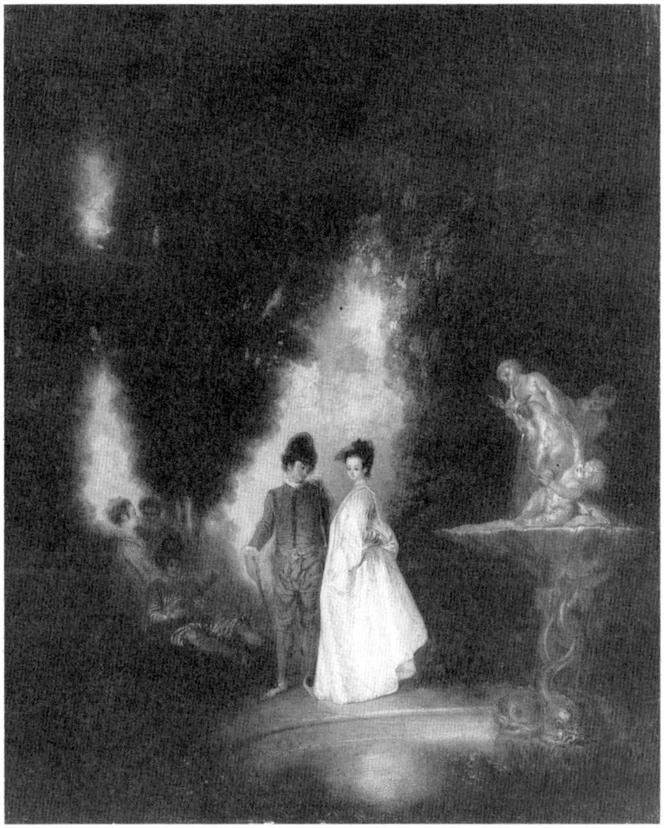

P395

After Watteau

P395 *The Fountain (La cascade)*

The man in pink, the lady in white.

Canvas, relined 45 × 35.5[1]

There are several damaged areas: on the man's right shoulder, below the fountain to the left, two areas above the lady, and along the bottom edge. There is a prominent craquelure on the right, and the uneven varnish is much discoloured.

P395 is an indifferent, full-size copy of *La cascade* by Watteau (CR133).[2] Though apparently attributed to Pater in the mid-nineteenth century (see Provenance) P395 was called Watteau between 1871 and 1913; MacColl published his doubts concerning this attribution separately in 1924.[3]

Provenance[4]

Lord Henry Seymour (1805–59); his sale, Paris, 2nd day, 14 February 1860 (113, *Pater, Promenade dans le parc*, 44 × 34), bt. Laboureau for the 4th Marquess of Hertford, 9,000 fr.;[5] rue Laffitte inventory 1871 (455, *'Pater, le rendez-vous'*); Hertford House inventory 1890.

Exhibition

Bethnal Green 1872–5 (422, as Watteau).

References General

All giving P395 as a copy: Zimmermann, no.130; DV, under 28; Réau, under no.81; Adhémar, under no.116; CR, under 133.

[1] P395 was catalogued between 1900 and 1928 as on panel.

[2] The original is not clearly identified. Two versions have recently been attributed to Watteau: Metropolitan Museum of Art (no.60.71.21), panel 21.6 diam., bequeathed by Lillian S. Timken 1959; New York, private collection 1961, panel 42 × 32, ex Lévy sale 1919. Adhémar, *loc. cit.*, mistakenly cites a copy in the Murray Scott sale 1913 (for which see Appendix III).

[3] D. S. MacColl, *The Burlington Magazine*, XLIV, 1924, pp.137–8.

[4] Adhémar, *loc. cit.*, mistakenly gave the provenance of P395 as *'sans doute coll. S. Rogers'*, and this was repeated by CR. P395 was also tenuously associated with the Grammont sale, Paris, 16 January 1775 (1920 catalogue).

[5] Described in the *Gazette des Beaux-Arts*, 1ère, V, 1860, p.309, as *'Pater, ou quelque autre . . . Peinture fatiguée et équivoque, représentant une promenade dans un parc'*. P395 has not previously been identified in the Seymour sale, but all Laboureau's other purchases at this sale were for the 4th Marquess of Hertford.

Appendices

Chronology of Acquisitions

Listing only those pictures catalogued in this volume.
In some cases the dates assigned are those of the last sale recorded.

Third Marquess of Hertford 1777–1842

1815
After Clouet P530

1822
Corneille de Lyon P532

1823
After Rigaud P130

date unknown
After Champaigne P645

Fourth Marquess of Hertford 1800–1870

1841
Fragonard P404

1842
Fragonard P471
Lancret P378

1843
Boucher P484, P487
Greuze P413
Prud'hon P272

1844
Lancret P436, P478

1845
Champaigne P134
Greuze P427, P441, P442
Ascribed to Greuze P434
Poussin P108

1846
Claude P114
Greuze P425, P440
Prud'hon P313
Watteau P381

1848
Ascribed to Boucher P390
Greuze P428
Watteau P389, P391

1849
Champaigne P129
Greuze P421

1850
Dughet P139

1851
Boucher P429, P432, P438, P444
Ascribed to Greuze P443
Lemoyne P392, P417
After Nattier P414

1852
Boucher P482, P489
Oudry P625, P627, P629, P631
Pater P472

1853
Lancret P465

by 1854
Raoux P128
Watteau P410

1855
Boucher P485, P486
Desportes P623
Jollain P488
Studio of L.-M. van Loo P477
Ascribed to Oudry P624
Pater P380
Taraval P483
C.-J. Vernet P480

1856
Ascribed to Watteau P377

1857
Boucher P445, P447
After Claude P125
Desportes P594, P628
Greuze P388, P407
Lancret P409
Prud'hon P295

1858
Greuze P403
Gros P303
Nattier P456

by 1859
Demarne P462, P469
Greuze P402
Pater P406, P426

1860
Boucher P431
After Watteau P395

1861
Boilly P435

1862
Vigée Le Brun P457

1863
Boilly P473, P479
Pater P460

1864
Greuze P398
Prud'hon P315

1865
Champaigne P119
Fragonard P382, P430
Greuze P384, P396, P454
Lancret P408
Pater P420, P424
Watteau P416

1865–9
Boucher P385, P399

1866
Mayer-Lamartinière P348

1867
Fragonard P379
Lancret P448 (?)
C. A. van Loo P451
Nattier P461
Prud'hon P264

by 1867
French School P122

1868
Lépicié P464, P466
Pater P405
Vigée Le Brun P449

1869
Boucher P418
After Nattier P437
C.-J. Vernet P135
Watteau P439

1870
Fragonard P394

dates unknown
Boucher P411, P423
Studio of Boucher P481, P490
Champaigne P127
Charlier P475
French School P599
Greuze P415, P419
Lancret P401, P422, P450
Nattier P453
Oudry P626, P630
Pater P383, P386, P397, P400, P458
Saint-Aubin P780

Sir Richard Wallace 1818–1890

1859
Watteau P387

1872
Boucher P446
After Boucher P433
Ascribed to Charlier P467, P468
Courtois P769
Fragonard P412, P455
Ascribed to Greuze P459
Lafrensen P772 (?)
Lancret P393
Pater P452
J.-F. de Troy P463, P470

1872–4
After Boucher P766
Charlier P474, P476

1875
Prud'hon P347

APPENDIX II

The 4th Marquess of Hertford's pictures in London and Paris

Listing only those pictures catalogued in this volume.

Paris

(95 oils)

Boilly P435, P473, P479

Boucher P385, P399, P411, P418, P423, P429, P431, P432, P438, P444, P445, P447, P482, P484, P485, P486, P487, P489

Studio of Boucher P481, P490

Champaigne P119, P127

Charlier P475

Desportes P594, P623, P628

Fragonard P379, P382, P394, P404(?), P430

French School P122, P599

Greuze P384, P388, P396, P403, P407, P415, P419, P454

Gros P303

Jollain P488

Lancret P401, P408, P409, P422, P448(?), P450

Lemoyne P392, P417

Lépicié P464, P466

C. A. van Loo P451(?)

Mayer-Lamartinière P348

Nattier P453, P456, P461

After Nattier P414, P437

Oudry P625, P626, P627, P629, P630, P631

Ascribed to Oudry P624

Pater P383, P386, P397, P400, P405, P420, P424, P458, P460, P472

Prud'hon P264, P272, P295, P313, P315

Raoux P128

Taraval P483

C.-J. Vernet P135

Vigée Le Brun P449, P457

Watteau P381, P391, P416, P439

After Watteau P395

London

(34 oils, 1 gouache)

Ascribed to Boucher P390

Champaigne P129, P134

Claude P114

After Claude P125

Demarne P462, P469

Dughet P139

Fragonard P471

Greuze P398, P402, P413, P421, P425, P427, P428, P440, P441, P442

Ascribed to Greuze P434, P443

Lancret P378, P436, P465, P478

Studio of L.-M. van Loo P477

Pater P380, P406, P426

Poussin P108

Saint-Aubin P780

C.-J. Vernet P480

Watteau P389, P410

Ascribed to Watteau P377

APPENDIX III

French pictures of before 1815 formerly in the Hertford-Wallace Collections

Compiled from the inventories of Hertford House, Bagatelle and the rue Laffitte, and from sale records, listing those pictures which did not form part of Lady Wallace's bequest to the Nation in 1897. The majority were left to her residuary legatee, Sir John Murray Scott (1843–1912), who also received the Paris properties, 2 rue Laffitte and Bagatelle. Pictures in the Murray Scott sale 1913 not identifiable in earlier inventories have been omitted. Dates are given only for those artists not represented in the preceding catalogue.

Abbreviations

In addition to the Abbreviations on pp.20–1.

Bagatelle c.1896	C. Yriarte, 'Mémoires de Bagatelle', *La Revue de Paris*, v, 1903, pp.380–414
rue Laffitte 1912	*inventaire après décès* of the possessions of Sir John Murray Scott found at 2 rue Laffitte, Paris, 16 February ff. 1912, P. Robineau *notaire* (typescript in Wallace Collection archives)
Murray Scott 1903	inventory of 5 Connaught Place, London, W1, 1903; the London residence of Sir John Murray Scott (Wallace Collection archives)
Murray Scott sale 1913	Christie's, 27 June 1913, 153 lots; following his death, Murray Scott's Executors sold a number of his pictures from Connaught Place
Petit 1883	*L'art du XVIIIe siècle*, exh. Georges Petit, Paris, December 1883–January 1884
Ragley sale 1938	Old Pictures, the property of the Fifth and Sixth Marquess of Hertford, deceased; removed from Ragley Hall, Alcester, Warwick (sold by Order of the Trustees, and by permission of the High Court), Christie's, 20th May 1938, lots 1–39 (entailed property, not acquired by the 4th Marquess or Richard Wallace)
Sackville sale 1923	By order of Victoria, Lady Sackville (1862–1936); 40 Sussex Square, Brighton, Wilson & Co., 4th day, 28 June 1923; Murray Scott bequeathed his Paris collections to Lady Sackville who sold them to Seligmann in 1914, except for some lesser items which appeared in this and the following sales
Sackville sale 1936	By order of the Personal Representatives of the Dowager Lady Sackville, deceased; White Lodge, Roedean, Brighton, Tansley, 21–3 October 1936
Scott sale 1942	By direction of Miss K. T. Scott, sister of the late Sir John Murray Scott; Willis's, 27 August 1942, lots 101–32

1 BOILLY
Le verrou (La surprise), 37 × 45; rue Laffitte 1871 (84); rue Laffitte 1912 (Harrisse, no.448)
Pasadena, Norton Simon Foundation

2 BOILLY
Le jaloux (Le retour), 37 × 45; rue Laffitte 1871 (387); rue Laffitte 1912 (Harrisse, no.554)
Pasadena, Norton Simon Foundation

3 BOILLY
Scène de carnaval (Le mardi gras au Boulevard Saint Martin), 61 × 107; Langlois sale, 8 April 1861 (92); rue Laffitte 1871 (834); exh. Petit, *Cent chefs d'oeuvre*, 1892 (1) lent Lady Wallace; rue Laffitte 1912 (Harrisse, no.497, as 55 × 75)
New York, S. H. Golding 1930

4 BOILLY — *Les chiens savants (La danse des chiens)*; Bagatelle 1871 (977); rue Laffitte 1912
New York, Mrs. George F. Clarke 1920

5 BOILLY — *Le saltimbanque*; rue Laffitte 1912
New York, Mrs. George F. Clarke 1920

6 BOILLY — *Femme se chaussant (La jarretière)*; Bagatelle 1871 (940); probably *La toilette*, 26 × 21, exh. Petit 1883 (3), lent Wallace; rue Laffitte 1912

7 BOILLY — *La marche incroyable (fragment)*; rue Laffitte 1912

8 BOILLY — *L'oiseau privé (Villageois dans un intérieur jouant avec un oiseau)*; rue Laffitte 1912

9 BOILLY — *Les galants surpris*; rue Laffitte 1912

10 BOILLY — *L'étreinte (La douce résistance)*, 45 × 37; exh. Petit 1883 (4, *Le baiser*); rue Laffitte 1912 (Harrisse, no.172)

11 BOILLY — *Les petits serins*; rue Laffitte 1871 (518)

12 BOILLY — *La statue cassée*; rue Laffitte 1871 (590)

13 BOILLY — *Le Palais Royal*, drawing; rue Laffitte 1912

14 BOILLY — *Etude de mains*, drawing; Bagatelle 1871 (974)

A *Group of Figures*, 15 × 20, by Boilly, was lot 895 in the Sackville sale 1923, and lot 628 in the Sackville sale 1936

15 BOUCHER — *Cupid and the Graces* 1738, 141 × 181 oval; Morny sale, 31 May 1865 (91), bt. by the 4th Marquess of Hertford; exh. boulevard des Italiens 1860 (75) lent Morny; used as a ceiling painting at Bagatelle (cf. *The Connoisseur*, XXVII, 1910, p.240); Bagatelle c.1896; rue Laffitte 1912 (A154)
Lisbon, Calouste Gulbenkian Foundation (no.433)

16 BOUCHER — *Diana and Endymion*, 92 × 135; rue Laffitte 1871 (438); exh. Petit 1883 (7); rue Laffitte 1912 (A36/6)
Washington, National Gallery of Art (no.1554, attributed to Boucher)

17–18 BOUCHER — *Jupiter and Callisto, Angelica and Medoro* 1763, a pair, 63.5 × 53 oval; Prousteau de Montlouis sale, 5 May 1851 (11), bt. by the 4th Marquess of Hertford; Bagatelle 1871 (?991, '*deux sujets mythologiques*', unattributed); exh. Petit 1883 (5 and 6, as *Venus and Adonis, Diana and Venus*); rue Laffitte 1912 (A575–6)
New York, Metropolitan Museum of Art (nos.1982.60.45–6)

19 BOUCHER — *The Muse Erato*, 93 × 132; possibly Cypierre sale, 10 March 1845 (14); Bagatelle 1871 (1008, '*Nymphe et amour*'); rue Laffitte 1912 (A488)
New York, Christie's, 9 May 1985 (14); exh. *Boucher*, Stair Sainty Matthiesen, New York, 1987 (41)

20–1 BOUCHER — *Drawing, Poetry*, a pair, 40 × 32.7 oval; Baudin sale, 9 January 1843 (35), bt. by the 4th Marquess of Hertford; Bagatelle 1871 (945); rue Laffitte 1912
New York, Frick Collection (no.16.1.16–17)

22 BOUCHER — *Girl with roses*, 54.6 × 42.5 oval; anon. sale 6 May 1857 (3), bt. by the 4th Marquess of Hertford; Bagatelle 1871 (?934 '*école française, jeune femme tenant une guirlande*'); rue Laffitte 1912 (A435)
New York, Frick Collection (no.16.1.18)

23 BOUCHER — *The Washerwomen*, 58 × 47; rue Laffitte 1871 (?550); Hertford House 1890; exh. Bethnal Green 1872–5 (454); Murray Scott 1903; Murray Scott sale 1913, lot 115, bt. Wertheimer, 1150 gn.; (A259)
New York, Newhouse Galleries 1953

24	BOUCHER	*Triumph of Venus*, 203 × 198; rue Laffitte 1871 (94); rue Laffitte 1912; New York, Metropolitan Museum of Art (no.28.163, Follower of Boucher) New York, Christie's, 5 June 1980 (138)
25	BOUCHER	*Lovers by a Statue*, 80 × 102; Hertford House 1870, 1890; Murray Scott 1903; Murray Scott sale 1913, lot 116, bt. McKay, 220 gn.
26	BOUCHER	*Shepherdesses*, 74 × 107; Hertford House 1870, 1890; Murray Scott 1903; Murray Scott sale 1913, lot 117, bt. Hodgkins, 1,600 gn.
27–8	BOUCHER	*Two overdoors, pastoral*; Hertford House 1870, 1890; [possibly P445 and P447, or] Murray Scott 1903
29	BOUCHER	*La cible des amours*, 63 × 91; Laperlier sale, 11 April 1867 (5), bt. by the 4th Marquess of Hertford; Bagatelle 1871 (944); rue Laffitte 1912
30	BOUCHER	*Pastorale*, gouache, oval; rue Laffitte 1912
31	BOUCHER	*Tête de jeune fille*, water-colour; rue Laffitte 1871 (491); Hertford House 1890 ('*Head of a girl with flowers in her breast*')
32	BOUCHER	*Etude de femme nue*, sanguine; rue Laffitte 1871 (854)
33–4	BOUCHER	*Une baigneuse*, *Les baigneuses*, drawings (two) rue Laffitte 1912
35–6	BOUCHER, school of	*Leda and the Swan*, *Jupiter and Callisto*, a pair, pastel 56 × 74; Bagatelle 1871 (970, '*d'après Boucher*'); rue Laffitte 1912 London, Sotheby's, 26 June 1963 (74)
37	BOUCHER, school of	*Danaë*, pastel, half-length; Bagatelle 1871 (969, '*école française*'); rue Laffitte 1912
38	BOUCHER, style of	*Femme assise*, drawing; rue Laffitte 1912
39	BOUCHER, after	*Naissance d'Adonis*; Bagatelle 1871 (1006)
40	BOUCHER, after	*Girl with a cushion*, pastel; possibly Cypierre sale, 10 March 1845 (175); rue Laffitte 1912 (AD415?)
41	CARESMES, J.-P. (1734–91)	*Faunes et bacchantes*, drawing 32 × 26; rue Laffitte 1912 (attributed to Clodion) New York, Parke-Bernet, 11 December 1948 (5)
42	CARESMES, after	*Bacchante*; possibly Wallace sale, 2 March 1857 (103); rue Laffitte 1912
43	CHARDIN, P.-J. (1731–68)	*Attributs des arts avec une tête de Mercure en plâtre*, 53 × 109; Laperlier sale, 11 April 1867 (28, Chardin *fils*, 54 × 112), bt. by the 4th Marquess of Hertford; Hertford House 1890 ('*Chardin fils*, Drawing *an emblematic panel* 109 × 53'); Murray Scott sale 1913, lot 119 (as Chardin), bt. Andrade, 270 gn. (Rosenberg, *Chardin*, 1983, under no.9)
44	CHARLIER	*Nymphs asleep*, gouache 44.5 × 37; rue Laffitte 1871 (408); 105 Piccadilly 1874; Hertford House 1890; Murray Scott 1903; Murray Scott sale 1913, lot 96, bt. Hodgkins, 210 gn.
45	CHARLIER	*Femme au bain*, gouache; Bagatelle 1871 (968)
46–7	CHARLIER, after	*Vénus et Amour*, *Flora et Zéphire*, a pair; rue Laffitte 1912
48	COYPEL, C.-A. (1694–1752)	*The pet Parrot with three Children*, 80 × 94 oval; Bagatelle 1866 (according to a label, *verso*); Murray Scott sale 1913, lot 120, bt. Nicholson, 900 gn.
49–50	DANLOUX, H.-P., attributed (1753–1809)	*Les cerises*, *Les prunes* (two); possibly Bagatelle 1871 (957, '*deux tableaux de jeunes filles*'); rue Laffitte 1912
51	DAVID, J.-L. (1748–1825)	*Napoléon Ier en costume de sacre* 1807, 87 × 58; Moreau Wolsey sale, 23 March 1869 (34); rue Laffitte 1912; possibly rue Laffitte 1871 (141, as Gérard); (cf. *Gazette des Beaux-Arts*, 6e, CII, 1983, pp.32–3 n.29) Cambridge, Mass., Fogg Art Museum (1943.228)

52	DEBRUCOURT, P.-L. (1755–1832)	*Promenade dans la galerie du Palais Royal*; rue Laffitte 1912
53	DESCOURTIS, C.-M. (1753–1820)	*L'amant surpris*, *Les espiègles*, a pair; rue Laffitte 1912
54–7	DESPORTES	*Chiens et faisans*, *Perroquets et fleurs*, a pair, 140 × 137; *Cygnes*, *Flamants*, a pair, 140 × 107; exh. Petit 1883 (29, 30); Bagatelle 1871 (1014); rue Laffitte 1912
58	DROUAIS, F.-H. (1727–75)	*Marie-Thérèse de Savoie, comtesse d'Artois, le duc d'Angoulême, le duc de Berry et la princesse Sophie*; exh. *exposition de Trianon*, 1867 (121) lent Hertford
59	DUSSAUX, J.-M. (fl. 1771–7)	series of decorative panels (*camées*) for the *grand salon* and boudoir doors at Bagatelle (including *Les noces de Psyché*, *Le temple des Graces*, *La baigneuse soutenue par des Naiades*); effaced by d'Artois in 1824, but restored by the 4th Marquess of Hertford
60	FRAGONARD, after	*A lady seated on a couch looking at a clock, a maid standing by the table*, 28 × 23; Hertford House 1890
61	FRENCH School	'*projet de plafond, le Triomphe d'amour, école française*'; rue Laffitte 1912
62	FRENCH School	*Les bains chinois, boulevard des Italiens*, water-colour 47.4 × 62.3; rue Laffitte 1912; exh. *Les grands boulevards*, musée Carnavalet 1985 (346) Paris, Musée Carnavalet (*rés.* T.G. Canon D6006)
63	FRENCH School	*Louis XI*; Orléans sale, 26 April ff. 1851 (283), bt. by the 4th Marquess of Hertford; rue Laffitte 1871 (372); cf. *The Connoisseur*, XXXIX, 1914, p.30
64	FRENCH School	*Homards, fruits, etc.*; rue Laffitte 1871 (380)
65	FRENCH School	*La nuit*; rue Laffitte 1871 (513)
66	FRENCH School	*Trianon*; rue Laffitte 1871 (586)
67–70	FRENCH School	*Scènes de cabaret* (two), *Jeune femme avec la poitrine découverte*, *Portrait de Louis XVI*; rue Laffitte 1912
71	FRENCH School	*Jeune femme pinçant de la guitare*, water-colour; Bagatelle 1871 (1015); rue Laffitte 1912
72	GERARD, F.-P. (1770–1837)	*Bélisaire*; rue Laffitte 1871 (140); rue Laffitte 1912
73–76	GERARD	Four portraits: *F. d'Imecourt*, *Mme. Bernadotte*, *Marie-Louise*, *Jérôme Bonaparte*, drawings; rue Laffitte 1912
77	GRANET, M. (1775–1849)	*Portique du couvent des Capucines à Rome*, drawing; Saint sale, 4 May 1846 (111), bt. by the 4th Marquess of Hertford
78	GREUZE	*Les oeufs cassés* 1756, 73 × 94; Demidoff sale, 21 February 1870 (107), bt. by the 4th Marquess of Hertford; rue Laffitte 1871 (364); exh. Bethnal Green 1872–5 (468); sold by Wallace to Lord Dudley in 1875 (Munhall no.9) New York, Metropolitan Museum of Art (no.20.155.8)
79	GREUZE	*Petite fille au chien*; rue Laffitte 1871 (663) Two *têtes de jeunes filles*, genre de Greuze, were in rue Laffitte 1871 (800), and a *Fillette à la colombe*, d'après Greuze, was in rue Laffitte 1912
80	GROS	*Portrait*; rue Laffitte 1871 (706)
81	GUERIN, F. (1774–1833)	*Diane et ses nymphes chassant le cerf*; rue Laffitte 1871 (512); rue Laffitte 1912
82	ISABEY, J.-B. (1767–1855)	*Plaisir et raison*, drawing; rue Laffitte 1871 (861); rue Laffitte 1912
83–4	LAFRENSEN	*L'assemblée au concert*, *L'assemblée au salon* (two); rue Laffitte 1912

85–8	LANCRET	*Concert champêtre*, *Baigneuses*, *Le petit déjeuner avant la chase*, *Hallali* (four), each c.61 × 132 lunette; rue Laffitte 1871 (825); exh. *Exposition de l'art français*, 1888 (18) lent Wallace; Bagatelle c.1896; rue Laffitte 1912 (WL743–6) San Francisco, Fine Arts Museums (nos.52.29.1–2, 53.2.1–2)
89	LATOUR, M.-Q. (1704–88)	*Mme. de Lareynière* 1751, pastel; Véron sale, 17 March 1858 (75), bt. by the 4th Marquess of Hertford
90	LEMOYNE	*Jupiter*; Bagatelle 1871 (998); possibly the '*plafond dans le boudoir de l'Est*' by Lemoyne at Bagatelle c.1896
91	LEMOYNE, attributed	*Leda and the Swan*, oval; rue Taitbout 1871 ('*école française*'); rue Laffitte 1912 Paris, Seligmann 1949
92	LEPICIE	*Portrait*; Bagatelle 1871 (1005)
93–4	LEPRINCE, J.-B. (1734–81)	*Paysanne orientale*, *Jeune femme coiffée d'un fichu bleu* (two), water-colours 28 × 20; rue Laffitte 1912 London, Agnew 1955
95	LEPRINCE	*Lady playing a mandoline*, panel 19 × 14; Hertford House 1890 (as artist unknown); Murray Scott 1903; Murray Scott sale 1913, lot 135, bt. Andrade, 280 gn.
96	LIOTARD, J.-E., after (1702–89)	*La chocolatière*; rue Laffitte 1912
97–8	LOO, A. van (1719–95)	*L'aveu*, *L'abandon*, a pair 116 × 90; rue Laffitte 1912; J. Seligmann sale, 18 May 1925 (42, 43)
99	LOO, C.A. van	*Tête de jeune femme*, pastel; rue Laffitte 1871 (849); exh. Petit 1883 (195); Scott sale 1942, lot 127
100	MALLET, J.-B. (1759–1835)	*Jeunes femmes dans un atelier de sculpture*; rue Laffitte 1912
101	MALLET	*Le corps de garde*; rue Laffitte 1871 (54); rue Laffitte 1912
102	MIGNARD, P. (1612–95)	*The marquise de Seignelay and two of her children* 1691, 194 × 155; exh. Paris, *exposition en faveur des Alsaciens et Lorrains*, 1874 (*supp.* 931) lent Wallace, and *Exposition de l'art français*, 1888 (27) lent Wallace; Murray Scott London, National Gallery (no.2967; Murray Scott bequest)
103	MIGNARD	*Portrait de femme*; bt. by the 4th Marquess of Hertford, 2 March 1847 (Hertford's account book in the Wallace Collection archives)
104–7	MOREAU, J.-M. (1741–1814)	*Four views of Bagatelle*; 1871 (1012)
108	MOREAU, J.-M.	*Vue de Bagatelle*, sepia; rue Laffitte 1912
109–10	MOREAU, L.-G. (1740–1806)	*Pair of Views of the garden at Bagatelle*; Bagatelle c.1896; rue Laffitte 1912
111	MOREAU, L.-G.	*View in a park*, water-colour, oval; rue Laffitte 1912
		Deux aquarelles et une sépia, représentant des vues de Bagatelle by Moreau, exh. Petit 1883 (188), lent Wallace
112	NATOIRE, C.-J.	*Trois figures*; rue Laffitte 1871 (381)
113	NATTIER	*Mme. Henriette en vestale*, 180 × 133; exh. boulevard des Italiens 1860 (212) lent Hertford; rue Laffitte 1871 (427); exh. Petit 1883 (105, *Mlle. Louise*); rue Laffitte 1912 Detroit Institute of Art (no.43.417)
		A *Mme. Henriette en vestale* 1749, 84 × 95, was with Murray Scott 1903, Murray Scott sale 1913, lot 133, bt. Wertheimer, 2,100 gn.; sold Sotheby's, 19 April 1967 (26); a portrait by Nattier of *Mlle. Victoire*, 190 × 98, was exh. Petit 1883 (104) lent Wallace

114–15	OUDRY	*Le lièvre, La tortue*, a pair; rue Laffitte 1871 (437)
116–17	OUDRY	*Chiens d'arret et faisan, Chiens près d'un bois gardant du gibier* (two); Barre sale, 29 January 1858 (35), bt. by the 4th Marquess of Hertford
118	PATER	*Fête champêtre*, 48 × 62; Hertford House 1870; exh. Manchester, *Art Treasures*, 1857 (saloon H, no.29); Bethnal Green 1872–5 (436); Murray Scott 1903; Murray Scott sale 1913, lot 134, bt. Agnew, 2,300 gn.; sold Christie's, 20 June 1930 (101) as Lancret Chicago, Art Institute (no.1954.295) A Pater '*tableau de Mr Collot*' was bt. by the 4th Marquess of Hertford, 13 April 1845, 5,800 fr. (Hertford's account book in the Wallace Collection archives)
119	PICARD, B. (1673–1733)	*Frontispiece*, drawing; rue Laffitte 1912
120	POUSSIN	*A Classical Landscape (The Death of Clytus)*, 147 × 109; Dorchester House 1842; Ragley sale 1938, lot 23
121	PRUD'HON	*Minerve conduisant le Génie des Arts à l'immortalité*, 49 × 30; Laperlier sale, 11 April 1867 (40), bt. by the 4th Marquess of Hertford (Guiffrey, no.875, has the buyer's name, in error, as Sabatier)
122	PRUD'HON	*Sleeping Nymph and Cupids*, a sketch, 20 × 10; exh. Bethnal Green 1874–5 (599); Hertford House 1890
123–4	PRUD'HON	*deux tableaux*, bt. by the 4th Marquess of Hertford, 18 February 1845, 1,366 fr. (Hertford's account book in the Wallace Collection archives)
125	PRUD'HON	*académie de femme*, drawing; rue Laffitte 1912
126	RAOUX	*Angélique et Medor;* Bagatelle 1871 (985); rue Laffitte 1912
127	REGNAULT, J.-B. (1754–1829)	*L'amour porté par les Graces;* rue Laffitte 1912
128	RIGAUD, after	*Louis XIV*, drawing 63.5 × 48.9; rue Laffitte 1871 (622); exh. Bethnal Green 1872–5 (62); Hertford House 1890; Murray Scott by whom given to G. Lockett Phoenix, Arizona, Art Museum (no.65.62)
129–30	TAUNAY, N.-A. (1755–1830)	*Paysage avec figures*, a pair; rue Laffitte 1871 (95); probably the *scène de chasse* and *bergers à la ruine*, pendants, rue Laffitte 1912 C.H. Geist, Philadelphia, 1950
131	TAUNAY	*Les saltimbanques*; rue Laffitte 1912; possibly the *scène de carnaval* in the Wallace sale, 2 March 1857 (74), bt. Laneuville
132	TOCQUE, L. (1696–1772)	*The duc de Chartres feeding Swans* 1775, 146 × 114; Bagatelle 1871 (1009, as Boucher, *Charles X enfant*); Bagatelle c.1896, as Boucher and Oudry; rue Laffitte 1912, as Desportes and Tocqué (Doria, *Tocqué*, 1929, no.255) Paris, Seligmann 1949
133	VALLIN, J.-A.	*Les baigneuses*; rue Laffitte 1912
134	VERNET, C. (1758–1836)	*Chevaux dans la prairie*; rue Laffitte 1871 (850); rue Laffitte 1912; probably sold Christie's, 4 June 1982 (243, dated 1812, 55 × 70)
135	VERNET, C.	*Bataille*; rue Laffitte 1871 (851)
136	VERNET, C.	*Le concert*; rue Laffitte 1871 (543)
137–8	VERNET, C.	*Chasse à cour*, water-colours, a pair; rue Laffitte 1912
139–41	VERNET, C.	*Cavalry*, water-colours, a pair; *Soldier's Farewell*, water-colour; Hertford House 1890

142	VESTIER, A. (1740–1824)	*Mlle. Duthé,* 167 × 118; bt. from Latapie, 24 April 1852, by the 4th Marquess of Hertford; Bagatelle c.1896; rue Laffitte 1912; exh. RA 1968 (703) Paris, Vieil-Picard sale, 14 March 1970 (22)
143	WATTEAU	*La perspective,* 47 × 55, Saint sale, 4 May 1846 (56), bt. by the 4th Marquess of Hertford; rue Laffitte 1871 (424); exh. Bethnal Green 1872–5 (440); RA 1889 (89); Hertford House 1890; Murray Scott 1903; Murray Scott sale 1913, lot 138, bt. Agnew, 6,200 gn. (DV172, CR196) Boston, Mass., Museum of Fine Arts (no.23.573)
144–5	WATTEAU	*'deux tableaux genre peint par Watteau',* bt. by the 4th Marquess of Hertford, Paris, 19 October 1827, 390 fr. (receipt for *le comte Yarmouth* in Wallace Collection archives)
146	WATTEAU, after	*L'accord parfait,* 27 × 23; Seymour sale, 14 February 1860 (126, Watteau, *L'accord parfait* as 35 × 28), bt. Van Cuyck; rue Laffitte 1912 (*'petit groupe pastoral L'Accord Parfait attribué à Watteau'*) (under DV23, CR196) London, National Gallery (no.2692, as After Watteau, Murray Scott bequest)
147	WATTEAU, called	*Figures in a Garden,* 37 × 28 ('man in a striped dress is seated; a lady reclines on the ground, while a youth with a guitar sits behind; two lovers recline on the ground to the right'); Hertford House 1870 (*'Watteau, Pastoral Landscape with Figures'*); Murray Scott 1903; Murray Scott sale 1913, lot 139, bt. Jones Bros., 110 gn.
148–9	WATTEAU, called	*Garden Scenes,* a pair, 81 × 58 oval; Hertford House 1890; Murray Scott 1903; Murray Scott sale 1913, lot 113 ('French School, *Fêtes Champêtres*'), bt. Cohen, 35 gn.
150–1	WATTEAU, called	*Astronomy, Music,* a pair, 86 × 58 oval; Hertford House 1890 (*'After Watteau'*); Murray Scott sale 1913, lot 53 (as A. Kauffman), bt. Tooth, 35 gn.

Indices

Attributions changed from the 1968 Catalogue and the 1978 Summary Illustrated Catalogue

Previous attribution	no.	Present attribution
BOUCHER	P390	Ascribed to BOUCHER
BOUCHER	P433	After BOUCHER
BOUCHER	P481	Studio of BOUCHER
BOUCHER	P490	Studio of BOUCHER
After BOUCHER	P467	Ascribed to CHARLIER
After BOUCHER	P468	Ascribed to CHARLIER
FRAGONARD	P483	TARAVAL
FRAGONARD	P488	JOLLAIN
GREUZE	P434	Ascribed to GREUZE
GREUZE	P443	Ascribed to GREUZE
GREUZE	P454	Ascribed to GREUZE
LARGILLIERRE	P122	FRENCH School c.1715–20
L.-M. van LOO	P477	Studio of L.-M. van LOO
NATTIER	P414	After NATTIER
OUDRY	P624	Ascribed to OUDRY
RIGAUD	P130	After RIGAUD
Attributed to F. de TROY	P122	FRENCH School c.1715–20
WATTEAU	P377	Ascribed to WATTEAU

Subject Index

Picture titles are given in italics

Index of previous Owners

Numerical Index

NOTE

These numbers (prefixed by the letter P for picture) were allocated according to the sequence of pictures exhibited when the Wallace Collection opened in 1900. The numbers appearing in this catalogue were then displayed as follows:

Numbers	*Location*
102–42	gallery 20
257–376	galleries 17 & 18
377–428	gallery 21
429–47	gallery 22
448–80	gallery 23
481–90	staircase and landing
525–56	gallery 3
590–622	gallery 11
623–31	gallery 12
780	gallery 12 (as no. XI 326)

Numbers 645 and 776–72 were not then on display.

Index of Artists

Arranged alphabetically by artist, the titles in numerical order
*Asterisk indicates a drawing or water-colour